SAGE was founded in 1965 by Sara Miller McCune to support the dissemination of usable knowledge by publishing innovative and high-quality research and teaching content. Today, we publish over 900 journals, including those of more than 400 learned societies, more than 800 new books per year, and a growing range of library products including archives, data, case studies, reports, and video. SAGE remains majority-owned by our founder, and after Sara's lifetime will become owned by a charitable trust that secures our continued independence.

Los Angeles | London | New Delhi | Singapore | Washington DC | Melbourne

Corporate Finance

Corporate Finance

Text and Cases

Vishwanath S. R.
Professor, School of Management and Entrepreneurship,
Shiv Nadar University

SAGE | TEXTS

Los Angeles | London | New Delhi
Singapore | Washington DC | Melbourne

First Edition published in 2000
Second Edition published in 2007
This Third Edition published in 2019 by

SAGE | TEXTS

SAGE Publications India Pvt Ltd
B1/I-1 Mohan Cooperative Industrial Area
Mathura Road, New Delhi 110 044, India
www.sagepub.in

SAGE Publications Inc
2455 Teller Road
Thousand Oaks, California 91320, USA

SAGE Publications Ltd
1 Oliver's Yard, 55 City Road
London EC1Y 1SP, United Kingdom

SAGE Publications Asia-Pacific Pte Ltd
18 Cross Street #10-10/11/12
China Square Central
Singapore 048423

Published by Vivek Mehra for SAGE Publications India Pvt Ltd. Typeset in 10/12 pt Berkeley by Zaza Eunice, Hosur, Tamil Nadu, India.

Library of Congress Cataloging-in-Publication Data Available

ISBN: 978-93-532-8289-9 (PB)

SAGE Team: Indrani Dutta, Amit Kumar, Madhurima Thapa, Ankit Verma and Kanika Mathur

To

My Parents, Priya, Mohith and Mythili

Contents

SECTION 4 THE FINANCING DECISION

SECTION 5 DIVIDEND POLICY

SECTION 6 FINANCIAL POLICY, COMPETITIVE STRATEGY AND SHAREHOLDER VALUE

TEACHING CASES

MODULE 1 RISK AND RETURN

MODULE 2 COST OF CAPITAL, CAPITAL BUDGETING AND CAPITAL STRUCTURE

MODULE 3 FINANCING YOUNG AND MATURE FIRMS

MODULE 4 PROJECT FINANCE

MODULE 5 DIVIDENDS AND STOCK REPURCHASES

MODULE 6 ACQUISITIONS AND CORPORATE RESTRUCTURING

Detailed Contents

SECTION 6 FINANCIAL POLICY, COMPETITIVE STRATEGY AND SHAREHOLDER VALUE

TEACHING CASES

MODULE 1 RISK AND RETURN

MODULE 2 COST OF CAPITAL, CAPITAL BUDGETING AND CAPITAL STRUCTURE

MODULE 3 FINANCING YOUNG AND MATURE FIRMS

Preface

Financial economics is the study of markets for real and financial assets. The past three decades have witnessed an unprecedented series of theoretical and empirical advances in our understanding of the markets, with major breakthroughs in capital asset pricing under uncertainty, portfolio theory, valuation of options and response of security prices to corporate financial behaviour. The practical implications of these breakthroughs, commonly known as modern finance theory, are widely accepted and applied by finance practitioners. Finance is concerned with the manner in which firms allocate resources across assets and over time. The developed body of financial knowledge deals with portfolio decisions of individuals, with investment and financing decisions by firms and with the implications of such behaviour for the pricing of capital assets in the marketplace.

The goal of this book is to provide a rigorous understanding of how and why firms make their financial decisions the way they do and their impact on shareholder value. The central theme of the book is value-based management, which assumes that maximizing shareholder value is the governing objective of a firm.

Corporate Finance: Text and Cases examines the role of finance in supporting other functional areas while fostering an understanding of how financial decisions can create value. Topics covered in this book are related to estimating divisional cost of capital, capital investments, executing a financing strategy, establishing debt and dividend policies consistent with the company's strategy and environment, choosing between dividends and stock repurchases, managing high growth and managing working capital.

This book explores the issues that are special to emerging economies such as India. These economies are the engine of growth opportunities in the world. However, these markets are prone to crises (e.g., East Asia in the late 1990s), which reinforces the importance of measuring risk in these markets. The book aims to develop a better understanding of how to do business in emerging markets. The book covers essential elements of emerging financial markets—emerging market valuation, portfolio diversification, project finance, capital structure, mergers and acquisitions and corporate restructuring. The objective of this book is to train highly skilled financial analysts and managers with strong theoretical background and practical knowledge about emerging markets.

TARGET AUDIENCE

This book is meant to be used in a corporate finance course in MBA programmes, although students of other professional programmes such as CFA/CA/ICWA would also find it useful. This book is suitable for those who are seeking a career in corporate finance, investment banking, general management, strategy consulting, securities analysis, turnaround management, commercial banking and investment management. It can also be used in executive education programmes in corporate finance.

Acknowledgements

Special thanks is due to Professor Campbell Harvey, J. Paul Sticht Professor of International Business, Fuqua School of Business, Duke University, USA, who contributed a number of excellent cases on emerging market firms.

I would also like to thank Professor Jaskiran Arora (BML Munjal University), Professor Durga Prasad (T. A. Pai Management Institute) and Professor Kulbir Singh (Institute of Management Technology, Nagpur) for co-authoring some of the cases.

About the Author

Vishwanath S. R. is a Professor of Finance, MBA Programme Chair and Faculty Director of Executive Education in the School of Management and Entrepreneurship at Shiv Nadar University. He is the author of two volumes of 80 case studies published by McGraw Hill (India) and four books published by Springer Verlag, SAGE and PHI Learning (formerly Prentice Hall of India), and several cases published by the *Asian Case Research Journal*, *The CASE Journal* and Harvard Business Publishing.

He has held academic appointments at the S. P. Jain Institute of Management in Mumbai, Emirates Institute for Banking and Financial Studies in Sharjah, T. A. Pai Management Institute in Manipal, Bharathidasan Institute of Management in Trichy, Tata Management Training Centre in Pune and Institute of Management Technology in Nagpur. He has two decades of experience in teaching graduate students and executives from a variety of industries.

Vishwanath S. R. was the Regional Editor of Emerald Emerging Markets Case Studies, UK, during 2012–2014. He received the Ruth Greene Memorial Award, the Best Workshop Case Award and Jonathan Welch Case Award from North American Case Research Association (NACRA) in 2010, 2012 and 2014, respectively. He was nominated for the CMA of Alberta Governance Award at NACRA in 2013 and Excellence in Case Writing Award in 2014 by the Case Association of the United States. He received the Hindustan Unilever Dewang Mehta Best Professor in Finance award in 2013.

His research papers examine the role of certification and anchor investors in initial public offerings (IPOs), performance of family firms, valuation effects of changes in dividend taxes, IPO price stabilization through call auctions, the impact of stock market reforms on capital allocation to IPO firms and economic growth, risk-taking in family firms, the value of executive directors, the impact of ownership of IPOs on liquidity and stock returns and offshore dollar-denominated convertibles issued by Indian firms. He has presented his research at major global conferences such as American Economic Association/ASSA meetings, Journal of Corporate Finance Special Emerging Markets Conference, Asian Finance Association meetings, EFMA meetings, Financial Markets and Corporate Governance Conference and North American Case Research Association meetings.

He has been enlisted in the Marquis Who's Who in the World and Madison's Who's Who among executives and professionals throughout the world.

SECTION 1

Building Blocks

CHAPTER

1

Introduction

LEARNING OBJECTIVES

- Introduction to the goal of financial management
- Competitors to wealth maximization rule and their limitations
- Factors affecting value creation
- Corporate governance around the world

Corporate financial management deals with the investment, financing and dividend decisions of a firm. To carry on the business, a firm invests in tangible assets such as plant and machinery, land and buildings, and in intangible assets such as goodwill and patents. For example, in July 2018, Samsung set up a plant in Noida, Uttar Pradesh, to manufacture 120 million mobile phones at a cost of US$716.57 million. The plant was the biggest in the world. This constitutes the 'investment decision'.

A firm has to arrange funding from a variety of sources to acquire assets. For instance, in February 2018, ICICI Securities, a subsidiary of ICICI Bank, obtained an approval from Securities Exchange Board of India to raise ₹30,000–₹40,000 million by way of an initial public offering (IPO) of shares to the investing public. In the prospectus, the company mentioned that the offering would provide liquidity to existing shareholders and enhance the visibility and brand image of the company. This constitutes the 'financing decision'.

The investment in projects generates revenues and cash flows in future years. The managers of the firm can either retain cash with the company for further investment or distribute it to shareholders who are owners of the firm. For example, for the year ending March 2018, Indian Oil Corporation declared an equity dividend of 210 per cent amounting to ₹21 per share. This constitutes the 'dividend decision'.

A finance manager is concerned with such financial decisions as: Which project should the company undertake and what are the financial implications? How should the company finance the project? What should be the mix of shareholders equity and debt at any given point in time? What fraction of net income generated from business should be returned to shareholders in the form of dividends?

We could think of investment decision as managing the right-hand side of the balance sheet and financing decision as managing the left-hand side of the balance sheet as shown below:

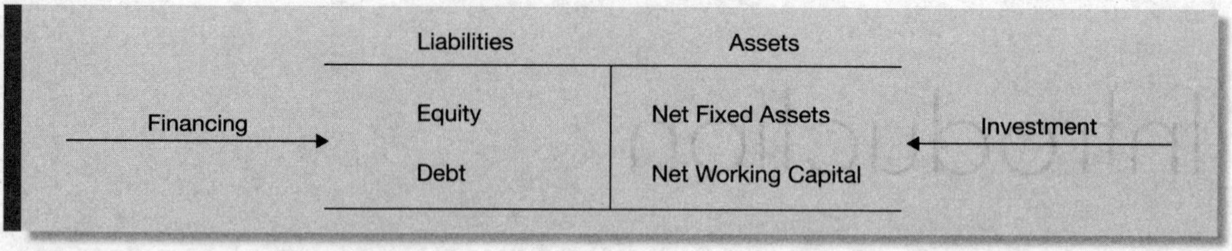

The relationship between these financial decisions is shown in Figure 1.1. The company decides to invest in a set of projects and approaches investors through financial intermediaries to raise capital in the form of debt and equity. Investors provide capital with the expectation that they will get a return commensurate with the risk assumed by them. The investor's expectation is the cost of capital to the company. Suppose a company borrows ₹100 million at an interest rate of 11 per cent. The company should earn more than 11 per cent on its investment to service the debt at all times. If earnings fall, a default will occur.

THE SEARCH FOR THE BEST CORPORATE OBJECTIVE

A firm is a group of claimants—shareholders, creditors, suppliers, customers and employees. Shareholders, as owners of the firm, appoint a board of directors to oversee the functioning and shape

FIGURE 1.1
Overview of Financial Decisions

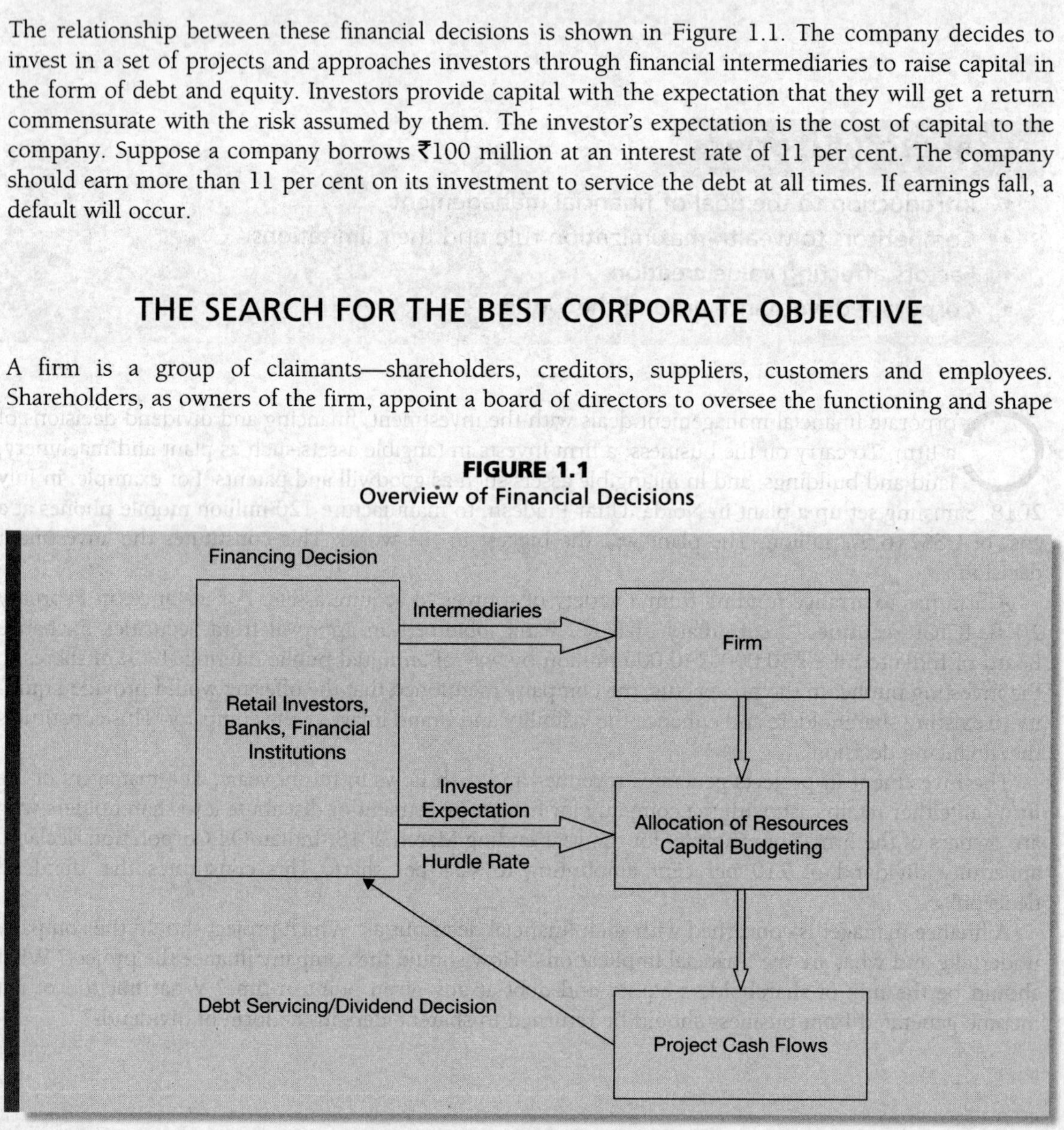

the strategic direction of the company. In theory, the board is supposed to act in the interest of claimants. Who should the managers serve? What should be the objective of a firm and, indirectly, its managers? Without an objective, one would not know if one has achieved what one set out to achieve. Corporate finance theoreticians generally agree that the objective of a firm is to maximize wealth although there may be some disagreement as to whether it should be the wealth of shareholders or the wealth of the firm, which includes bondholders and preferred stockholders. The shareholder wealth maximization rule requires managers to work towards a sustainable increase in the stock price.[1]

COMPETITORS TO THE SHAREHOLDER WEALTH MAXIMIZATION RULE

There are three principal competitors to the wealth maximization rule, namely profit maximization, social welfare and growth. These alternative objectives are supposed to be proxies for the wealth maximization rule. The underlying assumption is that an increase in any of these proxies results in an increase in shareholder value.

Profit Maximization: Profit is the excess of revenue over expenses. Profit maximization requires managers to keep all expenses low (including salaries and wages), extract the last rupee from the customer, sell spurious goods as long as it is legal, pay the lowest possible price to suppliers, that is, to hoodwink all the stakeholders for the sake of profit. If profit maximization is the objective, why do companies provide housing and health care to employees, spend millions on research and development? The message is that we do not see profit maximizing behaviour although some companies may claim that their objective is to maximize profits. Moreover, accrual profits are not a good proxy for shareholder value given the creativity of accountants when it comes to reporting income.[2]

Social Welfare: Businessmen are supposed to be socially responsible. They do not live in an ethical vacuum. Indeed Indian businesses have long been active in community development, higher education and health care services. Several of them have managed their businesses with less of an eye on shareholders. For instance, the Tata Group established the Indian Institute of Science in 1909 with active support from Jamsetji Tata. They were also instrumental in setting up the Tata Institute of Social Sciences, Tata Institute of Fundamental Research and the Xavier Labor Relations Institute. Many other business groups have followed suit. Although community development is laudable, the social welfare objective, often pursued by government organizations, has conceptual problems such as what constitutes society or social welfare? Can one section of the society be made better off without making somebody else worse off? The executive is an agent serving the interests of his/her principal, the shareholder. When executives start spending money for social purposes, they become public servants in effect even though they remain employees of the organization. In other words, social welfare itself cannot be the objective of a firm.

[1] See Hart and Zingales, 'Companies Should Maximize Shareholder Welfare Not Market Value' for a recent discussion on corporate objectives.

[2] Income statement and balance sheet are prepared on the basis of generally accepted accounting principles. Although accounting standards limit managerial discretion in the preparation of financial statements, managers still have leeway in the choice of accounting policies. They may be tempted to manage earnings.

The above argument notwithstanding, in India, the Companies Act, 2013, requires certain companies to spend at least 2 per cent on corporate social responsibility[3] (CSR) for the applicable financial year and report on these activities in the annual report. The CSR clause applies to any company, during any financial year, with (a) a net worth of ₹5 billion (about US$90 million) or more; (b) a turnover of ₹10 billion or more; or (c) a net profit of ₹50 million or more. The CSR clause will only apply to several thousand companies in India and is expected to generate a few billion dollars of CSR spending on local communities.

There is no penalty for failing to spend on CSR. But there are penalties for failing to report CSR activities or explain why CSR amounts were not spent. Failure to explain is punishable by a fine of not less than ₹50,000 and up to ₹25 lakh. Further, officers who default on the reporting provision could be subject to imprisonment and/or fine.[4]

The law requires companies to form a Corporate Social Responsibility Committee within the board of directors that will devise, recommend and monitor CSR activities, and report the amounts spent on such activities to the rest of the board. The CSR Committee must consist of three or more directors, at least one of which must be an 'independent director'. The composition of the CSR Committee must be disclosed in the annual board report.

Academic studies find that firms with high CSR disclosure quality are associated with lower costs of corporate bonds,[5] that is, these firms can borrow at cheaper rates. They may also exhibit less expensive equity financing.[6] These findings suggest that CSR and shareholder wealth maximization are complementary. A firm can be socially responsible without harming shareholders.

Corporate Growth: Emerging markets such as India and Korea are dominated by business conglomerates, some of which control as many as 90 (group) companies (e.g., the Tata group). The big businesses in Korea, the *chaebol*, typically owned 30–50 companies in all key business areas and the big five—Daewoo, Samsung, Hyundai, LG and SK—accounted for 20 per cent of all borrowing and contributed to almost 50 per cent of GDP. Debt ratios at the top 30 *chaebol* were in the range of 550 per cent in the late 1990s. They sucked up a major portion of the available credit and drove out smaller businesses. The *chaebol* borrowed to the maximum possible extent and focused on size or growth and not profit or productivity. They invested aggressively and acquired companies. The productivity in South Korea was about half the US levels. When earnings fell due to recession in the late 1990s, these companies crumbled. The lenders to these firms collapsed causing a systemic crisis.

Everything about business groups in Korea or India is not bad. In these countries, it appears, there are certain important benefits from being a part of a business group not available to other stand-alone companies.[7] Emerging markets are characterized by illiquid capital markets, scarce managerial talent and poor judicial system. These business groups often perform several useful institutional roles not available in the country. For instance, they act as venture capitalists to start-up ventures within the group; solve information problems of customers by attaching their group brand name to products manufactured by the group companies (i.e., assure a certain level of quality); and act as business school by providing high quality management education to managers. In other

[3] CSR is defined as 'the responsibility of enterprises for their impacts on society'.

[4] In July 2018, the government sent preliminary notices to 272 companies for not complying with CSR spending requirements. For 2014–2015, prosecutions against 254 were sanctioned of which 33 companies have filed applications for compounding. See *The Economic Times*, 'Government Issues Preliminary Notices to 272 Companies for CSR Violations'.

[5] Gong, Xu and Gong, 'On the Value of Corporate Social Responsibility Disclosure'.

[6] Dhaliwal, Li, Tsang and Yang, 'Voluntary Nonfinancial Disclosure and the Cost of Equity Capital'.

[7] Khanna and Palepu, 'Why Focused Strategies May Be Wrong for Emerging Markets'; Khanna and Palepu, 'The Right Way to Restructure in Emerging Markets'. Some of these arguments are less relevant today.

words, business groups that act as proxy market institutions create greater value for shareholders than do more focused, unaffiliated companies. Given this benefit, it appears, it is probably not prudent to dismantle them. Despite this benefit, several business groups create little or no value. This is probably due to the fact that liberalization of the economy has induced intense competition in most businesses. So what was unique to these business groups is no longer their domain. For instance, capital is more freely available to profitable companies. They may source capital from abroad if necessary. Likewise, the number of business schools has gone up from a few tens to a few thousand in the last 20 years. While growth is important, it need not necessarily lead to an increase in shareholder value.

WHY NOT PURSUE MULTIPLE OBJECTIVES?

Peter Drucker was one of the advocates of this view. In his words:[8]

> To manage a business is to balance a variety of needs and goals. This requires judgement. The search for one objective is essentially a search for the magic formula that will make judgement unnecessary. But the attempt to replace judgement by formula is always irrational; all that can be done is to make judgement possible by narrowing its range and available alternatives, giving it clear focus, a sound foundation in facts and reliable measurements of the effects and validity of actions and decisions. And this, by the very nature of business enterprise, requires multiple objectives.

Companies may simultaneously pursue objectives such as market standing, innovation, productivity, profitability and public responsibility. Pursuing multiple objectives is like serving many masters. Nobody will be served consistently. Worse, the wrong master might be served at the wrong time. What good is innovation if customers do not attach value to it? There are several examples in the past where innovation did not translate into profits because the customers were not willing to buy the product either because they did not like it or the product was way ahead of its times. Productivity is a relative concept, not absolute. If the improvement in productivity is less than the increase in productivity of competition, the company will be 'worse off'. Customer delight, employee satisfaction, maintaining good relationship with bankers and suppliers are all important. But they are not ends in themselves. Winning the Malcolm Baldrige Award by incurring an economic loss in the process is hardly a good idea.[9]

DO FIRMS PURSUE MULTIPLE OBJECTIVES?

The Balanced Scorecard[10] developed by Robert Kaplan and David Norton recognizes the fact that executives do not focus on one set of measures as no single measure can provide a clear performance target or focus attention on the critical areas of business. The balanced scorecard allows managers to look at their business from the perspective of customers, shareholders and employees. A typical balanced scorecard, shown in Figure 1.2 considers goals and measures from various perspectives and tries to bring all the elements of the business together in a single management report. The trouble with balanced scorecard is

[8] Drucker, *The Practice of Management*, 54.

[9] General Motors spent millions of dollars on the Saturn car project. The customers loved the car but the stock price plunged.

[10] Kaplan and Norton, 'The Balanced Scorecard'; Kaplan and Norton, 'Putting the Balanced Scorecard to Work'.

FIGURE 1.2
The Balanced Scorecard

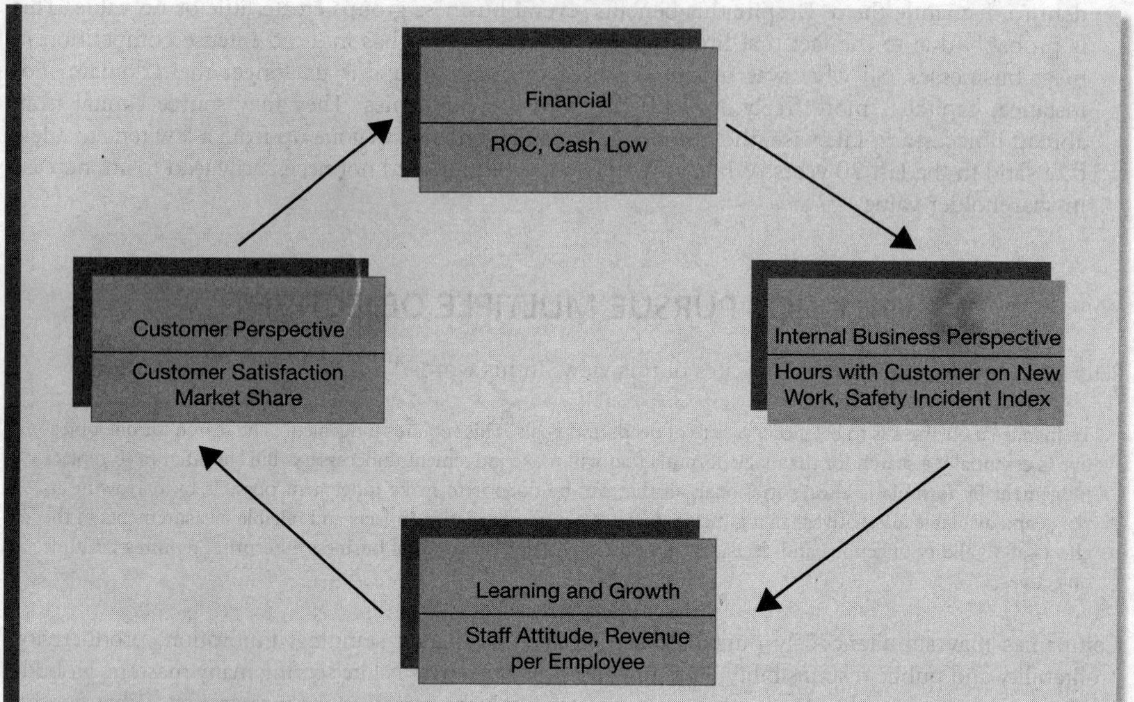

that it is not balanced in the sense that it does not tell us how the measures on the scorecard are to be weighted. In other words, the scorecard does not specify the trade-off among the measures. Further, it fails to provide a linkage between performance measurement and incentive system. However, managers can use balanced scorecard to drive results that lead to a sustained increase in shareholder value.

IMPEDIMENTS TO SHAREHOLDER WEALTH MAXIMIZATION

Shareholder wealth maximization rule is based on the assumption that other investor groups in the company are unaffected by the company's decisions. There could be potential conflict of interest between shareholders and bondholders, managers and shareholders, majority and minority shareholders. So maximizing wealth of one group could be achieved 'at the expense of' other groups.

Shareholders Versus Bondholders: Bondholders get a fixed contractual payment (interest) during the term of the bond but have a prior claim on the assets of the company, whereas equity investors have a residual claim on the cash flows of the company as they are owners. Since bondholders get a fixed slice of earnings pie regardless of the size of the earnings, they are more risk averse than shareholders who get to share the upside potential. Bondholders can suffer opportunity wealth loss due to the company's investment, financing and dividend decisions. A company making losses may be tempted to borrow and take on business gambles the benefits of which largely go to shareholders. If the project succeeds, shareholders enjoy the upside potential but bondholders get fixed interest payment and if the project fails, shareholders have nothing to lose. It's not their money anyway. Bondholders make an estimate of default risk at the time of lending and the price is set assuming that no further debt will be issued. The bondholders' claim gets diluted if additional debt is issued with same or higher priority. The increase in default risk leads to a decrease in the price of the bond. Potential conflicts can arise due to the firm's dividend decision as well. Bondholders lend money assuming that their money will be invested in profitable venture and the cash flows from the project would be used to service them. If the firm chooses to distribute that money to shareholders in the form of dividends, the bondholders will be left with an empty shell.

Managers Versus Shareholders: Investment in projects generates cash flows, which can either be reinvested in the business or returned to shareholders in the form of dividends who in turn can decide where to invest their money. Managers, as agents of shareholders, have discretion over investment of residual cash flow. Increasing dividends reduces the resources under the manager's control and limits growth. Since managers are appraised on the basis of growth, it is likely that they may pursue unprofitable projects that do not yield adequate returns leaving the shareholders in a lurch. This leads to conflict of interest between managers and shareholders. Conflict is more severe in those firms that generate substantial cash flows but do not have profitable investment avenues. Empire building may no longer be in fashion, but high growth is still in vogue. In theory, shareholders elect the board to oversee the chief executive on their behalf. But in practice, the chief executive, who chairs the board, exercises considerable influence on the board, including their remuneration. Typically, boards are populated with friends and relatives of the chief executive. Erring managers may be replaced if the market for corporate control (mergers and acquisitions) is active. The threat of acquisition by another company and the subsequent emotional upheavals keep managers on their toes. But takeovers are an expensive disciplining tool, entailing large administrative, legal and other economic costs.

Shareholder Versus Shareholder: In all but few advanced economies such as the USA, UK and Japan, most publicly traded firms are closely held with the majority shareholder playing an active role in management. The majority shareholder often serves as the chairman of the board. A study of the world's top 27 stock markets suggests that only 36 per cent of the largest publicly traded firms are widely held, that is, with no shareholder holding more than 20 per cent of the votes.[11] Most large publicly traded firms have a controlling shareholder, which may be a family, a state or another company. The 10 largest families in Indonesia, the Philippines and Thailand control half the corporate structure in terms of market capitalization, while the 10 largest in Korea and Hong Kong control about a third.[12] In the Philippines and Indonesia, the control of about 17 per cent of market capitalization can be traced to a single family. The Suharto family of Indonesia led by Suharto's children, relatives and business partners control 417 listed and unlisted companies. Control is defined as 20 per cent of voting rights and a widely held company is one in which no owner has significant rights. In many East Asian countries, control is enhanced through pyramidal structures and cross holdings.

A share is a share in the share capital of the company. Each share entitles the holder to exercise one vote at the annual general meeting. If this is true, then the value of the share should be the same

[11] La Porta, Lopez de Silanes, Shleifer and Vishny, 'Law and Finance'.

[12] Classens, Djankov and Lang, 'Who Controls East Asian Corporations?'

for all shareholders irrespective of how many shares one is holding—1 million or 100 shares. Glance through the financial dailies and magazines. Company after company is acquired by paying hefty premiums. Majority shareholders (i.e., promoters) control many of these firms. Why do they pay such premiums? Does the benefit accrue to all the shareholders? The answer lies in the benefits of being in control which accrue to the majority shareholder but not to minority shareholders.

The next logical question to ask would be what those benefits are and how minority shareholders are affected. The obvious benefits are the status bestowed upon the head of the company by the society, love and affection bestowed by family and friends, ability to buy larger than optimal size computer to play with, plush carpets, corporate jets and so on. The sum of these benefits will not add up to the premium paid. The less obvious benefits are the value of benefits arising out of access to information in related businesses and the ability to fix transfer prices between the company and its suppliers and customers.

An example will clarify the point. Let us suppose a foreign parent has two subsidiaries in India, one of which is a wholly owned subsidiary and the other, a 51 per cent subsidiary. If the foreign parent transfers profitable brands and businesses from a long established 51 per cent subsidiary to a newly formed 100 per cent subsidiary at low prices, the minority shareholders of the 51 per cent subsidiary suffer a loss. Another form of rip-off is to collect royalties for the use of a brand that the subsidiary has built through years of advertising. The parent takes the earnings pie away leaving the minority shareholders in dismay. Yet another form of expropriation is to acquire a more or less related business where the promoter has business interest through the holding company and further his/her interest without sharing any of those benefits with the minority shareholder. Academic studies suggest that the value of control is about 30 per cent of market value of equity in Italy, 10–20 per cent in Switzerland, the UK and Canada, and 4 per cent of firm value in the USA. The value of rip-off by majority shareholders is at least partly reflected in the premium paid for the target company.

When the risk of expropriation is high, investors either refrain from investing in closely held firms or demand a discount on the company's securities. But concentrated ownership in itself is not a bad thing. An obvious advantage of concentrated ownership is that it gives the owners better incentives to monitor firms and make necessary changes in management. Diffused ownership, in contrast, does not provide adequate incentives. If concentrated ownership indeed leads to better oversight by managers, we would expect positive correlation between ownership concentration and profitability and firm value. This is indeed the case in some central and Eastern European countries.[13] A study of 700 Czech firms finds that the more concentrated the ownership of a firm the higher is its market value and profitability.

INVESTOR PROTECTION

Shareholders provide equity in exchange for dividend and voting rights. Likewise creditors lend money in exchange for interest and principal payments and the right to possess collateral if the company defaults on its payments. The difference in governance in different parts of the world is partly due to the differences in the rights of shareholders and creditors.[14] A shareholder, as a residual claimant, has the right to attend annual general meetings and vote on various corporate matters such as asset sales, mergers and acquisitions, election of directors and so on. Often widely dispersed shareholders do not actively take part in the governance process. In those countries where voting by mail is not allowed, the

[13] Classens, Djankov and Pohl, 'Ownership and Corporate Governance'.

[14] La Porta et al. (1998); Shleifer and Vishny, 'A Survey of Corporate Governance'.

company's management can get away uncontested. In some countries such as Italy and Belgium whose legal systems are based on the French Civil law, shareholders are not allowed to vote by mail. In general, countries following the common law tradition (USA, UK, Australia, Canada and so on) provide the best investor protection. Likewise, the creditor rights vary from country to country. Some countries allow possession of collateral, whereas some do not. Again, the common law tradition provides the best protection to creditors. Further, in many countries companies can issue shares with different voting rights. The one-share, one-vote rule is followed in the USA, UK and many other countries. But it is common in countries such as Brazil and Chile to issue shares with different voting rights. Some companies restrict the voting rights of foreign investors. For example, some companies from Latin America and Europe have issued (depository) shares with differential voting rights.[15]

The shareholders of B class shares of Saga Petroleum, a Norwegian company, have no voting rights but holders of A shares have full voting rights. Mexican companies have issued L shares that provide limited rights to elect the number of directors and such other matters. Two Swedish firms—Astra and Scania—have issued two classes of shares—A and B. The A class shares have one vote each and B class shares carry one-tenth vote each. ABB has 24,345,619 shares with 0.1 vote per share and a par value of 5 SEK, as well as 66,819,757 shares with one vote per share and a par value of 5 SEK. Investors, in general, are better protected in countries where the one-share, one-vote rule is enforced. In the absence of such a law, the insiders of the company can have disproportionate control on the company in relation to their investment.

MAXIMIZE EQUITY VALUE OR FIRM VALUE?

There is a misconception that maximization of equity value and maximization of firm value are the same. They are not the same. Even though equity is a part of the firm's capital structure, there is also debt and many financial instruments with both debt and equity features that managers should take into account. As described in earlier sections, shareholders can increase their wealth at the expense of other investors. To illustrate, suppose there is a way in which managers could increase the value of equity by ₹1 if they could reduce the value of debt by ₹3. This would reduce the value of the firm by ₹2. What should the managers do now? Should they go ahead?[16] The answer is no, although managers are supposed to act on behalf of shareholders who have voted them to power.

CORPORATE GOVERNANCE

The term governance refers to exercise of power, authority, direction and control. A firm is a collection of physical assets that are jointly owned. Corporate governance refers to the allocation of ownership. It explains how power is shared, contracts are written and enforced, the role of the board of directors and chief executive, management compensation and so on. The root of the problem lies in the separation of ownership and control. Modern corporations are run by managers on behalf of shareholders. In many companies, the senior executives hold little or no equity stake. How do you make someone who has no stakes in a company behave like a true representative of the shareholders? The obvious answer is to force the top executives to buy the shares of the firm. In many companies, the board spends less than few hours in decision-making. The chief executive and other board members who are employees of the

[15] Pinegar and Ravichandran, 'The Idiosyncratic Nature of Sibling ADRs Issued by Mexican Firms'.

[16] Assuming that bondholders will not recognize this ex-ante and demand compensation for the loss of wealth.

company wield substantial power. The outside directors who have no experience in related businesses cannot make meaningful contribution to the company. It is important to appoint competent outside directors to balance the power and let the chief executive be responsible for decision-making. Further, the CEO is the only insider on the board in many companies. This need not necessarily be good for the company. Research shows that companies in which the CEO is the lone insider underperform.[17]

DOES CORPORATE GOVERNANCE MATTER?

Do good governance practices lead to an increase in market value of the firm? One set of studies conducted in the USA finds that the correlation between corporate governance attributes and firm performance is either weak or zero. For example, the proportion of independent directors on a company's board has no significant effect on performance. Likewise, other attributes like institutional shareholding or a firm's committee structure are not correlated with performance. This weak correlation between governance attributes and performance is probably because the differences in practices between firms (in the sample) are negligible. But we would expect the correlation to be much higher in a country where investor protection rights are weak, expropriation by insiders the maximum and so on. A study of correlation between performance and corporate governance in Russia suggests that a one-standard-deviation improvement in governance ranking[18] leads to eightfold increase in firm value, and a worst-to-best improvement in ranking leads to 600-fold increase in firm value.[19] Studies have shown that companies in which management has a stake tend to perform better than those in which it does not.[20] McKinsey surveyed 50 money managers representing about US$850 billion in assets and found they were willing to pay a premium of 11 per cent on average for good governance. Another survey by McKinsey of institutional investors from around the world suggests that investors are willing to pay a premium of up to 28 per cent for good governance.[21]

Some companies have embraced the shareholder wealth maximization philosophy in the recent years. But believing is not the same as achieving. Figure 1.3 presents the market price to book value (P/BV) ratios of stocks of some well-known companies.

If you were to give one buck to Aban Offshore, it was worth 15 paise in July 2018. Why is it that some companies trade below their book values (BVs)? Is it that investors do not recognize the intrinsic value of these companies? Finance theorists argue that stock markets react rationally to corporate strategies at least in the long run.

SHAREHOLDER ACTIVISM

Any large corporation is dependent on a large number of small investors for capital as it is not possible for any single investor or a small group of investors to provide the necessary capital because, by definition, large companies have large requirements. Further, the law in some countries prevents financial

[17] Zorn, Shropshire, Martin, Combs and Ketchen, 'Home Alone'.

[18] The ranking takes into account factors such as transparency, asset stripping, limits on foreign ownership and dilution through share issuance to construct an index.

[19] Black, 'Does Corporate Governance Matter?' Another study in the USA finds that a group of attributes are correlated with firm performance. Gompers, Ishii and Metrick, 'Corporate Governance and Equity Prices'.

[20] Branch, 'Corporate Objectives and Market Performance'.

[21] Coombes and Watson, 'Three Surveys on Corporate Governance'.

institutions (FIs, e.g., banks) from holding equity or cross a certain threshold (e.g., mutual funds are prevented from holding more than a certain percentage of shares in any one company). Due to the wide dispersion of shareholding, no single investor will have an incentive to monitor a company. Since diversification can be achieved by holding a dozen stocks, it is possible for institutional investors to hold a small number of stocks and actively monitor the portfolio companies.

FIGURE 1.3
M/B Ratios of Some Companies

Company	P/BV
Eicher Motors	14.11
Maruti Suzuki	8.20
CESC	0.90
Reliance Infra	0.50
Page Industries	37.46
Aban Offshore	0.15

Source: Money Control (24 July 2018).

Shareholder activism comes from two sources: institutional shareholders and wealthy individuals. Activism may take on two approaches:

- Presenting a proposal at a shareholders' meeting.
- Prod the company's management to change strategy and/or CEO.

Institutional investors discipline erring managers in the USA and now in some parts of Europe. This trend is spreading to other parts of the world. William Browder, the CEO of Hermitage Capital (a foreign institutional investor in Russia), for example, battled against Gazprom's (a Russian company) famously opaque bureaucracy for several years. Gazprom was accused of asset stripping and other irregularities. Is shareholder activism good? I mean does it lead to improvement in performance? The results of academic studies are mixed. One study in the USA reports positive long-term stock price returns to firms targeted by CalPERS, a large state pension plan.[22]

FIRM AND THE FINANCIAL MARKET

A financial market is a market where financial assets are traded. Financial assets are marketable financial claims issued by government and companies. Financial markets enable effective allocation of capital among competing uses. Financial markets perform four important economic functions. First, they enable individuals to choose more effectively between current and future consumption. Borrowing enables individuals to consume more, whereas lending enables them to postpone consumption. The interest rate is the price of exchange. The units that have a surplus of capital invest in those that have a deficit. This provides producers with resources in excess of those generated by income. Second, the interaction between buyers and sellers in a financial market determine the price of a traded asset, say stocks, or alternatively, return demanded by investors to invest in a company. Firms can raise capital if the return on their investment exceeds the return demanded by investors. Third, financial markets provide liquidity to investors, that is, the owner of the asset can sell off the asset in the marketplace to realize cash whenever required. The degree of liquidity may vary according to the nature of the asset and the financial market in question. Fourth, stock markets process the opinion of all market participants and place a value on the company's stock. If you wish to find the value of Hindustan Unilever's (HUL) equity, all you have to do is take out a financial daily, note down the prevailing price of HUL stock and multiply it by the number of outstanding shares. Thus, financial markets aid the process of price discovery. It would be very difficult to assess the performance of companies in the absence of active stock markets.

[22] Nesbitt, S. L., 'Long Term Rewards from Shareholder Activism'.

ARE FINANCIAL MARKETS SHORT-SIGHTED?

A manager is successful if he/she is able to raise the firm's stock price. The problem is that financial markets may not react rationally to corporate actions while setting the stock price. This could be due to non-availability of information or inefficiency of the stock market.

In many countries, the disclosure norms are less than adequate. It is quite possible that managers may not disclose adequate information or provide a biased picture. It is the job of security analysts to unearth information required for fair pricing. The usual argument is that investors and analysts are short-sighted, placing too much weight on current profits and dividends. This obliges managers to cut long-term investments. For, if managers invest in projects without an immediate pay-off, their profits and share price fall. As financial markets are myopic, managers should not pursue 'increase-the-stock-price' rule because long-term value maximization would be subordinated. If financial markets are indeed myopic, we should expect share price to fall when companies announce increases in capital expenditure (Capex). This, in general, does not happen. On the contrary, cuts in capital investments are considered bad news.[23] Perhaps financial markets are not too short-sighted after all. If the markets are not short-sighted, what is the real reason for underinvestment? Most executive incentive systems link rewards to short-term profits. If managers are rewarded on the basis of current profits, they would have little incentive to invest for the long run. There is a popular belief that US companies invest too little in intangible assets and capabilities required for competitiveness because of short-termism on the part of managers, shareholders, lenders and investment managers and the inability of the capital market to deploy capital to most productive uses.[24]

TYPES OF CAPITALISM

Broadly there are two types of capitalism—arm's length system (e.g., US, UK) and relationship-based system (e.g., Germany, Korea). In an arm's length (market-based) Anglo-Saxon system, a financier is protected by explicit contracts as opposed to a relationship-based system, which is largely self-governing; parties honour agreements to maintain their reputation. In market-based system, relationship matters less. In a relationship-based system, the lending bank has a close long-term relationship with the borrower. The lender often belongs to the same group. The *chaebol* in Korea or the *Keiretsu* in Japan exhibit close relationship with their lenders. For long, academicians have argued whether one type of capitalism is better than the other. Until the late 1980s, the East Asian economies were relationship-based systems. The relationship-based system works well when contractability is low and the amount of capital available is low. In other words, relationship-based systems are suitable if legal enforcement and investor protection norms in the country are weak and the amount of capital available relative to opportunities is low. Financiers (banks) in these countries tend to form long-term relationships with business. Over a period of time, many of these countries (e.g., Korea) attracted large amounts of foreign capital to fund opportunities created from opening up of the economy even when the institutional infrastructure was inadequate. The businesses in these countries needed capital, which the foreign investors readily supplied. Korean companies like Daewoo funded much of their investment with debt. The debt ratios of some Korean companies were more than 300 per cent. Most Korean companies had taken on huge amounts of debt to diversify into hi-tech businesses such as computers and telecom. Since the investors from Anglo-Saxon, market-based systems do not find extensive contracting and legal enforcement in these countries, they

[23] Marsh, 'Short Termism'.

[24] Porter, 'Capital Disadvantage'.

tend to lend short so that they can pull out if there is a problem. When the East Asian financial crisis was triggered in the late 1990s due to the depreciation of Thai Baht, Korean investors pulled out leading to a capital shortage. Relationship-based systems are now under attack for being inefficient and corrupt, and everybody is praising the merits of the arm's length system.[25]

ARE FINANCIAL MARKETS EFFICIENT?

News and information reach financial markets every hour of the day. Companies may report higher or lower earnings than what was expected, acquire companies, restructure assets and liabilities and so on. Investors and market intermediaries try to digest the information and price the share consistent with what they heard and understood. But do they react rationally? The Efficient Market Hypothesis (EMH) states that the price of a stock at any given point in time fully reflects all available information relevant to the value of the stock at that time. HUL's share, for instance, according to EMH, should fully reflect at all times the prevailing prospects for India and consumer goods industry as well as the prospects specific to HUL. The share price of HUL should equal its intrinsic value at all times. Is market efficiency a fact? If not, does this invalidate the wealth maximization rule? In other words, is maximization of shareholders wealth a concept that can be operationalized? If shares are undervalued, the managers of a company, acting in the interest of existing shareholders, will not sell stock cheaply. If the company has exhausted its borrowing capacity, the company may have to forgo profitable projects. Likewise, if shares were overvalued, managers would want to sell shares even when the project is unprofitable thereby transferring wealth from new shareholders to old shareholders. Ask any chief executive what he/she considers the stock price to be. Chances are that he/she thinks the stock is underpriced. It is possible that managers may have superior information compared to outside analysts. This does not imply that stock markets do not reward value-maximizing strategies. The difference of opinion between managers and investors is not on whether the company is profitable or not but 'how much profitable' and for 'how long'. The increase or decrease in share price at the time of annual earnings announcements is not due to the short-sightedness of investors. It is merely an indication of revision of investor expectations. Managers will benefit from interacting with prominent analysts and eliciting their views on the company's stock market performance. Even in countries like India, analysts do a fairly good job of price discovery. Financial markets may not be efficient at all times. It is enough if they are frequently efficient.

CONCLUDING COMMENTS

The objective of a firm should not be to make a profit or even maximize profit, increase market share or sales, but to maximize shareholders wealth. But this should not be achieved at the expense of other investor groups. Executives should quit complaining about the rationality of stock markets in pricing securities and work towards a sustainable increase in stock price. In any company of reasonable size, hundreds and thousands of decisions are taken every year. How should one establish a link between corporate decisions and stock prices? Are there some significant decisions, which if handled carefully would lead to increased shareholder value? In the chapters that follow, four major decision areas in corporate finance, namely capital investments, financing, dividend policy and working capital (WC) management, are described. There is plenty of potential for increasing shareholder value by improving project choice, debt and dividend policy, WC decision, and mergers and acquisitions.

[25] Rajan and Zingales, 'Which Capitalism?'

EXERCISES

1. What should be the goal of a governmental organization and that of an NGO?
2. What is the mechanism through which a firm can control managers' tendency to overstate earnings?
3. Put together a list of S&P 500 index companies that have the top performers in terms of shareholder value creation during the last decade. What explains their performance?
4. How can stock market regulators aid shareholder activism?

REFERENCES

Branch, Ben. 'Corporate Objectives and Market Performance'. *Financial Management* (1973 Summer).

Black, Bernard. 'Does Corporate Governance Matter? A Crude Test Using Russian Data, Stanford Law School' (Working Paper No. 209 [Undated]).

Classens, S., S. Djankov and Gerhard Pohl. 'Ownership and Corporate Governance—Evidence from the Czech Republic'. *Public Policy for the Private Sector* (1997 May).

Classens, S., S. Djankov and L. H. P. Lang. 'Who Controls East Asian Corporations?' *Public Policy for the Private Sector* (1999 September).

Coombes, P. and M. Watson. 'Three Surveys on Corporate Governance'. *The McKinsey Quarterly*, no. 4 (2000).

Dhaliwal, D. S., O. Z. Li, A. Tsang and Y. G. Yang. 'Voluntary Nonfinancial Disclosure and the Cost of Equity Capital: The Initiation of Corporate Social Responsibility Reporting'. *The Accounting Review* 86, no. 1 (2011): 59–100.

Drucker, Peter. *The Practice of Management*. New York: Routledge, 2011.

Gompers, P., J. Ishii and A. Metrick. 'Corporate Governance and Equity Prices'. *The Quarterly Journal of Economics* 118, no. 1 (2003): 107–156.

Gong, G., S. Xu and X. Gong. 'On the Value of Corporate Social Responsibility Disclosure: An Empirical Investigation of Corporate Bond Issues in China'. *Journal of Business Ethics* (2016 May).

Hart, Oliver and L. Zingales. 'Companies Should Maximize Shareholder Welfare Not Market Value'. *Journal of Law, Finance and Accounting* 2 (2017): 247–274.

Kaplan, Robert S. and David P. Norton. 'The Balanced Scorecard—Measures that Drive Performance'. *Harvard Business Review* (1992 Jan–Feb).

Kaplan, Robert S. and David P. Norton. 'Putting the Balanced Scorecard to Work'. *Harvard Business Review* (1993 Sep–Oct).

Khanna, T. and K. Palepu. 'Why Focused Strategies May Be Wrong for Emerging Markets'. *Harvard Business Review* (1997 July–August).

Khanna, T. and K. Palepu. 'The Right Way to Restructure in Emerging Markets'. *Harvard Business Review* (1999 July–August).

La Porta R., F. Lopez de Silanes, A. Shleifer and R. Vishny. 'Law and Finance'. *Journal of Political Economy* 106, no. 6 (1998 December).

Marsh, Paul. 'Short Termism'. In *The New Palgrave Dictionary on Money and Finance*, edited by P. Newman, M. Milgate and J. Eatwell. London: Macmillan, 1992.

Nesbitt, S. L. 'Long Term Rewards from Shareholder Activism: A Study of the CalPERS Effect'. *Journal of Applied Corporate Finance* (1994 Spring).

Pinegar, M. and R. Ravichandran. 'The Idiosyncratic Nature of Sibling ADRs Issued by Mexican Firms: A Clinical Study' (Unpublished Working Paper, Northern Arizona University, 2001 May).

Porter, M. E. 'Capital Disadvantage: America's Failing Capital Investment System'. *Harvard Business Review* (1992 Sep–Oct).

Rajan, R. and L. Zingales. 'Which Capitalism? Lessons from the East Asian Crisis'. *Journal of Applied Corporate Finance* 11, no. 3 (1998 Fall).

Shleifer, A. and R. Vishny. 'A Survey of Corporate Governance'. *Journal of Finance* 52 (1997).

The Economic Times, 'Government Issues Preliminary Notices to 272 Companies for CSR Violations'. 24 July 2018.

Zorn, M., C. Shropshire, J. Martin, J. Combs and D. Ketchen. 'Home Alone: The Effects of Lone-Insider Boards on CEO Pay, Financial Misconduct and Firm Performance'. *Strategic Management Journal* 38, no. 13 (2017): 2623–2646.

SUGGESTED READINGS

Anthony, R. 'The Trouble with Profit Maximization'. *Harvard Business Review* (1960 Nov–Dec).

Barclay, M. and C. G. Holderness. 'Private Benefits of Control of Public Corporations'. *Journal of Financial Economics* 25 (1989).

Cornell, B. and A. Shapiro. 'Corporate Stakeholder and Corporate Finance'. *Financial Management* (1987 Spring).

Donaldson, G. 'Financial Goals: Management vs Stockholders'. *Harvard Business Review* (1963 May–June).

Drucker, Peter. 'Business Objectives and Survival Needs'. *Journal of Business* 51 (1958).

Fama, E. and M. C. Jensen. 'Agency Problems and Residual Claims'. *Journal of Law and Economics* 26 (1983).

Friedman, M. 'The Social Responsibility of Business is to Increase Profits'. *New York Times Magazine* (13 September 1970).

Jensen, M. C. and W. Meckling. 'Theory of the Firm: Managerial Behavior, Agency Costs and Ownership Structure'. *Journal of Financial Economics* 3, no. 4 (1976).

Jensen, M. C. and W. Meckling. 'Reflections on the Corporation as a Social Invention'. *Midland Corporate Finance Journal* (1983 Fall).

Jensen, M. C. 'Agency Costs of Free Cash Flow, Corporate Finance and Takeovers'. *American Economic Review* 76, no. 2 (1986).

Jensen, M. C. 'Value Maximization, Stakeholder Theory, and the Corporate Objective Function'. *Journal of Applied Corporate Finance* 14, no. 3 (2001 Fall).

La Porta, Rafael, Florencio Lopez de-Silanes and Andre Shleifer. 'Corporate Ownership Around the World'. *Journal of Finance* 54 (1999).

Lewellen, Wilbur. 'Management and Ownership in the Large Firm'. *Journal of Finance* (1969 May).

Piper, Thomas R. and William E. Fruhan Jr. 'Is Your Stock Worth Its Market Price?' *Harvard Business Review* (1981).

Rappaport, Alfred. 'Stock Market Signals to Managers'. *Harvard Business Review* (1987 Nov–Dec).

Rappaport, Alfred. 'CFOs and Strategists: Forging a Common Framework'. *Harvard Business Review* (1992 May–June).

Shleifer, A. and R. Vishny. 'Large Shareholders and Corporate Control'. *Journal of Political Economy* 94 (1986).

Sundaram, Anant and Andrew Inkpen. 'The Corporate Objective Revisited' (Working Paper, Thunderbird, American Graduate School of Management, 2001, October).

Treynor, Jack L. 'The Financial Objective in the Widely Held Corporation'. *Financial Analysts Journal* (1981 March–April).

William, Oliver E. 'Corporate Finance and Corporate Governance'. *Journal of Finance* (1988 July).

Woolridge, J. R. 'Competitive Decline: Is a Myopic Stock Market to Blame'. *Journal of Applied Corporate Finance* 1 (1988).

Zingales, L. 'The Value of the Voting Right: A Study of the Milan Stock Exchange'. *Review of Financial studies* 7 (1994).

Zingales, L. 'What Determines the Value of Corporate Votes?' *Quarterly Journal of Economics* 110, no. 4 (1995): 1047–1073.

Zingales, L. 'Corporate Governance'. In *The New Palgrave Dictionary of Economics and the Law*, edited by Law, P. Newman. New York: Macmillan, 1998.

CHAPTER

2

Time Value of Money

LEARNING OBJECTIVES

- Calculate the future value (FV) of a single cash flow at a given interest rate
- Calculate present value (PV) of a single cash flow occurring at some point in time in the future
- Calculate the FV of a series of cash flow
- Calculate the PV of a series of cash flow
- Compare interests quoted on a different basis
- Prepare loan amortization schedule

Consider the following situations:

- You expect a liability of ₹100,000 in five years and you wish to know how much you should set aside today to meet the liability.
- Your car dealer offers you two schemes—A and B. Under the first scheme, you can borrow the entire amount at an interest rate of 15 per cent. Under the second scheme, the car dealer gives a discount of 10 per cent on the sticker price but the interest charged on the amount borrowed would be 19 per cent. You have to decide on the scheme.
- You come across advertisements inserted by two banks in a daily. Bank A offers 13 per cent interest per annum on deposits. Bank B offers 12 per cent semi-annual interest. You have to choose between these banks.

These are some of the financial decisions that you may have to take in your personal or executive life. This chapter answers questions such as why is a rupee available today not the same as a rupee available in the future; what amount should you set aside today so as to receive a specified amount in the future; when can you be indifferent between some amount available today and some amount available in the future.

BASIS FOR TIME VALUE OF MONEY

Intuitively, a cash flow available in the future is worth less than a similar cash flow today for several reasons:

Inflation: Due to inflation, the value of money decreases over time. The higher the inflation, the lower is the value.

Preference for Current Consumption: Individuals prefer current consumption to future consumption. So they have to be offered more in the future to give up current consumption.

Riskiness of the Cash Flow: The uncertainty of the cash flow reduces the value of the cash flow. The higher the uncertainty, the lower is its value of today.

Lastly, money can be invested profitably in some productive activity. In short, money has time value. A rupee available now cannot be compared with a rupee available, say, a year from now.

FUTURE VALUE AND COMPOUND INTEREST

Let us suppose you deposited ₹1,000 in ICICI Bank for one year and the bank pays 13 per cent interest.

$$\text{Interest} = ₹0.13 \times 1{,}000 = ₹130$$

$$\text{Amount at the end of 1 year} = \text{Principal} + \text{Interest}$$

$$= ₹(1{,}000 + 130) = ₹1{,}310$$

It is easy to see that the value of investment after one year = Initial investment × (1 + r) where r is the interest rate in decimal form.

Now, if you wish to keep the balance in the bank, the principal for the second year would be ₹1,310 (and not 1,000) and interest would be paid on this amount.

$$\text{Interest for the second year} = ₹0.13 \times 1{,}310 = ₹170.30$$

$$\text{Amount at the end of second year} = ₹(1{,}310 + 170.30) = ₹1{,}480.30$$

An investment of ₹1,000 grew to ₹1,310 in one year and ₹1,480.30 in two years. The amount available at the end of the investment horizon is called future value (FV) and the process of multiplying the investment is called compounding. Note that the interest earned in the first year also earned interest in the second year.

In general,

$$\text{FV of an amount} = \text{Amount } (1 + r)^n \qquad (1)$$

where r is the interest rate

n is the investment horizon

The term $(1 + r)^n$ is called Future Value Interest Factor or FVIF. It is the value of ₹1 interest at r per cent after n years. The FV of an amount A at the end of 1, 2, 3, …, n years is shown as follows:

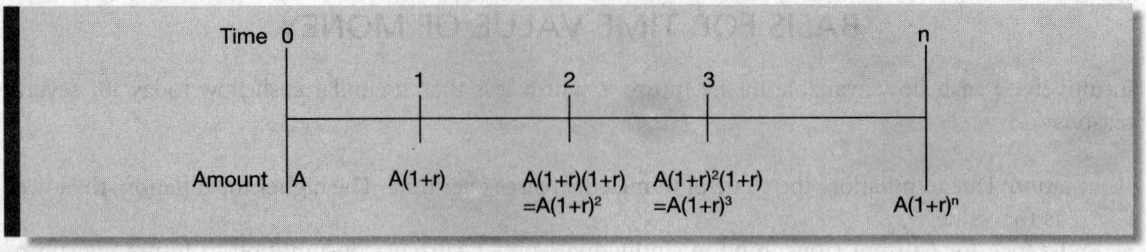

An investment 'A' made now grows to A $(1+r)$ in 1 year; $A(1+r)^2$ in two years; $A(1+r)^3$ in three years and so on.

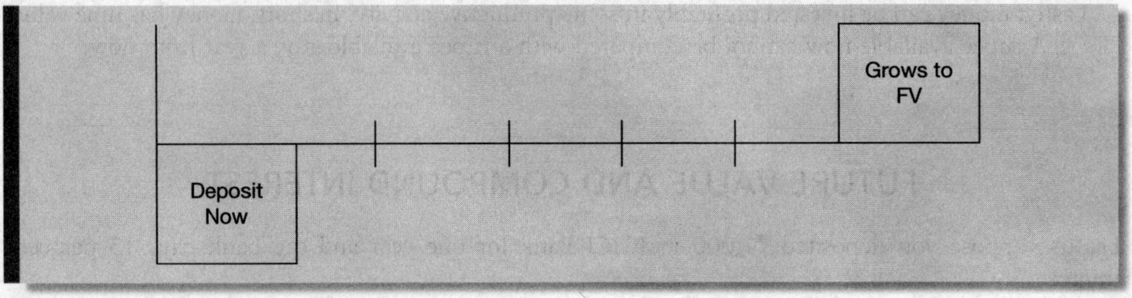

AN ILLUSTRATION

Suppose you open a bank account with ₹5,000. The bank pays 9 per cent interest per annum. What would be the account balance at the end of six years? Eigth years?

$$\text{Balance at the end of 6 years} = ₹5{,}000\ (1.09)^6 = ₹8{,}385.50$$
$$\text{Balance at the end of 8 years} = ₹5{,}000(1.09)^8 = ₹9{,}963$$

The concept of compounding could be used in several other areas. Here's one.

The current production of Steel Company of India is 3 million tons. The output is expected to grow at 8 per cent per annum. The output would grow to $3(1.08)^5 = 4.4$ million tons in five years. The annual growth rate is called compound growth rate. In the bank example, we calculated the interest on the outstanding balance and not on the original principal of ₹1,700. We assumed that interest receipts would also be reinvested. If interest were to be calculated on the original principal year after year, the amount would not compound. The interest in this case is called simple interest. Whenever we say interest, it is compound interest that we have in mind and not simple interest.

PRESENT VALUE

We saw that ₹100 grows to ₹108 at an interest rate of 8 per cent in one year. Let us do the reverse now. How much do we need to set aside today in order to produce ₹108 a year from now? The amount is referred to as present value (PV) of ₹108.

$$FV = A(1+r)^n$$

$$A = \frac{FV}{(1+r)^n}$$

that is,

$$PV = \frac{FV}{(1+r)^n} \quad (2)$$

The process of bringing a cash flow to the present is called 'discounting' and the rate of interest is called 'discount rate'. The discount rate is a rate at which PVs and FVs are traded off. The term $[1/(1+r)^t]$ is called Present Value Interest Factor or PVIF.

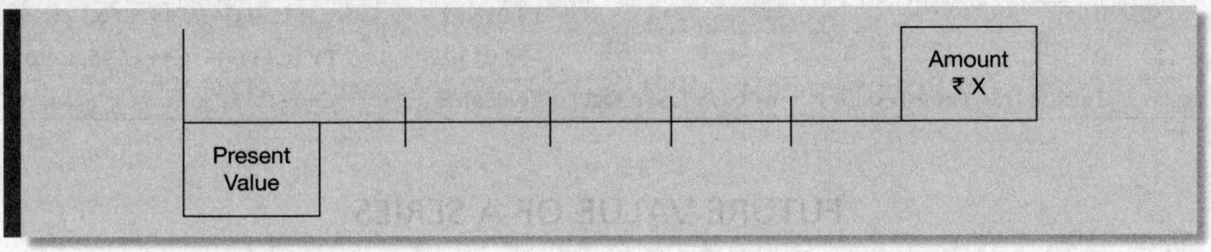

AN ILLUSTRATION

Let us suppose the second year fees for the MBA programme (which you are pursuing, say) is ₹45,000 and is not expected to change. The interest rate is 10 per cent.

$$PV = ₹[45,000/(1.10)] = ₹40,909$$

Now try discounting ₹1,000 available five years from now at 8 per cent.

$$PV = ₹[1,000/(1+0.18)^5] = ₹681$$

Another example is in order. ₹5,000 invested in a savings scheme grows to ₹10,000 in six years. The implicit interest rate, $r = ₹[(10,000/5,000)^{1/6}] - 1 = 0.122 = 12.2\%$.

A Spreadsheet Example[1]

How much would we have to invest today if we wish to accumulate ₹150,000 in 18 years (e.g., for daughter's education) if we can earn an annual interest rate of 4 per cent compounded daily?

[1] In Appendix 2A.2, we have provided a glossary of excel functions.

The solution is given as follows:

C43	'Annual Interest Rate'=Discount Rate (term used when doing PV calculations)=i	4.00%	
C44	No. of Compounding Periods per Year=n	365	
C45	Years=x	18	
C46	FV	150,000.00	
C47	Period Payment=PMT		
C48	Period Rate=i/n	0.000109589041	C43/C44
C49	Total Periods=n×x	6,570	C44×C45
C50	(1+i/n)^(n×x)	2.054352166	(1+C43/C44)^(C44×C45)
C51	0	73,015.72	C46/C50
C52	0	73,015.72	C46/ (1+C43/C44)^(C44×C45)
C53	0	–73,015.72	PV (C43/C44, C44×C45, C46)
C54	Total Interest Earned=Cash Put In–Cash Taken Out	76,984.28	C46+C53

FUTURE VALUE OF A SERIES

Till now we calculated the PV or FV of a single amount at some interest rate for some time period. Consider the following situation. You invest ₹500 today, ₹1,000 at the end of first year and ₹1,500 at the end of second year. You are required to find the FV at the end of second year. Assume 8 per cent interest. The FV of this series is nothing but the sum of FVs of each cash flow shown as follows:

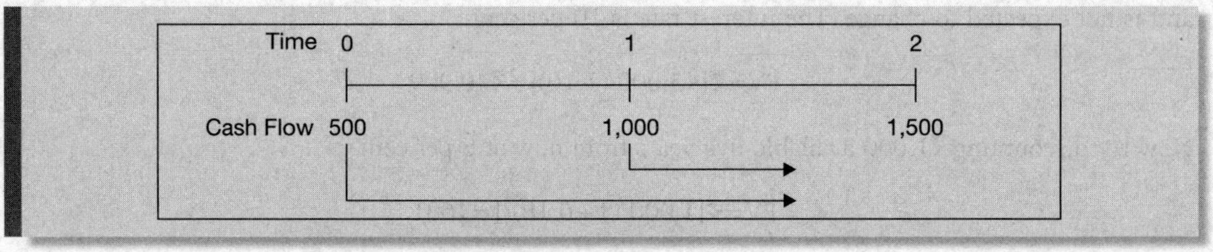

$$FV = FV \text{ of } ₹500 + FV \text{ of } ₹1{,}000 + ₹1{,}500$$

Note that 1,500 itself is the FV of the cash flow occurring at the end of second year.

$$\begin{aligned} FV &= ₹500\,(1.08)^2 + 1{,}000(1.08) + 1{,}500 \\ &= ₹500 \times FVIF_{8,2} + 1{,}000 \times FVIV_{8,1} + 1{,}500 \\ &= ₹3{,}163 \end{aligned}$$

What would happen to the FV if the cash flow were to occur at the beginning of the year? Beginning of year one is same as year zero (i.e., today) and beginning of year two is same as end of year one. The cash flow would be

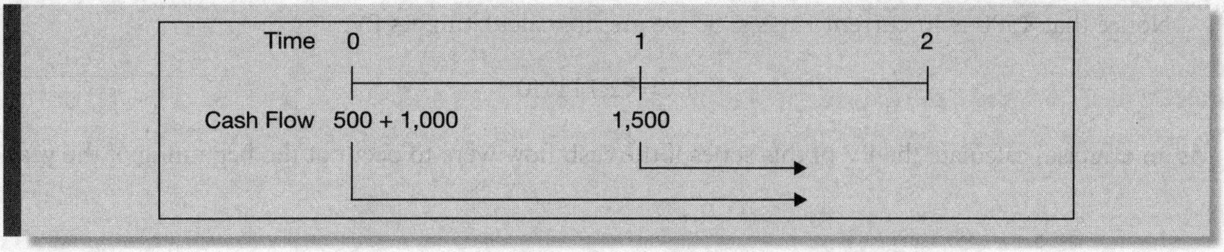

$$FV = ₹(500 + 1,000)(1.08)^2 + (1,500 \times 1.08) = ₹3,369$$

It should be clear by now that the time interval between two cash flows considered so far have been exactly one year and cash flows cannot be aggregated across years. But they can be moved to any particular year and then added.

A SPREADSHEET EXAMPLE

If you put ₹50 (PMT) in the bank each month for 50 years, how much will you have when you retire?

This exercise can be worked out using MS Excel. The solution is given as follows:

Periodic Payment ₹	50.00	PMT	Formula
Years	50		
# Compounding Periods per Year	12		
Annual Interest Rate	0.1		
Period Rate	0.008333333	Rate	B5/12
Total Periods	600	NPER	B3 × B4
FV ₹	866,219.54	FV	FV(B6, B7, –B2, 0)

PRESENT VALUE OF A SERIES

Consider the same cash flows again. The PV of this series is the sum of PVs of each of these cash flows.

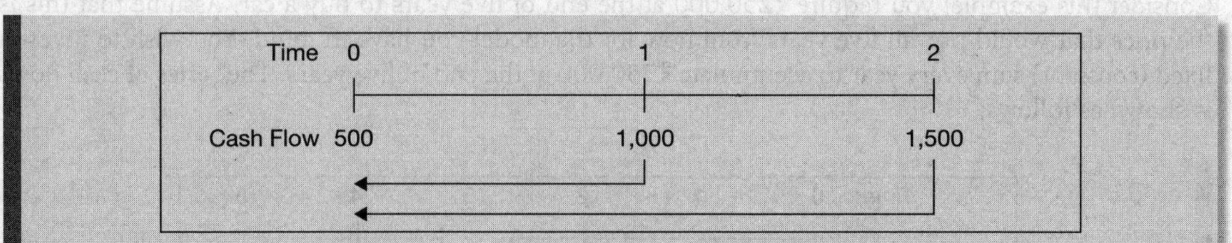

$$PV = 500 + \frac{1000}{1.08} + \frac{1500}{(1.08)^2}$$

Notice that ₹500 is in current rupees. So we are not calculating its PV.

PV=₹2,711.50

As an exercise, calculate the PV of this series if the cash flow were to occur at the beginning of the year.

A SPREADSHEET EXAMPLE

You have ₹7,500 balance in your credit card. If the annual percentage rate is 18 per cent and the minimum monthly amount is ₹125, how long will it take to pay off the credit card if you pay only the minimum amount?

The solution is given as follows:

Balance=	7,500.00	
APR=	18.00%	
Periods per Year	12	
Minimum Monthly PMT=	–125.00	
NPER=NPER Function=	154.6541086	NPER(B3/B12, B5, B2, 0)
Years=NPER/12	12.88784238	B6/B12

TYPES OF CASH FLOWS

Cash flows can exhibit different patterns. In the earlier example, the periodic amounts are different and the series had a finite life. A series of periodic flows of equal amounts is called an 'annuity' and a series of periodic flows of equal amounts but with an infinite life is called a 'perpetuity'. Thus, investing or receiving ₹500 as dividends forever is a perpetuity.

FUTURE VALUE OF AN ANNUITY

Consider this example; you require ₹250,000 at the end of five years to buy a car. Assume that this is the price that would prevail five years from now for the model you have in mind. You wish to invest a fixed (constant) sum every year to accumulate ₹250,000 at the end of five years. The series of cash flows is shown as follows:

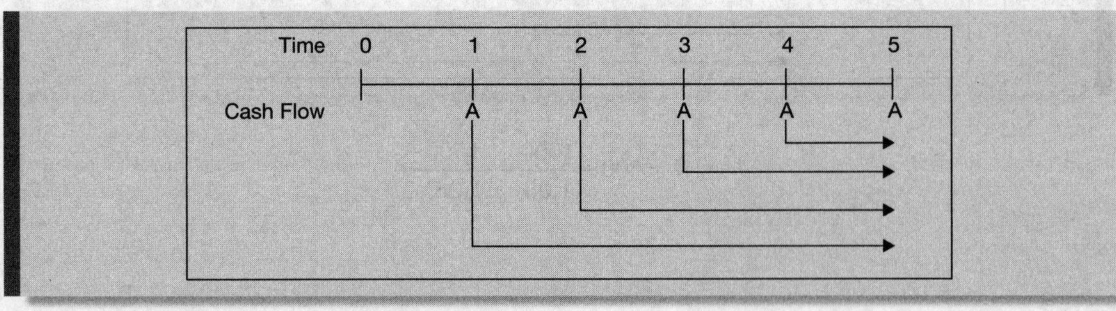

The FV of an annuity for a period of n years at a rate of interest r is given by

$$FVA_n = A\left[\frac{(1+r)^n - 1}{r}\right] \quad (3)$$

where

A = amount invested at the end of every year for n years
r = rate of interest in decimal form
n = time period in years

$$\text{The term in the brackets} = \frac{(1+r)^n - 1}{r}$$

is called the Future Value Interest Factor of an Annuity or FVIFA. It is the FV of an annuity of ₹1 for various values of r and n.

PRESENT VALUE OF AN ANNUITY

The PV of an annuity 'A' receivable at the end of each year for a period of n years at an interest rate of r is given by:

$$PVA_n = A\left[\frac{(1+r)^n - 1}{r(1+r)^n}\right] \quad (4)$$

$$\text{The term in the bracket} \left[\frac{(1+r)^n - 1}{r(1+r)^n}\right]$$

is called Present Value Interest Factor of an Annuity or PVIFA. It is the PV of an annuity of ₹1 for the given values of r and n. The PVIFA for 8 per cent and two years is 0.857. It should be noted that PVIFA is not the reverse of FVIFA although PVIF is the reverse of FVIF. Also, the cash flows in all the cases occur at the end of the year.

AN ILLUSTRATION

On 31 December, you buy a car for ₹200,000 paying 20 per cent up front and agreeing to pay the balance in five equal annual instalments. The rate of interest is 15 per cent.

$$\text{Amount payable} = ₹0.8 \times 200{,}000 = ₹160{,}000$$
$$PVA_n = A[PVIFA_{r,n}]$$
$$A = [160{,}000/3{,}352] = ₹47.73269$$

Sometimes annuities grow at a constant rate. Retirement and pension benefits, for example, increase every year with a cost of living adjustment. The PV of a series of growing annuity can be estimated using the following equation:

$$PV = \frac{A(1+g)}{r-g}\left[1-\frac{(1+g)^n}{(1+r)^n}\right]$$

If A = ₹6,600, r = 5%, n = 30 periods, g = 3.5%

PV = ₹154,251

LOAN AMORTIZATION

Consider an example similar to the previous example. Assume that you have borrowed ₹1 million from a FI at an interest rate of 14 per cent per annum. The loan is to be cleared in equal annual instalments.

Annual instalment = ₹1 million/PVIFA (14,5)

= ₹1 million/3433 = ₹291.290

This instalment contains interest and principal components. The principal is retired partially every year and the interest is paid on the outstanding balance. The loan amortization schedule is presented in Table 2.1.

TABLE 2.1
Loan Amortization Schedule

Year (1)	Annual Instalment ₹ (2)	Interest Component ₹ (3)	Principal Component ₹ (4)=(2)−(3)	Loan Outstanding ₹ (5)
1	291,290	140,000	151,290	1,000,000
2	291,290	118,819	172,470	848,710
3	291,290	94,673	196,616	676,239
4	291,290	67,147	224,142	479,622
5	291,290	35,767	255,500*	255,480*

Note: *These two figures do not coincide due to rounding off errors.

Working

Interest for 1st year = ₹0.14 × 1 million = ₹140,000

Principal Component for 1st year = Annual instalment − Interest for 1st year

= ₹151,290

Loan outstanding for 1st year	=₹1 million
Loan outstanding for 2nd year	=₹ (1 million − Loan repaid) = ₹1 million − 151,290
	=₹848,710
Interest for 2nd year	=₹0.14 × 848,710 = ₹118,819
Principal component	= Annual instalment − interest for 2nd year
	=₹291,190 − 118,819 = ₹172,371

All other entries could be similarly worked out.

AN ILLUSTRATION: MAKING SENSE OF HOUSING LOANS

Assume that you are in the process of borrowing ₹1 million to construct a house. The repayment period is 15 years. Bank A charges 14 per cent annually. Bank B charges 14.5 per cent. Verify that equated 'monthly' instalment is ₹13,600 for Bank A and ₹14,000 for Bank B. A 0.5 per cent reduction in interest will save ₹400 every month or ₹4,800 a year and ₹72,000 by the time the loan is cleared. Interest rates on housing loans are calculated either on a monthly reducing or an annual reducing basis. In the former case, interest is computed on the reducing outstanding balance on a monthly basis, whereas in the latter case, interest is levied on the annual principal, which reduces annually.

HDFC charges 15.5 per cent per annum on a ₹1 million loan and GIC Housing Finance 16.5 per cent.[2] On the face of it, HDFC is cheaper. However, since GIC HF calculates its interest on a monthly reducing basis, the EMI for a five-year loan works out to ₹24,585, against ₹25,200 for HDFC which calculates interest on an annual reducing basis.

NOMINAL AND EFFECTIVE RATES

In all the examples considered so far, compounding was done annually. This may not be true of all situations. For instance, a fixed deposit scheme may offer quarterly compounding, whereas a car dealer may quote an interest rate on a monthly basis. How should we compare interest rates that are quoted for different periods? Let us look at an example. A car dealer offers two schemes—A and B. Under the first scheme, you have to pay an interest of 12 per cent compounded monthly and under the second scheme you have to pay an interest of 12 per cent compounded annually. You are required to choose between the two. It is necessary to convert both of them into same basis. There is a simple formula to do this: $(1+\text{annual rate})=(1+\text{monthly rate})^{12}$.

For the first scheme, the annual rate is 12 per cent. So the rate per month is 12/12 = 1 per cent.

Substitute in the previous equation:

$$(1+\text{annual rate})=(1+0.01)^{12}$$
$$\text{Annual rate}=12.68\%$$

[2] This is a fictitious example.

From the example, it must be clear that the shorter the compounding period, the higher is the interest rate. The rate quoted on an annual basis (12%) is the simple annual rate and the rate that considers more frequent compounding is called the effective rate (12.68% in the previous example).

In general,

$$\text{Effective rate} = [1 + (r/m)]^m - 1 \tag{5}$$

where r is the nominal annual rate
m is the number of times compounding is done in a year

As an exercise, calculate the effective rate in the previous example when compounding is done daily, quarterly and semi-annually.

Let us present the idea a little bit. The following data are available for a fixed deposit scheme.

Investment = ₹5,000
Rate of interest = 13%
Compounding = Semi-annual
Term = 5 years

The FV would be

$$FV = A[1 + (r/m)]^{m \times n} \tag{6}$$

where n is the number of years.

$$FV = 5{,}000[1 + (0.13/2)]^{2 \times 5} = ₹9{,}385$$

Had the compounding been annual,

$$FV = ₹5{,}000(1 + 0.13)^5 = ₹9{,}212$$

The difference of ₹(9,385 − 9,212) or ₹173 is due to semi-annual compounding.

PERPETUITIES

Some investments make a regular income forever. Let us suppose the dividend per share (DPS) of company X is ₹2. It is expected to remain at this level forever (the firm is a going concern). If the appropriate discount rate is 13 per cent, the PV of this perpetual stream = (₹2/0.13) = ₹15.40.

In general,

$$\text{PV of a perpetuity} = \text{Periodic amount/Discount rate}$$
$$PV = A/K \tag{7}$$

If an amount is to grow at a constant rate forever, it is called a growing perpetuity. The PV of a growing perpetuity can be estimated using the following formula.

$$PV=\frac{A}{k-g}$$

where k is the discount rate and g is the growth rate.

CONCLUSION

1. Money has time value. It is to be explicitly recognized in financial analysis.
2. A rupee available today is more valuable than a rupee available sometime in the future because
   a. individuals prefer current assumption for future consumption
   b. of inflation
   c. of uncertainty in realization of future cash flows
3. A series of cash flows may be uneven or even. In the latter case, when the amount is the same, the series is called an annuity.
4. The PV of an uneven series of cash flows is the sum of the PVs of individual amounts.

$$PV(CF)_t=PV(CF_1)+PV(CF_2)+\cdots+PV(CF_n)$$

5. The PV of an annuity

$$PV(CF)=A\times[PVIFA_{r,n}]$$

6. The FV of an uneven series of cash flows is the sum of FVs of individual amounts.

$$FV(CF)=FV(CF_1)+FV(CF_2)+\cdots+FV(CF_n)$$

7. FV of an annuity $=A[FVIFA_{r,n}]$
8. PV of an amount is the discounted value at the given discount rate.
9. FV of an amount is the compounded value at the given compound rate.

APPENDIX 2A.1: DERIVATION OF FV OF AN ANNUITY (CASH FLOWS OCCUR AT THE END OF EACH PERIOD)

Let
A = constant periodic cash flow
r = interest rate
n = duration of the annuity
FVA_n = FV of an annuity
PVA_n = PV of an annuity

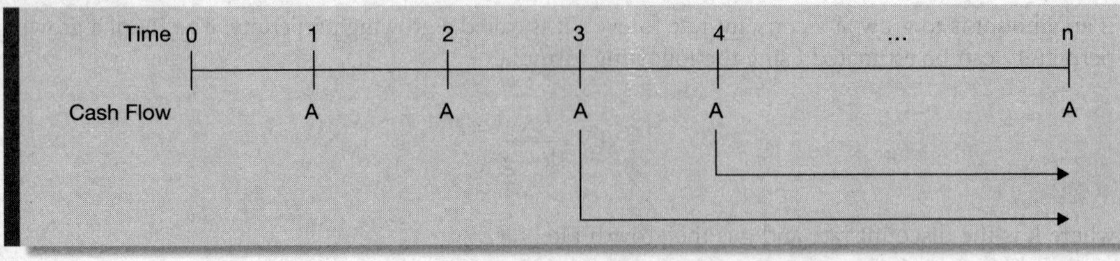

$$FVA_n = A(1+r)^{n-1} + A(1+r)^{n-2} + \cdots + A \tag{2A.1}$$

Multiply both sides of the equation by $(1+r)$

$$FVA_n\,(1+r) = A(1+r)^n + A(1+r)^{n-1} + \cdots + A(1+r) \tag{2A.2}$$

Subtract Equation (2A.1) from (2A.2):

$$FVA_n \cdot r = A(1+r)^n - A$$
$$FVA_n \cdot r = A\,[(1+r)^n - 1]$$
$$FVA_n \cdot r = A\left[\frac{(1+r)^n - 1}{r}\right]$$

Derivation of PV of an annuity (cash flows occur at the end of the period)

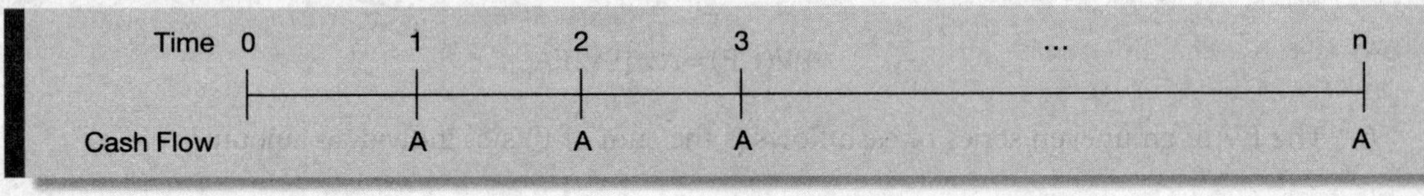

$$PVA_n = \frac{A}{(1+r)} + \frac{A}{(1+r)^2} + \cdots + \frac{A}{(1+r)^n} \tag{2A.3}$$

Multiply both sides of the equation by $(1+r)$

$$PVA_n(1+r) = A + \frac{A}{(1+r)} + \cdots + \frac{A}{(1+r)^{n-1}} \tag{2A.4}$$

Subtract Equation (2A.3) from (2A.4):

$$PVA_n \cdot r = A - \frac{A}{(1+r)^n}$$
$$PVA_n \cdot r = A\,[1 - \{1/(1+r)^n\}]$$
$$PVA_n \cdot r = A\left[\frac{(1+r)^n - 1}{(1+r)^n}\right]$$
$$PVA_n \cdot r = A\left[\frac{(1+r)^n - 1}{(1+r)^n \cdot r}\right]$$

Derivation of FV of an annuity when cash flows occur at the beginning of the period.

$$FVA_n = A(1+r)^n + A(1+r)^{n-1} + \cdots + A\,(1+r) \tag{2A.5}$$

Divide Equation (2A.5) by $(1+r)$

$$\frac{FVA_n}{(1+r)} = A(1+r)^{n-1} + A(1+r)^{n-2} + \cdots + A \tag{2A.6}$$

Subtracting Equation (2A.6) from (2A.5), we get

$$FVA_n\,[1-\{1-(1+r)\}] = A(1+r)^n - A$$

that is, $r/(1+r) \cdot FVA_n = A[(1+r)^n - 1]$

$$FVA_n = A\left[\frac{(1+r)^n - 1}{r}\right](1+r)$$

Note that the FVA of this series is FV of regular annuity multiplied by $(1+r)$

Derivation of PV of an annuity (cash flows occur at the beginning of the period).

$$PVA_n = A + \frac{A}{(1+r)} + \frac{A}{(1+r)^2} + \cdots + \frac{A}{(1+r)^{n-1}} \tag{2A.7}$$

Multiply both sides by $(1+r)$

$$\frac{PVA_n}{(1+r)} = \frac{A}{(1+r)} + \frac{A}{(1+r)^2} \cdots + \frac{A}{(1+r)^n} \tag{2A.8}$$

Subtract Equation (2A.7) from (2A.8):

$$PVA_n\left[1-\{1/(1+r)\}\right] = A - \frac{A}{(1+r)^n}$$

$$PVA_n\left[r/(1+r)\right] = A\left[\frac{(1+r)^{n-1}}{(1+r)^n}\right]$$

$$PVA_n = A\left[\frac{(1+r)^{n-1}}{r(1+r)^n}\right](1+r)$$

$$= \text{Present Value of a regular annuity Y } (1+r).$$

APPENDIX 2A.2: GLOSSARY OF EXCEL FINANCIAL FUNCTIONS

PMT function:

PMT function calculates the period payment for a loan (for the borrower or the lender).

Each PMT must be the same.
Time period between each PMT must be the same.
Interest rate must remain constant.

PMT function arguments:

rate=period rate (month, quarter, yearly and so on)
NPER=total number of periods
PV=amount of loan on the day it is issued (PV of future cash flows)
FV=value of loan on last day (balloon payment)
type=
End=omitted=1=payment at end of period
Begin=0=payment at beginning of period

Cash flow matters in finance:

Cash going out of the wallet is negative.
Cash coming into the wallet is positive.
PMT function Cash Flows:
For the borrower, the PV is positive, the PMT is negative and the FV is negative.
For the lender, the PV is negative, the PMT is positive and the FV is positive.

Be consistent with your unit of time!

If you are calculating monthly payment, you need monthly interest rate and total number of months!
The period can be monthly, quarterly, yearly or of any other length.

FV function:

Calculates the FV of an investment for either a lump sum or a savings plan.

Interest rate must remain constant.
Each PMT must be the same.
Time period between each PMT must be the same.

FV arguments:

rate=period rate (month, quarter, yearly and so on)
NPER=total number of periods
PMT=equal periodic payments
PV=amount of loan on the day it is issued (PV of future cash flows)
type=
End=omitted=1=payment at end of period
Begin=0=payment at beginning of period

RATE function:

Calculates the period rate.

Each PMT must be the same.

Time period between each PMT must be the same.

Interest rate will remain constant.

RATE arguments:

NPER=total number of periods

PMT=equal periodic payments

PV=amount of loan on the day it is issued (PV of future cash flows)

FV=value of loan on last day (balloon payment)

type=

End=omitted=1=payment at end of period

Begin=0=payment at beginning of period

NPER function:

Calculates the total number of periods.

Each PMT must be the same.

Time period between each PMT must be the same.

Interest rate must remain constant.

NPER arguments:

rate=period rate (month, quarter, yearly and so on)

PMT=equal periodic payments

PV=amount of loan on the day it is issued (PV of future cash flows)

FV=value of loan on last day (balloon payment)

type=

End=omitted=1=payment at end of period

Begin=0=payment at beginning of period

Concept Test

State whether the following statements are true (T) or false (F).

1. A series of periodic cash flows of equal amounts occurring at the end of each period is called an annuity.
2. The inverse of PVIF factor is FVIF factor.
3. The PV of a series of cash flows occurring at the beginning of the year is the same as that occurring at the end of the year.

4. The amount that must be set aside periodically to accumulate a stated amount in the future is called sinking fund.
5. Nominal rate of interest=Effective rate when compounding is done annually.
6. PVIFA/PVIF=FVIFA

EXERCISES

1. The current earnings per share (EPS) of the Hindustan Engineering Company is ₹3.80. Analysts expect it to grow at an annual rate of 8 per cent. What will be the EPS in 5 years?
2. You have the option of a lump sum today as against an annuity of ₹3,000 for 8 years. How large will the lump sum have to be to make you indifferent between the options if current interest rates are 12 per cent?
3. You know that the following liabilities must be satisfied:

Year from Now	Liability (₹ million)
1	2
2	3
3	4
4	5

How much should be invested today to satisfy this stream? You can earn an annual interest rate of 11 per cent on your investments.
4. Production target for 1997=5 million tons
Current production (for 1991)=2 million tons
What is the implied growth rate?
5. What annual percentage rate is equal to 12 per cent compounded monthly?
6. Suppose you open a savings account with ₹1,500. The account's stated interest rate is 12 per cent. Calculate the account's balance after two years if interest is paid (a) annually, (b) semi-annually and (c) quarterly.
7. You need ₹150,000 at the end of 15 years. You decide to make equal annual payments into a bank account. Current interest rate is 11 per cent (compounded annually). The first payment is to be made at the end of the first year.
   a. What must be your annual payment to meet your need?
   b. How would your answer change if the payments are made at the beginning of the year?

c. Instead of making annual payments if you were to decide to make a single payment today, how high should the lump sum be?

8. Your company has established a sinking fund to meet an obligation of ₹800,000 coming due in 10 years. If the fund can earn 10 per cent a year, what annual contributions must be made to accumulate the amount?
9. Bank A pays 13 per cent interest compounded annually on deposits. Bank B pays 12 per cent compounded monthly. In which bank would you prefer to deposit your money?
10. High Land Financial Services Company offers loans at an annual rate of 10 per cent. If the interest is compounded monthly, what is the effective rate?
11. You notice an advertisement by No Bank which claims that your money will double in six years. What is the implied interest?
12. You have taken a 30-year loan for ₹300,000. The annual interest on the loan is 12 per cent. Estimate your yearly payments.
13. Find the PV of the series. Discount rate = 10 per cent.

Year	Amount (₹)
1–5	125,000
6–10	28,000
11–15	136,000

14. You are 55 years old and expect to work for five more years saving ₹125,000 a year. Appropriate interest rate = 10 per cent.
    a. If you wish to withdraw ₹75,000 a year for the following 15 years, how much would you need in the bank five years from now?
    b. What is its current worth?
    c. If you already have ₹200,000 in your bank account, what would be your bank balance when you retire?
    d. From the above calculated bank balance, how much cash can you withdraw for 10 years?
    e. If current earnings are ₹250,000, how much of your income would you need to save each year for the next five years in order to be able to withdraw ₹75,000 a year for five years after retirement?
15. Find the FV of the following series at the end of fifth year at 13 per cent interest.

Year	Cash Flow (₹)
1	100
2	200
3	300
4	400

16. Find the PV of the cash flows at 13 per cent interest.

Year	Cash Flow (₹)
1	—
2	20,000
3	—
4	900

CHAPTER 3

Risk and Return

LEARNING OBJECTIVES

- How to measure security return for single and multi-periods
- The difference between risk for a single asset and a portfolio of assets
- The relationship between risk and return
- The intuitive reasoning behind the capital asset pricing model (CAPM)
- The competitors to CAPM

In Chapter 1, I pointed out that allocating capital to projects is one of the key decisions that a finance manager has to take. Conventional wisdom suggests that managers would want to maximize returns. At the same time, they may not want to take undue risk. This chapter is devoted to the exposition of risk and its relation to expected return from a shareholder's perspective. The company's perspective is just the mirror image.

MEASURING RETURN

Suppose an investor purchased 100 shares of a company at ₹120, received dividends amounting to ₹600 during the year and sold the shares at ₹140 at the end of the year. The rate of return an investor receives from buying shares and holding them for a given period of time is equal to the cash dividends received plus the capital gain (or minus the capital loss) during the holding period divided by the purchase price of the security.

Expressed as a formula, realized return

$$R = [D_1 + (P_1 - P_0)]/P_0 \qquad (1)$$

Where D_1 = Dividend received
P_1 = Selling price
P_0 = Purchase price

The rate of return on the investment = ₹ [((140 − 120) × 1,000)) + 600]/12,000 = 21.6%

Now consider a multi-period situation. The investor has a three-year investment horizon.
Purchase price = ₹200
Dividend receipts = ₹5, ₹6 and ₹10, respectively
Selling price = ₹225

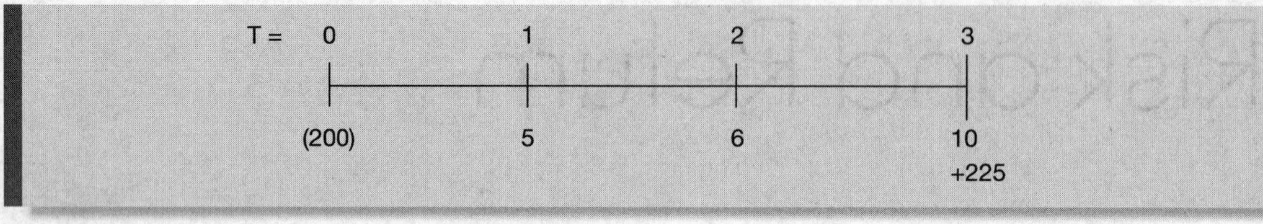

One measure of return is the arithmetic average of returns in these three years.

$$R = [R_1 + R_2 + R_3]/3$$

Where R is the investment return and R_1, R_2 and R_3 are periodic returns.

Another measure is the geometric mean of returns.

$$R_g = [(1+R_1)\ (1+R_2)\ (1+R_3)]^{1/3} - 1$$

In general, the geometric mean of returns

$$R_g = [(1+R_1)\ (1+R_2)\ (1+R_3) \ldots\ (1+R^N]^{1/N} - 1 \qquad (2)$$

In the equation, N is the number of periods. In the example, the investor had a three-year horizon. The holding period could be in months as well, say, January, February and March. The principle remains the same except that the rate of return will have to be converted to an annual rate. Table 3.1 presents the returns from all the Sensex stocks.

MEASURING PORTFOLIO RETURN

The return on a portfolio of stocks, as opposed to a single stock, could be written as

$$R_p = [D_p + (V_1 - V_0)]/V_0 \qquad (3)$$

Where R_p = Portfolio return
D_p = Dividend receipts
V_1 = Value of the portfolio at the end of the period
V_0 = Value of the portfolio at the beginning of the period

To illustrate, if an investor were to purchase shares of RIL, Colgate Palmolive and HUL at ₹1 million and sell them when the value of the portfolio is ₹1.2 million, the return on the portfolio (ignoring dividends) is:

$$(1.2 - 1)/1 = 20\%$$

TABLE 3.1
Annualized Real Returns on Major Asset Categories Around the World, 1990–2000 (%)

Country	Equities	Bonds	Bills
Australia	7.5	1.1	0.4
Belgium	2.5	–0.4	–0.3
Canada	6.4	1.8	1.7
Denmark	4.6	2.5	2.8
France	3.8	–1.0	–3.3
Germany	3.6	–2.2	–0.6
Japan	4.5	–1.6	–2.0
The Netherlands	5.8	1.1	0.7
Spain	3.6	1.2	0.4
Sweden	7.6	2.4	2.0
UK	5.8	1.3	1.0
USA	6.7	1.6	0.9

Source: Dimson, Marsh and Staunton, *Triumph of the Optimists*.

The previous formula is based on the assumption that the investor does not withdraw any portion of initial investment or inject fresh investment during the period or the dividend receipts are not reinvested. If any of these occur, the formula may have to be suitably modified. The portfolio return in case of a multi-period situation may be written as

$$V_0 = [D_1/(1+r)^1] + [D_2/(1+r)^2] + \cdots + [(D_N + V_N)/(1+r)^N] \quad (4)$$

where $D_1, D_2, \ldots, D_N$ are dividend receipts, V_0 and V_1 are values of portfolio at the beginning and end of the holding period. The rate r that equates cash inflows and cash outflows is the return on the portfolio. The concept is similar to the yield to maturity (YTM) of a bond.[1] The calculation is based on the assumption that dividend receipts are reinvested at r per cent. Although the previous example considers a stock portfolio, the concept can be extended to portfolio of other assets as well.

MEASURING RISK

Investors buy shares in anticipation of a particular return but the fluctuation in stock prices result in fluctuating returns. Therefore, shares are considered risky. As the returns from government securities such as treasury bills do not deviate from their expected returns, they are considered risk free. Financial theory defines risk as the possibility that actual returns will deviate from expected returns. The degree of potential fluctuation determines the risk. More specifically, the risk in holding a security is the

[1] YTM is the rate that equates periodic coupon receipts and principal repayments and the market price of the bond. YTM is explained later in the chapter on debt markets.

variance in expected returns. The variance in returns measures the disparity between actual and expected returns. Modern finance theory hypothesizes that investors choose securities on the basis of expected return and standard deviation (SD; square root of variance). Given a choice between two investments with the same expected return, an investor would choose the investment with lower SD. Two such investments are shown in Figure 3.1. Investment B is preferable as its variance is lower.

The mean and SD of returns of a few stocks are presented in Table 3.2. The past realized return is taken as a proxy for future expected returns. Obviously, forecast will almost never be accurate. So we need a measure of upside potential and downside risk. The variance of returns is supposed to measure how uncertain our forecast is. It is the breadth of the distribution of returns. In short, an investor is supposed to think of future returns as a probability distribution. The variance of such a distribution is the measure of risk. Another measure of variability is the square root of the variance—the SD. Note that the distribution of returns shown in Figure 3.1 is normal, that is, the upside potential and downside risk are of the same magnitude. In real-life situations, returns from securities may not be normal. To simplify, we assume normality.

One good thing about normal distribution is that it can be described with only two parameters—mean and SD. The SD captures both upside potential and downside risk. But the investor is considered with only the former. The downside risk is simply half the total variability. Hence, measuring SD serves our purpose. The annualized real returns on equities, bonds and bills in different countries is presented in Table 3.1.

TABLE 3.2
Mean and Standard Deviation of Daily Returns of Some Stocks, April 2016–March 2017

Axis Bank	0.026	1.81
Sun Pharmaceutical	–0.08	1.60
Bajaj Auto	0.05	1.29
Facebook	0.0015	0.01
Apple	0.001	0.011

FIGURE 3.1
Mean and Standard Deviation of Returns of Two Investments

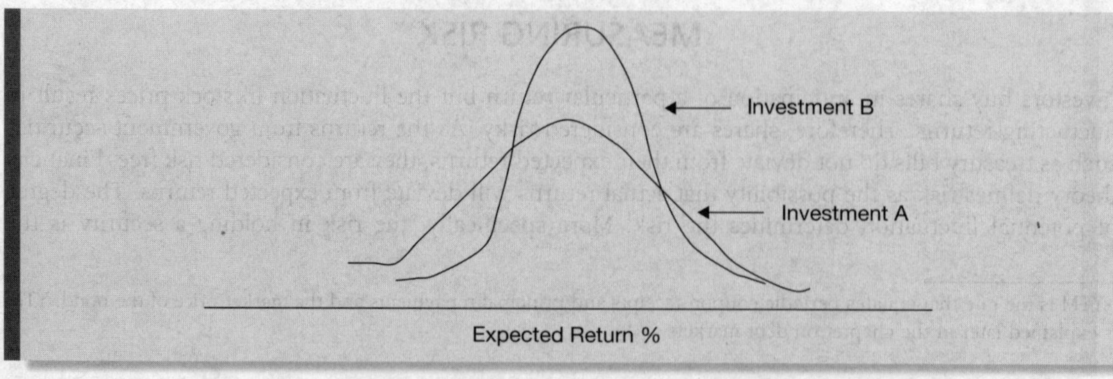

Notice that equities have outperformed bonds and bills in virtually every country. The annual stock returns in the USA is 6.7 per cent versus 1.6 per cent for bonds and 0.9 per cent for bills. That is not the end of the story. The SD of annual stock returns is usually more than that for bonds or bills, which suggests that returns are in line with risk.

TYPES OF RISK

The previous data suggest that the riskier the asset class, the greater the return. The argument is that investors are compensated with a risk premium for holding riskier securities. This relation does not hold true for the Sensex stocks. A scatter plot is displayed in Figure 3.2. This scatter plot does not indicate a positive relation between the mean monthly return and SD as would be suggested by the risk premium hypothesis. Some of the risk investors assume is specific to the individual stocks in their portfolio; for example, a company's earnings may come down due to a strike. On the other hand, because stock prices and returns move in tandem to some extent, even investors holding widely diversified portfolios are exposed to the risk inherent in the overall performance of the stock market. So the security's total risk can be divided into 'unsystematic risk', the portion specific to the company or a small group of assets, which can be diversified away, and 'systematic risk', the non-diversifiable portion that is related to the movement of the stock market.

$$\text{Total Risk} = \text{Unsystematic Risk} + \text{Systematic Risk}$$

FIGURE 3.2
Risk and Return of Sensex 30

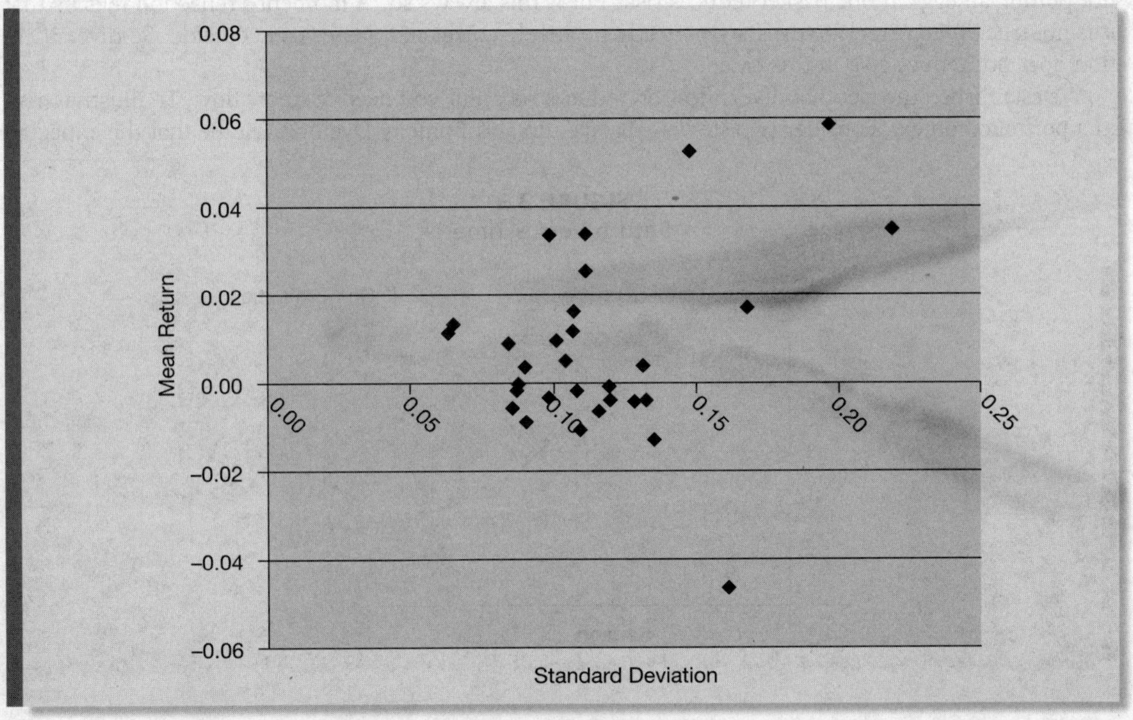

Examples of unsystematic risk factors are: a lower cost foreign competitor unexpectedly enters a company's product market or a labour unrest disrupting production in the company. Examples of systematic risk factors are: increase in long-term interest rates, RBI stepping up its restrictive monetary policy.

MEASURING PORTFOLIO RISK

The risk of a portfolio of securities is not the sum of variances of returns of individual securities. To demonstrate risk in a portfolio context, consider a primitive economy where there are only two firms—one makes umbrella and the other, sun tan lotion. Let us suppose the returns from these two stocks follow a cyclical pattern as shown in Figure 3.3.

The return from holding shares of both companies is the weighted average of returns from the two stocks.

$$R_p = \sum_{i=1}^{n} M_i R_i \qquad (5)$$

where X_i = proportion of money invested in asset i

R_i = expected return of asset i

But the risk of the portfolio is not the sum of individual variances. It would be smaller than that of holding individual stocks. As shown in Figure 3.3, the investor is 'assured' of return (the dashed horizontal line) however volatile individual stocks may be due to negative correlation between the returns. The returns from one stock exactly counterbalance the returns from the other stock. As the cliché goes, not putting all eggs in one basket reduces risk. But is this always so? A moment's reflection tells us that it is not true. When stock returns are perfectly positively correlated, losses can coincide. So diversification does not reduce risk in this case.

We established the fact that diversification reduces risk. But you need to know how. To illustrate risk in a portfolio context, consider two stocks—Bajaj Auto and Bombay Dyeing. Assume that the expected

FIGURE 3.3
Return Versus Time

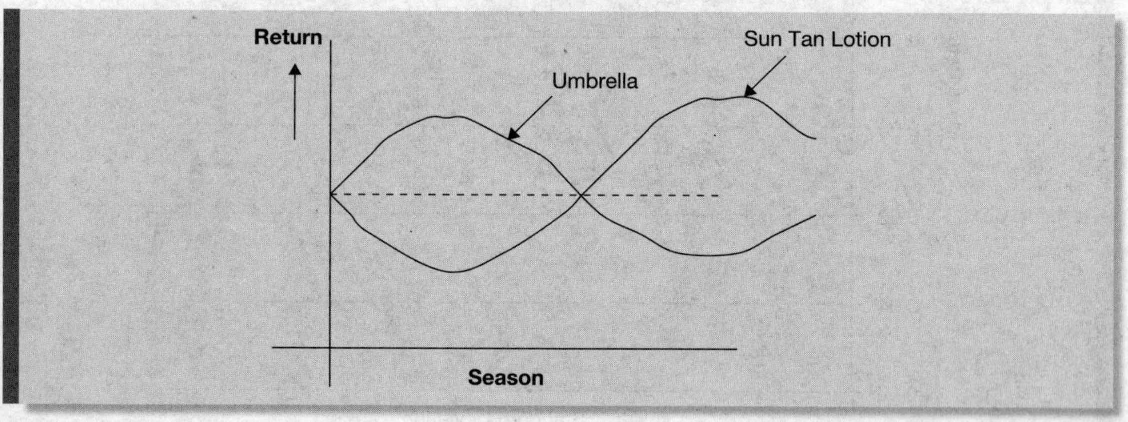

annual returns are 21.48 per cent and 16.56 per cent, respectively. Suppose that you invest 60 per cent of your initial investment in Bajaj Auto and 40 per cent in Bombay Dyeing.

$$\text{Expected Portfolio Return} = (0.6 \times 21.48) + (0.4 \times 16.56)$$
$$= 19.5\%$$

The SD of past returns is 18 per cent and 27 per cent, respectively. The portfolio variance is 'not' the weighted average of individual variances.

Portfolio variance,

$$\sigma_p^2 = X_1^2 \times \sigma_1^2 + X_2^2 \times \sigma_2^2 + 2X_1 \times X_2 \times Cov_{12} \tag{6}$$

where X_1 = Proportion of money invested in stock 1
X_2 = Proportion of money invested in stock 2
σ_1 = SD of returns from stock 1
σ_2 = SD of returns from stock 2

The portfolio SD is the square root of Equation (6). Note the third term in the equation. Covariance is a measure of the extent to which the two stocks covary. A positive covariance suggests that the returns (prices) move in the same direction and a negative covariance indicates that prices move in opposite direction most of the time.

$$Cov\ (1, 2) = \rho_{12} \times \sigma_1 \times \sigma_2$$

where ρ_{12} is the correlation coefficient

Three situations suggest themselves.

Situation 1: The stock returns are perfectly positively correlated, that is, ρ_{12} is 1.

$$\sigma_p^2 = (0.6 \times 18)^2 + (0.4 \times 27)^2 + 2 \times 0.6 \times 0.4 \times 1 \times 18 \times 27$$
$$= 466.56$$
$$\sigma_p = 21.6\%$$

Situation 2: ρ_{12} is –1

$$\sigma_p^2 = 116.64 + 116.64 - 233.28 = 0$$

Yes! The portfolio variance is 0. But it is unlikely that you will find perfectly negatively correlated stocks in real life.

Situation 3: ρ_{12} is less than 1 (say 0.5)

$$\sigma_p^2 = 349.92$$
$$\sigma_p = 18.7\%$$

Negative or less than perfect correlation (covariance) reduces the risk of the portfolio, positive covariance does not.

We have arbitrarily chosen 60 per cent and 40 per cent as weights. Suppose we alter it to 50 per cent and 50 per cent. Let ρ_{12} be 0.3.

$$\begin{aligned}\sigma_p^2 &= (0.5\times 18)^2+(0.5\times 27)^2+2\times 0.5\times 0.5\times 0.3\times 18\times 27\\ &= 336.15\\ \sigma_p &= 18.3\%\\ E(R_p) &= (0.5\times 21.48)+(0.5\times 16.56)\\ &= 19.02\%\end{aligned}$$

We can construct a large number of portfolios with different weighting schemes. But is there one best portfolio that minimizes portfolio variance?

$$\begin{aligned}\sigma_p^2 &= X_1^2\times\sigma_1^2+X_2^2\times\sigma_2^2+2X_1\times X_2\times Cov_{12}\\ &= X_1^2\times\sigma_1^2+(1-X_1)^2\times{\sigma_2}^2+2X_1\times(1-X_1)\times\rho_{12}\times\sigma_1\times\sigma_2\end{aligned}$$

Differentiating the previous equation with respect to X_1 and equating to zero

$$\begin{aligned}\delta\sigma_p^2\ \delta X_1 = 2X_1\times\sigma_1^2+(2X1-2)\ \sigma_2^2+2\rho_{12}\times\sigma_1\times\sigma_2\\ -4X_1\rho_{12}\times\sigma_1\times\sigma_2=0\end{aligned}$$

Solving for X_1

$$X_1=[\sigma_2^2-\rho_{12}\times\sigma_1\times\sigma_2]/[\sigma_1^2+\sigma_2^2-2\rho_{12}\times\sigma_1\times\sigma_2]$$

In the previous example,

$$\begin{aligned}\sigma_1 &= 18\%\\ \sigma_2 &= 27\%\\ \rho_{12} &= 0.3\end{aligned}$$

On substitution, we get $X_1=76\%$ and $X_2(=1-X_1)=24\%$

AN ILLUSTRATION

Figure 3.4 presents the average portfolio (weekly) return and SD for various compositions of HUL and Colgate Palmolive stocks. The correlation between the returns from the two stocks is 0.5. The portfolio variance is the least when 60.40 per cent of the money is invested in HUL stock. The portfolio variance decreases at a faster rate than the portfolio return in line with our expectation.

	HUL	Colgate
Average Weekly Return (%)	0.974	0.073
SD (%)	4.012	4.463
Covariance	8.743	
Correlation Coefficient	0.0493	

THREE ASSET AND N-ASSET PORTFOLIOS

The variance of a three-asset portfolio can be written as:

$$\sigma_p^2 = X_1^2 \times \sigma_1^2 + X_2^2 \times \sigma_2^2 + X_3^2\ \sigma_3^2 + 2X_1 \times X_2 \times Cov_{12} + 2X_2 \times X_3 \times Cov_{23} + 2X_1 \times X_3 \times Cov_{13}$$

where X_i are weights; σ_i^2 are variances.

Similarly, for an N-asset portfolio:

$$\sigma_p^2 = \Sigma\ \Sigma\ X_i\ X_j\ \sigma_1\ \sigma_j\ \sigma_{ij}$$

There are gains from diversification. But how large should the portfolio be? In other words, how many stocks should an investor hold before marginal costs exceed marginal benefits of diversification? As the number of assets in the portfolio increases, the variance of the portfolio approaches the covariance or the average systematic risk of the stocks, that is, unsystematic risk is diversified away. The marginal benefits from diversification diminish beyond a certain limit. Most textbooks conclude that 10 to 12 stocks are adequate to reap the benefits of diversification. The marginal costs (like transaction and information costs) offset the gains from diversification thereafter. For instance, Statman[2] shows that for a borrowing investor at least 30 stocks are required and for a lending investor at least 40 stocks are required. When one plots the distribution of historical returns of a diversified portfolio (e.g., 100 stocks) and compares it with the distribution of returns of a single security, one finds that the SD of returns of a single stock is much more than that of the portfolio; yet the average return of the stock is lower than that of the portfolio. What does this imply? Does the market not reward the higher risk of a stock with higher returns? The answer lies in the benefits of diversification.

FIGURE 3.4
Portfolio Return and Risk

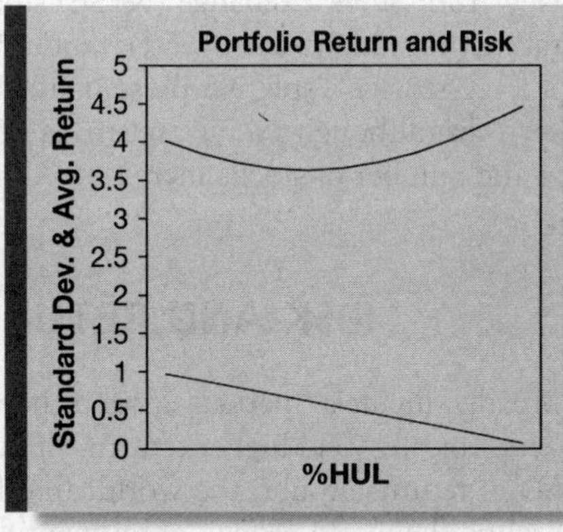

HUL (%)	Colgate (%)	Portfolio Std. Deviation (%)	Portfolio Return (%)
100	0	4.012	0.974
90	10	3.848	0.884
80	20	3.728	0.794
70	30	3.654	0.704
60	40	3.63	0.614
50	50	3.657	0.524
40	60	3.734	0.433
30	70	3.857	0.343
20	80	4.023	0.253
10	90	4.227	0.163
0	100	4.463	0.073

[2] Statman, 'How Many Stocks Make A Diversified Portfolio?'

TABLE 3.3
Effect of Diversification on Risk

No. of Stocks	Average Monthly Return (%)	SD (%) per Month
1	0.88	7.0
2	0.69	5.0
3	0.74	4.8
4	0.65	4.6
5	0.71	4.6
10	0.68	4.2
15	0.69	4.0
20	0.67	3.9

Realized returns will be more in line with systematic risk rather than risk. Wagner and Lau[3] divided 200 New York Stock Exchange (NYSE) stocks into six subgroups based on standard and poor stock quality rating (from highest to lowest); randomly selected portfolios from each of the subgroups containing from 1 to 20 stocks. Table 3.3 presents the average monthly returns and SD for the first subgroup. It can be seen that although average return is unrelated to the number of stocks in the portfolio, the SD declines as the number of stocks increases. Almost 40 per cent of risk can be eliminated by holding 20 stocks.

RISK AND RETURN: THE INTERNATIONAL EVIDENCE

Broadly, financial markets around the world can be classified as developed or emerging. Emerging markets typically yield higher returns. But their SD is higher as well. Table 3.4 presents the mean returns and SD of returns around the world. International investors have the option of investing in securities from around the world. A major argument for investing internationally is that it increases profit opportunities while providing risk diversification. Just as investors can diversify away unsystematic risk by holding a portfolio of stocks, they may also benefit from international diversification. As long as there are benefits from international diversification, a portion of what seems to be systematic risk in a domestic context may be diversifiable country risk at a global level. If markets are completely integrated, there would be no benefit from international diversification. Although the tendency of markets to move together has increased in the recent years, the correlation is still less than 1 (Table 3.5). So there are still opportunities to reduce risk. In other words, portfolios may be formed out of stocks from many countries to reduce risk further. As an assignment, construct an equal value-weighted portfolio of Japan and Germany.

MARKOWITZ MODEL

Modern portfolio theory is based on the premise that an investor chooses from all possible investments on the basis of expected portfolio return and portfolio variance. If an investor is rational, he/she will

[3] Wagner and Lau, 'The Effect of Diversification on Risk'.

TABLE 3.4
Characteristics of Emerging and Developed Markets

Country	Standard Deviation (%)	Mean Return Annualized (%)
Emerging Markets		
Argentina	93.1	42.0
Brazil	64	33.1
Colombia	31.4	39.7
India	29.5	17.4
Indonesia	30.8	3.3
Mexico	46.5	20.8
The Philippines	37.4	42.9
Developed Markets		
Australia	26.6	15.1
Canada	19.6	9.7
Germany	22.4	14.1
Japan	25.1	17.8
Switzerland	19.2	14.2
UK	21.5	16.4
USA	15.0	14.8

Source: Erb, Harvey and Viskanta, 'Expected Returns and Volatility in 135 Countries'.

TABLE 3.5
Global Correlations

Country	Correlation
USA/UK	0.67
Canada/Switzerland	0.59
Japan/Germany	0.34
Italy/France	0.69
India/Singapore	–0.18
Sweden/South Africa	0.35
Finland/Denmark	0.34

choose that investment which provides the highest return for a given level of risk or the least risky investment for a given level of return. Thus, these 'efficient' portfolios dominate other combinations. The curved line that connects all the efficient portfolios is called efficient frontier. Figure 3.5 depicts an efficient frontier.

Investment B is superior to Investment A as it offers higher return for the same level of risk. Similarly, Investment C is superior to Investment A as it offers the same return for lower level of risk. But how does an investor choose among the efficient portfolios? That depends on the risk-taking ability of the investor. To calculate the variance of a two-stock portfolio, we need individual variances and correlation between the stock returns. As the number of assets in the portfolio increases, the number of inputs increases considerably. For an N-asset portfolio, we would need N (N−1)/2 correlation estimates. This is the drawback of the Markowitz model.

FIGURE 3.5
Efficient Frontier

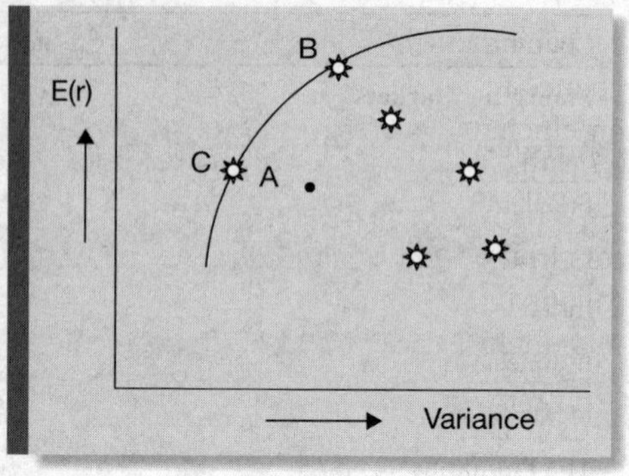

THE CAPITAL ASSET PRICING MODEL

The capital asset pricing model (CAPM) is an extension of Markowitz portfolio theory. The Markowitz technique involves too many calculations. The CAPM, on the other hand, tries to correlate the returns from the stock with a market index rather than with other stocks. For instance, for a portfolio of 30 stocks, we would have calculated 30 SDs and 30×29/2 correlations under the Markowitz technique but only 30 SDs and 30 correlations with the market under the latter technique. Both the methods help delineate efficient portfolios. The beauty is that both give same results.

FIGURE 3.6
Capital Market Line

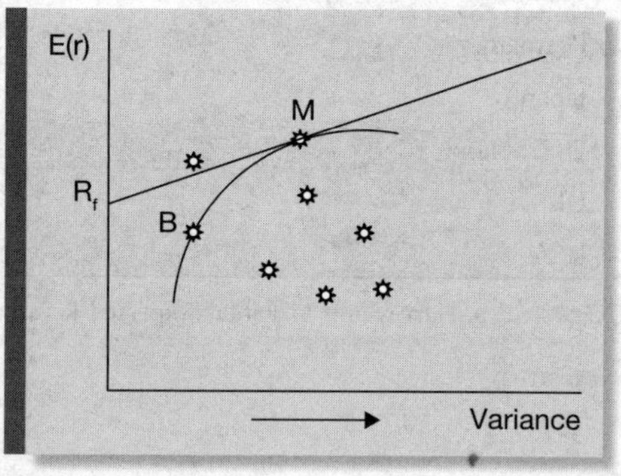

INTRODUCING RISKLESS LENDING

Suppose an investor has identified an efficient portfolio. Let us call it M. Further, the investor has the opportunity to invest in a risk-free asset. He/she can choose to invest in M or in the risk-free asset or in some combination. We can think of investing in risk-free asset as lending at risk-free rate (buying government securities). So the investor can take any position on the line R_f-M as shown in Figure 3.6. Note that the line is tangential to the efficient frontier meaning that the portfolio M gives the highest return per unit of risk.

All the points on the line R_f M are combinations of investment in risk-free asset and M. You might be wondering how or why this risk-free asset is significant. Let us go back to the two-stock portfolio case.

$$\sigma_p^2 = X_1^2 \times \sigma_1^2 + X_2^2 \times \sigma_2^2 + 2X_1 \times X_2 \times Cov_{12} \tag{7}$$

where X_1 = Proportion of money invested in risk-free asset
X_2 = Proportion of money invested in portfolio M
σ_1 = SD of returns from risk-free asset
σ_2 = SD of returns from M

By definition, the variance of returns from riskless asset is zero and the returns do not covary with the returns from other assets. So the first and the last terms become zero.

$$\sigma_p^2 = X_2^2 \times \sigma_2^2$$
$$= (1 - X_1)^2 \times \sigma_2^2$$

As is evident, by investing partly in a risk-free asset, the investor can reduce the risk further. Given a chance to invest in a riskless asset, an investor would always hold a combination of R_f and M, and not an efficient portfolio alone. The combinations yield higher returns for the same level of risk as shown in Table 3.6. In short, the efficient frontier has been transformed into a straight line.

What could be the 'composition' of M? If the investor has superior information vis-à-vis other investors in the market, then M is that portfolio which offers superior returns for its risk level (i.e., the portfolio is undervalued). Otherwise, it is that portfolio which any other investor can hold. The logical limit is to include all risky assets in the economy. The portfolio of all risky assets is called the market portfolio. Since the market portfolio is unobservable, a market index such as the BSE 30 index is taken as a proxy. The line joining R_f and M is called capital market line (CML).

DERIVING THE CAPITAL MARKET LINE

The expected return of a portfolio consisting of the risk-free asset and M,

$$R_p = X_1 R_f + X_2 E(R_M) \quad (8)$$

That is,

$$R_p = (1 - X_2) R_f + X_2 E(R_M)$$
$$= R_f + X_2 [E(R_M) - R_f] \quad (9)$$

We know that

$$\sigma_p^2 = X_2^2 \times \sigma_M^2$$

Or

$$\sigma_p = X_2 \times \sigma_M$$
$$\text{that is, } X_2 = \sigma_p / \sigma_M$$

Inserting in Equation (9)

$$= R_f + \sigma_p / \sigma_M [E(R_M) - R_f]$$

This is the equation for the CML. The slope of the line is given by

$$[E(R_M) - R_f] / \sigma_M$$

This is the market risk premium. It was pointed out earlier that the total risk consists of two components—systematic and unsystematic risk. Unsystematic risk can be diversified away by holding a portfolio of securities; what remains is the systematic risk. As well diversified investors are exposed to only systematic risk, the relevant risk in a CAPM universe is the systematic risk. Beta (β) is the standard measure of systematic risk. It measures the tendency of the returns of a security to move in line with the stock market as a whole. β gauges the sensitivity of security returns vis-à-vis market returns. A stock with a β of 1.0 rises and falls at the same percentage as the market. Stocks with a β greater than 1.0 (aggressive stocks) tend to rise and fall by a greater percentage than the market, that is, they are very sensitive to market swings. Stocks with β less than 1.0 (defensive stocks) are less sensitive to market swings. The market, by definition, has a β of 1.0.

$$\beta = [\text{Cov } R_j, R_m]/\sigma_M^2$$

Estimates of β for the Sensex stocks are presented in adjacent table.

Beta Estimates for Some BSE Stocks

Company	β
Divi's Lab	0.809
Asian Paints	0.067
Yes Bank	1.2
Escorts	1.72
Mahindra & Mahindra	0.865

SECURITY MARKET LINE

The CAPM establishes the relationship between risk and expected return. In a CAPM world, securities are priced such that

$$R_j = R_f + \text{Risk Premium}$$
$$R_j = R_f + \beta[E(R_M - R_f)]$$

This relationship between risk and expected return is called the security market line (SML). The risk premium of a security is a function of the risk premium on the market, $R_M - R_f$, and varies directly with β. The higher the β, the higher the expected return.

$$\text{Expected Return} = E(R) = R_f + \text{Amount of Risk} \times \text{Market Price of Risk}$$

In a financial market described by CAPM, no security can sell for long at prices low enough to yield more than its appropriate return on the SML. The security would then be very attractive compared with other securities of similar risk and investors would bid its price up until its expected return fall to the appropriate position on the SML. Conversely, investors could sell off any stock selling at a price high enough to put its expected return below its appropriate return. To reiterate, security return can be divided into components: one dependent, and the other independent of market return.

$$\text{Security Return} = \text{Systematic Return} + \text{Unsystematic Return}$$

Systematic return can be measured by multiplying the market return and the β of the stock.

The CAPM is based on certain assumptions:

- Investors make choices on the basis of risk (i.e., variance) and return
- Investors have homogeneous expectations of risk and return
- Investors have identical time horizons
- Information is freely available to investors
- There is a risk-free asset and investors can borrow and lend at risk-free rate
- There are no taxes or transaction. costs

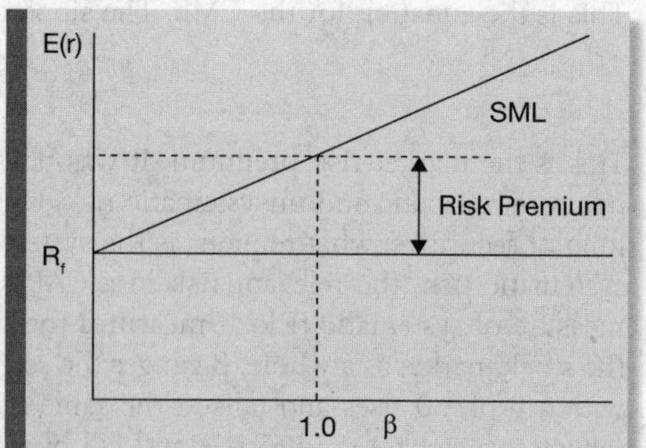

Application of CAPM in Fund Performance Measurement

Mutual fund managers would routinely want to measure the performance of a stock. To do the same, they will have to compare the stock's performance with the expected return. Assume that a stock's one-year return is 12 per cent. Is this adequate? We can answer this question only by comparing with the return on a benchmark stock market index. Assume that the stock has a β of 1.2 and the index return for the same period is 10 per cent. Although the raw return is more than that from the index, the β adjusted return (1.2 × index return) exactly equals the index return. In other words, the stock did as well as the index.

Another measure of security performance is the Jensen's alpha. The standard procedure for estimating β is to regress stock returns against market returns.

$$R_j = a + bR_m \tag{10}$$

where a = intercept from the regression
b = slope = β of the stock

The intercept of the regression provides a simple measure of performance during the period of the regression relative to CAPM.

$$\begin{aligned} R_j &= R_f + \beta(R_M - R_f) \\ &= R_f(1-\beta) + \beta R_m \end{aligned} \tag{11}$$

Thus, a comparison of the intercept (a) to $R_f(1-\beta)$ provides a measure of performance relative to CAPM (Jensen's alpha).

If $a > R_f(1-\beta)$, stock did better than expected during the period.
$a = R_f(1-\beta)$, stock did as well as expected.
$a < R_f(1-\beta)$, stock did worse than expected.

Jensen's alpha, thus, measures the difference between the actual returns on an asset and the return expected from it during the period.

DO INDIVIDUAL INVESTORS HOLD DIVERSIFIED PORTFOLIOS?

Studies conducted in the USA indicate that typical investor's stock portfolio contains only a small fraction of the available securities and the number of stocks in a portfolio range from 9 to 12. Why do investors forgo the benefits of diversification? Is it because they do not know the benefits of diversification? What does under diversification imply for pricing of risky financial assets? Some academicians observe that due to under diversification, even unsystematic risk may be priced in markets. Investors might not hold diversified portfolios; it is enough if they price securities as though they are diversified. This reinforces CAPM.

IS THERE A RISK-FREE ASSET?

Investors hold assets in anticipation of returns from them. The actual return may deviate from the expected return. The variance in actual return from the expected is the risk in holding that asset. For an asset to be risk free, the actual return from the asset should always be equal the expected return. For instance, an investor may buy a T-bond that promises to pay 12 per cent. Since sovereign governments are usually free of default risk, the actual return will be 12 per cent. For an asset to be classified as risk free, the first qualification is that it should be free of default risk. Even the highest rated companies will have some default risk in them. This precludes them from being classified as risk free. The second qualification is that the asset should not have any reinvestment risk. Reinvestment risk arises from reinvesting coupon payments at rates below that prevailed at the time of buying. To illustrate, if interest rates decline from 10 per cent to 8 per cent after buying, the investor can reinvest coupon payments only at 8 per cent. So he will not realize the YTM promised at the time of issue. For this reason, even treasury securities cannot be considered risk free.

SOME OBSERVATIONS ON RISK PREMIUM

The risk premium, $R_m - R_f$, is usually estimated by looking at the historical premium earned by stocks over government bonds over long periods (over 60 years in the case of the USA). In India, however, due to non-availability of data, 25-year period is used. The historical risk premium is used as proxy for the future. Table 3.6 presents the risk premium for countries around the world.

Some countries have low and some countries have negative risk premium. What factors affect risk premium? Why is the risk premium high in some countries? Can we expect future equity premium to be high as well? Can we predict short term (say, one month) and long term (say, 30 years) of equity premium?

TABLE 3.6
Risk Premium for Select Countries

Country	Annual Equity Return (%)	Bond Return (%)	Risk Premium (%)
Australia	8.47	6.99	1.48
Canada	8.98	8.30	0.68
France	11.51	9.17	2.34
Germany	11.30	12.10	–0.8
Italy	5.49	7.84	–2.35
Japan	15.73	12.69	3.04
Singapore	15.48	6.45	9.03
Hong Kong	20.39	12.66	7.73
Switzerland	13.49	10.11	3.38
UK	12.42	7.81	4.61

Several factors (such as the following) might affect risk premium.

Extent of Globalization: Due to increasing globalization of companies, the reliance on any one nation is decreasing leading to reduced sensitivity of economies and hence systematic risk. The flip side is that, due to increasing mobility of capital across national boundaries, stock markets are increasingly getting integrated. Due to integration of capital markets, volatility in one market gets propagated to other countries as demonstrated in the Asian financial crisis.

Market Sophistication: Individuals now invest in stock markets through professional investors like mutual funds. Fund managers, as informed investors, are better equipped to assess and manage risk. Consequently, stock market volatility in sophisticated markets is usually lower than underdeveloped capital markets.

Shareholder Activism: The pressure on managers to increase shareholder value is increasing. One way to increase value is to reduce systematic risk.

State-of-the-Stock Market: Larger stock markets such as the US market are more liquid, less volatile and hence less risky. The less developed markets like Latin American markets are more volatile and risky.

Riskiness of Stocks Relative to Bonds: Over time, the risk of investing in stocks may decrease while the risk of investing in bonds may increase thereby reducing risk premium. Since equity premia occupies an important place in modern finance theory, academicians are struggling to devise a method to estimate future premia.[4] Academic studies indicate that a simple regression predicting equity premia one year ahead with dividend yields works quite well.

DOES THE CAPM WORK?

The CAPM implies that each security's expected return is linear in its β. A possible strategy for testing the model is to collect securities' β at a particular point in time and to see if these βs can explain the cross-sectional differences in average returns. Consider the following cross-sectional regression.

$$R - R_f = \gamma_0 + \gamma_1\, \beta + \in$$

In this regression, R represents the returns of many securities at a particular cross-section of time and β represents the βs of many firms. According to the CAPM, γ_0 should be equal to zero and γ_1 should equal the expected excess return on the market portfolio. The earliest tests of the CAPM were carried out by Black, Jensen and Scholes,[5] and Fama and MacBeth.[6] Both of these tests were cross-sectional tests. To test the theory, Black, Jensen and Scholes created portfolios on the basis of β (high to low). A

[4] Campbell and Shiller, 'The Dividend–Price Ratio and Expectations of Future Dividends and Discount Factors'; Fama and French, 'Dividend Yields and Expected Stock Returns'.

[5] Black, Jensen and Scholes, 'The Capital Asset Pricing Model'.

[6] Fama and MacBeth, 'Risk, Return and Equilibrium'.

cross-sectional regression was run to see if the βs were able to explain the differences in the returns across securities.

$$R-R_f=\gamma_0+\gamma_1\,\beta+\in$$

The results were:

$$R-R_f=0.0036+0.0108\beta$$
$$[6.53]\ [20.77]$$

The t-statistics are in parenthesis. The CAPM suggests that $\gamma_0=0$ and γ_1 is >0 (and is equal to the expected market return less the risk-free rate). The regression evidence does not support this. More so in emerging markets such as India.

CRITICISMS OF CAPM

The CAPM is based on certain restrictive assumptions such as investors can borrow and lend at risk-free rate and so on. Clearly, some of these assumptions are unrealistic. It is not the assumptions that one should question but the predictive ability of the model. In a CAPM universe, high β portfolios should yield high returns than low β portfolios. But empirical evidence does not support this hypothesis, at least for the time period chosen by some researchers. A number of studies have found that βs of stocks do not adequately explain cross-sectional differences in stock returns. Instead, other variables with no presence in current asset (CA) pricing models seem to have a more significant predictive ability than β. The most prominent is the size effect noticed by Banz (1981). He finds that market equity adds to the explanation of the cross-section of average returns provided by βs. Average returns on small cap stocks are too high given their β estimates, and average returns on large stocks are too low. Another contradiction is the positive relation between leverage and average return. Eugene Fama and Kenneth French[7] argue that a multidimensional model of risk and return is necessary to explain differences in stock returns. Their model incorporates company size (as measured by market capitalization), the ratio of book to market value (BV of equity divided by market capitalization).

The Fama–French Three-Factor Model is estimated by running a time series multiple regression for each company. The dependent variable is the company's monthly excess stock returns over Treasury bill returns. The independent variables are as follows:

- The monthly excess return on the market over Treasury bills.
- SMB (small minus big)—the difference between the monthly return on small-cap stocks and large-cap stocks.
- HML (high minus low)—the difference between monthly returns on high book-to-market stocks and low book-to-market stocks.

In the Fama–French (FF) model, β measures the sensitivity of a stock to movements in the market.

The 'SMB premium' represents the return premium that companies with small market capitalization usually experience relative to companies with large capitalization. It is computed by multiplying the

[7] Fama and French, 'The Cross Section of Expected Stock Returns'.

coefficient for the SMB factor in the multiple regression by the difference between the historical average annual returns on the small-cap and large-cap portfolios.

The 'HML premium' represents the return that investors expect from companies that have a high book equity–market equity ratio. The FF model predicts that a company with a high book equity–market equity ratio has an excess return that is not captured in the market return. The number presented is the coefficient for the HML factor multiplied by the difference between the historical average annual returns on the high market-to-book and low market-to-book portfolios.

The β provided by the FF model is similar to the β provided by the CAPM; it is a measure of the risk of a stock relative to the market. By multiplying the FF β by the equity risk premium, and adding the HML and SMB premiums and the risk-free rate, the expected return for a company is obtained.

For the HML and SMB factors, the regression coefficients have been multiplied by the premium for each of the factors. The data presented are the per cent premium over the market return which each stock receives because of the small company premium and the value premium. An example is as follows.

$$\text{FF } \beta = 0.70,\ \text{SMB Premium} = 2.53\%,\ \text{HML Premium} = 4.17\%$$

$$\text{Expected Return} = \text{Risk-Free Rate} + (\text{Equity Risk Premium} \times \text{FF } \beta) + \text{SMB Premium} + \text{HML Premium}$$

The expected return for the company assuming a risk-free rate of 5.9 per cent and a risk premium of 7.8 per cent is:

$$5.9\% + (7.8 \times 0.70)\% + 2.53\% + 4.17\% = 18.06\%$$

THE CASE OF EMERGING MARKETS

The risk–return analysis presented so far is appropriate if the portfolio returns can be completely characterized by the mean and SD. A large number of studies have shown that emerging market returns are non-normal and hence cannot be described by mean and variance.[8] Figure 3.7 presents an example of Mexico. There are many small returns and a large number of negative returns in case of Mexico. If the Mexican returns were generated from a normal distribution, we would not expect so many negative returns of the magnitude shown in the graph. Thailand is similar to Mexico with some extreme negative observations. The same is true of many other countries. Emerging market returns are not only higher than returns from developed markets but also far more volatile due to economic shocks, military coups and many such factors. In addition, the mean and variance of returns change over time. One recent study of emerging market returns suggests that there is no relation between expected returns and β measured with respect to the world market portfolio.[9] Further, according to CAPM, expected return is a function of β. The β is measured by analysing the way the equity returns covary with a benchmark return. In many countries, β cannot be estimated because the equity market does not exist! One solution to this problem is to establish a relationship between expected returns and, say, country credit ratings (CCRs).

[8] Erb, Harvey and Viskanta, 'Expected Returns and Volatility in 135 Countries'.

[9] Harvey, Campbell R., 'Predictable Risk and Returns in Emerging Markets'. He found that the regression of average returns on average βs produces an R^2 of zero.

FIGURE 3.7
Monthly Returns from Mexican Stock Market

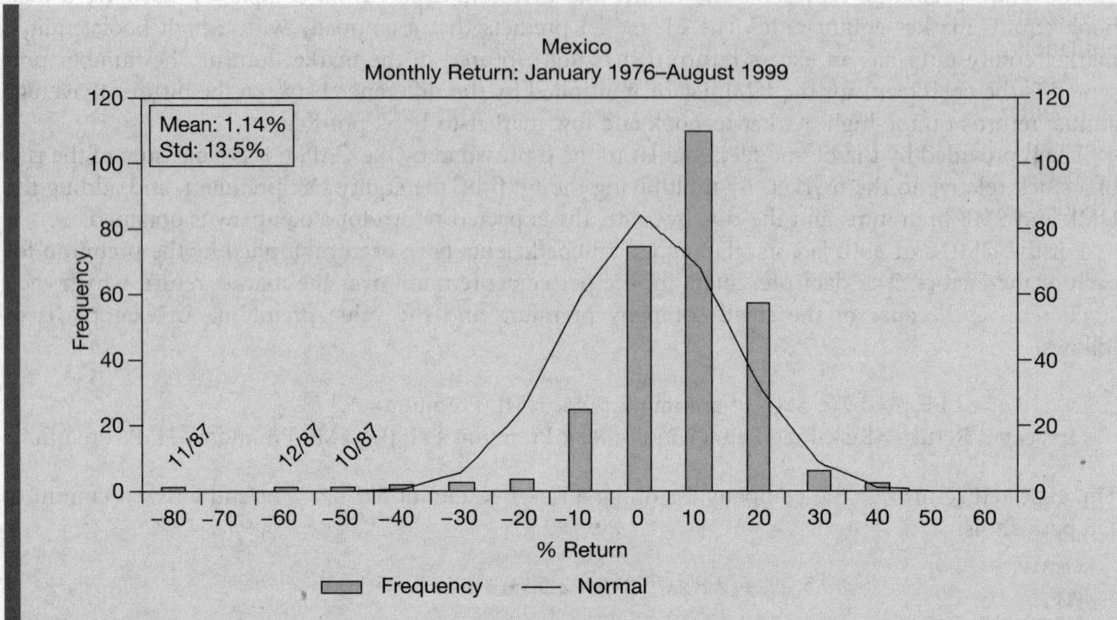

Source: Harvey, 'Predictable Risk and Returns in Emerging Markets'.

ARBITRAGE PRICING THEORY

CAPM is based on the concept of diversification. By holding sufficient number of stocks, an investor can diversify company-specific risk. Even if the investor were to hold all stocks in the market, he/she will still be exposed to market risk .The arbitrage pricing theory (APT), a competitor to CAPM, suggests that a small number of systematic factors affect the long-term returns of securities and the β alone does not explain differences in security returns. Consider two portfolios—one consisting of financial services companies stocks and the other, food products companies stocks. Would you expect both the portfolios to react in the same manner to rising interest rates and inflation? Obviously not. Financial services companies are more sensitive to increase in interest rates. The βs of the portfolios may be the same but investors may not expect the average returns from these portfolios to be the same due to their differential sensitivity to macroeconomic factors. The APT tries to capture these significant factors. The trick is to incorporate multiple sources of economic risk by having more than one β. Each β (called factor β) measures the sensitivity of the stock to the corresponding factor. The APT model does not tell us what those factors are. It assumes that the investor knows which systematic factors affect stock returns. The investor can construct his/her model unlike in CAPM where the β is thrust upon us. The APT model can be written as follows:

Expected return = Risk-free rate + [(sensitivity to factor 1) × (risk premium on factor 1)] + [(sensitivity to factor 2) × (risk premium on factor 2)] + ···

$$E(R) = R_f + \beta_1[E(R_{M1} - R_f)] + \beta_2[E(R_{M2} - R_f)] + \cdots.$$

If the stock market index is the sole factor explaining security returns, we would get back to our CAPM. Studies in the USA have shown that about five–six factors affect US stock prices. One important study by Chen, Roll and Ross suggests that growth in industrial production, unexpected changes in the term structure of interest rates, spreads between high and low grade bond portfolio returns and unexpected inflation determine security returns.

Assume that a portfolio's returns are dependent on two factors, for example, industrial production and inflation. Any unexpected change in the industrial production from current levels would change the expected returns in the same direction, while changes in inflation from current levels would change expected returns in the 'opposite' direction. Assume that there are four stocks whose returns and sensitivities are as follows:[10]

Stock	Expected Return (%)	Production Sensitivity	Inflation Sensitivity
1	13	0.2	2.0
2	27	3.0	0.2
3	16	1.0	1.0
4	20	2.0	2.0

This is not possible because one can buy the first two stocks and short sell the remaining stocks (so investment is zero) and still generate a positive return. This cannot happen in competitive markets. To construct an arbitrage portfolio, the following equations must be satisfied:

1. INV 1 + INV 2 + INV 3 + INV 4 = 0, that is, no investment
2. INV 1 (Sensit (P) 1) + INV 2 (Sensit (P) 2) + INV 3 (Sensit (P) 3) + INV 4 (Sensit (P) 4) = 0, that is, no production risk.
3. INV 1 (Sensit (I) 1) + INV 2 (Sensit (I) 2) + INV 3 (Sensit (I) 3) + INV 4 (Sensit (I) 4) = 0, that is, no inflation risk

Set the level of investment in Stock 1 at ₹1 and solve for the rest.

INV 1 = ₹1
INV 2 = ₹0.624857
INV 3 = –₹1.157143
INV 4 = –₹0.485714

The arbitrage portfolio would be:

Stock	INV	Exp. Return INV × Expret	Prod Sensitivity INV × Sensit (P)	Inf.Sensitivity INV × Sensit (I)
1	1.0	13.0	0.20	2.0
2	0.643	17.361	1.929	0.129
3	–1.157	–18.512	–1.157	–1.157
4	–0.486	–9.720	–0.972	–0.972
	0	**2.129**	0	0

[10] Bower, Bower and Logue, 'A Primer on Arbitrage Pricing Theory'.

The activity of buying the first two stocks will drive up their prices and bring their returns in line with their sensitivities. Similarly, short selling the remaining will drive down their prices. In other words, arbitrage will bring returns of stocks to their equilibrium levels. The factors that affect security returns themselves are identified through factor analysis.

BOND PRICING

Although the CAPM is used to estimate expected return from stocks, it is supposed to be applicable to any asset. What about bonds? Would the CAPM explain the cross-section of bond returns? William Gebhardt et al (2001) find that both bond market factors such as default risk β and term risk β, and bond characteristics such as bond rating and duration largely explain the variation in the cross-section of bond returns.[11] One source of risk for corporate bonds arises from unexpected changes in the term structure of interest rates. The other source of risk arises from changes in default risk in response to changing economic conditions. They take the difference between the monthly return on a portfolio of long-term government bonds and one month T-bill return as proxy for term risk and the difference between the monthly return on a value-weighted market portfolio of all investment grade bonds with at least 10 years to maturity and the monthly return on long-term government bonds as proxy for the default risk. To estimate default and term βs, they run the following two-factor regression:

$$r_{it} - r_{ft} = \alpha + \beta_d \, DEF_t + \beta_t \, TERM_t + u_t$$

where $r_{it} - r_{ft}$ = excess return on corporate bonds

DEF_t and $TERM_t$ are default risk and term risk factors.

β_d and β_t are factor loadings (β) for the two risk factors.

Their model also captures firm-specific default risk. They use bond ratings, Altman's Z-score and duration to measure default risk and maturity risk. Credit risk refers to the chance that the expectation will not be met. One approach to estimating default risk is to compute a composite risk measure based on a firm's financial ratios advocated by Altman.[12] His Z-score model combines select financial ratios to come up with a score as follows:

$$\begin{aligned} Z = \; & 0.012 \times \text{Net WC/Total Assets} \\ & + 0.014 \times \text{Retained Earnings/Total Assets} \\ & + 0.033 \times \text{EBIT/Total Assets} \\ & + 0.006 \times \text{Market Value of Equity/BV of Liabilities} \\ & + 0.999 \times \text{Sales/Total Assets} \end{aligned}$$

A high Z-score represents a low probability of default and a low Z-score represents a high probability of default. The model's classification accuracy was 95 per cent one year before bankruptcy and 72 per cent two years before. Accuracy of the model decreases as the time period is extended (it may also be unreliable in its predictive ability). Based on the study, it was concluded that firms with a Z-score less than 1.81 are all bankrupt, while those with Z-scores greater than 2.99 fall into the non-bankrupt

[11] Some of these concepts are discussed in the chapter on debt markets.

[12] Altman, 'Financial Ratios, Discriminant Analysis and the Prediction of Corporate Bankruptcy'. Financial ratios and bankruptcy prediction is discussed in greater detail in Chapter 5 on Financial Statements.

group. Those falling into the area between 1.81 and 2.99 require more analysis to determine their solvency status. The non-liquid asset ratios such as total debt to total assets and cash flow to total debt are, in general, better predictors of bankruptcy than the liquid assets ratios like quick ratio or net WC to total assets.

In sum, a model containing default β, term β, ratings and duration could be used to calculate cost of debt.

CONCLUDING COMMENTS

The CAPM is a forward-looking model although past returns and βs are taken as proxies for future. It is supposed to give us 'expected' return. In this chapter, different asset pricing theories were outlined. The simple CAPM is intuitive and easy to use. But it might not be the best. An analyst has the liberty to construct his/her asset pricing model.

A riskless asset is one whose actual return equals expected return, that is, variance is zero. Its covariance, by definition, with other assets is also zero. No asset is truly risk free in reality. Since government securities are default risk free, we take the T-bond rate as a proxy for risk-free rate. Variance is a measure of total risk. Total risk can be split into two components—systematic risk and unsystematic risk. The portion of risk which cannot be diversified is called systematic risk or non-diversifiable risk and that which can be diversified is called unsystematic risk.

The portfolio of all risky assets in the economy is called the market portfolio. The systematic risk of an asset is the risk it adds to the market portfolio. β is the standard measure of systematic risk. It measures the sensitivity of stock returns to changes in market returns. Since the market portfolio is unobservable, a broad stock market index such as the BSE Sensex is used as a proxy. By definition, the β of the market is 1.0. Stocks with βs greater than 1 are considered aggressive; those with βs less than 1.0 are considered defensive.

The risk of a well-diversified portfolio mainly reflects the market risk of individual securities because the unsystematic risk is diversified away. Portfolio β is simply the weighted average of individual stock βs.

Investing partly in a risk-free asset reduces risk for the same level of return as demonstrated by the CML.

EXERCISES

1. Refer to the following data.

	ACC	Indian Hotels
Mean Weekly Returns	0.52	0.08
SD	6.98	3.78

Correction coefficient=0.31

Covariance=8.30

Calculate portfolio return and SD for various compositions and plot a graph. Identify the minimum risk portfolio.

2. Calculate the expected return for a stock whose β is 0.8. The T-bond rate is 12 per cent. The monthly return on the market index is 1.7 per cent.
3. You are holding shares of Ashok Leyland, Tata Motors and Grasim. Their individual βs are 0.8, 0.96 and 0.81, respectively. Assuming equal investment, calculate the portfolio β.
4. List three stocks that you think are highly correlated. Explain the rationale.
5. What factors do you think affect the β values?
6. Suppose that the government defaults on sovereign borrowings. The T-bond rate cannot be considered risk free. How would you come up with a risk-free asset?
7. Suppose in a country only three–four stocks (in the index) account for 75 per cent of market capitalization. What would be its effect on β estimate?
8. What factors do you think affect market returns?
9. The following is the correlation matrix for three stocks.

	A	B	C
A	1.0	0.37	0.49
B	0.37	1.0	0.66
C	0.49	0.66	1.0

Other information:

E(R)	0.04	0.10	0.09
Variance	0.02	0.03	0.008
SD	0.14	0.17	0.089

Calculate the expected portfolio return and variance for various compositions.

10. The following are stock and market returns. Calculate mean and SD of returns, correlation and covariance.

Year	Stock Return (%)	Market Return (%)
1987	7.64	14.31
1988	16.98	–8.50
1989	–11.36	4.01
1990	21.12	18.98
1991	–30.01	–26.48
1992	–22.14	–14.66
1993	37.68	37.20
1994	28.27	23.84

11. The following data are available for three stocks.

Stock	Variance	Cov (i,m)	Corr. (i,m)
1	114.4	52.58	0.84
2	72.50	42.50	0.85
3	283.73	28.0	0.30

Market variance = 34.30

Which of the stocks is the riskiest? Rank them.

REFERENCES

Altman, Edward. 'Financial Ratios, Discriminant Analysis and the Prediction of Corporate Bankruptcy'. *Journal of Finance* 23 (1968).

Banz, R. 'The Relationship between Return and Market Value of Common Stocks'. *Journal of Financial Economics* 9, no. 1 (1981 March).

Black, F., M. C. Jensen and M. Scholes. 'The Capital Asset Pricing Model: Some Empirical Tests'. In *Studies in the Theory of Capital Markets*, edited by M. C. Jensen. New York: Praeger, 1972.

Bower, Dorothy, Richard Bower and Dennis Logue. 'A Primer on Arbitrage Pricing Theory'. In *The Revolution in Corporate Finance*, edited by Joel Stern and Donald Chew. Oxford: Basil Blackwell, 1992.

Campbell, John and Robert Shiller. 'The Dividend–Price Ratio and Expectations of Future Dividends and Discount Factors'. *Review of Financial Studies* 1, no. 3 (1988).

Chen, N. F., R. Roll, and S. Ross. 'Economic Forces and the Stock Market'. *Journal of Business*, 59, no. 3 (1986 July).

Dimson, Elroy, Paul Marsh and Mike Staunton. *Triumph of the Optimists: 101 Years of Global Investment Returns*. Princeton, NJ: Princeton University Press, 2002.

Erb, C., C. Harvey and T. Viskanta. 'Expected Returns and Volatility in 135 Countries'. *The Journal of Portfolio Management* (1996 Spring).

Fama, Eugene and James D. MacBeth. 'Risk, Return and Equilibrium: Empirical Tests'. *Journal of Political Economy* 81 (1973).

Fama, Eugene and Kenneth French. 'Dividend Yields and Expected Stock Returns'. *Journal of Financial Economics*, 22, no. 1 (1988).

Fama, Eugene and Kenneth French. 'The Cross Section of Expected Stock Returns'. *Journal of Finance* (1992).

Gebhardt W., C. M. Lee, and B. Swaminathan. 'Towards an Implied Cost of Capital, *Journal of Accounting Research* (2001 June).

Harvey, Campbell R. 'Predictable Risk and Returns in Emerging Markets'. *Review of Financial Studies* 8 (1995).

Statman, Meir. 'How Many Stocks Make A Diversified Portfolio?' *Journal of Financial and Quantitative Analysis* 22, no. 3 (1987 September).

Wagner, Wayne H. and Sheila Lau. 'The Effect of Diversification on Risk'. *Financial Analysts Journal* 26 (1971 Nov–Dec).

SUGGESTED READINGS

Berry, M. A., E. Burmeister and M. B. McElroy. 'Sorting Out Risks Using APT Factors'. *Financial Analysts Journal* (1968 March–April).

Bower, Dorothy, Richard Bower and Dennis Logue. 'Equity Screening Rates Using Arbitrage Pricing Theory'. In *Advances in Financial Planning*, edited by C. F. Lee. Greenwich, CT: JAI Press, 1984.

Bower, Dorothy, Richard Bower and Dennis Logue. 'Arbitrage Pricing Theory and Utility Stock Returns'. *Journal of Finance* 39, no. 4 (1984).

Chan, Louis K. C. and Josef Lakonishok. 'Are the Reports of Beta's Death Premature?' *Journal of Portfolio Management* 19 (1993 Summer).

Cochrane, John. 'New Facts in Finance' (NBER Working Paper No. 7169, 1999 June).

Divecha, A. B., J. Drach and D. Stefek. 'Emerging Markets: A Quantitative Perspective'. *Journal of Portfolio Management* (1992 Fall).

Fama, Eugene and Kenneth French. 'Size and Book-to-Market Factors in Earnings and Returns'. *Journal of Finance* 50, no. 1 (1995).

Gebhardt, W., S. Hvidkjaer and B. Swaminathan. 'The Cross Section of Expected Bond Returns: Betas or Characteristics?' *Journal of Financial Economics* 75, no. 1 (2005).

Kothari, S. P., J. Shanken and R. Sloan. 'Another Look at the Cross Section of Expected Stock Returns'. *Journal of Finance* 50, no. 1 (1995).

Modigliani, F. and G. Pogue. 'An Introduction to Risk and Return: Concepts and Evidence'. *Financial Analysts Journal* (1979).

Odier, Patrick and Bruno Solnik. 'Lessons for International Asset Allocation'. *Financial Analysts Journal* (1993 March–April).

Reinganum, Marc R. 'The Arbitrage Pricing Theory: Some Empirical Results'. *Journal of Finance* 34, no. 2 (1981).

Roll, Richard and Stephen Ross. 'An Empirical Investigation of the Arbitrage Pricing Theory'. *Journal of Finance* (1980 Dec).

Rosenberg, Barr and Andrew Rudd. 'The Corporate Uses of Beta'. In *The Revolution in Corporate Finance*, edited by Joel Stern and Donald Chew. Oxford: Basil Blackwell, 1992.

Ross, S. A. 'The Arbitrage Theory of Capital Asset Pricing'. *Journal of Economic Theory* 13 (1976).

Sharpe, William F. 'Capital Asset Prices: A Theory of Market Equilibrium Under Conditions of Risk'. *Journal of Finance* 19, no. 3 (1964).

Siegel, Jeremy. 'The Shrinking Equity Premium'. *Journal of Portfolio Management* (1999 Fall).

Siegel, Jeremy and Richard Thaler. 'The Equity Premium Puzzle'. *Journal of Economic Perspectives* 11, no. 1 (1997).

CHAPTER

4

Estimation of Cost of Capital

LEARNING OBJECTIVES

- Apply CAPM, discounted cash flow (DCF), risk premium and FF approaches to estimate cost of equity for firms
- Be aware of estimation issues in applying CAPM to estimate divisional required returns
- Estimate β, cost of debt, preferred stock and cost of capital for listed and unlisted firms

Chapter 3 provides a framework for pricing of risky assets. In a CAPM universe, only systematic risk as measured by β matters. This chapter describes the application of CAPM in estimating divisional required returns. The investor's expected rate of return on investment is the cost of equity (COE) for the firm. Thus, the expected return for the equity investor, $E(R) = R_f + \beta\ [E(R_M) - R_f]$, is also the COE for the firm.

It is important to understand that COE is not the same thing as dividends. The COE incorporates both dividends and capital gains expected by investors. Estimation of COE using CAPM involves estimation of risk-free rate, β and market risk premium.

ESTIMATION OF RISK-FREE RATE

The investor's expected rate of return consists of two components—the time value of money and risk premium. A risk-free asset rewards the investor for time value of money alone. Further, a risk-free asset is one whose returns are certain (i.e., variance is zero) and unconnected with that of the market (i.e., covariance is zero). Generally, finance theorists agree that long T-bond rate can be used as proxy for risk-free rate. Sometimes the 365-day T-bill rate is also used. Obviously, what you choose as R_f has a bearing on the COE estimate as it appears twice in the equation. As the T-bill rate tends to be volatile, the long-term T-bond rate might be chosen. It must be understood that there is no such thing as a risk-free asset. The government securities usually do not have default risk[1] but reinvestment risk remains.

Academic studies in the USA and Canada have shown that the long-term bonds are not completely riskless. The government bond returns are positively correlated with stock market returns, that is, government bonds have systematic risk (β). The β of T-bonds in the USA is about 0.25. To arrive at riskless rate, the systematic component of bond yield should be deducted from the prevailing bond yield. To illustrate, suppose risk premium=6.7 per cent, β of T-bonds=0.25 and current bond yield=5.5 per cent.

$$\text{True Risk-Free Rate} = \text{Current Bond Rate} - \text{Systematic Component}$$
$$= 5.5 - (0.25 \times 6.7) = 3.81\%$$

ESTIMATION OF BETA

In the CAPM, β is the sole company-specific factor. The estimates of risk-free rate and market premium are same for all stocks. β is the only link between investor's expected return from the stock with the expectations of market returns. So the estimate of β should be accurate. Often academics and practitioners estimate the historical β and use it as proxy for future. The CAPM is supposed to be a forward-looking model. So what we really need is ex-ante β. The standard practice is to regress stock returns against returns from an index representing the market portfolio. The plot of security returns versus market returns is called a security characteristic line. A typical characteristic line is shown as follows. Each dot corresponds to the stock return against the market return in that period. A line can be fitted to the array of points to explain the relationship. The line of best fit minimizes the distance from the dot and the line.

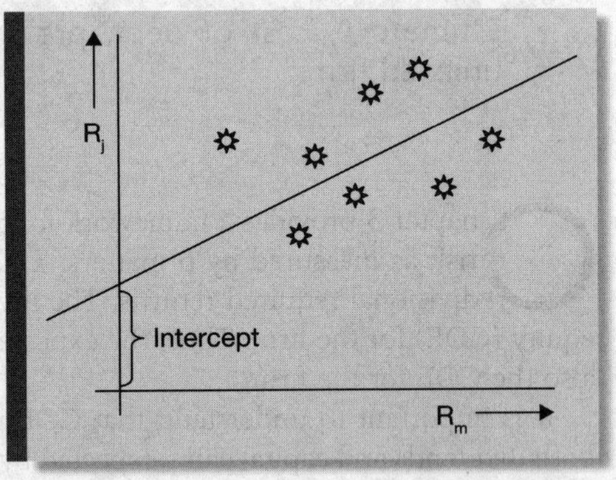

The regression equation we obtain is of the form

$$R_j = a + b\,R_m + \varepsilon$$

where a is the intercept, b is the β of the stock, R_j is the return on the stock, R_m is the return on the market index.

To estimate β, calculate the holding period return for both the stock and the market for some interval of time.

$$\text{Holding period return for the stock} = \frac{(P_t - P_{t-1}) + \text{Div}}{P_{t-1}}$$

where P_t and P_{t-1} are current and prior period prices, Div is the dividend received. Similarly,

[1] This is not true of those countries that default on sovereign borrowings. In such a situation, we can probably use a slightly lower rate than the interest rate on AAA-rated debt instruments, that is, deduct, say, 50 basis points, from the AAA rate and use it as risk-free rate.

$$\text{Index Return} = \frac{\text{Value of Index At the End} - \text{Value at the Beginning}}{\text{Beginning Value}} + \text{Div. Yield on the Index}$$

The β estimate depends on four factors:

- Estimation Period: The model does not specify the time period over which βs have to be estimated. An analyst has the liberty to choose an appropriate time period. Typically, analysts use two-year and five-year data. The latter is more popular. The longer the period, the more the number of observations and more meaningful is the estimate. But macroeconomic changes may be better reflected in recent data. Further, the company itself might have changed in risk complexion. So there is a trade-off between the number of data points and accuracy.
- The Starting and Ending Points of the Estimation Interval: One could randomly choose starting and ending points or choose some deliberate interval. There are no rules except that an analyst should avoid data that are abnormal. For instance, for some reason if the returns in January are consistently higher than returns in other months, one could avoid January data.
- The Market Proxy Used: A stock market index is generally used as a proxy for the market portfolio that is supposed to cover all risky assets in the economy. The β estimate is sensitive to the market proxy used. We could use the Bombay Stock Exchange (BSE) sensitive index (Sensex), National Stock Exchange 50 (NIFTY), BSE 100 or any other market proxy. As long as these indices are highly correlated, it does not really matter which index is chosen. But the problem is that none of these indices might be good proxies for the market portfolio. The β estimates of some well-known companies are shown in Table 4.1.

  The differences in β estimates are not dramatic although different proxies do give different results.
- The Choice of Return Interval: The analyst can choose weekly, monthly, quarterly or annual data to estimate β. The normal practice is to use weekly returns. The choice is made depending on whether weekly or monthly returns have significant correlation with β. CAPM can be applied only if there is correlation between holding period returns and β. A recent study suggests that there is significant correlation between quarterly returns and β. The β estimate is sensitive to the return interval chosen. Table 4.2 presents the β estimates of the same companies for various return intervals with Sensex as proxy. In case of SBI, the β estimate jumps from 1.30 to 2.72 when weekly returns are replaced with quarterly returns. Obviously, this affects the COE estimate.

TABLE 4.1
Beta Estimates with Different Market Proxies

Company	BSE 200	NIFTY	Sensex
Ashok Leyland	0.78	0.89	0.77
Bajaj Auto	0.90	0.92	0.85
SBI	1.59	1.20	1.30
ACC	1.28	1.23	1.23
Colgate Palmolive	0.76	0.68	0.68
Reliance Industries	1.42	1.24	1.38

The β estimates come with statistical noise. The quality of regression can be determined by some simple statistical parameters such as standard error and R^2. If the β estimate is 0.8 and the standard error of β is 0.30, we could be more than 99 per cent confident that the true β lies in the range of –0.10 and 1.7 (i.e., ± 3σ limit). R^2 provides an estimate of the proportion of risk

TABLE 4.2
Beta Estimates for Different Return Intervals

Company	Weekly	Monthly	Quarterly
Ashok Leyland	0.77	0.80	1.02
Bajaj Auto	0.85	0.86	1.18
SBI	1.3	2.04	2.72
ACC	1.23	1.31	1.18
Colgate Palmolive	0.68	0.54	0.35
Reliance Industries	1.38	1.60	1.67

(variance) of the stock that can be traced to the systematic factors. The balance $(1-R^2)$ is the unsystematic risk.

AN ILLUSTRATION

The daily returns of Escorts were regressed against Sensex returns for the period 2016–2017. The results of the regression are:

$$\alpha = 0.163$$
$$\beta = 1.72$$

Standard error of $\beta = 0.213$

$$2\sigma \text{ limit} = 1.72 \pm (2 \times 0.213)$$

So, we can be 95 per cent confident that the true β lies in the range 2.146 and 1.294. The R^2 of the regression is 0.23, that is, 23 per cent of total risk is systematic and the rest unsystematic.

The β of 1.72 suggests that Escorts stock is riskier than the average stock.

The holding period return is the sum of capital gains yield and dividend yield. Dividends are paid semi-annually or annually. To calculate returns, dividends are added to the capital gain/loss in the month in which the stock goes ex-dividend, that is, dividends are not added in all the months but only in that month in which dividends are announced.

ESTIMATION OF MARKET RETURN AND MARKET PREMIUM

Market return is the average of past realized returns from the market index. Weekly or monthly intervals are chosen to calculate average returns. The average could be the arithmetic mean or the geometric mean. Some theorists argue that arithmetic mean is consistent with the mean–variance framework of CAPM. There are some pitfalls in using the arithmetic mean. Suppose the price of an asset increases from ₹100 to ₹200 and then falls to ₹100. Holding period returns are 100 per cent and –50 per cent. The arithmetic mean is 25 per cent. Clearly, the return is zero.

TABLE 4.3
Historical Mean and Standard Deviation of Return on Indices, January–December 2016

	Mean Return (%)		SD (%)	
	Daily	Monthly	Daily	Monthly
BSE 100	0.017	0.94	0.96	4.92
Sensex	0.011	0.71	0.93	4.65
NIFTY	0.015	–0.01	0.95	4.28

Source: BSE and National Stock Exchange.

$$\text{The Geometric Mean} = [(1+1)(1-0.5)-1]^{1/2} = 0$$

Consequently, some suggest that the geometric mean of returns be used. Table 4.3 presents the historical mean and SD of returns of some popular indices in India.

The actual returns earned by stocks (i.e., index) over a long period of time over and above the actual return earned on a default-free security is the market premium, $R_m - R_f$. The arithmetic average of returns on government bonds is deducted from the average returns from stocks. This historical premium is used as proxy for future risk premium. The choice of index affects the market premium estimate. In India, Sensex is popular because it has the longest history. Sensex data are available for about 25 years, whereas other indices have a shorter history. The risk premium for several countries are presented in Tables 4.4 and 4.5.

Risk premium as measured by the historical difference between stocks and bonds usually suffers from statistical noise. Further, risk premiums may change over time. So adding a constant risk premium to the T-bond rate might be inappropriate. The CAPM parameters can be estimated individually, as demonstrated in the preceding sections, and then plugged into the CAPM to arrive at the COE.

AN ILLUSTRATION

The COE for Divis Lab in 2017 is estimated as follows:

- $R_f = 6.896\%$

Market premium, $R_m - R_f = 7.03\%$

$$\beta = 0.809$$
$$COE = 6.896\% + 0.809(7.03)\%$$
$$= 12.58\%$$

TABLE 4.4
Risk Premium Around the World

Country	Risk Premium (%)
Australia	5.08
Singapore	5.08
Taiwan	5.70
Malaysia	6.31
Hong Kong	5.59
Thailand	6.72
India	7.03
UK	5.59
USA	5.08

Source: Damodaran, 'Estimating Risk Premiums'.

OTHER APPROACHES FOR ESTIMATION OF COST OF EQUITY

There are two other popular methods for calculating COE—the risk premium approach and discounted cash flow (DCF) approach.

TABLE 4.5
Equity Premiums (%) US Data, 1802–1998

	Equity Premium with Bonds		Equity Premium with Bills	
Period	Arithmetic	Geometric	Arithmetic	Geometric
1802–1998	3.5	4.7	5.1	5.5
1802–1870	2.2	3.2	1.9	2.9
1871–1925	2.9	4.0	3.4	4.6
1926–1998	5.2	6.7	6.7	8.6
1946–1998	6.5	7.3	7.2	8.6

Source: Jeremy Siegel (1999).

DCF Approach

The price of a stock, P_0, on the day the most recent dividend, D_0, is paid, is the PV of future dividend stream.

$$P_0 = D_0 \sum_{t=1}^{\infty} (1+g)^t / (1+r)^t$$

where g = per period growth in dividends
r = investor's expected rate of return

The rate of return that equates the current market price and future dividend payments is the COE for the firm.

The model is based on certain assumptions:

- The future rate of growth, g, is constant
- The rate at which the investor discounts future cash flows, r, is constant
- Dividends are paid annually
- The COE is calculated on the day the most recent dividend is paid

If we assume that the dividends grow at a constant rate forever,[2]

$$P_0 = [D_1/k - g]$$
$$K = [D_1/P_0] + g$$
COE = Next Period Dividend Yield + Growth in Dividends

The normal practice is to use a two-stage dividend growth model as shown in the following text.

The expected future dividend stream can be split into two periods: non-constant growth period (say four years) and constant growth period thereafter.

[2] This is the famous Gordon model.

$$P_0 = \frac{D_1}{(1+k)^1} + \cdots + \frac{D_4}{(1+k)^4} + \frac{D_4(1+g)}{(k-g)}[1/(1+k)^4]$$

With a forecast of D_1, D_2, D_3, D_4 and g, the COE can be found by trial and error.[3]

The constant growth rate in dividends can be calculated by multiplying the expected retention ratio in year four with the return on equity (ROE).

$$g = (\text{retention ratio in year 4}) \times (\text{ROE})$$

The Gordon model could also be used to estimate the risk premium.

$$P = [D_1/(k-g)]$$

Extending the model to the market as a whole

$$\text{Market Value} = \frac{\text{Expected Dividends Next Year}}{\text{Required Return on Stocks} - \text{Expected Growth Rate}}$$

Given the current market value, expected dividends and growth rate in earnings and dividends in the long run, one can solve for the required ROE. The difference between the required ROE and the risk-free rate provides an estimate of risk premium.

To illustrate, if,

Index value = 3,500, dividend yield on the index = 8 per cent, expected growth rate = 7 per cent

$$3{,}500 = [(0.08 \times 3{,}500)/(r - 0.07)]$$

Required ROE = 15 per cent

If risk-free rate is 12 per cent, the premium is 3 per cent.

Risk Premium Approach

Under the risk premium approach, a risk premium is added to the YTM on the company's bonds (to reflect the higher risk borne by shareholders) to estimate the COE.

That is,

$$\text{COE} = \text{Bond Yield} + \text{Risk Premium}$$

The equity risk premium can be calculated in two ways: historic yield spread method and ex-ante yield spread based on DCF analysis.

The historic risk premium is the difference between the average of annual returns on a stock index in the past (say, 10 years) and the average of annual returns on a bond index over the same period.

$$\text{Historic Yield Spread} = \text{Average Return on Stock Index} - \text{Average Return on Bond Index}$$

The prevalent practice is to use geometric mean return on the indices. The historic premium is then added to company's bond yield to obtain the COE.

[3] Analyst forecasts of dividend and growth rate can be used as inputs to estimate the cost of equity.

Under the ex-ante (expected) risk premium method, the average expected future return on a group of stocks, say, index stocks, is calculated and the concurrent risk-free rate is subtracted from it. The yield on long-term T-bond could be taken as R_f.

$$RP_M = R_M - R_f$$

The DCF model may be used to estimate expected return on stocks. A survey of analysts' forecast of growth rate in dividends may be used as proxy for 'g' in the equation.

$$K_e = (D_1/P_0) + g$$

The simple logic behind the risk premium approach is that if the premium is expected to remain constant over time, then the constant premium may be added to the prevailing interest rate to calculate the COE.

ESTIMATION OF COST OF DEBT

Debt is of two types: term loans from FIs, and debentures sold to investors. The cost of debentures is the investor's required rate of return. The bond pricing equation suggests that:

$$P = \sum_{t=1}^{n} [C/(1 + k_d)^t] + [F/(1 + k_d)^n]$$

where P is price, C is coupon in rupees, F is redemption price and K_d is the investor's expected rate of return. The discount rate that equates the current market price, and coupon and principal payments is the cost of debt. Note that cost of debt is not the same thing as interest paid by the company. At the time of issue, the company would set the interest rate equal to the investor's expected rate, which is the yield on comparable instruments. As time passes, the YTM may increase or decrease. In other words, if you have to find the cost of debt, do not take the interest rate payable by the company. Call up your investment banker and ask him/her the prevailing yield on your company's bonds. You may point out that yields fluctuate. That is precisely the point. Why do yields change? Mainly for two reasons: changes in general interest levels, and changes in default risk of the issuer. When the interest rates in the economy increase, the investor's expected rate of return on this company's bond increases. This increases the cost of 'both' old and new bonds. Similarly, the required yield may change due to changes in default risk of the instrument. Bondholders would have set the interest rate at the time of issue after assessing the default risk. If the default risk increases later on, the required rate of return (or yield or YTM or cost of debt) also increases. In sum, the cost of debt is in the 'denominator' and not in the numerator. This is the pre-tax cost of debt. Since, interest payments are tax deductible, the post-tax cost of debt is k_d (1 – T), where T is the marginal tax rate.

Going by the previous reasoning, we should not take the interest rate on non-traded debt like term loans as the cost of debt. The interest rate on comparable debt instruments is the cost of debt (or the yield on traded debt, if the company has issued debentures).

Assume that a company issues ₹1,500 million of bonds due in 10 years. The bond carries a coupon of 12 per cent. The company's marginal tax rate is 35 per cent. Coupon on bonds is usually paid semi-annually. The effective after-tax cost of debt is:

$$[1+(0.12/2)\times(1-0.35)]^2=1.0795 \text{ or } 7.95\%$$

The semi-annual tax shield from interest expense on these bonds (in ₹ million) is:

$$0.35\times(0.12/2)\times ₹150 \text{ million}=₹31.5 \text{ million}$$

The PV of tax shields can be estimated by discounting semi-annual debt tax shields of ₹31.5 million at the pre-tax semi-annual cost of debt as the discount rate that best captures the riskiness of these tax shields.

$$=31.5 \text{ million}\times \text{PVIFA } (6\%, 10)$$

COST OF PREFERRED STOCK

Preference shares share characteristics of both debt and equity. The dividend on preference shares is fixed just as interest on bonds is fixed. But preference dividends are not tax deductible just as dividends on ordinary shares are non-tax deductible. Preference dividend is to be paid out of after-tax profits similar to ordinary dividends.

The cost of preferred stock could be found by calculating the discount rate K_p that equates current market price, and dividends and principal, similar to debentures.

$$P=\sum_{t=1}^{n}[D/(1+k_p)^t]+[F/(1+k_p)^n]$$

If the preferred stock is perpetual, the cost of preferred stock = Preference DPS/Market price of preferred stock = D/P

THE WEIGHTED AVERAGE COST OF CAPITAL

The weighted average cost of capital (WACC) is the weighted average of costs of various sources of finance.

$$\text{WACC}=K_e\,[E/V]+K_d(1-T)\,[D/V]+K_p\,[PS/V]$$

where

K_e = COE
K_d = pre-tax cost of debt
K_p = cost of preferred stock
T = tax rate

E, D and PS are amounts of equity, debt and preferred stock in the capital structure.

$$V=\text{market value of all securities } (E+D+PS)$$

Note that the weights used in WACC calculation are target, market value weights and not BV weights. Market value reflects the value of the firm better than the BV. BV reflects the historical value of assets in place, whereas market value reflects the value of both assets in place and PV of future growth opportunities. Moreover, securities are issued at market values and not at BVs. Further, the proportions are the target proportions the company intends to maintain.[4] The WACC is the hurdle rate to be applied to projects that have similar risk characteristics (and financing) as the firm, that is, investments should earn the hurdle rate to meet investors' expectation. Otherwise investors would be worse off.

AN ILLUSTRATION

Infosys Technologies stock had a β of 0.69 in 2018. The prevailing 10-year T-bond rate was 7.8 per cent. Using a market premium of 7.03 per cent, the COE for Infosys works out to 7.8+0.69 (7.03)=12.65%

Infosys does not have debt in its capital structure. So the cost of capital is the same as the COE.

Some companies use a single company-wide discount rate for all projects and divisions even though the divisions have different risk complexion. Obviously, this leads to inappropriate investment decisions.

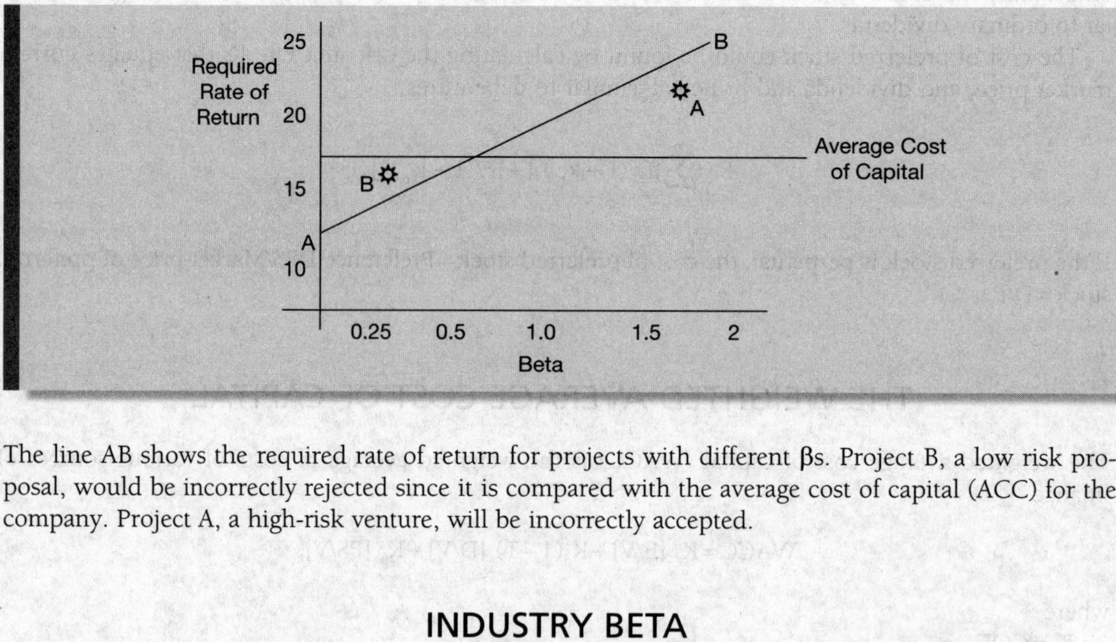

The line AB shows the required rate of return for projects with different βs. Project B, a low risk proposal, would be incorrectly rejected since it is compared with the average cost of capital (ACC) for the company. Project A, a high-risk venture, will be incorrectly accepted.

INDUSTRY BETA

The β of any individual asset is:

$$\beta_i = \frac{Cov(R_i - R_m)}{Var(R_m)}$$

Now consider a portfolio with weights W_p. The β of the portfolio is:

[4] Target capital structure is discussed later in Chapter 14 on capital structure.

$$\beta_p = \frac{Cov(R_p - R_m)}{Var(R_m)}$$
$$= \sum_{i=1}^{n} W_i \beta_i$$

The βs of individual stocks tend to be fickle. They change quite rapidly. Portfolio βs, on the other hand, are more stable. Their standard errors are generally lower than individual β values. The weighted average β of stocks in the same industry group is called industry β with the weights being market capitalization (number of shares outstanding multiplied by market price) of individual companies. What purpose does industry β serve? Let us suppose Reliance Industries is in the process of appraising a telecom project. So it needs an estimate of COE for the project. They can use either the Reliance β or the telecom industry β. Conventional wisdom suggests us that the banking industry β is more indicative of what investors expect from the telecom project. In other words, COE and cost of capital are project specific. The WACC for the company cannot be applied across the board to all projects. The COE estimated for the parent company can be applied only if the project has the same risk as the parent company.

FUNDAMENTAL BETA

Since firm characteristics change over a period of time, we would expect the β values to change. Consequently, placing too much emphasis on history might be unwise. Researchers have attempted to establish relationship between systematic risk and its determinants such as payout ratio, growth, leverage, liquidity ratio, size of the firm and EPS variability. Studies have shown that the β obtained from fundamental factors is more stable. About 54 factors in six categories are supposed to influence β.

A growth-oriented strategy implies large capital investment plans. Such long-term investments typically translate into higher uncertainty about the eventual outcome and hence risk. So we would expect growth to be a consistent predictor of β. Likewise, earnings variability is another important predictor of β. An important research by Robert Hamada[5] shows that the β of a stock depends on operating and financial leverage of a firm. An increase in either of them or both will lead to an increase in β, and hence the COE.

The relationship between levered and unlevered β is:[6]

$$\beta_L = \beta_U [1 + (1 - T)\ D/E]$$

where β_L = levered β (β at the current level of debt)
β_U = unlevered β (β when there is no debt in the capital structure)

We know that:

$$V = D + E$$

That is, the value of the firm equals the sum of values of debt and equity.

[5] Hamada, 'The Effect of the Firm's Capital Structure on the Systematic Risk of Common Stocks'.
[6] The effect of leverage on β is not too clear in the Indian context. But it is better to be vaguely right than precisely wrong!

Multiplying both sides by their respective β,

$$\beta_A V = \beta_D D + \beta_E E$$

Dividing both sides by V

$$\beta_A = \beta_D D/V + \beta_E E/V$$

That is, asset β is the weighted average of debt and equity β.

If the β of debt is assumed to be zero,[7]

$$\beta_A = \beta_E E/V$$

or

$$\beta_E = \beta_A (V/E)$$

The β that we estimate by regressing stock returns against the market returns should not be directly used in the CAPM. It should be re-levered using the aforementioned relationship at the target debt ratio and then used.

Assume that a company currently has a D/V ratio of 0.3 (or E/V is 0.7). The target D/V is 0.5. Let the current equity β be 0.50.

$$\beta_A = \beta_E E/V$$

Asset β = (0.50) (0.7) = 0.35

$$\beta_E \text{ at the target debt ratio} = \beta_A (V/E) = (0.35)(1/0.7) = 0.5$$

As you can see, the estimate is more than the current β.

COST OF CAPITAL FOR UNLISTED DIVISIONS

The CAPM is used to estimate the COE for a listed firm. An unlisted division, by definition, would not have stock market data. As a result, CAPM is not useful. The accepted procedure is to follow the 'pure play' method. Since the β of the division is unobservable, a proxy β derived from publicly traded firms whose operations are similar to the division and this proxy β is assumed to be the division's systematic risk. The pure play approach attempts to identify firms with publicly traded securities that are solely engaged in the same line of business as the division. These comparable firms are called pure play firms. A firm should satisfy the following characteristics to qualify as a pure play firm:

- The firm should have only one business line and no miscellaneous revenue.
- The pure play should be in the same industry or business line as the division in question.
- The revenues of the pure play should be roughly the same as those of the division.

[7] The β of debt is assumed to be zero because debt is priced on the basis of 'unsystematic', firm-specific, default risk.

- When more than one firm can be identified as a potential pure play, the firm with the median β could be chosen as pure play.

The important insight to be gained from the preceding discussion is that for multi-division firms, WACC is a meaningless concept. It is necessary to calculate the cost of capital for each division separately.

TABLE 4.6
Survey Responses to the Question: Does Your Firm Estimate the Cost of Equity Capital? If Yes, How?

	(%) Always or Almost Always
CAPM	73.49
Average Historical Return on Stock	39.41
Multi-β CAPM	34.29
Dividend Discount Model	15.74
Whatever Our Investors Tell Us	13.93
By Regulatory Decisions	7.04

SURVEY RESULTS

Graham and Harvey[8] conducted a survey of practices in 392 firms in the USA. Their survey had questions on how firms estimate the COE capital. Each question was to be rated on a four-point scale. They explore whether firms use the CAPM, a multi-β CAPM, average historical returns or a dividend discount model. They find that CAPM is by far the most popular method. The result of their survey is presented in Table 4.6.

LIQUIDITY AND THE COST OF CAPITAL

Although modern finance theory hypothesizes that only systematic risk matters for pricing risky assets, one study in the USA indicates that portfolios of less liquid stocks provide investors with significantly higher returns, on average, than highly liquid stocks even after adjusting for risk.[9] Why? Investors price securities after considering transaction costs. Given two stocks with same cash flows but with different liquidity, the less liquid stock will trade at lower prices. Thus, a liquidity premium is attached to illiquid stocks. What this implies is that managers of these companies must earn higher returns than that suggested by CAPM or any asset pricing model to increase shareholder value. This also means that managers can increase the value of their companies by increasing the liquidity of the company's stocks and bonds. But increasing liquidity is not costless. For instance, one way to increase liquidity is an IPO, which involves underwriting costs. Voluntary disclosure of information is another way to increase liquidity and lessen COE.

DISCLOSURE AND THE COST OF CAPITAL

CFOs considering whether they should gratuitously provide corporate information to the capital markets must weigh the costs and benefits of disclosure. Among the potential costs are the risks of a

[8] Graham and Harvey, 'The Theory and Practice of Corporate Finance'.
[9] Amihud and Mendelson, 'Liquidity and Asset Prices'.

shareholders' lawsuit or a weakened competitive position, which could impact the company's future earnings and the price of the stock. On the other hand, providing certain types of information may lower the COE capital for a given level of earnings, and thus enhance the stock price. Voluntary disclosure of information can also provide some benefits. It might lower investors' estimation of risk by defusing their uncertainty about the stock. Armed with adequate knowledge, investors feel more confident about their estimates of the company's value.

Only certain types of companies and certain kinds of information are able to lower the cost of capital. Research in the USA shows that companies with a high market β and larger analytical following generally pay more for the equity capital than others do.[10] Those results apply without regard to size or disclosure level. On the other hand, companies that have little or no analytical coverage and that maintain a generous disclosure policy enjoy a 9 per cent reduction in COE when compared to the firm with the least amount of disclosure. The results suggest that investors find the information a company provides to be most valuable when they cannot turn to any outside analytical coverage. Which kind of information lowers the cost of capital will depend largely on the extent of analytical coverage. Companies with little following enjoy the largest decrease in the COE when they disclose forward-looking information such as sales or earnings forecasts. Companies with low analyst coverage might consider disclosing the impact of industry trends on profits and sales, since these areas bear the greatest potential to improve the company's COE.

ESTIMATING COST OF EQUITY IN EMERGING MARKETS

Asset pricing models such as the CAPM break down in emerging markets due to non- availability of stock market data, non-normality of returns, small size of the market and such other factors. As a result, several models that explicitly sidestep the limitations of conventional asset pricing models have been proposed. In this section, I summarize four such models.

GODFREY–ESPINOSA APPROACH

The Godfrey–Espinosa[11] model for estimating COE in emerging markets suggests that:

$$K_i = R_{f,\,u.s.} + \text{Credit Spread}_i + 0.6\ [\sigma_i/\sigma_m]\ [\text{Risk Premium}_{u.s.}]$$

where $R_{f,\,u.s.}$ = risk-free rate in the USA, say, 6 per cent
σ_i = annualized equity market volatility of the country in question
σ_m = annualized equity market volatility of the USA
Credit spread = Difference in yields on the public debt of two countries denominated in a common currency

Table 4.7 presents the credit spread and other inputs to estimate the COE in several countries in 1996.[12]

[10] Botosan, 'Evidence that Greater Disclosure Lowers the Cost of Equity'.
[11] Godfrey and Espinosa, 'A Practical Approach to Calculating Cost of Equity for Investments in Emerging Markets'.
[12] These inputs are dated. As a result, the applicability of the model is limited unless the model inputs are regularly updated.

TABLE 4.7
Cost of Equity Using the Godfrey–Espinosa Approach

Country	Credit Spread (%)	Annualized Volatility (%)	Adjusted β	COE
Argentina	4	54.74	3.39	28.7
Brazil	4.1	53.75	3.33	28.4
Mexico	3.8	36.56	2.26	22.3
The Philippines	2.0	32.05	1.99	18.9
India	1.6	29.95	1.86	17.8
Indonesia	1.0	27.19	1.68	16.3

Source: Godfrey and Espinosa, 'A Practical Approach to Calculating Cost of Equity for Investments in Emerging Markets'.

Goldman Sachs Model

The Goldman Sachs model[13] is specified as:

$$R = R_{us} + \text{Premium}$$

where R_{us} = risk-free rate in the USA

They calculate premium in two steps:

- The country risk spread, R_s, the spread over treasuries for sovereign, dollar-denominated emerging market bonds of similar maturity
- A leveraged measure of the US equity risk premium (Eu) defined as the equity risk premium in the USA adjusted by the ratio of daily volatility (S_b) over the volatility of the US market (S_u).

$$\text{Premium} = R_s + (S_b/S_u)E_u$$
$$\text{So Cost of Equity } R = R_{us} + [R_s + (S_b/S_u)E_u]$$

The components of the risk premium are not independent leading to a problem of double counting. To obtain a realistic discount rate, the equity risk premium is adjusted by subtracting the correlation of dollar returns between the stock market and sovereign bond as follows:

$$\text{Adjusted premium} = [R_s + (S_b/S_u)E_u]\ [1 - \text{corr}(S,B)]$$
$$\text{And Cost of Equity} = R_{us} + [R_s + (S_b/S_u)E_u]\ [1 - \text{corr}(S,B)]$$

International Cost of Capital and Risk Calculator

The Erb–Harvey–Viskanta model, that is, the International Cost of Capital and Risk Calculator (ICCRC),[14] unlike the other models that calculate expected equity returns using stock market or

[13] Mariscal and Hargis, 'A Long-Term Perspective on Short-Term Risk'.

[14] Harvey, 'The International Cost of Capital and Risk Calculator'; Erb, Harvey and Viskanta, 'Expected Returns and Volatility in 135 Countries'.

TABLE 4.8
Cost of Equity Using the EHV Model

Country	Credit Rating (Sep 1995)	Expected Return (%)
Australia	71.2	18.1
Belgium	79.2	15.9
Brazil	34.9	33.0
China	57.0	22.8
Germany	90.9	13.0
Hong Kong	67.0	19.4
India	46.1	27.2
Indonesia	52.4	24.5

economic data, focuses on CCRs. The result of credit risk ratings of 75–100 bankers conducted biannually by Institutional Investor is the basis for their model.[15] Since the country ratings take into account macroeconomic factors such as political and expropriation risk, exchange rate volatility, sensitivity to global economic shocks, E–H–V take country risk ratings as proxy for fundamental risk and try to model equity data and associated credit ratings for some 135 countries.

That is,

$$R_j = a_0 + a_1 \text{ Log}(CCR_j) + \varepsilon_j$$

where R = semi-annual return in US dollars for the country
Log (CCR) = natural logarithm of the CCR
ε_j = regression residual

The log of the credit rating is used to capture non-linear relationship between CCR and expected return. Further, the E–H–V study indicates that CCRs also pick up country risk and that higher rating (lower risk) leads to lower expected returns.

Their study established the following regression model:

$$\text{Country Hurdle Rate} = \text{Risk-Free Rate} + 0.944 - 0.177 \text{ Log (CCR)}$$

Table 4.8 presents the risk ratings and expected returns for some countries. These data are updated every six months.

Aswath Damodaran's Approach

The risk premium for a company in a non-US country could be expressed as follows:[16]

[15] These bankers rate each country on a scale of 0–100, with 100 representing the lowest risk of default.
[16] Damodaran, 'Estimating Risk Premiums'.

TABLE 4.9
Country Ratings and Default Spread

Country	Long-Term Bond Rating*	Country Risk Premium (%)
Argentina	Ba3	4
Australia	Aa2	0.65
Austria	Aaa	0.00
Belgium	Aaa	0.00
Brazil	B2	5.5
Canada	Aa2	0.65
Chile	Baa1	1.2
China	A3	0.95
India	Ba2	3
Indonesia	B3	6.5
Japan	Aa1	0.60
Pakistan	Caa1	7.5
Sweden	Aa2	0.65
Switzerland	Aaa	0.00

Note: *Spread between interest on foreign currency country bond and that on US corporates with similar rating.

$$\text{Risk Premium} = \text{Base Premium for A Mature Market} + \text{Country Premium}$$
$$\text{COE} = R_f + \beta\ (\text{Base Premium for Mature Market Like the USA}) + \text{Country Premium}$$

where R_f = T-bond rate, a proxy for risk-free rate, base premium is the geometric average premium (i.e., $R_m - R_f$) earned by stocks over bonds over a long period of time, 6.1 per cent in case of the USA. The country premium is added on the assumption that country risk cannot be diversified due to cross-market correlation. Put differently, a major portion of the country risk is systematic. The equity risk premium of a country is a function of country default risk and the volatility of equity market relative to the country bond market.

$$\text{Country Equity Risk Premium} = \text{Country Default Spread} \times [\sigma_{\text{equity}}/\sigma_{\text{country bond}}]$$

The country risk can be measured by the credit rating given by international credit rating agencies like Standard & Poor's, and Moody's.[17] These agencies publish default spread over T-bond rate and spread over corporate bonds with similar rating in the USA. Table 4.9 presents the Moody's country ratings and the default spread (at the time of writing). Either the corporate spread or the country spread could be used as default risk premium. The default risk premium should be translated into equity risk premium.

$$\text{Country Equity Risk Premium} = \text{Country Default Spread} \times [\sigma_{\text{equity}}/\sigma_{\text{country bond}}]$$

[17] See www.moodys.com.

where σ_{equity} is the SD of returns on the country's stock market index and $\sigma_{country\ bond}$ is the SD of country bond prices.

The COE can be used to discount free cash flow to equity investors to value the company's equity.

The problem with some of these approaches is twofold: First, they yield a countrywide COE that cannot be applied at the company level. Second, the numerical values of ratings are highly subjective.

CONCLUDING COMMENTS

The cost of capital is an important idea in finance theory. This chapter introduced several approaches for estimation of cost of capital for both listed and unlisted firms. It is inappropriate to apply the WACC as the hurdle rate for all the projects and divisions across the board. Cost of capital is specific to the project in question. The methodology for estimating pure play βs and making appropriate adjustments for leverage will be introduced at a later stage.

The COE can be estimated in three ways.

- The CAPM approach
- Dividend discount model
- Risk premium approach

CAPM is the most widely used method.

The systematic risk of a stock, among other factors, depends on operating and financial leverage. The higher the leverage, the higher is the β.

The WACC is the hurdle rate for an average risk project undertaken by the company. It can be applied only if the project is a mirror image of the company's activities. Any project that deviates from the parent's operating and financial characteristics should be subjected to a different hurdle rate. WACC is a meaningless concept for well diversified groups like the Tata Group or the Birla Group.

The hurdle rate is the minimum return a project should earn to satisfy the investors' expectations.

EXERCISES

1. Using historical data available on the BSE website (https://www.bseindia.com/markets/equity/EQReports/StockPrcHistori.aspx?scripcode=512289&flag=sp&Submit=G and https://www.bseindia.com/indices/indexarchivedata.aspx) estimate ∝, β, standard error of ∝ and β, and R^2 for the following stocks. Establish 95 per cent confidence interval for β.

Company Name
Tata Chemicals
HUL
Cadbury's

Use monthly returns for the last five years and Sensex as market proxy.

2. Draw characteristic line for the same stocks. Interpret the line. Classify the stocks as aggressive, defensive and neutral.
3. Estimate BSE 30 returns (weekly and monthly) for the last two years. Convert them into annual returns.
4. Assuming equal investment estimate the β for the following portfolio.

Company	β
HDFC	1.35
CIPLA	0.93
BHEL	1.38
SBI	1.28
Dr Reddy's Lab	0.62
HDFC Bank	0.93
Hero MotoCorp	0.67
Infosys	0.69
Vedanta	1.28
ONGC	1.18

5. Using the following data, estimate cost of capital.
   $\beta=1.2$, $R_f=6.15$ per cent, market premium=8 per cent. The company has stated that it intends to maintain a debt to value ratio of 0.40. The yield on the company's bonds is 13.5 per cent. The company's marginal tax rate is 35 per cent.
6. Given the following book and market value data, calculate WACC based on BV weights and market value weights. Assume CAPM parameters as in the previous question.

	BV ₹	Market Value ₹
Long-term Debt (12%)	600,000	650,000
Preferred Stock (15%)	150,000	180,000
Equity	250,000	470,000

7. Sushil Shyam Sundar is the finance manager of a biotechnology company. His company shares characteristics of 'both' pharmaceutical and speciality chemicals companies. Hence, obtaining a pure play proxy β is difficult. He reasoned that the β of a company is dependent on fundamental factors such as sales growth, investment in R&D and so on. He ran a regression program between unlevered βs of publicly traded pharmaceutical, specialty chemicals and biotechnology companies and the determinants of β. The following regression result was obtained:

$$\beta_u = 2.348 + 0.214 \times \text{Sales growth} + 0.687 \times \text{R\&D/Sales} - 0.081 \ln(\text{capital}) + 0.394\ (\text{NOPAT margin}) - 0.205\ (\text{Sales/Capital}) + \varepsilon$$

His company has the following characteristics:

ln[18] Cap	Sales Growth	R&D/Sales	NOPAT Margin
10	25%	15%	25%

Estimate β for the company.

8. The Central Electricity Regulatory Commission is in the process of estimating COE for electric companies. The Commission regulates the price per unit of electricity the electric company can charge and hence the ROE (assuming that expenses are constant or increase in a definite fashion). The idea is to add a constant spread to the COE to calculate the allowable ROE and work backwards to calculate price per unit. The Commission decides to use the Gordon model. The model requires estimation of constant dividend growth in the long run. Either the historic dividend growth rate or a forecast might be used. The officials reasoned that the growth rate in earnings and dividends is a function of: CPI inflation, yield on long-term T-bond and growth rate in GDP. Using macroeconomic data, the Commission obtained the following regression results:

$$\text{Divgro} = 0.9671 + 0.7028 \text{ CPI inflation} + \varepsilon$$

The other factors were found to be uncorrelated. If the forecast of inflation is 7 per cent, what is the expected growth rate in dividends? Do you think this method is appropriate for other types of businesses?

[18] Natural log.

REFERENCES

Amihud, Y. and H. Mendelson. 'Liquidity and Asset Prices: Financial Management Implications'. *Financial Management* (1988 Spring).

Botosan, Christine. 'Evidence that Greater Disclosure Lowers the Cost of Equity'. *Journal of Applied Corporate Finance* 12, no. 4 (2005).

Damodaran, Aswath. 'Estimating Risk Premiums' (Working Paper, Stern School of Business, New York University), accessed 6 December 2018, from www.stern.nyu.edu/~adamodar

Erb, C., C. Harvey and T. Viskanta. 'Expected Returns and Volatility in 135 Countries'. *The Journal of Portfolio Management* (1996 Spring).

Graham, J. and C. Harvey. 'The Theory and Practice of Corporate Finance: Evidence from the Field'. *Journal of Financial Economics* 61 (2001).

Godfrey, S. and R. Espinosa. 'A Practical Approach to Calculating Cost of Equity for Investments in Emerging Markets'. *Journal of Applied Corporate Finance* 9, no. 3 (1996 Fall).

Hamada, R. S. 'The Effect of the Firm's Capital Structure on the Systematic Risk of Common Stocks'. *Journal of Finance* (1972 May).

Harvey, Campbell. 'The International Cost of Capital and Risk Calculator' (Unpublished Manuscript, Duke University, Fuqua School of Business), accessed 6 December 2018, from https://people.duke.edu/~charvey/applets/iccrc.html

Mariscal, Jorge and Kent Hargis. 'A Long-Term Perspective on Short-Term Risk' (Goldman Sachs Research, Oct 1999).

Siegel, J. The Shrinking Equity premium. *The Journal of Portfolio Management* 26, no. 1 (1999 Fall).

Much of research on behaviour of emerging market returns is by Professor Campbell Harvey. Some of his papers on the subject are as follows:

- Beakert, G. and C. Harvey. 'Emerging Equity Market Volatility'. *Journal of Financial Economics* 43, no. 1 (1997).
- Erb, C., C. Harvey and T. Viskanta. 'Political Risk, Economic Risk and Financial Risk'. *Financial Analysts Journal* (1996 Nov/Dec).
- Erb, C., C. Harvey and T. Viskanta. 'Risk in Emerging Markets'. *The Financial Survey* (1998 July–August).

SUGGESTED READINGS

Booth, Laurence. 'A New Model for Estimating Risk Premiums'. *Journal of Applied Corporate Finance* (1998 Spring).

Booth, Laurence. 'Estimating the Equity Risk Premium and Equity Costs: New Ways of Looking at Old Data'. *Journal of Applied Corporate Finance* (1999 Spring).

Bower, R. S. and Jeffrey M. Jenks. 'Divisional Screening Rates'. *Financial Management* (1975 Autumn).

Brigham, Eugene. 'Hurdle Rates for Screening Capital Expenditure Proposals'. *Financial Management* (1975 Autumn).

Brigham, E., D. Shome and S. Winson. 'The Risk Premium Approach to Measuring a Utility's Cost of Equity'. *Financial Management* (1985 Spring).

Chambers, D., R. Harris and J. Pringle. 'Treatment of Financing Mix in Analyzing Investment Opportunities'. *Financial Management* (1982 Summer).

Conine, T. E. and M. Tamarkin. 'Divisional Cost of Capital Estimation: Adjusting for Leverage'. *Financial Management* (1985 Spring).

Erhardt, M. C. *The Search for Value: Measuring the Company's Cost of Capital*. Boston, MA: HBS Press, 1994.

Fuller, R. Jr and K. Hickman. 'A Note on Estimating the Historical Risk Premium'. *Financial Practice and Education* (1991 Fall/Winter).

Fuller, R. J. and H. S. Kerr. 'Estimating the Divisional Cost of Capital: An Analysis of Pure Play Technique'. *Journal of Finance* (1981 December).

Gordon, M. J. and P. Halpern. 'The Cost of Capital for a Division of a Firm'. *Journal of Finance* (1972 May).

Gup, B and S Norwood. 'Divisional Cost of Capital: A Practical Approach'. *Financial Management* (1982 Spring).

Harrington, Diana. *Modern Portfolio Theory and Capital Asset Pricing Model*. Upper Saddle River, NJ: Prentice Hall, 1984.

Harris, R., T. J. O'Brien and D. Wakeman. 'Divisional Cost of Capital Estimation for Multi Industry Firms'. *Financial Management* (1989 Summer).

Petit, Justin. 'Corporate Capital Costs: A Practitioner's Guide'. *Journal of Applied Corporate Finance* (1999 Spring).

Rosenberg, B. and J. Guy. 'Prediction of a Beta from Investment Fundamentals'. *Financial Analysts Journal* (1976 May–June).

Siegel, Jeremy. 'The Application of the DCF Methodology for Determining the Cost of Equity Capital'. *Financial Management* (1985 Spring).

CHAPTER

5

Financial Statements and Firm Value

LEARNING OBJECTIVES

- Calculate all the significant financial ratios for a firm and interpret them
- Perform DuPont analysis
- Draw up cash flow statements
- Use financial information to predict financial distress
- Prepare financial and cash flow forecasts
- Understand the role of financial statement information in asset pricing

Financial statements are reports of financial performance of a company during the year. Financial statements are used by different stakeholders for different purposes. Lenders are interested in financial statements to assess the creditworthiness of the company; shareholders are interested in assessing the profit potential; bankers are interested in fixing the WC limit; and academic researchers are interested in the quality of disclosure. Nobody would be as much interested in the company as its managers simply because their personal fortune and jobs are tied to the performance of the company. For instance, they would be interested in assessing the indebtedness of the company or the impact of extending credit to customers. The set of analytical tools available is the same regardless of who you are. Only the emphasis changes.

A company's management is responsible for anticipating future imbalances in the company's financial system before its severity is reflected in the company's financial statements. The starting point for a financial forecast is the formulation of management goals and product market strategy, which in turn determines the outlook for sales. The firm's strategy and sales growth will determine the investment in fixed assets and WC to support these strategies. The effectiveness of these strategies coupled with competitive reaction will influence the company's financial performance and future need for finance. Obviously future profitability is necessary to access capital markets.

This chapter introduces introductory techniques such as ratio analysis, cash flow statement analysis and financial forecasting commonly used by managers and analysts to assess a firm's financial health.

FINANCIAL RATIOS AND FINANCIAL ANALYSIS

A ratio is a relationship between two numbers. Managers and analysts use a variety of balance sheet and income statement ratios to assess the financial health of a company. These ratios can be classified as:

- Liquidity ratios
- Coverage ratios
- Leverage ratios
- Operating ratios
- Profitability ratios

RATIOS MEASURING A COMPANY'S LIQUIDITY AND INDEBTEDNESS

Liquidity is a measure of the quality and adequacy of current assets to meet current obligations of the firm as they mature. Some liquidity ratios are discussed in the following text.

CURRENT RATIO

Computation: Total current assets divided by current liabilities.

$$\text{Current Ratio} = \frac{\text{Total Current Assets}}{\text{Total Current Liabilities}}$$

This ratio is a rough indication of a firm's ability to service its current obligations. Generally, the higher the current ratio, the greater is the cushion available to the firm. A higher ratio reflects the numerical superiority of current assets over current liabilities. However, it is prudent to look at the quality and composition of current assets in analysing the firm's liquidity. Bankers may prescribe certain minimum current ratio that a firm must maintain in order to be liquid at all times.

QUICK RATIO

Computation: Cash and equivalents plus trade receivables divided by total current liabilities.

$$\text{Quick Ratio} = \frac{\text{Cash \& Equivalents} + \text{Trade Receivables}}{\text{Total Current Liabilities}}$$

Quick ratio, a variant of the current ratio, measures the degree to which a company's current liabilities are covered by the most liquid current assets. Inventory is generally considered not too liquid and hence not included in the numerator. However, the portion of inventory that can be converted to cash fairly quickly can be included in the numerator. A ratio of less than 1 implies dependency on other current assets to liquidate short-term debt. This ratio is also called 'acid test' ratio. Highly liquid securities that can be converted to cash easily and bank deposits are considered cash equivalents.

COVERAGE RATIOS

These ratios measure the ability of the firm to service contractual financial commitments like debt. They make use of balance sheet and/or income statement numbers to estimate the cushion available (in earnings) to the firm before it defaults on contractual payments.

Interest Coverage Ratio

Computation: (EBIT) divided by interest expense.

Meaning: This ratio measures the firm's ability to meet its interest (expense) obligation. A high ratio indicates a comfortable position as regards debt servicing ability. The figure in the denominator is the actual interest expense extracted from the income statement. It is to be noted that this ratio does not measure the risk of default. The risk of default is measured by volatility of EBIT, which is dependent on the industry condition, profitability and such other factors. And so, a high ratio in one industry or during economic boom may be low in another industry or during economic recession. Put differently, this ratio is not forward-looking in nature.

Fixed Charges Coverage ratio

Computation: $\dfrac{\text{EBIT} + \text{Fixed charges such as lease payments and current portion of long-term debt}}{\text{Fixed charges}}$

Meaning: Fixed charges coverage ratio, a variant of interest coverage ratio, takes into account other fixed financial obligations of the firm while measuring the (financial obligation) servicing ability. It might be better to take cash flows rather than earnings in the numerator. Cash flow from operation = Profit after Tax (PAT) + Non-Cash Charges Such As Depreciation and Amortization

LEVERAGE RATIOS

These ratios measure the indebtedness of a firm. Firms with high amount of debt relative to equity are considered highly levered and are vulnerable to business downturns. It must be remembered that leverage ratios vary according to the capital requirements of the business, firm size, profitability and stability of earnings.

DEBT/NET WORTH

Computation:

Variant 1: Long-term debt divided by tangible net worth (share capital plus reserves and surplus)

Variant 2: Total liabilities divided by net worth

Meaning: This ratio measures the amount of debt employed by the firm. It is a measure of financial risk. A high ratio is generally viewed as risky because the firm is vulnerable to recession. When earnings fall, the firm may have difficulty in servicing debt. The higher the equity contribution (owner's capital), the greater is the protection provided to creditors.

DEBT/TOTAL ASSETS

Computation: Long-term debt divided by total assets (balance sheet total)

Meaning: This ratio measures the amount of debt as a fraction of total capital employed.

TOTAL ASSETS/EQUITY

Computation: Total assets (balance sheet total) divided by net worth

Meaning: This ratio measures the extent to which equity has been invested in total assets. A variant of this ratio is net fixed assets divided by equity.

Usually, only long-term debt is used in computation. A variant of this ratio incorporates short-term bank borrowings as well.

RATIOS MEASURING FUNDS MANAGEMENT (TURNOVER RATIOS)

These ratios are useful in ascertaining the efficiency of funds management. Some of the popular ratios are discussed in the subsequent section.

Sales/Receivables

Computation: Net sales divided by trade receivables.

This ratio measures the number of times trade receivables turn over during the year. The higher the turnover of receivables, the shorter is the time elapsed between sales and cash collection. Obviously, a firm should try to squeeze the lag between the two. If the ratio is less than the industry average, quality of receivables should be examined. When sales are seasonal, as in the air cooler industry, for instance, it may be inappropriate to use the value of receivables on any particular date as it may not be representative of the pattern during the entire year.

Days' Receivables

Computation: Number of days in a year divided by sales/receivables ratio.

$$\frac{365}{\text{Sales/Receivables Ratio}}$$

The resulting value expresses the average time in days that receivables are outstanding. Generally, the longer the time, the greater is the possibility of default. A comparison between the day's receivables ratio and the credit period offered by the company to customers will throw light on the efficiency of the collection process. As pointed out earlier, the ratio should not be calculated mechanically.

Cost of Sales/Inventory

Computation: Cost of sales divided by average inventory held.

This ratio measures the number of times inventory is turned over during the year. A higher ratio indicates better liquidity. A low inventory turnover ratio indicates poor liquidity and possible overstocking. It is to be noted that the value of inventory on a particular date may be inappropriate as it may not be representative of inventory held at other points in time. When the inventory figure is small (the denominator), the ratio will be high leading to wrong conclusions.

Days' Inventory

Computation: Number of days in a year divided by (cost of sales/inventory) ratio.

It measures the period of time for which the items are in inventory. It is expressed in days.

Cost of Sales/Payables

Computation: Cost of sales divided by trade payables

It measures the number of times payables turned over during the year. The higher the ratio, the shorter is the time between purchase and payment. Conversely, the lower the ratio, the longer is the time between purchase and payment. It could be either because the firm is enjoying good credit terms or deliberately extending the credit period.

Days' Payables

Computation: Number of days in one year divided by (cost of sales to payables) ratio.

$$\frac{365}{\text{Cost of Sales/Payables}}$$

Interpretation: It measures the average length of time for which payables (debt) are outstanding.

Sales/Working Capital

Computation: Net sales divided by (current assets minus current liabilities).

$$\frac{\text{Net Sales}}{\text{Net WC}}$$

Interpretation: It measures the efficiency with which WC is employed. A low ratio may indicate inefficiency and a high ratio may indicate efficient usage of WC or over trading.

OPERATING RATIOS: HOW EFFICIENT IS THE COMPANY?

These are measures of financial efficiency. They measure the efficiency with which the firm employs capital, be it shareholders equity capital or total capital. Accordingly, there are two commonly used measures: return on equity (ROE), and return on assets (ROA), depending on from whose viewpoint you are analysing.

RETURN ON EQUITY

Computation: Earnings available for shareholders divided by net worth.

$$\text{ROE} = \frac{\text{PAT} - \text{Preference Dividend (If Any)}}{\text{Net Worth}}$$

Interpretation: This ratio measures the efficiency with which the firm employs owners' equity. It estimates profits per rupee of shareholders' funds.

RETURN ON ASSETS

Computation:
Variant 1: EBIT divided by total assets
Variant 2: EBIT (1 – tax rate) divided by total assets

PROFITABILITY RATIOS

These ratios relate profit to sales. Some of the profitability ratios are as follows:

- Operating Profit Margin = EBIT ÷ Sales
- Net Profit Margin = PAT ÷ Sales

An Illustration

The balance sheet and income statements of Reliance Communications Ltd (RCL) are presented in Appendices 5A.1 and 5A.2. The key ratios for RCL are presented in Table 5.1.

Common Size Financial Statements

Common size balance sheet and income statements are prepared by dividing each item by a common denominator such as total assets or sales, respectively. The objective of preparing common size balance sheet and income statement is to ascertain the trends in proportions. For instance, if total currents have

TABLE 5.1
Key Ratios of RCL and Telecom Industry Peer Companies

							Domestic Industry Average	Global Industry Average
	2012	2011	2010	2009	2008	2007	2012	2012
Debt–Equity Ratio	0.98	0.81	0.79	0.87	0.8	0.76	0.63	0.42
Long-Term Debt–Equity Ratio	0.62	0.46	0.54	0.54	0.52	0.61	0.43	
Current Ratio	0.51	0.47	0.45	0.39	0.46	0.67	0.76	
Turnover Ratios								
Fixed Assets	0.23	0.29	0.29	0.38	0.47	0.4	0.1	
Inventory	40.87	46.91	43.96	52.15	46.41	31	9.53	
Debtors	6.03	7.05	6.57	7.4	9.05	8.16	2.46	
Total Asset Turnover Ratio	0.28	0.32	0.31	0.35	0.42	0.37	0.12	
Interest Cover Ratio	1.54	1.99	4.37	5.47	6.28	5.16	2.01	91.35
PBIDT Margin (%)	29.32	35.19	44.02	45.23	46.16	39.52	23.42	
PBIT Margin (%)	11.35	9.06	28.34	30.65	32.55	23.89	9.43	
PBDT Margin (%)	21.96	30.64	37.53	39.64	40.98	34.89	18.73	
Cash Profit Margin (%)	22.44	30.89	35.66	39.85	39.9	34.5	17.19	
PAT Margin (%)	4.46	4.77	19.99	25.26	26.28	18.87	3.2	10.52
ROCE (%)	3.15	2.9	8.69	10.88	13.74	8.85	1.13	
ROE (%)	2.5	2.78	10.99	16.8	19.91	12.3	0.64	13.68
Price Earning (P/E)	18.85	16.75	7.62	5.99	19.52	30.55	37.91	12.01
Price to Book Value (P/BV)	0.47	0.55	0.81	0.85	3.61	3.74	2.52	
Price/Cash EPS (P/CEPS)	3.5	2.78	4.15	3.67	10.96	13.36	4.67	
EV/EBIDTA	8.49	6.17	6.1	6.57	11.86	13.02	1.90	5.28
Market Cap/Sales	0.88	0.99	1.64	1.62	5.57	5	1.41	

Source: CMIE Prowess Database.

grown from 10 per cent of total assets to 15 per cent between the last year and the current year, one can investigate the reasons for changes in proportion.

DuPont Analysis

The ROI is a function of operating profit margin and turnover. By decomposing major ratios, a more meaningful analysis of the underlying business drivers can be made. For instance, the total assets figure can be broken down into its components such as current assets and fixed assets to investigate why these ratios are what they are.

$$\begin{aligned} ROE &= \frac{\text{Net Income}}{\text{Equity}} \\ &= \frac{\text{Net Income}}{\text{Sales}} \times \frac{\text{Sales}}{\text{Assests}} \times \frac{\text{Assests}}{\text{Equity}} \\ &= [\text{Profit Margin}] \times [\text{Asset Turnover}] \times [\text{Financial Leverage}] \end{aligned}$$

ROE can increase if any of these ratios increase. Decomposing ROE into its components throws light on the behaviour of each of the component ratios over a period. Increasing financial leverage is beneficial only up to a certain extent. Reckless borrowing destroys shareholder value.

$$ROE = [ROA + D/E\{ROA - i(1-T)\}]$$

where

i = interest rate on debt
T = tax rate
D/E = debt – equity ratio
$ROA = EBIT(1-T)/BV$ of Total Assets

Injecting debt increases the actual ROE as long as ROA is greater than the after tax cost of debt by an amount

$$D/E[ROA - i(1-T)]$$

This equation links ROE, ROA, D/E, Tax rate and the interest on debt.

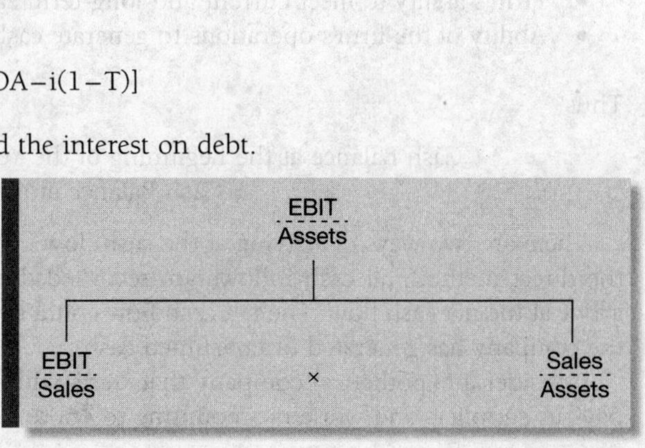

PREDICTING DISTRESS

Lenders lend money in exchange for interest and principal payments over a specified period of time. Credit risk refers to the chance that the expectation will not be met. The default risk can be estimated through a composite risk measure based on a firm's financial ratios as advocated by Altman (1968). His Z-score model combines select financial ratios to come up with a score as follows:

$$
\begin{aligned}
Z = & 0.012 \times \text{Net WC/Total Assets} \\
& + 0.014 \times \text{Retained Earnings/Total Assets} \\
& + 0.033 \times \text{EBIT/Total Assets} \\
& + 0.006 \times \text{Market Value of Equity/BV of Liabilities} \\
& + 0.999 \times \text{Sales/Total Assets}
\end{aligned}
$$

A high Z-score represents a low probability of default and a low Z-score represents a high probability of default. The model's classification accuracy was 95 per cent one year before bankruptcy and 72 per cent two years before. Accuracy of the model decreases as the time period is extended (it may also be unreliable in its predictive ability). Based on the study, it was concluded that firms with a Z-score less than 1.81 are all bankrupt, while those with Z-score greater than 2.99 fall into the non-bankrupt group. Those falling into the area between 1.81 and 2.99 require more analysis to determine their solvency status. The non-liquid asset ratios such as total debt to total assets and cash flow to total debt are, in general, better predictors of bankruptcy than the liquid assets ratios such as quick ratio or net WC to total assets. Managers may use distress prediction models as a first step to understand the solvency status of their firms. A low Z-score (below 1.81) itself does not suggest that bankruptcy will occur. A firm may avoid bankruptcy by cash infusion and/or waiving of loan covenants by lenders.

CASH FLOW STATEMENT

A cash flow statement tries to explain the change in cash position between two balance sheet dates. Thus, an increase in plant and machinery will be recorded as a use in funds flow statement but may not be recorded in cash flow statement if it does not involve a cash outlay during the period. In short, non-cash transactions do not enter the cash flow statement. The net cash flow is simply the net of all inflows and outflows during the period. The cash flow statement is helpful in a number of situations where cash flows are important. These include the following:

- Analysis of credit proposals
- Firm's need for external financing and the use of its long-term debt
- Firm's ability to meet current and long-term cash obligations
- Ability of the firm's operations to generate cash

Thus,

$$
\begin{aligned}
& \text{Cash Balance at the Beginning of the Year} + \text{Net Cash Flow During the Year} \\
& = \text{Cash Balance at the End of the Year}
\end{aligned}
$$

There are two ways of arriving at the cash flow from operations: direct and indirect methods. Under the direct method, all cash inflows are recorded during the period and all outflows are deducted to arrive at the net cash flow. The net cash flow could be either positive or negative depending on whether the company has generated or consumed cash.

Consider a hypothetical company that starts with ₹1,000 in hand. During the period, the company pays its suppliers and workers amounting to ₹600. Customers pay ₹700 during the period.

$$
\begin{aligned}
\text{Net Cash Flow} &= -₹600 + 700 = ₹100 \\
\text{Cash Balance at the End} &= ₹1{,}100
\end{aligned}
$$

The cash flow statement is usually prepared for the year although any other duration may be chosen. Net profit is not the same as cash flow. The financial statements are prepared on the basis of accrual concept. For instance, sales are recorded when products are sold even if customers do not pay cash immediately or salaries are recorded as expense even when in reality the actual cash outflow is in the next period (e.g., beginning of next month). The cash flow statement is designed to analyse the underlying cash flow position. Cash flow might be higher or lower than the net income. The direct method illustrated earlier is simple and straightforward but is time-consuming. Managers of the company who have intricate details of all transactions can use it. The indirect method arrives at the same result in a circuitous way. Starting with net income, a series of adjustments are made to transform net income into cash flow from operations.

Net income

Add back expenses that do not involve cash outflow (e.g., depreciation, amortization).

Subtract cash outflows not treated as expenses (e.g., capex [machines, land]).

Increase in inventory involves outflow but is not recorded as expense.

Subtract revenues that do not involve cash inflow (e.g., sales on credit, i.e., increase in accounts receivables).

Increase in accrued interest earned.

CASH FLOW FROM OPERATIONS

It is useful to classify cash flows on the basis of activities. The standard practice for preparing the cash flow statement is to classify activities into operating, investing and financing activities and record cash flow under each heading. A manager or an analyst can make useful interpretations such as: Where is the cash coming from? How is it being used? What are the levels of and trends in cash flows from the three types of activities?

The generic structure of a cash flow statement is as follows:

Cash Flow from Operations + Cash flow from Investment Activities + Cash Flow from Financing Activities + Net Effect of Exchange Rate Changes on Cash = Net Increase (Decrease) In Cash

Operating activities are related to the firm's ongoing ability to generate cash from operations. This includes information on cash receipts from customers for sales and service, cash payments related to vendors, employees, taxes and interest. The net of all these flows is the cash flow from operations. Investment activities relate to change in non-current assets. This includes information on capex to acquire fixed assets and proceeds from sale of non-current assets. This section also contains purchase and sale of short-term investments. Only cash transactions get reflected. Financing activities relate to changes in borrowings and owners' equity. This includes information on cash proceeds from issuing equity and short-term and long-term debt, and cash outflow due to repurchase of shares. Dividend payment is also a financing activity. The cash flow statements of RCL is in Appendix 5A.3.

The cash flow pattern depends on the nature of business and the life cycle of the company. Start-up companies in high growth industries would have negative cash flow because of high capex in relation to the level of earnings. The gap between the two is met by selling debt or equity. Established growth companies can meet their investment requirements from internally generated funds. Mature companies will have modest capex requirements.

Their cash flow from operations will be slightly more than reinvestment. Those firms in the declining phase would have surplus cash from operations which could be returned to shareholders, pay off debt for revitalize product lines. Turnarounds are characterized by cash inflows due to freeing up of assets and income statement losses. Thus, the cash flow pattern indicates the position of a company in its business life cycle and the business model. To start with, cash flow from operations should be positive and growing.

Second, see whether the company is investing to grow, that is, whether investments are more than depreciation. Healthy companies typically purchase more assets than they sell. Hence, cash flow from investing activities will be negative. To judge whether a company is doing well or not, one must use evidence from all pieces and put them together.

THE LINK BETWEEN CASH FLOWS AND FIRM VALUE

The value of a firm is equal to the PV of future cash flows.[1]

$$V=\sum_{t=1}^{\infty}(\text{Cash Flow}_t)/(1+k)^t$$

where cash flow = EBIT (1 − T) + Depreciation − (+) Increases (Decreases) in WC − Capex
k = discount rate = WACC

Since the value of the firm is determined by the cash flow it generates, an analysis of drivers of cash flow (see Figure 5.1) would be useful. The value of the firm can also be rewritten as PV of free cash flows discounted at cost of unlevered equity plus the PV of debt tax shields discounted at the cost of debt.[2] While sales growth, gross margin expenses and tax rate determine NOPAT, days' receivable, days' inventory and days' payable determine incremental WC investment. Investors care about the cash economics of the business because they determine the magnitude, timing and risk of future cash flows. Because new economy companies such as Amazon and Flipkart have dramatically different cash flows than old economy companies such as Unilever, we would expect them to have dramatically different valuations as well. This is indeed the case. Other things being equal, the larger the cash inflow from cash investments, the more valuable is the company. Conversely, a larger cash outflow from cash investments translates into lower valuation. Internet companies usually have significantly lower investment needs than their old economy counterparts.

FINANCIAL FORECASTING

Techniques like ratio analysis and cash flow statement analysis are used to evaluate past performance. Financial forecasting involves development of financial models to look into the future. There are three principal components of financial planning.

- Preparation of pro forma financial statement

[1] These concepts will be explained in greater detail in the following chapters.

[2] This is the adjusted present value method of valuation. It will be discussed later.

FIGURE 5.1
Drivers of Cash Flow

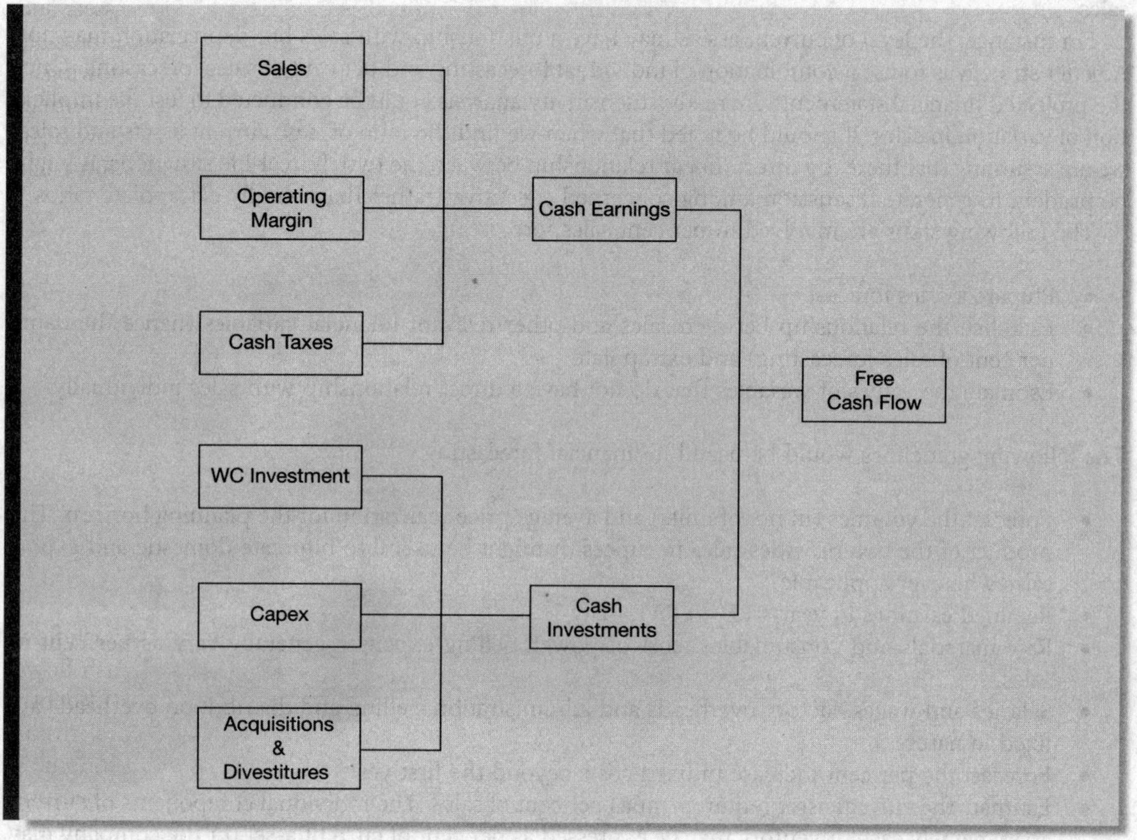

- Preparation of cash flow estimates
- Preparation of cash budgets

In this section, the first two will be discussed. Financial planning is essential to all companies regardless of size. Since the common denominator in business is money and money needs to be managed well, it is the responsibility of not only the finance manager but also all concerned executives to plan and prepare for the future. A financial plan is only one part of the story. The other components of the overall plan include marketing strategy, production plan and so on. A financial plan is supposed to throw light on the capital investment and financing needs of the firm given its growth objective. The preparation of pro forma financial statements is one of the most widely used financial forecasting techniques. As the name suggests, it is the projection of what the financial statements look like during the forecast period, say, one–five years. The projection (of financial statements) involves prediction of each of the variables that you find in the balance sheet and income statement. The simplest way to forecast financial statement would be to express all income statement and balance sheet numbers as per cent of sales and given the sales forecast for the next period find the values of all variables using the historic relationship between the variable and sales. Obviously, not all variables will have a strict, direct relationship with sales.

For instance, the level of current assets may have a relationship with sales but depreciation may not. A better strategy is to use a combination of individual forecasting and per cent of sales forecasting. Once the projected financial statements are ready, a sensitivity analysis could be conducted to test the implication of variation in sales. It should be noted that when we find the ratio of, say, current assets and sales, we are assuming that there is a direct, linear relationship between the two. In real-life situations, it might be prudent to generate discussion among concerned executives rather than blindly extrapolate ratios.

The following steps are involved in per cent sales forecasting:

- Prepare a sales forecast
- Establish the relationship between sales and other relevant financial variables (hence the name per cent of sales forecasting) and extrapolate
- Estimate the values of variables that do not have a direct relationship with sales individually.

The following guidelines would be useful in financial forecasting.

- Forecast the volumes (in no. of units) and average price realization for the planning horizon. The product of the two provides sales in rupees. It might be useful to bifurcate domestic and export sales wherever applicable.
- Retained earnings in $\text{year}_t = RE_{t-1} + PAT_t - Div_t$
- Raw materials and consumables, cost of power, selling expenses generally vary as per cent of sales.
- Salaries and wages, factory overheads and administration, selling and distribution overheads are fixed in nature.
- Forecast the per cent increase in fixed costs beyond the first year.
- Estimate the current asset requirement as per cent of sales. The individual components of current asset, namely cash, inventory may be expressed as per cent of current asset (or the company may have a policy of maintaining, say, 30 days inventory and so on. Use this information to forecast).
- Estimate current liabilities as a per cent of current assets.
- Depreciation schedule of fixed assets needs to be drawn up to estimate the amount of depreciation in each year.
- Use the marginal tax rate to calculate PAT.
- Ending Equity = Beginning Equity + Retained Earnings for the Year + Share Capital Issued If Any.
- Draw up the loan amortization schedule and then calculate the value of long-term liabilities for each year.
- Calculate interest on the outstanding amount at the stated per cent rate.

The per cent-of-sales forecasting model provides an estimate of the amount of external financing required in the coming year to support the expected level of activity.

External Funding Requirement = Increase in Assets Required to Support the Increase in Sales – [Additional Funds Provided by Spontaneous Current Liabilities Such as Accounts Payable + Pro Forma Increase in Retained Earnings]

$$= [(A_t/S_t)\Delta S_{t=1}] - [(L_t/S_t)(\Delta S_{t=1}) + E_{t=1} - D_{t+1}]$$

where A/S is asset intensity, $\Delta S_{t=1}$ = increase in sales, E is the expected increase in earnings after taxes, D is total dividends and $(L_t/S_t)(\Delta S_{t=1})$ is the additional funds provided by spontaneous current liabilities.

This equation assumes that a company's capital investment is closely associated with next year's sales. The capital budgeting process defines expected increase in fixed assets as the sum of capital expenditures plus other necessary expenditures and there need not be a proportional relationship between fixed assets and sales. Consequently, the equation can be rewritten as:

$$\text{External Funding Requirement} = [(CA_t/S_t)\Delta S_{t=1}) + \Delta FA_{t=1}] - [(L_t/S_t)(\Delta S_{t=1}) + E_{t=1} + Dep_{t+1} - D_{t+1}]$$

where $(CA_t/S_t)\Delta S_{t=1})$ is the forecast of change in current assets, $\Delta FA_{t=1}$ is the total capex planned for t+1 and Dep_{t+1} is the depreciation expense expected in the forecast period.

CASH FLOW FORECASTING

A cash flow statement is an ex-post statement of net cash flows from operating, investing and financing activities of a company prepared between two balance sheet dates. A cash flow forecast is a forward-looking financial planning tool. To prepare a cash flow forecast, predict the cash proceeds and cash disbursements during the period. The excess of cash outflow over cash inflow is the external funds requirement.

$$\text{External Fund Requirement} = \text{Total Uses} - \text{Total Sources}$$

Whether a company has external financing requirement depends on sales growth, length of cash cycle, future level of profitability and profit retention. Those companies with high sales growth, long cash cycle and low profitability will have to seek external financing frequently (Why?). High sales growth need not always result in a need for external finance. A company that extends no credit to customers or carry few current and fixed assets can experience rapid sales growth without seeking external finance as long as it is reasonably profitable. Because the company has fewer assets, the increase in total assets is largely offset by a corresponding increase in current liabilities. To fix the idea, consider an example. In order to equip itself with high-tech capabilities, a telecom company is making massive capital investments. The forecast of the same is given as follows:

(₹ million)

1995	1996	1997	1998–2001
121	115	89	270

The company currently earns ₹46.4 million PAT. The company expects PAT to grow at 25 per cent for the next three years and decline to 15 per cent for the next four years. The company is currently paying 80 per cent of its earnings as dividends and feels that the same payout should be continued. Assume the following values depreciation: ₹20 million, ₹26 million, ₹30 million for the next three years and ₹150 million for the following four years (cumulative).

$$\text{Sources of Funds} = \text{Net Income} + \text{Depreciation}$$

$$\text{Uses of Funds} = \text{Capex} + \text{Incremental Net WC} + \text{Dividends}$$

$$\text{External Fund Requirement} = \text{Sources} - \text{Uses}$$

The forecast of sources and uses of funds and the external funding requirement is given as follows:

Sources				
PAT	58	73	91	522
Depreciation	20	26	30	150
Total	78	99	121	672
Uses				
Capex	121	115	89	270
Inc WC[3]	15	20	30	50
Dividends[4]	46	58	73	418
Total	182	193	192	738
External Funding Need (Annual)	104	94	71	66

The company needs close to ₹335 million in the next seven years. Having estimated the future financing requirement, management must identify the sources of finance and establish financial policies that will ensure continuous access to capital markets on acceptable terms. The last step involves analysis of viability of the plan, determination of debt–equity mix consistent with the company's debt policy and stress testing the plan.

Sensitivity analysis refers to the analysis of sensitivity of profitability and other financial variables to changes in sales. Sensitivity analysis involves observation of changes in financial forecast for changes in underlying variables. For instance, if the growth in PAT for the company mentioned in the previous example were to be only 15 per cent throughout, what would happen to external funding requirement (EFR)? Financial ratios?

The steps involved in forecasting and planning is summarized in the following figure.

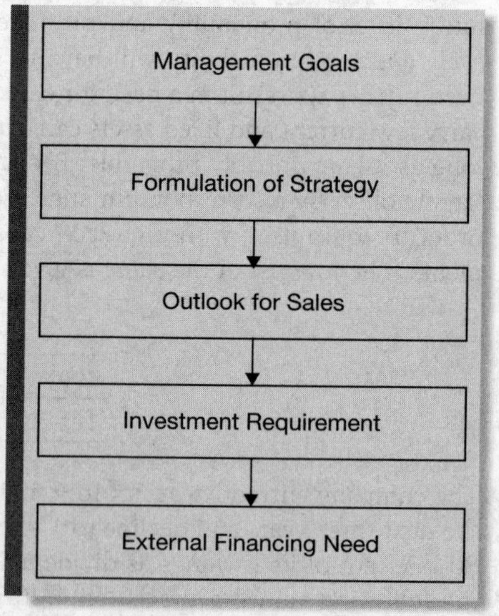

FINANCIAL STATEMENTS AND ASSET PRICING

The value of a company's equity is a function of cost of equity which in turn depends on β. As pointed out in Chapter 4, some studies in the USA and elsewhere have reported theoretical links between financial leverage and β. The higher the financial leverage, the higher is the β. Likewise, few other studies have shown that the higher the operating leverage (ratio of fixed to variable costs), the

3 Increase in WC. In real life, this is to be estimated on the basis of target current ratio, lending bank's norms and sales growth.

4 80 per cent of PAT.

higher is the β. Other ratios such as debt–equity ratio, preferred stock to equity ratio, sales to equity ratio, current ratio, SD of earnings to price ratio also seem to be highly correlated with estimates of β derived from security returns. Stock markets price a company's securities on the basis of financial information released to the market. A manager would be interested in knowing, for instance, how stock markets react to earnings announcements. Academic studies in the USA suggest that:

- The release of interim and annual earnings is associated with both increased trading volume and increased return variability.
- The sign and magnitude of the unexpected earnings change is positively correlated with the sign and magnitude of security returns in the two trading days immediately surrounding the earnings announcements.
- Significant positive association exists between magnitude of forecast deviation and magnitude of abnormal returns in the period immediately around forecast disclosure date.
- Firms that increase dividends or announce special or extra dividends or initiate dividend payments for the first time experience positive abnormal returns.

CONCLUDING COMMENTS

In this chapter, we introduced you to the use of ratio analysis, preparation of cash flow statements and financial forecasts. These tools find extensive application in appraising credit risk, capital structure planning and financial planning.

CONCEPT TEST

State whether the following statements are true (T) or false (F).

1. A firm with high ROE is necessarily better than the one with a low ROE.
2. ROA = Gross Profit Margin (%) × Asset Turnover
3. ROE = ROA × Financial Leverage
4. ROE measures the efficiency with which the firm employs total capital.
5. ROA is a basic measure of the efficiency with which a company allocates and manages its resources.
6. Asset Turnover = $\frac{\text{Sales}}{\text{Assets}}$
7. Financial leverage refers to employing debt in the capital structure.
8. ROE increases as long as the ROA is more than the post-tax interest cost of debt.
9. Interest or fixed charges coverage measures the cushion available to the firm in servicing fixed financial obligations.

EXERCISES

1. The balance sheets and income statements of Kingfisher Airlines are given as follows:

Income Statement

	2011	2010	2009
Sales Turnover	63,596	50,679.2	52,389.8
Excise Duty	380.3	706.9	0
Net Sales	63,216	49,972.3	52,389.8
Other Income	1,359	2,031.2	8,406.9
Total Income	**64,575**	**52,003.5**	**60,796.7**
Power and Fuel Cost	22,806	18,105.5	26,092.1
Employee Cost	6,760	6,887.6	8,254.2
Other Manufacturing Expenses	12,720	11,793.2	12,356.5
Selling and Administration Expenses	20,397	21,844.7	23,050.5
Miscellaneous Expenses	1,558.9	4,897.7	3,478
Total Expenditure	64,243	63,528.7	73,231.3
Operating Profit	331.9	–11,525.2	–12,434.6
Interest	13,129.4	11,025.9	7,785.5
Gross Profit	–12,797.5	–22,551.1	–20,220.1
Depreciation	2,410.4	1,628	1,332
Profit Before Tax	15,207.9	–24,179.1	–21,552.1
Tax	0	0	0
Fringe Benefit tax	0.03	–60.6	125
Deferred Tax	–4,943.2	–7,646.3	–5,588.8
Reported Net Profit	–10,274	–16,472.2	–16,088.3
Extraordinary Items	–918	–3,551.5	–6.6
Adjusted Net Profit	**–9,356**	**–12,920.7**	**–16,081.7**

Balance Sheet

	2011	2010	2009
Sources of Funds			
Share Capital	1,050.88	362.91	362.91
Reserves	–4,002.07	–4,240.86	–2,496.37
Total Shareholders' Funds	–2,951.19	–3,870.47	–2,125.35
Secured Loans	5,039.91	4,842.43	2,622.52
Unsecured Loans	1,986.31	3,080.17	3,043.04
Total Debt	7,026.22	7,922.6	5,665.56

Other Liabilities	33.19	0	0
Total Liabilities	4,108.22	4,052.13	3,540.21
Gross Block	2,254.26	2,048.13	1,891.8
Less: Accumulated Depreciation	682.37	493.62	316.28
Net Block	1,571.89	1,554.51	1,575.52
Capital Work-in-Progress	0	980.61	1,630.94
Investments	0.05	0.05	0.05
Current Assets, Loans and Advances			
Inventories	193.08	171.32	147.25
Sundry Debtors	440.53	322.48	274.23
Cash and Bank	252.36	206.47	171.87
Loans and Advances	871.57	1,936.9	1,606.34
Total Current Assets	1,757.54	2,637.17	2,199.69
Less: Current Liabilities and Provisions			
Current Liabilities	4,108.82	3,501.37	3,494.68
Provisions	41.61	53.2	45.55
Total Current Liabilities	4,150.43	3,554.57	3,540.23
Net Current Assets	–2,392.89	–917.4	–1,340.54
Miscellaneous Expenses not Written Off	0	0	4.51
Deferred Tax Assets	3,286.9	2,841.03	2,034.08
Deferred Tax Liability	359.12	406.67	364.35
Net Deferred Tax	2,927.78	2,434.36	1,669.73
Other Assets	2,001.39	0	0
Total Assets	4,108.22	4,052.13	3,540.21

Calculate all the ratios and interpret them.

2. Classify as sources and uses of funds

Fixed Assets	–500
Long-Term Debt	2,000
Cash	–300
Accounts Payable	1,000
Net Profit	–600
Cash Dividends	800
Public Issue of Shares	1,000

3. On 2 January 2018, Nitin, a young MBA set up a manufacturing unit. 500,000 shares were issued at par (₹10). During the period January through June, the company made the following expenditure.

- 15 Jan: Paid ₹7,500 in legal fees, printing expenses and so on associated with the incorporation of the company
- 15 June: Spent ₹62,500 for machining
- 20 June: Purchased ₹75,000 worth of plastics and chemicals for use in the production

During the second half of 2018, the company started full production. In early July, a consulting engineer was paid ₹23,750.

During July–December, the company sold goods worth ₹754,500. A big customer still owed ₹69,500 at the end of the year. All other customers paid in full. Additional chemicals and plastics were purchased for a total of ₹175,000. All of these purchases were paid in cash.

During the year, the company spent ₹22,500 on television and trade journal advertising.

The company expended ₹350,000 on direct labour and other manufacturing related overhead. An additional ₹80,000 was spent on corporate salaries and other corporate expenses.

In early July, a further ₹150,000 was spent on machinery.

During the year, the company had borrowed ₹50,000 for a short time and repaid the loan by the year end. The interest paid amounted to ₹750.

On 31 December, the company had ₹55,000 worth of plastics and chemicals in the warehouse. However, there were no finished goods. The machinery used in the production was expected to last 10 years, six months of which had already passed.

Prepare a summary of cash transactions and a statement of cash flows for the year.

4. The historical balance sheets of a company are given as follows:

Liabilities	2016	2017	2018
Equity	34,650	33,056	33,032
Long-Term Liabilities	13,542	11,909	18,143
Current Liabilities	15,554	11,915	15,647
Total	63,746	56,880	67,092
Assets	1,982	1,983	1,984
Net Fixed Assets	11,138	12,437	11,246
Others	736	1,571	2,066
Current Assets			
Total	63,746	56,880	67,092

If sales are ₹75,000, express all variables as (average) per cent of sales. If current assets grow at 14 per cent, current liabilities at 22 per cent and fixed assets at 21 per cent, forecast the balance sheet for the next year.

5. From the following data, calculate collection period, payables period and inventory turnover, respectively.

A.	Sales	₹150,000
	Accounts Receivable	₹12,000
B.	Sales	₹900,000
	Cost of Sales	₹500,000

	Purchases	₹360,000
	Ending Inventory	₹420,000
	Accounts Payable	₹90,000
C.	Sales	₹1,400,000
	Beginning Inventory	₹120,000
	Ending Inventory	₹310,000
	Cost of Sales	₹900,000

6. A company with a current ratio of 2.5 has current liabilities of ₹130,000. Indicate whether the transactions increase or decrease the current ratio, the WC and if yes, to what extent.
   - The company purchased ₹10,000 worth of goods on account.
   - The company collects accounts receivables amounting to ₹8,000.
   - The company purchases a machine worth ₹40,000 by paying ₹10,000 in cash and the balance on credit to be paid after 15 months.
   - Company pays dividends amounting to ₹10,000 in cash.
7. Calculate the ROA for the two companies given as follows:

	α	β
Net Sales	₹25,375,000	–
Total Assets	–	₹4,250,000
Net Profit on Sales	5%	20%
Turnover of Assets	6X	–
Gross Margin (%)	35	₹460,000 (25%)

SUGGESTED READINGS

Altman, E. 'Financial Ratios, Discriminant Analysis, and the Prediction of Corporate Bankruptcy'. *Journal of Finance*, (1968 September).

Barnes, P. 'The Analysis and Use of Financial Ratios: A Review Article'. *Journal of Business Finance & Accounting* 14, no. 4 (1987 Winter).

Firer, C. 'Driving Financial Performance Through the DuPont Identity: A Strategic Use of Financial Analysis and Planning'. *Financial Practice and Education* (1999 Spring/Summer).

Houghton, K. and D. Woodliff. 'Financial Ratios: The Prediction of Corporate "Success" and Failure'. *Journal of Business Finance & Accounting* 14, no. 4 (1987 Winter).

Hubbard, C., D. Walz and D. Walz. 'An Empirical Test of the Percent-of-Sales Financial Forecasting Model'. *Financial Practice and Education* (1997 Fall/Winter).

Matsumoto, K., M. Shivaswamy and J. Hoban. 'Security Analysts' Views of the Financial Ratios of Manufacturers and Retailers'. *Financial Practice & Education* (1995 Fall/Winter).

Taggart, R. 'Spreadsheet Exercises for Linking Financial Statements, Valuation and Capital Budgeting'. *Financial Practice & Education* (1999 Spring/Summer).

APPENDIX 5A.1

Income Statement of RCL (₹ million)

	2012	2011	2010	2009	2008	2007
Sales Turnover	221,330	248,980	239,021.5	247,360	206,055	186,842
Net Sales	196,770	224,310	214,963	222,505	188,273	171,903
Other Income	7,050	7,430	33,740	24,671.8	31,231	10,496
Total Income	**203,820**	**231,740**	**248,704**	**247,177**	**219,505**	**182,400**
Expenditure						
Power and Fuel Cost	16,620	15,790	15,094	8,418.5	5,443.3	3,960
Employee Cost	12,830	14,690	14,993	16,758	11,669.9	10,843
Other Manufacturing Expenses	72,280	72,460	72,821	69,039	56,527	63,420
Selling and Administration Expenses	36,480	35,920	40,166	38,387	28,736	23,896
Miscellaneous Expenses	710	1,340	417	2,680	7,631	6,448
Total Expenditure	**138,920**	**140,200**	**143,492**	**135,283**	**110,008**	**108,567**
Operating Profit	64,900	91,540	105,211	111,893	109,496	73,832
Interest	16,300	11,330	15,518	13,849	10,681	8,644
Gross Profit	48,600	80,210	89,693	98,044	98,815	65,188
Depreciation	39,780	65,040	37,4651	36,077	28,052	29,192
Profit Before Tax	8,820	15,170	52,228	61,967	70,762	35,995
Tax	–1,060	–2,800	3,725	327.6	1,644.9	529.1
Fringe Benefit Tax	0	0	0	162.3	189.7	191.6
Deferred Tax	0	2,920	728.9	–1,007.8	1,001.6	10.3
Net Profit	9,880	15,050	47,774	62,485	67,926	35,264
Minority Interest (After Tax)	610	1,500	1,192.5	2,051.7	13,900	–49.2
Profit/Loss of Associate Company	1	–100	–31.9	15.9	–14.7	0
Net Profit after Minority Interest and P/L Associate Company	9,280	13,450	46,550	60,449.3	54,011	35,313
Extraordinary Items	786	3,173	1,569	3,187	13,766	8.3
Adjusted Net Income	9,201.4	10,276.5	449,80.9	57,261.4	40,245.4	35,305.2
Equity Dividend (%)	5	10	17	16	15	10
DPS (₹)	0.25	0.5	0.85	0.8	0.75	0.5

Source: CMIE Prowess Database.

APPENDIX 5A.2
Balance Sheet of RCL (₹ million)

	2012	2011	2010	2009	2008	2007
Share Capital	10,320	10,320	10,320	10,320	10,320	10,223
Reserves	356,890	394,670	423,286	412,483	279,943	219,083
Total Shareholders' Funds	367,210	404,990	433,606	422,803	290,263	229,306
Minority Interest	8,600	8,240	6,583.9	6,549.2	24,309.3	56.1
Secured Loans	359,640	216,930	30,000	30,000	9,500	51,135.7
Unsecured Loans	23,390	173,780	267,154.2	361,622.5	248,717	123,247.6
Total Debt	383,030	390,710	297,154.2	391,622.5	258,217	174,383.3
Other Liabilities	20,410	14,180	0	0	0	0
Total Liabilities	**779,250**	**818,120**	**737,344.5**	**820,974.9**	**572,789.6**	**403,745.9**
Gross Block	1,045,710	868,380	836,629	807,316.4	499,041.8	376,029.1
Less: Accumulated Depreciation	331,100	273,400	190,671	141,144.2	89,561	55,192.1
Less: Impairment of Assets	0	0	0	0	0	733.9
Net Block	714,610	594,980	645,958	666,172.2	409,480	320,103
Capital Work-in-Progress	50,260	166,000	116,556.5	113,096	149,299.3	36,906.8
Investments	6,520	5,700	41,598.9	95,657	109,996.3	77,114
Current Assets, Loans and Advances						
Inventories	5,660	5,170	5,446.3	5,427.2	4,058.8	4,821.2
Sundry Debtors	35,840	37,530	33,116.7	39,617.7	27,223.7	18,316.1
Cash and Bank	5,500	48,660	8,185.4	16,829	8,781.8	72,006.4
Loans and Advances	73,260	68,600	74,824.5	85,270	65,752	35,986
Total Current Assets	120,260	159,960	121,572.9	147,144.7	105,817.2	131,130.4
Less: Current Liabilities and Provisions						
Current Liabilities	110,810	94,320	147,084.6	159,718.3	156,212.5	114,333.6
Provisions	26,660	31,120	40,266.7	41,095.7	44,563.7	47,148.8
Total Current Liabilities	137,470	125,440	187,351.3	200,814	200,776.2	161,482.4
Net Current Assets	**–17,210**	**34,520**	**–65,778.4**	**–53,669.3**	**–94,959**	**–30,352**
Deferred Tax Assets	6,450	6,800	7,553.0	121	1,298	178.8
Deferred Tax Liability	16,630	10,470	8,543.8	402	2,325.6	204.8
Net Deferred Tax	–10,180	–3,670	–990.5	–281	–1,027.6	–26
Other Assets	35,250	20,590	0	0	0	0
Total Assets	**779,250**	**818,120**	**737,344.5**	**820,974.9**	**572,789.6**	**403,745.9**

Source: CMIE Prowess Database.

APPENDIX 5A.3
Cash Flow Statements of RCL (₹ million)

	2012	2011	2010	2009	2008	2007
Cash and Cash Equivalents at Beginning of the Year	38,130	820	5,351.5	1,926.6	66,872.2	0.5
Net Cash from Operating Activities	**33,390**	**7,260**	**10,754.3**	**18,877.8**	**29,813.9**	**105,087.9**
Cash Flow from Operating Activities						
Net Profit Before Tax and Extraordinary Items	1,550	–8,600	6,194.7	48,150.7	26,040.9	24,208.5
Adjustment For						
Depreciation	17,410	15,940	15,112.4	19,335.1	18,436.6	18,361.2
Interest (Net)	6,690	700	5,360.2	3,914.7	8,247.3	2,949.2
P/L on Sales of Assets	–70	–4,260	0	–30,634.3	–0.7	50.3
P/L on Sales of Invest	–230	–190	–2.4	0	38.4	–217.8
Prov. and W/O (Net)	450	1,310	–817.4	1,050.4	1,465.8	1,385.8
P/L in Forex	–1,300	–2,410	–20,449.8	–2,469.9	–3,838.5	–1,011.7
Fin. Lease & Rental Charges	–30	–30	–29.2	0	0	0
Others	–50	–70	–311.4	–4,790.9	130.9	131.5
Total Adjustments (PBT and Extraordinary Items)	22,870	10,990	–1,137.6	–13,594.9	24,479.8	21,648.5
Op. Profit Before WC Changes	24,420	2,390	5,057.1	34,555.8	50,520.7	45,857
Adjustment For						
Trade and Other Receivables	1,330	–6,350	–6,486.3	–16,410.7	–4,253.6	32,309.9
Inventories	–230	–80	–452	–519.2	–1,027.1	–325.4
Trade Payables	7,210	10,980	12,978.2	3,336.6	–14,893	27,764.5
Total (OP before WC Changes)	8,310	4,550	6,039.9	–13,593.3	–20,173.7	59,749
Cash Generated from/(Used In) Operations	32,730	6,940	11,097	20,962.5	30,347	105,606
Direct Taxes Paid	650	320	–2,390	–2,113.8	–533.1	–518.1
Others	0	0	2,047.3	29.1	0	0
Total – Others	650	320	–342.7	–2,084.7	–533.1	–518.1
Cash Flow Before Extraordinary Items	33,380	7,260	10,754.3	18,877.8	29,813.9	105,087.9
Gain on Forex Exch. Tran	10	0	0	0	0	0
Net Cash Used In Investing Activities	**–21,150**	**–28,020**	**43,402.6**	**–79,505.4**	**–157,007**	**–150,466**
Cash Flow from Investing Activities						
Investment in Assets						
Purchase of Fixed Assets	–24,680	–87,460	–8,433.6	–43,826.2	–73,198.4	–27,278.3

	2012	2011	2010	2009	2008	2007
Sale of Fixed Assets	2,160	2,080	0	100	2.6	5.9
Financial/Capital Investment						
Purchase of Investments	–269,370	–175,730	–38,142.8	–1,748.3	–112,007	–84,174
Sale of Investments	272,140	198,910	28,420.5	230.5	72,749.4	91,604.9
Interest Received	4,230	4,820	5,818.6	102.5	777.6	1,013.5
Loans to Subsidiaries	–158,960	–285,130	–423,850	–380,301	–36,962.8	–31,000
Others	153,330	314,490	479,589.9	345,936.6	–8,368.9	–10,0638
Net Cash Used in Financing Activities	**–48,590**	**58,070**	**–58,686.6**	**64,052.5**	**62,347.5**	**46,062.4**
Cash Flow From Financing Activities						
Proceeds						
Proceed from Issue of Debentures	20,000	0	0	30,000	0	0
Proceed from Other Long-Term Borrowings	78,920	51,860	24,280.7	0	58,912.2	1,116.6
Proceed from Short-Term Borrowings	0	40,160	0	68,351.1	75,509.1	75,190.6
Payments		0	0	0	0	0
On Redemption of Debenture	–65,070	0	0	0	0	0
Of the Long-Term Borrowings	–14,840	–21,290	0	–9,500	–40,385.2	–5,671
Of the Short-Term Borrowings	–50,600	0	–69,502.3	–905.9	–22,343.1	–19,879.5
Dividend Paid	–1,190	–2,020	–1,911.2	–1,792.3	–1,182.8	0
Shelter Assistance Reserve	0	0	0	0	0	0
Interest Paid	–13,540	–10,640	–11,553.8	–10,911.5	–8,163.3	–4694.3
Others	–2,270	0	0	–11,188.9	0.6	0
Net Cash Used in Financing Activities	–48,590	58,070	–58,686.6	64,052.5	62,347.5	46,062.4
Net Inc/(Dec) in Cash and Cash Equivalent	–36,350	37,310	–4,529.7	3,424.9	–64,845.6	684
Cash and Cash Equivalents at End of the Year	1,780	38,130	821.8	5,351.5	2,026.6	684.5

Source: CAPITALINE Databases.

SECTION 2

Capital Investments

CHAPTER

6

Overview of Capital Budgeting

LEARNING OBJECTIVES

- The nature of capital investment appraisal
- The techniques available for evaluating capital investments
- The limitations of these techniques
- The capital budgeting practices in select countries

Some of the major responsibilities of top management are in the area of long-range planning. Allocating resources to competing uses is one of the most important decisions a manager has to take. Executives are constantly faced with such questions as:

- Which projects should a firm accept?
- How should the productivity of capital be measured?
- Should the company make investments that reduce costs or that enhance profitability?
- What happens to the risk profile and competitive position of the firm if the investment under consideration is accepted as opposed to not choosing it?

A typical capital budgeting decision involves commitment of large, initial cash outlay with the benefits spread out in time. The time to recoup the initial investment may be long. This makes it imperative for the firm to carefully plan capital investments to attain the corporate objectives. Capital investments are typically irreversible in nature or costly to get out. Unwarranted investments can jeopardize the financial well-being of the firm. Capital budgeting deals with investment in real assets. A project requires a large, upfront capital investment, and generates cash flows for a specified period of time at the end of which the project may be liquidated. The liquidation value of assets at the end of the project life is called salvage value. It should be noted that the term initial investment is a misnomer. The term is used even when the investment is spread over a number of years. It is indeed the case with many real-life capital-intensive projects (e.g., steel plants, atomic energy power plants). A project is shown on a timeline in the following figure.

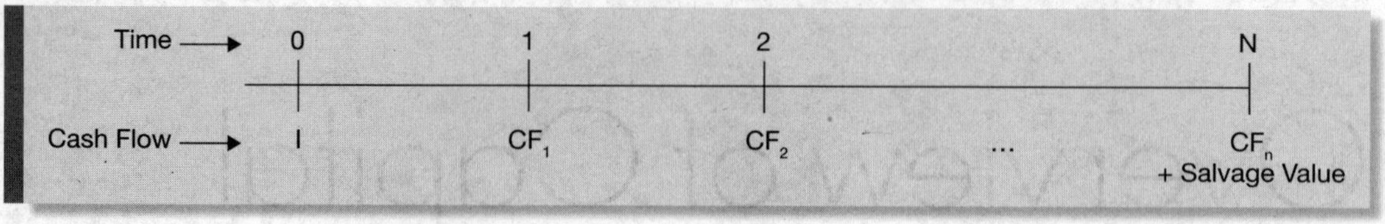

CLASSIFICATION OF INVESTMENTS

Investments can be classified on the basis of importance, size, functional activity, whether they are cost reducing or revenue increasing and so on. The most appropriate way is to classify projects on the basis of relationship between investments. The possible relationship between investments can be plotted on a continuum shown as follows.

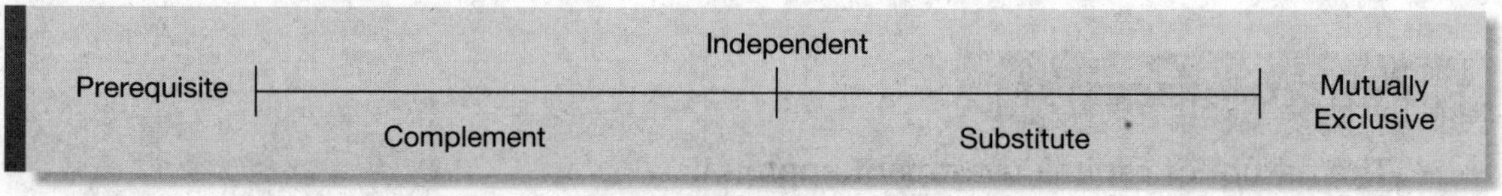

At one end of the spectrum, one investment might be a prerequisite for the other. At the other end, there are projects that are complete substitutes. Accepting one will result in the automatic rejection of the other. Two investments are said to be 'independent' if the cash flows from one investment would be the same regardless of whether the second investment is undertaken or not. Thus, buying a lathe for the machine shop and computerizing administration are independent investments. If the cash flows from one investment are affected by the decision to undertake another investment, they are said to be 'dependent'. Dependence can be of four types. If the decision to undertake the second investment increases the benefit expected from the first (or decreases cost), then the second investment is said to be a 'complement' of the first. For example, providing entertainment to visitors in a mall may enhance the attractiveness of a mall thereby increasing overall cash flows. If the decision to undertake the second investment decreases the benefit from the first investment (or increases costs), the second investment is said to be a 'substitute' of the first. For example, making air coolers and fans for the same market may lead to product cannibalization and erode profitability. In the extreme case, the benefits from the first may totally disappear if the second investment is accepted or it may be technically impossible to undertake both. Such investments are called 'mutually exclusive' investments. For example, it is not possible to build a plant in two locations. Accepting one will result in the automatic rejection of the other.

TECHNIQUES FOR EVALUATING CAPITAL INVESTMENTS

Companies spend a great deal of time and money on new investments. Executives need measures of productivity of capital, which can be applied to distinguish good ones from bad ones. There are broadly two types of measures: those that are based on accounting income, and those based on cash flows. The cash flow-based measures can be further categorized as those that consider time value of money and those that do not. Cash flow-based measures that consider time value of money are called DCF techniques.

RETURN ON INVESTMENT

ROI is essentially a single period measure. Income is computed for a specified period and then divided by the average book value (BV) of assets of the same year.

$$ROI = [EBIT(1-T)/\text{Average BV of Investment}]$$

where,

EBIT = Earnings Before Interest and Tax
T = Marginal Tax Rate
Average BV = {Beginning BV + Ending BV}/2

A variant of the aforementioned formula is:

$$ROI = \{\text{Net Income}/\text{Average BV}\}$$

ROI computed by the second method will be higher if equity financing is substituted for debt financing because lower interest expense increases net income (PAT). To separate investment and financing decisions, it is better to use the first method. Consider a one-year project with an investment of ₹1 million. The project is expected to generate ₹400,000 in pre-tax earnings. The applicable tax rate is 30 per cent and the salvage value of the project is ₹600,000.

$$ROI = [400{,}000(1-0.30)/800{,}000] = 35\%$$

Note that ROI is a per cent return measure. Now consider a multi-period project that has a life of five years.

Initial investment = ₹1 million
Salvage value = Nil
Life = 5 years
Depreciation is provided on straight line basis.

The project is expected to generate earnings of ₹40,000 (loss), ₹60,000, ₹100,000, ₹150,000 and ₹200,000. How should the ROI be computed in this case? Should the ROI be measured for each of the years and averaged out or the average earnings and average BV of assets be used? ROI computed under the two methods is shown as follows:

Method 1

1. After-tax Operating Earnings ₹	(40,000)	60,000	100,000	150,000	200,000
2. Beginning BV ₹	1 million	800,000	600,000	400,000	200,000
3. Depreciation ₹	200,000	200,000	200,000	200,000	200,000
4. Ending BV ₹	800,000	600,000	400,000	200,000	0
5. Avg. BV ₹	900,000	700,000	500,000	300,000	100,000
6. ROI = (1)/(5)	–4.5%	8.5%	20%	50%	100%

The ROI increases from –4.5 per cent in the first year to 100 per cent in the fifth year. The average ROI is 35 per cent.

Average ROI = [–4.5 + 8.5 + 20 + 50 + 100]/5 = 35%

Method 2

Average earnings = [–40,000 + 60,000 + 100,000 + 150,000 + 200,000]/5 = ₹94,000

Average BV of investment = [900,000 + 700,000 + 500,000 + 300,000 + 100,000]/5 = ₹500,000

ROI = (94,000 / 500,000) = 18.8%

It can be seen that ROI computed by the first method is almost twice that computed by the second method. The rule is to accept the project if ROI > cost of capital and reject if ROI is < cost of capital.

LIMITATIONS OF ROI

As is evident, ROI is a function of earnings and BV of investment. Both the numerator and the denominator are affected by accounting practices. Changing the method of depreciation or inventory valuation affects earnings and ROI. ROI is typically understated initially and overstated in later years because the asset base is depreciated. In fact, ROI can increase for the same or lower earnings simply because the asset is being depreciated and becomes infinite when the denominator is zero! ROI does not consider time value of money in case of multi-year projects. No distinction is made between earnings in the first year and earnings in the last year. Further, ROI is an accrual accounting return, whereas cost of capital is an economic return based on cash flows demanded by investors. The two cannot be compared.

CASH FLOW-BASED MEASURES

As the name itself suggests, these are based on cash flows rather than accounting income. Accounting earnings suffer from the credibility problem. In the absence of real performance improvement, accountants may accelerate revenues and defer costs, leading to overstatement of true profits. Earnings and cash flows, though related, measure different things. Cash flow is the net of cash inflows and outflows within a time period. Earnings, on the other hand, are the net of inflows and outflows from completed operating cycles. Cash flow measures inflows and outflows within a period regardless of the state of operating cycle. Earnings measure inflows and outflows from operating cycles that the business has completed regardless of when the cash flow occurs. Put another way, there may be no cash flow even when there is a profit because profit is recorded on accrual basis. It is inappropriate to value earnings per se. You must also take into account the investment in fixed assets and working capital required to generate a given level of earnings. It is for this reason cash flows are used to value projects.

To arrive at cash flow from earnings:

- Add non-cash charges such as depreciation and amortization that reduce net income but not affect cash flow.
- Deduct investment in working capital and capital equipment in that year.

These cash outflows are not reflected in the net income as they are carried to the balance sheet. For instance, investment in inventory is not charged off to the income statement. But there is a cash outflow to bring the inventory to its present position. Money would have been spent on raw materials, wages and so on. Since the inventory has not been sold, no revenue or profit is recorded.

Cash Flow = EBIT (1 − T) + Depreciation − Capital Expenditure − (+) Increase (Decrease) In Net Working Capital

Note that we have used NOPATs in the previous expression rather than PAT in order to separate investment and financing decisions, that is, interest expense is not deducted from EBIT. The discount rate, WACC, incorporates the after-tax cost of debt. The taxes applied are hypothetical taxes, not actual taxes because income tax is levied on profit before tax (PBT), not EBIT. However, for the purpose of valuation we estimate hypothetical taxes.

Assume that a project has the following characteristics:

Year	1	2	3	4	5
NOPAT ₹	(40,000)	60,000	100,000	150,000	200,000
Depreciation ₹	200,000	200,000	200,000	200,000	200,000

As there is no capital investment in any year, cash flow = NOPAT + Depreciation

The cash flow in the last year should include salvage value of land and buildings, plant and equipment, and working capital. In the previous example, salvage value is zero and is not considered.

Payback Period

This is one of the simplest ways of measuring an investment's worth. It is the length of time required to recoup the initial investment. Payback period is expressed in years. Thus, the payback period for an investment of ₹1,000 that generates cash flows of ₹250 for five years is four years. The payback period is determined by adding up the expected cash flows in successive years until the total equals investment.

Assume that you are investing in a project with an initial investment of ₹1 million. The cash flows from the project are given in the following table.

Year	Cash Flow ₹	Cumulative Cash Flow ₹
1	160,000	160,000
2	260,000	420,000
3	300,000	720,000
→ 4	350,000	1,070,000 ←
5	400,000	1,470,000

The payback period in this case lies in between third and fourth years. If we assume that cash flows occur uniformly over the year,

$$\text{Payback} = 3 + [(1{,}000{,}000 - 720{,}000)/(1{,}070{,}000 - 720{,}000)]$$
$$= 3.8 \text{ years or 4 years}$$

The rule is to accept those projects that have a payback period less than the limit set by the management. Although all textbooks on corporate finance have declared that using the payback period criterion is inappropriate, some managers continue to use it. Some use it as a secondary criterion.

Limitations of the Payback Rule

Although the payback period is based on cash flows, it ignores time value of money. Cash flow in year one is considered on par with cash flow in any other year. Payback considers cash flows till the investment is recovered. But it ignores cash flows that are realized later on. As a result, a project that generates substantial cash flows in later years may be discarded in favour of another project that generates higher cash flows in the initial years even if the former makes more economic sense. Often projects with shorter payback are considered less risky. There is usually not much correlation between risk and payback period. A project that has a shorter payback may be riskier than a project with longer payback.

DISCOUNTED CASH FLOW MEASURES

The rules considered so far do not consider the time value of money. DCF measures, on the other hand, are based on cash flows and explicitly consider time value of money. There are three DCF measures:

- Net Present Value (NPV)
- Internal Rate of Return (IRR)
- Discounted Payback

The NPV of a project is the sum of PVs of expected project cash flows and the initial investment.[1]

$$NPV = \sum_{t=1}^{n} [CF_t / (1+K)^t] - \text{Initial Investment}$$

where

CF_t = cash flow in any year t

K = Appropriate discount rate, usually the weighted average cost of capital

t = year 1, 2, ..., n

Thus, NPV is the excess of PV of cash inflows over the initial investment. It is an absolute number expressed in a currency (e.g., rupees). The rule is to accept the project if NPV is >0 and reject if NPV is <0. A firm accepting a negative NPV project will be financially worse off. If the NPV is zero, the firm is neither better off nor worse off. To calculate NPV:

- Estimate project cash flows
- Choose an appropriate discount rate
- Calculate PV of project cash flows and deduct the initial investment

The calculation of NPV is based on certain assumptions:

- Cash flows occur at the beginning or end of the period rather than continuously throughout the period
- Cash flows are certain

[1] The initial investment is negative. So it is subtracted from the PV of cash flows.

Consider a project that requires an initial investment of ₹1 million. The expected cash flows are shown as follows.

Year	Cash Flow (₹)
1	250,000
2	300,000
3	400,000
4	500,000

Assume that the appropriate discount rate is 15 per cent.

$$\text{NPV} = ₹[250{,}000/(1.15) + 300{,}000/(1.15)^2 + 400{,}000/(1.15)^3 + 500{,}000/(1.15)^4] - 1{,}000{,}000$$
$$\text{NPV} = ₹6{,}500$$

As the NPV is negative, the project should not be accepted.

A SPREADSHEET EXAMPLE

The NPV function in Excel allows you to calculate the NPV of an investment using a discount rate and a series of future cash flows.

The syntax is: = NPV (rate, value 1, value 2,......)

An example is given as follows:

Period	Cash Flow (₹)
0	–800
1	100
2	200
3	300
4	400
5	500
Required Return	10%
NPV	US$241.14

NPV has certain properties:

- It is in line with shareholder wealth maximization rule.
- It considers all cash flows unlike payback period.
- It is additive, that is, NPV (A+B)=NPV (A)+NPV (B). The NPV of two or more projects can be added.
- It considers time value of money.
- It assumes that all intermediate cash flows are reinvested at the discount rate (hurdle rate).

Limitations of NPV

Although the NPV rule is conceptually sound, it has some limitations:

- Since it considers all cash flows, it is biased towards long-term projects.
- NPV is an absolute number. One can make the mistake of rejecting a project that has a slightly lower NPV by not asking what the initial investment is. A project that has an NPV of ₹150 might be better when compared to another with an NPV of 200 if the latter requires much higher investment.

The IRR is the discount rate at which PV of cash flows equals PV of cash outflows or NPV=0. The discount rate is calculated by trial and error. Note the similarity between IRR and YTM of a bond. The YTM of a bond is the discount rate that makes the PV of coupon and principal repayments equal to the market price of the bond. IRR is the discount rate at which NPV=0.

$$\text{NPV}=\sum_{t=1}^{n}[\text{CF}_t/(1+\text{K})^t] - \text{Initial Investment}$$

The value of K in the aforementioned expression is the IRR.

The IRR for the previous example is shown as follows:

Investment	=₹1 million
NPV	=₹[250,000 × PVIF (r, 1)] + [300,000 × PVIF (r, 2)] + [400,000 × PVIF (r, 3)] + [500,000 × PVIF (r, 4)] – ₹1 million = 0
At r	= 14 per cent, NPV=₹15,950
At r	= 15 per cent, NPV=–₹6,500

IRR lies in the range 14 per cent and 15 per cent.

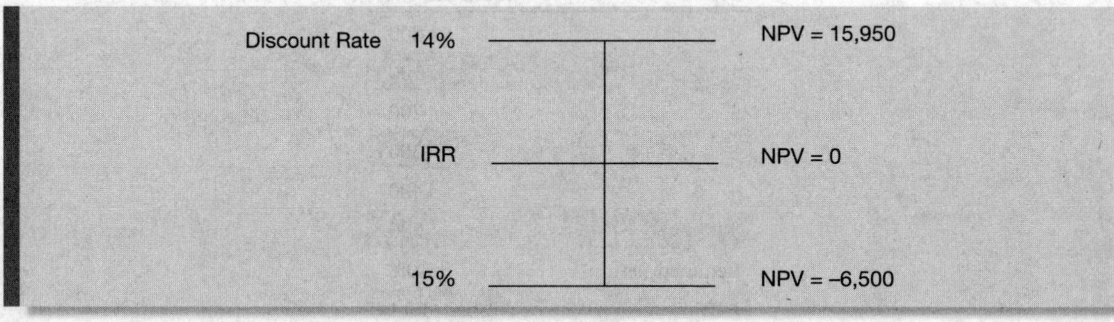

By trial and error, IRR = 14 + [15,950/(15,950 + 6,500)]% = 14.71%

A SPREADSHEET EXAMPLE

You can purchase a building for ₹350,000. The investment will generate ₹16,000 in cash flows (i.e., rent) during the first three years. At the end of three years, you will sell the building for ₹450,000. What is the IRR of this investment?

The solution is given as follows:

Period	Cash Flows	IRR	Formula
0	–350,000	13%	IRR(I7:I10)
1	16,000		
2	16,000		
3	466,000		

NPV PROFILE

The relationship between NPV and discount rate can be shown in a graph. The graph, called NPV profile, has NPV on the Y-axis and discount rate on the X-axis. The NPV profile for the previous example is shown in Figure 6.1. The point at which the profile cuts the X-axis is the IRR (NPV=0). Note the similarity between the bond price sensitivity to changes in YTM and the sensitivity of NPV to changes in discount rate. As can be expected, the NPV profile has a negative slope. The NPV decreases as the discount rate increases. There is an exception to this. All the examples considered so far were of the conventional kind—an initial outflow followed by inflows. When the sign of cash flows alternate or change during the life of the project, NPV can increase when discount rate increases.

Moral: NPV is dependent on timing, magnitude, the sign of cash flows, discount rate and investment. NPV can be increased by simply understating investment or discount rate and overstating cash flows. The rule is to accept the project if IRR is>cost of capital and reject if IRR<cost of capital. IRR, unlike NPV, is a scaled measure. It is expressed in per cent.

LIMITATIONS OF IRR

Since IRR is a scaled measure, it is biased towards smaller projects. IRR assumes that intermediate cash flows are reinvested at IRR (>COC) during the life of the project. Competition may drive down earnings

FIGURE 6.1
NPV Profile

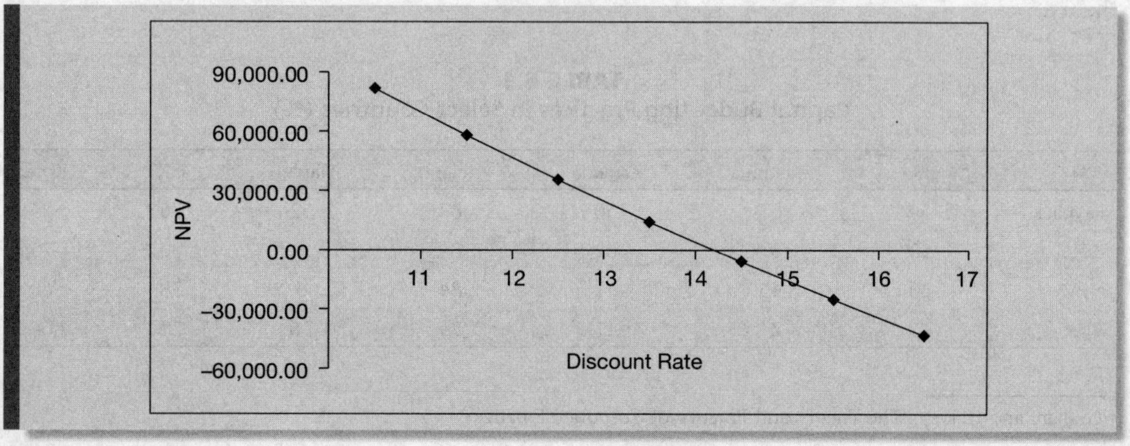

in the long run to normal levels. At times, more than one IRR is obtained because of which decision-making becomes difficult.

DISCOUNTED PAYBACK

It measures the time required for DCFs to cover the initial investment. Unlike the payback period, the discounted payback period considers the time value of money. The discount rate is the firm's cost of capital.

Consider a project has an initial investment of ₹700,000.

Year	Cash Flow ₹	PV @ 15%	Cumulative PV (₹)
1	160,000	139,200	139,200
2	260,000	196,560	335,760
3	300,000	197,400	533,160
4	350,000	200,200	733,360
5	400,000	198,800	932,160

Discounted Payback=4 years (approximately)

CAPITAL BUDGETING PRACTICES: SURVEY RESULTS

The results of an academic survey conducted in several countries are shown in Table 6.1. The survey results are dated and management practices might have changed. Nevertheless, they do throw light on what firms do in real life. Payback and IRR seem to be the favourite methods in the USA, Australia, UK, Canada and Japan.

IRR and average rate of return seem to be the favourite methods in the USA. More recently, Graham and Harvey conducted a survey of 329 CFOs in the USA.[2] The summary of their findings is presented in Table 6.2. They find that NPV and IRR are more popular than other approaches in line with the theory.

TABLE 6.1
Capital Budgeting Practices in Select Countries (%)

	USA	Australia	Canada	Ireland	Japan	UK	Korea
Payback	59	61	50	84	52	76	75
IRR	52	37	62	84	4	39	75
NPV	28	45	41	84	6	38	60
ARR	13	24	17	24	36	28	68

[2] Graham and Harvey, 'The Theory and Practice of Corporate Finance'.

TABLE 6.2
Survey Responses to the Question: How Frequently Does Your Firm Use the Following Techniques When Deciding Which Projects or Acquisitions to Pursue?[3]

			Company Size	
	% (Always or Almost Always)	Mean	Small	Large
IRR	75.61	3.09	2.87	3.41
NPV	74.93	3.08	2.83	3.42
Payback	56.74	2.53	2.72	2.25
ROI	20.29	1.34	1.41	1.25
Discounted Payback	29.45	1.56	1.58	1.55

Another survey of capital budgeting practices in the Asia-Pacific suggests that DCF techniques are considered important in Australia, Malaysia, the Philippines and Indonesia, whereas Payback and IRR are considered important in Singapore and Hong Kong.[4]

CONCLUDING COMMENTS

In this chapter, we considered several capital budgeting techniques. Each has its limitation. What are the characteristics of the 'right' technique?

- It should distinguish between good and bad investments.
- It should summarize what the investment will do to the profitability of the organization.
- It should factor in time value of money.
- It should be unambiguous.
- It should be in line with the corporate objective, that is, maximization of shareholders wealth.
- It should be applicable to a wide range of business situations.
- It should not be biased and permit realistic comparison of one investment proposal with another.
- It should permit simple adjustments to allow for ranges of uncertainty.
- It should take into account the life pattern of cash flows.

Clearly, NPV is the only criterion that satisfies most of these. Consequently, NPV is recommended. NPV is not an abstract concept. A company accepting a negative NPV project will really be worse off.[5] Managers are appraised on the basis of current earnings and profits. Naturally, any manager would be biased towards those projects that generate revenues during his/her tenure even if the NPV is negative. Why should anyone care about investments that are likely to generate returns during another executive's regime? Finally, note that the discount rate used in the NPV calculation is the divisional cost of capital. The investment decision is shown in the following flow chart.

[3] Respondents are asked to rate on a scale of 0 (never) to 4 (always). They report the overall mean as well as the per cent of respondents that answered 3 (almost always) or 4 (always).

[4] Kester et al., 'Capital Budgeting Practices in the Asia-Pacific Region'.

[5] This is not really the case when a project has options embedded in it. NPV has its limitations too. Chapter 9 on real options deals with real options analysis.

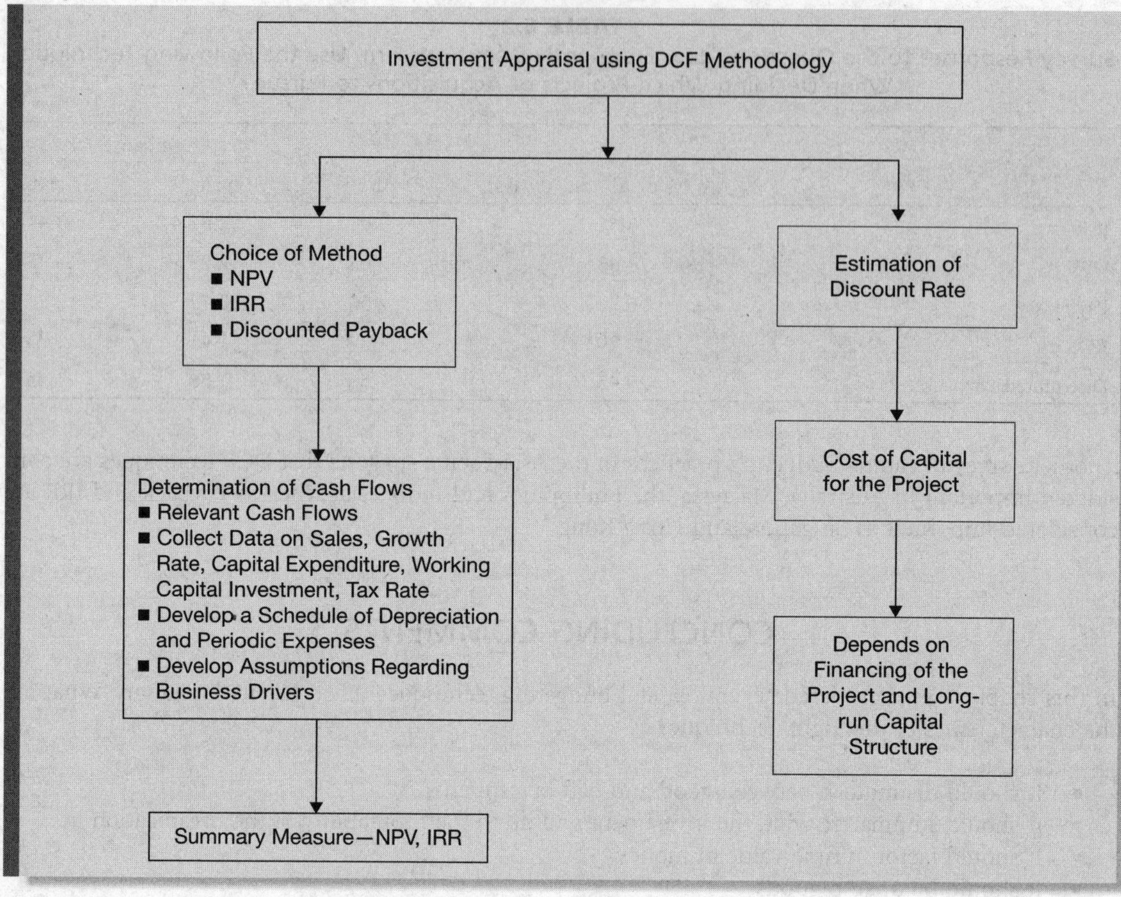

EXERCISES

1. A chemical company is planning to invest in a new plant. The team of analysts responsible for investment appraisal has arrived at the following information:

Estimated Investment		₹1 million
Estimated Life of the Plant		7 years
Annual Cash Flows:	Years 1–3	₹150,000
	Years 4–7	₹200,000
Appropriate Discount Rate		15%

   a. Find the PV of all cash flows.
   b. How would your answer change if cash flows were to grow at 40 per cent per year after third year until the seventh year?

c. Now reduce the life of the plant to six years. Keeping the other data constant, find the PV.
d. Recalculate the PV using a discount rate of 14 per cent.

2. A fuel injection company has four investments. Classify them as cost reducing, revenue expanding (related business) and revenue expanding (unrelated business).
   a. A project to implement ERP software in the company
   b. A proposal to start a software subsidiary
   c. Repairing an old assembly line
   d. A proposal to manufacture spark plugs
3. The initial investment (in rupees) and NOPAT for three projects is as follows:

		Years			
Investment	Outlay (₹)	1	2	3	4
A	10,000	2,000	3,000	4,000	4,000
B	7,500	1,500	2,000	2,500	5,000
C	5,000	2,000	1,500	1,000	500

   The salvage value is zero for all the projects. Depreciation is provided on a straight line basis. Calculate the average ROI for the projects. If the cost of capital is 20 per cent, which of the projects (if any) would you choose? Is it meaningful to calculate ROI for the projects? Why or why not? Calculate ROI by the second method and compare it that obtained from the first method.
4. Calculate the payback period for each of the investments. If the maximum acceptable payback period is three years, which of these investments would you accept?

	Years (₹)				
Investment	0	1	2	3	4
A	(1,000)	500	300	300	900
B	(1,000)	(100)	200	500	600
C	(1,000)	250	250	250	250

5. A project requires an initial investment of ₹1 million. The first year cash flow is expected to be ₹100,000. It is expected to grow at 20 per cent per annum for five years and remain at year six level for four more years. Calculate the payback.
6. An automotive company is evaluating a project that requires an initial investment of ₹2 million. The project cash flows are as follows:

Year	Cash Flow ₹
1	100,000
2–5	200,000
6–10	400,000

   Calculate the NPV if the discount rate is 14.5 per cent. Draw the NPV profile.

7. You are evaluating a project that has the following characteristics:
   Initial investment=₹2 million. Cash flows are expected to remain constant for five years, double in the sixth year and remain at that level for four years and then grow at 5 per cent per annum forever after that. The discount rate is 11 per cent. Calculate the cash flows that make NPV=0.
8. For the following two mutually exclusive projects, calculate IRR.

	Project A	Project B
Year	Cash Flow	Cash Flow
0	–500,000	–1,500,000
1–4	100,000	200,000
5–10	150,000	250,000

   If the cost of capital is 18 per cent, which of the projects (if any) would you choose? Calculate NPV if the cost of capital is 14 per cent.
9. Growth company has ₹40 million to invest in any or all of the following projects:

		(₹ 000)			
		Years			
Project	Type of Cash Flow	0	1	2	3
1.	Investment	(10,000)			
	Revenue		21,000		
	Operating Expenses		11,000		
2.	Investment	(10,000)			
	Revenue		15,000	17,000	
	Operating Expenses		5,833	7,833	
3.	Investment	(10,000)			
	Revenue		10,000	11,000	30,000
	Operating Expenses		5,555	4,889	15,555
4.	Investment	(10,000)			
	Revenue		30,000	10,000	5,000
	Operating Expenses		15,555	5,555	2,222

   Assume that all expenses are on cash basis. Tax rate=35 per cent. Depreciation is provided on a straight line basis. Ignore salvage value. Rank projects on the basis of payback, NPV, IRR and ROI. The cost of capital to the company is 15 per cent.

REFERENCES

Graham, John R. and Campbell Harvey. 'The Theory and Practice of Corporate Finance: Evidence from the Field'. *Journal of Financial Economics* 61 (2001).

Kester, G., R. Chang, E. Echanis, S. Haikal, M. Isa, M. Skully, K. Tsui and C. J. Wang. 'Capital Budgeting Practices in the Asia-Pacific Region: Australia, Hong Kong, Indonesia, Malaysia, Philippines and Singapore'. *Financial practice and Education* (1999 Spring/Summer).

CHAPTER 7

Free Cash Flow Valuation

LEARNING OBJECTIVES

- How to estimate truly incremental cash flows
- How to estimate free cash flow to firm and free cash flow to equity
- Some accepted principles in estimating free cash flow and NPV
- Impact of debt financing and inflation on NPV
- Why do alternate measures of project profitability such as NPV and IRR give conflicting results and how to deal with them
- How should projects with unequal lives be evaluated

As mentioned in Chapter 6, the DCF methodology is widely used to evaluate capital projects. In the DCF approach, the value of the project is the future expected cash flows discounted at a rate that reflects the risk of the projected cash flows. The DCF methodology is founded on the principle that it is inappropriate to capitalize earnings per se. One must also take into account the investment required to generate those earnings. Consequently, cash flows are obtained by deducting net capital expenditure (capex) and incremental WC investment from NOPAT. The steps involved in the valuation are as follows:

Step 1: Determine Free Cash Flow

Free cash flow is the cash flow available to all investors in the company—both shareholders and bondholders—after consideration for taxes, capex and WC investment.

$$\text{Free Cash Flow} = \text{NOPAT} + \text{Depreciation} - \text{Capex} - (+)\ \text{Increases (Decreases) in WC Investment}$$

where NOPAT = EBIT (1 − Tax Rate)

$$EBIT = Revenue - Cost\ of\ Goods\ Sold - Operating\ Expenses - Depreciation$$

Estimation of cash flows requires NOPAT, capex and net WC. In calculating NOPAT, interest is not deducted because the discount rate, WACC, incorporates the after-tax cost of debt.

The physical assets of a company depreciate and need to be replaced to maintain a certain level of growth in sales. Usually, capex is estimated as a constant percentage of revenues. Capex can be either positive or negative depending on whether the company is making or liquidating investments. If capex is negative, it is a source of funds. To gain an estimate of capital investment required per rupee of sales increase, take the sum of all capital investments less depreciation over the last five or 10 years in a similar project and divide this total by the sales increase from the beginning to the end of the period.[1]

Free cash flows thus obtained can be either positive or negative depending on whether the business is generating a surplus or a deficit under a specific plan of growth. Due care must be taken in estimating WC investment. Actual year-to-year balance sheet changes often do not reflect the average or normal needs of the business during the year.

Operating WC is defined as:

	Transaction Cash Balance
Plus:	Accounts Receivable
Plus:	Inventory
Plus:	Other Current Assets
Less:	Accounts Payable
Less:	Taxes Payable
Less:	Other Current Liabilities

$$CF_t = Cash\ Flow\ In\ Year\ t = S_{t-1}(1+g_t)(p_t)(1-T) - (S_t - S_{t-1})(C_t + W_t)$$

where S = Sales
p = Profit Margin = EBIT as a Percentage of Sales
T = Income Tax Rate
C = Capital Investment Required (Net of Depreciation) Per Rupee of Sales Increase
W = Net WC per Rupee of Sales Increase
g = Growth Rate

Estimate the most likely incremental cash flows to be generated by the project. Note that financing is not incorporated in the cash flows. Suitable adjustments for the specific financing will be made in the discount rate. The forecast of free cash flows requires the following inputs:

- Initial sales before the starting of the forecast period.
- Growth rate in sales for the entire forecast period. The growth rate may remain constant or change.
- The ratio of EBIT/sales (profit margin) for the entire period.
- The ratio of total operating capital (i.e., capex + WC investment) to sales for the period.

[1] The time duration should cover one business cycle to remove the effects of cyclicality.

Thus,

$$Sales_t = Sales_{t-1} \times (1+g_t)$$
$$EBIT_t = Sales_t\ (p_t)$$
$$\text{Asset Requirement} = a_t = [(FA+WC)/S]_t$$
$$(FA+WC)_t = Sales_t \times [(FA+WC)/S]_t$$

Step 2: Estimate a Suitable Discount Rate for the Project

A company can use its WACC based on its target capital structure only if the project has the same (systematic) risk as the parent. If the company has a different capital structure in mind, suitable adjustments for the discount rate should be made. The discount rate should reflect the capital structure of the project. To calculate the discount rate:

- Estimate the asset β for the project using the relationship.
- $\beta_A = \beta_E\ (E/V)$ where E/V is the equity-to-value ratio and β_E is the equity β. The asset β may also be obtained by taking the average asset βs of comparable firms in the industry.
- Re-lever the asset β at various debt ratios (say, from 0% to 60%) using the same relationship and find levered equity β for the project.
- Estimate the cost of equity at various debt ratios.
- Similarly, estimate the cost of debt at various debt ratios.
- Calculate WACC as the weighted average of costs of debt and equity, the weights being target, market value debt-to-value and equity-to-value ratios, respectively.

Step 3: Calculate the Present Value of Cash Flows

Since the project is usually a going concern,

Value of the Project = PV of Cash Flows During the Forecast Period + Terminal Value

We can set the forecast period in such a way that the project reaches a stable phase after that. In other words, we are assuming that the project will grow at a constant rate after the forecast period. The period of high growth can be anywhere from 3 to 20 years (may be even more for some computer software firms) depending on the type of business, size of the market, entry barriers, availability of substitutes, number of players in the market and so on.

Step 4: Estimate the Terminal Value

The terminal value is the present value of cash flows occurring after the forecast period. If we assume that cash flows grow at a constant rate after the forecast period, the terminal value

$$TV = [CF_t(1+g)]/(k-g)$$

where CF_t = Cash Flow in the Last Year
g = Constant Growth Rate
k = Discount Rate

Step 5: Add Present Value of Terminal Value

Step 6: Deduct the Value of Initial Investment to Arrive at NPV

One might calculate IRR given a forecast of free cash flows and initial investment.

ACCEPTED PRINCIPLES

Estimation of project cash flows involves some generally accepted principles.

After-Tax Incremental Cash Flows

The first principle in investment analysis is to consider only incremental cash flows. The idea is to arrive at cash flows, either inflows or outflows that can be traced to the project. To arrive at incremental cash flows subtract the expected cash flows without the project from the expected cash flows with the project. Thus, if you are evaluating two alternatives, subtract the cash flows from one alternative from the cash flows of the second alternative to arrive at incremental cash flows. The NPV of the incremental cash flows should be positive for the project to be accepted.

Income tax should be computed by applying the expected tax rate for each period to the taxable income, excluding interest charges of that period and all projects should be compared on the basis of after-tax cash flows and NPV. The tax rate used is the marginal tax rate applicable for the next rupee of earnings. The depreciation for the purpose of reporting taxable income is calculated on the written-down value (WDV) method, although straight line method (SLM) may be used for accounting purposes. It is likely that in the initial years a firm may incur losses and not absorb depreciation. The unabsorbed depreciation and losses may be carried forward and set off in later years.

Opportunity Cost

In many cases, some of the resources, including human, needed for a project may be a part of the already existing business. Such resources have alternative uses. These alternative uses create opportunity cost—the cost for the existing business due to the new project. For instance, some executives may be transferred to render analytical support to a project or the project may make use of already owned building. Are these resources cost free? Obviously they are not free. The project has to be charged for these. Assume that a company has transferred some executives to the new project temporarily. These executives have to be replaced by suitable personnel and incur an additional salary expenditure of ₹1.35 million. The opportunity cost for this resource is ₹1.35 million. Similarly, cost may be attached to other resources such as buildings, plant and equipment, vehicles and so on based on the next best use or expenses incurred. The opportunity cost charged should measure net cash flows that could have been earned had the project under consideration not been undertaken. In real-life situations, it may be difficult to attach opportunity cost to all resources, especially those that do not have an alternative use.

An example is in order. A project under consideration will use an already owned office space in a commercial complex for four years. The office could be let out for an annual rent of ₹125,000 and the depreciation tax shield lost per year is ₹1,400. Assume a discount rate of 15 per cent.

$$\begin{aligned}\text{Opportunity Cost} &= \text{PV of Rent Foregone} + \text{PV of Tax Shield Lost}\\ &= ₹[125{,}000 \times \text{PVIFA}(15,4) + 1{,}400 \times \text{PVIFA}(15,4)]\\ &= ₹360{,}872\end{aligned}$$

Note that the depreciation tax shield is simply depreciation expense per year multiplied by tax rate. The opportunity cost should be added to the initial investment.

Sunk Costs

Some expenses related to the project may be incurred before the investment analysis is considered. For instance, the sponsors of a project might have hired a consultant to assess the viability of the project and spent some money on the feasibility study. Such expenses are called sunk costs. Since sunk costs cannot be recovered if the project is rejected, they have to be ignored. Thus, outlays on research and development should be ignored. Then who should pay for sunk costs? The cumulative NPV of all successful projects should cover the sunk costs of all projects undertaken.

Working Capital Investment

Apart from investment in fixed assets, a firm will have to invest in current assets such as inventory and book debts for day-to-day running of the business. Part of current assets can be funded by non-interest bearing current liabilities such as accounts payable, and salaries and wages payable. The excess of current assets over current liabilities, which is to be funded by other sources, is called net WC. Often, executives either ignore or understate WC investment. The new project causes sales to rise which leads to higher accounts receivable and inventory; the NPV is overstated. Usually, the spontaneous rise in accounts payable and other accrued liabilities will not cover the increase in current assets. The gap comes from new debt, which increases risk. Executives usually do not notice this. Many projects end up with substantial cost over runs. As a rough estimate, WC can be expressed as a function of the level of activity, that is, number of units sold or sales revenue. To illustrate, WC for a project may be 15 per cent of revenues.

Impact of Depreciation

Cash Flow = EBIT − Tax on EBIT + Depreciation − Capex − (+) Increase (Decrease) In WC

NPV is a function of cash flows and cash flow is a function of depreciation. The higher the depreciation, the higher is the cash flow and hence NPV, other things remaining constant.

Assume the following data:
Initial Investment = ₹4,500
Project Life = 4 years
Salvage Value = 0
Discount Rate = 15%

	1	2	3	4
EBIT ₹	1,000	2,000	3,000	4,000
– Tax @ 35%	350	700	1,050	1,400
+ Depreciation ₹	1,125	1,125	1,125	1,125
Cash Flow ₹	1,775	2,425	3,025	3,725

NPV = –₹4,500 + PV of Cash Flows = ₹2,998.70

If the method of depreciation were to be changed:

	1	2	3	4
EBIT ₹	1,000	2,000	3,000	4,000
–Tax @ 35%	350	700	1,050	1,400
+Depreciation ₹ (at 33.3 % of WDV)	1,500	1,000	667	444
Cash Flow ₹	2,150	2,300	2,617	3,044

NPV=–₹4,500+PV of Cash Flows
=₹2,572

The total amount of depreciation might be the same in both the cases but there is a timing difference. In the second case, more depreciation is provided in the initial years. This results in a change in NPV.

The Tax Benefit of Depreciation

Depreciation is a tax deductible expense. The higher the depreciation (an expense), the lower will be the income and hence tax paid on income.

Assume the following data:

Investment =₹400
Tax Rate =35%
Discount Rate =12%
Tax Shield =D×T
=₹100×0.35=₹35

Year	Depreciation	Tax Shield
1	100	35
2	100	35
3	100	35
4	100	35

PV of Tax Shield=₹35×PVIFA(12,4)=₹106.30

If depreciation were to change

Year	Depreciation	Tax Shield
1	200	70
2	100	35
3	50	17.50
4	50	17.50

PV of Tax Shield=₹114

Increase in depreciation will result in higher NPV. But reported earnings come down as an expense item has increased. This may send wrong signals to the stock market resulting in lower stock prices. So, there is a trade-off between reported earnings and higher NPV due to higher tax benefits.

TABLE 7.1
Depreciation Rates as per Schedule II

Nature of Asset	SLM (%)	WDV (%)
Buildings (Other than Factory Buildings)	3.17	9.15
Factory Buildings	3.17	9.15
Furniture and Fittings	9.5	25.89

SCHEDULE II OF THE COMPANIES ACT, 2013

The Schedule II of the Companies Act, 2013, prescribes rates of depreciation for various classes of assets. An extract from the same is shown in Table 7.1. The Income Tax Act prescribes rates of depreciation for the computation of taxable income. The Act is amended by yearly Finance Acts that prescribe the rate to be applied.

SALVAGE VALUE OF INVESTMENT

The price at which fixed assets and WC can be liquidated, called salvage value, should be estimated and added to the last year cash flows. Excluding salvage value would understate the true NPV of the project. In real-life situations, it is difficult to extrapolate asset values far into the future. Typically, advice from professional estimators (engineering) is sought.

A subsidiary of Bharat Electronics Ltd was setting up a Black & White picture tube project in the early 1990s. The company had estimated the salvage value of fixed assets and net WC to be ₹80 million. The forecast of free cash flows for the project is given as follows.

Year	Cash Flow (million)
0	–1,410
1	128
2	180
3	389
4	365
5	342
6	307
7	288
8	268
9	248
10	227

NPV Without Salvage Value = –₹72.80 million
NPV with Salvage Value = ₹124 million

Much of the project's value comes from salvage value. Without it, the project would become unviable.

THE IMPACT OF DEBT FINANCING ON NPV

To arrive at cash flows, we did not deduct interest charges. The reason is that the discount rate (WACC) already considers debt financing. The WACC is calculated by taking the weighted average after-tax costs of equity and debt. The cost of debt in the WACC formula already accounts for project-specific debt financing. Deducting interest from EBIT would lead to double counting.

$$WACC = K_d(1 - T)(D/D + E) + K_e(E/D + E)$$

A project can be analysed from the perspective of all investors or just equity investors. In the former case, the cash flows do not consider interest charges and the discount rate is the WACC. While analysing from the equity investors' perspective, some changes need to be made. The initial investment would be equity investment and not the total investment; the discount rate would be the cost of equity and the cash flow would be the residual cash flow to equity investors.

Cash Flow to Equity = EBIT – Tax + Depreciation – Capex – Increase in WC – After-Tax Interest Payment – Principal Repayment + New Borrowing

Cash flow to equity is the residual cash flow after meeting investment requirements and contractual payments. It should be noted that cash flow to equity is more meaningful for a growing firm that borrows frequently to invest. For a typical growing firm, cash flow from operations would be negative.

Consider an example.

Investment = ₹3,000
Discount Rate (WACC) = 15%

(₹)

Year	Cash Flow	Interest Expense	Cash Flow after Deducting Interest
1	1,000	150	850
2	2,000	150	1,850
3	3,000	150	2,850

NPV Without Deducting Interest = –3,000 + [1,000 × PVIF (15,1) + 2,000 × PVIF (12,2) + 3,000 × PVIF (15,3)]
= ₹1356

NPV after Deducting Interest = –3,000 + [850 × PVIF (15,1) + 1,850 × PVIF (12,2) + 2,850 × PVIF (15,3)]
= ₹1,016

THE IMPACT OF INFLATION ON NPV

In Chapter 2, I introduced the concept of real and nominal rates of return which are linked by the equation

$$(1+k)=(1+i)\,(1+r)$$

where k = Nominal Rate
i = Inflation
r = Real Rate Expressed in Decimal Form

It is evident from the previous equation that the nominal discount rate used in calculating NPV would go up if the inflation rate increases. The increase in discount rate would lead to a lower NPV. An example is in order. An investment has the following cash flows.

Year	Cash Flows (₹)
0	−1,000
1	200
2	300
3	400
4	400

The firm uses a discount rate of 10 per cent, which includes an expected inflation of 4 per cent.

$$\text{Real Rate } r=[(1+k)/(1+i)]-1$$
$$=(1.10/1.04)-1$$
$$=5.76 \text{ per cent}$$

NPV of the Project Using a Discount Rate of 10% is −1,000 + [1,003.48] = ₹3.5

Suppose that the expected inflation is 8 per cent, nominal rate would be

$$(1+k)=(1.08)\,(1.0576)$$
$$k=14.22 \text{ per cent}$$

The NPV decreases due to an increase in discount rate.

REAL VERSUS NOMINAL CASH FLOWS

Cash flows can be stated either in nominal or real terms. If cash flows incorporate expected inflation, they are said to be nominal. Nominal cash flows can be adjusted for inflation and stated in real terms. The relationship between nominal and real cash flows is: Real Cash Flow = Nominal Cash Flow × [Price Index In Next Period/Price Index This Year]

An investment is expected to return ₹100 next year and the price level is expected to increase by 4 per cent during the period. Real cash flow = 100/1.04 = ₹96.10. Consider another example.

Year	Nominal Cash Flow ₹	Real Cash Flow ₹
1	1,000	952.3
2	2,000	1,818
3	3,000	2,593
4	4,000	3,292

Real cash flows have been calculated using an expected inflation of 5 per cent for all the years using the relationship

Real $CF_t = [\text{Nominal } CF_t/(1+i)^t]$. where t is the time period

Real Cash Flow In Year 2 = Nominal Cash Flow/$(1.05)^2$

Real Cash Flow In Year 3 = Nominal Cash Flow/$(1.05)^3$ and so on

It is to be noted that the nominal rate should be used to discount nominal cash flows and real rate to discount real cash flows. If there is a mismatch between cash flows and discount rate, the result will be flawed. Another subtle effect of inflation is that asset values get eroded very fast in high inflation environments. The depreciation provided on historical cost will be less than that on replacement cost leading to fictitious earnings.

Inflation is the rise in the average price level, generally measured as the increase in the consumer price index during the period. The increase in prices of goods and services that are of importance to the decision-maker may or may not have correlation with that in the general price rise. Hence, assuming the general inflation rate in the economy as proxy for increase in the price of the firm's inputs may be incorrect.

The implicit assumption in matching cash flow and discount rate is that the actual price increases equal the inflation rate included in the discount rate. The price behaviour may not have much correlation with general inflation in the economy as measured by the increase in consumer price index. Further, the tax shield arising out of interest and depreciation affects the value of the project. The amount of depreciation and interest charges under both the approaches might be the same but the relative value is higher with constant prices. So the project will be undervalued in the constant price approach. Similar difficulties arise when a company sells goods on credit and when dealing with hard currencies where inflation rates are not exactly offset by currency depreciation.

CONFLICTS IN RANKING

The recommendation in case of conventional projects is that if NPV > 0, accept; else reject. Similarly, if IRR is > cost of capital, accept; else reject. Both give similar results. But there are some situations in which conflicts arise. A project acceptable on the basis of NPV may have to be rejected on the basis of IRR. Consider the following example.

There are two mutually exclusive investments A and B. Investment A needs an outlay of ₹100,000 and returns ₹120,000 a year later. Investment B needs an outlay of ₹150,000 and returns ₹177,000 a year later. The cost of capital is 13 per cent.

$$NPV_A = [120{,}000/1.13] - 100{,}000$$
$$= ₹6{,}194.69$$
$$NPV_B = [177{,}000/1.13] - 150{,}000$$
$$= ₹6{,}637.16$$

Based on the NPV, Project B is better.

$$IRR_A = [120{,}000/100{,}000] - 1$$
$$= 20 \text{ per cent}$$
$$IRR_B = [177{,}000/150{,}000] - 1$$
$$= 18 \text{ per cent}$$

Based on the IRR, Project A is better. Why did this happen? The answer lies in the outlay (size) of the project. IRR does not control the size of the investment. The outlay for the second project is higher. To find out which investment is more profitable, we need to figure out if the incremental outlay of ₹50,000 on Project B is profitable.

(₹)

	Investment	Cash Flow
A	100,000	120,000
B	150,000	177,000
Incremental Cash Flow	5,000	5,700

$$IRR = [57{,}000/50{,}000] - 1$$
$$= 14\% > \text{cost of capital}$$

So investment B can be accepted. Since the two projects are mutually exclusive, A has to be rejected.

If the discount rate were to be 15 per cent,

$$NPV_A = [120{,}000/1.15] - 100{,}000$$
$$= ₹4{,}347.80$$
$$NPV_B = [177{,}000/1.15] - 150{,}000$$
$$= ₹3{,}913$$

Project A is better on both measures. The result can be plotted on a graph as shown in Figure 7.1.

For discount rates less than 14 per cent, Project B has a higher NPV and for discount rates greater than 14 per cent, Project A has a higher NPV. However, the NPV is a better decision rule and is recommended for decision-making.

FIGURE 7.1
NPV Versus Discount Rate

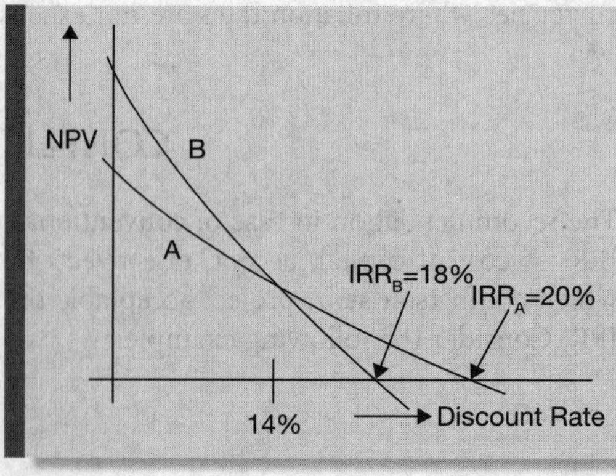

Reinvestment Assumption

Now consider an example where the cash outlay for both the projects is the same. Discount rate = 9 per cent

	Investment (₹)	Cash Flows (₹) 1	2	IRR (%)	NPV (₹)
A.	100,000	20,000	120,000	20	19,350
B.	100,000	100,000	31,250	25	18,045

Based on IRR rule, Project B is better while on the basis of NPV, Project A should be accepted. Why does this conflict arise? The answer lies in the reinvestment assumption. The NPV rule assumes that intermediate cash flows are reinvested at hurdle rate of 9 per cent, whereas the IRR rule assumes that intermediate cash flows are reinvested at IRR of the project. If the cash flows were reinvested at the IRR of the project, the balance at the end of the second year would be $I\,(1 + IRR)^2$.

For Project A, the balance would be ₹$100{,}000(1.2)^2 =$ ₹$140{,}000$
For Project B, the balance would be $100{,}000(1.25)^2 =$ ₹$156{,}250$

We are assuming that the firm will continue to reinvest at IRR (>cost of capital) year after year. We can relax this assumption and consider a reinvestment rate equal to cost of capital in the future periods. This is possible if we assume that super normal profits get wiped out in the long run due to entry of competitors.

Modified Internal Rate of Return

The IRR obtained by assuming that intermediate cash flows are reinvested at cost of capital is called modified internal rate of return (MIRR). To calculate MIRR:

- Find the future value of all cash flows by compounding at the hurdle rate
- Add the future value of all cash flows
- Find the implied return

Consider a project with the following cash flows:

Year	Cash Flow (₹)
0	–1 million
1	300,000
2	400,000
3	500,000
4	600,000

Discount rate = 15 per cent

1. Calculate the future value of project cash flows at the discount rate of 15 per cent

$$300{,}000 \times 1.15^3 = ₹456{,}262.50$$
$$400{,}000 \times 1.15^2 = ₹529{,}000.0$$
$$500{,}000 \times 1.15 = ₹575{,}000$$
$$600{,}000$$

2. Add them

$$= ₹2{,}160{,}262.50$$

3. Calculate the implied return

$$\text{Investment } (1+r)^n = \text{Future Value of Cash Flows}$$
$$1{,}000{,}000(1+r)^4 = ₹2{,}160{,}262.50$$
$$r = 21 \text{ per cent}$$

That is, MIRR = 21 per cent

MULTIPLE IRR$_S$

In a conventional project, a cash outflow is followed by cash inflows. Such projects will have a unique IRR. Consider the following example. A project requires an outlay of ₹100,000. The cash flows from the project are given as follows.

Year	Cash Flow (₹)
0	(100,000)
1	310,000
2	(220,000)

The project has a cash outflow in the second year. The project has two IRR$_s$.

$$IRR_1 = 10\%$$
$$IRR_2 = 100\%$$

When there is more than one change in sign of cash flows, there will be more than one IRR. The number of IRR$_s$ equals the number of sign changes. There are two ways to tackle the problem.

Approach 1

Discount the negative cash flows to year 0 and then to the initial investment. It becomes a conventional project. In the previous example, discount the last year cash flow of ₹220,000 to year 0 using the hurdle rate and add it to the initial investment of ₹100,000. If the IRR of the new series of negative cash flow followed by positive cash flows is greater than cost of capital, the project can be accepted.

Approach 2

Move the positive cash flows to the year in which the negative cash flow occurs so that it becomes a positive flow. The IRR of the conventional series is easy to find. In the previous example, move the positive flow to the second year and add it to the negative cash flow. Assuming that the hurdle rate is 12 per cent.

$$=₹310{,}000\ (1.12)-₹220{,}000=₹127{,}200$$

This is a conventional series with an initial outflow followed by a positive inflow of ₹127,200 in year two. Find the IRR of this series. If it is greater than the cost of capital, the project can be accepted.

$$\frac{127{,}200}{(1+r)^2}=₹100{,}000$$

CAPITAL RATIONING

In some circumstances, in choosing a set of investments, firms may be faced with limited amounts of capital. As a result, some projects with positive NPV may be rejected. The situation where companies are constrained to obtain funds to invest in all available positive NPV projects is called capital rationing. Capital rationing is of two types—internal and external. External capital rationing occurs due to capital market imperfections such as mispricing of securities, flotation costs and so on. Internal capital rationing occurs from self-imposed restrictions by top management. A company may decide not to raise additional capital—either debt or equity—and place an arbitrary limit on the amount to be invested. The reluctance to go to the capital market could be due to the fear of scrutiny by financial intermediaries or the fear of loss of control. In another type of internal capital rationing, the company sets a cut-off rate higher than the cost of capital due to which profitable projects may have to be foregone. A survey of Fortune 500 firms was conducted to find out whether capital rationing is internal or external, how firms decide on the budget amount and so on.[2] The results of the survey are shown in Tables 7.2, 7.3 and 7.4. Quite often, the profitability index (PI) is suggested as the solution to dealing with capital rationing. PI is a scaled measure. It is the NPV of an investment for every rupee of investment.

[2] Mukherjee and Hingorani, 'Capital Rationing Decisions of Fortune 500 firms'.

TABLE 7.2
Implementing the Capital Rationing Decision: Who Makes Allocation and Selection

Allocation and Selection Decisions	Frequency	Percentage
Capital is allocated to each division which then prioritizes investment opportunities within the allocation	35	54
Each division submits all positive NPV proposals and project selection is done at the central management level	26	40.6
A combination of the above two	4	6.0
Total	65	100.0

TABLE 7.3
Why Internal Capital Rationing?

Statement	SD	D	NS	A	SA	Score
Capital rationing is used to discourage biased cash flow forecasts	4	7	8	34	12	0.66
Rationing is more severe when managers have a job mobility	8	25	23	8	1	–0.48
When senior managers cannot trust project forecasts and when the project's downside risk is large	1	7	4	40	13	0.88
Firms are more likely to Reject a+ve NPV project when it is non-routine/unique in nature	2	16	5	33	9	0.48
Firms impose rationing and avoid low NPV projects in order to preserve borrowing capacity to finance potentially high NPV projects in the near future	1	8	6	40	10	0.78

Note: SD=Strongly Disagree, D=Disagree, NS=Not Sure, A=Agree, SA=Strongly Agree. Their points are –2, –1, 0, 1 and 2, respectively.

TABLE 7.4
Flexibility of the Investment Ceiling

Circumstances under which a firm would lower the original ceiling	Ceiling	Percentage
Never lower the ceiling	6	9
When it currently has low NPV projects	22	34
When it has better prospects in future	14	22
When actual cash flows are lower than predicted	18	27
Other reasons	5	8
Total	65	100

Circumstances under which initial allocation is increased		
	Ceiling	Percentage
Never raise the ceiling	6	9
When it has to give up high NPV projects	28	43
When it does not impair future ability to issue debt	14	22
When actual cash flows are better than predicted	8	12
Other reasons	9	14
Total	65	100

$$PI = NPV/\text{Initial Investment}$$

PI is sometimes specified as present value of cash inflows divided by present value of cash outflows.

To calculate a PI

- Estimate the investment required for each project.
- Identify the total amount of funds available for investment.
- Calculate PI for all projects and rank them from highest to lowest.
- Start from the project that has the highest PI and move downwards. Accept those projects that can be funded by available capital.

A company has a capital constraint of ₹10 million. The company has the following projects:

Project	Investment (₹)	NPV (₹)
1	1.0	1.0
2	2.0	2.2
3	3.0	3.3
4	3.0	2.4
5	1.0	0.7
6	4.0	4.8

The PI and ranking are shown as follows.

Project	PI	Ranking
1	1.0	3
2	1.1	2
3	1.1	2
4	0.8	4
5	0.7	5
6	1.2	1

Projects 6, 3, 2 and 1 can be chosen to exhaust the capital budget of ₹10 million. The cumulative NPV is ₹11.3 million.

LIMITATIONS OF PROFITABILITY INDEX

If the objective is to choose that investment whose PI is greater than one, calculation of PI is unnecessary as NPV is positive! PI is a function of NPV and investment. It penalizes those projects that have higher cash outlays even if the incremental investment is worthwhile. This 'scale problem' was demonstrated earlier. Further, the implicit assumption in calculating PI is that the capital rationing constraint applies to current period and not future periods. The cumulative investment need not exactly equal capital constraint. A portion may be left unutilized. The unutilized portion may be used to accept a fractional project (i.e., staggering the investment). Sometimes another combination of projects may yield a higher NPV.

PROJECTS WITH UNEQUAL LIVES

One of the limitations of the NPV rule is that it is biased towards long-term projects. So it is likely that a short-term project may be discarded without considering the fact that the proceeds of the project can be reinvested at termination. Consider the following example.

Project	Investment (₹)	NPV (₹)	Life
A	5 million	6.0	7 years
B	3 million	4.0	4 years

Based on NPV if we were to choose A, we would be ignoring the project lives.

Under the 'replacement chain' (RC) method, both the projects are replicated till their lives become equal. If, for example, two projects have lives of two years and three years, the first project is replicated thrice and the second project is replicated twice so that their lives become six years. Consider two projects given as follows:

	Project 1	Project 2
Year	Cash Flow (₹)	Cash Flow (₹)
0	−1,000	−1,500
1	750	800
2	750	800
3		800
NPV	337	489
Discount Rate	8%	10%

The NPV after replicating the projects are ₹875 and ₹857, respectively. Based on RC NPV, we would choose Project 1.

Under the equivalent annuity method, the NPV of the projects are converted into their annual equivalent and then compared. The equivalent annuity is the annuity that produces the same NPV as that of the project.

$$\text{Equivalent Annuity} = \text{NPV/Annuity Factor } (r,n)$$

where r = discount rate and n is the project life. Consider the two projects:

Project	Investment (₹)	NPV (₹)	Life
A	5 million	6.0	7 years
B	3 million	4.0	4 years

If the discount rate is 15 per cent, equivalent annuity for the two projects would be:

$$6.0/\text{PVIFA } (15,7) = 1.44$$
$$\text{and } 4.0/\text{PVIFA } (15,4) = 1.40$$

Based on the equivalent annuity, we would choose Project A. Note that this technique can be applied only if the projects can have the same risk complexion and hence the discount rate. What if the risk complexion is different? The correct way to implement equivalent annuity method is to find the annuity over the 'replicated life' of the project, 12 years in the example given before.

Consider the example given under RC method. The EA for the two projects are:

$$337/\text{PVIFA } (8\%, 2 \text{ years}) = ₹189 \text{ p.a.}$$
$$489/\text{PVIFA } (10\%, 3 \text{ years}) = ₹197 \text{ p.a}$$

The correct procedure is to calculate PVs of the EAs over the least common multiple of the project lives as in the RC.

$$189 \times \text{PVIFA } (8\%, 6 \text{ years}) = 875$$

And

$$197 \times \text{PVIFA } (10\%, 6 \text{ years}) = 857$$

CONCLUDING COMMENTS

In this chapter, I described the process of arriving at cash flows and discount rate. More specifically, in project evaluation only after-tax, incremental cash flows attributable to the project need to be considered. This is not a trivial exercise. Assume that a company is increasing its plant capacity from 125 tons to 250 tons. Current sales are 75 tons. The first two years sales are expected to be 90 tons and 120 tons. Since the increase in sales can be handled with existing capacity, one should not attribute the investment made to upgrade the capacity to the new project although the investment is made now. Further, in many situations, the investment itself is not made in one year at the beginning of the project, that is, the investment is not 'initial'. If the capital investment is spread over, say, three years, the same may be deducted in the year in which it occurs from cash flow from operations. Alternatively, the present value of capital investment may be deducted from present value of cash inflows to arrive at NPV.

EXERCISES

1. The cash flows from two investments are given as follows:

(₹)

	Years			
Investment	0	1	2	3
A	100,000	70,000	70,000	
B	120,000	60,000	60,000	60,000

Which of them would you choose if the cost of capital is 17 per cent?

2. A journal has the following subscription rates

1 year	₹215
2 years	₹395
3 years	₹540

Assuming that subscription rates do not change, which offer would you choose? Assume an opportunity cost of capital of 16 per cent.

3. A company has the following investments:

(₹ million)

Project	Investment	NPV
A	2.50	1.75
B	1.0	0.8
C	1.5	1.5
D	2.0	2.0
E	2.0	2.4

If the company has a capital constraint of ₹5 million, which set of projects would you choose?

4. You are evaluating two alternative machines for your machine shop. They have the following characteristics:

Machine	Cost (₹)	Operating Cost per Year (₹)	Expected Life
A	800,000	40,000	8 years
B	1,000,000	32,000	5 years

Which machine would you choose? Discount rate = 16 per cent

5. A project has the following cash flows:

Year	Cash Flow (₹)
0	(100,000)
1	80,000
2	100,000

Year	Cash Flow (₹)
3	(200,000)
4	120,000

Find the IRR. Would you accept the project at a hurdle rate of 16.5 per cent?

REFERENCE

Mukherjee, T. and V. Hingorani. 'Capital Rationing Decisions of Fortune 500 Firms: A Survey'. *Financial Practice and Education* (1999 Summer).

SUGGESTED READINGS

Beedles, W. L. and M. Joy. 'Mutually Exclusive Projects with unequal Lives, Reinvestment Plans and Unequal Required Rates of Return'. *Financial Practice and Education* (1997 Fall).

Dorfman, R. 'The Meaning of Internal Rates of Return'. *Journal of Finance* (1981 Dec).

Emery, G. W. 'Some Guidelines for Evaluating Capital Investment Alternatives with Unequal Lives'. *Financial Management* (1992 Spring).

Ehrhardt, M. C. and P. Daves. 'Capital Budgeting: The Valuation of Unusual, Irregular, or Extraordinary Cash Flows'. *Journal of Financial Practice and Education* (2000 Fall/Winter).

Lorie, J. H. and L. J. Savage. 'Three Problems in Rationing Capital'. *Journal of Business* 28 (1955 Oct).

Meyer, R. L. 'A Note on Capital Budgeting Techniques and the Reinvestment Rate'. *Journal of Finance* (1979 Dec).

Pilotte, E. A. 'Evaluating Mutually Exclusive Projects of Unequal Lives and Differing Risks'. *Journal of Financial Practice and Education* (2000 Fall/Winter).

Weingartner, H. M. 'Capital Rationing: n Authors in Search of a Plot'. *Journal of Finance* 32, no. 5 (1977 Dec).

CHAPTER

8

Risk Analysis in Capital Investments

LEARNING OBJECTIVES

- Discuss cash flow at risk, sensitivity analysis and best case/worst case analysis
- Learn to draw decision trees
- Introduce certainty equivalent cash flows and risk-adjusted discount rates
- Introduce simulation through Crystal Ball®
- Summarize issues in valuation in emerging markets

In our examples so far, we have assumed that cash flows are certain and known. This is unlikely in real-life situations. The value of NPV we computed in many of the examples is really one of the many values it can assume due to uncertainty in the underlying variables. In this chapter, I describe methods of assessing risk in investment decisions.

MEASURING RISK

Uncertainty about a situation can often indicate risk, which is the possibility of loss, damage or any other undesirable event. Most people desire low risk, which would translate to a high probability of success, profit or some form of gain. For example, if sales for next month are above a certain amount (a desirable event), then orders will reduce the inventory, and there will be a delay in shipping orders (an undesirable event). If a shipping delay means losing orders, then that possibility presents a risk. Almost any change, good or bad, poses some risk. Your own analysis will usually reveal numerous potential risk areas such as overtime costs, inventory shortages, geological survey results, unpredictable demand, changing labour costs, government approvals, fluctuations in personnel requirement and pending legislation.

Once the risks have been identified, a model can help you quantify the risks. Quantifying risk means putting a price on risk to help you decide whether a risk is worth taking. For example, if there is a 25 per cent chance of running over schedule, costing you ₹100 out of your own pocket that might be a risk you are willing to take. But if you have a 5 per cent chance of running over schedule, knowing that there is a ₹10,000 penalty you might be less willing to take that risk.

Firms worry about the absolute level of cash flow because it affects the firm's ability to service debt, invest and grow. To measure risk, a firm can forecast the distribution of cash flows. The firm can set a threshold below which the firm will experience financial distress and use the cumulative distribution of cash flows to find out the probability of a cash flow below this level. The cash flow shortfall corresponding to the probability level chosen by the firm is called 'cash flow at risk' at that probability level.[1] A 'cash flow at risk' of ₹200 million at 5 per cent means that there is a probability of 5 per cent that the firm's cash flow will be lower than its expected cash flow by at least ₹200 million. If there is a probability that the level of cash flow will be less than the threshold, the company should take actions to reduce the risk of cash flow and ensure that it earns the cash flow corresponding to the threshold level 95 per cent of the time.

There are two approaches to incorporate risk in capital budgeting. The first approach is to estimate the changes in decision criteria such as NPV and IRR to changes in underlying business drivers such as sales growth, market share and so on. The second approach is to adjust the cash flows or discount rate for the risk of the project. Before we go on to the measurement of risk, a brief description of risks is in order. There are essentially two types of risk—diversifiable and non-diversifiable. Risks can also be classified as business and financial. Some of the risks that affect a project are completion risk, raw material supply risk, technological risk, economic risk, financial risk, currency risk and political risk. Executives commonly make ad hoc adjustments to cash flows and discount rates to account for the unique risks in the project. Modern finance theory hypothesizes that only systematic risk is rewarded in stock markets, and project-specific risk is not relevant as investors can diversify their portfolio. In a CAPM world, only systematic factors such as changes in inflation and interest rates are relevant. But this does not mean that managers should not manage unsystematic or project-specific risk because systematic risk is a function of total risk. In the following sections, I describe some methods of assessing risk.

BEST CASE–WORST CASE ANALYSIS

A popular way of assessing risk is to assume conservative, most likely and optimistic values for key drivers of NPV such as sales growth rate, operating profit margin and incremental investment in fixed assets and working capital during the project life and compute NPV. The range of NPV represents the risk of the project. The most likely, pessimistic and optimistic values of the key variables for a hypothetical project are shown as follows: Cash flows are estimated for pessimistic, most likely and optimistic scenarios. The NPV is computed for the three scenarios, say, 50,000, 100,000 and 400,000. The limitation of best case–worst case analysis is that what constitutes worst case remains subjective. In real-life situations, worst case estimates tend to be optimistic because of executives' faith in the business and strategy. So the usefulness of the tool is limited.

---

[1] This concept is similar to value at risk for financial firms. A good book on the subject is Jorion, *Value at Risk*.

Variable	Years 1	2	10
Sales Growth Rate (%)			
Pessimistic	11	11	10
Most Likely	13	13	12
Optimistic	15	15	14
Operating Profit Margin (%)			
Pessimistic	11.5	11.5	11
Most Likely	12	12	11.5
Optimistic	12.5	12.5	12
Market Growth Rate (%)			
Pessimistic	10	10	9
Most Likely	11	10.5	10
Optimistic	12.5	12	11.15

Best case–worst case analysis does not tell us the likelihood of best case or worst case. The worst case, as many executives assume, is one in which competition is the greatest, input costs the highest, selling price the least and so on. The probability of all these happening together is very low.

SENSITIVITY ANALYSIS

The cash flows used for computation of NPV are dependent on assumptions relating to selling price, sales quantity, market share, market growth, capacity utilization and so on. The NPV corresponding to the most likely values of these variables is referred to as the base case. Due to uncertainty, the variables can take on a range of values rather than a single value. The sensitivity of NPV (or IRR or ROI) can be estimated for various likely values of selling price or any variable that can affect the decision rule significantly.

Sensitivity analysis refers to the process of changing variables or assumptions to determine their impact on a project's profitability. It does not involve the use of probabilities. To conduct a sensitivity analysis:

- Estimate the base case NPV or IRR based on most likely values of variables.
- Identify the key variables (those that are expected to affect the project profitability significantly).
- Change one variable, say selling price, at a time keeping all others unchanged and compute NPV or IRR. Carry out the exercise for all the possible values of the variable.
- Repeat for all variables.

Similarly, the sensitivity of NPV and IRR to changes in other variable such as sales growth rate, market growth could be ascertained individually and in combination. For instance, we can find the sensitivity of NPV to a combination of:

Project Life = 8 years
Price = ₹475 and 300, respectively
No. of Units Sold = 10% Less than the Base Case

The sensitivity of NPV for changes in operating profit margin and sales growth rate is shown in Figure 8.1 for a hypothetical project.

It is useful to show the results of sensitivity analysis in a graph. The graph can have the profitability criterion (say, NPV) on the Y-axis and the variable (expressed as a percentage of base case) on the X-axis. The sensitivity of NPV to changes in selling price for a hypothetical project is shown in Figure 8.2. It is to be noted that when the level of activity (no. of units produced) comes down, other related inputs such as WC, variable material costs and so on have to be changed before estimating cash flows. A greater slope indicates higher sensitivity.

The end result of sensitivity analysis is a range of NPVs. The management should take the decision to accept or reject the project based on the risk of the project. Sensitivity analysis gives us the range of NPV but it does not tell us which NPV is more likely to occur.

BREAK-EVEN ANALYSIS

As the name suggests, break-even point (BEP) refers to the level of activity at which profitability is zero. Depending on whether the measure of profitability is net income or NPV, the BEP is called accounting BEP or financial BEP, respectively. At the accounting BEP, net income is zero. The firm neither makes profit nor loss.

BEP is calculated for a single year.

FIGURE 8.1
Sensitivity of NPV

		Sales Growth Rate			NPV (₹ in million)
			Base Case ↓		
		–1%	0	+1%	
Operating Profit Margin%	+1%	9.50	17.5	25.5	
	0	2.6	10.6	18.6	← Base Case
	–1%	(4.3)	3.7	11.7	

FIGURE 8.2
Sensitivity of NPV to Changes in Selling Price

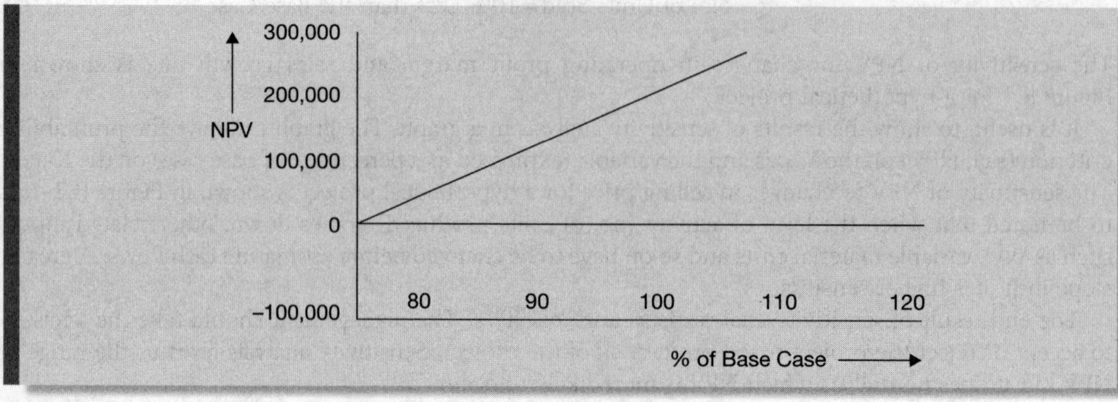

$$\text{Sales Revenue} = \text{Total Costs}$$

$$(\text{No of Units Sold} \times \text{Selling Price per Unit}) = \text{Fixed Cost} + \text{Total Variable Costs}$$

$$= \text{Fixed Cost} + (\text{Variable Cost/Unit} \times \text{No of Units Sold})$$

$$\text{No of Units Sold} = \frac{\text{Fixed Cost}}{\text{Selling Price per Unit} - \text{Variable Cost per Unit}}$$

Within the relevant output range, some expenses like depreciation or managerial remuneration remain whether the firm makes use of the capacity or not. Such costs are fixed costs. Some costs such as the raw material cost vary with the level of activity. Such costs are called variable costs. It should be noted that over an extended period of time, all costs are variable. For example, managers can be relieved from service or equipment could be disposed of. The denominator in the previous equation (Selling Price–Variable Cost/Unit) is called contribution (towards recovering fixed cost and profits). The accounting BEP for a hypothetical project is shown in Table 8.1. The higher the BEP, the higher is the risk that the firm will incur a loss.

$$\text{BEP} = \frac{\text{Fixed Cost}}{\text{Contribution}} \times \text{Capacity Utilization \%}$$

$$= \frac{368}{555} \times 100\%$$

$$= 66.33\%$$

A typical BE chart is shown in Figure 8.3. Financial BEP refers to the level of activity at which NPV=0. At that level, present value of revenues = present value of costs. Since at any level below the BEP the company will be financially worse off, BEP serves as a useful check.

DECISION TREES

Pharmaceutical companies like Merck typically license drugs from smaller companies. Under the agreement, the pharmaceutical company is responsible for approval of the drug from the concerned

TABLE 8.1
Accounting BEP as % of Installed Capacity
(Figures Relate to a Normal Year of Operation)

		(₹ million)
Sales		2,713
Less: Variable Costs		
– Raw Materials		
Dyes & Chemicals		
Stores & Spares	1,839	
– Utilities	127	
– Interest of WC Borrowing	101	
	2,158	
Contribution = Sales – Variable Costs		555
Fixed Costs		
– Wages & Salaries		82
– Factory & Plant Overheads		25
– Administrative Expenses		35
– Interest on Term Loan		101
– Other Bank Charges		7
– Depreciation		118
		368

FIGURE 8.3
Break-Even Chart

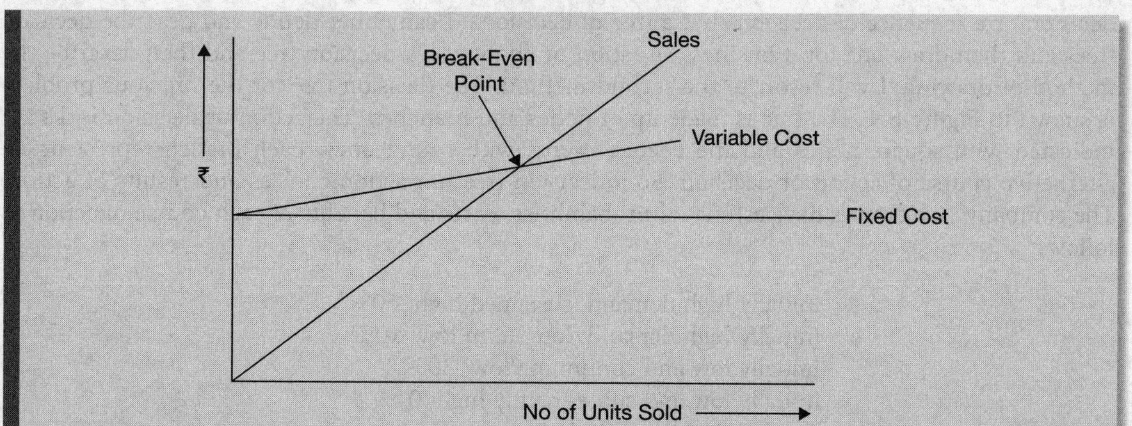

authorities, its manufacture and marketing. The company pays an initial fee, a royalty on all sales and makes additional payments as the licensor completes each stage of the approval process. In the USA, each drug goes through a three-phase approval process shown as follows.

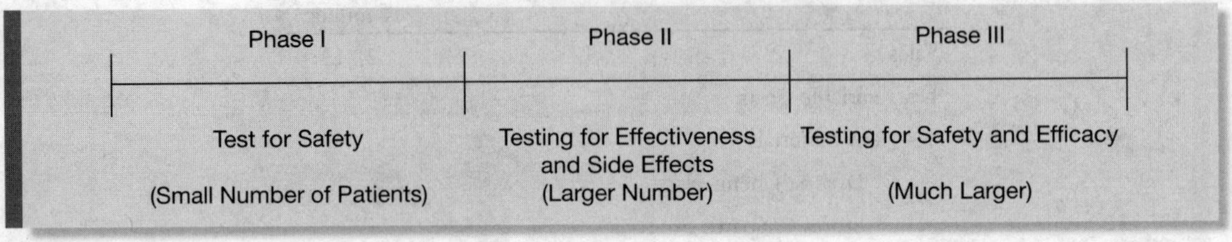

The whole process takes about seven years to complete. There is 60 per cent, 10 per cent, 85 per cent chance that the product will successfully complete Phase I, II and III, respectively.

Consider another business situation. The management of a company must decide whether to build a small plant or a large plant to manufacture a new product with an expected market life of 10 years. The decision depends on what the market size will be for the new product.

The demand for the product could be

- High during the first two years and then drop off to a low level if customers do not find the product satisfactory.
- High followed by sustained high demand if the product is well accepted.
- Low during the introductory period in which case the company can abandon the project.

The company has three options:

- Build a small plant during the introductory period and expand quickly if demand shoots up. Otherwise competitive product will eat into the company's market share.
- If the demand is low during the introductory period, maintain the small plant.
- Build a big plant whatever the market size. Furthermore, the new product is the company's first major breakthrough and management is not sure what course of action is optimal.

The previous example has an important message. The decision problem is not in terms of an isolated decision or a sequence of decisions but a tree of decisions. I can either define and describe decision trees and then draw one for a business situation or show you a decision tree and then describe the method of drawing. I will resort to the second method. The decision tree for the previous problem is shown in Figure 8.4. The tree is made up of nodes and branches. The action or decision forks are indicated with square nodes and the chance events with round ones. Each branch represents an alternative course of action or decision. So a decision tree has action choices and results of action. The company's executives have estimated probabilities, costs and benefits of each course of action as follows:

Initially high demand, sustained high: 60%
Initially high demand, long-term low: 10%
Initially low and continuing low: 30%
Initially low and subsequently high: 0

FIGURE 8.4
Decision Tree

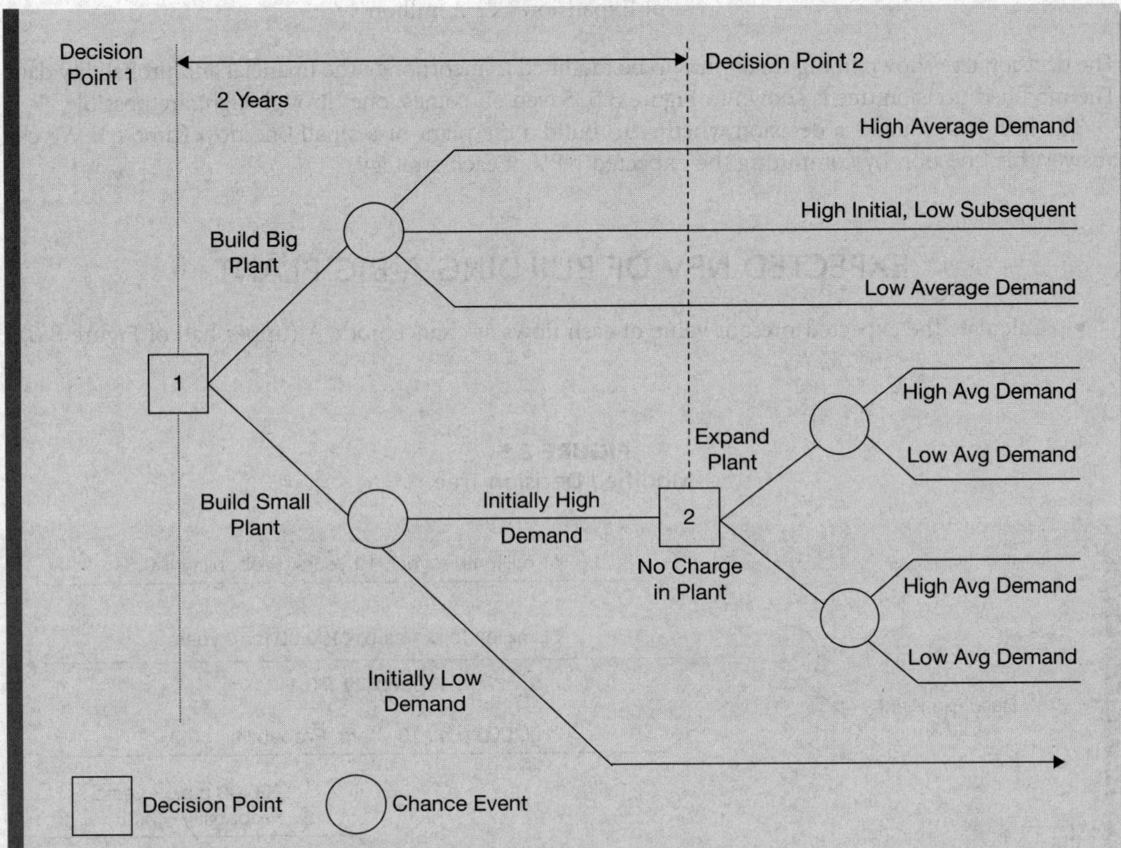

Source: Magee John (1964).

The cash flows for each alternative outcome are as follows:

- A large plant with high volume would yield ₹1 million annually in cash flow.
- A large plant with low volume would yield ₹100,000.
- A small plant with low demand would yield ₹400,000.
- A small plant during an initial period of high demand would yield ₹450,000 per year and drop to ₹300,000 p.a. in the long run because of competition.
- If the small plant were expanded to meet sustained high demand, it would yield ₹700,000 cash flow annually as it would be less efficient than a large plant built initially.
- If the plant were expanded but high demand were not sustained, estimated annual cash flow would be ₹500,000.

Cost of Large Plant=₹3 million
Cost of Small Plant=₹1.3 million
Cost of Expansion=₹2.2 million

The decision tree shown in Figure 8.4 has to be modified to incorporate the financial and probability data. The modified decision tree is shown in Figure 8.5. Seven outcomes, one through eight are possible.

The firm has to make a decision whether to build a big plant or a small one now (time t_o). We can answer this question by computing the expected NPV of each strategy.

EXPECTED NPV OF BUILDING A BIG PLANT

- Calculate the expected present value of cash flows at chance node A (upper half of Figure 8.6).

FIGURE 8.5
Modified Decision Tree

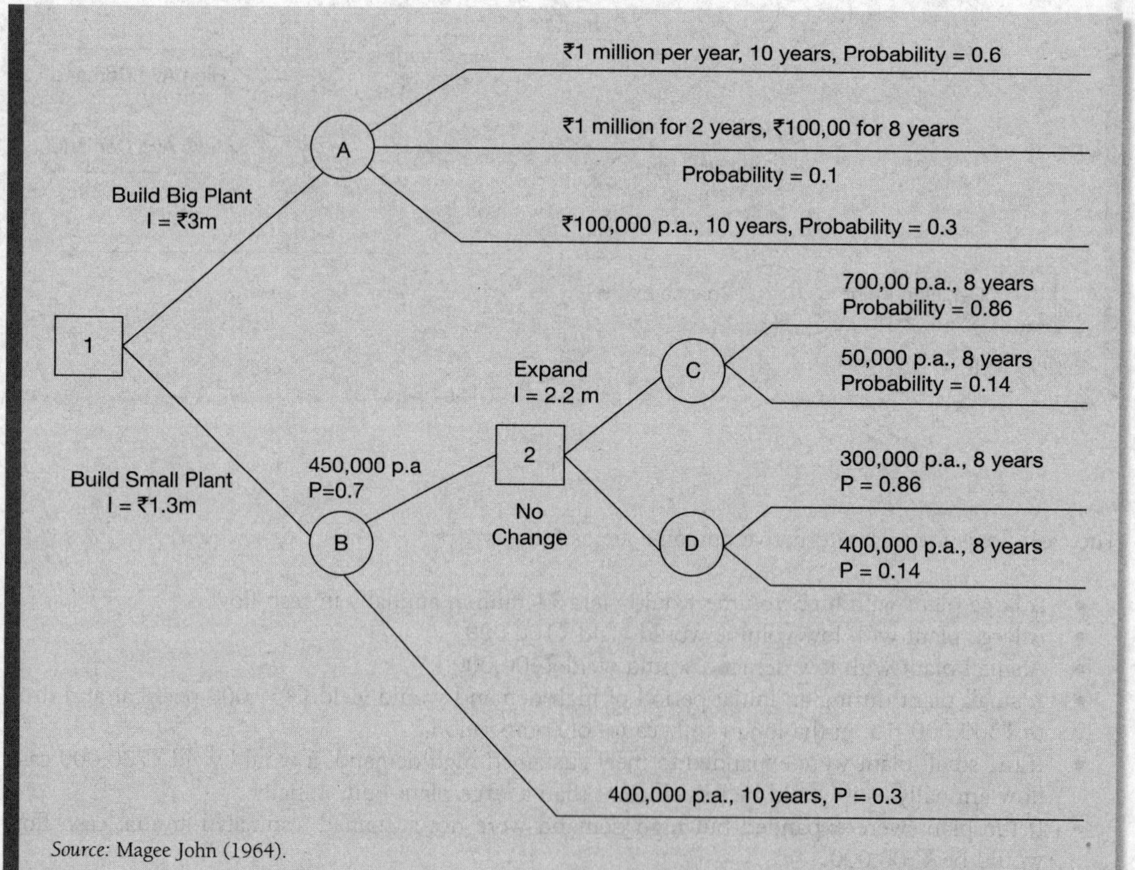

Source: Magee John (1964).

FIGURE 8.6
Uncertainty Profile

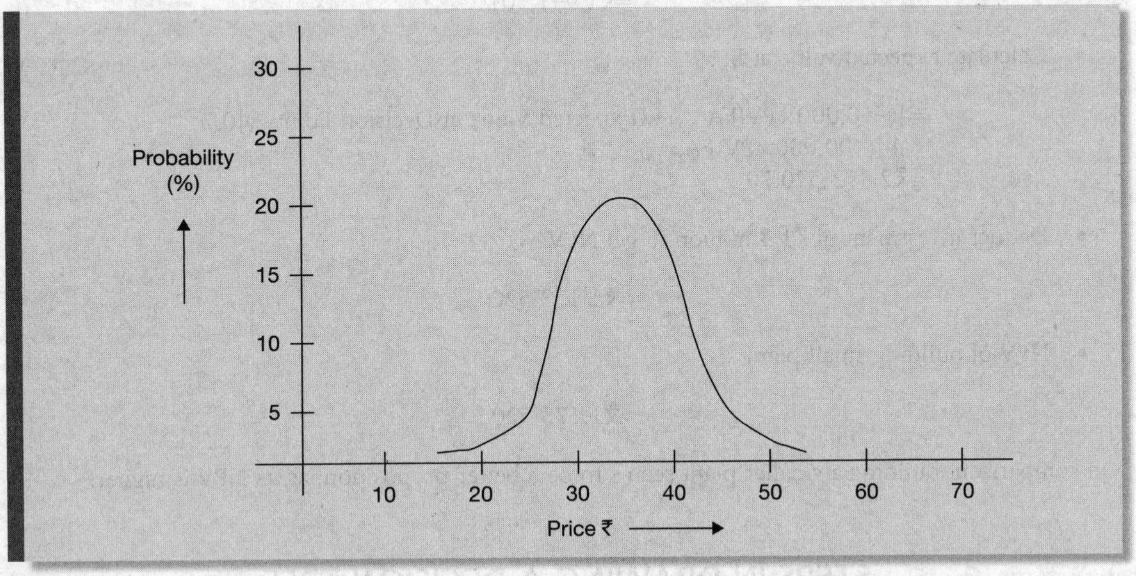

$$E(PV) = PV \times \text{Probability}$$

$$PV = [(1 \text{ million} \times PVIFA_{15,10})0.6 + \{1 \times PVIFA_{15,2} + 100{,}000 \times PVIFA_{15,8}\}0.1 + (100{,}000 \times PVIFA_{15,10}) \times 0.30]$$

$$= ₹2{,}164{,}880$$

- Deduct the initial investment of ₹3 million to get NPV.

$$= ₹2{,}164{,}880 - 3{,}000{,}000$$

$$= -164{,}880$$

EXPECTED NPV OF BUILDING A SMALL PLANT

- Calculate the expected value at C&D.

$$\text{Expected Value at C} = [(700{,}000 \times PVIFA_{15,8})0.86 + (50{,}000 \times PVIFA_{15,8})0.14]$$

$$= ₹2{,}732{,}583$$

Deduct investment of ₹2.2 million to get NPV

$$= ₹532{,}583$$

$$\text{Expected Value at D} = [(300{,}000 \times PVIFA_{15,8})0.86(400{,}000 \times PVIFA_{15,8})0.14]$$

$$= ₹1{,}408{,}918$$

Since there is no investment, NPV = ₹1,408,918

- Add the two to get the expected value at Decision Point 2

$$=₹1,941,501$$

- Calculate expected value at B.

$$\begin{aligned}&= [(450{,}000 \times PVIFA_{15,2}) + (\text{Expected Value at Decision Point 2})]0.7\\ &\quad + [(400{,}000 \times PVIFA_{15,10})0.13]\\ &= ₹2{,}473{,}520.70\end{aligned}$$

- Deduct investment of ₹1.3 million to get NPV

$$=₹1,173,520$$

- NPV of building small plant

$$=₹1,173,520$$

On comparison, building a smaller plant seems to be a better proposition, as its NPV is higher.

STEPS IN DRAWING A DECISION TREE

A decision tree is a presentation of various decisions, possible outcomes and their probabilities at various stages of a project. The steps involved in drawing a decision tree are as follows:

- Identify decision points and alternative actions available at each point.
- Identify the points of uncertainty and the range of alternative outcomes at each point.
- Estimate the probabilities, costs and benefits of various events and actions.
- Analyse and choose a course of action.

The information about investment requirements, market conditions and so on may come from many sources such as operations research, market research department, R&D, finance and sales personnel. A cross-functional team may be entrusted with the task of developing all alternatives and developing them. The team should identify what alternatives and uncertainties exist now and in the future, estimate costs, demand, prices and competitive action anticipated under alternatives. It may not be possible to identify all future possibilities. But a reasonable job can be done. In drawing decision trees, we assumed that the outcome could take on discrete values. In reality, the outcome may not be discrete but continuous. Also, it might be hard to estimate subjective probabilities for all the outcomes.

SIMULATION

Since each of the factors that enter into investment analysis is subject to some amount of uncertainty (in isolation and in combination). Simulation, a method of risk analysis, tries to combine the variability inherent in each of the factors under consideration and assess the odds of earning a healthy return. Monte Carlo simulation is a technique in which the uncertainty encompassing the main variable is processed in a forecasting model in order to estimate the impact of risk on the projected results. The model is subjected to a number of simulation runs usually with the aid of a computer. The following steps are involved in simulation.

Step 1: Construct 'uncertainty profile' for each key input factor such as market size, market share, price per unit, selling costs, variable costs and so on. The uncertainty profile is constructed by attaching probability of occurrence to different values it can take on. The profile has probability on Y-axis and values of factor on the X-axis. For instance, let us suppose, price can take any value ranging from ₹30–₹50. Further, let us suppose there is a 5 per cent chance of the realized price being ₹30, 10 per cent chance of price being ₹35, 20 per cent chance of price being ₹40 and so on. The uncertainty profile for the price factor could be constructed as shown in Figure 8.6. The probabilities are set subjectively based on expert opinion and past experience. Uncertainty profiles are constructed for all key factors similarly.

Step 2: One value is chosen from each of the profiles randomly and combined to compute NPV or IRR.

Step 3: The process is repeated several hundred times. Each time NPV and IRR are noted.

Step 4: Each result is listed from highest to lowest and the percentage of total situations falling within given range of NPV or IRR is determined shown as follows:

NPV Range (₹)	Percentage of Situations = Probability of Occurrence (%)	Cumulative Probability (%)
150,000–200,000	28	28
100,000–150,000	14	42
50,000–100,000	21	63
0–50,000	16	79
–50,000–0	21	100

Step 5: The risk profile for the decision rule could be plotted using the result obtained in Step 4.

Step 6: Risk profiles are constructed for all investments in hand. Those projects that offer a greater probability of achieving any level of return or NPV are chosen (within capital constraints).

Step 7: The expected value and standard deviation of the risk profile are computed and a summary is presented.

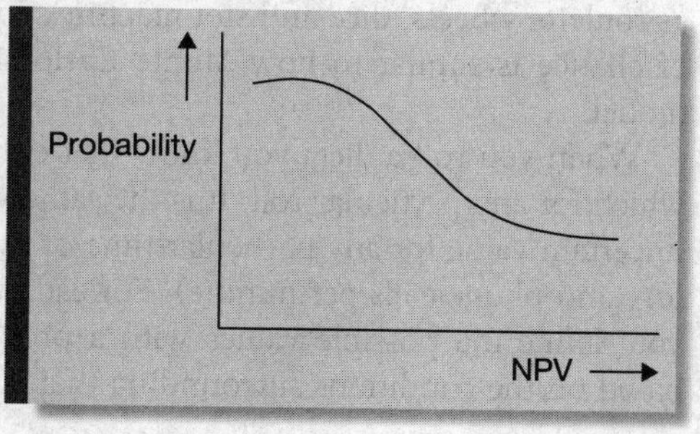

SIMULATION USING CRYSTAL BALL

Crystal Ball[2] 2000® works with spreadsheet models, specifically MS Excel spreadsheet models. A model represents a process with combinations of data, formulas and functions. Traditionally, spreadsheet

[2] This section is based on a product description prepared by Oracle, the producer of Crystal Ball software. Crystal Ball is the registered trademark of Oracle.

analysis tried to capture this uncertainty in one of three ways: point estimates, range estimates and what-if scenarios. Point estimates are when you use what you think are the most likely values (technically referred to as the mode) for the uncertain variables. These estimates are the easiest, but can return very misleading results. For example, try crossing a river with an average depth of three feet. Or if it takes you an average of 25 minutes to get to the airport, leave 25 minutes before your flight takes off. You will miss your plane 50 per cent of the time.

Range estimates typically calculate three scenarios: the best case, the worst case and the most likely case. These types of estimates can show you the range of outcomes, but not the probability of any of these outcomes.

What-if scenarios are usually based on the range estimates and calculate as many scenarios as you can think of. What is the worst case? What if sales are best case but expenses are the worst case? What if sales are average but expenses are the best case? What if sales are average, expenses are average, but sales for the next month are flat? As you can see, this form of analysis is extremely time-consuming, and results in lots of data, but still does not give you the probability of achieving different outcomes.

You can perform a risk analysis in several ways, but one method involves building a spreadsheet model. A good spreadsheet model can be very helpful in identifying where your risk might be, since cells with formulas and cell references identify causal relationships among variables.

One of the drawbacks of conventional spreadsheet models, however, is that you can only enter one value in a cell at a time.

Crystal Ball helps you define those uncertain variables with a range or a set of values. So you can define your business phone bill for future months as any value between ₹2,500 and ₹3,750, instead of using a single point estimate of ₹3,000. It then uses the defined range in a simulation. In addition, Crystal Ball keeps track of the results of each scenario for you.

When we use the word simulation, we refer to any analytical method meant to imitate a real-life system, especially when other analyses are too mathematically complex or too difficult to reproduce. Without the aid of simulation, a spreadsheet model will only reveal a single outcome, generally the most likely or average scenario. Spreadsheet risk analysis uses both spreadsheet model and simulation to automatically analyse the effect of varying inputs on outputs of the modelled system. One type of spreadsheet simulation is Monte Carlo simulation, which randomly generates values for uncertain variables over and over to simulate a model. Monte Carlo simulation was named for Monte Carlo, Monaco, where the primary attractions are casinos containing games of chance. Games of chance such as roulette wheels, dice and slot machines exhibit random behaviour. The random behaviour in games of chance is similar to how Monte Carlo simulation selects variable values at random to simulate a model.

When you roll a dice, you know that either a 1, 2, 3, 4, 5 or 6 will come up, but you do not know which for any particular roll. It is the same with the variables that have a known range of values but an uncertain value for any particular time or event (e.g., interest rates, staffing needs, stock prices, inventory and phone calls per minute). For each uncertain variable (one that has a range of possible values), you define the possible values with a probability distribution. The type of distribution you select is based on the conditions surrounding that variable. Distribution types include the following:

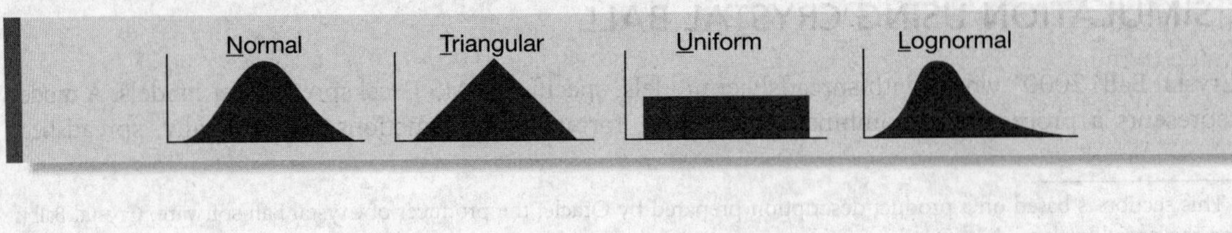

To add this sort of function to an Excel spreadsheet, you would need to know the equation that represents this distribution. With Crystal Ball, these equations are automatically calculated for you. Crystal Ball can even fit a distribution to any historical data that you might have. A simulation calculates multiple scenarios of a model by repeatedly sampling values from the probability distributions for the uncertain variables and using those values for the cell. Crystal Ball simulations can consist of as many trials (or scenarios) as you want—hundreds or even thousands—in just a few seconds. During a single trial, Crystal Ball randomly selects a value from the defined possibilities (the range and shape of the distribution) for each uncertain variable and then recalculates the spreadsheet. For every spreadsheet model, you have a set of important outputs, such as totals, net profits or gross expenses that you want to simulate and analyse. Crystal Ball lets you define those cells as forecasts. A forecast is a formula or output cell that you want to simulate and analyse. You can define as many forecasts as you need, and when you run a Monte Carlo simulation with Crystal Ball, it remembers the values for each forecast for each trial. During the simulation, you can watch a histogram of the results referred to as a frequency chart developed for each forecast. While the simulation runs, you can see how the forecasts stabilize towards a smooth frequency distribution. After hundreds or thousands of trials, you can view the statistics of the results (such as the mean forecast value) and the certainty of any outcome.

Crystal Ball is an easy-to-use simulation programme that helps you to analyse the risks and uncertainties associated with your Microsoft Excel spreadsheet models. Excel models are deterministic, which means that the inputs are fixed (one value to one cell). You can only see one solution at a time. If you want to view alternative results, you need to manually change the inputs in the model. Simulation is a way to quickly generate and analyse many possible results. Excel by itself cannot run simulations, so you need an add-in programme like Crystal Ball to make Excel do this. Because Crystal Ball is an analysis tool, you can use it to simulate existing or new spreadsheets in any industry and for any application.

INCORPORATING RISK INTO CAPITAL BUDGETING DECISIONS

There are two ways of incorporating risk into capital investment appraisal. One way is to adjust the discount rate to reflect the riskiness of the cash flow and other approach is to adjust the cash flow for risks and use a 'risk-free rate' as discount rate.

ADJUSTING DISCOUNT RATE

Under this approach, the discount rate is adjusted to reflect the riskiness of the project cash flows. The risk-adjusted discount rate is arrived at by adding suitable risk premiums to a risk-free rate of return to adjust the discount rate for each factor contributing to the riskiness of the project. The higher the risk, the higher is the discount rate. Modern finance theory tells us that only systematic risk (as measured by β of the stock) is relevant since all other forms of risk could be diversified away.

Thus, Return Expected by Equity Investors = Risk-Free Rate + Risk Premium = $R_f + \beta\ [E(R_m) - R_f]$

But investors may demand a premium for other risks like country and currency risk, project risk. So the discount rate may have to be adjusted upwards/downwards to reflect these as well. The net present value of the project

$$\text{NPV} = \sum_{t=1}^{N} \frac{E_t}{(1+k)^t}$$

where k = risk-adjusted discount rate
= I + Q, that is, risk-free rate + premium
E_t = risky cash flow in period t
N = life of the project

To calculate NPV, we used the firm's WACC as the discount rate. The underlying assumption is that the project has the same business and financial risk as that of the parent company. Stated in another fashion, WACC can be applied only when the project is a carbon copy of the firm's assets. At times, the project may have a different operating risk profile and more or less leveraged than the parent. So it is improper to apply the firm's WACC as the discount rate. To arrive at the project discount rate:

- Estimate the project β
- Plug it into the CAPM to arrive at cost of equity
- Estimate cost of debt
- Calculate the WACC for the project

Since the β for the project is unobservable in the marketplace, a proxy β derived from a publicly traded firm whose operations are as similar as possible to the project in question is used as the measure of the project's systematic risk. The pure play approach attempts to identify firms with publicly traded securities that are engaged solely in the same line of business as the division. These comparable firms are called 'pure play' firm. The characteristics of a pure play firm are as follows:

- The firm should have only one business line and no miscellaneous revenues.
- The pure play should be in the same industry or business line as the division in question.
- The revenues of the pure play should be roughly the same as those of the division in question.
- When more than one firm could be identified as a potential pure play, the firm with the median β could be chosen as the pure play.

After obtaining the proxy βs, estimate the asset βs for each of these firms. The idea is to remove the effect of capital structure on β. The asset β reflects only operating risk.

$$\beta_A = \beta_E \text{ (E/V)}$$

The average of these serves as an estimate of asset β for the project. Re-lever the project β to reflect the project's financing mix using the same equation. Assume that a company is setting up an engineering services company. The project will have a D/V ratio of 0.3. The company has identified four pure plays.

Pure Play	β_E	D/V
A	1.1	0.3
B	0.9	0.25
C	0.95	0.35
D	1	0.3

The asset βs these companies are as follows:

Firm	β_A
A	0.77
B	0.675
C	0.6175
D	0.7

Average $\beta_A = 0.7$. This is taken as proxy asset β of the project.

Now, levered β for the project $= \beta_E = \beta_A/(E/V) = 0.70/0.7 = 1.0$

If $R_f = 11\%$, $(R_M - R_f) = 10\%$,

Cost of equity for the project $= R_f + \beta_L[E(R_M) - R_f]$

$= 11 + 1.0[10\%]$

$= 21\%$

$$WACC = \frac{D}{V}K_d(1-T) + \frac{E}{V}K_e$$

The project's debt-to-value ratio is to be used in WACC calculation.

Certainty Equivalent

Under the certainty equivalent method, the risky cash flows are adjusted downwards by a risk adjustment factor and converted into a series of certain cash flows. The series is to be discounted using a 'risk-free rate'. The higher the uncertainty regarding the realization of the cash flow, the lower is its value today, that is, the lower the certainty equivalent

$$NPV = \sum_{t=1}^{N} \frac{L_t E_t}{(1+i_t)^t}$$

where L_t = certainty equivalent factor

$$= \frac{1+i_t}{1+K_t}$$

i_t = risk-free rate of return in period t

K_t = risk-adjusted discount rate in period t

The discount rate used in capital budgeting has the time value of money and an adjustment for risk. It is difficult to separate the two. So some finance theorists suggest that the certainty equivalent method is better (and hence be used). Instead of making ad hoc adjustments to cash flows and/or discount rate, an analyst can selectively choose the appropriate method as and when the situation warrants. For instance, political risk, in case of international projects, is one of the significant sources of risk. Most multinationals buy insurance from international agencies such as OPEC and Lloyds. In this case, it is easier to adjust cash flow than discount rate. In other words, the adjustment depends on the risk in question.

PROJECT VALUATION IN EMERGING MARKETS

The DCF methodology for evaluating a project involves estimation of cash flows and discount rate. Estimation of cash flows for a foreign project is just an extension of domestic counterpart except that the cash might be more variable or volatile. More specifically, international capital budgeting involves the following:

- Estimation of cash flows specific to that project
- Estimation of discount rate specific to that project

Managers evaluating an international project need to address two questions: Should the project be evaluated from the perspective of managers in the country in which the project is located or that of parent company? Should the cash flows be adjusted downwards or the discount rate be raised to account for differential political and economic risks? An international project can be evaluated in two stages. In the first stage, project is evaluated from the subsidiary's perspective. In the second stage, the amount and timing of profits repatriated (after paying taxes) to the parent company is estimated. It is a common practice to make ad hoc adjustments to cash flows or discount rates. For instance, if a company were to use 15 per cent discount rate for a domestic project, it might raise it to 20 per cent for foreign projects. Such adjustments, obviously, do not have a sound basis. Some academics suggest that it is better to adjust cash flows to account for risks (and not discount rate) because international risks are unsystematic in nature and hence diversifiable. Remember that only systematic risk matters in a CAPM universe. Whether or not the discount rate for foreign projects should be revised depends on how managers view risks in international projects. If the risks are adequately reflected in the project β, then it is inappropriate to add an additional risk premium to the discount rate. There are two alternative approaches for valuing overseas investments.

Approach 1

- Forecast foreign currency cash flows using host country tax rate and inflation rate.
- Estimate foreign currency discount rate using project-specific capital structure and β.
- Calculate PV of the free cash flows in foreign currency.
- Convert to home currency using spot exchange rate.

Approach 2

- Forecast foreign currency cash flows using host country tax rate and inflation rate.
- Forecast future exchange rates using parity relationships and convert cash flows to home currency.
- Estimate home currency discount rate using project-specific capital structure and β.
- Calculate PV in home currency.

The two approaches usually give the same answer.

ADJUSTING CASH FLOWS

The effect of international risk can be incorporated by charging a premium for political and economic risk against each year's cash flows, that is, incorporate the cost of buying an insurance to cover political risk from an agency like Overseas Private Investment Corporation or the Lloyd's of London and the cost of covering economic risk by a forward cover in the currency market. Another approach is to estimate the probability of expropriation and the expected value (mean) of cash flows. Once the cash flow in the host country's currency is estimated, probabilities are attached to different exchange rates (between local currency and home currency) forecasted by the analyst to translate cash flows into home currency.

ADJUSTING DISCOUNT RATE

Whether or not the discount rate for a foreign project should be adjusted depends on how one views international risk. Modern finance theory suggests that only systematic risk of a project matters as unsystematic risk can be diversified away. A multinational, due to its global focus, can diversify country-specific risk as long as cash flows from these countries are not perfectly positively correlated. The standard measure of systematic risk is β, which measures the sensitivity of asset returns to market returns. What is the appropriate proxy for the market portfolio in case of multinational investment? Is it the portfolio in country of operation or that in the home country? Or may be a 'global' portfolio? In many emerging countries, the stock markets lack depth. More than half the market capitalization is accounted for by a handful of companies. So the stock market index would be a poor proxy for market portfolio, which is supposed to represent the portfolio of all risky assets held by the marginal investor in the company. The resulting β estimate would be biased. The investor, in this case, is a multinational company. As there is no international index,[3] one could use the home country stock market index as market portfolio. If we assume that the systematic risk of a project in, say, Chile, is about the same as that elsewhere (which is not true), the problem boils down to finding the β in the home country.[4]

CONVERTING DISCOUNT RATES

Some academics suggest that the discount rate be calculated in the home currency and then translated to host currency. The conversion of home currency discount rate to host country discount rate involves application of interest rate parity condition. Interest rate parity stipulates that the expected rate of change in the spot exchange rate equals the ratio of the prevailing interest rates in the two currencies.

$$(1+\Delta s) = \frac{(1+R_1)}{(1+R_2)}$$

where Δ s = expected change in spot rate

R_1 and R_2 are yields on comparable government bonds denominated in the currencies in question. The WACC in one currency can be converted into another by multiplying by the expected annual change in the exchange rate. While changes in exchange rates may correspond with changes in the differential in national inflation rates in the long run, there are sharp deviations from this parity relationship for shorter intervals. The inflation rate in many emerging markets is much higher than that in stable

[3] We can probably take the Morgan Stanley Capital International Index as the best proxy.

[4] Shapiro (International Capital Budgeting) points out that the systematic risk would not be much higher for a project in LDC vis-à-vis that in industrialized countries.

economies. So discounting foreign cash flows with interest rate in that country would be inappropriate. Likewise, managers in low interest rate economies such as Japan should not use the Yen rate. This will inflate the NPV of the investment.

CONCLUDING COMMENTS

The risk of the project can be captured either by adjusting the cash flow or the discount rate. The discount rate should be adjusted if the risk is systematic in nature. The pure play technique might be employed to estimate the project discount rate. In any case, the corporate cost of capital should not be applied indiscriminately to all the projects. There are three principal methods for risk analysis. They are sensitivity analysis, simulation and best case–worst case analysis. An analyst has the freedom to choose from these methods.

EXERCISES

1. The ACME company is in the oil business. It has a transferable short-term option to drill on a certain plot of land. The company has three options.
   a. Drill immediately
   b. Pay to have a seismic test run in the next few days, and then, depending on the result of the test, decide whether or not to drill
   c. Let the option expire

   Draw a decision tree for the problem.
2. You are trying to decide whether to approve a development budget for an improved product. You are urged to do so on the grounds that the development, if successful, will give you a competitive edge, but if you do not develop the product, your competitor may seriously damage your market share. Draw a decision tree.
3. The following data are available for a project.

   Initial Investment = ₹100 million (including working capital of ₹25 million)
   Expected Life = 8 years
   Salvage Value = 50% of initial investment
   First Year Sales = ₹60 million
   Growth Rate in Sales = 7.5%
   Operating Profit Margin = 10%
   Tax Rate = 35%
   Cost of Capital = 17%
   Increase in WC = 5%

   Depreciation is provided on a straight line basis. Estimate cash flows and NPV. Conduct a sensitivity analysis by changing key assumptions.
4. Find the financial BEP for the previous example.
5. Find the accounting BEP for a project that has the following characteristics.

   Fixed cost = ₹500 million
   Sales Revenue/Unit = ₹1,000
   Variable Cost/Unit = ₹800

6. Given below are two mutually exclusive investments. The management of the company has developed pessimistic, most likely and optimistic estimates of cash flow.

(₹)

	A	B
Investment	5,500	5,500
Pessimistic	200	700
Most likely	800	800
Optimistic	1,400	900

Both projects have a life of 15 years. Cost of capital = 14 per cent. Which project is more risky? Recalculate NPV if the probabilities of the three situations are 30 per cent, 50 per cent and 20 per cent, respectively.

A Mini Case: Valuation of Foreign Divisions

In 2017, a US multinational requested an investment bank to value two of its divisions in Argentina and Brazil. Martin Smith, an analyst with the bank, was asked to forecast free cash flow and estimate suitable discount rates for each of these divisions. Table 8A.1 presents the forecast of free cash flow for the two divisions.

TABLE 8A.1
Forecast of Free Cash Flow

(US$ 000)

	2018	2019	2020	2021	2022
Argentina	6,930	7,117	7,331	7,617	7,990
Brazil	10,920	11,215	11,551	12,002	12,591

Cash flows are expected to grow at 6 per cent p.a. after 2022 in perpetuity. The cash flows from local currency were translated into US$ using the estimated exchange rate for each period. The only task remaining was the estimation of discount rate. Smith discovered that the businesses in Latin America had no pure play proxies. Most of the competitors were subsidiaries of large, diversified companies. So the determination of β for each country operation was difficult. In addition, the efficiency of the local stock markets was questionable and so was the estimate of risk premium. The analyst obtained the dollar borrowing rate, tax rates and target capital structure information from relevant sources. These are displayed in Table 8A.2.

TABLE 8A.2
Interest Rates, Tax Rates and Target Capital Structure

Subsidiary	Borrowing Rate (%)	Tax Rate (%)	Target D/V (%)
Argentina	8	35	20
Brazil	12	35	20

To calculate the cost of equity, he could choose between two approaches under the CAPM method. The first approach involved usage of local CAPM parameters. The second approach involved estimation of parameters (and cost of equity) for the USA and then this estimate was to be adjusted for individual country risk to yield estimates for these subsidiaries. The risk premium for the USA was 6.1 per cent. Other relevant data are given as follows:

Foreign currency debt rating:

	Moody's	S&P
Argentina	B1	BB–
Brazil	B1	B+

US treasuries were yielding:

	YTM (%)
1-year T-bill	5.92
10-year T-bond	6.80
30-year T-bond	7.0

Median β and capital structure information for comparable US industries are given as follows:

	1	2	3	4
Unlevered Median β[5]	0.86	0.79	0.74	0.76
Mean D/V ratio (Market Value)	0.2	0.18	0.17	0.19

Refer to other data provided in Chapter 4. Estimate an appropriate discount rate for and the value of each division.

[5] It is the value of β when leverage is zero. The relationship between levered and unlevered β is $\beta_L = \beta_U\ [1 + (1-T)\ D/E]$.

REFERENCE

Jorion, Philipe. *Value at Risk: The New Benchmark for Controlling Derivatives Risk*. New York, NY: McGraw Hill, 1997.
Shapiro, A. C. 'International Capital Budgeting'. *Midland Corporate Finance Journal* (1983 Spring).

SUGGESTED READINGS

Carter, Eugene. 'What Are the Risks in Risk Analysis'. *Harvard Business Review* (1972 July).
Gaddis, P. 'Analyzing Overseas Investments'. *Harvard Business Review* (1966 May/June).
Hammond, J. 'Better Decisions with Preference Theory'. *Harvard Business Review* (1967 Nov/Dec).
Hertz, David. 'Risk Analysis in Capital Investments'. *Harvard Business Review* (1964 Jan).
Hodder, J. E. and H. E. Riggs. 'Pitfalls in Evaluating Risky Projects'. *Harvard Business Review* (1985 Jan–Feb).

Lessard, Donald R. 'Evaluating Foreign Projects: An Adjusted Present Value Approach'. In *International Financial Management*, edited by Donald Lessard. New York, NY: Warren, Gorham, 1979.

Lessard, Donald. 'Incorporating Country Risk in Valuation of Offshore Projects'. *Journal of Applied Corporate Finance* (1996 Fall).

Lewellen, W. G. 'Some Observations on Risk-Adjusted Discount Rates'. *Journal of Finance* (1977 Sep).

Magee, John. 'How to Use Decision Trees in Capital Investments'. *Harvard Business Review* (1964 Sep–Oct).

Robichek, A. A. and S. C. Myers. 'Conceptual Problems in the Use of Risk Adjusted Discount Rates'. *Journal of Finance* (1966 Dec).

Savvides, Savvakis C. 'Risk Analysis in Investment Appraisal'. *Project Appraisal* 9, no. 1 (1994 March).

Shapiro, A. C. 'Capital Budgeting for the Multinational Corporation'. *Financial Management* (1978 Spring).

CHAPTE
9

A Real Option Perspective of Capital Budgeting

LEARNING OBJECTIVES

- Introduction to financial options
- Bring out the analogy between financial and real options
- Introduction to types of real options
- Valuation of real options

A derivative is a financial instrument or contract between two parties that derives its value from some underlying asset or reference price, interest rate or index. Options, futures, swaps and forwards are derivative instruments. Underlying assets include interest rates, exchange rates, commodities, stocks, stock indices and bonds. Derivatives are traded both on recognized exchanges and in the over-the-counter market. Companies, financial institutions, individuals and institutional investors use derivatives for a variety of reasons. Companies may use derivatives to manage interest rate and foreign exchange rate risk. Investors in stocks may trade in derivatives to manage exposure to equity prices. People may trade in derivative instruments either to hedge risk or to speculate. Derivatives enable individuals to allocate economic risks efficiently by transferring risks from risk-averse individuals to those who are willing to bear. Options are derivative instruments that can be used as a means to hedge or speculate. Options are written on both financial and real assets. Option contracts on foreign currency, stocks, stock indices, interest rates, commodities and treasury bonds.

An option is a contract between the buyer of the option and the seller (writer). The contract gives the buyer of the option the 'right' but not the 'obligation' to buy the underlying asset at a specified price (strike price) at a specified time in the future (expiration date or maturity date). The buyer of the option pays an option 'premium' to the seller for obtaining the right. The seller of the option is however obligated to honour the contract. The option to buy an asset is called a 'call' option and the option to sell an asset is called a 'put' option. An example of call and put options written on a stock as of 30 March 2018 is provided as follows.

Options Traded on the Stock	(Rupees per Share)
Stock Price	₹139
Exercise Price	₹135
Maturity Date	24/04/2018
Call Option Premium	₹5.15
Put Option Premium	₹2.70

The underlying asset in the case is a stock. Options are of two types: European and American. European options can be exercised only on the maturity date, whereas American options can be exercised any time up to maturity. The example presented here is an American type option. The buyer of a call option on the stock could have purchased it at ₹135 any time before the maturity date. Likewise, the holder of a put option could sell the stock at ₹135 by exercising the option.

Options have premium value and intrinsic value. The premium value of the call option mentioned above is ₹5.15 and that of the put option is ₹2.70. The premium is simply the market value of the contract, the price at which buyers and sellers of the option are willing to enter into a contract. Each option contract is for 100 shares. Therefore, an investor would have to pay ₹515 to buy a call option and ₹270 to buy a put option. The intrinsic value is the price an investor would pay for the option if it were to mature immediately. Assume that you buy a call option on the stock at ₹5.15. If the price of the stock were to decline to ₹132, you would not exercise the option because it is cheaper to buy the stock in the market rather than choose the option. So the option expires worthless. In other words, the value of an option can at worst be zero. Let us suppose the price increased to ₹140. The intrinsic value of the option is ₹5, the profit you make by exercising the option and selling the share simultaneously in the open market. In general, the intrinsic value of a call option is the maximum of zero and the difference between the current market price of the underlying asset and the option's exercise price.

The opposite is true of put options. They gain value when the price of the underlying asset decreases because the holder of the option can sell the asset at a higher price than the prevailing market price. The intrinsic value of a put option is the maximum of zero and the difference between the put option's exercise price and the current market price of the underlying asset. An option is 'in-the-money' if its intrinsic value is positive and 'out-of-the money' if its intrinsic value is negative. A call option is in-the-money if the price of the underlying asset exceeds exercise price. The converse is true for put option. An option is at-the-money when the asset price and the strike price are equal. If the asset price is far above the exercise price for a call option, the option is deep in-the-money. If the asset price is far below the exercise price for a call option, the option is deep out-of-the-money. The converse is true for put options. Assume that on 6 January 2018, you purchased a call option to buy 100 shares of a stock at a strike price of ₹180. Each option has a premium of ₹5. The options expire on 30 January 2018. At the time of entering into the contract, the buyer has to pay a premium of ₹5 × 100 for each contract. The value of the call option for various exercise prices is shown as follows.

Exercise Price	Stock Price	Premium	(₹) Value of Call Option
180	170	5	–5
180	175	5	–5
180	180	5	–5
180	185	5	0
180	190	5	5
180	195	5	10

The option is worthless as long as the strike price exceeds the exercise price by an amount equal to the premium paid. The pay-off can be plotted on a diagram shown as follows.

The maximum that an option holder loses is the premium paid, whereas the upside potential is unlimited. The value of the option increases one-to-one for any increase in price above the BE price. Since each option is for 100 shares, the strike price, exercise price and the premium have to be multiplied by 100 to arrive at the aggregate pay-off. If the holder of the option decides to exercise the option, he/she should pay ₹180 × 100 (i.e., exercise price × 100 shares). Those options worth exercising are called in-the-money and those that are not are considered out-of-the-money.

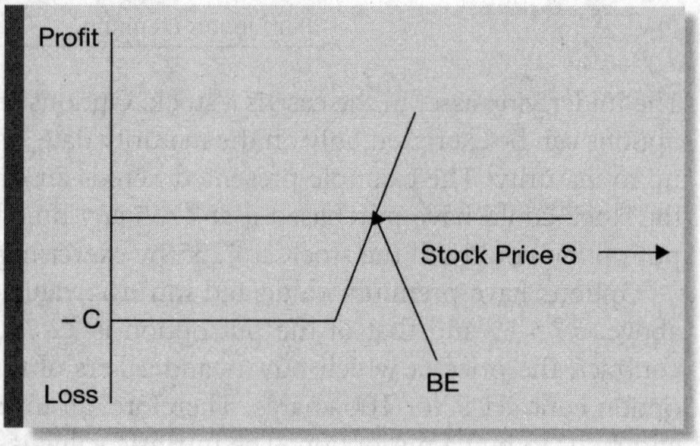

The pay-off from the perspective of a seller is shown as follows:

Note that the seller (writer) of the call option gets the premium as long as the strike price is lower than the exercise price. While the upside is fixed, the downside is unlimited. Also note that the pay-offs are mirror images—what the buyer gains the seller loses and vice versa—that is, they sum to zero (zero sum game).

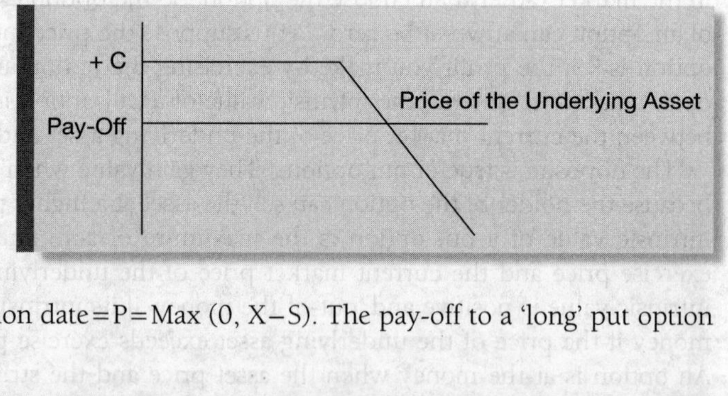

The value of put option on the expiration date = P = Max (0, X – S). The pay-off to a 'long' put option position is shown as follows:

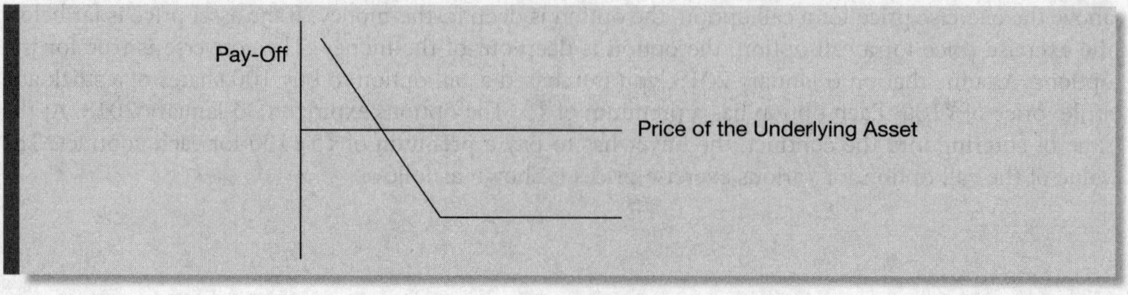

Note that the buyer of the put option makes money if the ending spot price of the underlying asset is lower than the exercise price. Likewise, the pay-off to the writer of a put option is shown as follows:

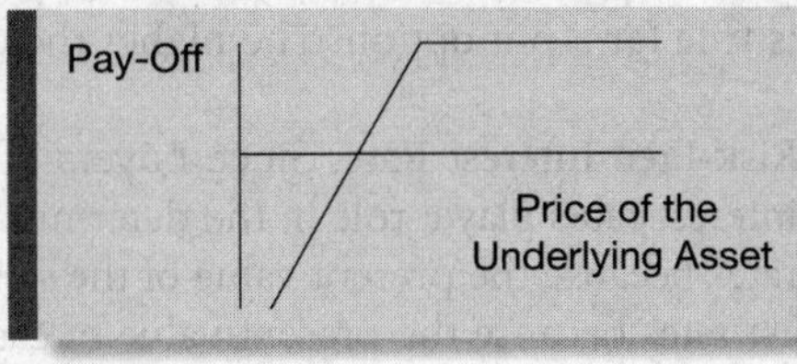

Like call options, the pay-offs for the put option holder and the writer sum to zero.

DETERMINANTS OF OPTION VALUE

Note from the data on prices of options on average cost of capital (ACC) stock that the market value of option is more than the intrinsic value, that is, the market value of the call option on 20 March was ₹5.15, whereas the intrinsic value was ₹4 (i.e., ₹139–₹135). Likewise, the put option was worthless (i.e., out-of-the-money). Yet it has value (₹2.70). This is true of all options that have time remaining to maturity. A graph of a call option's premium relative to intrinsic value is given in Figure 9.1.

How much the premium exceeds the intrinsic value depends on the following six factors:

- Underlying Asset Price
- Exercise Price
- Risk-Free Rate
- Volatility of the Asset Price
- Time to Expiration
- Cash Distributions from the Underlying Asset (i.e., Dividends in Case of Stock)

Asset Price: For a European or an American type call option, an increase in the asset price leads to an increase in the option's intrinsic value because the option becomes more valuable. The premium, therefore, increases with an increase in the asset price. The opposite is true for a put option. The higher the asset price, the less valuable is the put option.

FIGURE 9.1
Call Option Premium Relative to Intrinsic Value

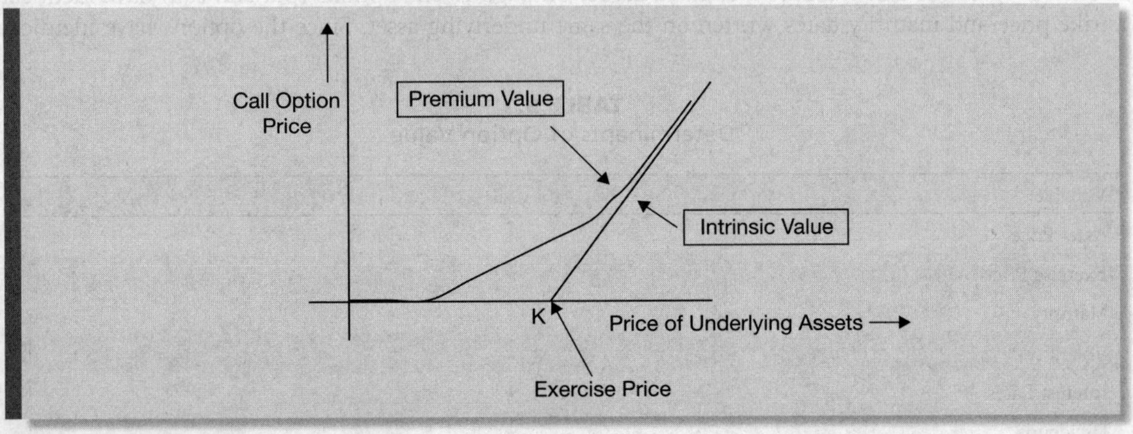

Exercise Price: An increase in a call option's exercise price decreases the intrinsic value. The higher the exercise price for an American or European type call option, the lower will be its premium. The opposite is true for a put option. The higher the exercise price, the more valuable is a put option.

Risk-Free Interest Rate: Since buyers of options do not receive the option's exercise price until later, interest rates play a role in the determination of option value. A call option value increases with interest rates because the present value of the strike price falls. A put option value falls with an increase in interest rates because the present value of cash received decreases.

Volatility of Asset Price: An increase in the volatility of asset price increases the value of call option because of asymmetrical pay-off of options, that is, the upside is unlimited, whereas the downside is limited to the premium paid. Although the holder of a put option experiences limited potential gains, the holder can limit loss by simply not exercising the option if the asset price rises above the exercise price. In sum, an increase in volatility leads to an increase in the value of call and put options.

Time to Expiration: For both American and European type call options, an increase in the time to expiration has a positive impact on the option value because the probability of the ending up in-the-money is more and the present value of exercise price is less. An American type put option also gains in value because of the chances of ending up in-the-money. For European type options, the impact of lengthening the time to expiration is not known. If the option is in-the-money, a longer time to maturity will have a negative impact because the present value of cash receipt from exercising falls. If the option is deep out-of-the-money, a longer time to maturity will increase the option value because a longer time provides a greater opportunity for the stock price to drop far enough to make the option valuable.

Cash Distributions (Dividend): A cash dividend paid on the stock decreases the stock price because of which the call option value declines. The opposite is true for put option because a fall in stock price increases the value of a put option.

A summary of the effect of each factor on option value is given in Table 9.1.

PUT–CALL PARITY

Consider again the first example illustrated earlier on page 1. The options (put and call) have identical strike price and maturity dates written on the same underlying asset. Since the options have identical

TABLE 9.1
Determinants of Option Value

Variable	Call	Put
Asset Price	↑	↓
Exercise Price	↓	↑
Maturity	↑	?
Volatility	↑	↑
Interest Rates	↓	↑
Dividends	↓	↑

characteristics, we would expect them to be related in some way. There's a condition known as 'put–call parity' that describes the relation between the call and put option values.

Assume that you have purchased a European call option and sold a European put option on the same asset (S) with the same exercise price X and expiration date T. The investment required to establish this position is the difference between call and put values.

That is, C–P

The pay-off to this position is S–X. On the expiration date if the spot price is less than the expiration price, the call option expires worthless and the put option will be exercised against the position. Consequently, the pay-off will be negative.

Consider another investment in which an investor borrows the present value of X to purchase the asset. The investment required is:

$$= S - \frac{X}{(1+r)^T}$$

and the pay-off to this position on the expiration date, T, is S–X since the investor owns the asset (S) and owes X.

Since the pay-off to these two investment positions is the same, their initial investment must also be the same to prevent arbitrage opportunities.[1]

$$C - P = S \frac{X}{(1+r)^T}$$

VALUATION OF OPTIONS

The Black–Scholes model is widely used in pricing options. The Black–Scholes formula values a European call or put option as follows:

$$\text{Value of a Call Option} = S\, e^{(b-r)T}\, N(d_1) - X\, e^{-rT}\, N(d_2)$$
$$\text{Value of a Put Option} = -S\, e^{(b-r)T}\, N(-d_1) + X\, e^{-rT}\, N(-d_2)$$

where:

S = stock price

X = strike price or exercise price

b = cost of carry defined as risk-free rate minus the dividend yield (q)

T = time to maturity in years

σ^2 = variance in returns from the underlying stock

$$d_1 = \frac{\text{Ln}(S/X) + (b + \sigma^2/2)T}{\sigma\sqrt{T}}$$

$$d_2 = d_1 - \sigma\sqrt{T}$$

[1] A standard text on derivatives would explain put–call parity in greater detail. See, for example, Hull, *Options, Futures and Other Derivatives*.

The function N (parameter) used in the formula is a mathematical notation for the cumulative normal distribution function.

AN EXAMPLE

A call option has the following properties:

$S = ₹50$

$X = ₹40$

$R_f = 5\%$

$q = 3\%$

$b = r - q = 0.05 - 0.03 = 0.02$

$T = 5$ years

$\sigma = 30\% = 0.3$

$e = 2.7183$, a constant

$$d_1 = \frac{\ln(50/40) + (0.02 + 0.3^2/2)5}{0.3\sqrt{5}} = 0.8171$$

$$d_2 = 0.8171 - 0.3\sqrt{5} = 0.5582$$

$$N(d_1) = N(0.8171) = 0.7931$$

$$N(d_2) = N(0.1463) = 0.5582$$

$$\text{Value of Call} = Se^{(b-r)T}N(d_1) - Xe^{-rT}N(d_2)$$

$$= 50\ e^{(0.02-0.05)5}\ 0.7931 - 40\ e^{-0.05\times 5}\ 0.5582$$

$$= ₹16.74$$

Note that the value of the option is more than its intrinsic value (50−40=10) because of time value.

A call option should be exercised if the stock price exceeds the strike price at expiration, that is, exercise if S>X. For the sake of convenience, let us express it as a ratio. The option has value if S/X>1. If S/X is less than 1, the option should not be exercised as it is out-of-the-money.

The variability (per unit of time) of returns is measured by variance. Multiplying the variance per unit of time by amount of time to maturity gives the cumulative variance. The higher the cumulative variance, the more valuable the option. The Black–Scholes value of a European call option as a percentage of value of underlying asset is available in a tabular form. A portion of the same is shown as follows.

Option Value (%)

	Annual σ × Square Root of Time			
Share Price/PV of Exercise Price	0.25	0.5	0.75	1.0
0.5	0	3	10	19
0.6	0	5	14	24
0.7	1	8	18	28
0.8	3	12	22	32
0.9	6	16	26	35
1.0	10	20	29	38

Consider the following data.

Stock Price = ₹50
Annual Volatility = 25%
r = 5%
Exercise Price = ₹60
T = 4 years
PV of Exercise Price = $60/(1.05)^4$ = ₹49.36
Share Price/PV (X) = 50/49.36 = 1.01

$$\sigma (\sqrt{4}) = 25\% \times 2 = 50\%$$

The cell at the intersection of row six and column two, 20 per cent, gives the call option value as percentage of value of underlying asset.

Option Value = 20% of Stock Price = 0.2 × ₹50 = ₹10

REAL OPTIONS

The traditional DCF methodology is based on the assumption that managers make an investment and then wait to see what happens.

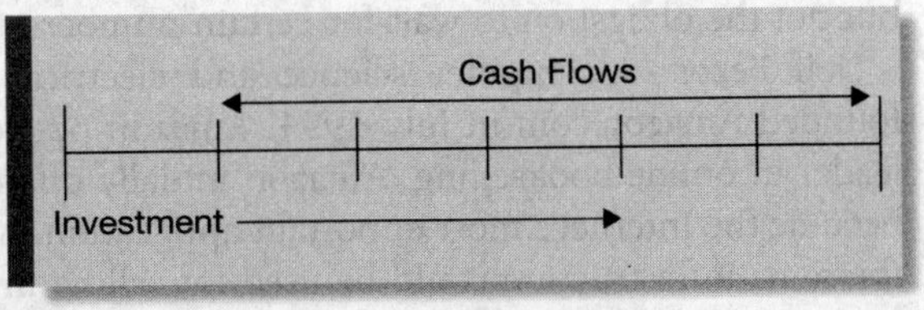

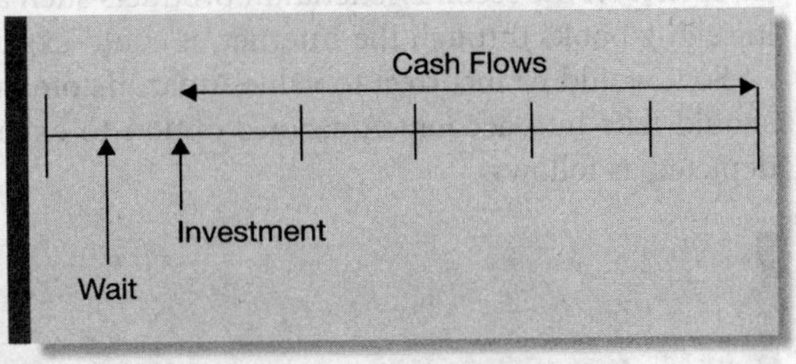

It does not, for example, consider why managers cannot wait and 'then' invest.

If the price for the product turns out weak, they may choose to abandon the project or wait for some time. The DCF methodology does not account for managerial flexibility in making mid-course corrections. For instance, the managers of a gold mining company could stop digging if gold prices fall. The NPV calculated using the DCF methodology is a complex average of many outcomes—both positive and negative. Managers, of course, have the option to avoid the downside by limiting investment. Real options are options on capital projects implicitly held by companies. Just as a bond–warrant[2] package is to be valued separately and added up, the option component of capital projects has to be valued separately and added to the DCF value.

Real options analysis extends financial option theory to options on real assets. Investment examples include new plants, line extensions, joint ventures and licensing agreements. Real options analysis is a

[2] A bond or a debenture is a debt instrument that entitles the holder to interest payments throughout the life of the bond and principal repayment at the end. The value of a bond is simply the present value of interest payments and principal repayment. A warrant is a call option that entitles the holder to exercise his/her option and purchase the shares of a company at a specified price on or before a certain date.

complement to DCF analysis, not a substitute. The DCF methodology falls short of real options analysis on several counts:

- Flexibility is the ability to defer, abandon, expand or contract an investment. Because the NPV rule does not factor in the value of uncertainty, it is less robust than the real options approach. For instance, a company may choose to defer an investment for some period of time until it has more information about the market. The NPV rule does not assign value to the investment, whereas the real options approach would.
- In standard finance, higher 'volatility' means higher discount rates and lower NPV. In options theory, higher volatility leads to higher option value because of asymmetric pay-off.
- In many situations, future investments are contingent on the success of current investments. Managers may make investments today, even if they are negative NPV projects, to access future investment opportunities. Pharmaceutical companies are a good example. Future spending on drug development is often contingent on the product clearing hurdles. This is valuable because investments can be made in stages, rather than up front.

Capital projects are like options in the sense that managers have the right but not the obligation to cultivate them. An R&D investment may, for example, may open up new markets and products. So a valuation of the R&D investment should take into account the value of future products as well. Likewise, while making natural resource investments (e.g., gold mining), managers may have the option but not the obligation to wait for certain number of years by paying a fee.

Jeff Bezos, a computer science and electrical engineering graduate from Princeton University, founded Amazon.com in July 1994. Amazon opened its doors in 1995 with the mission to become a leader in online bookselling. Amazon initially offered 1 million titles. Bezos believed that retail would become the Internet's most important application. Although Amazon.com started selling books initially, the same infrastructure could be used for selling music CDs and videos. In other words, Amazon held an option on the second-generation products such as music CDs and videos. If Amazon were successful in selling books through the Internet, it could expand the product offering to music and video.

So it would be incorrect to value Amazon.com on the basis of sales from books alone. The valuation should take into account Amazon's option to expand into music and video. The correct approach is depicted as follows:

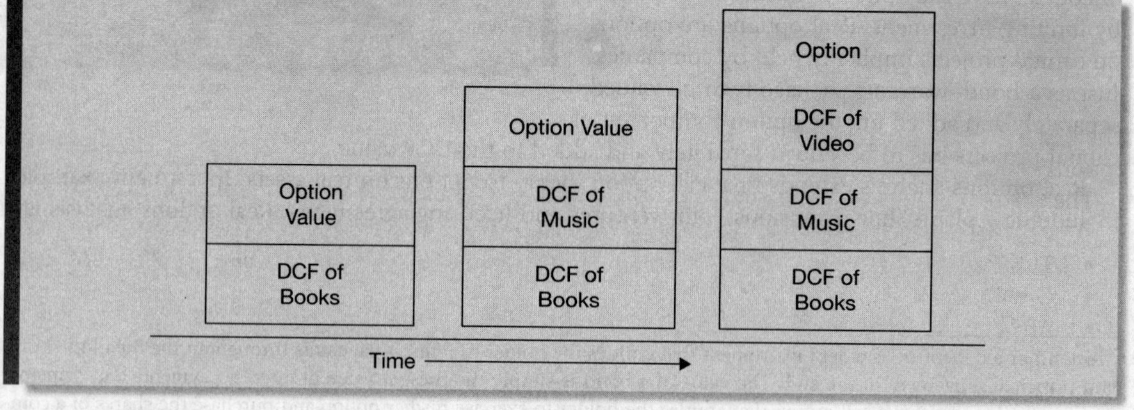

VALUATION OF REAL OPTIONS

The binomial option–pricing model is one of the most widely used real options valuation methods. The binomial model describes price movements over time, where the asset value can move to one of two possible prices with associated probabilities. Given below is a binomial process through a decision tree.

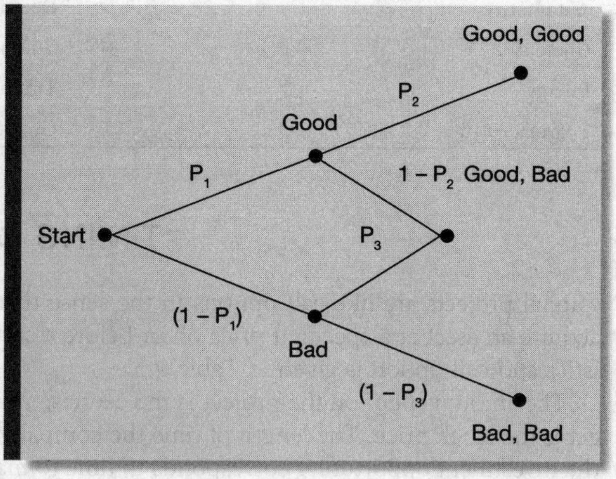

Consider a project that has a best outcome of ₹13 million and a worst outcome of ₹9 million. Each of these outcomes are equally likely to occur (probability is 0.5). The expected value of the project, the weighted average of outcomes, is ₹11 million. The discounted value at a discount rate of, say, 10 per cent, is ₹10 million. If the initial investment is ₹9.7 million, the NPV is ₹0.30 million. Based on NPV, most managers would go ahead with the project. But NPV does not deal with the management's ability to time the project. Suppose the management has the option to wait for 1 year at which time they can decide to invest. If the demand for the product turns out weak, the management can decide not to invest as it does not make sense to invest ₹ 9.7 million and receive ₹9 million a year later. However, if the product turns out to be popular, the project would yield ₹13 million for an investment of ₹9.7 million. The NPV in this case is ₹2.12 million. Since there is a 50–50 chance of a good outcome (NPV 2.12 million) and a bad outcome (do not invest; 0 NPV in year 1), the expected value is $(0.5 \times 2.12 + 0.5 \times 0)$ ₹1.06 million. The present value at year 0 is ₹9.6 million. The moral is that we must assign a value to the option to defer. By not considering the option, managers will miss out on a chance to add value by waiting. In other words, options are exercised only if they have value and are left unexercised if they are worthless. A brief study of the decision tree shows that time and the range of outcomes are key to option value. The Black–Scholes model is a narrow case of the binomial model. It applies when the limiting distribution on asset and assumes a continuous price process.

TYPES OF REAL OPTIONS

The first step in real options analysis is to identify them. Table 9.2 presents a list of some common real options.

There are six categories of real options. They are as follows:

- Timing option
- Growth option
- Abandonment option
- Option to expand scale
- Option to switch inputs and outputs
- Option to contract scale

TABLE 9.2
Typical Real Options by Sector

Aerospace	Valuing options in customer contracts
Banking and Securities	Valuing real estate leases
Automotive	Decisions to modify new car designs
Chemicals	Timing of investment
Energy	Timing the development of oil and gas fields/switching inputs
Pharmaceuticals	Growth options embedded in R&D projects

TIMING OPTION

Capital projects are like call options in the sense that both involve the right but not the obligation to acquire an asset at a specified price on or before a certain date. The analogy between project characteristics and call option is given in Table 9.3.

The amount spent on the project is the exercise price. The present value of cash flows from the project is the stock price. The length of time the company can defer the investment decision without losing the investment opportunity corresponds to time to maturity. The uncertainty in the project's cash flows corresponds to the standard deviation of returns. The cash flows lost due to competitors who have fully committed corresponds to dividends.

An analogy between capital projects and a call option is presented in Table 9.3.

The impact of changes in option variables on the value of the option is shown in the following table.

Variable	Value of Real Option
Increase in the PV of the project	Increase
A higher investment cost	Decrease
A longer time to maturity	Increase
Increase in uncertainty (volatility of cash flows)	Increase
Increase in risk-free rate	Increase
Increases in cash flow lost	Decrease

TABLE 9.3
The Analogy Between Capital Projects and a Call Option

Project Characteristic	Call Option
Expenditure required acquiring the asset	Exercise price (X)
PV of cash flows	Stock price (S)
Length of time decision may be deferred	Time to expiration (t)
Riskiness of underlying operating assets	Variance of stock returns (σ^2)
Time value of money	Risk-free rate of return (r_f)

Timing option enables managers to defer investment for a certain period of time without losing the opportunity. In other words, managers would always want to spend later rather than sooner. If an investment can be deferred for one year, one could put the investment in a bank for one year and withdraw it when the time is ripe to invest, that is, the investment X would be invested at r_f for one year. So the amount now is the present value of X discounted at r_f.

$$PV(X) = X/(1+r_f)^t$$

Since our objective is to refine NPV to incorporate other option variables like r_f, t and σ, lets redefine NPV as S−PV (X). As with financial options, this can be expressed as a ratio=S/PV (X).

Cumulative Variance=σ t² (Cumulative Volatility is the Square Root of Cumulative Variance)

We can use these two values to estimate the value of the option as percentage of value of underlying assets.

An example is in order. A company is investing ₹300 million in a project. The project is expected to generate cash flows of ₹75 million p.a for five years. A company has the option of investing in the project (i.e., develop the product) in the next five years, that is, the company can delay the project for a period of five years without seriously jeopardizing the value of the project. A simulation of project cash flows suggests that the standard deviation of cash flows is 40 per cent. The risk-free rate is 6 per cent and the cost of capital for the company is 12 per cent.

X=Investment=₹300 million
S=PV of Cash Flows @ 12 per cent
t=5 years
σ=40 per cent=0.4
PV(X)=300/(1.06)⁵=300/1.338=₹224.2
S=75×PVIFA(12%, 5 years)=75×3.605=₹270.375 cr

Traditional NPV=₹270.375 million−₹300 million=−₹29.625 million. This analysis does not take into consideration the possibility of deferring the investment and the volatility of the returns.

$$S/PV(X) = 270.375/224.2 = 1.2$$

$$\sigma\sqrt{t} = 0.4 \times \sqrt{5} = 0.89$$

The value of the call option as percentage of value of underlying asset from the table is 40.8%, that is, 0.408×270.375=₹110 million.

GROWTH OPTION

A growth option is characterized by an early investment (e.g., in R&D) which leads to a chain of interrelated projects opening up future new generation products and processes, access to new market, oil reserves and so on. Any investment that creates new investment opportunities can be characterized as a growth option. Companies derive their value from two sources: assets in place and present value of growth opportunities. Stock markets realize it when pricing securities.

Just as a package of bond and warrants are valued separately, the option component embedded in projects should be evaluated separately and then added to the value obtained from the DCF methodology. Assume that a project is expected to lead to a second-generation investment. The NPV of the entire proposal may be written as follows:

$$NPV = NPV(\text{Phase 1}) + \text{Call Value of Phase 2}$$

To evaluate growth options embedded in projects:

- Segregate discretionary expenditure and its associated cash flows of Phase two project from Phase one project.
- Find the NPV of phase using the traditional DCF approach.
- Discount the discretionary spending to the present using an appropriate risk-free rate. If the discretionary spending that leads to Phase two project is ₹300 million to be made in the third year, discount it to the present by using a three-year risk-free rate. This constitutes X.
- Find the present value of cash flows (net of inflows and 'routine' expenditure on WC and fixed assets) using WACC. This is S.
- Find S/PV(X).
- Estimate cumulative volatility ($\sigma\sqrt{t}$); t is three years in this case. Volatility can be estimated in several ways. One approach is to estimate the historical volatility of the company's stock and take it as proxy for the volatility of returns from the project undertaken by the company. Another approach is to use implied volatility of options on the company's stock traded in exchanges. The third approach is to simulate project cash flows and find the standard deviation of NPV using a standard package such as Crystal Ball.[3]
- Find the value of the call option and add it to the NPV of Phase one.

ABANDONMENT OPTION

If market conditions deteriorate severely, management can abandon operations and realize resale value of project assets in second-hand markets. Abandonment options are important in capital-intensive industries, financial services and new product introduction in uncertain markets.

In a competitive industry with over capacity, management has to continuously consider whether to stay or get out. The actual decision depends on the value of the project below which management may choose to abandon and the value above which extension could take place. An abandonment option is a put option.

$$\text{Value of Put} = -S\, e^{(b-r)T}\, N(-d_1) + X\, e^{-rT}\, N(-d_2)$$

The development of an oil field consists of sequential investments in test drilling, evaluation drilling and production capacity.

CONCLUDING COMMENTS

Corporate investments are like options. The DCF methodology invariably breaks down while evaluating investments that can be timed or phased out. But real options analysis is a complement to the DCF

[3] Crystal Ball is a product of Oracle.

approach, not a substitute. The examples cited in this chapter are simple call and put options. As shown in the case of oil exploration, for example, some investments are a series of options. These are compound options, that is, these are options on options. They cannot be treated as simple call or put options. Since compound options are complex, we do not deal with them here. The objective of this chapter was to provide a flavour of real options theory. Serious readers must refer to advanced books on real options cited under bibliography.

EXERCISES

1. A company is investing in a project. The project requires an outlay of ₹1,000 million and the present value of cash flows is ₹1,200 million. This project is expected to lead to a second-generation project in 5 years that requires an investment of another ₹2,000 million. The second generation would generate cash flows with a present value of ₹1,700 million if developed right now. The standard deviation of cash flows is 0.8. Assuming a risk-free rate of 6 per cent, estimate the value of option. Would you undertake the project?
2. A company has a project that requires an outlay of ₹1,000 million. The present value of cash flows from the project is ₹1,100 million. The company has the option to sell the stake in the project to the other sponsor of the project for ₹600 million any time in the next eight years. The variance in project cash flows is 0.6. What is the value of the option to abandon? What is the true NPV of the project?
3. Can equity be treated as an option held by shareholders? Why? Likewise, can debt be treated as an option held by creditors? Why or how?
4. A company is in the process of acquiring another company. The forecast of free cash flows are prepared on the basis of the following assumptions:
   - Current sales are ₹50 million.
   - Expected growth rate in sales is 6 per cent for the next 10 years.
   - Cost of goods sold is 65 per cent of sales.
   - Selling, general and administrative expenses are 15 per cent of sales.
   - Depreciation is 4 per cent of sales.
   - Capital investment to support sales is 8 per cent of sales.
   - Tax rate is 35 per cent.
   - WACC for the company is 9.5 per cent.
   - The book value of the company's debt is ₹10 million.

   The target has an excellent distribution system that has value to the acquirer. The acquirer plans to set up a new plant if the acquisition goes through. The new plant requires an initial investment of ₹6 million in year zero and ₹8 million one year later. If plant construction is delayed, construction costs are expected to increase 10 per cent p.a. Sales are expected to increase to 11 per cent p.a. from 5 per cent one year after the investment is made. Due to increased efficiency, cost of goods sold will decrease from 65 per cent to 60 per cent of sales. S, G&A, depreciation and capital investment remain the same. Capex required to maintain only the plant will equal depreciation expense of the plant. The new plant has the same risk complexion as the firm itself.

   The managers of the company have decided to wait for three years before building the plant. In other words, the managers have a three-year real option starting three years from now. The standard deviation of project returns and risk-free rate are 45 per cent and 5 per cent, respectively.

- Estimate the value of the target company's equity without the new plant.
- Estimate the value of the real option assuming managers defer the construction of plant for three, four and five years.

REFERENCE

Hull, John C. *Options, Futures and Other Derivatives*, 9th edition. London: Pearson, 2014.

SUGGESTED READINGS

Brennan, M. J. and E. Schwartz. 'A New Approach to Evaluating Natural Resource Investments'. In *The Revolution in Corporate Finance*, edited by Joel Stern and Donald Chew Jr. Oxford: Basil Blackwell, 1992.

Copeland, T. and P. Keenan. 'How Much Is Flexibility Worth'. *The McKinsey Quarterly*, no. 2 (1998a).

Copeland, T. and P. Keenan. 'Making Real Options Real'. *The McKinsey Quarterly*, no. 3 (1998b).

Copeland, T. and V. Antikarov. *Real Options: A Practitioner's Guide*. New York, NY: Texere LLC, 2001.

Damodaran, A. 'The Promise of Real Options'. *Journal of Applied Corporate Finance* 13, no. 2 (2000).

Dixit, A. and R. Pindyck. 'The Options Approach to Capital Investment'. *Harvard Business Review* (1995 May–June).

Edelson, M. 'Real Options: Valuing Managerial Flexibility' (HBS Case No. 9-294-109, 1994 March).

Imai, J. and M. Nakajima. 'A Real Option Analysis of an Oil Refinery Project'. *Financial Practice and Education* (2000 Fall/Winter).

Kemna, A. 'Case Studies on Real Options'. *Financial Management* (1993 Autumn).

Kester, C. 'Today's Options for Tomorrow's Growth'. *Harvard Business Review* (1984 March–April).

Leslie, K. and M. Michaels. 'The Real Power of Real Options'. *The McKinsey Quarterly* (1997).

Luehrman, T. and B. Wall. 'M W Petroleum (A)' (HBS Case No.9-295-029, 1994 November).

Luehrman, T. 'Capital Projects as Real Options: An Introduction' (Harvard Business School Case No 9-295-074, 1995 March).

Luehrman, T. 'Investment Opportunities as Real Options: Getting Started on the Numbers'. *Harvard Business Review* (1998 July–August).

Luehrman, T. 'Strategy as a Portfolio of Real Options'. *Harvard Business Review* (1998 Sep–Oct).

Martha, A. and N. Kulatilaka. *Real Options: Managing Strategic Investment in an Uncertain World*. Boston, MA: Harvard Business School Press, 1999a.

Martha, A. and N. Kulatilaka. 'Disciplined Decisions: Aligning Strategy with Financial Markets'. *Harvard Business Review* (1999b Jan–Feb).

Martha, A. and N. Kulatilaka. 'Uncertainty: The New Rules for Strategy'. *Journal of Business Strategy* (1999c March).

Martha, A. and N. Kulatilaka. 'Strategy and Shareholder Value Creation: The Real Options Frontier'. *Journal of Applied Corporate Finance* 13, no. 2 (2000 Summer).

McDonald, R. and D. Siegel. 'The Value of Waiting to Invest'. *Quarterly Journal of Economics* 101 (1986).

Robichek, A. and J. Van Horne. 'Abandonment Value and Capital Budgeting'. *Journal of Finance* (1967 March).

Sachdeva, K. and P. Vandenberg. 'Valuing the Abandonment Option in Capital Budgeting—An Option Pricing Approach'. *Financial Practice and Education* (1993 Fall).

Trigeorgis, L. and S. Mason. 'Valuing Managerial Flexibility'. *Midland Corporate Finance Journal* (1987 Spring).

Trigeorgis, L. 'Real Options and Interactions with Financial Flexibility'. *Financial Management* (1993 Autumn).

CHAPTER

10

A Follow-Up Note on Capital Budgeting

LEARNING OBJECTIVES

- Highlight potential pitfalls in capital budgeting
- Introduce the administrative process surrounding capital budgeting
- Discuss issues in selecting hurdle rates
- Discuss the link between capital budgeting and corporate strategy

The focus of capital budgeting should not be on the result of calculation but on the important assumptions on which the calculation is based. The use of unrealistic assumptions is a more significant source of bad investment decisions than the use of unscientific techniques. The project can still fail if the result is based on unrealistic assumptions, however refined the technique might be. Measures such as ROI and NPV do not consider the subtle behavioural aspects of capital budgeting or the problems of single point estimates. Quite often, the strategic aspects of individual investments are not considered or an ad hoc evaluation of alternatives is made. It is important to consider all alternatives before a decision is made. A firm can segregate its businesses into three categories—those in which it wants to expand, those in which it wants to maintain position and those which no longer fit into the firm's portfolio and, hence, need to be liquidated. The firm can set different standards for different businesses. The upshot is that one project may be accepted despite low returns and another project may be rejected despite high returns. The DCF approach breaks down when hurdle rates are arbitrarily chosen, especially while evaluating unconventional technology. Executives tend to focus on a set of numbers while trying to be practical in evaluation.

SELECTING HURDLE RATES

Often, the hurdle rate in investment analysis is the firm's cost of capital. The reason is quite simple; unless a firm can earn at least what it costs to raise the necessary capital, there is no justification for that investment. The problem lies in measuring the cost of equity. The cost of equity is the return expected by investors, which is their opportunity cost (the return they can earn on comparable investments). Theoretically, it is correct to take the investors' expected return as the cost of equity. An equity investor has many alternatives and can diversify in a broad range of investments. But a company cannot diversify, at least in the short run, from, say, paper to steel to aircraft manufacturing. In fact, it might not be possible to diversify at all due to technical reasons. So Donaldson[1] argues that the relevant opportunity cost for the company is not that of the shareholder but that of the company itself. The hurdle rate could be what the company can earn on the company's alternatives. It is often argued that if the company cannot find attractive investments it should return cash to stockholders. But this does not happen in reality. A company in a declining market will not return cash but strive to revitalize product lines and grow. It is useful to classify investments as tactical and strategic. Tactical investment decisions are concerned with near future, and strategic decisions are concerned with change for a major transformation. He suggests that a tier of hurdle rates be constructed and applied to investments depending on their nature. For tactical decisions, the appropriate standard could be the performance of the most efficient competitor. For strategic investments, the hurdle rate could be the return a competing division with the best track record is earning or the return the company can earn on new businesses the company is capable of launching.

ADMINISTRATIVE PROCESS IN CAPITAL BUDGETING

Success in investment decisions depends not only on techniques but also on people and process of generating, evaluating and implementing investments. The starting point for an organization is a long-term plan. The long-term plan can be exploded into investment ideas. The planning period is typically five years. The plan integrates sales and cost projections, operating and capital investment needs. Specific guidelines translate long-term goals into specific investment proposals. Guidelines provide a frame of reference for everyone in the organization. They reflect the organization's policy and strategic thrust, what the firm intends to do with regard to expansion, what product markets it intends to serve and so on. Guidelines should ensure adherence from all executives. At the same time, it should not discourage unconventional thinking. Guidelines can be classified as long term and short term. Long-term guidelines deal with growth objectives, whereas short-term guidelines deal with projections regarding sales, input prices and so on.

PREPARING BUDGETS

Executives are typically asked to put their ideas down on paper with specific capital investment plans. The result is a capital budget. It serves as an initial screening device and the ones that pass through the initial screen are taken up for greater scrutiny. If a time limit is given for capital expenditure plans, ideas that arrive later in the budget cycle may be rejected. So a budget should be flexible enough. Project proposals typically go through several levels before they are accepted. Decentralization reduces the time spent on project approval.

[1] Donaldson, 'Strategic Hurdle Rates for Capital Investments'.

Allocating Funds

Appropriate allocation of funds is essential as it decides the future of the company. So a sound basis for allocating funds should be evolved. The allocation could be based on mission, product portfolio, geographic area of operations and competence.[2] Mission is fundamental to any company. It reflects the fundamental purpose the company is trying to achieve. A firm can be viewed as a portfolio of products. This gives us another basis for allocation. Those products that hold promise would receive more funds than those that need to be milked. Geographic scope of operations can also be used as a basis as it defines the competitive arena within which a company intends to compete. An international company has a different set of competitive rules and problems when compared to a domestic company. Finally, competence could be a basis for allocation since success comes from abilities rather than product characteristics. Prahlad and Hamel[3] define core competencies as the collective learning in the organization, especially how to coordinate diverse production skills and integrate multiple stream of technologies. Core competence is not to be confused with core business. Core competence is communication, involvement and a deep commitment to working across organizational boundaries. Core competence is about harmonizing streams of technology. Sony's competence is in miniaturization and Philip's expertise is in optical media. Companies need to stop viewing themselves as portfolios of businesses. The successful companies, even while holding seemingly unrelated businesses, are integrated by a set of common skills.

POST-COMPLETION AUDIT

Post-completion audit is the most important phase in capital budgeting. It permits the comparison of projected and actual performance and the analysis of variance. Most importantly, it helps in judging whether the assumptions, policies and analyses have been sound. The advantages of post-completion audits are as follows:

- Management can learn from past mistakes.
- Management can identify weaknesses in the existing projects and revise estimates.
- The audit process can be used to distinguish between good and bad performance. Executive compensation can also be designed to encourage good performance.
- Post-completion audits discourage executives from being overoptimistic.
- They can lead to group learning due to identification of mistakes.

It should be noted that post-completion audits should not be used for petty politicking. A firm can set quarterly or half yearly reviews.

Communicating Investment Decisions

As organizations grow, it becomes increasingly difficult for the top management to have the technical knowledge of all the decision situations that arise at the branch or divisional level. The ideal situation

[2] Tiles, 'Strategies for Allocating Funds'.

[3] Prahlad and Hamel, 'The Core Competence of the Corporation'.

is one in which both the technical expert and the decision-maker are the same. This is rarely the case. Information flows upwards through many layers before it reaches the decision-maker. Senior management will have to rely on information provided by lower level executives who have first-hand knowledge of business drivers. Often top management may end up with information that executives never intended to convey. Distortions can occur due to the following:

- Difficulty in conveying uncertainty that surrounds an estimate
- Difference of opinion as to what constitutes uncertainty!
- Differences in risk-taking ability among executives
- Ad hoc estimation of risk

Executives report best estimates or expected values, say, for instance, sales of ₹300 million. The question is: what does the executive have in mind when he/she says—a best estimate of ₹320 million? Does he/she have a probability of 90 per cent or 75 per cent in mind? The argument can be extended to pessimistic or optimistic estimates as well. Moreover, executives might have reported what they considered a pessimistic estimate but the top management may misconstrue it as an expected value. The screen for accepting or rejecting investment proposals may be coarse or fine depending on the risk aversion of the top management. The normal practice is to accept those proposals that meet a predetermined financial standard such as 17 per cent ROI or 18 per cent IRR and so on. This policy is not effective since the range of tolerance is not specified. A better policy would be to specify how top management would prefer to trade off risk and return. An illustration will clarify the point. In the following text, there are two policies communicated by top management to executives:

Policy 1	Policy 2
1. All projects should be evaluated on the basis of IRR	1. All projects should be evaluated on the basis of IRR
2. Accept all projects with IRR > 17 per cent	2. Accept those projects that have anexpected value of 17 per cent or more a. A probability of 10 per cent that IRR will be greater than 16 per cent b. A probability of 90 per cent that IRR will be greater than 14 per cent

Clearly, Policy 2 is better since it articulates the risk-taking ability of top management. Policy 1 gives a point estimate, which is meaningless in an uncertain world.

CAPITAL BUDGETING AND CORPORATE STRATEGY

The emphasis in most capital budgeting analysis is on estimating and discounting future project cash flows. Projects with positive NPVs are accepted; those that fail this test are rejected. It should be understood that generating projects likely to yield positive excess returns is as important as the investment analysis. It is unlikely that a firm will encounter positive NPV projects by luck all the time; they have to be 'created'. Creating and taking advantage of product market imperfections is at the heart of corporate strategy. Top-down capital budgeting is not corporate strategy. Competitive strategy concerns how to create competitive advantage in each of the businesses a company operates. A good understanding of corporate strategy will help unearth potentially profitable projects. Shapiro[4] provides a framework for analysing the source of positive NPV projects. Successful investments involve creating, preserving and enhancing competitive advantage that serves as barriers to entry. There are five major sources of barriers to entry: economies of scale, product differentiation, cost disadvantages, access to distribution channels and government policy. Economies of scale exist whenever a given increase in the scale of production results in less than proportional increase in cost. The existence of scale economies means that there are advantages in being big. The more significant the scale economies, the greater the cost disadvantage faced by a new entrant to the market. Companies such as HUL take advantage of highly developed marketing skills to differentiate their products and keep out potential competitors by increasing entry costs. Investments aimed at achieving low cost position in the industry coupled with a pricing policy to expand market share are likely to succeed. Hero MotoCorp in two-wheeler industry follows this strategy.

Sound financial analysis ties the details of strategy to financial implications. It is hard to convince executives from non-financial backgrounds that it is possible to capture the value of any strategy in rupee terms and that it is nothing qualitative. Capital budgeting in many companies is simply an exercise in finding an input value that gives the required output.[5] Strategic investments usually open up 'options' that extend beyond the original projects. Options stemming from investment in R&D, brand names have value beyond the initial investment period as they open up opportunities to create subsequent products that complement existing ones. The usual DCF methodology breaks down when applied to multi-stage options on real assets. In fact, the option pricing formula does not resemble DCF formula in anyway. This explains why strategic investments, most of the time, fail to pass the DCF test leading to a conflict between marketing and finance.

Following a System

It pays to follow a well-defined system of capital budgeting. The following guidelines may be borne in mind while establishing a capital budgeting system.

- Start with the end in mind. The process of capital allocation should be driven by the strategic thrust of the company. Establish long-range and short-range plans and translate them into short-term objectives and specific capex proposals. Investments are to be evaluated in the context of company objectives and plans for the future.
- Personnel at all levels can often turn their experience into ideas for new and better ways of doing jobs. Management should not have monopoly on ideas. Be open for discussion, both formal and informal. The organization climate should be conducive for such an experiment. Involve operating personnel in preparing short-term guidelines. Prepare them for meaningful evaluation of capital projects. Inadequately trained executives often mix up expenses, capital expenditure and sunk costs. This leads to a bias in the estimation of initial investment and NPV.
- Avoid over centralization. Develop general definition of types of projects for which authority approval can safely be delegated to junior officials. For instance, a manager at the shop floor level

[4] Shapiro, 'Corporate Strategy and the Capital Budgeting Decision'.
[5] Patrick, Marsh and Wensley, 'Must Finance and Strategy Clash'.

could be authorized to spend up to ₹50,000. The amount and the degree of delegation depend on the size of the company and the importance of the project.

- Evolve your own methods of analysis and decision criteria. Estimating divisional hurdle rates is as much an art as a science. Evolve criteria for allocation of funds to projects with different risk levels.
- Avoid spending money on a first-come-first-serve basis. Be receptive to investment proposals throughout the year. A great investment idea that surfaces later in the budget period may not get funded if the budget is exhausted.
- Check whether a decision from one division affects other divisions, quantify the effect and factor it into the analysis. Incorporate product cannibalization, competitive advantages and disadvantages in the analysis.
- Use post-implementation appraisal as a feedback to fine-tune the analysis and administrative process. Continuous improvement in the capital budgeting system can be expected in companies where post-implementation appraisal is seriously implemented.
- Do not hold executives responsible for narrow deviations from forecasts. Establish a band of acceptable tolerances. Otherwise, there will be scope for downward biasing. Initially, the forecast will be set below the expected value resulting in 'happy surprises' later on.
- There should be as few guidelines as possible to ensure that they are well known and fully understood by everyone in the organization.
- Create an organization climate conducive for trying innovative product ideas and processes. The best way to drive home the message that the top management is serious about the strategy adopted by the company or ideas from employees is to 'spend' money on such projects.
- Finally, the objective of creating wealth for shareholders should be the guiding post for acceptance of project proposals. Executives prepare summary measures such as payback period and IRR for project evaluation. These measures along with ROI may be used for performance appraisal. But, from the shareholders' perspective, NPV is the most consistent measure. So there is a conflict of interest between managers and shareholders. Tying executive compensation to a measures of shareholder value can reduce the conflict.

Bringing Them All Together

Strategy, performance evaluation and corporate culture are three components of a value maximizing capital allocation system. The balanced scorecard popularized by Kaplan and Norton[6] could serve as the focal point for the organization's efforts in communicating priorities to managers, employees, investors and customers. It is important to understand that performance measurement is an important aspect of strategy. What gets measured gets done. The balanced scorecard tries to measure the capital allocation efficiency of executives from various perspectives. From a purely financial perspective, ROI, cash flow, project profitability and sales booking might be the relevant measures, whereas from a customer's perspective, customer satisfaction index, customer ranking survey, market share might be the relevant measures. A company can start by assessing its current position on these perspectives and arrive at the priority areas where attention is required. Companies can often create a lot of value for shareholders by fine-tuning project choice.

[6] Kaplan and Norton, 'Putting the Balanced Scorecard to Work'.

CONCLUDING COMMENTS

Capital budgeting rules like NPV are based on several questionable assumptions. For instance, NPV is calculated by discounting cash flows at WACC. The standard procedure for estimating cost of equity is the CAPM. As pointed out in Chapter 3, the CAPM has been challenged by many recent studies. Likewise, hurdle rates are calculated on the basis of market price of stock. The implicit assumption is that the market is efficient. So capital budgeting, when prices are inefficient and managers are fully rational, is more complex than in the rational world.[7] Modern capital budgeting suggests that only systematic risk matters. This approach ignores the impact of the new project on the firm's total risk and therefore leads to an inappropriate assessment of the value of the project. Total risk is often costly and it is necessary to take total risk into account in capital budgeting to make capital budgeting and capital structure decisions consistent.[8]

REFERENCES

Donaldson, Gordon. 'Strategic Hurdle Rates for Capital Investments'. *Harvard Business Review* (1972 March–April).

Kaplan, Robert and David Norton. 'Putting the Balanced Scorecard to Work'. *Harvard Business Review* (1993 Sep–Oct).

Patrick, B., P. Marsh and R. Wensley. 'Must Finance and Strategy Clash'. *Harvard Business Review* (1989 Sep–Oct).

Prahlad, C. K. and Gary Hamel. 'The Core Competence of the Corporation'. *Harvard Business Review* (1990 May–June).

Shapiro, A. C. 'Corporate Strategy and the Capital Budgeting Decision'. *Midland Corporate Finance Journal* (1985 Spring).

Stein, Jeremy. 'Rational Capital Budgeting in an Irrational World'. *Journal of Business* 69 (1996).

Stulz, Rene. 'What's Wrong with Modern Capital Budgeting?' *Financial Practice and Education* (1999 Fall/Winter).

Tiles, Seymour. 'Strategies for Allocating Funds'. *Harvard Business Review* (1966 Jan–Feb).

SUGGESTED READINGS

Hastie, Larry. 'One Businessman's View of Capital Budgeting'. *Financial Management* (1974).

Hertz, David. 'Investment Policies That Pay Off'. *Harvard Business Review* (1968 Jan–Feb).

Mathews, John. 'How to Administer Capital Spending'. *Harvard Business Review* (1959 March–April).

Myers, S. C. 'Finance theory and Financial Strategy'. *Interfaces* (1984 Jan–Feb).

Woods, Donald H. 'Improving Estimates That Involve Uncertainty'. *Harvard Business Review* (1966 July–August).

Welter, Paul. 'Put Policy First in DCF Analysis'. *Harvard Business Review* (1970 Jan –Feb).

[7] Stein, Jeremy, 'Rational Capital Budgeting in an Irrational World'.

[8] Stulz, Rene, 'What's Wrong with Modern Capital Budgeting?'

SECTION 3

Managing Current Assets

CHAPTER

11

Working Capital Estimation and Financing

LEARNING OBJECTIVES

- Discuss the components and determinants of WC
- Measure WC requirement and the length of operating cycle
- Highlight the link between operating cycle and sustainable growth
- Estimate the impact of WC investment on shareholder value
- Be able to apply the different methods of WC estimation
- Provide a working knowledge of non-bank sources of WC finance

A firm requires funds to acquire two types of assets: fixed assets and current assets (CAs). Fixed assets include land, building, plant and machinery, vehicles and equipment. These assets are relatively permanent in nature and are necessary for carrying on the business. CAs, on the other hand, are maintained to support day-to-day operations and keep changing during the course of the business. They are liquidated within a short period of time during the operating cycle of the company not normally exceeding one year. CAs include cash, debtors, inventory of raw material and finished goods. CAs constitute gross WC.

The excess of CAs over current liabilities (CLs) is the net WC or simply, WC. CLs are to be paid in the ordinary course of business (normally within one year) out of the profits generated by the company or from the proceeds from sale of CAs. Fixed assets are to be financed by owners' equity and long-term liabilities, while CAs are partly financed by long-term sources and partly by CLs and short-term loans given by banks. The concept of WC is shown as a diagram below:

Liabilities	Assets
Share Capital Reserves and Surplus Long-Term Liabilities	Net Fixed Assets
→ WC CLs	CAs

Net WC is also called liquid surplus. To sum up, WC is the funds required to carry the required level of CAs in order to carry on its operations at the expected level without any disruption. WC is a function of the level of activity (i.e., sales), and the type of business. WC for a trading company will be generally more than that for a manufacturing company because it carries a substantial portion of its assets in the form of inventory of finished goods.

$$\text{Net WC} = \text{CAs} - \text{CLs}$$

The deficit (CA−CL) is to be financed by bank borrowings and long-term funds.

$$\text{CAs} = \text{CLs} + \text{Margin from Long-Term Sources} + \text{WC Limit from Banks}$$

In the equation, CAs are more than CLs. Is this always true? When CLs are more than CAs, that is, WC is negative, one can infer that short-term funds have been diverted to long-term uses or the value of CAs have shrunk (may be due to obsolescence of stocks or book debts turning bad). Obviously this is not a desirable situation and the company is said to be facing liquidity crunch. It can also be possible that the company may receive cash from customers before goods are shipped (a current liability) but may ship goods from vendors, rather than its own warehouses, that is, the company would have substantial CLs but very little CAs. Amazon.com is an example of this type of situation.

We discussed financial ratios earlier. The current ratio and the quick ratio are measures of liquidity. How high should the liquidity be? Is a large liquid surplus a desirable situation? We will answer these questions as we go along. Before that, we will take a quick look at the components of WC.

COMPONENTS OF WC

The components of WC are as follows:

- Cash
- Inventory
- Accounts Receivable
- Marketable Securities
- Loan from Bank

Cash is the most liquid component of WC. Holding cash enhances liquidity. But this is not cost free. Cash can be invested in business to earn a return. There is an opportunity cost involved. But why do companies hold cash? Cash balance is necessary to meet day-to-day expenses such as payments for raw materials, wages, salaries; to meet (random fluctuation) contingencies and to take advantage of business opportunities that may arise. Accordingly, these motives are classified as: transaction motive, precautionary motive and speculative motive.

Marketable securities are temporary investments that a company can liquidate when cash is required. They are a substitute for holding idle cash balance. For instance, there may be a lag between raising and deployment of funds after the sale of long-term security. A company may wish to temporarily deploy the proceeds in liquid securities. Marketable securities can also be held to ride the seasonality of operations, that is, hold marketable securities during lean periods and sell off during the high demand phase to free up cash for normal business.

Inventory normally constitutes a major portion of CAs. Inventory is simple insurance against fluctuations in demand for the firm's product. Inventory is of three types, namely raw material, work-in-progress and finished goods. Inventory, like any other asset, needs to be managed well. Too much of inventory results in lower profitability as money is locked up in redundant assets, which earns no return and too little inventory results in loss of sales or customer goodwill. So there is a trade-off between profitability and liquidity.

Accounts Receivable: Most businesses sell goods on credit. When goods are sold, inventories are reduced and accounts receivable are created. A firm may not have much choice in its credit granting decision because it depends on the product market condition. In competitive industries, a company may be forced to match industry standards to protect sales. Thus, accounts receivable is an essential investment. Like other components of CAs, there is an optimal level of investment in accounts receivable beyond which profits deteriorate. In other words, the marginal profits from increased sales should be greater than the marginal cost of credit.

A firm's credit policy has the following four components:

- Credit Period
- Credit Standards
- Discount Policy
- Collection Policy

Each of these will be discussed in the subsequent chapters.

Accounts Payable: As the name itself suggests, it is the credit accepted from suppliers of raw material and components and so on. It is one of the sources of short-term financing. There is no explicit cost involved with trade credits although the supplier may load the cost of capital tied up into the price. It can be easily arranged unlike a loan but one should be careful not to stretch trade credit too far because it may result in loss of suppliers.

MEASURING WC

Net WC is defined as the difference between CAs and CLs. Consider the following figures:

Current Assets			Current Liabilities (₹ million)		
	2017	2018		2017	2018
Cash	10	29	A/C Payable	70	125
Receivables	140	196	Current Portion of Long-Term Debt	10	53
Inventory	170	306	Accrued Expenses	155	125
			Taxes Payable	15	20
	320	531		220	353

WC in 2017 = ₹(320 − 220) million = ₹100 million
WC in 2018 = ₹(531 − 353) million = ₹178 million

Change in WC between 2017 and 2018 = ₹(178 − 100) million = ₹78 million

The net WC, thus calculated, may be compared with other companies in the industry group to find out whether the company is generating adequate revenues for the investment in WC and take necessary action to correct the situation. Remember that cash flow from operations is affected by the investment in WC. The higher the investment in WC, the lower is the cash flow.

Cash Flow from Operations = PAT + Depreciation and Amortization –/+ Increases/Decreases in Net WC

Another subtle impact of WC is that the company will have a lower level of cash available for debt service because CADS = Cash Flow from Operations + Interest Expense

OPERATING CYCLE

A manufacturing activity is characterized by a cycle of operation consisting of the following:

- Procurement of raw material, components, stores and spares for manufacture of the product
- Conversion of raw materials into finished goods
- Storage of finished goods before they are sold
- Sale on credit to customers
- Collection of cash from customers

An operating cycle is shown in Figure 11.1. The time elapsed between cash outlay and cash realization by sale of finished goods is the length of the operating cycle.

Operating cycle is also called cash-to-cash cycle. At any given point in time, a firm will have several operating cycles at various stages of completion.

$$\text{Total WC} = \frac{\text{Total Expected Operating Expenses for the Year}}{\text{No. of Operating Cycles in a Year}}$$

Operating cycles will be relatively long in construction and shipbuilding industries and relatively short in trading.

To illustrate, if

Raw Material Holding Period = 40 days
Conversion Time = 10 days
Finished Goods Storage Period = 15 days
Average Collection Period = 30 days

Operating Cycles = 40 + 10 + 15 + 30 = 95 days. This means that there are (365/95 or) 3.84 operating cycles in a year.

If operating expense is ₹10 million,

FIGURE 11.1
Operating Cycle

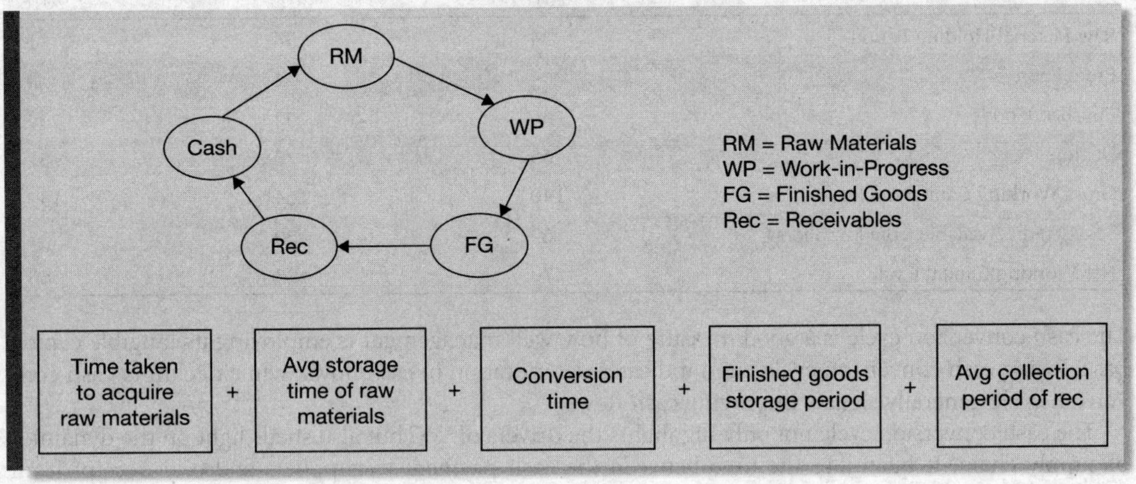

$$\text{WC requirement} = \frac{10\,\text{million}}{(365/95)} = ₹2.60 \text{ million}$$

As is evident from the previous illustration, WC is a function of operating expenses and the length of operating cycle. Reducing either of them (or both) will lead to reduction in WC requirement and hence increases efficiency. To illustrate, if the operating cycle is reduced to 75 days, the WC turnover ratio would be (365/75) 4.80

$$\text{WC Requirement} = \frac{10\,\text{m}}{4.80} = ₹2.10 \text{ million}$$

Managing the components of the operating cycle, namely raw material holding period, conversion time, finished goods storage period and average collection period more efficiently can reduce operating cycle.

If the accounts payable period is included, we get net operating cycle.

$$\text{Net Operating Cycle} = \text{Operating Cycle Time} - \text{Average Payables Period}$$

The calculation involved in the estimation of components of WC is shown in Appendix 11A.1.

AN ILLUSTRATION

The following is the estimation of net WC cycle for a company.

	(days)		
	2016	2017	2018
Raw Material Holding Period	34	38	41
Production	4	4	4
Finished Goods	36	52	39
Debtors	65	70	51
Gross Working Capital Cycle	140	164	135
Less: Credit Available from Suppliers	69	80	67
Net Working Capital Cycle	70	83	68

The cash conversion cycle is a good measure of how well management is employing its tangible capital base. Rising cash conversion cycle often indicates deterioration in cash flows, while declining cash conversion cycle generally signals improving cash flows.

The cash conversion cycle not only highlights the drivers of WC but also sheds light on the dynamics of supply chain. It quantifies the time between the cash payment to suppliers and cash receipt from customers. The three components of cash conversion cycle are:

- Days Sales Outstanding
- Days in Inventory
- Days Payable Outstanding

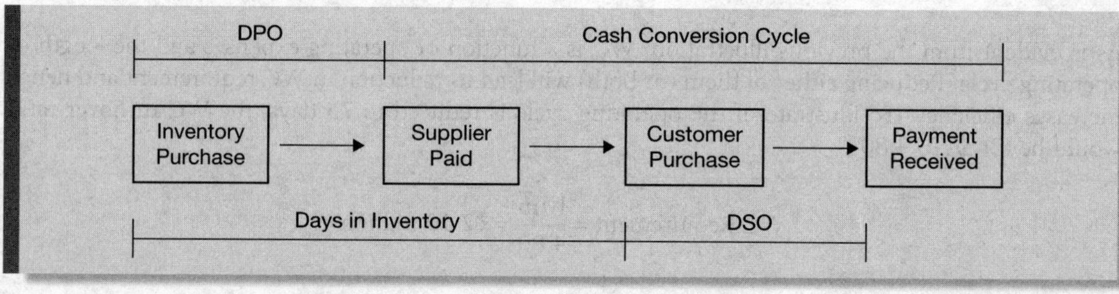

Dell manufactures and sells personal computers. The company started by marketing PCs directly to its customers. The company assembled computers 'after' receiving a customer order. This model enabled Dell to have much smaller investment in WC than its competitors. The efficient usage of WC helped in providing internal funding for growth and also avoided the cost of obsolete inventory that companies faced when the technology changed.

Amazon.com, an online retailer, like Dell, receives cash payments upfront for its products but pays its suppliers about two months later. When it was started, Amazon had modest inventory requirements because it carried only popular titles and its distributors such as Ingram and Baker & Taylor were responsible for carrying inventories of less popular items. Traditional booksellers like Barnes & Noble carry substantial inventories in warehouses and in each store. This was a source of competitive advantage for Amazon.

To illustrate the impact of reduced inventory on a company's competitive position, assume that a company's cost of sales is ₹1,000 million, its days' supply of inventory (DSI) is 30 days and that for the nearest competitor is 60 days. The additional inventory the company would have to hold if it were to have as long a DSI as its competitor

= (Cost of Sales) × (Competitor's DSI – Own DSI)/360 Days
= ₹1,000 (60 – 30)/360 million
= ₹83.3 million

Improvements in the components of the cash conversion cycle can be translated into cash equivalents by multiplying the improvements in the components (in days) by daily savings.

THE LINK BETWEEN OPERATING CYCLE AND SUSTAINABLE GROWTH

Neil and Mullins define sustainable growth rate as the rate at which a company can grow its revenues without seeking outside capital.[1] Operating cash cycle is the length of time a company's cash is tied up in WC before that money is collected from customers. Other things remaining constant, the shorter the cycle, the faster can a company redeploy its cash and grow from internal sources. The extra money generated from each rupee of sales over and above that invested in WC and operating expenses can be reinvested in additional WC and operating expenses to generate more revenue in the next cycle. There are three ways to increase growth rate.

- Speeding cash flow by accelerating receivables collection and improving inventory turnover
- Reducing cost of sales
- Raising prices without hurting demand

Theoretically, it is possible for the components of operating cycle to assume any value, including zero. This does not happen in practice. For instance, not maintaining any inventory or forgoing credit sales may not be advisable. So there is a trade-off between liquidity risk and opportunity loss. Liquidity risk refers to the non-availability of cash when a liability falls due. This may hurt reputation and in the extreme case, further credit may be stopped. Opportunity loss is the risk of losing potential sale due to non-availability of inventory or cash to support credit sales. The firm will be losing out on potential business.

Assume that the current sales are ₹1,000 million and the company expects the sales to increase to ₹150 million. CA efficiency (assets/sales) is 0.50. Therefore, additional assets required to generate an additional ₹500 million of sales equal 0.5 × 500 = ₹250 million. This can be partly funded by profits. Assume that the current return on sales is 5 per cent, the next year profit will be 0.05 × 1,500 = ₹75 million. Therefore, the funding shortfall is ₹(250 – 75) = ₹175 million.

[1] Neil and Mullins, 'How Fast Can Your Company Afford to Grow?'

The funding shortfall can be met by improving asset efficiency (because of which the actual assets required would be less), improving profit margins (because of which actual profits would be higher than expected) and incurring liabilities (including new equity).

THE IMPACT OF WC INVESTMENT ON SHAREHOLDER VALUE

The value of a company or a project is the present value of free cash flows discounted at WACC.

$$\text{Free Cash Flow} = \text{NOPAT} + \text{Depreciation} - \text{Capital Expenditure} - \Delta\text{NWC}$$
$$= [(\text{Sales in a Year})\,(1+\text{Sales Growth Rate})\,(\text{Operating Margin})\,(1-\text{Tax Rate})] - \text{Capex} - \Delta\text{NWC}$$

Since free cash flow is a function of net WC, reducing investment in WC for a given level of sales increases cash flows and hence the stock price. An illustration will clarify the point. A company currently has sales of ₹17 million. Sales are expected to grow at 15 per cent for the next five years; profit margin is expected to be 12 per cent; tax rate is 35 per cent; incremental capital expenditure and WC are expected to be 25 per cent and 15 per cent of the increase in sales, respectively. Free cash flows are expected to grow at 7 per cent after the fifth year in perpetuity. WACC is 12 per cent.

Sales	(₹ million)					
	1	2	3	4	5	6
Sales	17	19.55	22.50	25.90	29.80	34.30
Op. Profit	2.35	2.70	3.10	3.58	4.12	
Taxes	0.82	0.95	1.08	1.25	1.44	
Capex	0.64	0.74	0.85	0.975	1.125	
NWC	0.384	0.444	0.51	0.585	0.675	
Free Cash Flow	0.506	0.566	0.66	0.77	0.88	

The Value of the Firm = PV of Free Cash Flows During the First Five Years + PV of Terminal Value of Free Cash Flows

Value of Equity = Value of Firm – Value of Debt Outstanding

Value of a Share = (Value of Equity/Number of Shares Outstanding)

Assume that WC investment increases to 20 per cent, cash flows will be reduced to that extent and stock price will fall.

DETERMINANTS OF LEVEL OF WC

Bankers provide finance to hold an acceptable level of CAs to achieve a predetermined level of production and sales. So each of the components of WC needs to be estimated to quantify the funds required for WC.

Raw Materials: A company has to necessarily stock a minimum quality of raw materials to ensure smooth running of operations. The factors that should be considered in estimating the required inventory of raw materials are:

- Average Consumption of Raw Materials
- Availability of Raw Materials
- Lead Time Between Ordering and Receipt of Materials
- Cost of Holding Stocks
- Transportation Charges
- Seasonality of the Item in Question

Work-in-Progress: There is generally a time lag only after which raw materials get converted into finished product. The time taken for processing varies from industry to industry. The factors affecting the inventory of WIP are:

- Processing Time
- Batch Quantity—The Average Quantity of Each Product Processed
- Number of Shifts in a Day and Plant Capacity

Finished Goods: Normally a certain quantity of finished goods may have to be held in inventory awaiting sale. The quantity to be stored depend on the following:

- Variation in Demand
- Transportation Delay
- Nature of Business—Manufacture Against Order (e.g., Machine Tools) or Manufacture Against Anticipated Sales (e.g., Soaps and Detergents)
- Seasonality

Accounts Receivable: Goods or services may be sold either against advance payment (e.g., airline) or against cash (e.g., fast food) or on credit (e.g., shipbuilding). In the first two cases, there is no investment in accounts receivable. But in the third case, a company will have to invest in book debts. The extent of credit granted to customers depends on the following:

- Industry Practices
- Market Condition
- Quantity Purchased by the Customer

While arriving at the average credit period, the transit time should also be taken into account.

Expenses: Normally one month's expenses (direct and indirect) are included in the WC requirement to provide a cushion to take care of temporary bottlenecks. When the operating cycle is relatively short, the provision may be reduced. Similarly, when the operating cycle is relatively long, the provision may be increased. The credit available on purchases and advance payment received from customers will have to be deducted from the WC as estimated earlier to arrive at the net required WC. The WC requirement varies from industry to industry, size and, of course, productivity. The format for assessment of WC is shown in Appendix 11A.2. The WC requirement calculated as earlier will have to be financed from long-term source (such as capital and borrowings) and short-term borrowings from banks. Banks provide WC finance by way of advance against stocks and debtors. They, however, do not provide the full amount and normally insist that the promoter (or founder) of the company brings in margin money to ensure that the promoter has a stake in the business. The permissible limit of bank finance can be derived from the WC requirement as shown in Appendix 11A.3.

APPROACHES TO LENDING

Historically, banks in India have adopted three methods for assessing WC limit.

- Operating Cycle Method for WC Limits up to ₹25,000
- Tandon/Chore Committee Norms for WC Limits above ₹1 million
- Cash Budget Method for Seasonal Industries such as Shipbuilding

The first method has been explained earlier. The Tandon Committee was set up in 1974 by the RBI to study the defects of the prevailing system of bank lending. The cash credit/overdraft system wherein the borrower paid interest only on the amount drawn and not on the cash credit limit was tilted towards the borrower rather than the banks. Many borrowers misused the system to acquire inventory more than that warranted and the prevailing system made credit planning extremely difficult for the lending bank. The terms of reference of the Tandon Committee were:

- To prescribe norms for assessing WC to be financed by banks
- To prescribe norms for carrying CAs in different industries
- To make recommendation for obtaining operational data, business forecasts, production plans and credit needs
- To make recommendation as regards the criteria to be used to measure a unit's financial health

The Committee norms for inventory for receivable were initially applicable to 15 major industries but later on the scope was enlarged and norms substantially revised. The norms were applicable to all units in the specified groups of industries including small-scale industries with fund-based WC limits in excess of ₹1 million and public sector units were also covered. The norms cover major industries accounting for 50 per cent of industrial advance by banks. The norms take geographical location of the units and seasonality of demand into account. They represent the levels of units with average efficiency. There can be temporary deviations from inventory norms for reasons such as bunched receipt of raw materials, power cuts, strikes and transport delays.

The group suggested that the level of bank finance may be determined by the WC gap arrived at after taking into account the projected levels of CAs and CLs (other than bank borrowings). So the items that can be classified under CAs and CLs need to be defined. The classification of WC and the list of items to be included in CAs and CLs are presented in Appendices 11A.4 and 11A.5. CAs comprise cash and other assets or resources commonly identified as those which are expected to be realized in cash, or sold or consumed or turned over during the operating cycle of the business usually not exceeding one year. CLs include items payable or expected to be turned over within one year from the date of balance sheet and the item is used principally to designate obligations whose liquidation is reasonably expected to require the use of existing resources properly classified as CAs or the creation of other liabilities.

NORMS FOR LENDING

The Tandon Study Group recommended norms for inventory and receivables for 15 major industries. The norms suggested by the Tandon Study Group are reviewed from time to time by a Committee set up by the RBI. Bank lending norms were given for raw materials, stock-in-progress, finished goods and receivables. These norms indicated maximum levels for holding inventory and receivables in each industry and were not to be taken as entitlements to hold inventory or receivables up to the prescribed levels. Inventory and receivables suggested by the RBI from time to time were only broad indicators and banks were free to decide the norms based on their own experience.

COMPUTATION OF MAXIMUM PERMISSIBLE BANK FINANCE

Once the estimation of the reasonable level of CAs required for the operation of the unit is completed, the source of financing the same is decided. A part of the total CAs can be financed by credit for purchases and other CLs. The funds for financing the WC gap are bridged from the borrower's own funds and long-term borrowings and partly from bank borrowings.

The Tandon Study Group suggested the following three alternatives for arriving at the Maximum Permissible Bank Finance (MPBF):

- The first method of lending allows a bank to finance a maximum of 75 per cent of the WC gap (total CAs minus total CLs other than bank borrowings), with the balance coming from long-term funds.

$$\text{MPBF} = 0.75\ (\text{CA} - \text{Other CLs})$$

  This method ensures a current ratio of 1.
- The second method of lending requires the borrower to provide a minimum of 25 per cent of total current assets from their long-term funds. Credit for purchases and other CLs will be available to finance a part of the remaining amount of CAs with banks financing the remaining portion. Thus, total current liabilities inclusive of bank borrowings will not exceed 75 per cent of the current assets.

$$\text{MPBF} = (0.75 \times \text{CA}) - \text{CL}$$

  This method ensures a current ratio of 1.33.
- The third method of lending is similar to the second method of lending except that core current assets are excluded from total current assets. Core current assets are expected to be financed by long-term funds. Under this method, long-term funds are required to finance core current assets and an additional 25 per cent of the remaining current assets. RBI did not accept this method for implementation.

$$\text{MPBF} = 0.75\ (\text{CA} - \text{CCA}) - \text{CL}$$

  The borrower's contribution from long-term funds would be 25 per cent of WC gap under the first method of lending and 25 per cent of total CAs under the second method of lending. The borrower's contribution of long-term funds described is called the minimum stipulated net working capital (NWC), which comes from equity and term borrowings.

Banks generally calculated MPBF using the second method of lending.

Other methods of assessing WC requirements are:

Turnover Method

Under this method, the WC requirements are estimated at 25 per cent of the projected turnover. Of the WC requirement, banks cane finance to the maximum extent of 20 per cent of the projected turnover and the balance 5 per cent is the net WC to be brought in by the borrower as his margin.

Cash Budget Method

Under this method of assessment, the borrower submits cash budgets for the future period. Bank finance is limited to cash deficit, that is, the excess of payments over receipts. While assessing under this method, the profitability statement, balance sheet for the future period is taken into account to prepare the cash budget. The operating cycle is also considered for cash flow assessment. Generally, this method of assessment is used for seasonal industries such as tea, sugar, construction and so on.

STYLE OF LENDING

Tandon Committee suggested that the total credit limit be bifurcated into a loan component and cash credit component. The loan component corresponds to the minimum level of borrowing that the party will use during the year. The fluctuating part is the cash credit component. The obvious reason for bifurcating credit limit was to ensure financial discipline from the borrower. The Committee also suggested that bill financing, wherever possible, be encouraged.

Another working group was set up under the chairmanship of KB Chore in 1979 to recommend modification to the existing system. The summary of the Committee's recommendation is given as follows:

- The three types of lending—loan, cash credit and bill finance to continue.
- The dependence of medium and large size borrowers to be reduced by inducing them to use surplus cash generated by the unit.
- Second method of lending is to be made compulsory for all units with fund-based WC limit of ₹50 lakh and above.
- Projected statement of production/sales/CA/CL to be submitted quarterly within a week prior to commencement of quarter. This statement is used for fixing the quarterly drawing level.
- Actual statement of production/sales/CA/CL to be submitted quarterly within six weeks from the closure of the quarter it relates to.
- The actual and projected operating statement for the earlier half-year and the current half to be submitted within two months after the close of the earlier half-year.
- The actual and projected funds flow statement for the earlier half-year and the current half-year to be submitted within two months after the close of the earlier half-year.

The Quarterly Information Statements one and two are given in Appendix 11A.6.

Under the old system, the borrower could draw upon the sanctioned limit at his own option. Under the new system, quarterly operative limits are fixed on the basis of quarterly budget and performance data. The RBI introduced two forms. Form one contains estimates of production, sales, level of CAs and CLs for the ensuing quarter based on which operative limits are fixed for the quarter. Form two contains actual achievement of production, sales and level of CAs and CLs. In addition, half-yearly operating and fund flow statements are to be submitted.

The WC assistance provided by banks can broadly be classified on the basis of fund and non-fund. The difference between the fund and non-fund-based assistance lies mainly on the cash outflow. Fund-based assistance involves an immediate cash outflow. The latter may or may not involve cash outflow from the bank. The grant of any of the fund-based facilities to a borrower would result in depletion of actual liquidity of the bank, whereas grant of non-fund-based facility may or may not affect the bank's liquidity.

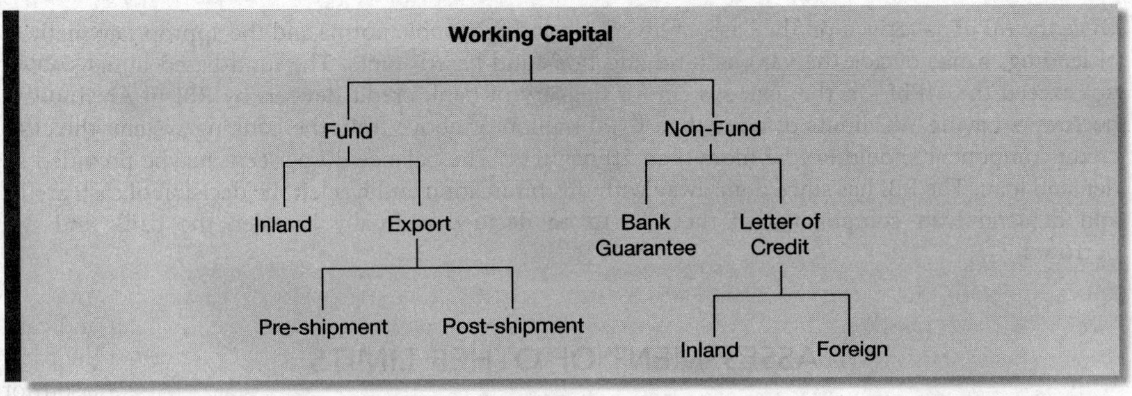

Consistent with the liberalization of the financial environment in the country, greater operational freedom has been progressively provided to banks in dispensation of credit. In April 1997, RBI decided to withdraw the prescription with regard to assessment of WC needs based on the MPBF concept. Banks are required to lay down, through their boards, a transparent policy and guidelines for credit dispensation. However, banks are free to follow the erstwhile RBI guidelines based on the concept of MPBF to assess WC requirements of borrowers.

CREDIT MONITORING ARRANGEMENT

In 1975, the RBI prescribed the format to obtain the necessary data from borrowers, assess WC requirement under the Credit Authorization Scheme. This scheme was changed to Credit Monitoring Arrangement (CMA) in 1988. Banks continue to obtain CMA forms for funded WC limits as these facilitate computation of MPBF.

The CMA comprises of six forms:

Form I: This form contains particulars of existing credit from the entire banking system including term loan facilities availed from banks/financial institutions (FIs).

Form II: Also called operating statement, Form II contains data relating to gross sales, net sales, cost of raw materials, power and fuel, direct labour, selling and administration expenses, interest and so on. It also covers information on operating profit and net profit.

Form III: A complete analysis of various items of last year's balance sheet, current year's estimate and following year's projections are given in this form. The details of CLs, term liabilities, net worth, CAs, fixed assets, non-CAs as per classification accepted by banks are included.

Form IV: This form provides details of various items of CAs and CLs as per the classification explained earlier. The figures given in this form must tally with those given in Form III, where details of all liabilities and assets are given.

Form V: On the basis of the details of CAs and CLs provided in form IV, the calculation of MPBF is done in this form to obtain the fund-based credit limits to be granted to the borrower.

Form VI: This form provides the details of fund flow of long-term sources and uses to indicate whether long-term funds are sufficient to meet the borrower's long-term requirements. The increase/decrease of CAs is also indicated in the form.

Once the MPBF is arrived on the basis of inventory and receivable norms and the appropriate method of lending, banks decide the various fund and non-fund-based limits. The fund-based limits should not exceed the MPBF. In the loan system for delivery of bank credit devised by RBI in April 1995, borrowers having WC limits of more than ₹100 million or above from the banking system, the cash credit component should not be more than 20 per cent. The balance 80 per cent maybe provided as demand loan. The RBI has since done away with this bifurcation and has left the decision of cash credit and demand loan components of the WC to be decided mutually between the bank and the borrower.

ASSESSMENT OF OTHER LIMITS

Letter of Credit

While sanctioning the letter of credit (LC) limits, the following particulars are required to be estimated:

- Value of raw materials projected to be consumed during the year
- Value of raw materials to be purchased on credit out of the above
- Time taken for advising establishment of LC to the beneficiary
- Time for shipment and the consignment to reach the location of the customer for whom the LC is to be opened
- Credit (usance) period agreed between the beneficiary and the customer
- Credit period projected as available by the borrower in the CMA format and reckoned for calculation of MPBF during sanction of fund-based limits

Bank Guarantee

There is no standard formula for assessment of bank guarantee limits. The details pertaining to nature of guarantee, purpose, particulars of the contract, period for which the bank guarantee is sought and the amount of guarantee are to be obtained. This information, along with the view on creditworthiness of the borrower and the relationship with the bank, would comprise the major inputs towards deciding the sanction of limits required by the borrower.

MARGINS

Bank, in its assessment of WC requirement of the borrower, stipulates limits up to which it would extend finance against each component of WC. This is done after the assessment of levels of raw material, stock-in-process, finished goods and bills receivable to be held at any one point by the borrower to reach the desired production. Banks thus stipulate margins, which the borrower should bear as its contribution to finance WC. The bank's objective in demanding a margin from the borrower are:

- To ensure a degree of stake of the borrower in its own enterprise.
- To ensure commitment of the borrower in times of adversity.
- To hedge against price level changes in the event of distress sale to recover advance.

Margins applied by banks vary but the range of margins on different kinds of WC assets is usually 10 per cent to 40 per cent. They basically convey the extent of marketability of the particular asset in event of distress sale.

BANKING ARRANGEMENT

The assessed WC is made available to the borrower under the following arrangements:

Consortium Banking Arrangement: The RBI, till 1997, made it obligatory for availing WC facilities beyond a threshold limit, through the consortium arrangement. The objective of the arrangement was to jointly meet the financial requirements of big projects by banks and also share the risks involved. While the consortium arrangement is no longer obligatory, some borrowers (especially large ones) continue to avail WC finance under this arrangement. The major features of this arrangement are as follows:

- Bank with maximum share of the WC limits usually takes the role of 'lead bank'.
- Lead bank, independently or in consultation with other banks, appraises the WC requirements of the company.
- Banks at the 'consortium meeting' agree on ratio of sharing the assessed limits.
- Lead bank undertakes the joint documentation on behalf of all member banks.
- Lead bank organizes collection and dissemination of information regarding conduct of account by borrower.

Multiple Banking Arrangement: Multiple banking arrangement is an open arrangement in which no bank takes the lead role. Most borrowers are shifting their banking arrangement to multiple banking now. The major features of this arrangement are as follows:

- Borrower needs to approach multiple banks to tie up entire requirement of WC.
- Banks independently assess the WC requirements of the borrower.
- Banks independent of each other do documentation, monitoring and conduct of the account.
- Borrower deals with all financing banks individually.

SYNDICATION

A syndicated credit is an arrangement between two or more lenders to provide a borrower credit facility using common loan agreement. It is an internationally practised model for financing credit requirements, wherein banks are free to syndicate the credit limits irrespective of the quantum involved. It is similar to a consortium arrangement in terms of dispersal of risk but consists of a fixed repayment period.

Under this arrangement:

- The borrower intending to raise resources awards mandate to a bank to raise the resources (referred to as lead manager).
- Lead manager prepares an information memorandum and distributes the same amongst prospective lenders. Information memorandum provides basis for each lending bank for making independent valuation of borrower.
- A meeting of prospective lenders is convened by lead manager to finalize deal timing, cost of credit, share of participating banks and so on.
- Loan agreement is prepared and signed by all participating banks. The borrower gives prior notice to lead manager for drawing loan amount (to enable tie-up disbursement with other lending banks).

It is easy to arrange syndication for borrowers that are rated strong by rating agencies regarding payment of principal and interest.

NON-BANK SOURCES OF WC FINANCE

Commercial Paper

Commercial paper (CP) is a short-term usance promissory note with a fixed maturity period issued by financial or non-financial companies with a high credit rating. The RBI guidelines relating to issuance of CP is discussed as follows:

Eligible Issuers:

- Companies, including Non-Banking Finance Companies (NBFCs) and All India Financial Institutions (AIFIs), are eligible to issue CPs subject to the condition that any fund-based facility availed of from bank(s) and/or FIs is classified as a standard asset by all financing banks/institutions at the time of issue.
- Other entities such as cooperative societies/unions, government entities, trusts, limited liability partnerships and any other body corporate having presence in India with a net worth of ₹100 crore or higher subject to the condition as specified under 3 (a) above.
- Any other entity specifically permitted by the RBI.

End Use

The exact end use shall be disclosed in the offer document at the time of issue of a CP.

Eligible Investors:

- All residents, and non-residents permitted to invest in CPs under Foreign Exchange Management Act (FEMA), 1999, are eligible to invest in CPs; however, no person can invest in CPs issued by related parties either in the primary or secondary market.
- Investment by regulated financial sector entities will be subject to such conditions as the concerned regulator may impose.

Form of the Instrument, Mode of Issuance, Rating and Documentation Procedures
Form

- A CP shall be issued in the form of a promissory note and held in a dematerialized form through any of the depositories approved by and registered with SEBI.
- A CP shall be issued in minimum denomination of ₹5 lakh and multiples thereof.
- A CP shall be issued at a discount to face value.
- No issuer shall have the issue of a CP underwritten or co-accepted.
- Options (call/put) are not permitted on a CP.

Rating Requirement
Eligible issuers, whose total CP issuance during a calendar year is ₹1,000 crore or more, shall obtain credit rating for issuance of CPs from at least two CRAs registered with the SEBI and should adopt the lower of the two ratings. Where both ratings are the same, the issuance shall be for the lower of the two amounts for which ratings are obtained.

The minimum credit rating for a CP shall be 'A3' as per rating symbol and definition prescribed by the SEBI.

Documentation Procedures
Issuers, investors and Issuing and Paying Agents (IPAs) shall follow the standard procedures and documentation prescribed by Fixed Income Money Market and Derivatives Association of India (FIMMDA) as 'Operational Guidelines on CPs'.

Issue of CP–Credit Enhancement, Limits And So On

- A CP shall be issued as a 'stand-alone' product.
- Banks and FIs may, based on their commercial judgement, choose to provide standby assistance/credit, backstop facility and so on by way of credit enhancement for a CP issue.
- Non-bank entities (including corporates) may provide unconditional and irrevocable guarantee for credit enhancement for CP issue provided the offer document for CP properly discloses the net worth of the guarantor company, the names of the companies to which the guarantor has issued similar guarantees, the extent of the guarantees offered by the guarantor company and the conditions under which the guarantee will be invoked.

Buyback of CP

- The buyback of a CP, in full or part, shall be at the prevailing market price.
- The buyback offer should be extended to all investors in the CP issue. The terms of the buyback should be identical for all investors in the issue.

- The buyback offer may not be made before 30 days from the date of issue.
- CPs bought back shall stand extinguished.

DUTIES AND OBLIGATIONS

The duties and obligations of the Issuer, IPA and credit rating agency (CRA) are set out as follows:

- Issuer—The issuer of CP shall
    - Appoint an IPA for issuance of a CP.
    - Comply with all relevant requirements under these directions and furnish a declaration in this regard to the IPA.
    - Ensure that the proceeds from CP issues are for declared end uses.
    - Furnish the board resolution authorizing the company to borrow through issuance of a CP to the IPA.
    - Keep the bank(s) from whom it has outstanding fund or non-fund-based credit facility(ies) informed of its market borrowings, including through CPs, latest by the end of the month in which a CP was issued.
    - Arrange for crediting the CP to the demat account of the investor with the depository through the IPA within seven days of issue.
    - Route all subscriptions/redemptions/buybacks/payments and default details through the IPA.
    - Submit a certificate from the CEO/CFO to the concerned IPAs on quarterly basis that CP proceeds are used for disclosed purposes, and certifying adherence to other conditions of the offer document and the CP directions. The certificate may be provided within 15 days from the close of the quarter.
    - Inform the CRA and IPA on the same day about any default/delay in CP-related payments.
    - The issuer who has defaulted on a CP shall not be allowed to access the CP market for six months from the date of repayment of the defaulted obligation.
- IPA—The IPA for a CP issuance shall
    - Ensure that the borrower is appropriately authorized to borrow through CPs.
    - Verify all information disclosed in the offer document before issuance.
    - Verify all documents submitted by the issuer and ensure that they are in order and issue a certificate to this effect.
    - Make available the IPA certificate in electronic form on the website of the depositories for the CPs. IPAs are encouraged to shift to issue of digital signature certificates.
    - Verify and hold certified copies of original documents and/or digitally signed documents in its custody.
    - Report the details of issuance of a CP, or its buyback and instances of default.
- CRA
    - A CRA must act responsibly in rating CP issuances and continuously monitor the rating assigned to an issue and disseminate rating revisions, if any, to public through its publications and on its website.
    - A CRA must publicly disseminate the ratings of the CP and any subsequent change in the ratings, on the date of rating or change in rating, as the case may be.

The steps involved in issuing a CP are shown as follows.

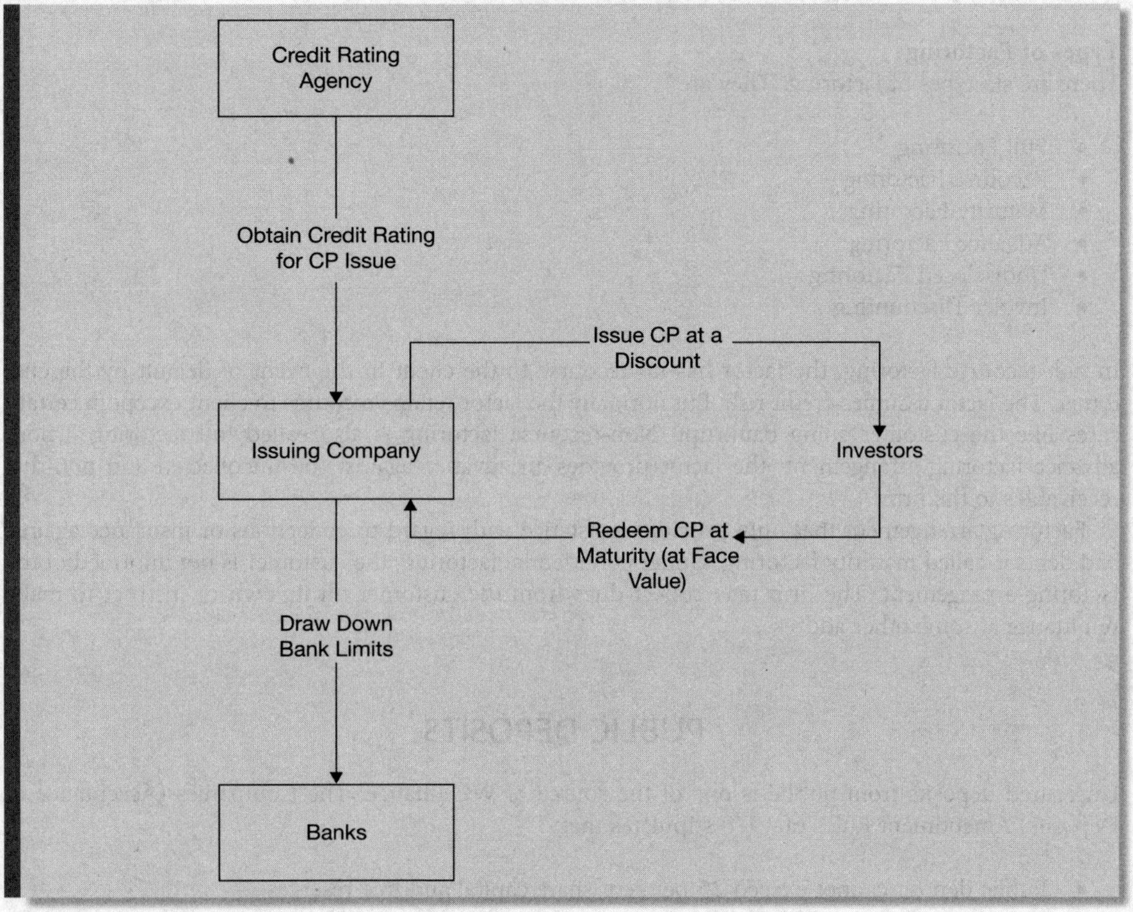

The cost of issuing CP can be calculated as:

$$\text{Cost of CP} = \frac{\text{Face Value} - \text{Net Amount Realized}}{\text{Net Amount Realized}} \times \frac{360}{\text{Maturity Period}}$$

The advantages of issuing CP are its lower cost and flexible maturity. Further, the borrower does not provide a charge on the asset.

FACTORING

Factoring involves a continuing arrangement between the company and an FI, called factor, to assume the credit and collection functions of the company. The factor purchases the client's receivables as and when they arise, maintains the sales ledger, attends to other bookkeeping duties relating to accounts receivable and performs other auxiliary functions.

Types of Factoring

There are six types of factoring. They are:

- Full Factoring
- Recourse Factoring
- Maturity Factoring
- Advance Factoring
- Undisclosed Factoring
- Invoice Discounting

In non-recourse factoring, the factor has no recourse to the client in the event of default by the customer. The factor assumes credit risk. But normally the factor retains recourse to client except in certain cases like the customer going bankrupt. Non-recourse factoring is also called full factoring. Under advance factoring arrangement, the factor provides an advance against the uncollected and non-due receivables to the firm.

Factoring arrangement that only provides assistance with regard to collections or insurance against bad debts is called maturity factoring. Under confidential factoring, the customer is not informed of the factoring arrangement. The firm may collect dues from the customer on its own or instruct to make remittance at some other address.

PUBLIC DEPOSITS

Unsecured deposits from public is one of the source of WC finance. The Companies (Acceptance of Deposits) Amendment Rules of 1978 stipulates that:

- Public deposit cannot exceed 25 per cent share capital and free reserves.
- Maturity period should be between six months and eight years. However, a minimum maturity period of three months is allowed for deposits amounting to 10 per cent of share capital and free reserves.
- The company should provide for repayments in its balance sheet 11 months before the maturity date.
- The company's financial health should be disclosed in the notice inviting public deposits.

The advantages and disadvantages of public deposits are listed as follows.

Advantages	Disadvantages
Simple Procedure	Limitation in Volume
No Restrictive Covenants	Shorter Maturities
Unsecured Borrowings Fair Post-Tax Cost	

CONCLUDING COMMENTS

It should be understood that the focus of WC management should not be on ratios but on the important, underlying business drivers. The WC policy should be aligned with the strategic thrust of the company. A decision to pursue product differentiation strategy may be frustrated if the executives are forced to cut inventory and/or credit period. Likewise, a firm pursuing cost leadership strategy should make an all-out effort to squeeze the extra flab of inventory to stay competitive. Some of the action areas have already been mentioned earlier under different components of WC such as lot size, batch run and so on. WC management is not the job of finance managers alone. It is the joint effort of production, marketing and finance departments. The finance function will only provide required (decision-making) financial inputs. The actual implementation rests with other line executives.

APPENDIX 11A.1: ESTIMATION OF COMPONENTS OF WC

1. $$\left.\begin{array}{l}\text{Average Raw Material, Stores \& }\\ \text{Spares Storage Period in Days}\end{array}\right\} = \frac{\text{Average Stock of Raw Material}}{\text{Average Monthly Consumption of Raw Material}}$$

   where

$$\text{Average Stock of Raw Material} = \frac{\text{Opening Stock} + \text{Closing Stock}}{2}$$

$$\text{Average Monthly Consumption of Raw Materials} = \frac{\text{Opening Stock} + \text{Total Purchases} - \text{Closing Stock}}{12}$$

2. $$\text{Conversion Time in Days} = \frac{\text{Average Stock of WIP}}{\text{Average Daily Cost of Production}}$$

   where

$$\text{Average Stock of WIP} = \frac{\text{Opening WIP} + \text{Closing WIP}}{2}$$

$$\begin{aligned}\text{Cost of Production} = {} & \text{Opening Stock WIP} + \text{Consumption of Raw Materials, Stores \& Spares}\\ & + \text{Other Manufacturing Costs} - \text{Closing WIP}\end{aligned}$$

$$\text{Average Daily COP} = \text{COP}/360$$

3. $$\text{Finished Goods Storage Period} = \frac{\text{Average Stock of Finished Goods}}{\text{Average Daily Cost of Sales}}$$

   where

$$\begin{aligned}\text{Annual Cost of Sales} = {} & \text{Opening Stock of Finished Goods} + \text{COP}\\ & + \text{Selling \& Distribution Expenses} + \text{Administrative Expenses}\\ & + \text{Financial Charges}\\ & + \text{Excise Duty} - \text{Closing Stock of Finished Goods}\end{aligned}$$

$$\text{Average Daily Cost of Sales} = \text{Cost of Sales}/365$$

$$\text{Average Stock of Finished Goods} = \frac{\text{Opening Stock} + \text{Closing Stock}}{2}$$

4. $$\text{Average Collection Period} = \frac{\text{Average Balance of Sundry Debtors}}{\text{Average Daily Credit Sales}}$$

where

$$\text{Average Balance of Sundry Debtors} = \frac{\text{Opening Balance} + \text{Closing Balance}}{2}$$

$$\text{Average Daily Credit Sales} = \text{Annual Credit Sales}/365$$

5. $$\text{Average Accounts Payable Period} = \frac{\text{Average Balance of Sundry Creditors}}{\text{Average Daily Credit Purchases}}$$

where

$$\text{Average Daily Credit Purchases} = \text{Annual Credit Purchases}/365$$

$$\text{Average Balance of Sundry Creditors} = \frac{\text{Opening Balance} + \text{Closing Balance}}{2}$$

APPENDIX 11A.2: FORMAT FOR ASSESSMENT OF WORKING CAPITAL

______ Month's Raw Material Requirement	₹______
______ Week's/Month's Consumable Stores & Spares	₹______
______ Week's Stock-in-Process at Any Time	₹______
______ Month's Finished Goods at Cost	₹______
______ Week's/Month's Receivables	₹______
One Month's Manufacturing & Administrative Expenses	₹______
Total WC Requirement	₹______
Less: Credit Available on Purchase	₹______
Advance Payment Received from Customers	₹______
	₹______

APPENDIX 11A.3: ESTIMATION OF PERMISSIBLE LIMIT

		Permissible Limit
Raw Materials	₹	
Less: % Margin	₹	
	______	______ (A)

Stock-in-Progress	₹	
Less: % Margin	₹	
	______	______ (B)
Sundry Debtors	₹	
Less: % Margin	₹	
	______	______ (C)
Finished Goods	₹	
Less: % Margin	₹	
	______	______ (D)
Total Permissible Limit	(A+B+C+D)	

The Margin Varies from 25–40%.

APPENDIX 11A.4: CLASSIFICATION OF WC

Fund-Based: Fund-based facilities maybe categorized into advances towards meeting domestic (inland) WC requirement of a borrower and funding WC required for exports. The assessed bank finance is made available to borrowers through any one of the following facilities.

- **Cash Credit**: It is a running account facility and is extended for a short period, usually not more than 18 months and the same is reviewed. It is a pre-sale finance against stock of inventory consisting of raw materials, semi-finished goods and finished goods of a borrower. This also constitutes the primary security for the bank. The bank fixes the limit under the cash credit account after application of security margin over the value of the stock declared in the monthly statement given by the borrower. The security margin is determined at the time of assessment of WC, taking into account the margin contribution expected of the borrower. The borrower is at his/her liberty to draw funds under the limit, subject to availability of stock and maintenance of security margin. Withdrawals from the cash credit account are made by means of cheques issued from the account. The borrower is also required to deposit its sale proceeds into the cash credit account. Therefore, in a cash credit account, there would be a number of transactions (both debits and credits) in a single day and the balance outstanding would fluctuate on a day-to-day basis.

  The principle advantages of cash credit account are:
  - Enables the borrower to operate the account within the stipulated limit, as and when required.
  - Helps the borrower to reduce interest payment by reducing the debit balance in the account as and when it is able to do so.
  - Lender can monitor by tracking the debits and credits in the account.
- Working Capital Demand Loan (WCDL): Under cash credit system, by allowing the borrower to draw and replenish the cash credit account at will, the burden of the borrower's cash management is thrust on the bank. Also, on account of the nature of facility, banks incur a carrying cost, as the funds have to be made available, irrespective of the borrower utilizing the sanctioned limit or not.

In order to bring some financial discipline and free the banks from having to take care of the borrower's cash management, RBI, in 1995, modified the loan delivery system. Under the new delivery system, wherever the WC (fund-based) limits of ₹10 crores or above were granted, to borrowers, it was mandatory to bifurcate into loan component and cash credit component in the ratio of 80:20. The loan component was designated as 'WCDL' as it was repayable on demand, unlike a term loan, which gets paid at the scheduled points of times fixed.

For the fund-based limits below ₹10 crores, RBI did not fix the level of loan and cash credit components, which may be settled between the bank and the borrower. Banks are also allowed to price cash credit and demand loan components differentially.

In tune with the liberalization in the financial sector, the RBI has since done away with the bifurcation of WC limits and has left the decision of loan delivery to individual bank's discretion. However, most banks continue to use the bifurcation system in their loan delivery system to borrowers.

- Overdraft: It is a form of credit akin to cash credit. It is also a running account facility where the borrower could remit and draw funds freely, subject to the limit granted. The credit limit is normally granted against lien/pledge of assets, such as government securities, units of mutual funds, shares and debentures, bank's fixed deposits. Overdraft facility could be temporary or regular. It may be secured or unsecured. Interest is charged in the overdraft account based on the debit outstanding at the end of each day, at regular (monthly, quarterly) intervals. Borrowers are free to repay by means of deposits into the account. They can overdraw again up to the sanctioned limit.
- Bills: It is a means of payment used by companies to finance trade transactions. It is an instrument in writing containing an unconditional order, signed by the maker, directing a certain person to pay a specified amount of money only to or to the order of a certain person or to the bearer of the instrument. The maker of the bill is the drawer and the person on whom the bill is drawn is the drawee who has to discharge his/her liability under the bill.
- Demand/Usance Bills: Bills are mainly of two types, namely demand bills and usance bills. Demand bills are payable at sight and usance bills are payable after a certain period.

Other forms of lending cash credit are documentary/clean bills, provide for an advance against bills, commercial paper, short-term loans, Foreign Currency Non-Resident (Bank) FCNR (B) loans, export finance, advances against receivable from government and so on.

Non-Fund-Based: There are two ways that a bank offers non-fund-based credit facilities to banks. They are:

- **Letters of credit**: A letter of credit is a banker's undertaking on behalf of a constituent to pay to a third party against compliance of stipulated conditions. A letter of credit facilitates settlement of trade payments and is used for both local and international trade. The seller is promised payments in his/her own country and the buyer is assured that seller makes the payment against submission of universally acceptable title to goods.

  Types of Letters of Credit

  Revocable Letter of Credit: It is a credit that can be revoked, that is, cancelled or amended by the bank issuing the credit without the notice of other parties. Revocable letter of credit is rarely used.

  Irrevocable Letter of Credit: Irrevocable letter of credit is a firm undertaking on the part of the issuing bank and cannot be cancelled or amended without the consent of the parties to LC, particularly the beneficiary.

Confirmed Letter of Credit: Confirmed letter of credit is an LC to which another bank has added its confirmation or guarantee. Thus, there is a double guarantee in such credit and it is more favourable to beneficiary.

Sight Credit and Acceptance Credit: Sight credit is a demand draft drawn by the exporter that is paid on presentation to the negotiating bank, provided all the terms of the credit have been strictly adhered to. In case of an acceptance credit, drafts are drawn on the issuing bank or the correspondent bank at specified usance period.

Red Clause Letter of Credit: It is also called countervailing credit. When an LC is opened with security of another LC, the credit thus opened is termed as back-to-back letter of credit. The practical purpose is that when an LC is opened by the ultimate buyer in favour of a particular beneficiary who may or may not be the actual supplier or manufacturer, the beneficiary may open another LC with near identical terms in favour of the actual supplier/manufacturer offering the main credit opened in his/her favour, as security and will be able to obtain reimbursement by presenting the documents received under back-to-back credit under the main LC.

Transferable Letter of Credit: The original beneficiary in favour of a second beneficiary or several second beneficiaries can transfer this type of credit.

Standby Letter of Credit: These credits are generally used as a substitute for performance guarantee or for securing secured loans.

Effectiveness of LC as an Assured Payment Mechanism: LC deals only with documents. If the documents are submitted exactly as per the LC terms, the LC opening bank is duly bound to make the payment.

Payment of LC Liability: The payment for the LC on the due date is the responsibility of the customer and has to take place through his own sources. However, in case the customer is unable to arrange for the payment on the crystallization date, the LC is deemed as 'devolved'. The bank has to pay-off the LC amount and recovers the same from the customer.

- **Bank Guarantee:** A contract of guarantee is a contract to perform the promise or discharge the liability of a third person in case of his/her default. There are three parties to a contract of guarantee. The person who guarantees the performance of a promise or the liability of a third person is called the guarantor (surety). The person, on whose behalf the guarantee is given, is the principal debtor and the person to whom the guarantee if given is called the creditor.

  The obligation of the surety under a guarantee issued arises when there is a default to perform the promise by the person on whose behalf the guarantee is given. The liability of a surety runs parallel to the liability of a principal debtor towards the creditor. On failure of the principal debtor to perform the obligation under the contract, the liability of the surety with respect to the guarantee starts. The bank may be called to perform its obligation under a bank guarantee issued by it the moment the customer, on whose behalf the guarantee is given, defaults. Therefore, though bank guarantees are non-fund credit supports initially, the probability of their turning into fund-based credit is high.

  In order to ensure that the guarantee executed by the banker does not remain in force for an indefinite period, it is stipulated that the guarantee would remain in force for the period specified therein, on the expiry of which no claims would be entertained by the banker.

Types of Bank Guarantees

Bank guarantees issued by banks are principally of three types:

- Financial Guarantee: Under this type of guarantee, the bank undertakes only the financial liability. The bank undertakes to pay the beneficiary of the guarantee, an amount not exceeding the sum stated, on default of promise by the customer. These are guarantees issued in respect of purely monetary obligations.

- Performance Guarantee: The bank guarantees that the customer, on whose behalf the guarantee is given, will perform the contract undertaken. If the customer fails on performing the same, the banker shall make good the loss caused to the beneficiary, by limiting him financially to a sum not exceeding the amount undertaken in the guarantee.
  - The important difference between the financial and performance guarantees lies in the additional factor, that is, performance by the customer guaranteed by the banker in case of the latter. The commonality between the two is that both result ultimately in financial liability only.
- Deferred Payment Guarantee: The banker guarantees payment by his/her customer of the amount to be paid by his customer, which has been spread or deferred over a period of time. This type of guarantee is normally required when the customer when he/she desires to purchase machinery or goods on credit. Deferred payment guarantees are usually the non-funded substitutes for term loans.

APPENDIX 11A.5: CLASSIFICATION OF CURRENT LIABILITIES AND CURRENT ASSETS

Current Liabilities

- Short-term borrowings including bills purchased and discounted from banks (and others).
- Unsecured loans.
- Public deposits maturing within one year.
- Sundry creditors for raw material and consumable stores and spares.
- Interest and other charges accrued but not due for payment.
- Advance/progress payments from customers (see Note 6).
- Deposits from dealer, selling agents and so on (see Note 7).
- Instalments of term loans, deferred payment credits, debentures, redeemable preference shares and long-term deposits payable within one year.
- Statutory liabilities.
  - Provident fund dues.
  - Provision for taxation (see Note 2).
  - Sales tax, excise and so on.
  - Obligation towards workers considered as statutory.
  - Others.
- Miscellaneous current liabilities.
  - Dividends (see Note 2).
  - Liabilities for expenses.
  - Gratuity payable within one year.
  - Other provisions.
  - Any other payments due within 12 months.

Current Assets

- Cash and bank balances.
- Investment (see Note 3).

- o Government and other trustee securities other than for long-term purposes.
- o Fixed deposits with banks.

- Receivables arising out of sales other than deferred receivables, including bills purchased and discounted by banks.
- Installments of deferred receivables due within one year.
- Raw materials and components used in the process of manufacture including those in transit (see Note 4).
- Stocks-in-process including semi-finished goods.
- Finished goods including goods in transit.
- Other consumable spares (see Note 4).
- Advance payment for tax.
- Prepaid expenses.
- Advances for purchase of raw materials, components and consumable stores.
- Monies receivable from contracted sale of fixed assets during the next 12 months.

Notes:

1. The concept of current liabilities would include estimated or accrued amounts which are anticipated to cover expenditure within the year for unknown obligations, namely taxes, accrued bonus payments, provisions and so on.
2. In cases where specific provisions have not been made for these liabilities and will be eventually paid out of general reserves, estimated amounts should be shown as current liabilities.
3. Investments in shares and advance to other firms/companies, not connected with the business of the borrowing firm, should be excluded from current assets.
4. Slow moving or obsolete items should not be classified as current assets.
5. Amounts representing interconnected company transactions should be treated as current only after examining the nature of transactions and merits of the case. For example, advance paid for suppliers for a period more than the normal trade practice, in spite of any other considerations such as regular and assured supply should not be considered as current.
6. Advance payments from customers are to be classified as current liabilities where deposits are required.

APPENDIX 11A.6: QUARTERLY INFORMATION SYSTEM (FORM I)

Name of Borrower ______________________ (₹ Hundred Thousand)

A. Estimates for the Current Accounting Year Indicated In Annual Plan	(a) Production:	
	(b) Gross Sales:	
	(1) Domestic ______	
	(2) Exports ______	
		______
	(c) Net Sales:	
		______

B. Estimate for the Ensuing Quarter Ending ________	(a) Production :
	(b) Gross Sales:
	(1) Domestic ________
	(2) Exports ________
	(c) Net Sales:

C. Estimates of Current Assets and Current Liabilities for the Ensuing Quarter Ending.

Quarterly Information System (Form II)

A. Estimates of Current Accounting	(a) Production:
	(b) Gross Sales:

B. Actual Production/Sales	During the Quarter	Cumulative
1st quarter ________		
2nd quarter ________		
3rd quarter ________		
4th quarter ________		

C. Data Relating to the Latest Completed Quarter Ending	Estimate	Actuals
(a) Production:		
(b) Gross Sales:		
(c) Total:		

D. Current Assets and Current Liabilities	Estimate	Actuals

Exercises

1. Refer to the data given below and calculate MPBF.

	(₹ Hundred Thousand)
A. Inventory:	
Raw Materials	35.00
WIP	90.00
Finished Goods	285.00
Stores & Spares	61.00
B. Book Debts	300.00
C. Other Current Assets	90.68
D. Current Liabilities Other Than Bank Borrowings	245.00
E. Minimum NWC is 25% of Current Assets	

2. Calculate operating cycle

Raw Materials	0.96 months
Stock-in-Progress	1.44 months
Finished Goods	5.27 months
Stores & Spares	3.63 months
Receivables	4.66 months

3. What are the drawbacks of the cash credit and overdraft system?
4. Describe the four methods used by banks for WC lending.
5. What are the limitations of the cash budget approach to WC lending?
6. The current assets and current liabilities of a company are ₹300 million and ₹180 million, respectively. Calculate the maximum permissible bank finance under the three methods assuming that the core component of current assets is ₹240 million.
7. A company stores three weeks of raw material (₹1 million), two weeks of work-in-process (₹1.5 million), four weeks of finished goods (₹2 million). The company has ₹2.5 million of outstanding credits. One month expense is ₹300,000. The company does not receive any credit from suppliers. Assume appropriate margin on each of the components and calculate WC requirement and bank finance.

CHAPTER 12

Cash Management

LEARNING OBJECTIVES

- To know the determinants of corporate cash holdings
- To measure cash flow timeline
- To be aware of cash management techniques
- To prepare cash forecasts and budgets
- To be aware of cash management services available in India

Executives worry about the cash balances they hold. This is not without a reason. Holding 1 million excess cash balance amounts to not investing in other available profitable opportunities. To illustrate, a company would be incurring a cost of ₹150,000 at a cost of capital of 15 per cent on 1 million. Cash is an asset only when it used. Idle cash is a liability. To borrow ₹1 million for a day at 12 per cent costs ₹333. In addition, the borrower will have to maintain a compensatory balance of, say, 10 per cent. So the cost of holding cash is higher. Cash management involves control and analysis of cash flows during a particular period. Corporate cash management aims to

- Track and control cash flows
- Provide adequate liquidity
- Optimize usage of cash, manage short-term borrowing and investment activities

This chapter has three parts:

- Measuring and managing cash flow timeline
- Strategies for accelerating cash receipts and decelerating disbursements
- Cash forecasting and cash budgeting

Cash management can be viewed as a system with interrelationships between a company and its banks as well as the headquarters (treasury function) and different operating units.

WHY DO FIRMS HOLD CASH?

John Maynard Keynes wrote in the *General Theory of Employment, Interest and Money*, 'There is no necessity to hold idle cash to bridge over intervals if it can be obtained without difficulty at the moment when it is actually required'. Yet we do not see it in actual practice. Companies continue to hold cash (see Table 12.1). In a perfect market case, it does not matter whether the firm retains the cash or disburses it to shareholders through dividends or cuts debt since there is no difference between cash inside the firm and that outside. When markets are not perfect, cash inside and outside are not equivalent. One of the most commonly cited reasons for holding cash is the transaction motive. A firm may hold cash to enable it to fund projects if the cash flow in that period is low. Transaction motive refers to requirement of cash for the day-to-day running of the business. Companies may also hold cash to meet contingencies. This is known as precautionary motive. Companies may also hold cash to speculate in business opportunities. This is the speculative motive.

TABLE 12.1
Corporate Cash Holdings in 2018

Company	Cash in Hand and Bank Balance (₹ crore)
HUL	3,373.00
Infosys	16,770.00
Reliance Industries	2,731.00
Tata Motors	39,700.00
Tata Steel	4,696.00

Source: Prowess.

The company may raise external finance if available. This is not possible for firms that face information asymmetry or agency costs. A cash reserve would enable the company to tide over the deficit. In other words, firms that have volatile cash flow are more likely to hold greater amounts of cash. Likewise, firms that are subject to higher distress costs may hold greater amounts of cash to act as buffer. The length of the cash conversion cycle also determines the amount of cash a company holds. Firms with relatively shorter cash conversion cycles are likely to hold less liquid assets. Other determinants of scope and nature of cash management in an organization include:

- Extent of decentralization of operations
- Size of the company
- Geographical scope

Size: Larger companies can justify the cash management efforts by the magnitude of savings, whereas smaller companies cannot. Larger companies, almost by definition, have larger cash flows to track and have greater number of bank relationships. This calls for sophisticated cash management practice. This is especially true of businesses that are cash intensive. For instance, the need to hold cash is more in companies that sell through retail outlets such as FMCG companies than in those that sell on a wholesale basis.

Extent of Decentralization: If the company has a decentralized structure, it might delegate at least a part of the cash management responsibility to the operating units. In many companies, the corporate treasury function is restricted to headquarters with minimal freedom given to divisional units. The headquarters may exercise control on short-term investing and borrowing activities, whereas divisions may be responsible for cash flow they generate. This type of allocation of responsibilities leads to sub-optimization of efforts. The philosophy is to let someone do what one is good at. This is not an easy process. Excessive centralization of key activities leads to dissension from managers.

Geographical Scope: A global company would have a different set of reporting needs vis-à-vis a domestic company. A global company, due to its dispersion of activities beyond national boundaries, is affected by economic and political risks as local regulations on repatriation of income and exchange rate risk. So a cash manager needs to have a global view of cash management function, the reporting relationships among different operating units and the choice of currency.

State-of-the-Art Banking System: Cash managers can reduce time involved in transferring funds only if the banking system is developed and if bankers are willing to extend cash management services. The check clearing system exerts considerable influence on the controllability of cash. Without technological upgradation, there is little a cash manager can do. Innovations such as electronic fund transfer, automated payment system are possible due to technological advances. Corporate cash management essentially involves policy decisions regarding disbursement of funds and use of bank services. The corporate philosophy regarding disbursements has the most significant impact on cash management. Centralized handling of payables would provide greater control on outflow as opposed to a decentralized system. The cash management process is shown in Figure 12.1.

CASH FLOW TIMELINE

Cash flows can be categorized into three types—inflows, outflows and intra-firm flows. Examples of inflows are cash collected from customers, cash received on sale of investments and so on. Outflows go to suppliers, creditors, government (tax), employees and shareholders. Intra-firm flows refer to movement of funds from bank to head office, between divisions and special account. Cash management

FIGURE 12.1
Cash Management Process

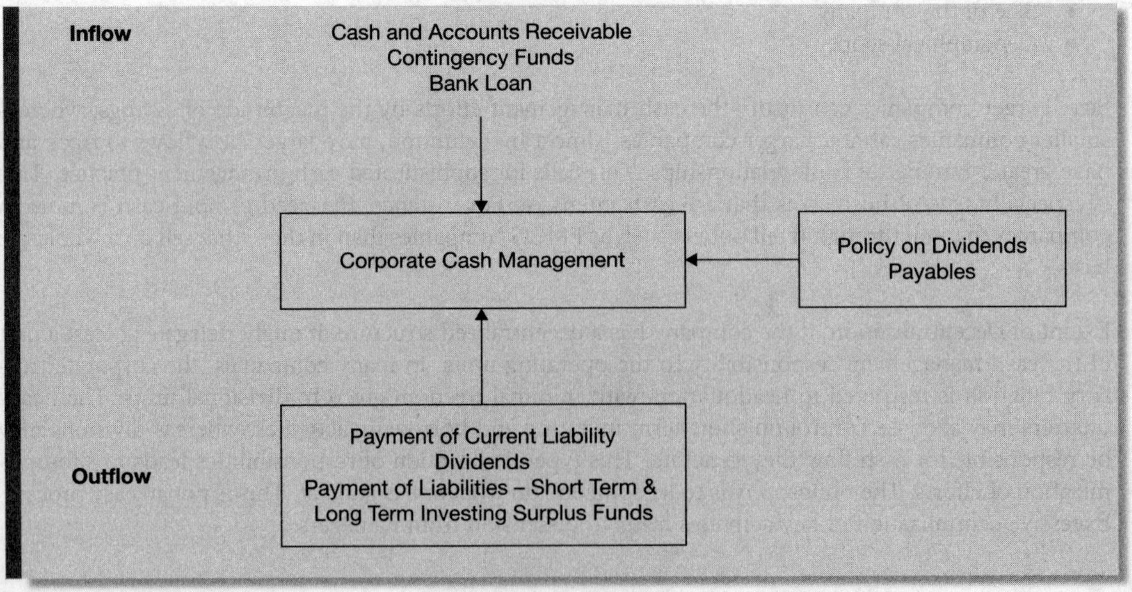

FIGURE 12.2
Cash Inflow Timeline

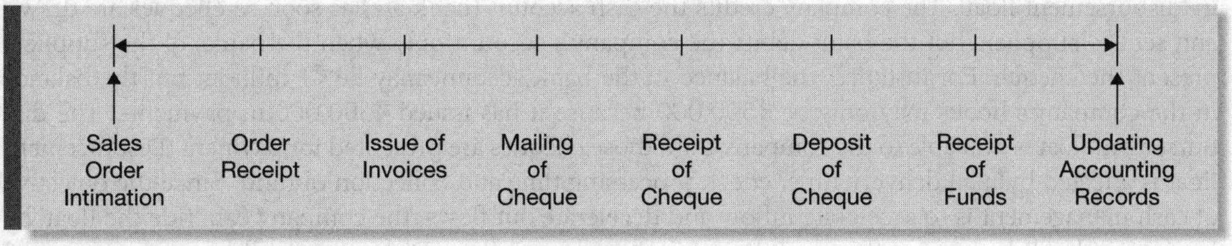

FIGURE 12.3
Cash Outflow Timeline

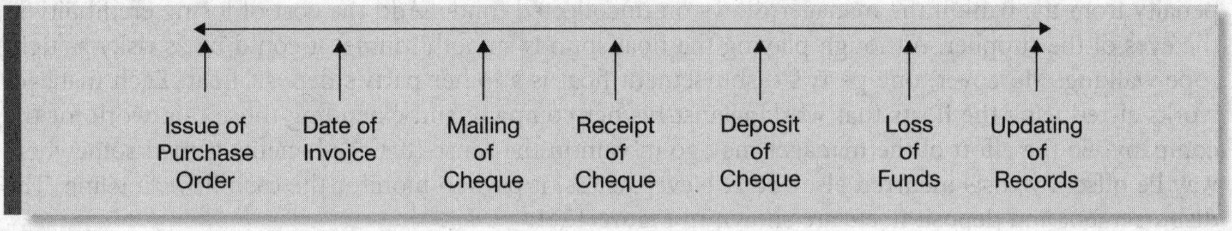

involves accelerating inflows and decelerating outflows. Cash inflow is shown on a timeline diagram in Figure 12.2.

The length of the components of cash flow timeline could range from few minutes to days or even months. For instance, the production and billing interval could range from a few hours to several months depending on the business of the company. Cash managers typically concentrate on accelerating the receipt of cheque and encashing it. With technological improvements, the savings in the activity decreases. The real savings come from managing the other components of the timeline such as sales order processing and production billing process. Obviously, they do not come under the domain of the cash manager. Coordination among departments leads to improved efficiency and savings. The other strategy is to decelerate outflows.

The outflow timeline is shown in Figure 12.3.

The cash outflow timeline begins with the initiation of the purchase requisition. Again, the focus of managing disbursements should not be on the banking activities involved but on the other segments. The objective of cash flow timeline management is to reduce the overall cost.

FLOAT

The cash balance shown in the books of accounts of the company and the balance in the books of the bank need not coincide. The reason could be that the bank has not collected the cheques presented by the company or the customers have not yet presented the cheques issued by the company. As soon as the cheques are deposited in the bank, the company debits the cash account. But the bank credits the account only when the amount is realized from the bank of the customer. This time lag is called deposit float. The deposit float is the time lag between drawing of the cheque by the customer and the receipt of funds by the company. The deposit float consists of mail float, processing float and check clearance float shown as follows. It is important to monitor all the three components of the deposit float for accelerating receipts. Similarly, check issued by the company but not yet presented by the suppliers results in 'disbursement float'. The company credits the cash account (bank a/c) as soon as cheques are drawn and sent to suppliers but the bank debits the company's account only when the banks of the suppliers present the cheque. For instance, the balance in the bank account may be ₹1 million, but the balance in the company's books may only be ₹500,000 because it has issued ₹500,000 in payments. The disbursement float is available to the company until those cheques are presented for payment. Disbursement float is affected by mail delivery time, check processing time and collection of fund. Since the objective of cash management is to accelerate inflow and decelerate out flows, the company can 'ride the float' by increasing the disbursement float and decreasing the deposit float. Disbursement float can be increased by issuing the payables checks against a distant bank or mailing from a remotely located post office! Playing the float requires the cash manager to think in terms of bank balance in the bank books and not that in the company's book of accounts. A cash manager should be careful not to overdo it and incur penalty from the bank if the manager draws on uncollected funds. Add the cost of losing credibility in the eyes of the supplier. Although playing the float sounds smooth sailing, it could be as risky as tight rope walking. Moreover, one party's disbursement float is another party's deposit float. Each manager works at reducing the floats that work against his/her company and extending those that work for the company. So the effort of the manager may go in vain in the sense that the benefits gained somewhere way be offset by costs incurred elsewhere. Nevertheless, it pays to monitor the cash flow timeline. The disbursement and deposit floats are shown in Figure 12.4.

FIGURE 12.4
Deposit and Disbursement Float

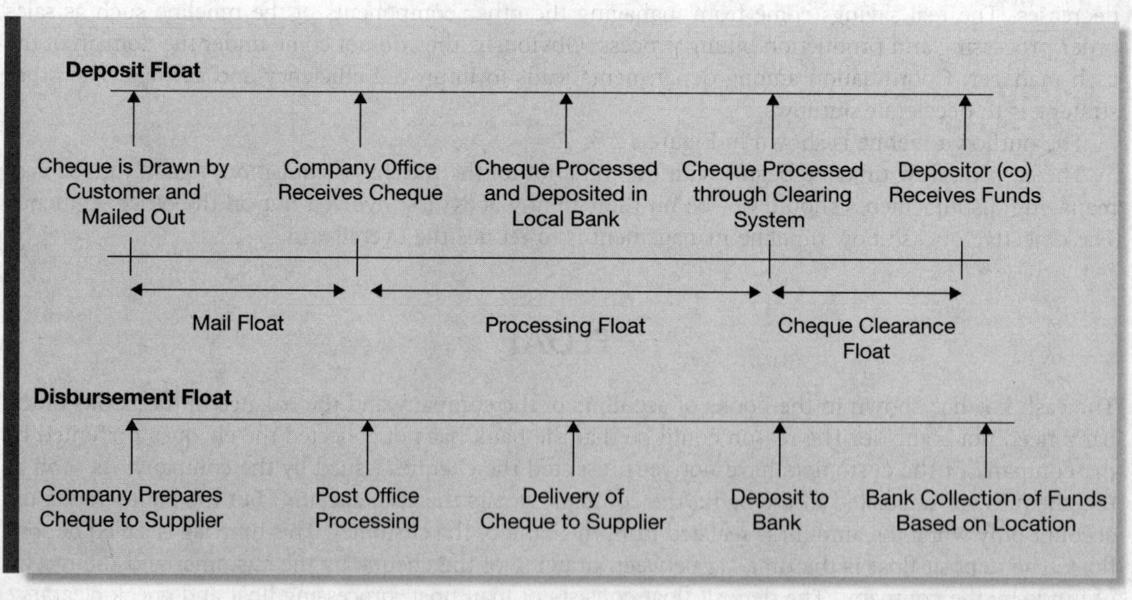

ACCELERATING INFLOWS: LOCK BOX SYSTEM

Lock boxes are centrally located collection post office boxes meant for intercepting receivables from customers. In a lock box system, the customers mail their remittances to a post office box number rather than to the company. The company's bank collects the lock box receipts from the post office several times a day and processes them on behalf of the company. The bank deposits the checks received directly to the company's account. The obvious advantage of lock box system is that the mail processing and check collection time is drastically reduced provided the lock boxes are located at optimum distance from the customers. The company receives a hard copy of detailed information regarding customer name, a/c no., amount paid and the funds processed by the bank at regular intervals. Figure 12.5 gives a graphical representation of the lock box system. Lock box system is efficient in accelerating receivables and reducing clerical work for the company. Since the processing work is delegated to a bank, the company may have to follow up from time to time to reconcile any differences. It might be uneconomical to operate a lock box if high value transactions are not experienced. The choice of a new lock box location depends on the cost of lock box service, number and frequency of daily mail pickups, and the bank's expertise in operating the box and the presence or absence of allied services.

FIGURE 12.5
Lock Box System

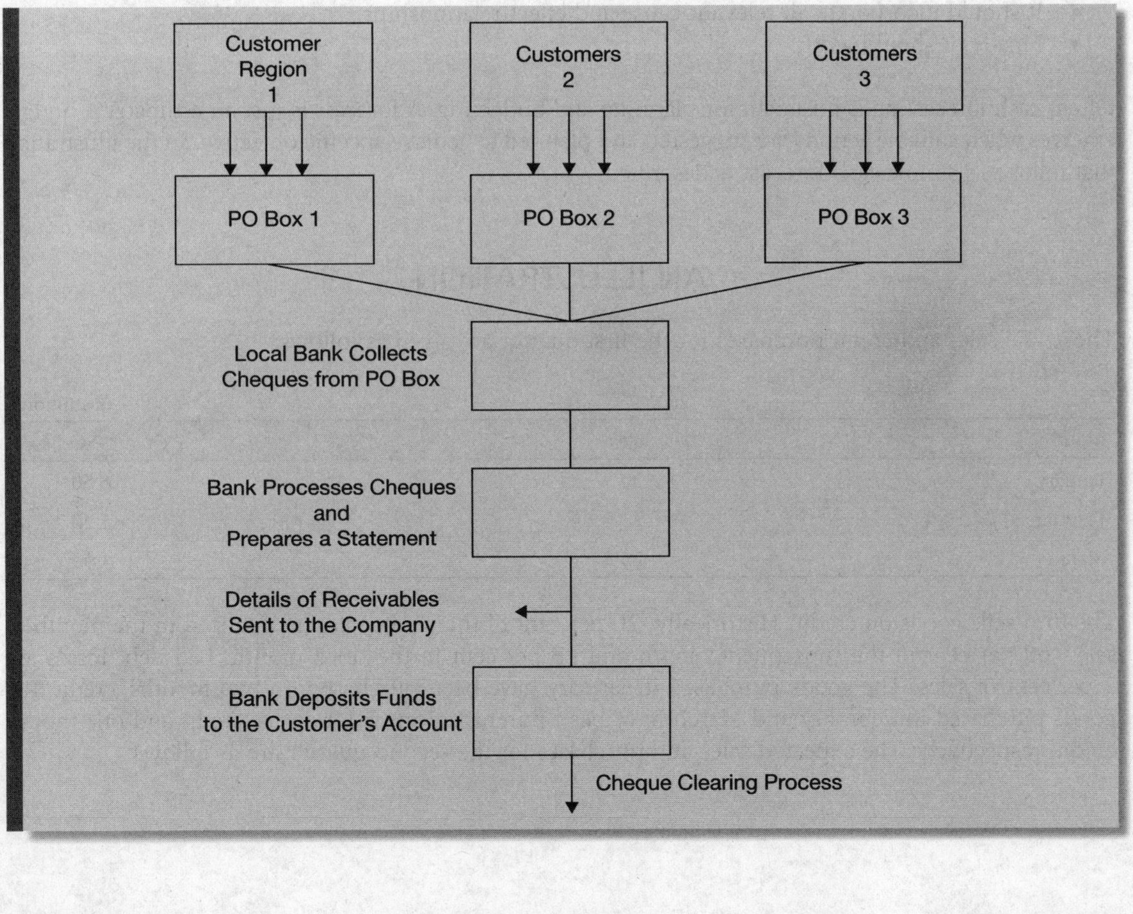

CASH FORECASTING

Since cash management is a forward-looking activity, sound predictions of demands and trends are a necessity to cope with seasonality in demand. Forecasting can be qualitative or quantitative. Qualitative forecasting involves eliciting expert opinion on the future states of the world and their influence on the item under consideration. Qualitative forecasting is usually restricted to identifying basic long-term trends rather than short-term and intermediate forecasts. Moving averages, exponential smoothing and regression analysis are some of the quantitative techniques used in forecasting. Forecasting techniques vary in their costs, as well as in scope and accuracy. The cash manager must decide what accuracy is required or what inaccuracy is tolerable. This allows for a trade-off between cost and the value of accuracy. Increased accuracy may lead to lower cash levels and hence carrying costs. One should weigh the savings against the cost of more sophisticated and expensive techniques.

The following guidelines might prove useful while selecting a forecasting technique.

- The forecasting technique should be relevant for decision-making. It should not rely too much on past.
- It should make best use of available data with reasonable degree of accuracy.
- It should not be too expensive vis-à-vis the benefit arising out of the analysis.
- It should not require maintenance of large amount of data.
- It should incorporate all relevant cause and effect relationships.
- Finally, it should work.

Often, cash forecasting is mistaken for planning and budgeting. A forecast is just an estimate. A budget emerges when suitable actions are suggested and planned to achieve specific objective. In the illustration that follows, a simple cash forecast is described.

AN ILLUSTRATION

The actual sales and credit purchases for the first quarter are given as follows:

(₹ million)

Month	Sales	Credit Purchases
January	20	6.50
February	22	5.20
March	25	3.0

The firm sells goods on credit. Historically, 20 per cent of the credit sales are realized in the month of sales, 60 per cent in the subsequent month and 18 per cent in the third month. Bad debt losses are 2 per cent of sales. The goods purchased in January have been purchased on two months' credit; the goods purchased in February and March have been purchased on two months' credit and one-month credit, respectively. The expected sales and purchases for the second quarter are as follows:

(₹ million)

Month	Sales	Cash Purchases	Credit	Credit Period
April	24	1.2	3.7	2 months
May	23	1.7	3.5	1 month
June	26	2.0	4.0	1 month

Other details are as follows:

- Salaries for April through June: ₹4.5 million, ₹5 million, ₹5.5 million
- Interest on term loan to be paid in April: ₹750,000
- Principal repayment in June: ₹10 million
- Utility charges: ₹80,000 p.m.

(₹)

	Month		
	April	May	June
Inflows:			
Sales Collections:			
20% of April	4.8 million		
60% of March	1.5 cr.		
18% of February	0.4 cr.		
20% of April		46L	
60% of March		1.44 cr.	
18% of February		45L	
20% of April			0.52 cr
60% of March			1.38 cr
18% of February			0.432 cr
	2.38 cr.	2.35 cr.	2.332 cr.
Outflows			
Cash Purchases	1.2 million	1.7 million	2 million
Credit Purchases			
February Purchases	5.2 million		
March Purchases	3.0 million		
April Purchases			3.7 million
May Purchases			3.5 million
Salaries	0.45 cr	0.5 cr	0.44 cr
Interest	0.075 cr		
Principal Repayment			1.0 cr
Utility Charges	80,000	80,000	80,000

The summary of inflows and outflows is given below.

	April	May	June
Inflow	238	235	233
Outflow			
Purchases	94	17	92
Salaries	45	50	55
Interest	7.5		
Principal Repayment			100
Utility Charges	0.8	0.8	0.8
Net (₹ Lakhs)	90.70	167.2	(14.8)

CASH BUDGET

Cash forecasting involves estimation of cash inflows and cash outflows for a future period. From the forecast of all cash receipts and payments, cash surpluses or shortages are determined for each sub-period (say, a month). Once the estimate is in place, the concerned executive is expected to initiate appropriate action to synchronize inflows and outflows. It is unlikely that they will balance on their own. This imbalance necessitates appropriate action to tide over cash deficit whenever there is one (by borrowing) and plan short-term investments whenever there is a surplus. A cash budget is a document prepared after effecting these adjustments. The primary distinction between a cash forecast and cash budget is that the former is an as-is document, while the latter reflects the actions that management plans to take in order to manage future events. The cash budget contains forecasted figures of receipts and disbursements of cash over a certain period of time, usually one year. A typical cash budget has four sections—receipts, payments, deficit/surplus and adjustments.

The receipts section lists out all anticipated cash receipts from all sources such as cash collected from customers, sale of plant and equipment, scrap sales and advance payment by customers. The payment section records all anticipated cash payments such as repayment of term loans, salaries and wages, purchase of raw material, fuel and excise duty. The deficit or surplus section gives the difference between receipts and payments. If the inflow is more than outflows, a surplus results else a deficit results. The cash budget also reveals the opening cash balance, ending cash balance and the desired cash balance. The adjustment section reveals the actions the management intends to take in periods of deficit or surplus.

AN ILLUSTRATION

The cash budget for a company is given in Table 12.2. The company prepares cash budget for the entire year (only a portion is shown in Table 12.2). Reviews are conducted every quarter and remedial actions are taken. The cash budget suggests that it is a cash-rich company.

The contents of the cash budget could be grouped into the following: operating, financing and investment activities just like the cash flow statement.

TABLE 12.2
Cash Budget

Budget	Cash Budget for the Year 2017–2018 (₹ Hundred Thousand)								
	Full Year	Apr	May	Jun	Jul	Aug	Sep	Oct	Nov
Opening Cash and Bank Balance as on 01.04.17	654	654	654	654	654	654	654	654	654
Unutilized Cash Credit Limit with Banks	32	32	32	32	32	32	32	32	32
Receipts									
Sale of Cement	23,000	1,790	3,691	5,593	7,450	9,418	11,342	13,020	14,586
Sale of Scrap Materials	50	5	9	14	10	30	34	40	45
Sale of Unserviceable Assets	1	1	1	1	1	1	1	1	1
Others	10	1	2	3	4	5	6	7	8
Term Loan from Banks	1,800	0	0	1,000	1,000	1,000	1,500	1,500	1,500
Interest Receipts	15	2	4	6	8	10	12	14	16
Total (A)	25,562	2,485	4,393	7,303	9,158	11,150	13,581	15,268	16,842
Payments									
Additions to Fixed Assets (Land, Building Machinery)	1,500	5	15	25	125	500	700	900	1,100
Repayment of Term Loans	330	75	75	75	150	150	150		
Salaries, Wages and Benefits to Employees	1,450	120	240	360	480	615	735	850	1,000
Purchase of Raw Materials	1,050	85	165	245	331	412	503	587	670
Purchase of Packing Bags	1,300	107	215	322	428	536	642	749	857
Purchase of Fuel (Coal Lignite and so on)	3,600	302	608	909	1,213	1,515	1,819	2,121	2,424
Purchase of Stores and Spares	700	55	112	168	216	278	328	390	441
Payment of Electricity Board (Power)	2,400	201	406	594	791	968	1,188	1,486	1,680
	Cash Budget for the Year 2017–2018								
Budget	Full Year	Apr	May	Jun	Jul	Aug	Sep	Oct	Nov
Excise Duty	3,000	232	479	725	957	1,218	1,479	1,711	1,885
Sales Tax	3,600	296	583	884	1,177	1,449	1,732	1,909	2,192
Other Taxes	125	9	19	27	35	42	51	61	69
Interest	500	0	0	80	80	123	203	203	302
Advertisement Expenses	150	5	10	15	25	65	70	85	105
Repairs and Maintenance	125	12	20	33	41	50	59	66	72

(Continued)

TABLE 12.2
(Continued)

	Cash Budget for the Year 2017–2018 (₹ Hundred Thousand)								
Budget	Full Year	Apr	May	Jun	Jul	Aug	Sep	Oct	Nov
Royalty for Limestone	425	35	70	105	141	181	216	250	285
Insurance Premium	30	14	14	14	14	14	26	26	26
Travelling Expenses	60	5	11	14	19	23	28	33	39
Freight and Transportation	1,300	102	209	317	421	515	630	735	820
Expenses on Export Sales	70	0	0	9	18	28	36	42	50
Depot Maintenance Expenses	325	25	58	81	108	135	161	186	209
Donations	30	5	8	12	17	19	19	21	25
Bank Charges	30	2	4	5	8	10	12	14	16
Legal Expenses	25	1	5	7	7	9	11	11	18
Postage, Telegram, Telephones and Telex	65	4	7	15	21	24	30	33	38
Conveyance Expenses	35	3	7	10	13	15	18	21	24
Business/Sales Promotion Expenses	20	1	3	5	8	11	11	12	14
Other Expenses	150	13	28	36	49	58	71	89	102
Surplus Remitted to Head Office	2,500	200	400	800	1,300	1,500	1,800	2,000	2,100
Total (4+5) (B)	24,895	1,839	3,696	5,892	8,118	10,388	12,728	14,741	16,713
Closing Cash and Bank Balances (A) – (B)	667	646	697	1,411	1,040	762	852.5	527	129

Note: The first column gives the total amount for the particular item for the entire year.

Operating activities are the principal revenue producing activities of an enterprise (and those activities that are not investment and financing activities). Examples of operating activities are:

- Cash receipts from the sale of goods and the rendering of services
- Cash payments to suppliers of goods and services
- Cash payments to and on behalf of employees
- Income tax

Investing activities include acquisition and disposal of long-term assets required to facilitate operating activities. Examples of investing activities are:

- Cash payments for acquiring fixed assets
- Cash receipts from disposal of fixed assets
- Cash payments to acquire shares, warrants and debt instruments of other companies
- Cash receipts from disposal of warrants and debt instruments of other companies

Financing activities are activities that result in changes in the size and composition of the owners' capital and borrowings of the enterprise.

Examples of financing activity are:

- Cash proceeds from issuing shares or other similar instruments
- Cash payments to owners to acquire or redeem the enterprise's share
- Cash repayments of amounts borrowed
- Cash proceeds from issuing debt instruments

CASH MANAGEMENT SERVICES IN INDIA

Management of cash flow is an important function for every business organization. An efficient cash flow management requires faster conversion of receivables into cash. Banks play a crucial role in cash management of companies. Indeed banks are partners in managing working capital. Many banks offer cash management services to companies. A bank's main activity is collection and payment of cheques. The introduction of electronic banking services has provided faster delivery mechanism. The general requirements for the cash management system to succeed are that cheques deposited at the bank should be realized faster, the collected funds should be pooled at a required centre for better utilization and a strong MIS support should be there for reconciliation.

The traditional banking system requires an organization to open accounts at various locations, deposit cheques in these accounts, monitor collections, transfer excess funds to corporate treasury on regular basis, reconcile accounts and control operations.

Some of limitations and disadvantages of traditional system are outlined as follows:

- Organizations are deprived of timely access to funds of their own for profitable deployment, for reasons such as delay in realization, funds not cleared, irregularity in carrying out standing instructions
- Poor monitoring of collections
- Higher cost of operation
- Hassles of operating multiple accounts at various locations
- Hassles of reconciliation
- Poor MIS support

Cash management service offered by banks is an effective solution for corporates to overcome the inefficiencies, constraints, costs and hassles involved in traditional collection system. Banks play a critical role in providing the faster turnover of receivables, given the complexity of clearing system (read banking system) in India; hence, it is very important for a cash manager to understand the payment system in India.

The payment or clearing system in India can be understood in the following contexts:

- Paper-based payment system
  - Local cheque clearing system
  - Outstation clearing system
- Electronic payment system

PAPER-BASED PAYMENT SYSTEM

Payments in India are mainly paper-based, and cheques are the widely accepted method of funds transfer. Clearing of these instruments are done at respective clearing centres at over 990 locations across India. The RBI conducts the clearing at 17 centres; at about 975 centres SBI conducts the clearing and rest are being managed by the associate banks and other public sector banks.

High Value Clearing: The RBI offers high value clearing facility at selected centres within a certain geographical limits of that centre. High value clearing represents the instruments of value more than ₹100,000 issued and deposited within that limited area of the clearing location. High value instruments are of significant importance to the cash manager as he/she gets credit for the amount in his/her account on the same day.

Local Clearing: At certain identified clearing centres, having large volume of transactions, the RBI has made mandatory magnetic ink character recognition (MICR) clearing for automated processing. Cheques that cannot be deposited in high value are processed in MICR clearing. The cycle for MICR clearing is 48 hours.

At centres where MICR clearing is not followed, clearing process takes place in traditional manual method with the same 48-hour clearing cycle.

The timeline for local clearing of cheques is as follows:

Day 0: Company deposits the cheques in the CMS bank branch before the stipulated clearing cut-off time.

Day 1: The bank branch presents the cheque in local clearing. Paying bank credits funds to the presenting bank on uncleared basis to allow time for returns.

Day 2: If the cheque is not cleared, paying bank returns the instrument to the presenting banker. If the cheque is cleared, the presenting bank makes the funds available to the depositor.

In case the depositor is availing CMS, the banker makes funds available on Day 1 on clear funds basis. In case of high value clearing, the entire procedure takes place on the same day, that is, Day 0.

The case can be narrated with an example:

The Hyderabad branch of XYZ Ltd deposits cheques (drawn in Hyderabad) in Hyderabad branch of his CMS banker—Corporation Bank on 1 January. The bank sends the cheque for clearing to the local clearing house and without waiting for the funds to be cleared, Corporation Bank credits the amount to the account of the XYZ Ltd on 2 January at Mumbai. Thus, clear funds are made available to the cash manager for effective utilization.

OUTSTATION CLEARING

Cheque not drawn on the same location where it is deposited becomes outstation cheque. In such cases, the banker of the company sends the cheque to the drawee bank on a collections basis. The collection (realization) of these cheques generally takes 5 to 20 days. To improve the collection cycle, the CMS banker arranges for tie-up with other banks for correspondent banking.

However, the CMS banker makes available the funds to the corporate immediately without waiting for the cheque to be realized, on the strength of the creditworthiness of the company. The CMS banker discounts the cheque and gives credit to the client on Day 0–Day 1 basis, thus providing liquidity to the cash manager.

An Example

The Hyderabad branch of XYZ Ltd deposits a cheque drawn on Anantapur at the Hyderabad branch of his CMS banker—Corporation Bank on 1 January. The bank discounts the cheque and gives credit to the central account of the company at Mumbai on 2 January. The Hyderabad branch of Corporation Bank sends the cheque to its Anantapur branch for realization through courier. The Anantapur branch receives the cheque on 4 January and presents the same in the local clearing on the same day. If the cheque is not returned by the paying banker within the stipulated period, on 6 January (i.e., Day 2 considering 4 January as Day 0—the day on which cheque is deposited for local clearing) Anantapur branch of Corporation Bank passes on the credit to Hyderabad branch. Hyderabad branch marks the cheque as realized. In case the cheque is dishonoured, Anantapur branch returns the cheque to Hyderabad branch and the bank debits the account of the company.

ISSUES CONCERNING THE CASH MANAGER

The CMS banker charges a fee to the corporate for the service rendered. The fee for collection of local cheques is very minimum, which could range from 5 paise to 50 paise per ₹1,000 collected. The fee varies from location to location, metro and RBI clearing centres being the cheapest. In case of outstation cheques, the fee could range from ₹2 to ₹10 per ₹1,000 collected. The fees are often negotiable on the basis of volume of business provided to the CMS banker. Understanding this complexity of clearing system is very important to a company. A corporate with a marketing strategy of rural penetration often collects large volume of outstation cheques. The collection of these cheques are more costly, and fate of these cheques need to be carefully monitored by the company. A corporate with the strong brand and with the demand pull strategy can dictate terms to its clearing and forwarding (C&F) agents or dealers and can get payments done by way of demand drafts. Thus, the company can avoid utilizing outstation cheques clearing facility to reduce the cost of collection. A corporate can implement an effective cash management system only with the effective coordination of its marketing, finance and accounts functions.

ELECTRONIC PAYMENT SYSTEM

There are two prevalent modes of electronic payment service: electronic clearing service (ECS) and electronic funds transfer, both introduced by the RBI. In ECS (credit clearing), the corporate makes multiple payments (single debit, multiple credits) electronically instead of issuing large volume of paper instruments. The system is well suited for transactions such as issuing of dividend warrants, interest payments and so on. The minimum volume for payment is ₹2,500 per transaction and the maximum limit is ₹50 lakh per transaction. The service is available at 46 Indian cities. The ECS (debit clearing) is well suited for utility companies, where they collect large volume of small value payments (single credit, multiple debits) from their customers. The maximum limit for such transaction is ₹50 lakh. This service is available in 15 Indian cities.

CONCLUDING COMMENTS

Cash management is a worthwhile activity. This needs to be explicitly incorporated in the day-to-day functioning of a company. The following guidelines could be useful:

- Measure the cash flow timeline and assess the magnitude of savings that could result from alternative management strategies.
- Conduct an ongoing analysis of whether or not to take cash discount offered by suppliers.
- Release cheques according to payables policy.
- Exploit mail and presentation float by judiciously choosing the day of the week, time of the day and location of release.
- Resolve billing problems quickly.
- Develop regular schedule to follow up delinquent accounts.
- Computerize wherever required.
- Accelerate issue of invoice.
- Improve credit management.
- Negotiate better payment terms.
- Compare the length of timeline with that of other companies in the industry or standards set by the company.
- Assign responsibility to specific individuals and hold them responsible for unfavourable deviation from standards.
- Do not permit cash to stand idle for as much as a day.
- Banks are an important part of the cash system. Develop long-term relationships with them.
- Make every effort to speed up the flow of funds.
- Pay bills only when they fall due and instruct personnel in field offices to do the same.

EXERCISES

1. Prepare a cash forecast.
   The sales forecasts for Jan, Feb, March and April are given below:
   Jan ₹260 million
   Feb ₹280 million
   March ₹240 million
   April ₹300 million
   The company has historically experienced the following collection pattern: 50 per cent in the month of sales, 30 per cent in the following month and 15 per cent in the second month. Bad debt losses are 5 per cent. Raw material expenses are 50 per cent of sales with 40 per cent paid in the month of consumption and the rest in the following month. Salaries and wages are ₹10 million per month. Selling, administration and general expenses are ₹15.5 million per month.
2. A company receives cheques worth ₹800,000 every day and issues cheques for ₹200,000. If the cheque realization periods are eight days and five days, respectively, what will be the cash balance after 15 days? Assume that the initial cash balance is ₹1.2 million.
3. How would you quantify the benefits of operating a lock box system?
4. Explain the terms deposit float, disbursement float, riding the float and cash flow timeline.

5. How is a cash forecast different from a cash budget?
6. Explain the salient features of a lockbox system.
7. A company collects ₹8 million every day on average. The company is contemplating on instituting a lock box system. The new system could reduce its overall collection time by three and a half days. The system costs ₹240,000. Would you recommend the implementation? What is the saving under the new system? The company can make 15 per cent on its investment.
8. A company had sales of ₹40,000 in February and ₹60,000 in March. Forecast sales for April, May and June are ₹70,000, ₹100,000 and ₹90,000, respectively. The current cash balance as on 1 April is ₹5,000. Refer to the following data and estimate ending cash balance after three months.
    - Ten per cent of sales is for cash, 60 per cent of receivables to be collected one month later, 30 per cent after two months.
    - Other income in each month is ₹3,000
    - Purchases were ₹50,000, ₹80,000, ₹100,000 and ₹90,000, respectively, for February through June. Thirty per cent of purchase is for cash, 60 per cent will be paid in the following month and 10 per cent after two months.
    - Wages and salaries represent 5 per cent of the previous month's sales.
    - Monthly rent=₹2,500
    - Dividends amounting to ₹3,400 to be paid in May.
    - Taxes of ₹5,800 to be paid in April.
    - Capital expenditure of ₹500 to be incurred in June.
9. Excellent Manufacturing receives ₹40 million worth checks from its customers every day and takes about three days to clear them. It pays out ₹30 million every day and the customers take four days to clear them. Estimate processing and disbursement float for the company.

SUGGESTED READINGS

Beehler, Paul. *Contemporary Cash Management*. Hoboken, NJ: John Wiley and Sons, 1978.

Blanchard, O., F. Lopez-de-Silanes and A. Shleifer. 'What Do Firms Do with Cash Windfalls'. *Journal of Financial Economics* 36 (1994).

Harford, J. 'Corporate Cash Reserves and Acquisitions'. *Journal of Finance* 54 (1999).

Hill, N. C. and W. L. Sartoris. *Short-Term Financial Management*. New York, NY: Macmillan, 1988.

Kallberg, J. G. and K. L. Parkinson. *Current Asset Management: Cash, Credit and Inventory*. Hoboken, NJ: John Wiley and Sons, 1984.

Kallberg, J. G., K. L. Parkinson and J. R. Ochs, eds., *Essentials of Cash Management*. Newtown, CT: National Corporate Cash Management Association, 1989.

Mehta, Dilip. *Working Capital Management*. Upper Saddle River, NJ: Prentice Hall, 1974.

Opler, Tim, Lee Pinkowitz, Rene Stulz and Rohan Williamson. 'The Determinants and Implications of Corporate Cash Holdings'. *Journal of Financial Economics* 52 (1999).

CHAPTE

13

Receivables Management

LEARNING OBJECTIVES

- Highlight the motivations for credit sales and their impact on profit
- Discuss how to assess the risk of selling goods on credit
- Describe the components of credit policy and how to manage them

Credit facilitates sales. It is valuable to customers as it augments their resources. Accounts receivables arise out of selling goods on credit to customers. The value of goods sold on credit appears as accounts receivable under the current assets in the balance sheet at the end of the accounting year. Many companies sell goods on credit. Given below is an extract from the balance sheet of Lanco Infratech Ltd Lanco had ₹29,883 million worth of receivables in 2015–2016.

(₹ million)

Year	2016
Inventories	33,652.2
Sundry Debtors	29,883.4
Cash and Bank Balance	6,342.5
Loans and Advances	26,332.8
Total Current Assets	96,210.9
Current Liabilities	61,451.1
Provisions	992.1
Total Current Liabilities	62,443.2
Net Current Assets	33,767.7

In many companies, receivables management is restricted to phone calls by follow-up executives in the sales department. It is important to understand that a sale unpaid has an implicit cost. If it costs 13 per cent for a company to borrow, an unpaid sale of ₹1 million costs ₹13,000 p.a. in interest expense or ₹13/12 × 1 million per month. Yet receivables management may not receive the attention it deserves. The reason is simple. Sales executives focus on closing a sale, whereas credit information rests with the accounting staff. They live in different worlds.

MOTIVATIONS FOR CREDIT SALES

Three major motivating factors may be traced to the credit granting decision. First, selling on credit usually induces customers to buy more. The growth in sales revenue is usually considered a healthy situation. Second, as sales increase, profits generally increase as long as the benefits of granting credit exceeds costs. Third, credit sales could be a potential marketing tool. Other things remaining constant, credit terms could be used to differentiate from competitors or match the industry norms. In this chapter, we discuss how to estimate the impact of extending credit on profit, design a credit policy and assess the credit risk.

COST OF EXTENDING CREDIT

Three types of costs are involved in maintaining receivables, namely the cost of financing receivables, administrative and collection expenses and bad debt losses. Receivables must be financed from current income or new debt or equity. There is a cost attached to these. Firms will have to incur capital expenditure on computing equipment to maintain sales ledger and bear operating expenses such as salaries to staff, rent and so on. In addition, all customers may not pay on or before the due date. Some collection effort is required to prompt them, which involves additional expenses. Some of the accounts may turn bad resulting in bad debt losses. The effect of granting credit on profits is explained in the following text. Consider three companies. Company A sells on 60-day credit, B on 90-day credit and C on 120-day credit. As demonstrated in this example, net profit decreases when the credit period is extended to 120 days because the cost of financing outweighs the increase in profit on additional sales.

	A	B	C
Sales	120,000	180,000	210,000
Credit Period	60 days	90 days	120 days
Debtors	20,000	45,000	70,000
EBIT	6,000	9,000	10,500
Cost of Financing @13% p.a.	2.16%	3.25%	4.33%
i.e., 1.08% p.m. ₹	432	1,463	3,033
PBT ₹	5,568	7,537	7,967

DETERMINANTS OF CREDIT TERMS

One could think of a number of factors that might affect the credit terms of a company.

- Nature of Product and Industry: In capital equipment businesses (e.g., industrial boilers), customers typically make an advance payment to the company to manufacture a custom-built boiler. At the other extreme in some businesses, customers may get two months' credit or deferred payment. Most companies fall in this continuum. In case of hotels, customers pay concurrently as and when they consume service.
- Credit Terms of Suppliers: Companies that get generous credit from suppliers would be able to pass on at least a part of the benefit to the customers.
- Cash Flow Position: A company facing cash crunch would be working towards accelerating receipts rather than decelerating. So we would expect a company facing cash flow problems to enforce stricter credit terms.
- Structure of the Industry: In a buyer's market, other things remaining constant, a company may be guided by industry practices in granting credit.
- Volume of Sales Involved: The higher the offtake, the more generous would be the credit terms.
- Cost of Capital: A company can offer credit if the cost of capital is less than the benefits of sale. A higher cost of capital would discourage a company from offering credit.
- Character of the Customer: Prior experience with a customer gets reflected in credit terms offered by a company. Customers who make prompt payments get better terms than delinquent customers.

The sale may require a company to make payment in advance, or on receipt of invoice or delivery of goods or after the delivery at some specified point in future. Cash discounts are generally offered on invoice price if payment is made within the specified period. For instance, 2/10 net 30 implies that 2 per cent of discount is offered if the payment is made on or before 10 days; otherwise the payment is due in 30 days. The benefit of receiving early payment should outweigh the cost of cash discount offered. Put another way, the consideration in offering the cash discount is the financing cost saved on the 20 days against the cost of cash discount.

ASSESSING CREDIT RISK

In competitive markets, it might not be possible to confine to AAA-rated customers. As a result, it is necessary to define risk parameters and the conditions under which a company can trade with these marginal customers. Sound credit risk measurement leads to a fair assessment of probability of loss and the extent of follow-up action required. Companies spend substantial time and money in follow-up activities. These efforts can be saved if credit risk assessment procedure is rigorous. Usually, sales executives are appraised on the basis of volume of sales generated rather than realized cash.

Some of the elementary ways of assessing credit risk are:

- Obtaining bank reference (without the customer's knowledge)
- Obtaining reference from other reliable third parties
- Financial statement analysis
- Obtaining formal credit rating from agencies such as Dun & Bradstreet.

An analysis of profitability, solvency and activity ratios can also provide useful insight into the financial performance of the customer.

BAD DEBTS

Delinquent accounts are called bad debts. When there is reasonable certainty that a customer will not pay dues, it is prudent to write off the amount as bad debt loss. A company may have a policy of charging off a fixed percentage of credit sales as bad debt at the end of the accounting year. Selling goods on credit to high-risk customers may increase sales but it will also depress profits if the accounts turn bad. Of course, it is possible that a bad debt may be recovered at a later point in time. But conservatism requires a company not to book profits until they are reasonably certain.

The impact of bad debt on profit will not be the same for all companies. It depends on the cost structure, that is, the operating leverage. A company with high fixed costs can gain by selling to marginal customers (assuming that fixed costs have been recovered already) as the next rupee of sales has to recover only the variable costs. A company with high variable costs does not profit much from selling to marginal customers. Any bad debt loss will offset the increase in revenue.

Aging Schedule

		Aging in ₹ Hundred Thousand (%)			
Month	Receivables (₹ million)	0	1	2	3
May	3.5	21 (60)*	3.5 (10)	7 (20)	3.5 (10)
June	4.0	26 (65)	6 (15)	5 (12.5)	3 (7.5)
July	4.2	25 (59)	7 (16)	6 (14)	4 (9.5)
August	4.5	28 (62)	9 (20)	5 (11)	3 (7)

Note: *Figures in bracket indicate receivables as percentage of total receivables outstanding in that month.

The aging schedule provides a snapshot of receivables outstanding for various periods. As shown in the aging schedule, the total receivables outstanding in May was ₹3.5 million out of which 10 per cent was overdue for three months, 20 per cent for two months and 10 per cent for one month.

For the purposes of monitoring, the data available in the aging schedule could be converted into measures of effectiveness of credit policy such as average collection period (ACP) and DSO.

If the company has an annual sales of ₹48.6 million, average daily sales is ₹133,000 (=486/365)

$$\text{DSO in May} = 35/1.33 = 26.3 \text{ days}$$
$$\text{DSO in June} = 40/1.33 = 30 \text{ days}$$

If the DSO is within the normal limits specified by the company, the situation is considered normal. Otherwise, follow-up action needs to be taken. A variant of DSO, the ACP, measures the average number of days required to realize cash.

$$\text{ACP} = (\text{Proportion of Customers Taking Cash Discount} \times \text{Discount Period}) + (\text{Proportion of Customers Not Taking Cash Discount} \times \text{Credit Period})$$

Thus, under a 1/10 net 30 credit policy, if 30 per cent of customers take discount,

$$ACP = (0.3 \times 10 + 0.7 \times 30) = 24 \text{ days.}$$

CLASSIFICATION OF CUSTOMERS

Customers can be classified into various risk categories on the basis of creditworthiness. Customers may be placed into five or six categories so that appropriate credit limit may be fixed. A company could follow a credit rating system adopted by rating agencies such as CRISIL. To illustrate, five risk categories may be constructed as shown in Table 13.1.

Each customer may be awarded a symbol as shown earlier. It is quite possible that customers may jump from one category to another due to improvement or deterioration in financial condition. This calls for reclassification at periodic intervals. Formal guidelines may be developed to guide executive decision-making. For instance, a company may restrict itself to the top two or four categories based on its risk-taking ability. It is important to communicate the company's policy to executives who actually transact. In the absence of guidelines, executives may grant credit to companies with dubious record. The amount involved in each trade may be small at the individual level. At the aggregate level, the amount involved could be substantial forcing a company into distress.

COMPONENTS OF CREDIT POLICY

A firm's credit policy has four variables. They are: credit period, cash discount, credit standard and the collection effort. Changing any of these variables will require additional investment. For instance, lengthening the credit period from 30 days to 45 days with the objective of increasing sales involves additional investment in receivables. Some of the customers may not pay dues resulting in bad debt losses. So an analysis of the credit policy essentially involves comparison of incremental benefits and incremental costs of the new policy. Initially, we will treat the four variables as independent and ascertain their impact on profit. Once the impact of altering any of these variables is clear, we would be in a better position to understand their combined impact.

TABLE 13.1
Classification of Customers

Category	Symbol	Explanation
Negligible risk	AAA	Companies with reputation for prompt payment Strong market and financial position Cash rich Governmental organizations
High safety	AA	Credit risk marginally lower than AAA customers
Adequate	BBB	Companies that are normally prompt
Risky	BB	Companies in extreme volatile businesses, profitability based on dubious schemes and so on
High risk	C	Companies in distress, financial reorganization

CREDIT PERIOD

Lengthening the credit period will generally induce new customers to buy. Existing customers may increase their offtake. The increase in credit period requires additional investment in receivables. There will be an increase in profits due to an increase in sales. There may or may not be additional bad debt losses depending on the creditworthiness of customers. If we assume that fixed costs have already been recovered or no additional fixed costs will be incurred, each rupee of sales contribute to recovery of variable cost and profit. Consider the following data.

$$\text{Current Sales} = ₹1{,}000 \text{ million}$$
$$\text{(ACPo) Credit Period} = 30 \text{ days}$$
$$\text{Cost of Capital} = 15\%$$
$$\text{(ACPn) Proposed Credit Period} = 45 \text{ days}$$
$$\text{Anticipated Increase in Sales} = 10\% = ₹100 \text{ million} \quad (1)$$
$$\text{Contribution/Sales} = 0.2$$
$$\text{Additional Profit on New Sales} = \text{New Sales} \times \text{Contribution/Sales}$$
$$= ₹100 \times 0.2 \text{ million}$$
$$= ₹20 \text{ million}$$

Increase in Receivable on Existing Sales:

$$\frac{(\text{ACPn} - \text{ACPo})}{360} \times \text{Current Sales}$$
$$= ₹15/360 \times 1{,}000 \text{ million} \quad (2)$$
$$= ₹4.2 \text{ million}$$

$$\text{Investment in Receivable on New Sales} = \text{New Receivables} \times \frac{\text{Variable Cost}}{\text{Sales}}$$
$$= \text{New Sales} \times \frac{45}{360} \times \frac{\text{Variable Cost}}{\text{Sales}}$$

But
$$V/S = (1 - C/S)$$

$$= ₹100 \text{ million} \times \frac{45}{360} \times 0.8 \quad (3)$$
$$= ₹10 \text{ million}$$

$$\text{Total New Investment in Receivables} = \text{Increase in Receivables} \times \text{Cost of Capital}$$
$$= ₹52 \times 0.16 = ₹8.32 \text{ million}$$

Since the additional profit (₹20 million) is greater than the additional cost of maintaining receivables, the lengthening of credit period should be considered.

CASH DISCOUNT

The purpose of offering cash discount was briefly discussed earlier. A credit term of 1/10 net 30 implies that 1 per cent discount is offered if the payment is made by the 10th day, otherwise the payment is due by the 30th day. The benefits of offering higher discount are:

- Customers may pay up early to avail cash discount. So the cost of maintaining receivable decreases.
- Additional sales may be generated resulting in profits.

The costs are:

- Additional cash discount to be paid
- Additional investment in receivables arising out of new sales.

Suppose a company has a cost of capital of 16.5 per cent, the average credit sales is ₹100 million. The terms of sale are: 2/10 Net 45.

The seller will receive

- ₹100 million less discount of 2 per cent on day 10 or
- ₹100 million on Day 45

The PV of (a) is:

$$\frac{100 \text{ million } (1-0.02)}{[1+(10/365)\times 0.165]} = ₹97.56 \text{ million} \tag{4}$$

The PV of (b) is:

$$\frac{100 \text{ million}}{[1+(45/365)\times 0.165]} = ₹98 \text{ million} \tag{5}$$

Net Benefit = (5) − (4) = ₹0.44 million

Consider an extended example.

Current Sales = ₹1,000 million
Current Credit Policy = 1/10 Net 30
C/S Ratio = 0.2
Cost of Capital = 16%
New Credit Policy = 2/10 Net 30
Anticipated Increase in Sales = 10%
= ₹100 million

Forty per cent of customers are availing cash discount now. Sixty per cent of customers are expected to avail cash discount after the introduction of the new policy. Assume that the average collection period remains the same at 20 days.

$$\begin{aligned}\text{Profit on New Sales} &= \Delta\,\text{Sales} \times \text{C/S}\\ &= ₹100 \text{ million} \times 0.2\\ &= ₹20 \text{ million}\end{aligned} \qquad (6)$$

$$\begin{aligned}\text{Current Discount} &= ₹1{,}000 \times 0.4 \times 0.01\\ &= ₹4 \text{ million.}\end{aligned} \qquad (7)$$

$$\begin{aligned}\text{New Discount} &= ₹1{,}100 \times 0.6 \times 0.02\\ &= ₹13.2 \text{ cr.}\end{aligned} \qquad (8)$$

$$\text{Additional Cash Discount} = (8) - (7) = ₹13.2 - 4 = ₹9.2 \text{ million} \qquad (9)$$

Cost of capital tied up in new receivables:

$$\begin{aligned}&= ₹100 \text{ million} \times \frac{20 \text{ days}}{360 \text{ days}} \times 0.6 \times 0.16\\ &= ₹0.53 \text{ million}\end{aligned} \qquad (10)$$

Incremental Cost $= (9) + (10) = ₹9.2$ million $+ ₹0.53$ million $= ₹9.73$ million
Benefit $= ₹20$ million

Since the benefit exceeds cost, the new policy should be adopted. The increase in profit and reduction in collection period should be significant to justify a change in policy. The benefit of offering a discount, from the seller's perspective, is receiving the funds earlier, while the cost is the discount given to the buyer to encourage early payment. A company offering cash discount would want to know the likely outflow due to cash discount.

Outflow Due to Cash Discount (In Rupees) = [Percentage of Customers Opting for Cash Discount × Credit Sales × Percentage Discount]

One could look at past data to assess the percentage of customers opting for cash discount. Suppose, historically 40 per cent of customers have opted for cash discount, on a sale of ₹10 million, a 2 per cent discount would lead to an outflow of $0.4 \times 10\text{m} \times 0.02 = ₹80{,}000$

BUYER'S PERSPECTIVE

Let us suppose the credit terms are 2/10 net 45. The cost of short-term funds for the company is 11 per cent. The terms imply that the buyer can either make payment in 10 days and receive a 2 per cent discount or pay within 45 days, thereby forgoing cash discount.

$$\text{Cost of forgoing discount in ₹} = \text{Discount} \times \text{Selling Price} \qquad (11)$$

$$\text{Financing Received if Discount is Taken} = (100 - \text{Discount})\ \text{Price} \tag{12}$$

$$\text{Rate per Period} = \frac{\text{Rupee Cost}}{\text{Financing Received}}$$

$$= \frac{d \times P}{(100 - d)P}$$

$$= \frac{d}{100 - d}$$

$$\text{Financing Period} = \text{Payment Period} - \text{Discount Period} \tag{13}$$

$$\text{No. of Periods per Year} = \frac{\text{Days per Year}}{\text{Financing Period}}$$

$$= \frac{365}{\text{Payment Period} - \text{Discount Period}} \tag{14}$$

$$\text{Annual Interest Rate} = \text{Rate per Period} \times \text{No. of Periods}$$

$$= \frac{d}{100 - d} \times \frac{365}{\text{Pay Period} - \text{Discount Period}}$$

$$\text{Effective Cost of Discount} = \frac{d}{1 - d} \times \frac{365}{n - t}$$

where d = discount in decimal form
n = credit period
t = discount period

$$\text{Effective Cost of Discount} = \frac{0.02}{1 - 0.02} \times \frac{365}{45 - 10}$$
$$= 21.2 \text{ per cent}$$

The company should accept the discount as the cost of not taking the discount (21.2%) is much higher than the cost of short-term funds (11%). The company will be better off by borrowing short term at 11 per cent and taking the discount.

CREDIT STANDARDS

Credit standards are norms prescribed by the company with respect to the creditworthiness of the customers. A company may have the policy of extending credit to only these customers with highest credit rating. Another company may be relatively generous in extending credit to marginal customers. Extending credit to the less creditworthy increases sales volume. But the probability of bad debt loss increases. The increase in profit on new sales should outweigh the cumulative bad debt losses to justify the relaxation of credit standards. To illustrate, a company that currently restricts it to the first two categories (described earlier) could relax the standards by selling to customers under the next two categories.

The consequence of relaxing standards are:

- The incremental profit on incremental sales
- New investment in additional receivables
- Increase in bad debt losses

Consider the following data.

Current Sales = ₹1,000 million
Anticipated Increase in Sales = 10 per cent
C/S = 0.2
Cost of Capital = 16 per cent
Anticipated Bad Debt Loss = 10 per cent of New Sales
Average Collection Period = 30 days

- Incremental Profit on New Sales

= New Sales × C/S
= ₹100 million × 0.2 = ₹20 million

- Cost of Financing Increment Receivables

= Cost of Capital × Investment in Receivables
= Cost of Capital × (Receivables × V/S)
= Cost of Capital × ΔSales × ACP/360 × V/S
= 0.16 × ₹100 million × 30/360 × 0.8
= ₹106 million

- Additional Bad Debt Loss

= ₹0.1 × ₹100 million
= ₹10 million
Incremental Cost = ₹11.06 million
Incremental Benefit = ₹20 million

Therefore, the new policy should be accepted.

A COMPREHENSIVE ILLUSTRATION

A company currently has a 2/10 net 35 policy. The marketing executives of the company propose to change the credit policy. Details of current policy are given below.

Current Sales = ₹1 million
Current Credit Terms = 2/10 net 35
Current Bad Debt Loss = 1 per cent of Gross Sales

Sixty per cent of customers who pay take the discount, that is, 0.99×0.6=0.594 or 59.4 per cent of all customers

ACP=20 Days
Variable Costs=70 per cent of Sales, that is, V/S=0.7 [1–V/S=C/S=0.3]
Cost of Capital=15 per cent

There is productive capacity to support 40 per cent increase in sales.

New Policy

The new policy involves more liberal attitude towards granting credit. The summary of the new policy is given as follows.

- New Credit Term=3/10 net 60
- More Liberal Attitude Towards Granting Credit
- Anticipated Increase in Sales=20 per cent (₹200,000 p.a.)
- New ACP=35 Days
- Fifty per cent of the Paying Customers Will Take the Discount
- Bad Debt Loss=5 per cent of Total Sales

New Sales=₹1.2 million

The desirability of moving towards a new policy can be assessed by comparing the costs and benefits of relaxing credit standards.

- Profit on New Sales=₹200,000×C/S=₹200,000×0.2=₹40,000
- Current Cash Discount=₹1 million×0.594×0.02=₹11,880

Cash Discount under Proposal Policy=(0.95×12 L)×0.5×0.03=₹17,100
Increase in Cash Discount=₹17,100–₹11,850=₹5,220

- Current Bad Debt Loss=1 per cent of ₹1 million=₹10,000

New Bad Debt Losses=5 per cent of ₹1.2 million=₹60,000
Increase in Bad Debt Losses=₹50,000
Old Credit Period=35 Days
New Credit Period=60 Days
Old ACP=20 Days
New ACP=35 Days

- Additional Receivables = Increase in Revenue × $\frac{\text{Collection Period}}{360}$

$$=₹200{,}000\times\frac{35}{360}$$

$$=₹19{,}444$$

$$\text{Investment in Receivables} = \text{Receivables} \times \text{V/S}$$
$$= ₹19{,}444 \times 0.7 = ₹13{,}610$$
$$\text{Cost of Financing} = ₹13{,}610 \times 0.15 = ₹2{,}041$$

Increase in Receivables on Existing Sales:

$$= (ACP_N - ACP_0) \times \text{Sales}/360$$
$$= 15/360 \times ₹1 \text{ million}$$
$$= ₹41{,}666$$

Cost of Financing the Increase in Receivables on Existing Sales = ₹41,666 × 0.15 = ₹6,250
Cost of Proposed Policy = Increase in Cash Discount + Increase in Bad Debt Loss + Cost of Financing Additional Receivables + Cost of Financing the Increase in Receivables on Existing Sales

$$= ₹5{,}220 + ₹50{,}000 + ₹2{,}041 + ₹6{,}250 = ₹63{,}511$$
$$\text{Profit} = ₹40{,}000$$

Since the profit is less than the costs, the new policy should not be accepted.

Let us suppose there is a compromise policy.

New Credit Terms = 3/10 net 45
Increase in Sales = ₹110,000 or New Sales = ₹1,110,000
Bad Debt Loss = 3 per cent of Sales

Fifty-five per cent of paying customers will take the discount and the remaining 45 per cent will pay on 45th day.

$$\text{Average Credit Period} = (0.55 \times 10) + (0.45 \times 45)$$
$$= 25 \text{ days}$$

- Profit on New Sales = New Sales × C/S = ₹110,000 × 0.2 = ₹22,000
- Current Cash Discount = ₹11,880

$$\text{Cash Discount under Compromise Policy} = (0.97 \times 1{,}110{,}000) \times 0.55 \times 0.03$$
$$= ₹17{,}765.55$$
$$\text{Incremental Cash Discount} = ₹5{,}885.55$$

- Current Bad Debt Losses = ₹10,000

$$\text{On Compromise Policy} = 0.03 \times 1{,}110{,}000$$
$$= ₹33{,}000$$
$$\text{Incremental Bad Debt Loss} = ₹23{,}300$$
$$\text{Old ACP} = 20 \text{ days}$$
$$\text{New ACP} = 25 \text{ days}$$

- Increase in Receivable on Existing Sales

$$= (ACP_N - ACP_o) \times \frac{\text{Sales}}{360}$$

$$= (5 \text{ days}) \times \frac{₹1 \text{ million}}{360}$$

$$= ₹13{,}000$$

Cost of Financing $= ₹13{,}000 \times 0.15 = ₹2{,}000$

- Additional Receivables $=$ Increase in Revenue $\times \frac{\text{Average Collection Period}}{360}$

$$= ₹110{,}000 \times \frac{25}{360}$$

Investment in Additional Receivables $= [7{,}638.88] \times V/S = [7{,}638.88] \times 0.7$
$= ₹5{,}347.20$

Cost of Financing Additional Receivables $= (5{,}347.20) \times 0.15$
$= ₹802$

Since the costs of policy exceed benefits, the policy should not be accepted.

RECEIVABLES SECURITIZATION

Companies short of cash due to credit sales may resort to securitization of receivables to realize cash. Securitization is a process by which illiquid assets can be transformed into liquid form and distributed to a broad range of investors through the capital market. It involves packaging of loans and receivables and the underwriting and sale of these packages to investors in the form of securities that are collateralized by the underlying assets and their associated income stream. A number of homogeneous receivables are pooled together to form a basket and then sold or passed through to another institution called special purpose vehicle (SPV). The assets are removed from the balance sheet of the originator. The SPV then unbundles these units and sells them to investors. These securities are called pass-through certificates (PTC). The PTC is designed in such a way that the cash outflow in the form of interest and redemption of PTC synchronize with the aggregate inflow of interest and principal of the basket of loans. The securitization of hire purchase (HP) portfolio of automotive manufacturers and non-bank finance companies by banks such as Citibank is an example of HP securitization.

CONCLUDING REMARKS

It is important to understand the strategic role of credit policy in marketing. Other things remaining constant, credit policy could be used as a differentiating tool to achieve sales objectives. This chapter provides an analytic framework for analysing the impact of changing credit policy on profit. Of course, real-life situations could be more complex than what is illustrated here. Many things can go wrong in real world. For instance, bad debt losses may be higher than anticipated; the increase in sales may not meet projections; the ACP may deviate significantly from the estimate and so on. The important message is that executives must work towards making things happen. That calls for communication with all concerned executives. The best way to obtain their consent is to involve them in the credit granting decision.

EXERCISES

1. Explain the term: 2/10 net 30
   1/10 net 45
   Net 30
2. Refer to the data in the comprehensive illustration in the chapter. What should be the level of sales to justify a switch to the new credit policy? At what cost of capital can the company switch to the new policy? Hold other variables constant. Come up with a new policy for the company assuming that the increase in sales will be the same as that under the new policy given in the question. Conduct an analysis of sensitivity of profits to changes in underlying policy variables.
3. What financial ratios would help the most in assessing creditworthiness?
4. Explain the terms: average credit period, aging schedule, cash discount and bad debt loss.
5. What does the aging schedule not tell you?
6. What factors affect the choice of credit policy variables such as cash discount, credit period and credit standards?
7. A firm currently sells 10,000 all-terrain bicycles each at a price of ₹4,000. The variable cost per cycle is ₹3,520. The firm makes all sales on credit and ACP is 36 days. If the firm adopts a more relaxed policy, sales would increase by 10 per cent and the ACP will increase to 60 days. If the cost of capital is 15 per cent, would you recommend the relaxed policy?
8. A company currently sells goods on credit but offers no cash discount. The company is contemplating on offering a 2 per cent cash discount for payment prior to 15 days. The current ACP is 60 days, sales are 20,000 units, selling price is ₹22 and the variable cost is ₹18. The company expects 70 per cent of its customers to take cash discount if it initiated the new policy, sales to increase to 21,000 units, the ACP to drop to 45 days and bad debt expenses to remain at zero. If the cost of capital is 20 per cent, should the company offer discount?
9. A company is contemplating a change in its credit policy that is expected to increase its bad debt expense from 1 per cent to 3 per cent of sales. Current sales are 25,000 units; selling price per unit is ₹11 and the variable cost per unit is ₹7. The firm expects to sell 27,000 units.
   a. Calculate bad debts under the present and proposed plan.
   b. If the firm expects savings of ₹3,500 from the proposed plan, would you recommend its implementation?
10. A company is considering lengthening its credit period from 30 to 60 days. The firm currently sells 15,000 units @₹3. The ACP is 40 days; bad debts are ½ per cent; variable cost is ₹2.30. The change in credit period is expected to increase sales to 17,000 units; the bad debt expense to 2 per cent and increase ACP to 72 days. If the cost of capital is 18 per cent, would you recommend the change?

11. A company currently sells 72,000 units @ ₹32. Other data is given as follows:

Current Bad Debt Expense = 3 per cent
Collection Expenditure = ₹20,000
ACP = 58 days
Variable Cost = ₹25

The firm is contemplating on spending an additional ₹40,000 on collections to reduce bad debt expenses to 1 per cent and ACP to 40 days. As a result of stricter collection policy, sales is expected to decrease to 71,000 units. If the cost of capital is 19 per cent, would you recommend the new policy?

SUGGESTED READINGS

Beckman, T. N. and R. S. Foster. *Credits and Collections: Management and Theory*, 8th ed. New York, NY: McGraw Hill, 1969.

Brennan, M., V. Makismovic and J. Zechner. 'Vendor Financing'. *Journal of Finance* (1988 December).

Cole. *Consumer and Commercial Credit Management*, 8th ed. Homewood, IL: Richard D Irwin Inc., 1987.

Edwards, H. *Credit Management Handbook*, 2nd ed. Surrey: Gower Publishing Co Ltd, 1985.

Mian, S. and C. Smith. 'Accounts Receivable Management Policy: Theory and Evidence'. *Journal of Finance* 47, no. 1 (1992).

Petersen, M. and R. Rajan. 'Trade Credit: Theories and Evidence'. *Review of Financial Studies* 10, no. 3 (1997).

SECTION 4

The Financing Decision

CHAPTER

14

Optimal Capital Structure

LEARNING OBJECTIVES

- How do managers make financing decisions?
- Does debt policy matter?
- Relation between capital structure and capital costs
- Impact of taxes on debt policy
- Impact of debt on investment, financing and dividend decisions of a firm
- How does debt policy vary across countries?
- Impact of changes in capital structure on security prices

Debt ratios vary across industries and companies. For instance, in 2018, ITC did not have any debt, whereas Tata Motors had significant amount of debt (see Table 14.1).[1] Is there an optimal level of debt for a company? What are the consequences of borrowing? How do firms figure out whether they have too much or too little debt? The theory of capital structure attempts to explain the mix of securities and financing sources used by corporations to finance investment.

Consider a firm that has no debt in the capital structure, that is, it is all equity financed. The ROE for this company now and at various debt levels is shown in Table 14.2. As can be seen from Table 14.2, the ROE increases as debt ratio increases. But is this increase without a cost?

[1] At the time of writing.

TABLE 14.1
Debt/Equity Ratios

Company	Sector	2015	2016	2017	2018
Ashok Leyland Ltd	Automotive	0.82	0.45	0.35	0.14
Bajaj Auto Ltd	Automotive	0.01	0.01	0.01	0.01
Hero MotoCorp Ltd	Automotive	0	0	0	0
Mahindra & Mahindra Ltd	Automotive	0.19	0.13	0.11	0.1
Tata Motors Ltd	Automotive	1.44	0.71	0.92	0.92
Britannia Industries Ltd	FMCG	0.01	0.01	0	0.01
Dabur India Ltd	FMCG	0.06	0.03	0.08	0.07
Emami Ltd	FMCG	0.02	0.43	0.26	0.15
Future Consumer Ltd	FMCG	0.59	0.61	0.35	0.42
Hindustan Unilever Ltd	FMCG	0	0	0	0
ITC Ltd	FMCG	0.002	0.001	0.001	0

Source: Prowess Database.

DOES DEBT POLICY MATTER?

The theory of capital structure starts with the Modigliani and Miller theorem that debt policy does not matter. The market value balance sheet of a company is given in Table 14.2.

Liabilities	Assets
Equity	Assets in Place
Debt	Present Value of Future Growth Opportunities
Firm Value	V

Franco Modigliani and Merton Miller (MM hereafter) were among the first to rigorously analyse the capital structure decision. They analysed the effect of a change in the firm's capital structure on the market value of the firm, first in a hypothetical world with no corporate taxes and then in a world with corporate taxes. They proved that the value of the firm, V, is independent of the debt policy of the firm, that is, V is constant regardless of the mix of D and E as long as the right-hand side of the balance sheet (i.e., real assets or projects) is held constant. Their theorem is based on certain assumptions.

- Investment opportunities of the firm remain fixed. Corporate real investment and operating decisions are not affected by capital structure.
- The business risk of a firm can be measured by the standard deviation of earnings and firms can be grouped into distinct business risk classes.
- Investors have homogeneous expectations about future corporate earnings and the volatility of these earnings.
- Capital markets are perfect. There are no transaction costs and taxes. Investors can borrow at the same rate as companies.
- Debt is risk free and the interest rate on debt is the risk-free rate.
- There are no bankruptcy and reorganization costs.

TABLE 14.2
ROE at Various Debt Levels

	Debt/Capital (₹)			
	0 %	10%	20%	30%
Equity	10,000	9,000	8,000	7,000
Debt	0	1,000	2,000	3,000
Total Capital	10,000	10,000	10,000	10,000
EBIT	3,000	3,000	3,000	3,000
Interest @15%	0	150	300	450
PBT	3,000	2,850	2,700	2,550
Tax @35%	1,050	997.50	945	892.50
PAT	1,950	1,852.50	1,755	1,657.50
ROE (%)	19.5	20.5	21.90	23.60

MM argue that the market value of the firm is determined by the magnitude and risk of cash flows generated by the firm's assets. The firm's capital structure merely indicates how this stream of cash flows is divided between shareholders and bondholders. Stated in a different fashion, it is the magnitude and risk (volatility) of cash flow stream and not it is partitioning between shareholders and bondholders that determines the market value of the firm. Whether you cut a pizza into six or eight slices will not 'increase' the size of the pizza. The same is true of companies as well. In other words, companies can make money by good 'investment' decisions and not good 'financing' decisions.

Since the company has already decided on which projects it should undertake and all investors agree upon the expected cash flows and the appropriate discount rate to discount these cash flows, the firm must sell for the present value of project cash flows whether it is 50 per cent debt financed or all equity financed.

Size of the Corporate Pie = PV of Cash Flows
100 per cent Equity = 50 per cent Debt

Consider two firms that are similar in all respects except for their capital structure. One firm is all equity financed and the other has 50 per cent debt carrying an interest of 12 per cent. Both the companies employ ₹500,000 and generate earnings of ₹125,000. There are no taxes. The effect of injecting debt on firm value is shown in Table 14.3. In a world without taxes, the decision to borrow will not affect firm value. Let us suppose, the optimal capital structure for a company is 70 per cent equity (30% debt) that maximizes the firm value, say, PV. But managers resort to a sub-optimal capital structure due to which the firm value is only 0.9 PV. If this happens, investors can buy the firm for 0.9 PV, repackage securities to attain the optimal capital structure, sell the company for PV. The difference of 0.1 PV is the riskless profit. Under competitive conditions, it is not possible to make riskless profit as demonstrated in the previous example.

The WACC for a firm is:

$$r_A = r_D \cdot (D/V) + r_E(E/V) \qquad (1)$$

TABLE 14.3
Effect of Leverage on Firm Value

		(in ₹)
	Firm A	Firm B
Equity	500	250
Debt	0	250
Total Capital	500	500
EBIT	125	125
Interest @12%	0	30
PBT	125	95
Tax	0	0
PAT	125	95
Income to Investors		
Dividends	125	95
Interest	0	30
Total	125	125

Since equity investors bear financial risk in addition to business risk, the cost of equity will be more than the cost of debt. Will the inclusion of debt, which has a lower cost, not reduce the WACC? MM argue that an increase in financial leverage increases the systematic risk (of the firm's stock) that equity investors have to bear. Being risk-averse, equity investors will demand a corresponding increase in the ROE. The increase in the cost of equity will exactly offset the effect of lower cost of debt. Likewise, decrease in financial leverage will not increase the WACC, as the reduction will result in an offsetting decrease in the cost of equity due to lower systematic risk. So the WACC is the same at all debt levels.

To prove the proposition, let us rewrite Equation (1):

$$r_E = r_A + (r_A - r_D)D/E \tag{2}$$

This equation suggests that the cost of equity increases with D/E and the spread between r_A and r_D.

Yogi Berra on the M&M Proposition[2]

When a waitress asked Yogi Berra (Baseball Hall of Fame Catcher for the New York Yankees) whether he wanted his pizza cut into four pieces or eight, Yogi replied, 'Better make it 4, I don't think I can eat 8'. Yogi's quip helps convey the basic insight of MM. The firm's leverage choice 'slices' the distribution of the firm's future cash flows in a way that is like slicing a pizza. MM recognize that if you fix a company's investment activities, it is like fixing the size of the pizza; no information costs means that everyone sees the same pizza; no taxes means the Internal Revenue Service (IRS) gets none of the pie and no 'contracting' cost means nothing sticks to the knife. And so, just as the substance of Yogi's meal is unaffected by whether the pizza is sliced into four pieces or eight, the economic substance of the firm is unaffected by whether the liability side of the balance sheet is sliced to include more or less debt.

[2] Barclay, Smith and Watts, 'The Determinants of Leverage and Dividend Policies'.

FIGURE 14.1
Debt Policy and the Cost of Capital

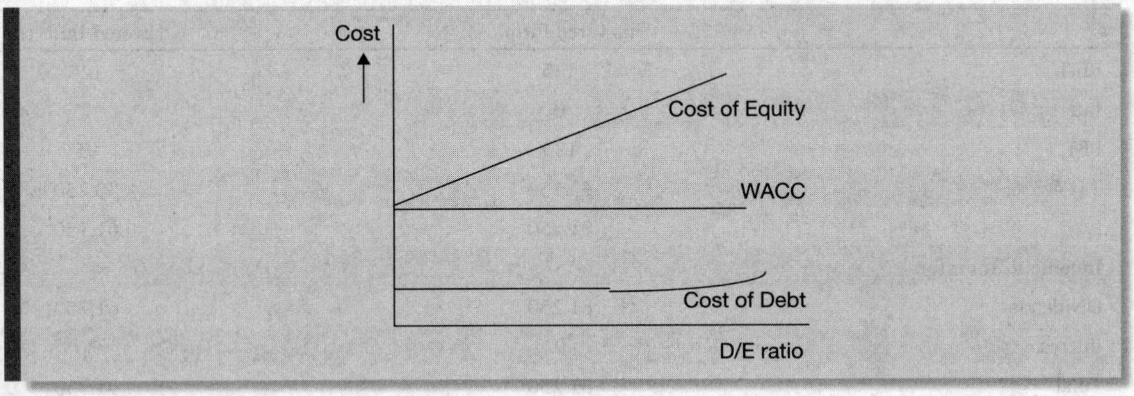

FIGURE 14.2
Non-Linear Relation

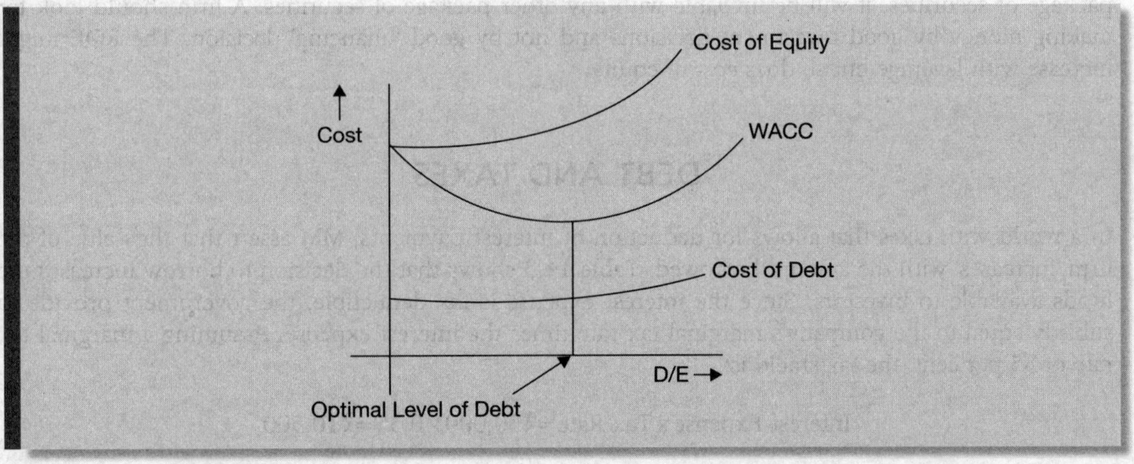

MM's Proposition II on the impact of debt policy on the cost of capital is shown in Figure 14.1. The argument sounds plausible. But is it credible? If financing is indeed irrelevant, why do companies hire management graduates paying them hefty salaries to manage the left-hand side of the balance sheet? Why do they see so many new securities? Their critics argue that injecting debt into the capital structure will cause an increase in the cost of equity that is less than that predicted by MM. As the firm borrows more, the increase in cost of equity will be greater than that predicted by MM. As a result, the graph of cost of capital versus debt ratio is U-shaped. Figure 14.2 illustrates this point.

In sum, the WACC is independent of leverage in a MM world without taxes. How you finance a project is only a matter of detail. It has no bearing on firm value. If a project is unviable with one

TABLE 14.3
Debt and Taxes (₹)

	Unlevered Firm (A)	Levered Firm (B)
EBIT	125	125
Interest @12%	0	30
PBT	125	95
Tax @35%	43.750	33.250
PAT	81.250	61.750
Income to Investors		
Dividends	81.250	61.750
Interest	0	30
Total	81.250	91.750

package of securities, it will be unviable with any other package of securities. A firm should look for making money by good investment decisions and not by good 'financing' decision. The ROE might increase with leverage but so does cost of equity.

DEBT AND TAXES

In a world with taxes that allows for deduction of interest payments, MM assert that the value of the firm 'increases' with the amount borrowed. Table 14.3 shows that the decision to borrow increases the funds available to investors. Since the interest expense is tax deductible, the government provides a subsidy equal to the company's marginal tax rate times the interest expense. Assuming a marginal tax rate of 35 per cent, the tax shield is:

$$\text{Interest Expense} \times \text{Tax Rate} = ₹30{,}000 \times 0.35 = ₹10{,}500$$

The difference in value of ₹10.50 as shown in Table 14.3 is the tax advantage of debt. The return to shareholders increases and the market value of the firm rises. The increase in market value is the present value of tax savings generated by debt.

$$\text{Tax Shield per Year} = \text{Interest Expense per Year} \times \text{Corporate Tax Rate}$$
$$= r \times D \times T_c$$

where r = interest rate on debt

D = amount borrowed

T_c = marginal tax rate

If debt is permanent, present value of tax shield

$$PV = [(r \times D \times T_c)/r]$$
$$= T_c \times D$$

The present value is obtained by discounting the perpetual stream of interest tax shield at the cost of debt. We have used cost of debt as the discount rate on the assumption that tax shields are about as risky as interest payments generating them. The idea is that the discount rate should be commensurate with the riskiness of the cash flow. Assume that a firm borrows ₹4 million at 15 per cent. The marginal tax rate for the firm is 35 per cent. The present value of tax shields assuming perpetual debt is

$$V = [(0.15 \times 4 \times 0.35)/0.15]$$
$$= ₹1.4 \text{ million}$$

Likewise, if the debt has a tenor of seven years, the present value of tax shields can be estimated as follows:

$$PV = (0.15 \times 4 \times 0.35) \text{ PVIFA}(15, 7) = ₹800{,}000$$

Extending the previous reasoning, the value of a levered firm will exceed that of the unlevered firm by an amount equal to the present value of tax shields. If debt is permanent (or rolled over forever),

$$V_L = V_U + T \times D$$

where V_L = value of a levered firm
V_U = value of an unlevered firm

The value of the firm increases with debt and reaches a peak when the debt ratio is 100 per cent. Of course, this is a hypothetical situation. If debt is so valuable, why is it that firms do not resort to 100 per cent debt financing? The answer lies in the problems of debt—agency and bankruptcy costs. These are discussed later.

THE IMPACT OF LEVERAGE AND TAXES ON WACC

Since interest is a tax deductible expense, the after-tax cost of debt is much lower. To illustrate, if the interest is 14 per cent and tax rate is 35 per cent, the after-tax cost of debt is 14 (1−0.35). In the absence of debt, shareholders are subjected only to business risk as measured by the volatility of operating earnings. The addition of debt to a firm's capital structure increases the risk borne by the shareholders. The additional risk premium is the financial risk premium.

The expected return

$$E(R) = \text{Risk-Free Rate} + \text{Business Risk Premium} + \text{Financial Risk Premium}$$

If a firm has no debt, the stock's beta reflects just the business risk. This (version of) beta is called unlevered beta. With financial leverage, the stock's beta reflects both business and financial risk. This (version of) beta is called levered beta.

The cost of levered equity can be expressed as the sum of cost of unlevered equity and a premium for additional financial risk

= Cost of Unlevered Equity + Premium Based on After-Tax Differential Between Cost of Unlevered Equity and Cost of Debt and Leverage

Let Cost of Levered Equity = K_{LE}
Cost of Unlevered Equity = K_{UE}
Cost of Debt = K_d

$$K_{LE} = K_{UE} + (K_{UE} - K_d)(1 - T)D/E \quad (3)$$

The cost of equity increases as leverage increases but at a slower rate. The increase in cost of equity is due to the increase in volatility of stock returns. An important research by Robert Hamada shows that the relationship between levered and unlevered beta is:

$$\beta_L = \beta_U\ [1 + (1 - T)D/E] \quad (4)$$

where β_L = levered beta (beta at the current level of debt)
β_U = unlevered beta (beta when there is no debt in the capital structure)

Stated in another fashion, the systematic risk of a stock depends on operating and financial leverage of a firm. An increase in either of them will lead to an increase in beta and hence the cost of equity.

The revised formula for WACC would be:

$$WACC = K_{LE} \times E/(D + E) + K_d\ (1 - T)\ D/(D + E)$$

The WACC decreases initially as debt is employed, reaches at a low point and increases thereafter as the increase in cost of equity offsets the tax advantage of debt similar to the traditionalists' argument.

PERSONAL TAXES

The investor who receives coupon payments or dividends must pay personal tax and therefore cares about after-tax receipts. Hence, managers should try to arrange their firms' capital structure to minimize total taxes paid after earnings are distributed to their owners. In real life, not all investors face the same tax rate. Low tax investors pay no or low personal taxes on dividends or interest receipts. High tax investors pay lower taxes when they receive income as capital gains instead of as interest. Since the capital gains tax is applied only when the investor realizes it, the investor can defer the tax payment. The combined effect of corporate and personal taxes is that there should be 'tax clienteles'. Consider a hypothetical situation where both debt and equity are taxed at 30 per cent at the investors' hands. Table 14.4 illustrates the effect of personal taxes on distributable funds.
It can be verified that

$$V_L = V_U + [1 - \{(1 - T_c)\ (1 - T_{PE})/(1 - T_d)\}]\ D \quad (5)$$

where, V_L = value of a levered firm
V_U = value of an unlevered firm
T_c = corporate tax rate
T_{PE} = personal tax rate on equity income
T_d = personal tax rate on interest income
D = amount of debt in rupees

TABLE 14.4
Effect of Personal Taxes on Firm Value

	Firm A	Firm B
EBIT	125	125
Interest @12%	0	30
PBT	125	95
Tax @35%	43.75	33.25
PAT	81.25	61.75
Income to Investors		
Dividends	81.250	61.750
Personal Tax @30%	24.375	18.525
After-Tax Dividend	56.875	43.225
Interest	0	30,000
Personal Tax @30%	0	9,000
After-Tax Interest	0	21,000
Total	**56.875**	**64.225**

We have assumed that the only source of equity income is dividends. We do know that capital gains realized on sale of shares are also a source. The tax rate T_{PE} is a blend of the tax rates on the two. When companies do not pay dividends and investors never sell shares, $T_{PE}=0$. The term in brackets in Equation (5) is the gain from leverage after considering both corporate and personal taxes. The point is that debt is beneficial if $(1-T_d)$ is more than $(1-T_c)(1-T_{PE})$; otherwise it is not. The relative advantage of debt is:

$$(1-T_d)/(1-T_c)(1-T_{PE})$$

Three scenarios follow from Equation (5):

Situation 1:

$$\text{If } T_{PE}=T_d=T_c$$

$V_L=V_U$ as in the original MM proposition without taxes. Debt is irrelevant

Situation 2:

$$\text{If } T_{PE}=T_d$$
$$V_L=V_U+[1-(1-T_c)]\ D$$
$$V_L=V_U+T_c\ D$$

This is the MM proposition with corporate taxes.

Situation 3:

$$T_c = 35\%$$
$$T_d = 35\%$$

TCG=20% (tax on capital gains). The company does not pay dividends

$$\text{Relative Advantage of Debt} = (1-0.35)/(1-0.35)\ (1-0.2) = 1.25$$

Suppose,

$$T_c = 0$$
$$T_d = 35\%$$
$$T_{PE} = 0$$
$$\text{Value of the Firm} = V_U + [1 - \{1/(1-0.35)\}]D$$
$$= V_U - 0.53D$$

Borrowing will 'reduce' firm value in this case. When the tax rate on income from shares is less than the tax on income from bonds, the gain from leverage will be less than T_cD.

DO MM PROPOSITIONS WORK?

MM propositions are static in nature. If a firm borrows to buyback equity, keeping the balance sheet size constant, the firm value is supposed to increase by an amount equal to present value of tax shields (Tc D). The framework can be applied only if the firm is continuing in the same line of business. MM propositions have been criticized on various grounds.

- Investors may not have access to funds to undo corporate leverage and replace it with 'home-made' leverage. Also, they may not be able to borrow at the same rate as a creditworthy company.
- They ignore transaction costs that could be substantial in real-life situations, thereby making arbitrage unattractive.
- MM propositions neglect agency and bankruptcy costs.

The most important assumption underlying MM proposition is that corporate investment and operating decisions are not affected by capital structure and dividend policies. Regardless of whether the company operates at 10 per cent debt or 80 per cent debt and whether the company pays all of its earnings or none as dividends, MM assume that a company's investment policy and thus the cash flows of the organization do not change. When companies make drastic changes in debt or investment or dividend policies, there could be dramatic changes in the performance and value of these companies.

BANKRUPTCY COSTS

The costs of bankruptcy are of two kinds: direct and indirect. Direct costs include lawyers' and accountants' fees, other professional fees and the value of managerial time spent on administering bankruptcy.

Indirect costs include lost sales (and hence lost profits), the possibility that the firm may not be able to obtain additional credit or to issue securities except under strict terms. A firm may lose sales rapidly if it is a manufacturer of long-lived products that require continuous servicing or replacement parts as customers may use their 'perception' of the financial condition of the company to make their purchase decisions. For instance, the value of a computer is not only determined by its hardware but also by the manufacturer's continued provision of hardware and software support. An obsolete software or hardware is worthless. So a customer may settle for an inferior alternative with a lower probability of bankruptcy based on the perception that this firm is risky. Software firms may refuse to support computer firms that have high probability of bankruptcy because these companies are unlikely to be around for long, thereby accelerating distress. Likewise, airlines depend on frequent flier plans to attract business travellers. No amount of advertising may bring credibility to the claim made by those companies. Similarly, retailing companies may not obtain goods or credit from wholesalers. Since these firms do not get credit, their competitiveness will be lost. The indirect cost of bankruptcy can arise from the bankruptcy process itself. The bankruptcy trustee, as an agent of the court, may not run the firm in a value maximizing way as he/she has no incentive to do so. The firm incurs an opportunity loss due to the sub-optimal decision-making of the agent. Another possible indirect cost of bankruptcy is the higher compensation that the managers of a highly levered firm will receive because of the higher probability of unemployment they may face. Because the indirect costs are mainly lost opportunities, it is difficult to measure them.

Based on the foregoing discussion, we would expect firms with large intangible assets to keep their leverage low to reduce the probability of future bankruptcy. Thus, Infosys Technologies, which derives much of its value from growth opportunities, should keep the debt level low. The presence of bankruptcy costs places an upper bound on the debt ratio of a company. Leverage is beneficial as long as the present value of tax shields is more than the expected bankruptcy costs.

From the perspective of a firm choosing a capital structure, it is the expected cost of bankruptcy at the time of decision-making that matters.

$$\text{Expected Cost of Bankruptcy} = \text{Probability of Bankruptcy} \times \text{Bankruptcy Cost (in rupees)}$$

To illustrate, let probability be 0.3, and the bankruptcy cost be 20 per cent of the current market value of the company (e.g., ₹1,000 million)

$$\begin{aligned} \text{E (bankruptcy)} &= 0.3 \times 0.2 \times 1{,}000 \\ &= ₹60 \text{ million} \end{aligned}$$

Therefore,

$$V_L = V_U + T_c\, D - \text{PV (Bankruptcy Costs)}$$

The bankruptcy cost is not constant obviously. It rises with leverage. The debt level at which present value of tax shields outweighs expected cost of bankruptcy is the optimal debt ratio for the company. The relationship between firm value and leverage when bankruptcy costs are considered is shown in Figure 14.3.

HOW DO MANAGERS MAKE FINANCING DECISIONS?

There are four theories that attempt to explain how managers make their financing decisions.

FIGURE 14.3
Firm Value with Bankruptcy Cost

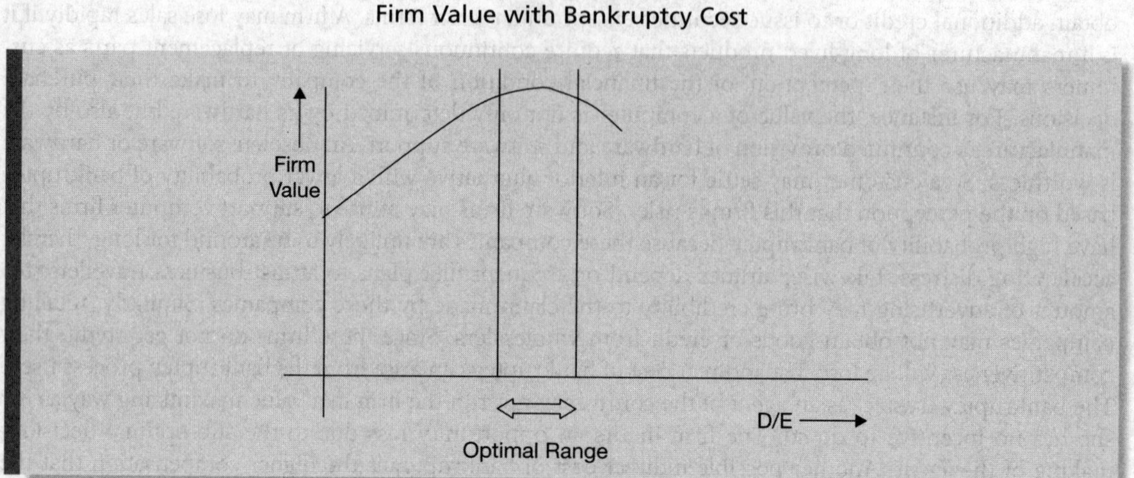

The 'static trade-off' theory suggests that firms trade off tax shields and bankruptcy costs and move towards an optimal debt ratio, that is, they stop borrowing when the present value of bankruptcy costs exceed present value of tax shields. In other words, profitable firms that can avail tax shields will borrow relatively more than less profitable firms. But some academic studies conducted in the USA and elsewhere do not support this hypothesis. Profitable firms, on the contrary, borrow less. Other studies have found positive relation between taxes and financing decisions.

Asymmetric Information Theories

Information asymmetry occurs when the management of a company has valuable information about the earning prospects which investors do not have may be because managers are unwilling to disclose information due strategic reasons or the information is too technical and complex to be communicated. These theories explain 'changes' in leverage, not 'amounts' of leverage.

Consider an all equity firm whose current market value is ₹2 million (100,000 shares @₹20). The management believes that the intrinsic value is ₹2.2 million (100,000 @₹22). The company is undervalued to the extent of ₹200,000. The company encounters a project that requires an investment of ₹800,000 and NPV is ₹10,000. The benefit of raising ₹800,000 is ₹10,000, the NPV of the project and the cost is that the firm has to sell the securities for 'less than they are really worth'. The company will have to sell 40,000 (i.e., 800,000/20) shares in order to raise ₹800,000. Let us suppose the information asymmetry is removed soon after the issue. The new stock price would be:

$$\frac{\text{New Market Value} + \text{Investment} + \text{NPV}}{\text{Total Number of Shares}}$$

$$= [2.2 \text{ million} + 800{,}000 + 10{,}000]/140{,}000 = ₹21.50$$

$$\text{New Shareholders Gain} = ₹21.50 - ₹20.0 = ₹1.50$$

Old shareholders also gain ₹1.50 but this is less than what they would have gained (₹2 per share) if the project were not taken up and information asymmetry were removed later on. In this sense, the loss to old shareholders is ₹0.50.

In the earlier situation, managers had favourable information. Now consider a situation where managers have unfavourable information.

Current market price is ₹20. But the managers think it is overvalued and worth only ₹18. The company decides to sell 100,000 shares at ₹20. The information asymmetry is removed soon thereafter.

$$\text{New Price} = \frac{\text{New Market Value} + \text{Investment}}{\text{Total Number of Shares}}$$

$$= [1.8 \text{ million} + 2 \text{ million}]/200{,}000 = ₹19$$

Old shareholders gain. New shareholders lose.

The moral of the story is that if managers act in the interest of 'existing' shareholders, they would rather pass up positive NPV projects rather than issue undervalued shares when the inside information is favourable and always issue shares when the inside information is unfavourable even if the project has 0 NPV. So the general strategy would be to issue debt when investors undervalue the firm and issue equity when they overvalue. In this sense, issuers send signals to financial markets by the security they choose. Debt is good news. Equity is bad news. The better the firm's projects are, the more senior the security the managers will offer for sale.

The pecking order theory predicts that:

- Firms prefer internal to external finance.
- If the internal cash flow is less than the investment requirement, companies issue the least information sensitive security first and work downwards,[2] that is, issue debt, convertibles, preferred stock and then equity in that order.

The 'free cash flow' theory suggests that debt enforces discipline on managers because of the contractual nature of interest and principal payments. According to the theory, the higher the debt ratio the better in those industry groups where future growth opportunities are limited and the most optimal strategy is to return cash to shareholders by repurchasing shares from borrowed money.

AGENCY COSTS

So far, we have assumed that the interests of managers and investors are perfectly aligned. But is it reasonable to assume that managers are totally altruistic? The shareholder wealth maximization rule is based on the assumption that other investors in the company are unaffected. An agency relationship is a contract under which one or more persons (the principal/s) engage another person (agent) to perform some service on their behalf that involves delegating some decision-making authority to the agent. If both are utility maximizers, there is good reason to believe that the agent will

[2] When companies issue securities, they have to meet the disclosure norms prescribed by the regulator. The disclosure norms are more for equity than for debt. Consequently, equity is considered more information sensitive.

maximize his/her utility. So the principal may have to incur monitoring costs to check his behaviour and limit divergences. The principal may suffer reduction in welfare due to this divergence of interest. Agency cost is the sum of monitoring costs and residual loss. Agency cost can arise whenever there is a cooperative effort between individuals even when there is no strict agency relationship such as costs due to conflict of interest between managers and shareholders, and shareholders and bondholders.

CONFLICTS BETWEEN SHAREHOLDERS AND BONDHOLDERS

The agency cost associated with debt consists of wealth loss caused by the impact of debt on the investment, financing and dividend decisions of the firm. Suppose a firm raises debt for some stated purpose of engaging in business activity. The bondholders would have set the price of the bond after making an assessment of the riskiness of the project. If the firm were to invest in riskier project later on, bond price decreases because of increase in default risk. The bondholders' loss is the shareholders gain.

To illustrate, assume that a company has a project that can return either ₹50 or ₹150 with equal probability. So the expected value today is ₹100. The company has ₹60 worth bonds plus equity. If the project bombs bondholders get ₹50, whereas shareholders get nothing; if the project clicks, bondholders get ₹60, their claim, whereas shareholders get ₹90. The summary of pay-offs is shown as follows.

Project	Bombs	Clicks	
Probability	0.5	0.5	Expected Value (Today)
Pay-Off	50	150	100
Bonds	50	60	55
Equity	0	90	45

Now suppose the managers of the company encounter a project that pays either ₹40 or loses ₹50 with equal probability, that is, the expected value of the project is –₹5. The risk of the project is largely borne by bondholders. If the project clicks, shareholders make fixed payment to bondholders, and keep the surplus, whereas, if the project fails, they have nothing to lose. It is not their money anyway. The bondholders lose ₹5 and shareholders gain ₹5. Bondholders realize the potential expropriation of wealth by shareholders at a later stage. Although expropriation per se is good for shareholders, it is bad for both shareholders and firm ex-ante, because bondholders make estimate of such behaviour and demand a premium payment from managers.

The second source of conflict is the firm's financing decision. Bondholders would have priced the bond, at the time of issue, with an assumption that no additional debt will be issued with the same or higher priority. If the firm sells bonds with higher priority, the bondholders' claim gets diluted as they have to share the proceeds of bankruptcy with another set of bondholders. The old bondholders lose, shareholders win and new bondholders get a fair deal.

The third source of conflict is the firm's dividend decision. Bondholders price their issue after making an assessment of the firm's dividend policy. If dividends are increased or investment is reduced, the collateral value of assets falls and bondholders suffer capital losses. In the extreme case, if the company sells all its assets and pay a liquidating dividend, bondholders would be left with worthless claims.

UNDERINVESTMENT

Managers acting on behalf of shareholders will ignore positive NPV projects when shareholders have no chance of receiving any proceeds when debt falls due. Because bondholders receive all the proceeds when their payment falls due, managers reject projects thereby reducing firm value. This reduces the value of bondholders and hence the price bondholders would be willing to pay 'today'. This is another cost of debt.

Smart bondholders realize the incentives faced by the stockholders and make estimates of the behaviour of stockholders. Bondholders may demand higher interest rates to reflect the possibility of subsequent wealth transfers to stockholders. Bondholders try to protect themselves with restrictive covenants. The loan covenants may affect the firm's efficiency leading to a lower firm value. But covenants cannot describe all possible ways of wealth transfer. Further, some good projects may be lost if they do not satisfy the covenants. Writing and monitoring loan covenants entail cash outlay. Add the bankruptcy cost associated with debt. The sum total of all these constitute agency cost of debt.

CONFLICTS BETWEEN MANAGERS AND SHAREHOLDERS

Free cash flow is cash flow in excess of that required to fund all projects that have positive NPV. Corporate managers, as agents of shareholders, have discretion over spending the residual cash flow. They can increase payout or invest in projects. Increasing payout will not only reduce the resources under their control but also limit growth. Since managers are appraised on the basis of growth from year to year, it is likely that they may invest residual cash flow in projects that do not yield adequate returns. This leads to conflict between shareholders and managers. Conflicts are severe in those organizations that generate substantial free cash flow.

Jensen[4] argues that forcing managers to borrow could reduce the agency costs of free cash flow. The threat caused by failure to make contractual debt payments serves as an effective motivating force to make organizations more efficient. The 'control' hypothesis holds well for those firms that generate large free cash flows but have poor investment opportunities and not for growth firms that have profitable investment opportunities but no free cash flow.

MANAGERIAL ENTRENCHMENT

Managers have discretion over the level of debt they choose in the absence of corporate control mechanisms such as monitoring by the board, threat of dismissal or takeover and stock option-based incentive plan. Left to their own device, they may resort to less leverage than is optimal (thereby foregoing increase in firm value) to keep the risk of failure low. The point is that managers are worried about 'their' welfare rather than that of shareholders. Often, the personal wealth and career of executives is tied to the performance of the company. This may motivate them to behave in sub-optimal ways. The degree to which managers are not subject to discipline is called managerial entrenchment. At the other extreme form of entrenchment, managers may increase leverage beyond the optimal level in order to keep the volume of floating stock low and reduce the possibility of take-over attempt.

[4] Jensen, 'Agency Costs of Free Cash Flow'.

Summing up

Debt has certain benefits and costs shown as follows.

Benefits	Costs
Tax Shield	Bankruptcy Cost
Disciplining Ability	Agency Cost
	Underinvestment Problem
	Loss of Flexibility

Debt payments generate valuable tax shields, and leverage keeps managers on their toes. But debt also has certain disadvantages—the direct and indirect costs of going bankrupt. Debt is beneficial as long as advantages are more than disadvantages.

Highly leveraged companies that have exhausted their debt capacity may have to forgo profitable projects whenever encountered. Further, the stricter loan covenants that come with high leverage may restrict their investment activity. For this reason, executives do not borrow to the theoretical limit. They would want to maintain a slack. If those projects never come up, which is generally the case, a company will be losing valuable tax shields.

SOME FACTS ABOUT FINANCING

Based on the foregoing discussion, we would expect the following relationship to hold:

- The higher the variability of earnings (business risk), the higher is the probability of default, other things remaining constant. Such firms with volatile earnings should borrow less.
- The greater the separation of ownership and management, the lower the debt ratio.
- A firm derives its value from both tangible assets in place and intangible future growth opportunities. Those firms that have substantial assets in place can borrow more vis-à-vis those that derive value from growth opportunities.
- If tax shelter is the sole motive, those firms that already have other tax shelters should borrow less.

Academic studies in the USA[5] have shown that

- Companies are heavily influenced by market conditions and past history of security prices in choosing between debt and equity, and companies make their choice of financing instruments based on the target level of debt in mind. The target level of debt is a function of company size, bankruptcy risk and asset composition.
- Companies with specialized assets have relatively low debt ratio; smaller companies tend to use significantly more short-term debt than larger firms.
- Debt ratio is unrelated to a firm's expected growth, volatility of earnings or non-debt tax shields.

The most direct way to find out how managers make their capital structure choice is to ask them. Graham and Harvey[6] conducted a survey of practices in 392 firms in the USA. Their survey had

[5] Marsh, 'The Choice Between Debt and Equity'.

[6] Graham and Harvey, 'The Theory and Practice of Corporate Finance'.

questions on what factors affect the choice of a security. Each question was to be rated on a four-point scale. A large number of respondents consider financial flexibility, volatility of earnings, cash flows and credit rating as important determinants of capital structure, whereas tax advantage and bankruptcy costs are considered relatively less important. The same survey also asked CFOs what factors affect issuance of common stock. The respondents indicated that EPS dilution, under or over valuation of common stock and recent stock price history were important.

INTERNATIONAL COMPARISON

There is a popular belief that companies in bank-oriented economies such as Germany and Japan enjoy close relationships with financial institutions and banks. Often, the borrower and the bank belong to the same group of companies. So these institutions stand behind the companies when they get into financial trouble and also take active interest in investment decisions. As a result, the bankruptcy costs are lower for these companies while the benefits of debt remain, thereby giving them a competitive advantage. Companies in these countries can, therefore, borrow more and add more value than their counterparts in market-oriented economies such as the UK and the USA. However, Rajan and Zingales[7] find that:

- Japanese companies are no more highly levered than companies in the USA.
- German companies are significantly less leveraged than those from all the other G-7 countries, with the exception of the UK.
- UK companies raise almost equal amounts from equity and debt issuances.
- UK companies are next only to Japan in the amount they raise externally.

They observe that the differences could be due to differences in creditor rights and tax codes in these countries and that well-regulated markets are adequate substitutes for close relationships between companies and financial institutions.

The summary of their findings is presented in Table 14.5.

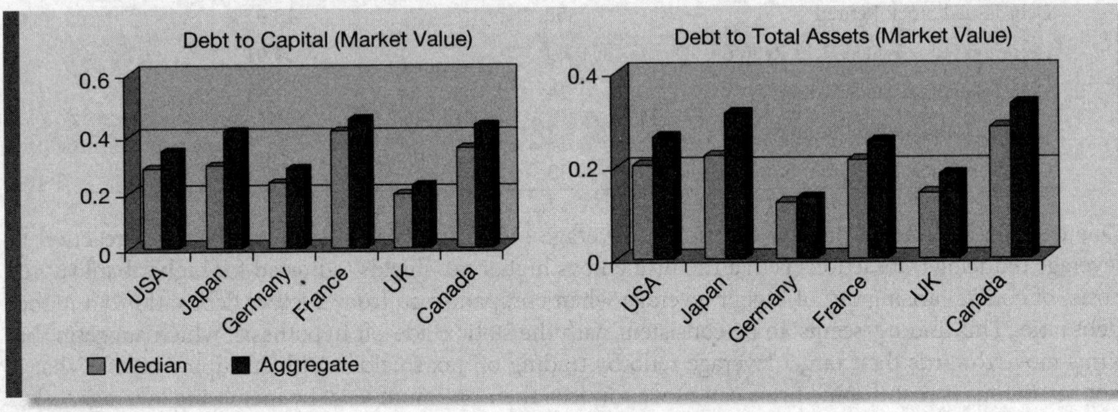

[7] Rajan and Zingales, 'What Do We Know about Capital Structure?'

TABLE 14.5
Leverage in the G-7 Countries[8]

	Debt to Total Capital (%)	
	Book	Market
Canada	39	35
France	48	41
Germany	38	23
Italy	47	46
Japan	53	29
UK	28	19
USA	37	28

THE IMPACT OF CAPITAL STRUCTURE CHANGES ON FIRM VALUE

In an exchange offer, the firm offers to trade freshly issued securities for seasoned securities in the hands of investors. Thus, a firm that wanted to move to a higher debt ratio could offer to trade new debt for outstanding shares. A firm that wanted to move to a more conservative capital structure could offer to trade new shares to outstanding debt securities. Ron Masulis[9] was one of the earliest to analyse the stock price impact of exchange offers of debt for equity or vice versa. He found that debt for equity exchanges were good news (stock price increased on announcement) and equity for debt exchanges were bad news. The summary of his findings are as follows:

Type of Capital Structure Change	No. of Offers	Primary Announcement Period Returns
Debt Issued/Stock Retired	52	13.97%
Common Stock Issued/Debt Retired	9	–9.91
Debt Issued/Pref Stock Retired	24	3.53
Pref Stock Issued/Debt Retired	9	–7.72
Common Stock Issued/Pref Stock Retired	23	–2.57

One explanation for the positive reaction to leverage increasing transactions and negative reaction to leverage reducing transactions is that the firm enjoys higher tax shields (adjusted for higher bankruptcy costs, of course) arising out of higher leverage when companies go from a lower debt ratio to a higher debt ratio. This finding 'seems' to be consistent with the static trade-off hypothesis, which suggests that firms move towards their target leverage ratio by trading off tax shields and bankruptcy costs. What is not so obvious is that if some firms can move towards their optimum level by increasing leverage, other

[8] Ibid.

[9] Masulis, 'The Impact of Capital Structure Change on Firm Value'.

firms may move towards their optimal debt ratio by 'decreasing' leverage. So it is not too clear why stock markets react positively when debt ratio goes in one direction and not in the other. Ronald's findings are, however, consistent with information asymmetry theory which suggests that debt is good news and equity is bad news.

CONCLUDING COMMENTS

Firms that have large intangible assets should have lower debt ratios vis-à-vis companies that have substantial tangible assets in place, as the bankruptcy cost for the former is more. Firms that have taxable income will be better off by borrowing as the company gets valuable tax shields. A casual observation reveals that firms that have specialized assets keep leverage very low. The trade-off theory hypothesizes that firms have target debt ratios and they move towards the target by trading off tax shields and bankruptcy costs. The survey by Graham and Harvey lends moderate support to it, that is, firms consider interest deductions moderately important, expected bankruptcy costs as not important and 44 per cent of the firms in the sample have strict or somewhat strict target/range.

The pecking order theory suggests that firms use securities in the reverse order of asymmetry—use internal funds first, debt second, convertible security third, equity last. To avoid need for external funds, firms may prefer to store excess cash. The survey finds that firms value financial flexibility, issue debt when internal funds are not sufficient. The survey does not support the free cash flow theory or the underinvestment problem or asset substitution.

APPENDIX 14A.1: MILLER'S THEOREM

Consider a company with constant expected EBIT. The company has a policy of paying out 100 per cent of its earnings as dividends. If the company has no debt, then the earnings available to investors as dividends are EBIT $(1-T_c)$. After paying personal tax of T_{PE}, investors will have EBIT $(1-T_c)(1-T_{PE})$.

Where T_c = Corporate Tax Rate on the Marginal Rupee of Earnings
T_{PE} = Tax Rate on Marginal Income as Dividends

Now let us suppose the company borrows ₹D at an interest rate i. Let the personal tax rate on interest income be T_d. The company distributes dividends and interest to investor.

$$\text{Distribution} = (\text{EBIT} - iD)(1 - T_c) + iD$$

The first term is the profit after tax distributed as dividends to shareholders and the second term is the interest paid in Rupees.

After payment of personal taxes, investors will have an amount equal to

$$(\text{EBIT} - iD)(1 - T_c)(1 - T_{PE}) + iD(1 - T_d)$$

Expanding terms, we get:

$$(\text{EBIT})(1 - T_c)(1 - T_{PE}) - iD(1 - T_c)(1 - T_{PE}) + iD(1 - T_d)$$

The first term is similar to the funds available from an unlevered company. Thus, the value of a levered company is equal to the value of an unlevered company plus the present value of an annuity of $-iD(1-T_c)(1-T_{PE})+iD(1-T_d)$ with the discount rate being the cost of debt adjusted for personal taxes, that is, $i(1-T_d)$.

If the annual flow is assumed to be a perpetuity,

$$\begin{aligned} PV &= \text{Amount/Discount Rate} \\ &= iD[(1-T_d)-(1-T_c)(1-T_{PE})]/i(1-T_d) \\ &= [1-\{(1-T_c)(1-T_{PE})/(1-T_d)\}]D \\ V_L &= V_U+[1-\{(1-T_c)(1-T_{PE})/(1-T_d)\}]D \end{aligned}$$

Concept Test

State whether the following statements are true (T) or false (F).

1. The agency cost of debt is borne by shareholders.
2. Maximizing firm value is same as minimizing WACC.
3. Maximizing shareholders wealth is same as maximizing firm value.
4. The cost of equity increases linearly with leverage.
5. The cost of debt increases with debt ratio.
6. A hybrid financial instrument like convertible bond that gives a bondholder an option to buy shares of the company is essentially designed to address the agency problem.
7. There is as much money to be made on the left-hand side of the balance sheet as there is on the right-hand side.
8. If the tax rate on debt and equity are same and the company does not pay taxes, then there is no advantage to debt.
9. Companies that generate lots of cash suffer from free cash flow problem.
10. Companies that derive much of their value from future growth opportunities should use relatively less debt.

Exercises

1. The Government of India introduced dividend distribution tax in 1998. Under the new law, dividends would be taxed at a flat rate of 10 per cent at the corporate level.[10] What could be its impact on capital structure and cost of capital?
2. Marginal tax rate, variability of operating cash flows, creditors' difficulty in monitoring a firm and need for flexibility are some of the factors that affect capital structure. What relationship between these variables and debt ratios do you expect to hold?

[10] It was repealed in 2002 and reintroduced in 2003.

3. Suppose the government makes only half the interest expense tax deductible. What will be its impact on capital structure?
4. Borrowing can make an unviable project viable. Explain.
5. Conventional lending gives recourse to the promoter in case of project failure. Can there be a type of debt where there is no recourse? How would your analysis change in case of such a project?
6. Borrowing enforces discipline on the company's management. Explain.
7. A project is expected to generate net operating income of ₹10,000. The cost of unlevered equity is 18.6 per cent and tax rate is 35 per cent, what is the value of the project?
8. If the project is financed with debt and equity, what is the value of the project if the increase in debt capacity is ₹18,000?
9. Is it possible to reduce the risk of insolvency by acquiring a project whose cash flows are less than perfectly correlated with that of the firm?
10. Unlevered beta=1.4, risk-free rate=8 per cent and risk premium is 10 per cent. What is the unlevered cost of equity?
11. Cost of unlevered equity=18.6 per cent, cost of debt=12 per cent, tax rate=35 per cent. The project will be financed with ₹18,000 of debt and ₹17,600 of levered equity. Calculate cost of equity.
12. Calculate levered betas at various debt levels

Beta	____	0.8	____	____
D/E	0	0.5	0.6	0.7

13. Calculate cost of equity at all the debt levels assuming suitable CAPM parameters.
14. You are analysing the debt policy of Ashok Leyland. You have obtained debt ratios of other companies in the automobile industry group. You notice that debt ratios vary among companies. Is it correct to compare debt ratios? Why or why not? What would you do?
15. Explain the terms managerial entrenchment and underinvestment.

REFERENCES

Graham, John R. and Campbell Harvey. 'The Theory and Practice of Corporate Finance: Evidence from the Field'. *Journal of Financial Economics* 61 (2001).

Jensen, Michael C. 'Agency Costs of Free Cash Flow, Corporate Finance and Takeovers'. *American Economic Review* 76, no. 2 (1986).

Marsh, P. 'The Choice Between Debt and Equity: An Empirical Evidence'. *Journal of Finance* 37, no. 1 (1982 March).

Masulis, Ronald. 'The Impact of Capital Structure Change on Firm Value: Some Estimates'. *Journal of Finance* (1983 March).

SUGGESTED READINGS

Altman, Edward. 'A Further Empirical Investigation of the Bankruptcy Cost Question'. *Journal of Finance* 39, no. 4 (1984): 1067–1089.

Barclay, Michael J., Clifford Smith and Ross Watts. 'The Determinants of Leverage and Dividend Policies'. *Journal of Applied Corporate Finance* (1995 Winter).

Barclay, Michael J. and Clifford Smith. 'The Capital Structure Puzzle: Another Look at the Evidence'. *Journal of Applied Corporate Finance* (1999 Spring).

Berger, Philip and Eli Ofek. 'Managerial Entrenchment and Capital Structure Decision'. *Journal of Finance* (1997 September).

DeAngelo, Harry and Ronald W. Masulis. 'Optimal Capital Structure under Corporate and Personal Taxation'. *Journal of Financial Economics* 8, no. 1 (1980).

Fama, Eugune and Kenneth French. 'Taxes, Financing Decisions and Firm Value'. *Journal of Finance* (1998 June).

Graham, John R. 'How Big Are the Tax Benefits of Debt?' *Journal of Finance* (2000 October).

Harris, Milton and Artur Raviv. 'The Theory of Capital Structure'. *Journal of Finance* 46, no. 1 (1991 March).

Haugen, Robert A. and Lemma W. Senbet. 'The Insignificance of Bankruptcy Costs to the Theory of Optimal Capital Structure'. *Journal of Finance* 33, no. 2 (1987).

Jensen, Michael C. and William H. Meckling. 'Theory of the Firm, Managerial Behavior, Agency Costs and Ownership Structure'. *Journal of Financial Economics* 3, no. 4 (1976).

Miller, M. H. 'Debt and Taxes'. *Journal of Finance* 32, no. 2 (1977).

Miller, M. H. 'Leverage'. *Journal of Finance* (1991 June).

Miller, M. H. 'The M&M Propositions 40 Years After'. *European Financial Management* 4, no. 2 (1998).

Modigliani, Franco and Miller M. H. 'The Cost of Capital, Corporation Finance and the Theory of Investment'. *American Economic Review* 48, no. 3 (1958).

Modigliani, Franco and M. H. Miller. 'Corporate Income Taxes and the Cost of Capital: A Correction'. *American Economic Review* 53, no. 3 (1963).

Myers, S. C. 'Determinants of Corporate Borrowing'. *Journal of Financial Economics* 5 (1977 November).

Myers, S. C. 'The Search for Optimal Capital Structure'. *Midland Corporate Finance Journal* (1983 Spring).

Myers, S. C. 'The Capital Structure Puzzle'. *Journal of Finance* 39, no. 3 (1984).

Myers, S. C and Nicholas S. Majluf. 'Corporate Investment and Financing Decisions When Firms Have Information that Investors Do Not Have'. *Journal of Financial Economics* 13 (1984 June).

Myers, S. C. 'Capital Structure'. *Journal of Economic Perspectives* 15, no. 2 (2001 Spring).

Rajan, R. and L. Zingales. 'What Do We Know about Capital Structure? Some Evidence from International Data'. *Journal of Finance* 50 (1995): 1421–1460.

Ross, Stephen A. 'The Determination of Financial Structure: The Incentive Signaling Approach'. *Bell Journal of Economics* 8 (1977).

Shyam Sunder, L. and S. C. Myers. 'Testing Static Trade Off Against Pecking Order Models of Capital Structure'. *Journal of Financial Economics* 51 (1999).

Smith, C. and J. B. Warner. 'On Financial Contracting, An Analysis of Bond Covenants. *Journal of Financial Economics* 7 (1979).

Titman, S. 'The Effect of Capital Structure on a Firm's Liquidation Decision'. *Journal of Financial Economics* 13, no. 1 (1984).

Titman, S. and R. Wessels. 'The Determinants of Capital Structure Choice'. *Journal of Finance* 43, no. 1 (1988 March).

Warner, J. B. 'Bankruptcy Costs: Some Evidence'. *Journal of Finance* 26 (1977 May).

CHAPTER 15

An Overview of Financing Choices

LEARNING OBJECTIVES

- Introduction to convertibles as a class of financial instruments
- Provide a rationale for financial innovation
- Introduction to warrants and preferred stock
- Estimate the impact of a financial instrument on the financial health of the firm

One of the primary responsibilities of a finance manager lies in selection of an appropriate source of funding. The objective of a financing strategy is to support a long-term business strategy. It is the responsibility of the CFO to maintain contact with public and private sources of capital to make sure that the company has adequate cash to invest and grow. In this chapter, I provide an overview of different types of securities that firms issue and the impact of a security on the financial health of a firm.

Companies have access to a wide array of instruments, the most prominent being straight debt and equity. The last 20–30 years have witnessed unprecedented advances in the type and the manner in which securities are offered to the investing public. Debt, as opposed to equity, entitles investors to contractual interest and principal payments. The interest payment may be at a fixed rate or at a floating rate. The interest rate in case of floating rate debt gets reset at specified intervals (e.g., three months or six months) according to a formula. The London InterBank Offered Rate (LIBOR) is the commonly used benchmark rate in international capital markets. The interest rate on a loan could be specified as, say, LIBOR+10 basis points.[1]

[1] 100 basis points = 1 per cent.

SECURITY DESIGN OBJECTIVES

The last two decades have witnessed unprecedented innovation in the range of and manner in which firms issue securities. Just as engineers apply scientific principles to design new products and services, financial engineers apply principles of financial economics for the purpose of structuring, pricing and managing the risk of financial contracts. Financial engineering involves the design, development and implementation of innovative financial instruments and processes, and the formulation of creative solutions to problems in corporate finance. Innovative instruments make financial markets more complete and efficient. For instance, greater efficiency could be achieved by reducing transaction costs. Financial markets can be made more complete by designing a new security whose contingent after-tax returns cannot be replicated by any combination of existing securities. Financial engineering involves three types of activities—design of new financial instruments, development of new financial processes and providing creative solutions to problems in corporate finance. Index-linked bonds, online trading of securities and project finance are examples of the three activities, respectively.

Some academics consider financial innovations 'unpredictable improvements' that come into being as a result of regulatory and tax impulses, while others consider innovative instruments and processes as attempts by companies to lessen the financial constraints they face. The factors responsible for financial innovation can be classified into 11 categories as shown in Table 15.1.[2] Financial engineering can be used not only in reducing financing costs and creating customized financial instruments but also in advancing a company's strategic goals.[3] For instance, a company could control the volatility of output prices using financial engineering principles to differentiate its products when customers attach importance to reduced uncertainty in prices. Similarly, a company could hedge its exchange rate exposure and hence the volatility of the expected revenue stream to reduce uncertainty in returns to shareholders.

New instruments can be classified into debt, equity, convertible or preferred stock categories. New securities can add value in several ways:[4]

TABLE 15.1
Factors Affecting Financial Innovation

1. Tax asymmetries that can be exploited to produce tax savings for the issuer, investors or both.
2. Transaction cost.
3. Agency cost.
4. Opportunities to reduce some form of risk or to reallocate risk from one market participant to another who is either less risk-averse or else willing to bear the risk at a lower cost.
5. Opportunities to increase an asset's liquidity.
6. Regulatory and legislative changes.
7. Level and volatility of interest rates.
8. Level and volatility of prices.
9. Academic work that resulted in advances in financial theories or better understanding of the risk–return characteristics of existing class of securities.
10. Accounting benefits.
11. Technological factors and other factors.

[2] Finnerty, 'Financial Engineering in Corporate Finance'.
[3] Tufano, 'How Financial Engineering Can Advance Corporate Strategy'.
[4] Finnerty, 'An Overview of Corporate Securities Innovation'.

Reduction in Agency Cost: Puttable bonds, for instance, enable investors to sell the bond back to the issuer if the issuer increases leverage beyond a certain level or when the control changes. Similarly, rating sensitive notes bear interest rates that change with the credit standing of the issuer.

Managing Exchange Rate Risk: Dual currency bonds (DCBs) are bonds offered in one currency while the interest payments and redemption are made in another currency. The issuer offers to make interest and principal payments in some specified list of currencies. The investor has the option to choose the currency DCBs, thus reallocating currency risk. DCBs can be issued in India after the rupee becomes fully convertible on the capital account.

Likewise, commodity-indexed bonds, bear coupon and principal payments tied to the price of a commodity to which the issuer has an exposure. The issuer's revenue declines when the price of the commodity falls. So does debt service. In other words, such bonds increase the debt capacity of the company.

Reducing Transaction Costs: Corporate bonds usually include a call provision that enables the issuing firm to redeem the issue before maturity. When interest rates fall, managers have the option of redeeming the issue and replacing it with a new issue. Because of the call provision, the issuer pays a premium over face value called the call premium. The call premium typically follows a declining schedule falling to zero a few years before maturity. Issuers are typically prohibited from redeeming the issue for few years after the issue (call protection period).

Two reasons are commonly cited for including the call provision:[5]

- It enables managers to increase shareholder value by refunding the bond when interest rates decline
- It enables companies to redeem when covenants become too restrictive.

The first reason assumes that managers have special expertise in forecasting interest rates, which is questionable. If they do, bondholders will recognize this over a period of time and price the call option accordingly. Since any gains to issuer from refunding is a loss to the bondholder (because he/she has to accept a lower interest bond), we would expect bondholders to demand higher interest rates on callable bonds when compared with non-callable bonds. If the higher interest payment cancels out the value of the call option, the issuer can be indifferent between paying a higher interest and including a call provision and issuing a non-callable bond. Further, lower quality bonds are more likely to have call provisions because the issuer can replace the bond when credit quality improves (because of which the interest is lower).

Most bond covenants restrict the issuer's investment and financing decisions. For instance, covenants prohibit the issuer from selling another secured bond or a merger. Due to such restrictions, a firm may have to pass up a positive NPV project in future. One way to get around the covenants is to include a call provision.

Callable bonds are derivative embedded securities. A callable bond can be viewed as a non-callable bond on which the bondholder has written a call option to the issuer. From the issuer's perspective:

$$\text{Callable Bond} = \text{Non-Callable Bond} - \text{Call Option}$$

The option embedded in the bond can be viewed as a call option (sold by the investor to the issuer) on the price of the bond with a strike price equal to the call price with an expiry date equal to the call dates.

[5] Kraus, 'An Analysis of Call Provisions and the Corporate Refunding Decision'.

As is evident, the call option has multiple exercise dates prior to the final maturity of the option. So it is a 'Bermudan style' option. The call option in case of a callable bond is an embedded option that cannot be separated from the bond. The value of the call option depends on the current and future levels of interest rates, slope of the term structure, volatility of interest rates, length of the call protection period, bond maturity and prepayment penalty.[6] Once an issuer has decided that it will include a call provision, it must then decide on the design of the call features such as the (schedule of) call price and length of the call protection period because the required coupon (the spread over non-callable bonds) depends on these.

Bond refunding involves significant transaction costs. In 1998, Tennessee Valley Authority issued an instrument called ratchet bond that captures the advantages of callable bonds while at the same time eliminating the undesirable feature—transaction cost.[7] The coupon on the ratchet bond indexed to the yield on a specified T-bond resets as long as the resulting rate is lower than the current rate, that is, ratchet bonds 'ratchet' only downward (the coupon can only decrease or remain the same). Since the coupon resets automatically, the issuer need not have to worry about the call decision or the transaction costs involved.

Reducing Inflation Risk

There are many securities whose cash flows are tied to an index such as a currency index or a general price index. Inflation-indexed securities are designed to provide protection against increases in prices. Usually, they are tied to a broad measure of prices such as the consumer price index (CPI) although the GDP deflator or a wholesale price index may be used. The choice depends on the needs of the issuer and the investor. The real return on these bonds is certain, whereas in an ordinary bond, the nominal return is certain. In other words, inflation indexed bonds offer a fixed real return. There are two common types of bonds—capital-indexed bonds and interest-indexed bonds. Capital-indexed bonds pay a fixed real coupon rate and a nominal principal that rises with inflation. Interest-indexed bonds pay a fixed coupon and an indexation of the fixed principal every year.

Floating rate instruments are debt securities whose coupon rates vary over time according to a pre-determined formula. The coupon rate is pegged to a reference rate such as the prime rate or LIBOR or T-bill rate. The coupon rate equals the reference rate plus a markup to reflect the credit risk of the issuer. The coupon rate is reset at regular intervals, say, three months. Thus, the coupon on floating rate instruments 'float'. The coupon is generally semi-annual. The premium over the reference rate may decline over time. For instance, the coupon might be reference rate plus 1.05 per cent for the first five years, 1 per cent for the next five years and so on. There is a maximum and minimum within which the coupon can fluctuate. They can also have call and conversion features, which enable the issuer to redeem the issue on or after a pre-specified date at pre-specified prices and enable the investor to exchange the instrument to a fixed rate instrument with predetermined coupon and maturity.

Floating rate notes make coupon payments that increase with the level of interest rates, while inverse floaters make coupon payments that decrease with the level of interest rates. Inverse floaters or bull

[6] Pricing of Interest rate derivatives is beyond the scope of this book. Interested readers may refer to Ho and Lee, 'Term Structure Movements and Pricing Interest Rate Contingent Claims'; Heath, Jarrow and Morton, 'Bond Pricing and the Term Structure of Interest Rates' and Black, Derman and Toy, 'A One-Factor Model of Interest Rates and Its Application to Treasury Bond Options'.

[7] See Kalotay and Abreo, 'Ratchet Bonds'.

floaters have reset formulas at some fixed rate minus the reference rate. The coupon on the instrument rises when LIBOR falls. For instance, the reset formula may be 15 per cent – LIBOR. These securities attract investors who are bullish on bond prices because the coupon rate moves inversely to the market rate. Bear floaters, on the other hand, reset at a multiple of the reference rate minus some fixed rate. For instance, the reset formula could be twice LIBOR – 9.12 per cent. Investors who are bearish on bond prices would be attracted to such securities because the coupon rate rises by more than the increase in the market rate.

One characteristic of inverse floaters is that their prices rise more than those on fixed rate bonds of same maturity. Likewise, when rates increase, investors receive lower coupon. Who would issue inverse floaters? Those companies that have a floating rate exposure (e.g., finance companies that are exposed to deposit rates) would want to issue an inverse floater to smooth out the cost of funds. Combining a floater and an inverse floater cancels the variable reference rate giving rise to a fixed rate liability. Investors and issuers in inverse floaters often hedge the risk by entering into a swap agreement.[8]

Addressing Investor Clienteles

Limiting availability of securities to only certain classes of investors usually restricts demand and hence price. State Bank of India offered Resurgent India Bonds amounting to US$4.2 billion and US$5.5 billion in multiple rounds of capital-raising to Indians living abroad at 150 basis points below comparable benchmarks leading to savings of US$1.08 billion.[9] Ownership restriction could enhance value by eliminating the dead weight costs of prolonged negotiation, particularly when a security is restricted to a homogeneous clientele that values the underlying collateral higher than other investors. Restricting the ownership ensures that investment is limited to a homogeneous class of investors that the issuer cares about. It thus serves as a pre-commitment to ensuring an efficient ex-post bargaining renegotiation in the potential default states, resulting in a lower ex-ante offering yield.

Convertible Securities

A convertible bond provides the performance attributes of a common stock and a bond. These securities typically pay a semi-annual coupon of 4 per cent–5 per cent. The security is typically a subordinated debenture with a fixed principal amount and time to maturity with a right to convert into common stock based on its conversion ratio. The upside of the convertible comes from its common stock component, while the downside protection comes from the cash coupon on the bond component.

A convertible preferred stock also has features similar to a convertible bond. However, convertible preferred stock is subordinated to debt of the issuing company. It typically offers a coupon of 6 per cent–7 per cent. A convertible preferred typically pays a cash coupon on a quarterly basis and is also perpetual (or long tenor).

Mandatory convertibles are equity-linked securities that pay a higher dividend (compared to the company's common stock) for a certain number of years and then get converted into common shares on a specified date. These securities have limited capital appreciation potential. In other words, the

[8] An interest swap is an agreement between two parties to exchange liabilities denominated in fixed rate to floating rate or vice versa.

[9] Gande and Puri, 'Can Ownership Restrictions Enhance Security Value?'

issuer puts a cap on the appreciation by specifying the conversion terms. Participating equity preferred shares (PEPS), a type of mandatory convertibles, are designed to provide investors with high current income with high equity-like participation in the underlying stock. PEPS usually provide a coupon which is usually paid quarterly. These securities mature in three–five years, are typically listed and are usually call protected for most of their life.

Convertible bonds are hybrid instruments. A convertible bond gets converted into shares of the company at a specified price after a specified period of time at one stroke or in instalments. The holder of a convert is entitled to receive interest on the convertible portion till conversion. Thus, a convert is a package of straight debt and equity option. The option to convert is usually at the discretion of the holder and will only be exercised when and if the holder finds such an exercise desirable. The features (terminology) of a convertible bond are discussed further.

The stated value or par value of a convertible security is typically US$1,000 in the USA, whereas preferred stocks have much lower par values—US$50 or US$25.

The number of shares a holder will receive on exercising the option is called conversion ratio.[10] The price paid to acquire the underlying shares through conversion is called conversion price.

$$\text{Conversion Ratio} = \text{Par Value of Security/Conversion Price}$$

To illustrate, if the par value were to be ₹100 and conversion price, ₹20, the investor will receive five shares.

The conversion value of a convert is the value of the bond if it is converted immediately.

$$\text{Conversion Value} = \text{Market Price of Shares} \times \text{Conversion Ratio}$$

Conversion premium is the difference between the conversion price and the current market price of the stock at the time of issue. The premium is expressed in percentage. To illustrate, if the conversion price is ₹50 and the current market price of the stock is ₹40.

$$\text{Conversion Premium} = \frac{50 - 40}{40} = 0.25 = 25\%$$

$$\text{Conversion Premium may also be calculated as} = \frac{\text{Convertible Price} - \text{Conversion Value}}{\text{Conversion Value}}$$

Although conversion premiums range from 10 per cent–70 per cent, a premium in excess of 30 per cent is considered too high to attract the traditional convertible band investors.

The 'current yield' of a convert is the coupon payment on the bond expressed as fraction of the current market price. Thus, if coupon payment is 4 per cent and market price is US$100, yield is 4 per cent. The current yield is usually set higher than the dividend yield on the company's stock. Breakeven measures the time it would take for the added return on the convert to equal the premium paid for the security in excess of its parity.

[10] There is a class of convertibles called death spiral convertibles which convert into a fixed dollar amount of common stock (equal to the convert's price). They derive that name from the fact that when stock price falls, the death spiral owners receive more shares because of which shareholders face severe dilution. The terms of these bonds are so onerous that only companies desperately in need of cash would consider them. Some 23 companies issued death spirals and raised US$123 million in 2001 in the USA.

$$\text{Breakeven} = \frac{\text{Convertible Market Price} - \text{Conversion Value}}{\text{Convertible Coupon} - (\text{Stock Dividend} \times \text{Conversion Ratio})}$$

The coupon payments on convertibles are tax deductible for the issuer and rating agencies assign varying degrees of equity content depending on the structure of the instrument. Coupon typically ranges from 4 per cent to 6 per cent.

Convertible price is the current market price of the security quoted as a percentage of par for bonds and an actual dollar price for preferred stocks. The price of the convert changes as the common stock price changes depending on the relationship between the convertible price and its equity value.

The credit spread (over treasuries) reflects the investor perception relating to how likely the issuing company will be able to make timely interest payments and pay off the principal at maturity. The larger the spread, the more concern investors have regarding the issuing company's ability to make timely interest payments. The smaller the spread, the less concern investors have.

Since a convertible is a hybrid instrument consisting of bond and option components, we would expect the value of the convertible to increase as the underlying stock price increased and decrease whenever the stock price declined. Although theoretically the price of the stock can be anything, including zero, the downside in case of convertibles is limited because of the straight bond component that provides contractual coupon payments. This serves as an investment floor.

The fixed income component of the convert is determined by discounting coupon and principal payments at an appropriate discount rate. The discount rate is usually the yield on a straight bond of similar maturity and credit rating. This value is termed investment value. The investment value premium is the amount that the market price of the convertible is above its investment value, expressed as a percentage.

All convertible bonds and preferred stock with premium over investment value less than or equal to 10 per cent are considered credit sensitive.

All convertible bonds and preferred stock with conversion premium less than or equal to 10 per cent or delta greater than or equal to 75 per cent are considered equity sensitive.

The sensitivity to changes in the stock price is called delta. It expresses the change in the convertible price per unit change in the underlying common stock price. The change in delta per unit change in stock price is called gamma.

Convertible bonds also come with call provision that enables the issuer to repurchase the bond from security holders at the option of the issuer. Converts also come with a call protection period during which the issuer cannot call the bond. A bond's call schedule sets out the dates and prices at which the bonds could be called. If the call price is below the conversion value, the issuing company can force conversion by calling the bond. The investor would be forced to convert the bond because he/she gets more by converting than redeeming. Converts also come with what is known as soft call protection which stipulates that a bond be called only if the underlying stock price is at a pre-specified level, say 125 per cent of the conversion price.

It is estimated that the global convertible bond market has a market capitalization several hundred billion dollars with Europe accounting for one-third of issuance. The USA alone accounts for more than US$200 billion in market value. Issuance in Europe has grown considerably over the last decade. The US convertible bond market is dominated by high growth, hi-tech, start-up firms (e.g., Internet and telecom companies), whereas the European market is dominated by large-cap, blue-chip companies. This trend is changing now. A large number of stable companies with investment grade rating from the USA have started issuing convertibles in the recent years.

A fully convertible debenture gets converted into shares of the company at a specified price after a specified period of time at one stroke or in instalments. In case of partly convertible debentures (PCDs), on the other hand, only a portion of the principal gets converted into shares with the remaining portion being redeemed at maturity. The holder of PCDs is entitled to receive interest on the convertible portion till conversion and up till maturity on the remaining portion.

RATIONALE FOR CONVERTIBLES

Why do companies issue convertible bonds? Often convertibles are viewed as delayed equity. If the managers of a company expect the firm's stock price to rise and expect investors to exercise their option of conversion, a convertible, as opposed to an outright equity issue will result in lower dilution. Since the investor has an option of conversion, the coupon on convertibles tends to be lower than their non-convertible counterparts. For this reason, some managers consider convertibles 'cheap'. The coupon on convertibles is lower because of the valuable option (of conversion) given to the investor. The option of conversion is a sweetener attached to straight debt.

Moral Hazard: Straight debt suffers from the moral hazard problem, that is, the company's risk can be shifted from equity to debt by taking on riskier projects. Since shareholders have limited liability, they enjoy all the upside potential but lose nothing in case of project failure. Smart bondholders realize this and demand higher coupon. The cost of moral hazard problem is borne by shareholders. Since holders of a convertible have a choice to convert debt into equity, the agency problem is reduced.

Risk Insensitivity: Suppose the managers and investors of a company disagree about the riskiness of a company. If investors believe that the company's risk is higher than that projected by managers, they will demand higher interest rates. The equity option in case of a convertible bond makes the value of the convertible insensitive to risk shifting. This is because the value of the straight bond component decreases as risk increases but the value of the equity component 'increases'. Thus, the package as a whole is risk neutral. By issuing convertibles, the managers and investors come to an agreement so that the value of the instrument is insensitive to riskiness of a company. Convertibles are often issued by high growth, risky firms for this reason.

Information Asymmetry: At times, the managers of a company may have better information than outside investors about the company's prospects. If the market undervalues the company's shares, the managers of the company have a disincentive to issue equity. They may issue debt. But debt increases the probability of bankruptcy. Convertibles fall in between. Based on this analysis, we would expect convertibles to be issued by those companies that are undervalued but not to a large extent, straight debt by undervalued companies and equity by overvalued companies.

High growth firms may not find straight debt attractive as they may not have an investment grade rating. So the interest expense will be high. Defaulting on interest payments may lead to restrictions on investment activities of the firm, which curtails growth. Equity financing will be expensive as high growth firms may have to sell equity at lower prices than that implied by growth opportunities. Those managements that have confidence in the future of the company can issue convertibles and use the call provision to force conversion when the stock price rises in the future.[11]

[11] Brennan and Schwartz, 'The Case for Convertibles'.

What is the best way to find out why managers issue convertible bonds? Ask them! This is precisely what academic surveys do. A recent survey by Graham and Harvey (2001) finds that most issuers consider convertibles delayed equity and issue them when the stock is undervalued.

Over time the stock price, and hence, conversion premium change. Holding the convertible bond enables the investor to earn interest on the bond component while at the same time retaining the option of conversion if it is desirable. Given this advantage, an investor would prefer to hold the bond rather than convert it into shares. While an investor prefers to hold the convertible bond rather than convert because of the downside protection offered by the bond, the opposite is true for the corporation. Issuers would want to force conversion so that the legal obligation to pay interest and principal is replaced by the non-contractual, more flexible commitments (dividends) to common stock.

One of the prime assumptions in issuing convertibles is that the company's stock price will rise in future. If, for some reason, the stock price falls after issuing the convertible, investors will not convert and straight debt remains. This situation is called 'debt overhang'. Often managers cite the debt overhang problem for not issuing convertibles. If the company issues convertibles when the chief alternative is debt, one need not crib when investors do not convert because the interest rate on convertibles is lower than that on straight debt resulting in cash savings. In fact, an issuer should rejoice. But the overhang problem is not solved. One should fix the root cause of a problem, not its consequences. Managers are constantly under pressure to get the best immediate financing deal. This prompts them to take a short-term view. Companies implicitly hold valuable growth options. So a company's financing should be structured in such a way that financial flexibility to exercise its growth options in future is maintained. The financial plan should ensure future access to capital even if it means a higher price for capital today.[12] Going by this reasoning, high growth, start-up firms should choose between convertibles, straight bonds and equity not just on the basis of current cost of capital and debt ratio but also on the basis of future financing needs and cost of capital. Even though convertibles ordinarily make sense to high growth firms, a company with high operating leverage, high (current) debt ratio and uncertain product market conditions should issue equity even if it implies selling stock at a discount.

Issuers of convertibles face uncertainty in future capital structure of the company in the sense that the company receives equity only if investors convert the bond into shares. To make sure that the company receives shares if and when it is desirable, that is, to 'control' investors, issuers can do two things:

- Insert a call option
  Since the objective of management is to maximize the value of the stock (and not the value of convertible), the bond could be called as soon as the conversion value reaches the call price. The investor is coaxed to convert because he/she gets more by converting than by holding the bond. In short, the management places a lid on the value of the convertible. Usually investors have 30 days to decide whether to surrender the bond or convert.
- Increase dividends making conversion more attractive
  At the time of issue, the coupon on convertible is set higher than dividends on the shares (otherwise the investor will immediately convert). As long as the coupon is higher than dividends, the investor enjoys higher income while at the same time retaining the option of conversion. The issuer can induce investors to convert by raising dividends. When dividends are sufficiently high, bondholders voluntarily decide to convert. But conversion exposes the investor to the risk of common stock.

[12] Willigan, 'The Case of the Expensive Expansion'.

FIGURE 15.1
The Value of Convertible at Various Stock Prices

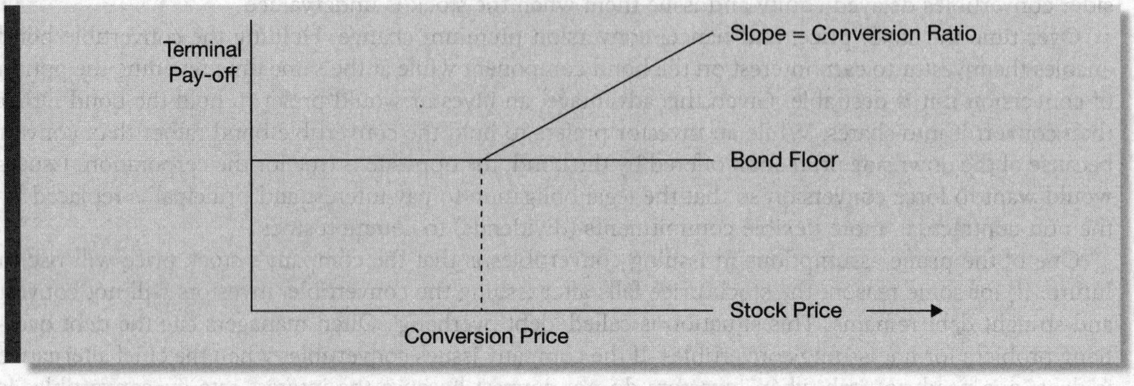

A diagram of convertible bond value against stock price is shown in Figure 15.1.

At the time of the issue, a finance manager should decide on the features of the bond such as convertibility, coupon rate, call and put options, exercise price and so on. Investors pay attention to both conversion premium and interest on the bond. The higher the conversion premium, the less attractive is the bond. Conversely, the lower the conversion premium, the more attractive is the bond and lower can be the interest. Increasing the coupon raises the bond floor and makes the convertible more attractive, other things remaining constant. Likewise, decreasing the coupon lowers the bond floor.

The higher the coupon, the lower can be the conversion premium and vice versa.

The actual features of the convertible depend on the particular financing problem the company is facing and the general market conditions.

- Interest on convertibles is a tax deductible expense. So firms with predictable taxable income could issue 'bond-like' instruments to take advantage of tax deductibility of interest expense and issue 'equity-like' instruments when the prospects of stock price rising is high.
- Companies suffering from asset substitution and risk shifting can give higher conversion, that is, issue equity-like securities to reduce the agency cost.

High growth companies could issue convertibles with shorter maturities and less call protection and force conversion when stock price rises. The call schedule should be designed to provide maximum flexibility to the issuer in forcing conversion as and when it is desirable. Issuers benefit from the call feature because it gives them the opportunity to strengthen their balance sheets by replacing debt by equity.

VALUATION OF CONVERTIBLE BONDS

A convertible is a combination of debt and equity option. So the value of a convertible is the sum of the straight debt and option components. The option embedded in a convertible is an American type option, not European because the investor can convert any time up to maturity. The Black–Scholes model takes into account the terms of the convertible, including its coupon, maturity, conversion ratio, call protection and credit spread. The underlying stock's volatility and stock dividends are also taken into account. To find the value of the straight bond component, one may use a single discount rate (equal to the yield on comparable bonds) for all the years or one may use the yield curve to calculate spot rates. The Black–Scholes model modified to account for continuous dividends can handle a convertible bond without a call provision. The presence of the call provision makes valuation difficult.

An Example

The terms of convertible bond issue are given below:

Maturity = 5 years
Currency = US$
Coupon = 5 per cent
Conversion Price = ₹62.21 = US$1.98 (at the prevailing exchange rate)
Conversion Premium = 5 per cent
Conversion Right = Any Time Until Maturity

Call Provision: Company can call the bond at any time after two years if dollar price of Essar shares exceeds 130 per cent of the conversion price. Bondholder can opt for conversion. Otherwise, the bond would be redeemed at par.

Valuation of this instrument requires inputs into the Black–Scholes model, namely volatility, risk-free rate, dividend yield and so on.

The relevant data is given below:

Volatility of stock returns of Essar stock (in dollars) = 40 per cent
5 year yield on US t-bonds (in dollars) = 6 per cent
Dividend yield on the underlying stock = 5 per cent
Yield on comparable straight bonds = 8.5 per cent

The value of the straight bond component can be calculated as:

Present Value of Coupon Discounted at 8.5% for 5 Years + Present Value of the Principal Discounted at 8.5%.

$$\frac{5.5 \text{ (Face Value)}}{100} \times \text{PVIFA}(8.5\%, 5) + \frac{\text{(Face Value)}}{(1+0.085)^5}$$

The value of the option (ignoring call and put provisions) can be estimated using the Black–Scholes formula.

$$\text{Value of Call} = Se^{(b-r)T}N(d_1) - Xe^{-rT}N(d_2)$$

Where:

S = Stock Price
X = Strike Price or Exercise Price
b = Cost of Carry Defined as Risk-Free Rate Minus the Dividend Yield (q)
T = Time to Maturity in Years
σ^2 = Variance in Returns from the Underlying Stock

$$d_1 = \frac{Ln(S/X) + (b + \sigma^2/2)T}{\sigma\sqrt{T}}$$

$$d_2 = d_1 - \sigma\sqrt{T}$$

X = US$1.98
S = ₹59.24 = US$1.88
σ = 40%
T = 5 years
r = 6%
q = 5%
e = 2.7183

The option value can be estimated by plugging the inputs into the model. As mentioned earlier, the Black–Scholes model does not capture early exercise and call provision. These will not be discussed here as they are beyond the scope of the book.

WARRANTS

A warrant is an option that gives the holder the privilege of buying a specified number of shares of the company at a specified exercise price at any time on or before the expiration date. Warrants usually come as attachments to bonds to make a bond issue more attractive to investors. The debenture holder can exercise a warrant. Warrants can also be detached and separately listed on a stock exchange for trading purposes. The issuer of the warrant receives the price of the warrant at the time of issue and the exercise price when the option is exercised. The company gets equity investment if the investor exercises the option. The uncertainty in the investor's reaction can affect further debt issuance by the company. In other words, if warrant holders do not exercise the option, the company may have to postpone further debt issuance due to inadequate equity base. A company contemplating on issuing equity to build equity may issue debentures with warrants instead of issuing straight equity if the shares are fully priced because issuing shares at a discount to the current market price will result in underpricing of 'all' shares subsequently. The exercise price is determined by market conditions. As a thumb rule, the conversion price may be fixed at a premium of 10–15 per cent of the prevailing market price. An issue of warrant at a strike price lower than that expected by the company's management will not affect a growing company much in the sense that the value of foregone capital in present value terms will not be high.

A comparison between convertibles and warrants is in order.

- The conversion rights are inseparable in case of convertibles. Warrants are separable from the bond and are usually listed on stock exchanges for trading.
- A warrant gives additional cash to the issuer when the holder exercises the right. A convertible does not.
- When convertibles are converted into shares, the associated debt is not repaid unlike in the case of a debt–warrant package.
- Convertibles frequently come with call provision. The issuer can force conversion when situation so demands. Warrant holders cannot be coaxed to exercise. They may or may not exercise their option depending on what happens to the underlying share price in the interim. The warrant

holders will not exercise if share price declines. So there is an element of uncertainty regarding the amount of equity the issuer gets. If cheap debt is the objective regardless of what happens to equity, warrant with debt is a better choice.

Warrants can be exercised with cash or with bonds valued at face value. The units are generally designed so that investors will exercise warrants by turning in debt. Bonds are worth the face value (₹1,000, say) in exercising warrants; bonds are worth less than ₹1,000 as debt instruments because of low coupon, which ensures bonds will be turned in to exercise warrants. Thus, when warrants are called, bondholders will sell their bonds to warrant holders or bondholders will purchase warrants. In either case, the bonds will be turned in to exercise the warrants.

Warrants are also callable so that the company can force investors to exercise warrants. For example, if the call price is ₹5 per warrant and the company's stock price rise to ₹65, the warrant holder gets ₹10 by exercising if the strike price is ₹55. He would get only ₹5 by receiving the call. Faced with this choice, investors are forced to exercise the warrants.

Unlike convertibles, the total issue value (of a bond–warrant package) is split between debt and equity. The accounting rule is that when the warrants are detachable, value is allocated to equity account for the warrants. Assume that the issue size is ₹10,000 million. Further, the bond carries a coupon of 7.5 per cent to yield the going rate on straight debt—12 per cent. The result is an original issue discount debt of ₹7,500 million. If the warrant is not exercised, the debt liability rises to ₹10,000 million over the life of the issue and the net worth is reduced by ₹2,500 million.

In sum, at the time of the issue, equity and debt are apportioned. The unit is designed to behave like a synthetic convertible. If the company's stock price rises, it calls the warrants, the bonds are turned in to exercise the warrants and the company is left with ₹10,000 million in equity. If the stock price falls, the warrants expire worthless and the company has to pay off ₹10,000 million in debt at the time of maturity.

PREFERRED STOCK

A preference share, as opposed to ordinary shares, entitles investors for fixed dividend payments. The preference dividend paid by the company is not tax deductible. It is paid out of after-tax profits. Often, preferred stock is compared with debt as both preference dividends and interest payments are fixed in nature. Since interest is tax deductible, whereas preference dividend is not, preference shares are less popular than straight debt. Executives tend to forget that there is an important distinction between interest payments on bonds and dividend payments on preference shares. While suspension of preference dividend might be unpleasant, default on a legal contract such as bonds can drive a company to insolvency. Management will be more comfortable with preferred dividends than it will be with the same amount of interest. Some favour preferred stock because rating agencies and analysts may view preferred stock as 'equity-like'. But this benefit is at best illusory.

Preferred stocks often trade at lower yields than straight bonds because preferred stocks are tax advantaged in the sense that corporate investors in the USA are taxed on only 30 per cent of income from preferred stocks. Even in the absence of taxes, other factors like differences in liquidity, the frequency of cash flows (semi-annual versus quarterly) and credit risk account for differences in yield. A preferred stock is more like debt than equity because it does not provide upside potential like equity. In terms of seniority, preferred stock ranks below debt but above common stock. The credit risk of a preferred stock is not the probability of default because issuers can omit dividends without triggering default, unlike debt. Since preferred stock ranks lower than debt in capital structure, it has greater risk of not making scheduled cash flows. This risk will be reflected in a higher yield on preference shares relative to yield on corporate bonds. The credit risk premium over straight bonds will be more for low rated bonds than for high rated bonds. In Chapter 17, I will discuss the estimation of default risk premium in greater detail.

An Extended Example

A company is in the process of investing ₹24 million in the next two years. The managers of the company are in the process of selecting a security to be issued. The balance sheet of the company is given below:

	2017	2018	(₹ million)
Liabilities			
Equity	90.6	92.7	
Long-Term Debt	12.4	12.4	
Current Liabilities	19.8	18.8	
Other Liabilities	9.3	9.6	
	132.1	133.5	
Assets			
Property, Plant and Equipment	32.6	33.3	
Investments	43.0	39.3	
Current Assets	55.8	59.5	
Other Assets	0.70	1.40	
	132.1	133.5	

The company has the following choices:

- Straight bond with a coupon of 12 per cent and four-year maturity
- Convertible bonds with the coupon rate of 9.5 per cent, four-year maturity and a conversion price of ₹834 (the current market price of the company's stock is ₹814).
- A bond–warrant package with a coupon rate of 8.5 per cent, with four-year maturity and a warrant that entitles the holder to subscribe the same amount of stocks as the bond's par value at the exercise price of ₹834.

The current cost of debt is 11.5 per cent and tax rate is 35 per cent. The company's stock has a beta of 0.8. Risk-free rate is 7 per cent; market risk premium is 10 per cent. The company currently has an equity/total assets ratio of 69 per cent. They intend to bring it down to 60 per cent. So there is room for some debt. Evaluation of alternatives involves calculation of debt ratio and cost of capital for all the alternatives. The cost of equity for the company is $7+0.8(10)=15$ per cent. The calculation can be made under two scenarios: No conversion of convertibles into shares and with conversion. The calculation for the second scenario is shown as follows.

Alternative 1		Alternative 2		Alternative 3	
Value of Debt	Cost %	Value of Debt	Cost %	Value of Debt	Cost %
₹12.4 million	11.5	12.4	11.5	12.4	11.5
₹24 million	12.0				
New Debt					
Value of Equity	Cost %	Value of Equity	Cost %	Value of Equity	%
₹92.7	15	92.7	15	92.7	15
		24.0	15	**24.0**	15
		(New Eq)		**(New Eq)**	
Total Assets	₹157 million		157 million		157 million
Equity/Assets	58.8%		74.12%		74.12%

WACC

$$K_d(1-T)\times D/V + K_e \times E/V$$

Compare the cost of capital for the three alternatives. Note that the balance sheet soon after issuing bond–warrant or any time before maturity may not (and does not) resemble the one shown before. Recollect the discussion of bond–warrant package. In other words, one should recast balance sheet in a more dynamic setting under various scenarios.

CONCLUDING COMMENTS

The choice of a security depends on current and future capital structure and cost of capital. It is important to understand that one of the key objectives of a financing programme is to maintain financial flexibility. A company strapped for cash or saddled with heavy debt may get into financial distress and lose valuable investment opportunities. The objective of this chapter was to provide a good understanding of the choice between debt, equity, convertibles and bond–warrant units. Chapter 16 on Initial Public Offerings discuss the mechanics of equity issuance.

EXERCISES

1. In December 1988, American Express, Dow Chemical, Pfizer and Sara Lee announced plans to offer 'unbundled stock units' (USU). Holders of shares in these companies could surrender their shares in exchange for USUs. In exchange for shares, the shareholders would get three certificates representing ownership of USUs. The units could be unbundled and traded separately. For each USU, the three different claims were: an equity appreciation certificate (EAC), an incremental dividend preferred (IDP) share and a priority income claim (PIC). The PIC was entitled to quarterly dividends equal to the current dividend on the common. This dividend was

to be continued even if the dividend on the common was increased or decreased. The IDP was entitled to dividend equal to any amount by which the common dividend was raised above the current amount. If the dividend on the common was cut, the IDP received no dividends. The equity appreciation certificate received no dividend. The trust was to be dissolved after 30 years. At that time, the PIC entitled to a balloon specified in the contract. The IDP holders were paid a nominal sum. The EAC holders would receive excess of the stock price above the PIC and IDP guarantees. The cash flows for the three claims are given below:

PIC For the 30 years, the PIC would receive quarterly interest payments equal in amount to the current common dividend. It would also get a balloon payment at the end of 30 years. The interest on PIC would be tax deductible for the company.

IDP For 30 years, the IDP was entitled to quarterly dividend payments equal to the excess of common dividend over the current dividend. After 30 years, the IDP would receive a small residual payment.

EAC No payment for 30 years. After 30 years EAC would receive the amount by which the stock price exceeded the payments to the PIC and IDP shares.
The American Express USU had the following features. Before the announcement of the issue, American Express shares were trading at US$26.875 and had an annual dividend of 84 cents per year (or 21 cents per quarter). The balloon payment was US$75. The IDP terminal payment was US$2 at the end of 30 years.

Other information:
Annual Interest Rate=9.8 per cent compounded semi-annually; annual log standard deviation of stock returns=33 per cent

1. The PIC is entitled to quarterly payments of 21 cents for 30 years and a final payment of US$75. What is the value of USU? Would you buy it?
2. A company needs ₹1,000,000 of new long-term financing. The firm is considering the issue of shares or convertibles. The current market price of the stock is ₹20. The new issue could be sold for ₹19. An alternative would be to issue 11 per cent, ₹1,000 face value convertible at a conversion price of ₹25 per share. The company currently has 200,000 shares outstanding. Current profit after tax is ₹400,000. Calculate EPS for the two alternatives before and after conversion assuming that earnings remain same.
3. Calculate the conversion price of a ₹1,000 face value bond convertible into 50 shares.
4. Calculate the conversion ratio if the bond can be converted to shares at ₹20 per share.
5. Calculate the conversion premium for the same bond if conversion ratio is 12.5 and the current market price is ₹75.
6. The value of a convertible is the sum of the values of the straight bond component and the conversion option (equity component). The value of the straight bond component can be calculated by discounting the coupon (of the convert) at the prevailing yield on comparable straight bonds. An 8 per cent, ₹100 face value convertible has a tenor of 20 years. If the yield on comparable straight bonds is 9 per cent, calculate the value of the bond component of the convertible.

7. On 1 September 1986, Salomon Brothers issued Standard & Poor's 500 indexed note (SPIN) to the public at par for a total of US$100,000,000.[13] The SPIN is a four-year 2 per cent (payable 1 per cent every six months), coupon bond which at maturity pays its holder:
   - The principal amount of US$1,000 per bond and accrued interest plus
   - The excess, if any, of the S&P 500 index value over the initial (exercise) value of the index times some determined multiplier.

The exercise price of the call option and the multiplier were fixed at 270.38 and 3.6985. The multiplier represents the number of call options on the S&P 500 index that the investor receives for every US$1,000 in bond principal held. The option is European type.

SPIN = Bond + (Call option × Multiplier)

Yield on Comparable Bonds = 8 per cent p.a.

S&P 500 Price Volatility = 18.4 per cent p.a.

X = 270.38

r = Risk-Free Rate = 6.5 per cent

S = Current Value of the S&P 500 index, adjusted for the present value of the expected dividends over the remaining life of the option.

Dividend on S&P 500 Index = US$8.28

Estimated Average Annual Growth in Dividends = 5.4 per cent

Current Value of S&P Index = 250

Estimate the value of SPIN. Use the Black–Scholes dividend adjusted model to calculate the value of call option.

[13] Chen and Sears, 'Pricing the SPIN'.

REFERENCES

Black, F., E. Derman and W. Toy. 'A One-Factor Model of Interest Rates and Its Application to Treasury Bond Options'. *Financial Analysts Journal* (1990 Jan–Feb).

Brennan, M. J. and E. Schwartz. 'The Case for Convertibles'. *Journal of Applied Corporate Finance* 1, no. 2 (1988).

Chen, K. C. and Stephen Sears, 'Pricing the SPIN', *Financial Management* (1990 Summer).

Finnerty, John D. 'Financial Engineering in Corporate Finance: An Overview'. *Financial Management* (1988 Summer).

Finnerty, John D. 'An Overview of Corporate Securities Innovation'. *Journal of Applied Corporate Finance* 4 (1992).

Gande, Amar and Manju Puri. 'Can Ownership Restrictions Enhance Security Value? Evidence from a Natural Experiment'. *Financial Management* 34, no. 4 (2005): 35–64.

Graham, J. and C. R. Harvey. 'The Theory and Practice of Corporate Finance: Evidence from the Field'. *Journal of Financial Economics* 60, (2001: 187–243).

Ho, T. and S. B. Lee. 'Term Structure Movements and Pricing Interest Rate Contingent Claims'. *Journal of Finance* 41 (1986).

Kalotay, Andrew and Leslie Abreo. 'Ratchet Bonds: Maximum Refunding Efficiency at Minimum Transaction Cost'. *Journal of Applied Corporate Finance* 12, no. 1 (1999 Spring).

Kraus, Alan. 'An Analysis of Call Provisions and the Corporate Refunding Decision'. *Midland Corporate Finance Journal* 1 (1983).

Heath, D., R. Jarrow and A. Morton. 'Bond Pricing and the Term Structure of Interest Rates: A Discrete Time Approximation'. *Journal of Financial and Quantitative Analysis* 25 (1990).

Tufano, Peter. 'How Financial Engineering Can Advance Corporate Strategy'. *Harvard Business Review* (1996 Jan–Feb).

Willigan, Geraldine. 'The Case of the Expensive Expansion'. *Harvard Business Review* (1989 Jan–Feb).

SUGGESTED READINGS

Alderson, M. J. and D. Fraser. 'Financial Innovations and Excesses Revisited: The Case of Auction Rate Preferred Stock'. *Financial Management* (1993 Summer).

Alderson, M. J., K. Brown and S. Lummer. 'Duction Auction Rate Preferred Stock'. *Financial Management* (1987 Summer).

Arzac, E. 'PERCS, DECS and Other Mandatory Convertibles'. *Journal of Applied Corporate Finance* (1997 Spring).

Brennan, M. J. and E. Schwartz. 'Convertible Bonds: Valuation and Optimal Strategies for Calls and Conversion'. *Journal of Finance* (1977 Dec).

Brigham, E. 'An Analysis of Convertible Debentures: Theory and Some Empirical Evidence'. *Journal of Finance* 21 (1966).

Carow, K., G. Erwin and J. McConnell. 'A Survey of Corporate Financing Innovations'. *Journal of Applied Corporate Finance* 12, no. 1 (1999).

Chacko, G. and E. P. Strick. 'Convertible Securities' (Harvard Business School Case No. 9–202–129, 2002 June).

Crabbe, Leland E. 'Estimating the Credit-Risk Yield Premium for Preferred Stock'. *Financial Analysts Journal* (1996 Sep–Oct).

Ganshaw, T. and D. Dillon. 'Convertible Securities: A Toolbox of Flexible Financial Instruments for Corporate Issuers'. *Journal of Applied Corporate Finance* 13, no. 1 (2000).

Houston, A. and C. Houston. 'Financing with Preferred Stock'. *Financial Management* (1990 Autumn).

Jen, F. C., D. Choi and S. H. Lee. 'Some New Evidence on Why Companies Use Convertible Bonds'. *Journal of Applied Corporate Finance* 10, no. 1 (1997).

Kim, Yong-Cheol and R. M. Stulz. 'Is There a Global Market for Convertible Bonds?' *Journal of Business* 65 (1992).

Mason, S., R. C. Merton, A. Perold and P. Tufano. *Cases in Financial Engineering: Applied Studies of Financial Innovation*. Upper Saddle River, NJ: Prentice Hall, 1995.

Miller, M. H. 'Financial Innovation: The Last Twenty Years and the Next'. *Journal of Financial and Quantitative Analysis* (1986 Dec).

Philips, George. *Convertible Bond Markets*. London: MacMillan, 1997.

Smith, Donald. 'The Pricing of Bull and Bear Floating Rate Notes: An Application of Financial Engineering'. *Financial Management* (1988 Winter).

Stanhouse, B. and D. Stock. 'How Changes in Bond Call Features Affect Coupon Rates'. *Journal of Applied Corporate Finance* 12, no. 1 (1999).

Stein, J. 'Convertible Bonds as Back Door Equity Financing'. *Journal of Financial Economics* 32 (1992).

CHAPTER

16

Initial Public Offerings

LEARNING OBJECTIVES

- Provide an overview of the security issuance process and the securities market in India
- Types of equity offers: general and rights offerings
- Role of intermediaries
- Types of issuance—fixed price versus book building
- Discuss methods of pricing of initial public offerings (IPOs)
- Summarize empirical findings on the performance of IPOs

Companies finance part of their investment from retained earnings and sell new equity or debt to make up any shortfall. Companies sell new securities in a number of ways. They can raise money by placing their securities with a small group of sophisticated investors or sell them to the public (including existing shareholders). The former is called private placement and the latter is a public issue. Public issues can be made in a variety of ways. At one end of the spectrum, securities may be sold to the highest bidder and at the other end, securities may be sold at a fixed price. Historically, first-time issues, called initial public offerings (IPOs), were fixed price offers. In a fixed price sale, the company advertises the number of shares on sale and the price. The investors then decide how many shares they wish to apply for. If the investors consider the price attractive, they may apply for more shares than on offer in which case the issue will be oversubscribed. The company then has to decide on an allotment rule, such as proportionate allotment. In many countries, now IPOs take the form of tender offers. Investors are invited to submit a sealed bid stating how many shares they wish to buy and at what price. The company then determines the price at which the total issue would be sold and all the successful bidders receive shares at that price.

Table 16.1 presents the estimate of funds raised during 2014–2017 by way of public issues.

Private placements of securities with institutional investors such as insurance companies are ideally suited for companies that do not find public markets attractive in terms of valuation. The IPO activity is partly dependent on the performance of the stock market. When returns from the market (index) are high, we would expect investors to be more confident of investing in stocks.

RIGHTS OFFERS

Instead of offering securities to the general public, a company may restrict the offering to existing shareholders who are then free to resell the securities to other investors. These are known as rights issues. Suppose a company has issued 8 million shares at ₹20 each. If the company intends to raise ₹80 million, it can offer its shareholders the right to buy two new shares for each share they currently hold at a price of ₹5. In other words, it is a 2:1 rights issue.

TABLE 16.1
Resource Mobilization During 2014–2017

Year	No. of IPOs	Amount Raised (₹ million)
2014	5	12,009
2015	21	113,623
2016	26	263,724
2017	38	754,753

Source: www.chittorgarh.com.

In many countries, the law requires the company to offer shares to existing shares before offering them to the general public. For instance, Sec 62(1) of the Companies Act, 2013, in India provides that when a company wants to raise further capital from the public, it has to first offer the same to the existing shareholders before issuing shares to other parties. This is based on the principle that the current owners should be given the option to decide whether they want to include new shareholders into the company or not. The company will first specify the size of the issue and the rights ratio. The ratio indicates the number of shares that a shareholder can apply for every share already held by him or her in the company. For example, a rights issue in the ratio of 1:4 means that for every four shares already held by the shareholder in the company, he or she can apply to buy one new share at the rights price.

The share price before the issue is called cum rights price and the price after the issue is called ex-rights price.

Let us assume that the company is all-equity financed.

$$\text{Current Value of Equity} = \text{No. of Shares Outstanding} \times \text{Cum Rights Price} = 80 \times ₹20 = ₹160 \text{ million}$$

The company issues 16 million shares at ₹5 to raise ₹80 million.

The total number of shares outstanding = 8 + 16 = 24 million

$$\text{Ex-Rights Price} = [\text{Value of the Firm/No. of Shares}] = [(160+80)/24] = ₹10$$

$$\text{Price of Right} = \text{Ex-Rights Price} - \text{Rights Price} = 10 - 5 = ₹5$$

To illustrate the effect of rights issue on wealth position of a shareholder, consider a shareholder who currently holds 10 shares. His or her investment is worth ₹200. At the time of the rights issue, he or she is entitled to receive 20 new shares for ₹5 each. After the issue, his or her investment is worth $(10\times10)+(20\times5)=$ ₹200. The shareholder is in the same position.

Let us suppose the company sells twice as many shares at half the price, that is, 32 million shares at ₹2.50. The shareholder is entitled to receive 40 new shares. The amount raised is the same. The ex-rights price will be ₹6 each.

$$\text{Value of Right} = 6 - 2.50 = ₹3.50$$

$$\text{Value of Shares Without Rights} = 10 \times 6 = ₹60$$

$$\text{Value of Shares with Rights} = 40 \times 3.50 = ₹140$$

Total Value = 60 + 140 = ₹200. The investor is in the same position. The message is that the shareholder does not benefit from the discount (to face value) given to him or her. Nor is he or she affected from the fall in price after the issue as long as there are no information effects on the stock price. The estimation of theoretical value of a right is derived in Appendix 16A.1.

FINANCIAL MARKETS

A financial market is a market where financial assets are traded. Financial assets are marketable financial claims issued by government and companies. Financial markets enable effective allocation of capital among competing uses. Financial markets perform four important economic functions. First, they enable individuals to choose more effectively between current and future consumption. Borrowing enables individuals to consume more, whereas lending enables them to postpone consumption. The economic units that have a surplus (investors) invest in those that have a deficit (borrowers). This provides capital to companies in excess of those generated out of business income. Second, the interaction between buyers and sellers in a financial market determines the price of the asset, say shares, or alternatively, the return demanded by investors to invest in the company. Firms can raise further capital if the return on their investments exceeds the return demanded by investors. Third, financial markets provide liquidity to investors, that is, the owner of the financial asset can sell off the asset in the market place to realize cash whenever required. The degree of liquidity may vary from asset to asset and market to market. For instance, shares of blue-chip companies like HUL are highly liquid. Fourth, financial markets can discipline underperforming managements. The prevailing stock price of a company reflects the opinion of all market participants regarding the outlook for the company under current management. If another company believes that the company is underperforming, then this company can buy the securities of the underperforming company and put the assets of the company to better use. Without a stock market, it would be difficult to value the performance of the company.

Financial markets are classified as capital market and money market. Capital market provides resources for long-term investment purposes, whereas money market provides resources for short-term purposes such as working capital investment. Commercial paper, certificate of deposits, T-bills issued by government are some of the instruments in the money market. Debentures, shares and preferred stocks are some of the instruments in the capital market. The capital market serves the function of channelizing resources from savers of capital to users of capital. The capital market consists of primary market and secondary market. The primary market creates long-term instruments through which companies raise capital. The secondary market provides liquidity to these instruments.

In the pre-liberalization period, raising money through public issues was regulated by the office of the Controller of Capital Issues (CCI). The process of going public took a very long time and the legal formalities were very cumbersome. All these changed in 1992 when the CCI was abolished and the SEBI was set up under an act of parliament. The SEBI has gone through various changes since then. The whole process of going public has been made simple and the government encouraged the companies to tap the capital markets. The government also recognized the need for a strong secondary market to support the primary markets. The setting up of the National Stock Exchange (NSE) in 1992 was the first step in this regard. Foreign equity participation was also encouraged by progressively relaxing the foreign direct investment (FDI) limits in Indian companies and by bringing in full current account convertibility of the Rupee. Today, public issue and private placements are the two most popular ways of raising capital. An issue by an already listed company is termed as a seasoned equity issue and an issue by a new company for the first time is termed as an IPO. This chapter will focus on IPOs. Given below is a small list of some recent IPOs.

Company	Issue Date	Offer Price (₹)	Current Price[1]	Listing Price (₹)
Add: Shop Promotions	10-09-2018	26.00	27.50	28.20
Supreme Engineering	06-09-2018	32.00	28.00	27.10
HDFC Asset Management	06-08-2018	1,100.00	1,610.00	1,739.0
Powerful Technologies	28-08-2018	51.00	28.60	48.00

Source: www.chittorgarh.com.

Financial markets around the world can be broadly classified as pre-emerging, emerging, established and mature. Countries such as Vietnam would be considered pre-emerging, whereas India, Korea and Thailand would be considered emerging markets. Similarly, Singapore and Hong Kong are established markets and the USA and UK are mature markets. The definition of emerging market itself is not very clear. If age is the basis of differentiation, India would be considered mature. The most widely accepted definition of an emerging market is that market which has begun a process of change and is growing in size and sophistication.

WHY DO COMPANIES GO PUBLIC?

It seems obvious that companies eventually grow big over a period of time and, consequently, the need for capital increases because of which they go public. The fact that many large companies in the world are unlisted suggests that going public is a choice, which a company may or may not exercise. So why do some companies go public? In other words, what are the benefits and costs of going public?

Moral Hazard: Due to information asymmetry between a company's managers and investors, it is likely that the mangers possess more information about the earnings prospects of the company. This asymmetry is an obstacle for young companies without a track record in going public. Indeed regulators in many countries prevent companies without a certain number of years of operating history from going public. Due to the adverse selection problem, we would expect bigger companies to go public.

Investment Opportunity Set: One of the commonly cited reasons for going public is to get access to an alternate source of capital (compared to bank debt or venture capital). So we would expect companies with high investment requirements to go public. Getting a listing on a stock exchange opens up a large source of capital. Subsequent to a public issue, a company may return to the market for additional capital through secondary offerings of shares or bonds, or convertibles. Listed companies can often bargain better terms and amount of finance from banks. This is another advantage of going public.

Increase Employee Commitment and Recruiting Power: By instituting a stock purchase plan for employee, companies may concentrate ownership in the hands of employees, which gives them an additional reason to deliver goods. Such plans tend to elicit a stronger employee commitment to productivity and quality.

[1] At the time of writing.

Facilitate M&A Activity: Because public companies may be able to raise additional cash through a secondary offering, they are generally better positioned to finance cash acquisitions. Alternatively, public companies may also be able to finance acquisitions with their own stock. For acquisitions financed by an exchange of stock, public companies can offer a valuation determined by the market, avoiding the complications of calculating the value of a private company.

Issue Costs: Public issue of securities involves underwriting and other issue expenses. The issue expenses can be broken down into fixed and variable components. The fixed costs are as high as US$250,000 and variable costs are about 7 per cent of issue expenses in the USA. Apart from underwriting fees and registrar's fees, a company will have to pay an upfront listing fees and an ongoing annual fees to renew listing every year. The principals must consider the ongoing expenses of producing information for shareholders and regulatory entities, and continuing fees to lawyers and accountants as the company grows. Companies may have to appoint chartered accountants and company secretaries for various audits and certifications. Although not always required, a company may also need a public relations firm to help promote the offering. All these entail cash outlay. A study conducted in India finds that the costs for both debt and equity issues decline as the gross proceeds of the offering increases, suggesting substantial economies of scale. The direct expenses are higher for equity issues as compared to debt issues. Given further is a rough estimate of the total issue expenses.

	(% of Net Offer to Public)
Lead Managers Fees Including Underwriting and Selling Commission	3–4
Other Expenses Like Advertising, Printing	1–2

The actual cost to a company will however work out less than the aforementioned percentages because of tax benefits. Issue expenses are treated as deferred revenue expenditure under the Indian tax laws and are deductible over a period of five years. Therefore, tax savings is available for the immediately following five years from date of issue. If, suppose, the total net offer to the public is about ₹1 billion, then the total fees will work out to about say ₹30 million (assuming 3% fees and cost). This can be written off over a period of five years from the date of issue. Hence, tax savings to the tune of 0.30 × ₹6 million = ₹1.8 million will be available for the issuing company in each of the five years. The benefits in real terms can be obtained by discounting the savings at a rate that reflects the risk of the project in which the capital is expected to be used.

The presence of (high) issue expenses suggests that only those companies that can afford to bear them would go public.

Information Disclosure: A public issue of securities brings fiduciary responsibilities to a company. The company's managers, as agents of shareholders, have an ongoing responsibility to provide timely information to investors. This results in a loss of confidentiality. So we would expect companies that are R&D intensive and hence, information sensitive, not to go public (in general). They may prefer private placement instead.

Sharing Corporate Control: By selling stock to shareholders, the original owners of a public company are, in essence, relinquishing exclusive control of the company's future. Once public, most companies need shareholder approval to take certain corporate actions such as increasing the number of shares outstanding or creating a new class of common stock. Shareholder approval is also required to institute stock option plans, mergers and so on. Even when an explicit approval is not required, companies must keep shareholders' interest in mind.

FIXED PRICE OFFERS VERSUS BOOK BUILDING

Conventional wisdom suggests that issuers and investment bankers would do well to assess market demand conditions before setting the terms of an IPO. Yet in several countries, fixed price offerings advertise the number of shares and offer price several days before the acceptance date. The issue price may become attractive or unattractive depending on stock price movement in the interim period. If the market declines after the price is set, the issue becomes overpriced. So issuers tend to underprice the issue. The public issue process in many countries suffers from numerous shortcomings such as inordinate delay between pricing of the issue and date of opening of the issue. To overcome these shortcomings, many countries have allowed book building in line with practices in the USA. In essence, book building involves little more than polling institutional investors before pricing the offering in an attempt to gauge market demand. This demand information is then used to determine the size, price and allocation of the offering.

In book building, a syndicate of investment banks brings an issuer's equity to the market. One of the investment banks acts as arranger with the rest of the members acting as underwriters. The arranger gives notice of a possible price range. The underwriters sell equity on a 'best efforts' basis. Orders for equity over the stated price range are collected by underwriters and returned to the arranger. Thus, book building assesses not only price but also volume at each price level. The arranger has the final responsibility of setting the actual price at which equity will be issued and its allocation to investors. The price, thus, reflects market demand. The issue has two components—placement portion and public portion. The placement portion is targeted at institutional investors like mutual funds. The book runner drafts the preliminary prospectus and files the prospectus with the concerned authority (SEBI) for approval. The preliminary prospectus does not contain the issue price. On obtaining the authority's approval, the book runner circulates the preliminary prospectus with intermediaries such as merchant banks and brokers inviting them to join the syndicate. The revised version of the prospectus indicates the price range. The intermediaries in turn circulate the prospectus among their clients and place one order for the total quantity on behalf of all clients. The book runner 'builds the book', records information such as name of the intermediary, number and price at which the buyer is willing to buy and so on. The book is kept open till the issue gets enough orders. The book runner then, in consultation with the issuer, prices the issue, decides on the amount of underwriting and allocation of securities. The final prospectus is filed with the concerned authority (SEBI). The issuer advertises the prospectus announcement in the newspaper the next day. The issue opens few days after the announcement and is kept open for three days. Syndicate members send their completed application. Allotment is made partly on a firm basis and partly on the basis of public subscription. If the public portion is undersubscribed, the syndicate members will receive allotment in the public portion also. Likewise, if the issue is oversubscribed, the syndicate member gets a refund. Securities are allotted and listed on stock exchanges for trading purposes.

Because of better price discovery, book building generally results in lower underpricing. Often critics of book building point out that investment banks make disproportionately large allocations in hot issues to their favoured clients and the market is rigged against the average investor. Cornelli and Goldreich[2] examined the books of investment banks for 39 international equity issues and find that the investment banker awards more shares to bidders who provide information in their bids and that regular investors receive favourable allocations, especially when the issue is heavily oversubscribed.

[2] Cornelli and Goldreich, 'Bookbuilding and Strategic Allocation'.

SEBI permits 100 per cent, one-stage, book building with bidding centres at all cities with stock exchanges. The allocation of 100 per cent book building is as follows:

- Not more than 60 per cent of the book built portion to be allocated to institutional investors, that is, banks, FIIs, mutual funds and other financial institutions on a discretionary basis. The maximum bid by these categories is restricted to the investment limit prescribed in the respective regulations/guidelines as applicable to these institutions.
- At least 10 per cent of the book built portion to be allocated on proportionate basis to non-institutional investors applying for more than 1,000 shares.
- The remaining 30 per cent of the shares would be available to the retail investors to be allocated on a pro rata basis.

Procedure for Bidding

The method and process of bidding is subject to the following:

- Bid shall be open for at least three days.
- The advertisement for inviting bids contain the following:
  - o The date of opening and closing of the bidding
  - o The names and addresses of the syndicate members as well as the bidding terminals for accepting the bids.
  - o The method and process of bidding.
- Bidding is permitted only if an electronically linked transparent facility is used.
- The syndicate members shall be present at the bidding centres so that at least one electronically linked computer terminal at all the bidding centres is available for the purpose of bidding.
- The number of bidding centres should not be less than the number of mandatory collection centres specified in the guidelines. Also, the same norms as applicable for collection centres shall be applicable for the bidding centres.
- Individual as well as institutional investors place their bids only through the 'syndicate members' who shall have the right to vet the bids.
- The investors shall have the right to revise their bids.
- Bidding form
- There is a standard bidding form to ensure uniformity in bidding and accuracy.
- The bidding form contains information about the investor, the price and the number of securities that the investor wishes to bid.
- The bidding form before being issued to the bidder is serially numbered at the bidding centres, and date and time stamped.
- The bidding form shall be issued in duplicate signed by the investor and countersigned by the syndicate member, with one form for the investor and the other for the syndicate member(s)/ book runner(s).

BOOK BUILDING AT NATIONAL STOCK EXCHANGE

NSE has set up nationwide network for trading whereby members can trade remotely from their offices located all over the country. The NSE trading network spans more than 400 cities and towns across India. NSE decided to offer this infrastructure for conducting online IPOs through the book building process. NSE operates a fully automated screen-based bidding system called National Exchange for Automated Trading, NEAT IPO, which enables trading members to enter bids directly from their offices through a sophisticated telecommunication network.

Book building through the NSE system offers several advantages:

- The NSE system offers a nationwide bidding facility in securities.
- It provides a fair, efficient and transparent method for collecting bids using latest electronic trading systems.
- Costs involved in the issue are far less than those in a normal IPO.

There are two IPO sessions on weekdays, one session from 11:00 a.m. to 2:00 p.m, while second session from 2:00 p.m. to 4:00 p.m. On Saturdays, the timings are from 11:00 a.m. to 3:00 p.m. On the last day of the IPO, the book running lead manager can extend the session timings up to 9:30 p.m. on specific request.

To use NSE's online IPO system, a company has to comply with the following procedure:

- Submit a written request as per the prescribed format for usage of electronic facilities and software of NSE.
- Give details regarding book running lead manager, co book running lead managers and syndicate members.
- Pay the requisite charges to NSE.

NEAT IPO is a fully automated screen-based bidding system that allows bidding in several issues concurrently. The system has the facility of defining a hierarchy amongst the users of the system. The book running lead manager can define who will be the syndicate member and who will be the other participating members in the issue. The syndicate member and other members also have a facility of defining a hierarchy among the users of the system as corporate manager, branch manager and dealer. Investors interested in trading through Neat-iXS must approach the brokerage and register. Once registered, the broker will provide a login name, password and a personal identification number (PIN).

An order can be placed by using the place order window and can be done in two ways:

- By entering the symbol, series of the stock and other parameters such as quantity and price of the stock on the place order window.
- By filling in the symbol, series and the default quantity. The investor then has to review the order placed by clicking the review option. He/she can also reset to clear values.

After reviewing, the order has to be sent by clicking on the send option. The investor will next receive an order confirmation message along with the order number and the value of the order. If the order is rejected by the stock exchange or the broker for reasons such as invalid price limit, an appropriate message will appear at the bottom of the screen.

Making Payments: Different brokerages will have different modes. Some will take an advance payment from investors and set trading limits. And after executing the trade, they will ask for transfer of funds from the investor's accounts to their own. One method which most large brokerages are likely to follow is to ask the investor to open an account in a pre-designated bank through which electronic transfer of funds can be done.

Order Book: As and when valid bids are received by the system, they are first numbered, time stamped and stored in the book. Each bid has a distinctive bid number and a unique time stamp on it.

All the bids placed in the system will remain outstanding till the last day of the book building process. Trading members can modify/cancel all the bids placed in the system from the start till the last day of the book building process. Some of the large banking companies that are venturing into Internet trading (e.g., ICICI) are providing the complete facility to investors. For example, when an investor executes a trade on the Internet, money is automatically credited or debited to his/her account that he/she has opened in a specific bank. Since this facility is available only in stocks in the dematerialized category, the stock is also transferred from one account to another by the brokerage that either has its own depository or through the depository with which it has a tie-up. The cost of transaction also varies between brokerages and between clients.

UNDERWRITING

In case of private placement, the issuing company will have to negotiate with a small group of potential investors. But in case of a public issue the company will have to employ intermediaries to ensure subscription. The underwriters have several roles to play. They bring credibility to the issue by attaching their name to the issue. Because they have to be in business, they would be concerned about the quality of the issue they handle. They also buy securities from the issuer at a discount and resell to other investors at a later stage thereby assuming risk. Underwriters have access to a network of retail investors to whom they can sell the issue. They also assist the issuer in pricing as they have valid market knowledge.

The registrar collects application from the collecting banks, scrutinizes application forms, classifies them, assists in finalization of basis for allotment, dispatches allotment letters and certificates, and refunds unsuccessful applicants. There are two types of underwriting contracts: firm commitment and best efforts. In a firm commitment contract, the underwriter guarantees the sale of securities at an agreed upon price. If the issue fails, the underwriter has the obligation to purchase the securities and keep them in inventory (and sell them later at an available price). Obviously this is in the interest of the issuer. In a best efforts contract, as the name suggests, the underwriter does not have an obligation to take up the issue if it devolves. Since the risk faced by the underwriter is less in a best efforts contract, the underwriting commission is also less. Often issues are underwritten by a group of underwriters when the issue size is large to limit the risk of failure. The lead underwriter identifies a group of underwriters (investment banks) to sell the issue. The underwriting compensation is shared on the basis of underwriting commitment and responsibility. Before taking the company public, top company executives must spend substantial time in preparing to go public, and ultimately, in being public. Selection of an IPO team deserves careful consideration: the company must be confident of sharing information with all team members. Before going public, a company must establish an investor relations programme and set aside resources for the same. Because the public issue process involves substantial investment in time and efforts, a company may appoint one or more executives to coordinate.

PROSPECTUS AND THE IPO TIMELINE

In India, SEBI clearance is required to sell securities. The SEBI guidelines requires all companies to prepare a prospectus for distribution of securities to investors. The contents of the prospectus and supplemental financial information are governed by the SEBI regulations. The prospectus is an important document. The company and its management team are liable for information provided in the prospectus and for omission of any material information. The company's investment banker drafts the prospectus after conducting due diligence investigation of the firm in consultation with the accountant and the legal counsel. The prospectus gives the details of the company's business and management, names of principal shareholders and their level of ownership, audited financial statements, underwriting agreement, information on the use of proceeds, dividend policy and capitalization. A discussion of management's perception of all risk factors and competitive position is also included. The company has to file the draft prospectus with SEBI through a merchant banker. After the preparation of prospectus, the merchant banker along with the due diligence certificates and other compliances sends the same to SEBI for vetting. On receiving the same, the Board scrutinizes it and may suggest changes within a certain number of (stipulated) days of receipt of prospectus. A company can come out with a public issue any time within 365 days from the date of the letter from SEBI or if no letter is received from SEBI, within 365 days from the date of expiry of 21 days of submission of prospectus with SEBI. A prospectus is also filed with the concerned stock exchanges along with the application for listing its securities. After making changes, if any made by SEBI/stock exchanges, the final prospectus duly signed by all the directors (or by authorized representatives through its power of attorney) must be filed with the Registrar of Companies (ROC) along with the copy of all material documents. The ROC may suggest changes which should also be reported to SEBI/stock exchanges. The date on which ROC card is obtained is the date of the prospectus. The draft offer document filed with the SEBI shall be made public for a period of 21 days from the date of filing the offer document with the SEBI. Once the registration statement is approved by the SEBI, the marketing of the offering begins.

THE IPO PROCESS

The following diagram lists out the typical activities in an IPO process.

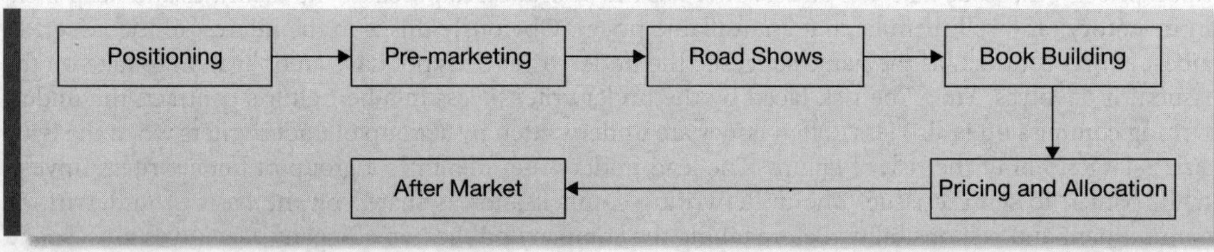

A typical road show lasts a few weeks. A detailed timeline diagram of the IPO process is given in Appendix 16A.2. Once the stock is listed, the underwriter has the obligation to stabilize the price (not mandatory in India), provide analyst recommendations and make a market in the stock.

PRICING OF IPOS

In determining the IPO price, the factors that will be considered are the prevailing market and general economic condition, the history of and prospects for the company and industry, an assessment of the company's management and its operating results and the market prices of securities and certain financial and operating information as they relate to market valuations of companies engaged in activities similar to those of the company. There are two approaches for valuing the equity of a company undertaking the IPO: DCF approach and peer comparison approach. The DCF approach involves forecasting of cash flows to equity and estimation of appropriate discount rate to discount cash flows. The value of equity thus arrived is divided by the number of shares outstanding to arrive at the intrinsic value. Valuation is both an art and a science. The issuer can come up with a price range and assess the likely market reaction to each of the prices. The final price is set in consultation with the lead manager.

Peer comparison approach requires identification of a set of comparable companies; obtaining for the latter their average price/earnings and price/book value ratios and application of these multiples to the earnings of the issuer to estimate the price. The obvious difficulty in this methodology is that it is hard to find peer companies due to differences in product life cycle, size, capital structure and so on. Further, estimation of future revenues and earnings based on short history of the firm's existence is difficult. Some examine the pricing of recent comparable issues in pricing the next issue. The difficulty in this approach is that P/E multiples fluctuate rapidly between quarters or days rendering this approach useless. The final pricing typically takes place the day the company is likely to get the SEBI clearance.

THE EMPIRICAL EVIDENCE ON IPOS

The cost of issuing securities includes the cost of underwriting and administrative expenses involved in the public issue process. In addition to these, there is a hidden cost of selling securities below their intrinsic values. A number of studies have recorded widespread underpricing of IPOs. The issue is said to be underpriced if an investor can make quick money upon listing of the issue.

The return on a stock from the day of offer to the day of listing is:

$$R = [(P_1/P_0) - 1] \times 100$$

where P_1 = price of stock on listing day and P_0 = Offer Price

To remove the effect of market, market-adjusted return could be calculated by subtracting the market return.

$$\text{Market-Adjusted Return} = \text{Raw Return} - \text{Market Return}$$

$$\text{Market Return} = [(\text{Market Index on Listing}/\text{Market Index on Offer}) - 1] \times 100$$

Table 16.2 presents the evidence on average underpricing in countries around the world.

Underpricing is not specific to the USA. Numerous studies replicated around the world confirm these findings. Why are so many issues underpriced? Many plausible reasons have been suggested. The underwriter, because of his/her superior experience in marketing IPOs and knowledge of the market can often coax an issuer to set a price low enough to sell the issue. This is obviously in the interest of the underwriter. But an underwriter's ability to set unduly low prices is limited by his/her desire to protect his/her reputation. Another explanation is based on information asymmetry between different groups of investors. If underwriters have no superior skills in accurately pricing all issues, we would expect some issues to be overpriced and some issues to be underpriced. If the informed investors are able to identify overpriced issues, we would expect them to avoid such issues and invest only in underpriced issues. The uninformed group realizes the incentives faced by the informed group and demand a discount on all issues. Another plausible explanation for short-run underpricing and long-run overpricing is that analysts tracking IPOs are overly optimistic about the earnings potential of these companies and investors pay attention to analyst forecasts.

TABLE 16.2
Average Underpricing Around the World[3]

Country	Sample Size	Time Period	Av. Underpricing (%)
Australia	381	1976–1995	12.1
Brazil	62	1979–1990	78.5
China	432	1990–2000	256.9
Denmark	117	1984–1998	5.4
France	448	1983–1998	9.5
Germany	407	1978–1999	27.7
Hong Kong	334	1980–1996	15.9
India	98	1992–1993	35.3
Korea	477	1980–1996	74.3
New Zealand	143	1979–1999	23.0
The Philippines	104	1987–1997	22.7
Switzerland	42	1983–1989	35.8

Studies in the USA have shown that although there is short-run underpricing, there is considerable 'overpricing' in the long run. Over the five-year period following the IPO, new issues produce significantly lower returns than similar public companies. Between 1970 and 1990, an average new issue in the USA produced annual returns of just 5 per cent, while investing an equal amount at the same time in a non-issuing firm would have produced an annual return of 12 per cent. Other studies have found that firms going public exhibit a substantial decline in post-issue operating performance. Over a six-year period extending from the year prior to the IPO until five years after the offering, the performance of IPO firms decline significantly relative to their pre-IPO levels. Some studies have documented the operating performance of firms after the IPO. These studies have noted the change in operating return on assets, operating cash flows/total assets, sales and asset turnover from one year prior to the IPO to three years after the IPO and document a decline in operating metrics.

Usually, the terms under pricing and undervaluation are used interchangeably. But are they? Undervaluation refers to the difference between the price and fair value. In other words, price and value are not the same. As discussed in the section on pricing, IPOs are priced on the basis of multiples of comparables and the DCF approach. If IPOs were priced too high compared to the valuations of comparable companies, we would expect prices of IPOs to revert to their intrinsic value in the long run. In other words, is the long-run underperformance of IPOs due to overvaluation at the time of time of offering? The answer appears to be yes. One study finds that in a sample of more than 2,000 relatively large capitalization IPOs from 1980–1997, the median IPO firm is overvalued by about 50 per cent relative to its industry peers. Studies have found that an IPO, on average, leaves US$9.1 million on table. Yet issuers and shareholders of the issuing company rarely complain. Why? The reason is that the

[3] Loughran, Ritter and Rydqvist, 'Initial Public Offerings'.

shareholders receive the bad news—that the issue was underpriced—and the good news—that their wealth is much higher than they had anticipated simultaneously!

IPO FEATURES UNIQUE TO INDIA

The SEBI has introduced certain features that are unique to India and potentially contribute to price discovery and reduce the underpricing of IPOs. We discuss them further.

Anchor Investors: The SEBI allows qualified institutional buyers (QIBs) to act as anchor (lead) investors in IPOs to boost investor confidence in IPOs.[4] This legislation went into effect on 9 July 2009. Earlier laws required that pre-IPO placement of shares to other investors, such as hedge funds and private equity funds, to be locked up for one year, which prohibited investors from exiting. Furthermore, issuers were compelled to issue shares at a discount to compensate investors for illiquidity. Under the legislation, a company can carve out a maximum of 30 per cent of the QIB section and offer it to anchor investors. The minimum application size for each anchor investor is ₹100 million. An anchor investor applies for shares like a regular investor at the price it deems fit. The offer to these investors opens and closes one day before the offer opens to other categories of investors. Allocations to anchor investors are made on a discretionary basis subject to a minimum of two investors for allocations of up to ₹2.5 billion and five investors for allocation of more than ₹2.5 billion. The number of shares allocated to anchor investors and the price at which the allocation is made are disclosed by the investment bank before the opening of the issue. These investors face a lock-in period of 30 days (on the shares allotted to them) from the date of allotment. The law prohibits entities related to the lead manager or founders of the company from acting as anchor investors. Typical anchor investors are public financial institutions, commercial banks, mutual funds, foreign institutional investors, multilateral and bilateral institutions, venture capital funds, insurance companies, provident funds and pension funds.

PRE-OPENING TRADING OF IPOS

In January 2012, the SEBI introduced a call auction mechanism for freshly listed IPOs. Under the law that came into effect on 20 January, there is a pre-trading session before the normal trading begins. The pre-trading session has a duration of 60 minutes from 9:00 a.m to 10:00 a.m. This session is conducted for IPOs only on the first day of trading, that is, the day of listing of the IPO on the exchange. This pre-market session helps in better price discovery with certain trade controls in a normal trading session. SEBI mandated that the normal trading session should commence only after the conclusion of call auction session for stocks on stock exchanges. From the next trading day onwards, trading of the stock follows the normal trading cycle of existing pre-open session (from 9:00 a.m.–9:15 a.m.) followed by continuous trading session. Pre-open sessions are available at the NSE of India and the Bombay Stock Exchange (BSE). On stock exchanges not eligible to offer call auction, the reference price for price bands for the first day would be the equilibrium price discovered in the call auction at NSE and BSE. The purported advantages of call auction market are (a) reduced price volatility due to multiple matching of orders at a single price, (b) greater liquidity due to deeper demand supply schedule, (c) better price discovery and (d)

[4] The 2007 crisis had eroded investor confidence in stock markets.

reduced market impact. This research is also motivated by the concern of stock exchanges, regulators and market participants about the initial price discovery and volatility of IPOs. Price discovery is particularly important and difficult for the opening of IPOs because no trading history exists. The initial trading and price discovery in these stocks can be noisy and has become a cause for concern. For example, Facebook, a social networking company's stock fell below the IPO price and the investment banks had to buy shares in the market to stabilize the price. This phenomenon is not unique to Facebook or the USA. Academic researchers have raised questions about the efficacy of traditional firm commitment offerings because of underwriters' inability to value firms facing valuation uncertainty. These studies document substantial volatility in IPO initial returns and note that alternate mechanisms such as auctions could result in better price discovery. Underpricing in emerging markets is not only much higher than the developed markets but also more volatile. For instance, underpricing in India during 1990–2014 was 88 per cent and in China it was 113.5 per cent during the same period.[5] Furthermore, underpricing has varied considerably through the 1980s, 1990s and the 2000s. The regulatory interference in India is in response to wide-spread underpricing and listing day volatility in IPO prices.

The Indian experiment conducts an auction after the offer price is set but before trading begins on the listing day. This feature combines the benefits of book building in the pre-market and auctions in the aftermarket. Guidelines by the SEBI impose trading controls and allow prices of freshly listed firms to fluctuate within specified price bands for 10 days after listing. SEBI guidelines require that in the normal trading session the prices of IPO firms fluctuate within a price band of ± 5 per cent of the 'equilibrium' price for IPOs with proceeds less than ₹2.5 billion and ± 20 per cent of the 'equilibrium' price for IPOs with proceeds more than ₹2.5 billion. This feature could potentially reduce the volatility of IPO initial returns.

CONCLUDING COMMENTS

Going public is a significant decision in the history of a company. Once public, a company will have to spend considerable time and resources in maintaining investor relations. For every seller, there has to be a buyer. To decide whether or not to invest in an IPO, one may rank the issue on several criteria, say, on a scale of four (with four being the best). Some of the potential criteria for raking include:

- Business model (company's products and services, future potential)
- Financial strength
- Reputation of underwriters
- Management and its experience in the business
- Superiority of the issuing company's technology over its competition
- Shareholding base (are the original shareholders successful venture capitalists or institutional shareholders?)
- Intended use of proceeds
- State of competition
- Trading comparables
- Major customers and their position

One may calculate an aggregate score for the company by summing up scores on each component and decide to purchase or not.

[5] https://site.warrington.ufl.edu/ritter/files/2015/05/Initial-Public-Offerings-International-Insights-2015–05-21.pdf

APPENDIX 16A.1: VALUATION OF A RIGHT

Consider a stock trading rights-on.[6] Each share gives the holder one right and n rights are needed to buy one share. For the sake of convenience, assume that the stock does not pay dividends until after the right's expiration date T. Let the subscription price be X and the stock price at time t be S_t. An approximate value of a right before ex-rights date is given by $(S_t - X)/(n+1)$.

This formula does not take into account the right's time to expiration, the stock's volatility and the risk-free rate of return. This equation ignores the option value embedded in a right and the time value of the subscription price. The arbitrage-free value of a right before the ex-rights date is given by the following equation:

$$[S_t N(d_1) - Xe^{-rf\,(T-t)} N(d_2)]/(n+1)$$

where

$$d_1 = [\ln(S_t/X) + (r_f + \sigma^2/2)(T-t)/[\sigma\sqrt{(T-t)}]$$
$$d_2 = d_1 - [\sigma\sqrt{(T-t)}]$$

σ is the volatility of the firm's equity value, which consists of its stock and rights.

The time to maturity could range from, for example, 2–100 days.

The ratio of a right's subscription price and the stock price at ex-rights date could be, for example, 0.5 to 1.0.

The volatility could be assumed to be 20–40 per cent or actually estimated.

When $S_t = X$, the value of a right is zero;

To value a right on or after the ex-rights date, S_t should be replaced by S_t + value of right in the previous equation.

To illustrate, assume the following data:

Rights-on stock price = ₹35
$N(d_1) = 0.4$
Subscription price = ₹30
$N(d_2) = 0.2$
Time to expiration = 20 days
$\sigma = 50\%$

The shareholders get 1.3 rights for every share held and each right can be exercised for one share. Let risk-free rate be 9 per cent. The traditional formula would give a value of:

$$(35-30)/(1+1.3) = ₹2.17$$

The option pricing approach would give a value of:

$$[35(0.4) - 30e^{0.09(20/365)} N(0.2)]/(1+1.3)$$

The value of the right can be estimated by referring to cumulative normal tables.

[6] Alexander and Baptista, 'A Note on the Valuation of Rights Formula Commonly Presented in Finance Text Books'. Also, see Smith, 'Alternative Methods for Raising Capital'.

APPENDIX 16A.2: IPO CALENDAR

	Day No.	No. of Days	Event	Remarks/Notes
A				
1	T – 0	1	Share transfer to increase number of members to seven	Inform the existing shareholders the reason and fix the transfer price for more members required.
2	T – 1	1	Board meeting and resolution	Resolution for conversion and authorization for convening AGM/EGM
3	T – 2	21	Notice for shareholders meeting	21 days' notice to shareholders for the AGM/EGM
4	T – 23	1	Shareholders meeting and special resolution	Resolution with three-fourths majority.
5	T – 24	1	Filing of Form 23 with ROC	Within 30 days—notice, explanatory statement, resolution.
6	T – 25	1	Filing of statement in lieu of prospectus with ROC	Draft copy can be kept ready before itself.
7	T – 26	1	Amendment of MOA and AOA	Delete certain clauses applicable only to a private company. File with the ROC the corrected copy
8	T – 27	5	Conversion into a public limited company	ROC will issue fresh certificate with the word 'Private' deleted.
9	T – 32	1	Notice for statutory meeting	21 days' notice to shareholders.
10	T – 33	30	Statutory meeting and statutory report	Anytime, after one month but before six months from date of conversion.
11	T – 63	1	Copy of statutory report to ROC	Copy to be filed with ROC immediately after circulating to members.
B			*Preparation and Regulatory Approvals*	
1	T – 64	1	Board resolution for issue of shares	Approving issue of shares and draft prospectus
2	T – 65	21	Shareholders' resolution	Sec 81 (A) of the Companies Act to be fulfilled. 21 days' notice for the meeting to be conveyed
3	T – 86	1	Filing Form 23 with ROC	Copy of special resolution, explanatory statement and notice to be filed.
4	T – 87	10	Appointment of merchant banker	MoU with the merchant banker, fixing terms and conditions, appointment of share registrars, underwriters, bankers to the issue and so on.
5	T – 97	30	Due diligence audit by the merchant banker	Financial statements, minutes, business profile, management study and so on.
6	T – 127	10	Preparation of prospectus	Legal requirements, contents, expert comments and risk factors.
7	T – 137	5	In principle approval for listing	Filing of statutory documents with regional and other stock exchanges
8	T – 142	25	Vetting of prospectus	Filing the prospectus with SEBI along with due diligence and compliance certificates.

	Day No.	No. of Days	Event	Remarks/Notes
				21 days available with SEBI for corrections. Practically takes more than 21 days most of the time.
9	T – 167	7	SEBI compliance	Terms and conditions put by SEBI. Corrections in the initial prospectus before obtaining ROC card.
10	T – 174	5	ROC card	Corrected final copy of prospectus duly attested by the Directors to be filed with the ROC
				Then ROC issues the ROC card. No specified time limit for the same.
11	T – 179	2	1% security deposit and promoters' contribution	Deposit to be paid to regional stock exchange and contribution to be kept in a separate Escrow account
C			*Marketing & Research*	
1	T – 181	3	Investor targeting	Identification of potential investors. Classification and segmentation of the targeted investors
2	T – 184	7	Research and sales calls	Conducting detailed analysis and research into company background and past performance.
				Identification of plus points and positioning the issue accordingly.
3	T – 191	7	Marketing efforts	Includes investor road shows, press conferences, statutory advertisements, printing prospectus and application forms and distribution of marketing materials.
D			*Execution*	
1	T – 198	10	Book open and close for book building	Bidding should be open for at least five days.
2	T – 208	3	Price discovery	In consultation with the merchant banker.
3	T – 211	10	Public offer opens	Minimum three days and maximum 10 days. Issue monitoring.
E			*Post-Issue Obligations*	
1	T – 221	10	Registry works	Collection of application forms and processing with the help of the merchant banker and registrars
2	T – 231	7	Allotment of shares	As per statutory rules in consultation with merchant bankers and regional stock exchange.
3	T – 238	5	Administrative duties	Post-issue advertisement, dispatch of share certificates and refund orders.
4	T – 243	3	Return of allotment	Form No. 2 to be filed with ROC within 30 days of allotment.
5	T – 246	5	Listing and trading of securities	Listing agreement with exchanges, listing fees.
6	T – 251	–	Commencement of trading	Trading of securities in stock exchanges.
7	–	–	Investor grievance handling	Includes 78-day monitoring report to be submitted to the SEBI.
8	–	–	Refund of security deposit	Application to the SEBI after completing all legal requirements.

EXERCISES

1. Explain the terms book building, underpricing, fixed price offers and private placements.
2. How are best efforts underwriting contracts different from firm commitment contracts?
3. Summarize the empirical evidence on short- and long-term performance of IPOs.
4. How are IPOs priced? Discuss.
5. Underpricing does not remain constant through time. They are highly volatile. What might explain the volatility of underpricing across time?

REFERENCES

Alexander, G. and A. Baptista. 'A Note on the Valuation of Rights Formula Commonly Presented in Finance Text Books'. *Journal of Applied Finance* (2001).

Cornelli, F. and D. Goldreich. 'Bookbuilding and Strategic Allocation'. *Journal of Finance* 56, no. 6 (2001).

Loughran, T., J. Ritter and K. Rydqvist. 'Initial Public Offerings: International Insights'. *Pacific Basin Journal* 2 (1994).

Smith, Clifford. 'Alternative Methods for Raising Capital: Rights Versus Underwritten Offerings'. *Journal of Financial Economics* 5, no. 5 (1977).

SUGGESTED READINGS

Aggarwal, R. and S. Dahiya. 'Capital Formation and the Internet'. *Journal of Applied Corporate Finance* 13, no. 1 (2000).

Beatty, R. B. and J. R. Ritter. 'Investment Banking, Reputation, and the Underpricing of Initial Public Offerings'. *Journal of Financial Economics* 15 (1986).

Benveniste, L. and P. Spindt. 'How Investment Bankers Determine Offer Price and Allocation of Initial Public Offerings'. *Journal of Financial Economics* 24 (1989).

Benveniste, L. and W. Wilhelm. 'A comparative Analysis of IPO Proceeds Under Alternative Regulatory Environments'. *Journal of Financial Economics* 28 (1990).

Benveniste, L. and W. Wilhelm. 'Initial Public Offerings: Going by the Book'. *Journal of Applied Corporate Finance* 10, no. 1 (1997).

Ibbotson, R. G., J. Sindelar and J. R. Ritter. 'The Market's Problems with the Pricing of Initial Public Offerings'. *Journal of Applied Corporate Finance* 7 (1994).

Jain, B. and O. Kini. 'The Post-Issue Operating Performance of IPO Firms'. *Journal of Finance* 49 (1994).

Levis, M. 'The Long-Run Performance of Initial Public Offerings: The UK Experience 1980–88'. *Financial Management* 22 (1983).

Loughran, T. and J. Ritter. 'The New Issues Puzzle'. *Journal of Finance* 50 (1995).

Loughran, T. and J. Ritter. 'Why Don't Issuers Get Upset about Leaving Money on the Table in IPOs?' *Review of Financial Studies* 15, no. 2 (2002).

Pagano, M., F. Panetta and L. Zingales. 'Why do Companies Go Public? An Empirical Analysis'. *The Journal of Finance* 53, no. 1 (1998).

Purnandam, A. and B. Swaminathan. 'Are IPOs Underpriced?' *Review of Financial Studies* 17, no. 3 (2004).

Ritter, J. 'The Long Run Performance of Initial Public Offerings'. *Journal of Finance* 46 (1991).

Rock, Kevin. 'Why New Issues Are Underpriced'. *Journal of Financial Economics* 15 (1986).

Smith, Clifford. 'Investment Banking and the Capital Acquisition Process'. *Journal of Financial Economics* (1986).

CHAPTER

17

Bank Loans

LEARNING OBJECTIVES

- Banks as a class of financial institutions
- Commercial bank lending products
- Evaluating creditworthiness from the perspective of a banker
- Syndicated loans

Bank loans are an important source of funding for a business. Banks and financial institutions provide at least a quarter of new funds raised by all corporations. Banks provide short-term WC loans and long-term loans to businesses in addition to other products like revolving credit facilities. Companies may borrow for a variety of reasons such as purchase of plant and machinery or repayment of other debt or meeting WC requirements and repay such loans from cash generated by business or sale of assets and/or infusion of new capital. This chapter describes the various products offered by banks and the methodology adopted by banks to evaluate the creditworthiness of borrowers.

COMMERCIAL BANK LENDING PRODUCTS

Although increased competition is forcing banks to design new, innovative products, the traditional products like short-term and long-term loans, and revolving credit facility continue to be the mainstay of banks. The credit facilities sanctioned by a bank to its corporate clients can be broadly classified into two categories:

- Working Capital Loans: These loans are provided for meeting the day-to-day expenses such as purchase of raw materials, consumable stores/spares, fuel and other essential needs. They are of a continuing nature and renewed every year.
- Term Loans: These are sanctioned for acquiring block or fixed assets such as land, building, plant and machinery and also to meet long-term WC. They are repayable over a period of time, say

three–five years, depending upon the profit generation capacity of the unit. Short-term loans are also granted for meeting temporary cash flow mismatches.

The banks fix a margin on the value of the security and drawing power for each facility. The unit can draw money to the extent of the limit or drawing power whichever is lower. WC gap is defined as current assets less current liabilities (other than bank borrowings) and NWC is defined as excess of current assets over all current liabilities. The borrower has to provide at least 25 per cent of current assets out of long-term funds. Total of current liabilities (including bank finance) should not exceed 75 per cent of current assets, that is, current ratio should be a minimum of 1.33:1.

CALCULATION OF PERMISSIBLE BANK FINANCE

Banks are required to make their own assessment of credit requirements of borrowers based on a total study of borrowers' business operations, that is, taking into account the production/processing cycle of the industry as well as the financial and other relevant parameters of the borrowers. Accordingly, the bank decides the levels of holding of each item of inventory, and receivables, which in its view would represent a reasonable build-up of current assets for being supported by bank finance. The RBI has discontinued the practice of prescribing detailed norms for each item of inventory and receivable for each industry. Earlier, the level of credit to a corporate was determined on the basis of MPBF to fix the eligible limits of credit. The Tandon Committee gave three methods as follows:

Method I: 0.75 (CA−CL)
Method II: 0.75 (CA)−CL
Method III: 0.75 (CA−CCA)−CL

where CA is current assets, CL is current liabilities and CCA is core current assets.

This mandated system was abolished and banks now have total freedom to decide on the methodology of assessing WC requirements. It is up to the companies to convince banks about their unique working capital needs.

CREDIT FACILITIES

The total credit requirement of an organization is usually catered to as a combination of various types of facilities discussed further.

FUND-BASED LIMITS

Fund-based limits involve extending funds or money to the borrower. There are four types of fund-based limits.

- **Cash Credit**
  It is an operating account from which the borrower can withdraw funds as and when needed up to a predetermined credit limit. The security for cash credit is inventory.

The banker takes the following precautions under cash credit accounts:

- o Valuation of stocks of raw material accepted as security is done on the basis of cost price or market price whichever is lower.
- o Stocks in process are valued as in the case of raw materials.
- o Finished goods are valued at cost of production or list price less trade discount and profit margin or market price whichever is the lowest.
- o Drawings in the account are regulated to the extent of drawing power or limit, whichever is lower.
- o The goods charged are properly stored to avoid any deterioration.
- o The goods are inspected every month to verify quantity, quality, age, saleability and value, and so on.

The cash credit permits the borrower to borrow up to a specified limit. The interest is charged only on the utilized portion but a service charge is levied on the unutilized portion. The customer (borrower) is also expected to maintain a minimum balance, called compensatory balance, in the cash credit account. The security offered by the customer is in the nature of hypothecation or pledge. Borrower's inventory and receivables are hypothecated to the bank in a cash credit arrangement. The amount that can be borrowed at any point in time is lower than that of the sanctioned limit and the value of security less margin. The following table gives an illustration of this.

(₹ in million)

	Situation A	Situation B
1. Sanctioned Limit	2	2
2. Value of Security	2	3
3. Margin Requirement	20% (i.e., 0.40)	20% (i.e., 0.60)
4. Value of Security Less Margin	1.6	2.4
5. Drawing Power (Minimum of 1 & 4)	1.6	2

The overdraft arrangement is similar to the cash credit arrangement. Under this arrangement, the borrower is permitted to overdraw up to a specified limit. Interest is charged on the amount drawn subject to a minimum. The drawing power is also determined as in case of cash credit arrangement. However, there is a minor technical difference between these two arrangements. Cash credit account operates against the security of the inventory and accounts receivables in the form of hypothecation or pledge. Overdraft account operates in the form of pledge of shares and securities, and sometimes even mortgage of fixed assets. The obvious shortcoming of these arrangements is that the customer can misuse the facility by keeping the limit higher than that warranted. It is tilted more towards the customer than the bank.

Packing credit

This is a credit given for exports only. It has a lower rate of interest because of various incentives. It is of two types:

- Pre-shipment Packing Credit: In this case, the loan is provided against a firm (definite) order or a letter of credit that is opened by the foreign buyer in favour of the Indian manufacturer. The Indian manufacturer's banker gives finance against hypothecation of raw material. The borrowed funds will be used to meet the expenses incurred for production, that is, raw material and labour.

- Post-shipment Packing Credit: In this case, the manufacturer already has finished goods, which are to be exported. The finished goods are evaluated based on sale value and there is usually no margin required to be paid to the banker. The banker provides finance based on the sales invoice and shipping documents.

The packing credit can be in the form of Packing Credit Foreign Currency (PCFC) or Rupee Packing Credit (RPC). PCFC has a lower interest rate and it is based on LIBOR. RPC has higher interest rate but the borrower can hedge the currency risk by booking forward contracts or by options.

In case the company uses PCFC, then it stands to gain on two fronts:

- The interest, which it pays, is substantially lower than that paid in case of RPC. In case of PCFC, interest is linked to LIBOR. This turns out to be quite lower than the Indian rate of interest even after converting to Indian currency.
- When it takes credit in foreign currency and converts it into ₹, it has to pay the extra spread between the selling quote and buying quote. This can be avoided by letting the foreign currency remain in the same denomination.

- **Bills Purchased/Discounted**

Under this facility, a banker purchases/discounts the bills and credits the amount in the customer's (seller of goods) account after deducting the discount. The term 'bills purchased' is used for allowing advance against demand bills which are payable on presentation before the drawee. The bills purchased can be clean or documentary. Under discounting of bills, advance is allowed against those bills that mature after a certain period of time. A banker realizes the amount of bill from the drawee on the due date but credits the customer's account by the amount of the bill less discounting charges immediately on receipt of the bill for discounting. Discounting charges also take care of the interest on the amount of bill for the discount period. In case a bill is dishonoured, the amount due, which includes the original amount, interest and other charges and so on, is debited to the drawer's account.

- **Term Loans**

These are sanctioned for acquiring block assets such as land, building, plant/machinery and other equipment for setting up a new industrial undertaking or expansion, modernization and so on of the existing one or for NWC. Term loans are normally granted for periods varying from three to five years, depending upon the profit generation capacity of the unit. The unit's repayment capacity is examined before sanctioning term loans. Term loan can be classified into two types based on the purpose and nature of the assistance:

Project loans are normally provided to finance the cost of establishment, modernization or expansion of industrial concerns. Project loans typically fund purchase of land, building, plant and machinery, preoperative and preliminary expenses including interest during construction period and margin money for WC.

Project loans are generally provided for periods ranging from five to seven years, depending upon the anticipated cash flow of the project. In the majority of cases, the project loan is repayable in quarterly instalments after a moratorium period for construction and early operational phase of the project.

Term loans are also provided to companies for their requirements of long-term funds for acquisition of equipment or investment in other capital assets such as captive power generation system, pollution control and effluent treatment and so on. The main difference over project loans is that in these cases, the investment may or may not result in increases in cash flow or profitability. Such investments are generally made by companies to maintain their productivity, upgrade their facilities or comply with regulatory requirements.

Corporate loans are non-project general purpose loans extended for the following purposes:

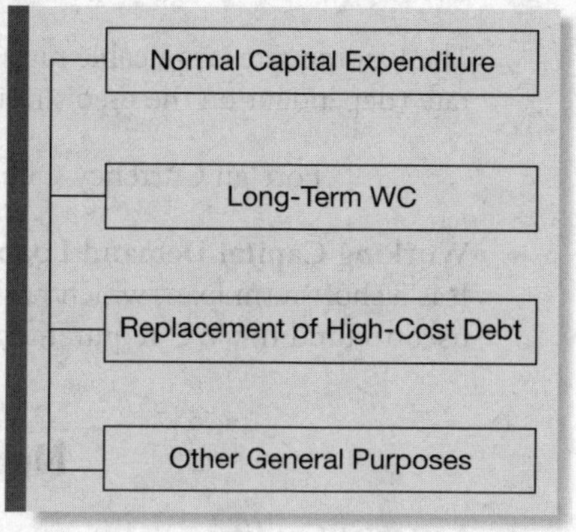

Corporate loans are normally advanced on the basis of the company's balance sheet strength and are generally extended to existing companies with good financial standing, a good credit rating and comfortable financial ratios.

The amount of corporate loan to be provided depends upon the company's credit rating, its debt servicing capacity and its refinancing capability. The tenure of corporate loan depends on specific requirements of the company and its future cash flow projections. The maturity of corporate loans is generally short to medium term, ranging normally from one to five years.

Since corporate loans are essentially balance sheet funding, it is necessary to keep track of changes in the balance sheet over the life of the loan. It is therefore essential to stipulate and monitor financial covenants such as maintaining a minimum debt service coverage ratio, interest coverage ratio, debt–equity ratio, security cover, restrictions on undertaking new projects or raising fresh borrowings to safeguard the lending institution's interest.

Most financial lending institutions while pricing their credit products follow the following three benchmarks:

- Short-term prime rate (STPR) for one-year bullet loans or loans of longer maturities with an annual repayment and annual reset values.
- Medium-term prime rate (MTPR) for loans with a final maturity between 12 and 36 months.
- Long-term prime rate (LTPR) for loans with a final maturity of greater than 36 months.

There are two options for pricing terms loans. They are:

- Benchmark pricing:

$$\text{Lending Rate} = \text{LTPR/MTPR/STPR} + \text{Appropriate Risk Charge}$$

The appropriate rate is calculated by adding an appropriate risk charge to the benchmark rate (STPR or MTPR or LTPR). The risk charge for term loan varies on three dimensions, namely the credit rating of the company, loan amount and the repayment schedule. The markup over the benchmark rate (risk charge in this case) remains fixed during the drawdown of the loan.

- Yield curve pricing:

$$\text{Lending Rate} = \text{Offer Rate} + \text{Appropriate Risk Charge}$$

The lending rate (applicable rate) is calculated by adding the appropriate risk charge to the offer rate (i.e., the cost of funds for the lending institution). Each disbursement has to be re-priced based on the cost of funds prevailing at the time of disbursement. On the date of each disbursement, the client has to be informed of the composite lending rate (applicable rate) based on the yield curve pricing methodology. In both pricing methods, the interest rate for the loan gets fixed on the date of disbursement and continues till the maturity irrespective of the change in the benchmark rate or the cost of funds. Banks also offer floating rate foreign currency loans. Pricing of foreign currency loans is similar to yield curve pricing for rupee term loans.

Lending Rate = Offer Rate + Appropriate Risk Charge

The lending rate (applicable rate) is determined by adding an appropriate risk charge to the offer rate (dependant on the credit rating).

Foreign Currency Offer Rate = Benchmark Floating Rate + Offer Rate Spread

- **Working Capital Demand Loan**
  It is a short-term loan, which has a minimum repayment period of three months and is generally used to fund the WC requirements of firms.

Non-Fund-Based Limits

- **Letter of Credit**
  It is an arrangement by means of which the bank acting at the request of the customer undertakes to pay to a third party a predetermined amount by a given date, according to agreed stipulations and against presentation of stipulated documents.

  There are four parties to a letter of credit. They are:

  - Applicant (or opener), who is the importer and who approaches the bank for opening a letter of credit
  - Issuing bank, which opens the letter of credit
  - Beneficiary, who is the exporter and in whose favour the letter of credit is opened
  - Advising bank, which informs the exporter about the letter of credit being opened, at the behest of the issuing bank. It is generally based in the same place as the exporter

  Letter of credit is opened by a bank in favour of its customer undertaking the responsibility to pay to the supplier in case the customer defaults on the payment for the goods purchased from the supplier within the due date. The bank does not provide finance but only assumes responsibility for its customer's behaviour. LC plays an important role in import transactions. LC can be of two types: clean and documentary. When the evidence of movement of goods is present, the LC is termed documentary LC. Another classification of LCs is on the basis of whether it can be revoked or not. Accordingly, they are called revocable, irrevocable or confirmed LC. In an irrevocable LC, the terms of the LC cannot be revoked/cancelled/amended without the prior consent of all the parties. Unless otherwise stated, LC is revocable. If the beneficiary is not satisfied about issuing bank, he/she may ask for a confirmation by a known bank (called advising bank). The advising bank adds its own confirmation to the LC. So the beneficiary (seller) gets two undertakings. Such an LC is called confirmed LC yet another classification of LCs is on the basis of method of payment. If the beneficiary gets immediate payment upon presentation of correct documents as per LC, then the LC is termed sight (demand) LC. The beneficiary may draw a usance draft on the issuing bank, confirming bank or buyer. The draft is accepted by the buyer, issuer bank or confirming bank and no payment is made immediately. Such an LC is called acceptance credit. The seller can wait till maturity or get it discounted but the buyer has to pay only on maturity.

  An LC contains:

  - Particulars of import licence if any
  - The full address of the beneficiary

- Brief description of goods
- Price and value of goods in words and figures
- Origin of goods
- Mode of transport
- Port of shipment/destination
- Payment terms
- Expiry date of LC
- Instructions regarding, negotiation of documents and reimbursement

- **Guarantee**

  This is a non-fund-based facility, that is, it does not involve extending any funds or money to the borrower. It, however, involves a commitment by the bank on behalf of the customer to pay to the parties in the event of default by the customer.

EVALUATING CREDITWORTHINESS

Before a bank agrees to commit its funds, it has to assess the creditworthiness of the borrower. Evaluation of a borrower's ability and willingness to repay a loan at maturity involves financial analyses, character and capability and so on. A number of variables are considered by banks while evaluating a loan proposal.

The loan evaluation procedure followed by banks involves the following steps:

- Determining the 'purpose of the loan', cash requirements of the borrower, type of advance to be made
- Collateral or security given by the borrower to safeguard the loan
- Covenants: These are conditions imposed upon the borrower to:
  - Preserve the financial strength of the borrower
  - Maintain the borrower's ability to refinance itself
  - Control the assets
  - Ensure that the borrower does not do something that would be detrimental to the lender

Covenants may be either positive or negative.

- Industry Analysis: To study the prospects for the industry, an industry-level credit analysis needs to be performed, which includes the study of the following:
  - Industry cycle
  - Entry barriers
  - Threat of substitutes
  - Shifts in consumer demand
  - Regulatory environment
- Operational Efficiency: The company level credit evaluation is conducted to assess the operational efficiency of the client company.

The critical aspects that are to be evaluated in this process fall into the following categories:

- Operating margins
- Stability and growth of market share

- Access to key raw materials
- Benefit from economies of scale

- Financial Efficiency: Repayment of the loan by the clients depends greatly on their financial soundness. Thus, financial analysis becomes an imperative part of credit risk analysis. It includes the analysis of the following:
    - Capital structure
    - Cash flow statements
    - Ability to raise funds
    - WC management
    - Projections and sensitivity analysis
    - Comparison of actual and budgeted performance
    - Asset/liability position
    - Asset quality
    - Profitability
    - Sensitivity to interest rate structures, tax policies and so on

Banks are concerned about the credit risk of not only individual transactions but also that of the entire loan portfolio. Credit risk is the risk of loss due to the default by a borrower or counterparty in meeting his/her obligations. The default could be due to inability, incapacity or unwillingness to honour commitments in relation to lending, trading, hedging, settlement and other financial transactions. This default gives rise to low quality assets which in turn leads to credit risk.

Credit risk is monitored intensively at transactional level and extensively at a portfolio level by any bank. Credit risk can be broadly divided into two types:

- Default Risk (includes Probability of Default and Actual Default)
  This is the main risk for a banker and this risk becomes evident on the counterparty missing an instalment/interest due or breaking a financial covenant or entering into a legal procedure. Some of the important types under this category for a bank could be:
    - Direct Lending Risk: This is the risk that actual customer obligations will not be repaid on time. This occurs in products ranging from advances/overdrafts to bill discounting. It exists for the entire life of the transaction
    - Contingent Lending Risk: This is the risk that potential customer obligations will become actual obligations and will not be repaid on time. This risk occurs in products such as LC and guarantees, and exists for the entire life of the transaction.
- Recovery Risk
  Some of the types of this category of risk are:
    - Sovereign Risk: Risk is dependent on a country's current financial standing vis-à-vis foreign exchange controls, economy, political stability and focuses across the ability of the country to repay its obligations.
    - Collateral Risk: The risk of the collateral offered as security to a transaction eroding in value or not being monetized.

QUALITATIVE ASSESSMENT

While evaluating a credit proposal, the bank should assess not only the ability of the client to pay back the loan but also its willingness to repay.

These refer to an analysis of the 'Five Cs of credit'.

- Character: The willingness of the customer to honour his obligations. It reflects integrity and moral attribute that are very important considerations for credit managers.
- Capacity: The ability of the customer to meet credit obligations from the operating cash flows.
- Capital Structure: The financial reserves of the customer. If the customer has difficulty in meeting his/her credit obligations from its operating cash flow, the focus shifts to its capital.
- Collateral: The security offered by the customer in the form of pledged assets.
- Coverage refers to business insurance or 'key man' insurance that is often required when management ability is concentrated in a few individuals. In the event of the death or disability of a key manager, such coverage ensures that the bank will be repaid if the business cannot meet its obligations.

Credit risk management is difficult due to variety of available methods, degree of sophistication and element of subjectivity involved in some areas. Many banks adopt credit scoring/rating which is essentially a default risk analysis or assessing the creditworthiness of the borrower for the purpose of granting/rejecting his/her credit proposal and fixing interest rate based on rating. Under this process, each type of risk is again divided under few key parameters and each parameter is assigned scores as per their degree of presence or absence over a scale. To make the process simple and practicable at field level, many banks have devised credit scoring/risk rating on selected parameters. Further, all the parameters are not truly objective. Some of them are subjective. Accordingly, in order to instil objectivity in the assessment, all the parameters need to be quantified against a benchmark or a scale (say, 0–4 or 0–5) depending upon predefined range of variation from the benchmark or degree of attributes. The output of the credit–appraisal process, specifically the financial ratios, is directly compared with the specified benchmarks for a particular risk category. In these cases, the risk rating is fairly standardized and credit rating model allocates a grade or a numeric value for the overall risk profile of the proposed exposure. For instance, assume a scale from '1' to '5', with '1' representing extremely low financial risk. The credit rating model may specify that for the risk-rating exercise:

If gross revenues are between ₹800 to ₹1,000 crores	Assign a score of	2
If operating margin is 20% or more	Assign a score of	2
If ROCE is 25% or more	Assign a score of	1
If debt/equity is between 0.60 and 0.80	Assign a score of	2
If interest cover is 3.50 or more	Assign a score of	1

The next step would be to assign weights to these risk parameters. Higher weights may be placed on size (as measured by gross revenues), profitability of operations (operating margins), financial leverage (debt/equity) and debt servicing ability (interest cover). Assume that the rating assigns a 25 per cent weight to each of these two parameters—gross revenues and the operating margin; a 20 per cent weight to financial leverage and debt servicing ability and ROCE is given a 10 per cent weight. The weighted-average score for the financial risk of the proposed exposure is 1.70, which would correspond with the low risk/high safety level category of the model (category 1–2). Similarly, the business and the management risk of the proposed exposure are assessed and an overall risk rating is assigned.

In case of some parameters where no benchmark is available like profit margin and so on, time series analysis may reveal a trend and accordingly score may be assigned. Aggregate credit rating score signifying creditworthiness of risk rating score reveals degree of risk in the unit and it helps the bank in the following aspects:

- To assess the borrower's credit risk
- To make distinction between good and bad borrowers
- To take a decision whether to lend or not on the basis of cut-off score
- To fix the interest rates, margin requirement, collateral security and also to prescribe the non-monetary terms in sanction.

The credit scoring sheet used by a major private sector bank is given in Appendix 17A.1. Overall risk can be measured on a 10-point scale as shown in Table 17.1.

Credit approval is done through a multi-tier credit approving system. Credit committees, formed for different quantum of exposures, approve the loan proposals. The head of corporate risk management or his/her nominee is necessarily a member of this committee. The committee members base credit approval only on a unanimous decision. Each committee is delegated specific powers for sanction of credit limits, within set guidelines, under a scheme of delegation of powers. In respect of high risk and

TABLE 17.1
Credit Rating of Loans

Grade	Degree of Safety with Regard to Servicing Debt Obligations	Comments
Grade I	Very High	The fundamentally strong debt servicing capacity of such companies is most unlikely to be adversely affected by changes in circumstances
Grade II	High	Adverse business conditions are unlikely to affect debt servicing capacity. Such companies differ in safety from those in Grade I only marginally
Grade III	Adequate	Changes in circumstances are more likely to affect debt servicing capacity than for higher grades
Grade IV	Average	Debt servicing capacity could weaken in view of changing circumstances
Grade V	Below Average	While such companies are less susceptible to default than those in lower grades, uncertainties faced by them could adversely affect debt servicing capacities
Grade VI	Inadequate	Uncertainties faced by the issuer could lead to inadequate capacity to make timely debt repayments
Grade VII	Low	Debt servicing capacity is highly vulnerable to adverse changes in circumstances
Grade VIII	High Risk	Adverse business or economic conditions are likely to lend to lack of ability or willingness to service debt obligations
Grade IX	Substantial Risk	Timely payment of debt would continue only in favourable circumstances continue
Grade X	Default	Debt servicing capacity is in default and returns from this may be realized only on reorganization or liquidation

delinquent assets, lower levels have no powers to sanction credit limits. Powers exercised by each committee is subject to reporting to the next level.

STRUCTURING THE CREDIT FACILITY AND LOAN AGREEMENT

Once creditworthiness is ascertained and the bank decides to lend, the bank and the borrower structure a suitable credit facility. The loan agreement contains the following sections:

- Amount and maturity of the loan
- Purpose of loan
- Sources of repayment
- Rate of interest
- Bank fees
- Loan covenants
- Security requirements and collateral guarantees
- Events of default
- Use of ancillary bank products

AMOUNT

The first section of a standard loan agreement describes how much and when the borrower may borrow, the interest provisions, repayment terms, fees and the intended use of the proceeds and any security taken by the bank.

WC requirements of a borrower are assessed in two stages.

Stage I: Fixing of Yearly Sanctioned Limits

At this stage, assessment of the WC is made for the entire year and permissible bank finance is sanctioned based on the projected financials of the entity for that year. The limits sanctioned during this process are called as sanctioned limits. This assessment for a borrower is made at the beginning of the year. The borrower's requirement for WC credit at no point during the year should exceed the sanctioned limit.

Stage II: Fixing of Operating Limits

To ensure that borrowers are provided need-based credit, borrowers are required to submit to the bank quarterly information system reports at the end of each quarter in the prescribed formats (monthly in case of some industries). These reports highlight the actual financial figures for the last quarter (quarter to which they relate to). Based on these reports, the operating/drawing power limits are defined for the borrower for the next quarter. This means that operating limits can vary across different quarters. However, the operating limit can never exceed the sanctioned limit for the year. The sanctioned limit should first be bifurcated into cash credit component and loan component.

Period of Loan

The period of the loan component of the WC credit limits is based on the appraisal and the cash flow projections. Considering the need for smooth availability of bank credit for WC purposes, the period of the short-term loan for WC purposes is kept at not less than one year. However, for seasonal industries, the minimum period is six months. The bank is free to decide the maximum period for the short-term loan for working capital purposes

Security/Collateral

Banks are free to decide the nature, type, margin and quantum of security to be obtained from borrowers. Where commodities are covered by the directives issued by the RBI under the Selective Credit Control Policy, banks must observe the regulatory framework as prescribed. However, banks are required to limit their unsecured advances and guarantees in such a manner that 20 per cent of bank's outstanding unsecured guarantees plus the total of its outstanding unsecured advances should not exceed 15 per cent of its total outstanding advances.

Mortgages are also given as security for the loans apart from hypothecation of stock and personal guarantees.

The time frame for arriving at a decision on a credit proposal does not normally exceed three months. All loan application for small-scale units are dealt with and disposed of within eight to nine weeks of application.

LOAN PRICING

When a bank decides to extend lending support on the basis of risk/credit score, the next step should be to set risk-based loan pricing, that is, interest rates on the basis of basic principle of risk–return trade-off. In acquiring assets, banks should use the pricing mechanism in conjunction with product/geography/industry/tenor limits. For example, if a bank believes that construction loans for suburban malls are unattractive from a portfolio perspective, it can raise the price of these loans to a level that will act as a disincentive to borrowers and an incentive to the lender, that is, the bank. This is an instance of 'marginal cost pricing'—the notion that the price of an asset should compensate the institution for its marginal cost as measured on a risk-adjusted basis. The more a product increases a lender's portfolio concentration, the higher its marginal cost to that lender. Marginal cost pricing may not always work. A bank may have idle capacity—a large cost base and capital that has not been deployed. While such an institution clearly would not invest in a negative spread, it would probably view even a small positive spread as worthwhile as long as the added risk was acceptable.

Institutions tend to book unattractively priced loans when they are unable to allocate their cost base with clarity or to make fine differentiations of their risks. If a bank cannot allocate its costs, then it will make no distinction between the cost of lending to borrowers that require little analysis and the cost of lending to borrowers that require a considerable amount of review and follow-up.

Traditional pricing for credit risk has followed the cost-plus-profit approach as, shown in Figure 17.1. A cost-plus-profit pricing strategy will work in the short run, but in the long run borrowers will baulk and start looking for alternatives. Cost-plus-profit pricing will also work when a bank has some flexibility to compete such as on an array of other services rather than exclusively on price.

The steps involved in and the considerations for pricing loans is depicted in Figure 17.1.

The base rate, that is, the rate available to the prime borrowers having negligible credit risk is the prime lending rate (PLR) and as the risk increases, a risk premium is added to the PLR to determine the rate applicable for the unit.

$$\text{Interest Rate Chargeable} = \text{PLR} + \text{Risk Premium}$$

FIGURE 17.1
Loan Pricing

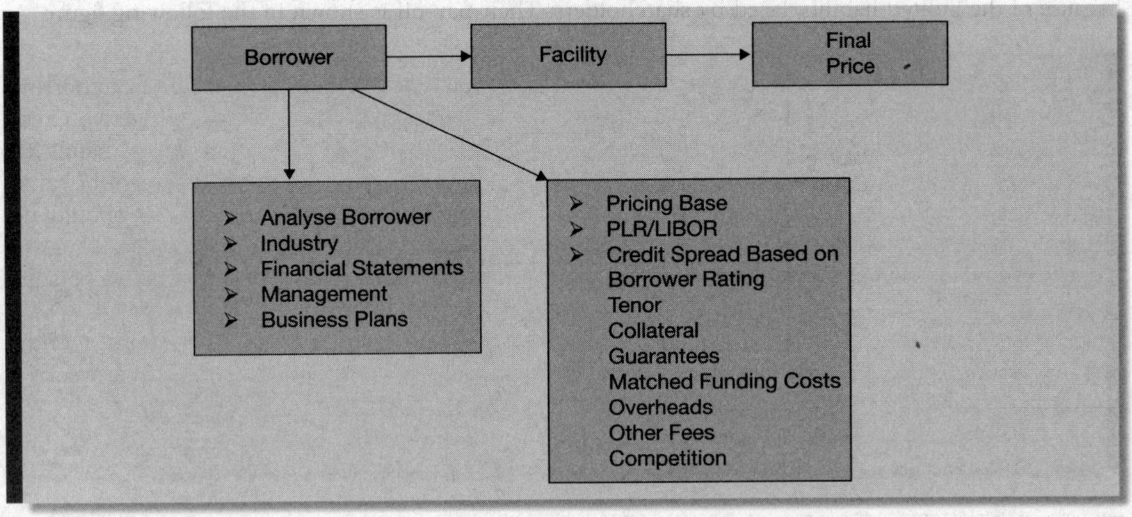

The higher the aggregate credit score, the better is the creditworthiness and lower is the risk. Accordingly, interest rate becomes higher with decline in score. The scoring is reviewed with each annual review of the account.

The interest rate charged on the loan takes into account a number of factors such as operating costs, profitability targets, credit risks and the competitive environment. The PLR is the rate given to the best customer of the bank. It is defined as such because it is almost (default) risk free. It covers the cost of funds and transaction costs of the bank. The risk premium is therefore the spread of the bank and is directly proportional to the creditworthiness of the corporate client and also the uncertainty attached to the future cash flows of the company. This uncertainty relates mainly to the amount of cash inflows and the timing of the cash flows. In such uncertain situations, the bank can arrive at the probability of repayment/default and also the extent of recovery in case of a default. While the probabilities can be assessed from the past data, the recovery rate can be computed by considering the guarantees and value of collateral attached to the loan.

Thus, the pricing is based on the borrower's risk rating, tenor, collateral and guarantees, and so on. A capital charge is applied based on a hurdle rate and a capital ratio. The historic loan loss rate used for each of the risk-rating categories is used to calculate the expected loss allowance to be built into the price. Other inputs are the capital ratio and the required rate of return on capital. Using these assumptions, the rate to be charged for a loan to a customer with a given rating could be calculated. This relatively simple approach to credit pricing works well as long as the assumptions are correct, especially those about the borrower's credit quality.

Shareholders, as residual claimants, are entitled to profits left over after meeting interest and principal payments. Thus, from the shareholders perspective, equity can be viewed as a call option on the value of the company's assets.[1] If the value of the assets is more than the amount to be repaid to lenders

[1] The option has more value when the firm is highly leveraged than when it is moderately leveraged because the probability of default is low.

at the end of the year, they get to keep residual profits, whereas if the value of assets falls short of the amount owed, they hand over the company to the lenders and walk away. The downside is limited because of the limited liability faced by shareholders. Their pay-off is shown in the following figure.

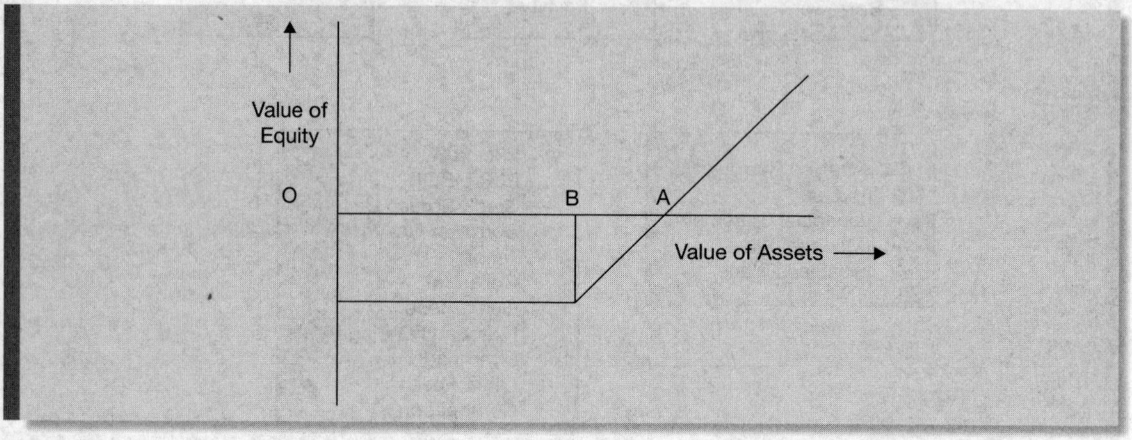

Thus, as long as the value of assets is more than OB, they get to retain profits. Similarly, the lenders position can be thought of as writing a put option on the firm's assets.

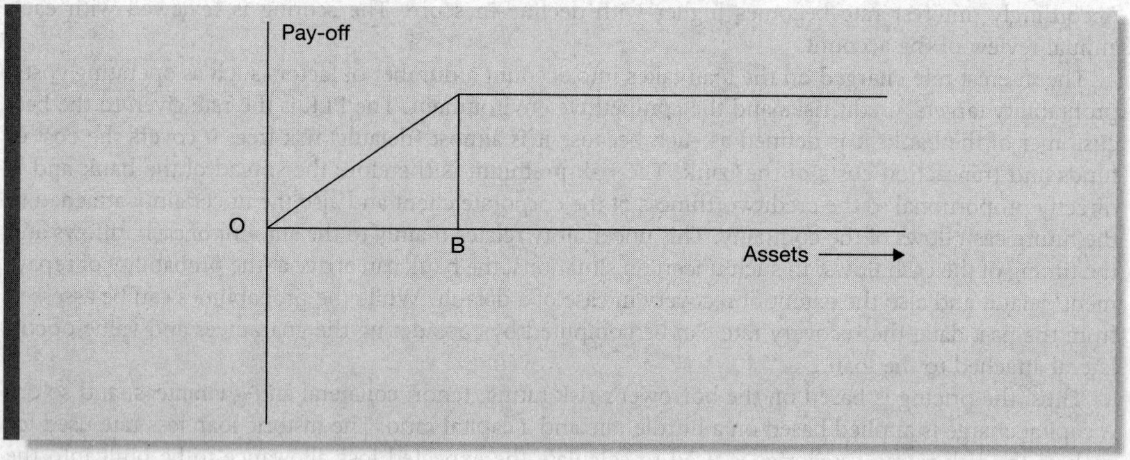

If the value of assets is greater than OB, the bank gets its payment, otherwise the firm's shareholders default. The bank's return is fixed, whereas it can lose its entire investment.

Professor Merton in a seminal paper[2] noted the equivalence between lending and writing a put option on the firm's assets. Just as option on stocks can be valued using the five variables that enter into the Black–Scholes model (S, X, r, t and σ), the value of a risky loan can be found using five similar parameters: A, B, r, t and σ_A.

[2] Merton, 'On the Pricing of Corporate Debt'.

Where,

A = Market value of firm's assets

σ_A = Volatility of the market value of a firm's assets

B = Market value of debt

Given these five parameters, it is possible to solve for the value of default option and the observed interest spread between a firm's risky bonds and a matched risk-free treasury rate.[3]

The relationship between the yield on risky debt and risk-free rate (on debt) of equivalent maturity is given by:

$$k(\tau) - i = (-1/\tau)\ \ln\ [N(h_2) + (1/d)\ N(h_1)]$$

where,

$k(\tau)$ = The required yield on risky debt

i = Risk-free rate on debt of equivalent maturity

τ = Length of time remaining to maturity

d = Firm's leverage ratio as $Be^{-r\tau}/A$

$N(h)$ = A value computed from standard normal tables. It reflects the probability that a deviation exceeding the calculated value of h will occur.

$$h_1 = -[1/2\sigma^2\ \tau - \ln(d)]/\sigma\sqrt{\tau}$$
$$h_2 = -[1/2\sigma^2\ \tau + \ln(d)]/\sigma\sqrt{\tau}$$

Bankers often calculate risk-adjusted return on capital (RAROC) and compare it with a hurdle rate such as return on equity or WACC while pricing individual loans.[4] It incorporates risk and funding sources and translates it into required returns pricing of assets. The ratio is based either on the size of the asset or the size of the capital allocated to it. When an institution observes asset prices directly (infers risk from observable asset prices), then it can determine how much capital to hold based on the volatility of the asset. This is the essence of the mark-to-market concept. If the return from the asset is less, relative to the capital held, the bank will not acquire it. If the asset is already in the bank's portfolio, it may be sold off. Bankers Trust introduced RAROC in the late 1970s. It is based on a mark-to-market concept. As defined by Bankers Trust, RAROC allocates a capital charge to a transaction or a line of business at an amount equal to the maximum expected loss (at a 99% confidence level) over one year on an after-tax basis. RAROC is a powerful risk measurement tool that assists banks and financial institutions both in measuring solvency and evaluating performance of different business activities. The RAROC process estimates the asset value that may prevail in the worst-case scenario and then equates the capital cushion to be provided for the potential loss.

$$\text{RAROC} = \frac{\text{Adjusted Income}}{\text{Capital at Risk}}$$

where Adjusted Income = Spread + Fees − Expected Loss − Operating Costs

[3] Interested readers may refer to Saunders, *Credit Risk Measurement*.

[4] A useful article on the topic is Zaik, Walter, Kelling and James, 'RAROC at Bank of America'.

$$\text{Spread} = \text{Loan Rate} - \text{Bank's Cost of Funds}$$

and Capital at Risk $= -D_L \times L \times (\Delta R/1 + R_L)$

D = Duration of the loan

L = Loan amount

$(\Delta R/1 + R_L)$ = Expected discounted change in the credit premium

A loan is value adding if RAROC > ROE.

Establishing the maximum expected loss in each product line and linking the capital to this loss makes it possible to compare products of different risk levels by stating the risk side of the risk–reward equation in a consistent manner. Performance measures such as ROA and ROE do not consider the different sources of risk or capital requirements of different activities of a bank.

RAROC is an improvement over the traditional approach in that it allows one to compare two businesses with different risk (volatility of returns) profiles. Using a hurdle rate, a lender can also use the RAROC principle to set the target pricing on a relationship or a transaction. Although not all assets have market price distribution, RAROC is a first step towards examining an institution's entire balance sheet on a mark-to-market basis, if only to understand the risk return trade-offs that have been made.

COVENANTS OF THE BORROWER

Since the borrower can expropriate wealth from the lending bank, the borrower's behaviour is contained by loan covenants that are heavily negotiated between the borrower and the bank. Covenants set minimum standards for a borrower's future conduct. There are two types of covenants: positive and negative.

Positive covenants are requirements made on the borrower to do certain acts. Negative covenants are those that do not force the borrower to perform certain acts but require him/her to ensure certain things and restricts him/her from doing certain acts. They are designed to protect the lender from the dissipation of assets, to protect his/her security and to an extent preserve the financial strength of the borrower. If credit risk is high, covenants may be directly tied to detailed financial projections provided by the

TABLE 17.2
Loan Covenants

Affirmative covenants that include promises that the borrower will	Negative covenants stipulates promises that the borrower will not
Submit annual, audited financial statements	Permit debt–equity ratio to exceed specified maximum
Submit periodic unaudited, interim financial statements	Permit the interest coverage ratio to be less than the minimum
Submit periodic certificates signed by an officer of the company stating whether the company is in compliance with the loan agreement	Permit additional borrowings
	Permit the current ratio to fall below a specified minimum.
	Permit NWC to fall below a specified minimum.
	Pledge its assets to another creditor, merge with or acquire another company or sell its assets.

borrower. If credit risk is low, a few general financial benchmarks may be sufficient. Table 17.2 presents a sample list of covenants.

The bank has a right to recall WC credit facility including short-term loan(s) for WC purposes, if the performance of a borrowing unit is not satisfactory, or where a borrowing unit is found to have used the amount for purposes other than for which the short-term loan is sanctioned or for any other reasons considered necessary.

LOAN SYNDICATION

In case of consortium, member banks will have to share the cash credit component and the loan component on a pro rata basis. In case of multiple banking and/or syndication, each bank must restrict sanction of cash credit component to a maximum of 40 per cent of its share of the loan. For this purpose, the banks should evolve an arrangement for sharing of information about the borrowing unit periodically. Where the facility is sanctioned by more than one consortium, either voluntary or obligatory, or through syndication, the reporting is done by the lead bank/lead manager, as the case may be. The lead bank will be responsible for preparation of appraisal note, its circulation, convening meetings, documentation and so on. The lead bank is vested with the responsibility of arranging for sanction and disbursal of credit, monitoring of the borrower's account and advising shares of member banks in the monthly/quarterly operative limits. Lead bank in a consortium will also be responsible for submitting prescribed data/information to the RBI on behalf of the consortium (syndicate). For various services rendered, lead bank can charge a suitable fee per annum to be borne by the borrower.

There is no ceiling on the number of banks that can participate in a consortium (whether in obligatory or voluntary consortium). It is open to a borrower to choose his/her bank for obtaining credit facilities as also for the bank to take a credit decision on the borrower. However, once a consortium (obligatory or voluntary) is formed, entry of a new member into a consortium should be in consultation with other member banks. An existing member bank can withdraw from the consortium only after two years of its joining. This is subject to the condition that other existing member banks or a new bank is willing to take its share by joining the consortium. In cases where the other existing member banks or a new bank are unwilling to take over the entire outstanding of withdrawing member, such bank may be permitted to leave the consortium by selling its debt at a discount and/or furnishing an unconditional undertaking that the repayment of its dues would be deferred till the dues of other members are repaid in full.

ARE BANK LOANS UNIQUE?

As pointed out in Chapter 15, academic studies in the USA have recorded neutral to negative responses to almost all kinds of securities offerings: private placement of debt, straight public debt, preferred stock, convertible debt, convertible preferred and common stock. Announcements by public firms of new bank lending agreements, in contrast, elicit, on average, a significantly positive reaction from the stock market.[5] This stark difference between the market reaction to announcement of bank loans and public securities raises the question 'what's different about banks?' One plausible explanation for the neutral to negative reaction to sale of debt or common stock is the information asymmetry between the company's management and investors. Since bank loans can be considered 'inside debt', the information

[5] James, 'Some Evidence on the Uniqueness of Bank Loans'.

asymmetry problem is resolved. In other words, since banks have an advantage in gathering information when compared to outside investors and because they actively monitor the conduct of the borrower, they are better able to price a loan. Further, banks have an incentive to monitor the borrower because they have their money at stake and take the initiative in resolving financial distress. This is a positive signal to 'other' investors in the company.

CONCLUDING COMMENTS

Bank credit is among the cheapest sources of finance to an entrepreneur. But getting it is not easy. Bankers are conservative because they operate on thin margins. If a banker is readily willing to lend, it is said, you probably do not need money! Just as bankers evaluate your business, it is important for you to evaluate your banker. More specifically, it is important to assess your banker's risk-taking appetite. Some banks are more conservative than the rest. As the relationship develops, educate the banker on your business, your needs, trends in your industry and encourage periodic visits. A good relationship with a bank would prove valuable to carry out business without interruptions arising out of shortage of funds.

EXERCISES

1. Describe fund-based and non-fund-based limits provided by banks.
2. Write a note on loan pricing.
3. Discuss the credit grading procedure in the context of bank loans.
4. What are the different types of LC?
5. List down the parameters considered for the qualitative assessment of a borrower.

REFERENCES

James, Christopher. 'Some Evidence on the Uniqueness of Bank Loans'. *Journal of Financial Economics* 19 (1987).

Merton, R. C. 'On the Pricing of Corporate Debt: The Risk Structure of Interest Rates'. *Journal of Finance* (1974 June).

Saunders, Anthony. *Credit Risk Measurement: New Approaches to Value at Risk and other Paradigms*. Hoboken, NJ: John Wiley, 1999.

Zaik, E., J. Walter, G. Kelling and C. James. 'RAROC at Bank of America: From Theory to Practice'. *Journal of Applied Corporate Finance* 9, no. 2 (1996).

APPENDIX 17A.1: SAMPLE CREDIT GRADING SHEET

There are two groups of parameters:

Group V: Veto score parameters consist of Financials & Business and must secure minimum score of 21 (minimum score for Financials is 12 and minimum score for Business is 9). Proposals without these minimum scores are not considered.

Group N: Normal score parameters consist of General, Management & Account. No minimum veto score is stipulated.

Name of the Account: ______________________ **Branch:** ______________

CG Branch: ______________________ **CG (Corp. Office):** ______________

Legend: B: Branch Score; C: Corp. Office Score

Negative Veto Score: Proposals with negative score in credit rating, profitability, liquidity and integrity are rejected.

I. General		B	C			B	C
1)	**Ownership/Constitution:**			**2)**	**Credit Rating by Rating Agencies:**		
a)	Limited & Listed	2	2	a)	'AAA' and 'AA' category	3	3
b)	Limit—Unlisted	1	1	b)	'A' category	2	2
c)	Private Ltd.—Closely held Ltd Co	0	0	c)	'BBB' category/not rated	0	0
d)	Partnership/Proprietorship	–1	–1	d)	Speculative grade	–2	–2
3)	**Age of Business:**			**4)**	**Priority Sector:**		
a)	Well established—over 10 years	6	6	a)	Export under priority	5	5
b)	New but well established—5–10 years	4	4	b)	Domestic under priority	3	3
c)	Recently established—3–5 years	2	2	c)	Domestic	2	2
d)	New, experienced promoters, synergies with existing business	1	1	d)	Export & others	0	0
e)	New project, no group support	–3	–3				
II.	**Business**						
1)	**Market Position:**			**2)**	**Buyer Profile:**		
a)	Diverse product range and markets, strong brands, low competition, one of the strongest players or single/double, enjoys the first or second market share, products enjoy premium in the market, would not be affected by growing competition.	5	5	a)	Large number of buyers for whom this product/service input is critical. Increasingly wide product applicability. Buyer has fewer options of suppliers. Imports not competitive, buyback arrangements. Large captive consumption.	4	4
b)	Same as above but a medium to large-size player, has a national brand, even if a strongest player now, could stand to lose with increasing competition.	4	4	b)	There are quite a few suppliers. Players are increasingly going for backward integration. Week buyback arrangements/captive use.	2	2
c)	Medium-size player, has a strong regional presence, no specific brand strength, but is a strong competition in the market place. Well positioned to take advantage to growing market. Even if a strong player now, could be adversely affected by competition.	3	3	c)	Sales seasonal, offtake dependent on government spending. Product substitutes available and gaining acceptance.	–2	–2

(Continued)

(Continued)

d)	Medium- to small-size player, has an average regional presence, can show consistent growth in medium term, even if a strong player now, could be badly affected by increasing competition.	2	2				
e)	Small and marginal player, can grow to become a regional player, no brand strength and so on.	1	1				
f)	Weak player, would get marginalized soon.	0	0				
3)	**Growth Plans, Capex, Diversification:**			**4)**	**Mix of Business:**		
a)	Company's business standing is high. Company is cash rich, can approach capital markets successfully, can well sustain a diversification and improve its overall position	4	4	a)	Net forex earner	2	2
b)	Company is an average player, can fund the diversification with low overall risk, going for synergistic diversification.	2	2	b)	Large exports but exports are less than imports	1	1
c)	Company is an average player, going for synergistic diversification.	1	1	c)	Purely domestic presence/only imports	0	0
d)	Any company diversifying into non-synergistic businesses.	0	0				
5)	**Technology:**	**B**	**C**	**6)**	**Raw Material Dynamics:**	**B**	**C**
a)	State-of-the-art technology, has strong technology-oriented principals, spends large amounts on own R&D.	3	3	a)	Raw material easily available, multiple sources, flexibility to import, good credit periods available.	2	2
b)	Stable technology, overall impact of change in technology marginal, company can adopt to changing technology	1	1	b)	Single source/poor RM quality in India, imports possible but costly. Avg. to good manufacturing facilities.	1	1
c)	Outdated technology, technological obsolescence is frequent.	–1	–1	c)	No major advantage or disadvantage in RM dynamics and average manufacturing facilities	0	0
				d)	High dependence on single source/ high imports	–2	–2
7)	**Manufacturing Facilities:**						
a)	Well laid out and clean mfg. area, ample space available for expansion at same location.	2	2				
b)	Average to good mfg facilities, space available for expansion.	1	1				
c)	Average manufacturing facilities.	0	0				

d)	Congested and poorly kept manufacturing area.	−2	−2				
III.	**FINANCIALS**						
1)	**Profitability:**			**2)**	**Liquidity:**		
a)	Steadily growing with stable profitability record during last 3 years	8	8	a)	Positive GCFO during last 3 years	5	5
b)	Steady growth with some fluctuations in profitability. Company is fundamentally strong and profitable.	6	6	b)	Liquidity strong with minor variations during last 3 years.	3	3
c)	Recently established, with inconclusive profit/track record operations so far have been profitable.	4	4	c)	Acceptable liquidity with +ve GCFO during last year. +ve GCFO expected to continue during the next one year.	1	1
d)	Company has suffered setback in to profitability in the last 1–2 years, but is expected to turn up.	0	0	d)	Liquidity acceptable—marginally negative GCFO. Company supporting liquidity through external term borrowings.	0	0
e)	Losses. No hope except in medium term #	−5	−5	e)	Negative GCFO. Company supporting liquidity with short-term borrowings.	−2	−2
				f)	Company illiquid—default situation/ diverts funds to group or other ventures.	−4	−4
3)	**Inventory Turnover:**			**4)**	**Debtors Period:**		
a)	More than 4	2	2	a)	Below 60 days	4	4
b)	2–4	0	0	b)	60–120 days	3	3
c)	Below 2	−1	−1	c)	120–180 days	1	1
				d)	180 days and above	−1	−1
5)	**Current Ratio:**			**6)**	**Gearing:**		
a)	1.30 and above	3	3	a)	TOL/NW less than 2	3	3
b)	1.00 to 1.30	1	1	b)	TOL/NW between 2–3	2	2
c)	0.75 to 1.00	0	0	c)	TOL/NW between 3–4	0	0
d)	Below 0.75 and more than 2.00	−2	−2	d)	TOL/NW more than 4	−1	−1
7)	**Interest Coverage:**			**8)**	**NCA to Debt**		
	PBDIT/Int. & Financial Charges				**(Net Cash Accruals to Term Debt)**		
	DSCR in Case of Term Loans						
a)	More than 3	3	3	a)	More than 0.33	2	2
b)	More than 2 and less than 3	2	2	b)	0.20 to 0.33	1	1
c)	Less than 2	0	0	c)	Less than 0.20	0	0
IV.	**Management**	**B**	**C**			**B**	**C**
1)	**Competence:**			**2)**	**Integrity:**		

(Continued)

(Continued)

a)	Highly qualified professionals working as a team. Clarity in goals and strategies and has capability of implementing the strategies, achieving the goals. Have implemented projects in time. There is a good degree of delegation.	10	10	a)	Management has maintained high standards of integrity and profession-alism. Integrity and character is beyond reproach.	4	4
b)	Professionals in key areas under overall control of owners, who function indepen-dently. Delegation levels are low.	7	7	b)	Apparently no adverse reason to doubt the integrity of the promoters. The management is reportedly reliable and of good integrity.	3	3
c)	Company is now inducting professionals in key areas which were hitherto looked after directly by the promoters. Decision-making highly centralized.	4	4	c)	Management is of acceptable integrity.	1	1
d)	No long-term vision and low on technical capabilities	−3	−3	d)	Management is of dubious integrity. Proven reports which point to malpractices in business.	−10	−10
3)	**Succession:**						
a)	Succession is well planned, second line of management is strong and qualified.	1	1				
b)	Succession is not an issue currently.	0	0				
c)	Group of promoters, succession could become an issue in medium term.	−2	−2				
V.	**Account**						
1)	**Limit:**			**2)**	**Trade Reports:**		
a)	More than `2 crore	1	1	a)	Good market/trade reports	3	3
b)	Less than `2 crore	0	0	b)	No adverse trade reports	1	1
				c)	Report of cautionary nature	−3	−3
3)	**Collateral:**			**4)**	**Documentation:**		
a)	Available for 100%/more than 100%	4	4	a)	Completed to satisfaction before release	2	2
b)	Available for 50–75%	2	2	b)	Completed within 6 months of release/new account	0	0
c)	Available for *Pari passu* with other banks	1	1	c)	Irregularities	−2	−2
d)	No collateral.	−2	−2				
5)	**Business Prospects:**			**6)**	**Finance Information:**		
a)	Good medium-term/long-term prospects of association in form of cross selling of products, group business/new project.	2	2	a)	Information is up to date. QIS and so on submitted timely	2	2
b)	Influential promoters new and liability business possible.	1	1	b)	Information asked for is given.	0	0

c)	Association to grow with usual growth.	0	0	c)	Difficulty in obtaining information	–2	–2
7)	**Conduct of Account:**						
a)	No irregularities for more than 6 months	3	3				
b)	New account	0	0				
c)	Devolvement/Dishonour of TODs/Excess drawing and so on.	–3	–3				

Score

	GROUP V		GROUP N			
Parameters	Business	Financials	General	Management	Account	Total
Minimum Score	9	12	-	-	-	21
Maximum Score	22	30	16	15	17	100
Score: Branch						
Corporate Office						

Credit Grade Guide:

Score	Credit Grade
Over 80	A2
71–80	A3
61–70	A4
51–60	A5
41–50	A6
Below 41	A7

CHAPTER 18

A Follow-Up Note on Financing

LEARNING OBJECTIVES

- Demonstrate the application of capital structure theory in real-life settings
- Outline the sequence of decisions in a financing programme
- Recent advances in capital structure theory
- Introduce the concept of adjusted present value

One of the primary responsibilities of a Chief Financial Officer is to estimate the external funding requirement over the planning period and maintain contact with financial institutions and capital markets to ensure a steady supply of funds to support the company's business strategy. This involves the following steps:

- Estimate the external fund requirement
- Decide whether to issue debt or equity or some combination of securities
- If the company already has adequate equity, issue the right type of debt

Corporate treasures have the following options:

- Public and private debt
- Fixed rate and floating rate debt
- Short-term or medium-term or long-term debt
- Domestic or foreign currency debt
- Issue the securities in the right 'sequence' and at the right time

EXTERNAL FUNDING REQUIREMENT

The first step in the sequence of decisions is to establish a planning horizon. How long should the planning horizon be? The planning horizon is the period over which the characteristics of the business are expected to change and within which strategic decisions can be made. For mature companies the planning horizon may be a few years, whereas for a company operating in a rapidly evolving industry the horizon may be one year. The objective of this analysis is to arrive at an ordered sequence of investment and financing activities to support the company's strategy. As pointed out in Chapter 9 on real options, a business is essentially a portfolio of projects that can be viewed as options: some projects are in-the-money, whereas some are out-of-the-money. The manager is required to cultivate promising projects and harvest those that are ripe. Any company would have competing strategies to achieve its objectives. Once a strategy is chosen from the available alternatives, a manager is required to estimate minimum financial requirements. Having determined the sequence of investments, a financing strategy that satisfies a given set of corporate objectives such as reasonable debt and dividend payout ratio and good liquidity is to be evolved. Companies commonly prepare pro forma statements consisting of income statement for the period under study and a balance sheet as of the end of the period. Preparation of pro forma statements requires common sense and judgement. The end product of the analysis is the cumulative funding requirement and the sequence of instruments to be issued (debt, converts or equity or preferred stock). A forecast of sources and uses of funds for a hypothetical company is given below.

Years				(in ₹ million)
Sources	1	2	3	4
Net Income	300	340	450	600
Depreciation	150	210	300	360
Uses				
Increase in WC	25	0	0	0
Total Capital Expenditure	500	1,300	1,200	1,500
External Fund Requirement	75	750	450	540
Cumulative Fund Requirement	75	825	1,275	1,815

The company needs ₹1,815 million in the next four years. The company may sell debt or equity, or convertibles or some combination of securities.

DEBT VERSUS EQUITY VERSUS CONVERTIBLES

The choice of the instrument depends on the financing problem the company is facing. Undervalued companies may want to issue debt, whereas overvalued companies may want to issue equity. In other words, companies choose a security not only on the basis of perceived need but also market conditions. If the company already has adequate equity, it may issue debt. Assume that the company issues debt. Whenever a company sells debt, it should get its issue rated by a credit rating agency such as CRISIL, CARE or ICRA. The issuer approaches the agency to rate its issue and update the rating throughout the life of the issue. For this service, the agency is paid a fee. The foundation of credit ratings was laid when

Moody's introduced the first bond ratings as a part of Moody's Analyses of Rail Road Investments in 1909. Since then, credit ratings have blossomed into a full-blown business, providing investors with an impartial measure of an issuer's creditworthiness. Most financial institutions today have guidelines on investment based on the ratings issued by the major credit rating agencies. Standard & Poor's started operations in 1916. These two agencies have today come to be acknowledged as the two most influential agencies in the business. S&P was the first analytical organization to publish its ratings criteria and procedures, and has been the pioneer in rating a large variety of financial instruments. It continues to be the most open organization about its ratings methodology, which is extensively documented. Figure 18.1 depicts the rating process adopted by S&P.

In India, credit ratings first began with the Credit Rating Information Services of India Limited (CRISIL) in 1987. ICRA and CARE were later set up. The rating process followed by CRISIL is illustrated in Figure 18.2. The rating process of CRISIL is more or less similar to that of S&P. In both the illustrations, the rating process starts with a rating request from the issuer, followed by assigning teams and basic research, management meetings, assignment of ratings and appeal, and surveillance and annual review. CRISIL employs a multi-layered decision-making process in assigning a rating. It assigns a team of at least two analysts who interact with the company's management.

After a rating has been assigned, CRISIL monitors the ongoing performance of the issuer and the economic environment in which it operates. Surveillance also enables analysts to stay abreast of current developments, discuss potential problem areas and be apprised of any changes in issuer's plan. Table 18.1 presents a brief description of credit rating symbols used by CRISIL. The credit rating is an attempt to judge the probability of default. The highest rating of AAA is given to those companies that have negligible default risk. A debt rating is not an evaluation of the issuing company but is security specific. It is supposed to assess the credit risk of a particular debt security. The rating agencies consider a variety of financial and non-financial factors to arrive at a rating. The agencies consider industry growth, global competitive position of the industry, availability of raw material supply, degree of regulation and the direction of change in regulation, economic cyclicality among other factors while assigning a rating.

FIGURE 18.1
Rating Process of S&P

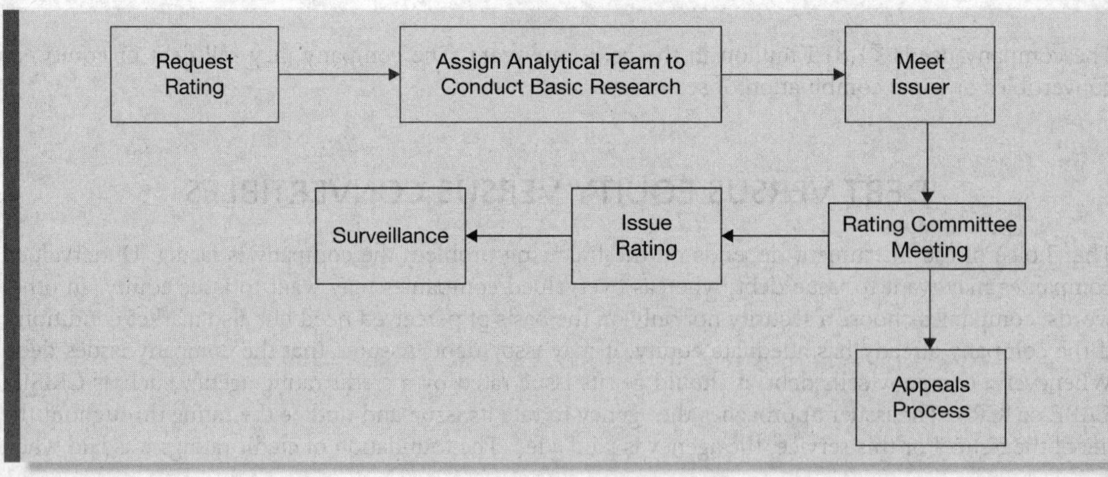

FIGURE 18.2
The Credit Rating Process

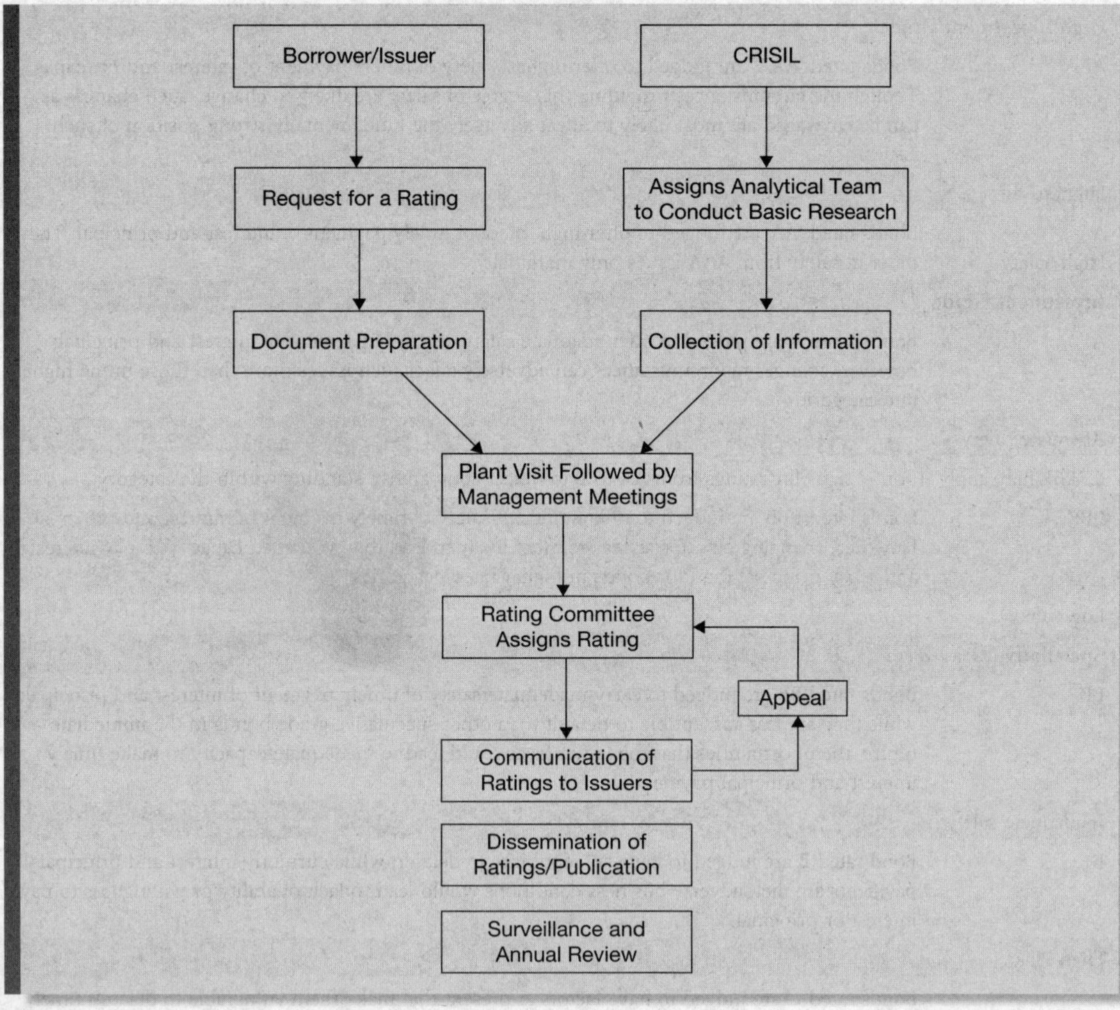

They also look at a number of financial ratios such as interest coverage, cash flow as a per cent of total debt and long-term debt as a per cent of capitalization to rate an issue. The amount of debt a project can support depends on the amount of cash flow the project can generate to service debt, credit support available to the project and the lender's coverage requirements. Two ratios are widely used to measure a project's ability to service debt; interest coverage ratio and debt service coverage ratio (DSCR).

$$\text{Interest Coverage Ratio} = \text{EBIT}/\text{Interest}$$

It measures the adequacy of operating profits to cover interest charges. A ratio less than 1.0 indicates that earnings are not adequate to meet interest charges and hence cannot support that level of borrowing. Lenders may typically insist that interest coverage ratio never fall below 1.25.

TABLE 18.1
Credit Rating Symbols

High Investment Grade	
AAA	Bonds rated 'AAA' are judged to offer highest safety of timely payment of interest and principal. Though the circumstances providing this degree of safety are likely to change, such changes as can be envisaged are most likely to affect adversely the fundamentally strong position of such issues.
Highest safety	
AA High Safety	Bonds rated 'AA' are judged to offer high safety of timely payment of interest and principal. They differ in safety from AAA issues only marginally.
Investment Grade	
A	Bonds rated A are judged to offer adequate safety of timely payment of interest and principal; however, changes in circumstances can adversely affect such issues more than those in the higher rate categories.
Adequate safety	
CRISIL may apply '+' or '–' signs for ratings from AA to B to reflect comparative standing within the category.	
BBB	Bonds rated BBB are judged to offer sufficient safety of timely payment of interest and principal. However, changing circumstances are more likely to lead to a weakened capacity to pay interest and repay principal than for bonds in higher rated categories.
Low safety	
Speculative Grades	
BB	Bonds rated BB are judged to carry inadequate safety of timely payment of interest and principal; while they are less susceptible to default than other speculative grade bonds in the immediate future, the uncertainties that the issuer faces could lead to inadequate capacity to make timely interest and principal payments.
Inadequate safety	
B	Bond rated B are judged to have susceptibility to default; while currently interest and principal payments are met, adverse business conditions would lead to lack of ability or willingness to pay interest or principal.
High Risk	
C	Bonds rated C are judged to have factors at present that make them vulnerable to default; timely payment of I&P is possible only if favourable circumstances continue.
Substantial Risk	
D	Bonds rated D are in default and in arrears of interest and principal payments or are expected to default on maturity.
In Default	Such bonds are extremely speculative and returns from these bonds may be realized only on reorganization or liquidation.

$$\text{Debt service coverage ratio (DSCR)} = \frac{\text{EBIT}}{\text{Interest Expense} + \dfrac{\text{Principal Repayment}}{1 - \text{Tax Rate}}}$$

While interest coverage ratio tells us how comfortable a company is in making interest payments, the firm's ability to make principal repayment is ignored. DSCR considers both. The principal repayment is not tax deductible and is to be paid out of after-tax earnings. Principal payment is adjusted to make numerator and denominator consistent (i.e., before tax). The higher the DSCR, the better is the financial position, all else equal. A DSCR of less than 1.0 indicates that earnings are not adequate to meet interest and principal payments. DSCR can be further extended to include other fixed charges such as lease rentals and preference dividend.

The second important ratio is the leverage as measured by debt to total capitalization. The higher the leverage, the higher is the proportion of operating income that should be used to meet contractual obligations like interest payments. These agencies measure leverage in a variety of ways. For instance, another measure of leverage is (long-term debt+net worth) divided by total debt. The third important ratio is cash flow from operations to long-term debt. Debt is after all serviced from cash flows, not accounting earnings. All extraordinary sources and uses of cash are excluded to determine the overall trend in cash flow coverage. Managers often target coverage ratios. The problem with setting target ratios is that they do not tell us how much the risk of default has increased when, say, debt-to-value ratio increases from 20 per cent to 30 per cent. Moreover, it is hard to relate the amount of debt to historical asset values (used in the denominator). There may be substantial changes in asset values due to inventory valuation and depreciation policies and consequently changes in capitalization ratio that have no bearing on the capacity to meet fixed claims. So their usage is limited.

Assume that a company currently has very little debt, say 1 per cent. The managers of the company are evaluating the option of introducing debt into the capital structure. Debt is added to the capital structure by issuing debt and using the proceeds to repurchase common stock. The company's stock is currently trading at ₹30. The company has a cash balance of ₹296.6 million. The company's executives intend to bring down the cash level to that of its nearest competitor (₹180.15 million). The excess cash of ₹116.5 million would be used to repurchase stock. The new debt (used to repurchase stock) is expected to carry an interest rate of 14 per cent. The company intends to maintain a payout ratio of 60 per cent. The current and the pro forma financial details are presented in Table 18.2. The impact of the repurchase on the stock price and bond rating is given further:

Reduction in Shares		9.9	4.2
Additional Debt ₹ million		181.1	125.35
EPS ₹	3.98	4.16	4.26
P/E	7.53	Same	Same
Stock Price if P/E is	7.53	31.32	32.07
EBIT/Interest		17.5	10.50
Rating Based on CRISIL Interest Coverage Medians		AAA	AAA

TABLE 18.2
Pro Forma Financial Forecast, Bond Rating for Alternate Capital Structures

(₹ million)

	Actual	30% Debt/Total Cap	50% Debt/Capital
Sales	2,065.6	2,065.6	2,065.6
EBIT	477.4	461.1[1]	461.1
Interest	1.15	26.35	43.9
PBT	476.25	434.75	417.2
Tax @ 35%	166.68	152.16	146.02
PAT	309.56	282.58	271.18
Dividends @ 60%	185.7	169.5	162.7
No. of Shares Outstanding in Million	77.75	67.85	63.65
Cash	296.65	180.15	180.15
Total Debt	6.95	188.05	313.4
Net Worth	736.4	438.8	313.45

This analysis suggests that the company is relatively safe even at high debt ratios and would probably get AAA rating. One may also benchmark debt ratio or cash flow coverage ratio. Alternatively, competitors in the same industry group may be benchmarked. Surprisingly, the increase in stock price is negligible even when the debt ratio is 50 per cent. This is in stark contrast to the notion of optimal capital structure, which suggests that increasing leverage creates shareholder value. Why is the increase in stock price so small? The reason is that the company is already trading at a high M/B (market value of equity/ book value of equity) ratio. The stock price will go up only if the market assigns a higher P/E multiple for a given level of earnings. The managers can also assess the impact of leverage on sustainable growth, risk (sensitivity of net income to a reduction in EBIT) and so on. The value of tax shields can be as estimated as follows:

$$= \text{Tax Rate} \times (\text{Additional Debt} + \text{Reduction in Cash})$$
$$= 0.35 \times (\text{Additional Debt} + \text{Reduction in Cash})$$

If this analysis is right, that is, the expected increase in stock price is negligible; we would expect the company not to increase leverage because the benefits are relatively small.

[1] When excess cash is returned to shareholders, the company forgoes interest income. Assume that the interest on excess cash is 14 per cent. So the reduction in EBIT = 0.14 × excess cash of ₹116.5 million.

SEQUENCE OF RAISING DEBT AND EQUITY

Modern[2] finance theory hypothesizes that companies have a target debt to value ratio in mind and they move towards the optimum capital structure by trading off tax shields and bankruptcy costs. Assume that you have just set up a project and you have 40 per cent debt ratio in mind. There are at least three ways in which you can attain the target.

Option 1: Start with 100 per cent debt and add equity slowly to bring down the debt ratio to 40 per cent over a period of time. But is this path feasible? Bondholders/lenders will not lend 100 per cent of the project cost because it provides wrong incentives to shareholders of the borrowing company in the sense that they can take on business gambles. It is not their money anyway. This is the agency cost of debt. In addition, the probability of going bankrupt would be very high. For all these reasons, shareholders would not resort to this path.

Option 2: Start with equity, add debt frequently and then again equity probably. This path gives rise to the underinvestment problem suggested by Myers (1977). His theory is that firms prefer internal capital to external capital because it is costly due to information asymmetry. So companies would want to sell debt, convertibles and equity in that order. Adding debt frequently is probably in the interest of shareholders but bondholders would not allow it.

Option 3: Start with equity; add some more equity and debt later. This path reduces the probability of distress because debt is added only when the company has stable earnings. It also reduces the agency costs of debt.

All the three options are shown in Figure 18.3.

Returning to the example that I gave at the beginning of the chapter, the company needs ₹1,815 million in four years. The schedule of external funding requirement is as follows:

External Fund Requirement (₹ million)	75	750	450	540
Cumulative Fund Requirement (₹ million)	75	825	1,275	1,815

The company has virtually countless options as far as the sequence of securities is concerned. Consider some of them:

- All debt finance amounting to ₹700 million in Year 1, ₹700 million in Year 2 and the rest in Year 3
- Debt initially followed by equity issue in Year 2 and debt again in Year 3
- Equity initially followed by two debt issues
- Equity issues in Years 1 and 2 followed by a debt issue in Year 3
- All equity issues

In case you wish to make it more complicated, add some more instruments such as convertibles, bond–warrant package, preferred stock and so on. To decide on the instrument, amount and sequence, one should ascertain the impact of a particular financing strategy on debt ratio, bond rating, cost of capital, control and risk. Assume that a company has the following capital structure:

[2] This line of analysis was motivated by Esty, Qureshi and Olson (2001).

FIGURE 18.3
Sequence of Raising Capital

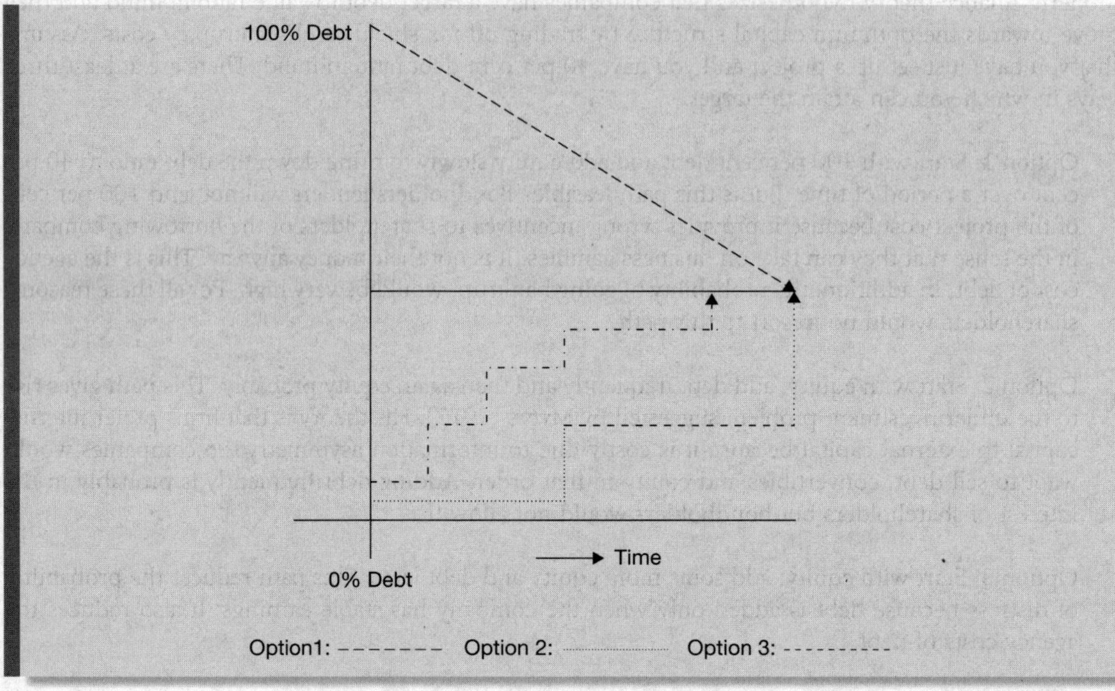

Debt	900
Equity	750
Total	1,650
Debt Ratio	54%

Assume that the company is thinking of issuing equity amounting to ₹400 million and the next year's retained earnings are expected to be ₹200 million. The next year's debt ratio will be:

Debt	900	
Equity	1,350	(750 Existing 200 Retained Earnings 400 New Issue)
Total	2,250	
Debt Ratio	40%	

Similar calculation can be made for other combination of instruments and sequence of issue. The central message of the discussion so far is that it is important to get the instrument and the sequence right. Otherwise, a company may get into financial distress. Assume, for example, that the company has convertibles outstanding and the company issues debt assuming that the outstanding convertibles would be converted providing some equity cushion. If the stock price falls, both convertibles and bonds will remain outstanding leading to a debt overhang.

PUBLIC VERSUS PRIVATE DEBT

For many companies, private debt from banks and financial institutions remain the main source of funding. Private debt comes from two sources: bank loans and private placement of securities with institutional investors. Private placement of securities continues to be the main source of funding for many companies even in the USA. Life insurance companies dominate the private placement market in the USA. These companies provide long-term (up to 20 years), fixed rate debt. Since the privately placed debt is usually illiquid, we would expect institutional investors to charge a liquidity premium.[3] In other words, is a privately placed debt costlier than public debt? A recent study in the USA finds that private placement yields compare favourably with public market benchmarks. The reason is that institutional investors have greater information and due diligent opportunities than individual investors. In addition, they enjoy greater covenant protection. Further, firms with high distress costs may find private debt more attractive since it is easier to resolve distress in case of private debt (it is easier to negotiate with few lenders).

MATURITY STRUCTURE OF DEBT

So far, we behaved as though there is only one, homogeneous, class of debt. In real life, companies have access to an array of instruments that differ in many important characteristics such as cash flow rights, maturity of the instrument and so on. According to modern finance theory, companies with many investment opportunities can be expected to issue short-term debt to preserve financial flexibility and to protect lenders against greater uncertainty in the company's future.[4] Further, growth firms ought to use relatively less debt to prevent the underinvestment problem. Conversely, for mature companies whose value comes mostly from assets-in-place, the costs of bankruptcy are likely to be low. Such firms can afford to have high leverage ratios to prevent wastage of free cash flow by managers.

OPERATING AND FINANCIAL LEVERAGE

All companies have fixed and variable operating costs. Fixed operating costs do not change when volume changes in the short run. Fixed costs include depreciation on plant and equipment, buildings and so on, insurance, and managerial remuneration. Variable costs, on the other hand, vary directly with the level of output. These include raw materials, direct labour costs and certain administrative expenses. Consider two firms that have the following cost structure.

[3] The Rule 144 A in the USA permits trading of privately placed instruments among qualified institutional investors.

[4] The cost of long-term debt will be unacceptably high for growth firms because of uncertainty in their future.

(₹ million)

	Firm A	Firm B
Sales	2,047	7,736
Variable Costs	1,642	6,186
Fixed Costs	144	1,089
Depreciation	54.60	164.44
EBIT	205	296
If sales were to increase by 30%,		
Sales	2,660	10,056
Variable Cost	2,134	8,041
Fixed Cost	144	1,089
Depreciation	54.60	164.44
EBIT	327	761
% Change in EBIT	58.90	157

For the same percentage change in sales, percentage change in EBIT for firm A is much lower than that for firm B. This is due to different cost structures. Firm B has substantial fixed costs. The percentage change in EBIT for a given percentage change in sales is called operating leverage. The impact of operating leverage is that there is more than proportional change in profits when sales change in either direction. The degree of sensitivity of a firm's operating profit to changes in sales is called degree of operating leverage.

$$DOL = \%\ \text{Change in EBIT}/\%\ \text{Change in Sales}$$

The operating leverage should be measured over a long period of time rather than on the basis of one-year data. DOL changes from year to year. An average of DOL for recent past may be estimated. Many tend to believe that operating leverage is the same as business risk. They are not the same. The volatility in sales and expenses gives rise to business risk. Other things remaining constant, the higher the DOL, the higher the business risk. Just as the presence of fixed operating costs can boost earnings above the BEP, the presence of fixed cost financing can boost earnings per share and return on equity. Consider two firms A and B. A is all equity financed, whereas Firm B has 40 per cent debt. Both employ ₹500,000. Both generate earnings before interest and tax of ₹150,000. The interest rate on debt is 14 per cent.

	Firm A	Firm B
Equity ₹	500,000	300,000
Debt ₹	—	200,000
BIT ₹	150,000	150,000
Interest	—	28,000
Tax@35%	52,500	42,700
Profit after Tax	97,500	79,300
No. of Shares	50,000	30,000
EPS	1.95	2.64

The previous example illustrates the effect of leverage on EPS. EPS increases when debt is injected to the capital structure. This is because Firm B has issued fewer shares. Extending the example further, it can be verified that the volatility of EPS increases when firms resort to debt financing due to the presence of fixed interest cost. When earnings are high, debt financing boosts EPS and when earnings are low, debt financing depresses EPS. The level of EBIT at which EPS is zero is called break-even EBIT. The earnings per share under different financing plans can be estimated and the financing plan that gives the highest EPS may be chosen. It is to be understood that the increase in EPS may not be free of cost.[5] The investors may expect higher returns as risk has gone up. A manager should consider the expected earnings and its volatility before choosing an option. As long as earnings are higher than the break-even point, EPS increases with leverage. But so does volatility of EPS. The degree of sensitivity of a firm's EPS to changes in operating profit is called the degree of financial leverage (DFL).

$$DFL = \% \text{ Change in EPS} / \% \text{ Change in EBIT}$$

Other things remaining constant, the higher the DFL, the higher is the financial risk.

TOTAL LEVERAGE

The product of DOL and DFL is called degree of total leverage (DTL). It is the ratio of percentage change in EPS and percentage change in sales that causes the change.

$$DTL = \% \text{ Change in EPS} / \% \text{ Change in Sales}$$

The central message of the foregoing analysis is that a firm can combine operating and financial leverage in such a way that the total leverage is in manageable limits. Those firms which have high operating leverage should have relatively low financial leverage and vice versa.

Operating leverage is the ratio of contribution to EBIT. The operating profit is the closest approximation of contribution and therefore used in our calculation. Similarly, financial leverage has been calculated as the ratio of EBIT to PBT.

Conventional wisdom suggests that companies should avoid combining high operating leverage (which leads to high business risk) and high financial leverage (which leads to high financial risk). Earnings are boosted in good times because of the presence of fixed costs and debt; but (earnings) get depressed in bad times for the same reason, namely presence of interest payments on debt and other fixed costs. Massey Ferguson, a multinational producer of farm machinery, industrial machinery and diesel engines sought to increase its market share by turning to the Third World for growth. Massey manufactured its products in UK and Canada, and sold the output to less developed countries (LDCs) in the late 1970s. This strategy worked quite well in the initial years. Compared to its competitors, Massey had an aggressive debt policy and an aggressive product market strategy. It was unwise to couple a risky strategy in a cyclical industry with high (short-term) debt.[6] When short-term interest rates shot up and the demand (and hence revenue) dried up for its products for various reasons, Massey was thrown into distress. John Deere, its major competitor, however, had moderate debt ratio because of which it had the financial flexibility to make capital investments. When Massey and another

[5] In well-functioning markets, investors may see through the increase in EPS (i.e., focus on cash flows) while making investment decisions. In other words, the increase in EPS may not have value relevance.

[6] Customers in LDCs are more risky compared to customers in developed countries.

competitor—International Harvester—were busy resolving distress, Deere pursued aggressive tactics to lock up market share.

Whether a particular issue of debt should be short term or long depends on various factors like:

- Current Capital Structure: If the company already has significant short-term debt, it may issue for medium or long term.
- Availability and access to markets.
- Cost of Alternate Maturity Debt Issues: Finance theory hypothesizes that investors expect a maturity premium. In other words, longer tenor instruments carry a higher rate of interest compared to shorter tenor instruments because investors have to lock in their instrument for a longer period. Even if they have the option of selling the instrument, the fact that longer term instruments are more sensitive to changes in interest rates suggests that they ought to demand a premium.
- The Extent to Which the Firm is Willing to Expose Itself to Interest Rate Risk and Refinancing Risk: When a short-term debt comes due, the firm will have to replace it with another issue or liquidate assets to pay off debt. The second option is usually not possible. Consequently, firms should issue short-term debt only when it is used for short-term purposes or when they are confident of replacing it with another debt issue at an acceptable price.

Executives commonly prepare a business plan that spells out the company's growth target, product market strategy, market evaluation, design and development plans and so on; accept all investment proposals that the top management considers worthwhile to exhaust the earnings. If some more projects are in the queue, choose securities on the basis of some pecking order. This works fairly well in case of small companies. In large companies that have cash flows in different currencies and service half a dozen debt and equity markets, the need for proactive steps is essential. Sub-optimal financing decision for one project could jeopardize the profitability of other projects by increasing the risk of cash flows. The first step in assessing debt capacity and default risk is to prepare a repayment schedule of existing debt.

The forecast is usually prepared with a standard set of assumptions such as constant average credit period, cost of goods sold as a constant fraction of sales and so on. A worst-case analysis is usually done to assess the impact of various business scenarios on financial statements. Worst-case analysis involves preparing a pessimistic cash flow forecast to determine if operations can generate enough cash to repay debt according to its contractual terms. The problem with worst-case analysis is that executives tend not to acknowledge the worst case. A sensitivity analysis provides useful insight into the magnitude of adversity when trouble comes. Executives assume that when a financial emergency arises, they can cut down inventory and book debts, divest fixed assets and lay off workers. While some of these measures are practical, some are not. When sales revenue declines, companies do not cut down inventory, they try to maintain it so that service to the existing customers is not harmed.

PRIORITY STRUCTURE

Lenders are entitled to contractual interest and principal payments. Default on promises made in lease or debt contracts generally give the claimholders the right to force the firm into bankruptcy. Default on lease payments gives the lessor the right to repossess the leased asset. In short, all financial claims do not have the same priority in bankruptcy. The characteristics of different corporate liabilities are given in Table 18.3.

TABLE 18.3
Priority Structure of Corporate Liabilities

Type of Liability	Capitalized Leases	Secured Debt	Ordinary Debt	Subordinated Debt	Preferred Stock	Common Stock
Priority of Claim	Highest →					Lowest
Can Trigger Bankruptcy?	Yes	Yes	Yes	Yes	No	No
Control Right	Rights to Restrict Use of Asset	Specified in Loan Covenants				

Growth firms, by definition, will have growth opportunities. Such firms may prefer to issue unsecured or subordinated debentures to maintain as much operating flexibility as possible.[7] Lenders to such firms demand security as well as lend short because of the uncertainty in payoff from growth opportunities. Further, such firms should avoid complicated capital structures because the competition between different claimholders when in distress will destroy whatever value is left out. In sum, growth firms will not be usually successful in selling low priority claims because of which they will have to sell high priority claims. The choice of priority is not independent of other variables like tax advantage or disadvantage, and floatation costs.

FIXED RATE VERSUS FLOATING RATE DEBT

Companies often have the choice of borrowing on a floating or fixed rate basis. Usually short-term debt is floating, whereas long-term debt is fixed. A finance manager is required to decide the mix of floating rate and fixed rate debt. Most companies will have rules of thumb regarding the mix. For instance, a company may maintain the fixed–floating rate mix at 60/40. There are countless other alternatives like:

- Only fixed
- Only floating
- Ten per cent floating and 90 per cent fixed and so on

What sort of companies should issue floating rate debt? Those companies that have floating rate assets may want to issue floating rate liabilities to match fluctuations. For instance, financial firms like banks that lend on a floating rate basis would want to issue floating rate debt. In general, companies with stable operating margins can use floating rate debt to take advantage of lower cost, and companies in volatile businesses may issue fixed rate debt to protect against the confluence of high business risk and high financial risk. Companies also have the option of dynamically shifting between fixed and floating rate debt. In general, it pays to shift to fixed rate debt when long-term treasury yields are low or when the spread over treasuries is low.

[7] Subordinated debt is repaid only after all creditors have been repaid.

CHOICE OF CURRENCY

Often companies (especially multinationals) have the option of choosing a currency in which it is cheaper to borrow. While the interest expense on the foreign currency borrowing might be lower, it exposes the company to foreign exchange risk—the risk that the foreign currency may appreciate against the domestic currency making debt service expensive. Companies may manage the currency exposure through several instruments such as a swap, a forward contract or a foreign currency option. Assume that a company has the option of borrowing in dollars or in rupees. Should this firm time the market? That is, should this firm borrow selectively in dollars and rupees when it is cheaper to borrow in a particular currency and minimize borrowing costs? The all-in-cost of borrowing in a particular currency is simply the IRR of the series of cash outflows and the initial cash inflow, similar to a bond. The company may incur transaction costs to arrange the loan. This should be deducted from the initial amount borrowed or amortized over the life of the loan. In other words, the presence of transaction costs increases the all-in-cost of borrowing.

Assume that a company borrows in dollars for five years and swaps the proceeds to rupees. This transaction involves the following steps:[8]

1. Borrow in US$ and swap the proceeds to rupees now.
2. Convert the interest payment every six months or one year (as the case may be) into US$ to service debt.
3. Repay the principal at the end of five years by swapping rupee into dollars.

The foreign exchange market is divided into two segments: spot and forward market. The spot market allows for buying and selling of foreign exchange with settlement in two business days, known as the value date. The forward market allows companies to establish the exchange rate between the two currencies for settlement at a fixed future date. The forward rate is fixed at the time the contract is made but payment and delivery are not made until the delivery date.

Many factors influence the exchange rate between two currencies. But they are most affected by relative interest rates and inflation rates. The covered interest parity suggests that the forward rate and the spot rate are linked by the difference in nominal interest rates on the two currencies.

$$F = S\frac{(1+R_h)}{(1+R_f)}$$

where F = forward exchange rate expressed as units of domestic currency per foreign currency

S = spot exchange rate expressed as units of domestic currency per foreign currency

R_h and R_f are interest rates at home and abroad

The purchasing power parity theory suggests that the percentage change in spot rate equals the difference in inflation rates in the two countries.

That is,

[8] Alternatively, the company may get into a forward contract to procure dollars to service debt. But forward markets are not liquid beyond a few years.

$$\frac{S_{t+1} - S_t}{S_t} = I_h - I_f$$

where I_h and I_f are inflation rates in the home country and the foreign country, respectively.

These parity conditions ensure that borrowing costs are equalized across currencies. While there may be some arbitrage opportunities, they are not likely to persist over long periods of time. Therefore, a CFO would be better off by borrowing in the home currency.

SIMULATING CAPITAL STRUCTURE

Interest on debt is a fixed obligation that should be met regardless of the firm's profitability at the time of payment. A default can lead to, in the extreme case, bankruptcy. Normally, only debt is considered a fixed obligation. To stay competitive, a firm may have to maintain R&D expenditure, invest in working capital and fixed assets and these are largely determined by product market conditions. In this sense, investment in fixed assets and working capital can also be considered fixed obligation. The debt level a firm can maintain is the level at which the cash flow from operation is adequate to service debt and maintain investment in fixed assets, working capital, and R&D.

$$\text{PAT} + \text{Depreciation} + \text{Borrowing} = \text{Interest Payment} + \text{Principal Repayment} + \text{Capital Expenditure} + \text{Increases in Working Capital}$$

The cash flow from operations coupled with external borrowing is used to pay interest, invest in fixed assets and working capital. We have assumed that a firm can borrow if cash flow from operations is not adequate to cover interest payments, capital expenditure and working capital. Extending this logic, external equity can be included as well.

$$\text{PAT} + \text{Depreciation} + \text{Borrowing} + \text{Equity} = \text{Interest Payments} + \text{Principal Repayments} + \text{Capital Expenditure} + \text{Working Capital}$$

We see in real life that firms hate to cut dividends. They would prefer to maintain or increase dividends. So dividend payment can also be considered a fixed payment.

$$\text{PAT} + \text{Depreciation} + \text{Borrowings} + \text{Equity} = \text{Interest} + \text{Principal Repayment} + \text{Capital Expenditure} + \Delta\text{WC} + \text{Dividends}$$

If we know for sure what the firm will earn in the foreseeable future, the exercise is quite straightforward. In an uncertain world where earnings and cash flow fluctuate, a finance manager needs probabilistic thinking. Simulating capital structure involves the following steps:

- First, analyse past changes in operating income and cash flow. Draw a frequency distribution of past changes in operating income. Find its mean and standard deviation.
- Estimate the interest and principal repayment to be made based on the amount of debt being raised.
- Estimate the probability of default.
- Choose that level which has an acceptable probability of default.

Opler, Saron and Titman[9] present a computer simulation model which tries to locate that capital structure which minimizes the discounted sum of future tax payments, financial distress costs and funding costs. Their model, a sophisticated extension of the model just discussed, proceeds in nine steps.

- The first step involves projecting a company's future interest expense based on its assumed capital structure and mix of fixed and floating rate debt. The amount of interest expense is obtained under several thousand interest rate scenarios over a 20-year horizon by simulation. The model also takes into account options, such as features and sinking fund requirements built into the bond, possibility of denominating in multiple currencies and so on.
- The second step involves measurement of historical volatility of earnings or EBITDA/assets.
- The third step involves generation of many paths of future earnings for the company (both good and bad).
- Calculate the tax payment under each scenario using the statutory tax rate after accounting for tax loss carry forwards and so on.
- For each earnings scenario, check if the firm is financially distressed, that is, earnings after interest is below a certain minimum.
- Calculate the PV of future tax payments and distress costs for the distribution of future earnings with a given capital structure.
- Holding total debt constant, account for any funding cost/pricing advantages of different ways of structuring debt.
- Try different capital structures by altering the amount, type and currency of debt and compute earnings and repeat all the steps.
- Find the optimal capital structure.

A simplified flow chart is presented as follows:

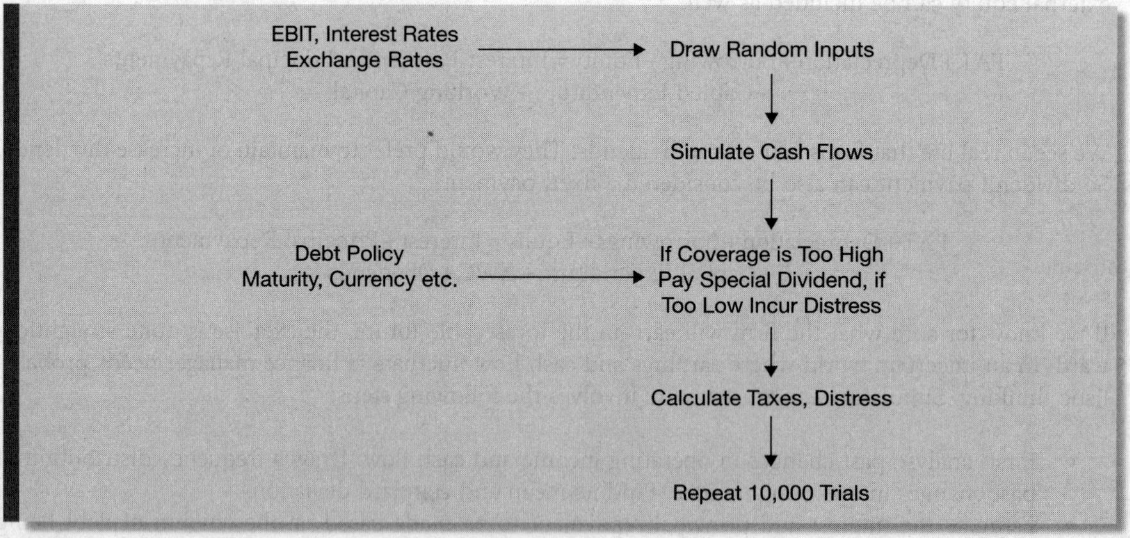

[9] Opler, Saron and Titman, 'Designing Capital Structure to Create Shareholder Value'.

The model suggests a target interest coverage ratio. A disadvantage of the model is that it does not factor in the value of financial flexibility. In other words, it is quite rigid. Further, one of the inputs to the model, the distress cost, is hard to estimate. One might make an intelligent guess however.

ADJUSTING FOR BANKRUPTCY COSTS

When companies borrow, the probability of their going bankrupt increases. Bankruptcy cost is the cost associated with going bankrupt. It includes the direct, deadweight costs such as administrative and legal expenses and indirect costs such as lost sales, lost investment opportunities, interest paid on emergency loan (if any), higher salary for chief executive (due to increased riskiness of leverage) and so on. There is no formula to estimate the bankruptcy cost. It is to be noted that it is the expected bankruptcy cost (i.e., present value at the time of borrowing) that we are interested in and not the actual expenses incurred in the year of going bankrupt. We also need to estimate the probability of going bankrupt.

$$\text{PV of Expected Bankruptcy Costs} = \text{Probability of Going Bankrupt} \times \text{PV of Bankruptcy Costs}$$

The proportion of companies that have gone bankrupt in your rating class can be taken as proxy for probability. Generally, expected bankruptcy cost is taken as 20–30 per cent of firm value. A practical way of adjusting for risk of disruption, impact on capital rationing, impact on morale, efficiency and effectiveness of spending programmes would be to:

- Take the cost of bank credit agreement as proxy for cost of disruption
- Take the NPV of projects cancelled as proxy for capital rationing
- Assume a subjective sum for lost efficiency, say, ₹500,000 a year
- Subjectively set a value for loss in sales

An academic study in the USA examined the industry-adjusted change in sales, operating income and market value of highly levered firms in industries experiencing downturn.[10] Industry downturns were defined as drops in sales and market values of 30 per cent or greater. After controlling for industry performance, the studies found that highly levered firms lost an additional 14 per cent, 12 per cent and 7 per cent of sales, operating income and market value relative to the average firm in the industry, and 26 per cent, 27 per cent and 15 per cent more than the least levered firm in the industry. This study provides a pointer to the magnitude of distress costs.

A RELOOK AT WACC: MARKET VALUE VERSUS BOOK VALUE PROPORTIONS

To estimate WACC, we use market value proportions rather than book value. Book values reflect the historical cost of tangible assets in place, whereas market value reflects the economic value of assets in place and present value of future growth opportunities. Market values predict the earning power of assets better than book values. Many managers use book value proportions while arriving at WACC. It

[10] Opler and Titman, 'Financial Distress and Corporate Performance'.

is unlikely that book values coincide with market value. Let us suppose your balance sheet reads like this

Liabilities		Assets	
Equity	50	Fixed Assets	70
Debt	50	Current Assets	30
	100		100

Debt to Value Ratio = 50/100 = 0.5

The market value of equity is 75. The market value balance sheet is:

	Liabilities	Assets
Equity	75	
Debt	50	
	125	125

Debt/Value = 50/125 = 0.4

You wish to raise ₹50 more. If you have a target D/E of ½ in mind, you would sell ₹25 of debt and ₹25 in equity to maintain book value proportion. To balance capital structure based on market value, you have to sell ₹12.5 of equity and ₹37.5 of debt. Obviously, the WACC depends on the weights you choose. You encounter a project that requires ₹50. The project has an NPV of ₹10. The market value of firm's equity increases by ₹10 (NPV) upon announcement of the firm's intention to invest in the project. To negate the resulting reduction of the firm's debt to equity ratio, the company needs to issue ₹10 additional debt (D/E is 1). There then remains only ₹40 of the ₹50 initial outlay to be financed in a 1:1 ratio between debt and shares. Preserving the firm's prevailing 1:1 ratio therefore involves the issuance of ₹20 debt and ₹20 equity.

If the management mistakenly assumes that by issuing ₹25 new debt and ₹25 new equity it will preserve its debt ratio, it has to needlessly issue ₹5 too much equity and ₹5 too little debt and the firms D/E ratio will deviate from the target value.

The commonly encountered argument is that the market value weights are more volatile (as market value of debt and equity change) than book value weights. And so book value weights, which are stable, should be used. The weights are not the current proportions (on the B/S) but target proportions. There is no reason why future book values should be any less volatile than market value proportions.

A RELOOK AT CAPITAL BUDGETING

Modern[11] capital budgeting, the way it is taught in business schools, suggests that volatility of cash flows of a project or how the cash flows are correlated with the cash flows of the firm does not matter because

[11] Stulz, 'What's Wrong with Modern Capital Budgeting?'

total risk does not affect value. Consequently, systematic risk is reflected in the discount rate. Assume that a firm has a project which has equity of ₹120 and a cash balance of ₹110. The firm encounters a project with a payoff of ₹100 in the upstate and a payoff of ₹20 in the downstate with equal probabilities, that is, it has an expected payoff of ₹1. Would a firm take a gamble that has large volatility but a small expected gain? Unlikely. Why? Because volatility matters as financial distress is not trivial—a distressed firm may not be able to raise funds at an acceptable price or be able to retain employees or suppliers. In other words, the cost of increases in total risk associated with new projects should be taken into account. When total risk matters, companies can enhance the value of either the firm or the project by hedging.

VALUATION IN PARTS: ADJUSTED PRESENT VALUE

Modern capital budgeting suggests that free cash flows be discounted by WACC to estimate NPV. The WACC is a tax-adjusted discount rate. It is supposed to capture the tax advantage of debt (we have used post-tax cost of debt as you know). The cost of debt and cost of equity are both opportunity costs, each consisting of time value and risk premium. WACC is a catch-all for risk and tax advantage of debt. The common practice is to increase the discount rate if the project is more risky. WACC is suitable when the capital structure is static. Quite often either the debt ratio or the absolute level of debt changes every year makes implementation of WACC cumbersome. An alternative approach is the adjusted present value (APV) method. Under the APV approach, a project is treated as though it is all equity financed and then this base case value is adjusted to account for financing effects such as interest tax shield, bankruptcy costs, issue costs and so on. APV unbundles all the components of NPV and analyses each one separately, whereas WACC bundles all financing side effects into the discount rate.

	Base Case Value		Value of Financing Side Effects
APV =	Value of Project if All Equity Financed	+	Interest Tax Shields, Bankruptcy Cost, Subsidy, Issue Cost, Other Cost

An Example

A project to manufacture cooling units for electrical cabinets requires an investment of ₹1.5 million. The project is expected to generate after-tax cash flows of ₹100,000 p.a. forever. The discount rate for the project is 15 per cent (compensation for business risk only). The project will have a D/E of 1.0. T=35 per cent, i=14 per cent

$$\text{Base Case NPV} = -1.5 \text{ million} + \frac{100{,}000}{0.15}$$
$$= -₹833{,}333$$

The discount rate is the cost of 'unlevered' equity. Since the project is debt financed to the extent of ₹750,000 adjustments for tax shields and bankruptcy costs should be made.

The project's APV is calculated by adding the base case NPV (all equity) and the financing side effects.

$$\text{APV} = \text{Base Case NPV} + \text{Interest Tax Shield}$$

$$\text{Interest Tax Shield p.a.} = i \times t_c \times D$$

$$\text{PV if Tax Shields Are Perpetual} = \frac{i \times t_c \times D}{i} = t_c \times D$$

$$= 0.35 \times 750{,}000 = ₹262{,}500$$

Adjustments for bankruptcy costs may be made by taking suitable proxies.

$$\text{APV} = V_u + t_c D = -₹833{,}333 + ₹262{,}500 = -₹570{,}833$$

Now, let us suppose the debt and equity issues cost ₹300,000 (towards underwriting, printing of prospectus, legal fees and so on)

$$\text{APV} = -₹570{,}833 - ₹300{,}000 = -₹\ 870{,}833$$

Similarly, adjustments for other costs and benefits can be made. The beauty of APV is that it not only tells you how much money you are making but also how (and from where).

COST OF UNUSED DEBT CAPACITY

Unused debt capacity is like excess cash or inventory (financial inventory). Just as a purchase manager should know the cost of holding raw material inventory, a finance manager should know the cost of holding financial reserves. The decision not to use ₹1 million of debt capacity is equivalent to holding ₹1 million more equity than needed. Using equity instead of debt has an implicit cost. If the cost of new equity is 18 per cent and after-tax cost of debt is 8.45 per cent, the cost of not borrowing is (18−8.45) 9.55 per cent. In rupee terms, this works out to (9.55% of 1 million) ₹95,500.

MANAGEMENT INCENTIVES AND DEBT CAPACITY

It is generally difficult to convince managers that debt is something beneficial and that free cash flow needs to be returned to shareholders when debt is available and/or the company is underleveraged. The willingness of managers to borrow is a function of the compensation plan. If managerial remuneration is tied to stock market performance, they would be forced to stay close to the optimal level of debt.

BRINGING THEM ALL TOGETHER

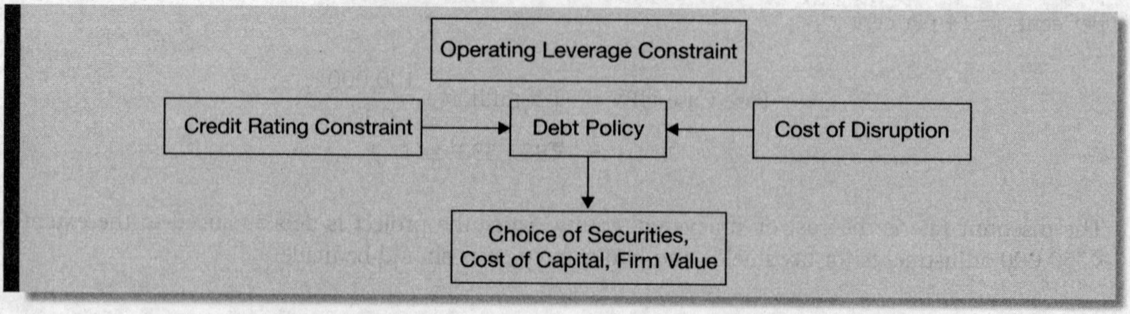

The sequence of decisions is shown in a decision tree:

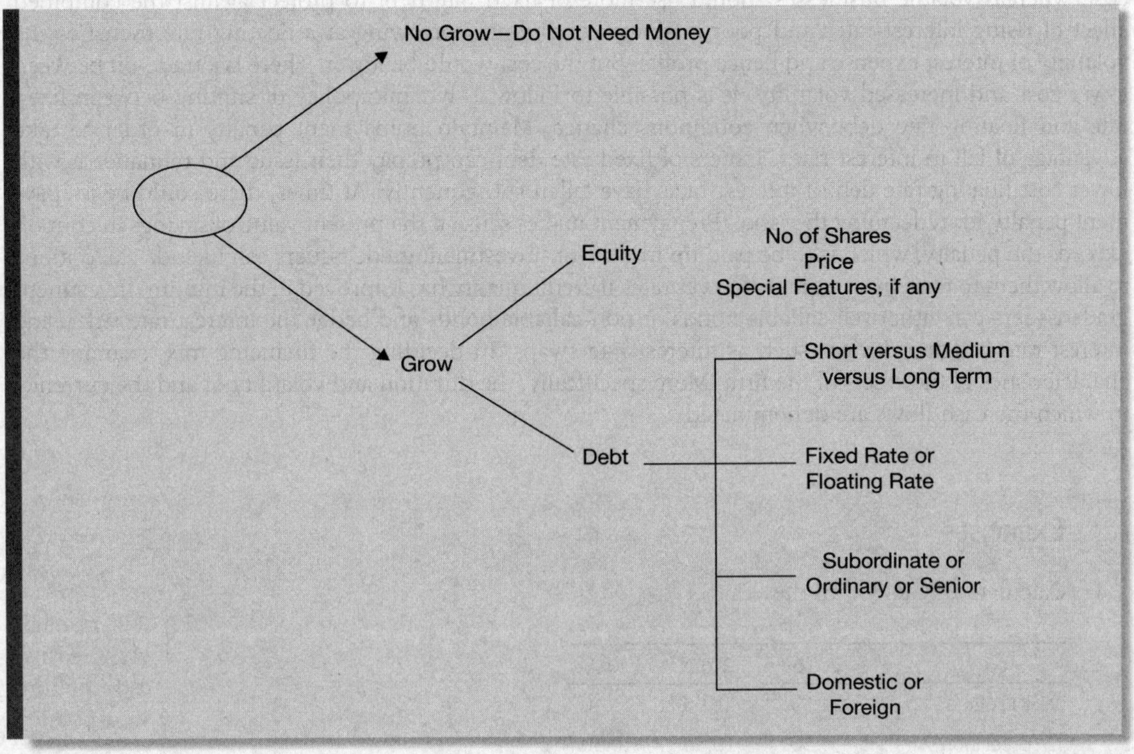

CONCLUDING COMMENTS

The objectives of financing strategy are to minimize the after-tax cost of financing, reduce the risk of default and reduce the potential agency costs. The trade-off involved in borrowing is not between high risk and no risk but between high risk and low risk. The analysis should not be done with balance sheet and income statement numbers. The analysis should incorporate the underlying cash flow behaviour. Debt policy is not the job of top management alone. It is a company-wide problem. Establish expected cash flow limits, maybe with subjective probabilities attached to them. The following factors need consideration while establishing a firm's debt policy.

- Projected cash flow from the project under consideration
- Variance of operating cash flows
- Loan covenants
- Corporate tax rate
- Personal tax rate on debt and equity income
- Bankruptcy costs
- Dilution of control
- Non-debt tax shields
- Pricing of the company's securities
- Information asymmetry

Businesses with stable operating margins could use more of floating rate debt to take advantage of lower cost, whereas volatile businesses should use more of fixed rate debt to protect against the combined effect of rising interest rates and poor business conditions. Borrowing at a floating rate increases the volatility of interest expense and hence profits. But the cost would be lower. There is a trade-off between lower cost and increased volatility. It is possible to follow a dynamic policy of shifting between fixed rate and floating rate debt when conditions change. Maintain prepayment penalty in order to take advantage of fall in interest rates. Issuers of fixed rate debt can prepay their issue and refinance it with lower cost floating rate debt if interest rates have fallen subsequently. At times, there could be prepayment penalty for redeeming the issue. Prepayment makes sense if the present value of savings in coupon exceeds the penalty, which is to be paid up front. Non-investment grade issuers can include call options to allow them to raise fresh capital at lower rates if credit quality has improved in the interim. Investment grade issuers can either sell callable bonds or non-callable bonds and hedge the interest rate risk using interest rate-hedging devices such as interest rate swaps. In deciding the financing mix, examine the characteristics of the assets of the firm. More specifically, the duration and volatility of and the currency in which the cash flows are denominated.

EXERCISES

1. Calculate DSCRs for all the years.

	2016	2017	2018
Net Profit	14.59	24.95	25.40
Depreciation	5.50	10.50	10.50
Loan Repayment	—	20.08	13.39
Interest	6.00	10.63	7.86

2. APV works when WACC does and when it does not. Explain.
3. Two rating agencies give two different ratings to a bond. Is this an indication of incompetence of one of the agencies?
4. There is this wall street adage—use it or lose it—which means companies should make use of their debt capacity or be prepared to be taken over. How can anyone make money from such a transaction?
5. If a company has issued convertibles, how would you estimate debt ratio?
6. Given the following book and market value data, calculate WACC based on book value and market value weights and compare them. Assume suitable CAPM parameters and tax rate.

	Book Value	Market Value
Long-Term Debt @ 12.5%	600,000	650,000
Preferred Stock @ 10 %	150,000	180,000
Equity	250,000	450,000

7. The cash flows from a project are given below:

Year	Cash flow
0	(1,000)
1	200
2	200
3	200
4	200

The cash flows are expected to grow at 8 per cent after year four. The project will be financed with 40 per cent debt. Assuming that debt is permanent, calculate APV with the following information.

Unlevered Beta = 0.9
Risk-Free Rate = 12%
Risk Premium = 10%
Cost of Debt = 12.5%

REFERENCES

Esty, B., Qureshi and Olson. 'Iridum LLC'. (Boston MA: Harvard Business School Publishing Case, 2001).

Myers S. 'Determinants of Corporate Borrowing'. *Journal of Financial Economics* 5, 1977: 147-175).

Opler, T. and S. Titman. 'Financial Distress and Corporate Performance'. *Journal of Finance* (1994 July).

Opler, T., M. Saron and S. Titman. 'Designing Capital Structure to Create Shareholder Value'. *Journal of Applied Corporate Finance* 10, no. 1 (1997 Spring).

Stulz, Rene. 'What's Wrong with Modern Capital Budgeting?' *Financial Practice and Education* (1999 Fall/Winter).

SUGGESTED READINGS

Barclay, M. and C. Smith Jr. 'The Maturity Structure of Corporate Debt'. *Journal of Finance* 50, no. 2 (1995).

Barclay, M. and C. Smith Jr. 'The Priority Structure of Corporate Liabilities'. *Journal of Finance* 50, no. 3 (1995).

Bhide, A. 'Why Not Leverage Your Company to the Hilt?' *Harvard Business Review* (1988 May–June).

Emerick, D. and W. White. 'The Case for Private Placements: How Sophisticated Investors Add Value to Corporate Debt Issuers'. In *The New Corporate Finance: Where Theory Meets Practice*, edited by Don Chew. New York, NY: McGraw Hill, 1999.

Luehrman, T. A. 'Note on Financial Programming Over Long Horizons' (Case No 9–294–087, Harvard Business School, 1994 Jan).

Luehrman, T. A. 'Using APV: A Better Tool for Valuing Operations'. *Harvard Business Review* (1997 May–June).

Myers, S. C. 'Interactions of Corporate Financing Decisions—Implications for Capital Budgeting'. *Journal of Finance* (1974 March).

Patrick, S. 'The Balanced Capital Structure'. *Journal of Applied Corporate Finance* (1998 Spring).

CHAPTER 19

Project Financing

LEARNING OBJECTIVES

- Provide an overview of the project finance market
- Introduction to project financing as a means to achieve financial objectives
- Provide a rationale for project finance
- Provide an overview of sources of project finance and the role of multilateral agencies
- Sensitize students to valuation issues in project finance settings

Project finance is a method of financing an economically viable project on the basis of the cash flows it is expected to generate. The project is a separate legal entity and its cash flows are segregated from the sponsoring organization. The sponsor may be the main user of the project's output, contractor or supplier, a consortium or a government. The revenue generated from the project should be adequate to cover all operating expenses, debt servicing burden and provide an adequate return to equity investors. This enables the sponsors to shift the operating risk and debt servicing burden to the project entity while retaining some benefits from the project. Project finance is usually restricted to large-scale, capital-intensive projects and often involves a high proportion of debt finance provided by a group of lenders. Toll roads, tunnels, bridges, ports and power projects are general candidates for project financing.

Project finance is not dependent on the credit support of the sponsors of the project but on the expected cash flows and/or the collateral value of project assets. Typically, lenders have no recourse to the sponsor in case of project failure. As a result, lenders should have a high degree of confidence in the performance of the project. Accordingly, extensive feasibility studies are necessary so that cash flow projections are accurate. As one project is not like the other, project finance package should be custom-built, and careful financial engineering is required to allocate risks and rewards among the participants. Project financing is ideal when the project's output has a strong demand, and parties are willing to enter into long-term contracts. A typical project structure is shown in Figure 19.1.

FIGURE 19.1
Project Structure

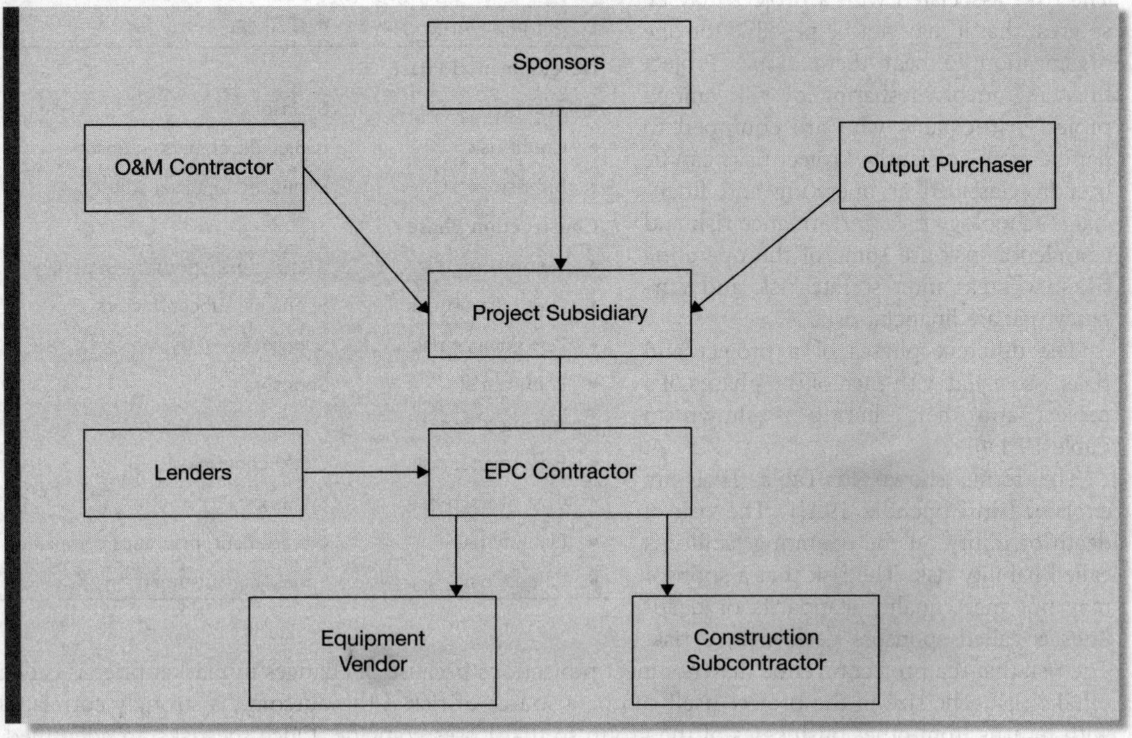

The construction and operation & maintenance contractors are responsible for timely completion and effective maintenance, respectively. The project sponsor undertakes bidding, financing and implementing. The complexity of the documentation necessitates the retention of a law firm, at least in case of large-scale international projects. The Hub Project in Pakistan, Petrozuata in Venezuela and the Mozal project in Mozambique are some of the prominent project finance transactions.

BENEFITS OF PROJECT FINANCING

Project financing provides certain advantages vis-à-vis conventional financing. Some of these advantages are:

- Sharing of risk
- Reduced agency cost of debt
- Reduced agency cost of free cash flow
- Expansion of sponsor's debt capacity
- Reduction in costs of information asymmetry

Sharing of Risk

The risks associated with a project may be so great that it may not be possible for one organization to bear them alone. Project financing involves sharing of risk among project participants who are equipped to handle them efficiently. Project risks can be broadly classified as operating and financial. Technology risk, performance risk and completion risk are some of the operating risks, whereas interest rate risk and currency risk are financial risks.

The different phases of a project and risks associated with each of the phases of a project and their sharing is shown in Table 19.1.

TABLE 19.1
Risk Sharing among Project Participants[1]

Project Phase/Risk	Participant
Developmental Phase	
• Technology risk	Sponsors
• Credit risk	Banks, developers, sponsors
• Bid risk	Sponsors, financial advisors
Construction Phase	
• Completion risk	Contractors, sponsors, suppliers
• Cost overrun risk	Sponsors, subcontractors
• Performance risk	Sponsors
• Political risk	Sponsors
Operating Phase	
• Performance risk	O&M contractor
• Cost overrun risk	Sponsors
• Liability risk	Government, insurance companies
• Offtake risk	Sponsors, consumers

The terms shown in Table 19.1 are explained in Appendix 19A.1. The risk of death or injury on the operating facility is called liability risk. The risk that a sponsor may not meet quality standards or deadlines is called sponsors performance risk. The risk that the project revenue may not meet projections because of changes in market price is called offtake risk. The size of the project itself can be a source of risk if the outcome is strongly correlated with returns from other businesses of the group so that losses coincide. Once the risks are identified, suitable mechanism should be evolved to cover each of them. For instance, sponsors may be asked to subscribe to equity to cover technology risk during the developmental phase. A major source of risk in a project is the completion risk which refers to the actual costs of constructing the project which may exceed the estimated costs; the completion date may be subject to unexpectedly long delays, the facility may be incapable of producing the output in the right quantity and quality as originally planned. Project level risks are usually mitigated through contractual agreements. Sponsors minimize revenue exposure to changing market conditions through sales or revenue contracts. A summary of the risks, participants and mechanism (to cover risk) is shown in Table 19.2. Risks can vary according to the nature of the project. For instance, market demand and interconnectivity charges are sources of risk in case of telecommunication projects, whereas low asset coverage and low toll collections are the risk factors in case of road projects.

Agency Cost of Debt

An agency relationship is a contract under which one or more persons (the principal/s) engage another person (the agent) to perform some service on their behalf, which involves delegating some decision-making authority to the agent. If both are utility maximizers, then there is good reason to believe that

[1] Biedelman, Carl R et al (1990).

TABLE 19.2
Mechanism to Cover Risk[2]

Project Phase/Risk	Participant	Mechanism
Developmental Phase		
• Technology risk	Sponsors	Equity or Subordinated debt
• Credit risk	Banks, developers	Letter of credit
	Sponsors	Credit rating
• Bid risk	Sponsors	Equity
	Financial advisors	Success fee
Construction Phase		
• Completion risk	Contractors	Performance guarantee
	Sponsors	Turnkey contracts
	Suppliers	Performance guarantee
• Cost overrun risk	Sponsors	Fixed price contracts
		Completion bonds
	Subcontractors	Fixed price contracts
		Completion bonds
• Performance risk	Sponsors	Performance guarantee
• Political risk	Sponsors	Joint venture with public partner
Operating Phase		
• Performance risk	O&M contractor	Equity, performance guarantee
• Cost overrun risk	Sponsors	Fixed price contracts
• Offtake risk	Sponsors	Take or pay, take and pay
	Consumers	Advance payments

the agent will maximize his/her utility. So the principal may have to incur monitoring costs to check his/her behaviour and limit divergence. The principal may suffer reduction in welfare due to divergence of interest. Agency cost is the sum of monitoring costs and residual loss. Agency cost arises whenever there is a cooperative effort even when there is no agency relationship. Agency cost can arise due to conflict of interests between shareholders and managers, shareholders and bondholders. Bondholders suffer opportunity wealth loss due to a firm's investment, financing and dividend decisions. If the firm sells bonds, and the bonds are priced assuming that no additional debt will be issued, the bondholders' claim gets diluted if the firm issues additional debt of the same or higher priority. Due to claim dilution, bondholders suffer capital loss. There is another form of agency cost. A company suffering losses may be tempted to take on business gambles, the gains from which largely go to shareholders, whereas if they fail, shareholders have little to lose and it is the lenders who suffer. It is a heads-I-win, tails-you-lose situation. Smart bondholders recognize the incentive faced by shareholders and make estimates of the behaviour of shareholders. The price bondholders pay for the issue will be lower to reflect the possibility

[2] Ibid.

of subsequent wealth transfers to stockholders. Bondholders try to protect themselves with restrictive loan covenants. The loan covenants may lead to reduced efficiency and lower firm value. Since the nature and boundaries of project in case of project finance are clear, lenders are less exposed to agency cost. This may result in lower interest cost and higher firm value.

Free Cash Flow Problem

Free cash flow is the residual cash flow available to managers after meeting the normal investment and debt servicing needs. Managers have discretion over the use of free cash flow in the sense that they can return it to shareholders or reinvest in some other business. Left to their own device, managers may pursue negative NPV projects for the sake of growth leaving the shareholders in lurch. Project financing can give investors control over free cash flow. Since the project has a finite life, the free cash flow is typically redistributed to shareholders who in turn decide where to invest their money (agreements prevent the siphoning of project cash flows through dividends or other channels). Moreover, heavy debt financing in case of project finance enforce financial discipline on managers.

Expansion of Sponsor's Debt Capacity

As pointed earlier, project finance is not dependent on the credit support of the sponsors of the project but on the strength of the contractual arrangement between parties and expected cash flows. This means that the sponsor who does not have a high credit rating can also lever up on the basis of the project related contracts—more specifically, the one with the output purchaser. This enables the sponsor to avail the benefit of debt—the tax shield, and hence, higher firm value. The projects undertaken by project companies generally have low bankruptcy costs, as their assets are largely tangible assets that are not affected by the bankruptcy process.[3] For instance, a change in ownership in case of a power project or toll road is not likely to affect its efficiency. Further, if the bankruptcy costs of the sponsor are higher than that for the project company, it is beneficial to isolate the debt in the project company.

Inside Information

Information asymmetry occurs when the management of a company has valuable information about the earning prospects that investors do not have, maybe because the managers are unwilling to disclose information due to strategic reasons or the information is too technical and complex to be communicated. Project financing reduces the cost of information asymmetry particularly in the case of large-scale, high-risk projects as project finance involves a small group of investors.

OTHER ADVANTAGES

Project financing can provide clearer information to investors' as the project is separately identifiable. Consequently, the effect of the project's failure on the share price of the parent company may be less.

[3] Brealy et al., 'Using Project Finance to Fund Infrastructure Investments'.

The performance of the project's managers can be assessed more accurately in case of a stand-alone project. More important, managerial incentives can be tied to the performance of the project.

TYPES OF CONTRACTS

Long-term agreements relating to purchase and sale are a characteristic of project finance. Some of the widely used types of contracts are:

- Take-or-pay contract
- Take-if-offered contract
- Hell-or-high water contract
- Throughput agreement
- Put-or-pay contracts

In a take-or-pay contract, the purchaser is obligated to pay for the output regardless of whether the purchaser takes delivery or not. But the purchaser has the option to take delivery. Also, the purchaser is not obligated to pay if the project is unable to deliver the output. Payments under take-or-pay contracts may be set to cover all fixed costs or may cover only a part of the project's capacity.

A take-if-offered contract is similar to the take-or-pay contract except that the purchaser has the obligation to take delivery.

In a hell-or-high water contract, as the name suggests, the purchaser has the obligation to pay for the output regardless of whether the output is delivered or not. Obviously, such a contract is in the interest of the lenders as they get more protection.

Many oil pipeline loans involve a throughput agreement. In a throughput agreement if other companies do not make sufficient use of the pipeline, the owners themselves should ship enough oil through it to provide the pipeline company with the cash it needs to service the loan.

Put-or-pay contracts provide for a secure supply of project raw materials. If the supplier is unable to provide the inputs, it agrees to indemnify the project company for excess cost incurred in securing the inputs from third parties, or, if third party supply is unavailable, for revenue losses due to the project's inability to comply with the offtake agreements.

FINANCIAL AGREEMENTS

Although project finance, in its pure form, involves lending with no recourse, we do not see it in reality. Lenders look for financial agreements and guarantees for comfort. A financial guarantee could take the form of a letter of credit or a guarantee from a financially sound third party such as bank. Some of the ways in which a sponsor can provide guarantee are:

- Cash Deficiency Agreement: Under this agreement, the project's owners agree to provide the operating company with enough funds to maintain a certain level of working capital.
- Capital Subscription Agreement: Under the capital subscription agreement, one or more creditworthy parties are required to purchase securities for cash when the project company experiences cash shortfall.

- Clawback Agreement: Under the clawback agreement, the sponsors are required to return cash benefits back to the project when there is a shortfall. The amount depends on the dividends and other benefits received by the sponsors (from the project).

Clawback agreements, also called cash traps, ensure that lenders continue to receive timely payments. For example, if the project were not able to maintain the DSCR no dividend distributions would be allowed. If the non-compliance persists, the project may be considered in default and lenders may seize all cash flow to prepay debt.

The concession agreement between sponsors, SPV and the local authority gives the SPV the right to recover the project costs and O&M costs through the levy of fees over the concession period (say 30 years). The base fee rate set in the concession agreement is indexed to the consumer price index to protect the revenue potential from being eroded by inflation.

The shareholders agreement specifies the inter se rights and obligations of the shareholders. It includes understanding between shareholders in relation to their shareholding, management of the company, constitution of the board, reorganization of the company, dividends, capital expenditure, material amendment to the project document and so on.

PUBLIC–PRIVATE SECTOR PARTNERSHIPS

Until recently, much of the financing of infrastructure development in many countries came from government sources, multilateral institutions and export financing agencies. Quite often, governments in emerging markets lack the financial capacity or creditworthiness to support the volume of infrastructure projects required to develop their economies. In case of large infrastructure projects, it is becoming inevitable for public and private sector to come together and jointly apply their skills and strengths to develop the project more quickly and efficiently. The joint venture between Railtrack and British Rail in the UK to set up a high-speed rail project is an example of such a partnership. Such partnerships try to involve the private sector in the process of designing, building, financing and operating public utilities. The government defines the services required, makes arrangements that enables the private sector to be the service provider and ensures that public services will be delivered at a specified quality at competitive prices. A number of public–private financing structures exist. Some of the schemes that can achieve the objectives are:

- Build–Operate–Transfer (BOT) Model
- Build–Transfer–Operate (BTO) Model
- Buy–Build–Operate (BBO) Model

In a BOT model, a private entity gets the mandate to finance, build and operate the project (which is otherwise a public sector project) for a specified period of time (say 25 years) at the end of which ownership reverts to the local government. Typically, the sponsoring organization makes an equity investment of 20 per cent to 30 per cent of the project cost and the rest is raised from international banks, multilateral agencies and domestic financial institutions. The host government generally gives a concession to carry out the construction and operation of the project and credit support for project borrowings. The licence agreement clearly spells out the commercial and financial terms. The BOT concept has been used in transportation (e.g., roads), energy (power projects), sewage and water treatment plants and hospitals.[4]

In a BTO model, the private entity transfers the facility to the government soon after the project clears the completion test and leases it back for a specified period of time. The project company runs the facility and collects revenues during the lease term. At the end of the lease term, the title passes on to the government (or the public sector entity).

In a BBO model, a private entity buys an existing facility, modernizes it and operates it as a for-profit, public-use facility. In many developing countries where existing facilities require modernization/expansion, BBO model is ideal. Roads and bridges are candidates for this model.

A typical project goes through the following phases:

- Planning
- Implementation
- Construction
- Operation
- Transfer

During the planning phase, the government identifies the need for a service, identifies the quality and quantity of service required upon identification of the project, the government invites bids from qualifies service providers. The most cost-efficient bid is awarded the contract. Once the contract is awarded, the contractor begins detailed engineering, design and construction work, usually under a fixed price contract. Upon completion, the project is tested for its suitability. If the project clears the hurdle, the private sector participant gets to run the project for a specified period of time after which it reverts to the public sector entity (or government). Table 19.3 presents the different phases in a BOT scheme.

FINANCING SOURCES

Although the financing package for a project is tailor-made, the basic form of funding remains the same, namely equity and debt. Project debt is either of the non-recourse or limited recourse type. Commercial

TABLE 19.3
BOT Scheme

A. Identification and Definition	Preliminary feasibility study and tendering
B. Selection	Bid evaluation and project award
C. Development of the Project	From project company, negotiate contracts and agreements
D. Financing	Equity contribution from promoters, financial closure
E. Actual Construction	
F. Completion	Testing and acceptance
G. Operation	Operation and maintenance
H. Transfer of Assets to the Government	

[4] See Table 19.3 for a brief description of different phases in a BOT scheme.

banks remain the most important source of project financing. Some banks have set up subsidiaries to serve the growing need of infrastructure. Bank loans can be either secured or unsecured. They may involve a single bank or a syndicate of banks. These loans are either fixed rate or floating rate and have tenors ranging from 5 to 10 years. In addition to the contractual arrangements between the parties, government may provide supplemental counter guarantee to comfort the lenders. Traditionally the multilateral agencies such as Asian Development Bank (ADB) and International Finance Corporation (IFC), Washington, have been active in funding infrastructure projects. For instance, IFC has financed CESC's 250 mw coal-fired power station in Budge and GVK Industries' 235 mw gas-based combined cycle power station in Andhra Pradesh in India. The ADB is a multinational development finance institution dedicated to fostering economic growth and cooperation in the Asia-Pacific region and to contributing to the economic development of its developing member countries. The Bank was established in 1966 with its headquarters in Manila, Philippines. The Bank is an infrastructure-oriented institution. The Bank has financed the Bangkok Expressway in Thailand, Hopewell Power Project in the Philippines, Port Qasim in Pakistan and Guangzhou Power Project in People's Republic of China among others. The bank provides both loan and equity capital. Infrastructure funds such as Global Power Investments of GE Capital, Asian Infrastructure Fund have come up to provide equity to infrastructure projects. The Asian Infrastructure Fund has been set up with equity contributions from IFC, ADB, Peregrine Investments Holdings, Frank Russell Company and Soros Fund Management. Export credit agencies (ECAs) finance imported equipment from reputed international suppliers such as GE, ABB, Siemens and so on.

The syndicated credit market is an important source of project finance. Transactions with loan amount of US$750 million–US$1 billion are not uncommon. A syndicated credit is one in which two or more banks contract with a borrower to provide credit on common terms and conditions governed by a common document. Syndicated loans are floating rate loans—the interest being reset after 1, 2, 3 or 6 months. The borrower chooses the interest rate reset period. One member of the group of banks (syndicate) is appointed to act as the agent for the syndicate. The agent bank coordinates all negotiations, payments and administration between the parties. A syndicated credit is usually of medium-term maturity, that is, 3–10 years, although transactions with maturities ranging from six months to 25 years could be arranged. Dual currency loan, term loans, standby letter of credit are some of the instruments in the syndicated credit market. Bank loans have a number of disadvantages such as short maturity, floating interest rate and restrictive loan covenants. Insurance companies such as AIG provide both equity and debt to infrastructure projects. They can also provide both subordinated and senior debt and can provide credit enhancement to make a non-investment grade transaction an investment grade transaction. Some of the insurance companies manage emerging market funds that contribute equity to projects in emerging markets.

Sometimes 'equity kickers', such as convertible debentures and stock warrants are also issued to allow investors to share in the upside potential of the project while limiting downside risk. Though small, the public bond market is also an important source of finance. Project bonds, unlike bank loans, have longer maturity, carry fixed interest rate and less restrictive covenants.

Leasing is often a viable alternative in power project financing. Leasing can be arranged to fund equipment, real estate and industrial facilities. Power plants are good candidates for leasing because of their long useful life, predictable salvage values and well-known operating characteristics.

ECAs like US Exim Bank offer funding if the borrower buys equipment, or technology or services from a source in the ECAs' country. Loans are offered in the form of buyer credit. Since the ECAs are expected to promote export from their respective countries, the interest on these loans are generally low: 1–1.25 per cent above LIBOR. These loans carry a maturity of 7–12 years with a moratorium of two years.

ECA credits can be either in the form of direct loan or as a guarantee to another lending institution. The following is a small list of projects funded by ECAs.

Export Credit Agency	Project
US Exim Bank	Dabhol (Enron)
	Roza (A V Birla)
	Hazira (Essar)
KfW, Germany	Gujarat Torrent (Torrent)
	Neyveli Lignite Corporation
	Bhadravati (Ispat)
	Vizag (Hinduja)
COFACE, France	Bhadravati
EXIM Bank, Japan	Vizag
	Bakreshwar Project

CREDIT RATING CONSTRAINTS

Issuing project bonds is a viable alternative only if the issue gets an investment grade rating. Companies in emerging markets are often constrained by their sovereign rating even though the project's economics are robust.[5] A sovereign's rating on its foreign currency obligations has been regarded as the ceiling on ratings for all issuers domiciled in the country. The assumption is that a sovereign default will force all domestic issuers to default.

For the purpose of rating project finance transactions, rating agencies like Standard & Poor's and Moody's review the technical and construction risks, financial projections, political risk and currency market volatility. S&P bases its evaluation on:

- Engineering and design, choice of technology, operating history of similar projects and experience with other rated projects
- Independent engineer's report on the technical feasibility of the project
- Political and legal support to the project
- Controls for management of construction funds
- Achievability of construction schedule and budget
- Creditworthiness of the engineering, procurement and construction (EPC) contractor to honour contingent liabilities
- Construction contractor's experience and reputation
- Testing and commissioning procedure
- O&M expertise, planning, budgeting and staffing details
- Quality of cash flows, financial and sensitivity analyses

[5] Esty and Millet, 'Petrolera Zuata, Petrozuata C.A'.

THE ROLE OF BILATERAL AND MULTILATERAL ORGANIZATIONS

The World Bank Group provides a variety of support to infrastructure projects in developed and developing countries. The group consists of the International Bank for Reconstruction and Development (IBRD), the International Development Association (IDA), the International Finance Corporation and the Multilateral Investment Guarantee Agency (MIGA). The IBRD provides loans to middle-income countries, whereas IDA supports poorer developing countries. IBRD lends at rates slightly higher than those available to AAA borrowers. IBRD can either lend to the project entity directly or to the host government, which in turn can on lend to the project. Within the World Bank Group, the IFC and MIGA are active in supporting private sector projects. IFC supports both equity and debt financing. It assists companies through the syndicated B loan programme, security and underwriting. MIGA provides political risk insurance primarily for equity. Other multilateral agencies such as ADB, European Development Bank and European Bank for Reconstruction and Development also provide guarantees. Bilateral agencies like Exim Bank often provide guarantee in association with the World Bank.

WORLD BANK GUARANTEE PROGRAMME

The guarantee programme of the World Bank tries to address the need to offer political risk mitigation products to enable implementation of infrastructure projects in developing countries. The Bank offers three types of guarantees: partial credit guarantees which cover debt service defaults on a specified portion of a loan or a bond; partial risk guarantees which cover debt service defaults on a loan to a private sector project caused by a government's failure to meet its contractual obligations related to a private project. They are 'partial' in that they cover the minimum number of risks and the smallest amount of debt consistent with successful implementation of the project. And, policy-based guarantees (PBGs) which cover a portion of debt service on a borrowing by an eligible member country from private foreign creditors. The Bank also has PBGs.[6]

PBGs help crisis-stricken countries to re-enter international markets. PBGs are a class of partial credit guarantees that cover defaults on long maturity interest or principal payments. Partial risk guarantees are likely to be useful to infrastructure projects located in countries that are about to attract international investors. The presence of a World Bank guarantee helps accelerate investment. Partial credit guarantee is likely to be needed where the failure to refinance as well as the pricing of loans and guarantees can be determined on the basis of the Bank's knowledge of the financing market place. IFC is the largest multilateral source of debt and equity financing for private sector projects in developing countries. IFC offers a syndicated loan programme (known as B loan programme) along with some 280 commercial banks and financial institutions. IFC invests through debt, equity and quasi-equity (subordinated loans and convertible loans). IFC loans have a tenor of eight years or more, and interest rates range from 0.5 per cent to 4 per cent above LIBOR. IFC also lends from its own resources (A loan) apart from providing equity and quasi equity.

MIGA guarantees cover risks of expropriation or breach of contract by host government, war and civil disturbance in developing member countries. MIGA guarantees are long term in nature (up to 15–20 years) and non-cancellable. MIGA's coverage for equity and equity-related investments are in addition to the World Bank guarantee products outlined earlier.

[6] World Bank, 'Bidding for Private Concessions'.

In sum,

- IBRD provides loans and guarantees.
- IFC provides A and B loans, equity and quasi-equity.
- MIGA provides political risk insurance.
- IDA lends to poorer countries.

All four organizations may work together in a project.

BENEFITS OF GUARANTEES

The World Bank guarantees benefit to both borrowers and sovereign governments in the following ways:

- By covering risks that the market cannot assume, guarantees facilitate access to financing that would not otherwise be available to certain projects.
- Guarantees can extend the maturity of the loan beyond loan period that would not be possible without a guarantee.
- Partial risk guarantees reduce host governments' exposure to a project.
- Credit guarantees enable borrowers to select the currency, interest rate basis (fixed or floating) and maturity to best match the project's requirements.
- The presence of Bank guarantee obviates the need for a country premium usually charged by lenders.

For providing guarantee, the Bank charges a standby fee, a guarantee fee and a front-end fee. In addition, the Bank may also charge an initiation fee and a processing fee for a particular project. Charges differ from one guarantee structure to the other. The fee is usually charged in advance of each interest period and non-payment of fees results in the lapse of the guarantee. The 1,292 mw Hub Power Project in Pakistan was the first private sector project to receive a World Bank guarantee. The Bank's guarantee protects commercial lenders from sovereign risks associated with the project. The project achieved financial closure in 1995. A special purpose project company, Hub Power Company, has been set up to own and operate the power station. The project cost of US$1.8 billion of which 80 per cent is debt mobilized on a project finance basis.

PROJECT FEASIBILITY STUDIES

Because of the non-recourse feature, extensive project feasibility studies are conducted. Elaborate projections are made for each of the cost and revenue items for the life of the project, profitability measures such as NPV and IRR are calculated. Accounting measures such as ROI and ROE are quite popular in infrastructure projects. For instance, a 16 per cent return on equity is allowed in case of power projects in India. ROE is a single-period measure. The actual IRR of the project might be much lower. ROE is a function of timing of equity investment and timing of returns in case of multi-period projects. It might not be meaningful to calculate ROE as it is an accounting-based measure. It suffers from the same pitfalls as ROI.

The DCF methodology requires estimation of equity cash flows or total cash flows.

Free Cash Flow = EBIT − Cash Taxes + Depreciation − Capital Expenditure − ΔWorking Capital
Equity Cash Flow = Free Cash Flow − Debt Service + New Borrowings

Typically, lenders expect the sponsor to maintain a debt service reserve account equal to six months of interest and principal payment. This amount should be deducted to arrive at equity cash flows.

If the NPV of the project is positive, the project can be accepted. This approach assumes two things:

- The capital structure remains the same throughout the life of the project and therefore a single discount rate (WACC) be used for all the cash flows.
- The discount rate can be estimated using book value weights instead of market value weights as the latter is typically not available.

Both the assumptions are questionable.[7] In most project finance situations, the leverage rises from 0 per cent to 60–80 per cent and then falls back to 0. Therefore, using a single discount rate (WACC) is inappropriate. A project can be evaluated either from the equity investors' perspective or from the perspective of all investors. The cost of equity, which is the discount rate in the former approach, is a function of systematic risk, which depends on leverage.[8] Calculating the project's cost of equity using the maximum leverage or average leverage gives erroneous answers. So it is necessary to calculate a different discount rate for each year based on leverage in existence in that year.

The equity beta

$$\beta_E = \beta_A\,(V/E)$$

where β_A = asset beta, V and E are values of firm and equity, respectively.

The asset beta can be estimated using regression analysis and a set of comparable, publicly traded companies. To illustrate, if asset beta is 0.8, V and E are 100 and 35, equity beta = 0.8 (100/35) = 2.28.

If risk-free rate is 12 per cent, market premium is 10 per cent, cost of equity = 12 + 2.28 (10) = 34.8 per cent.

Beta and cost of equity can be estimated for each year by using actual leverage. Quite often, the capital structure is measured using book value. According to modern finance theory, investors demand returns based on market values and not book values. The two values rarely coincide. Unfortunately, measuring market value of equity is difficult. The market value of equity is the present value of equity cash flows but the discount rate used to discount equity cash flows (ECFs) itself is supposed to be based on market value of equity, that is, there is a circularity problem. We can get over this problem by using the quasi-market valuation (QMV).[9] Further, DCF is unsuitable for projects characterized by varying degrees of risk resolution.[10] For example, in case of oil exploration projects or pharmaceutical R&D projects, the exploration/research phase differ from development and production phases in terms of risk.

---

[7] See Esty, 'Improved Techniques for Valuing Large-Scale Projects'.

[8] Cost of equity also goes into WACC under the latter approach.

[9] For more on QMV, see Esty, 'Improved Techniques for Valuing Large-Scale Projects'.

[10] Mandron, Alix, 'Improved Techniques for Valuing Large Scale Projects'.

CONCLUDING COMMENTS

Project financing is likely to be successful if there is no significant correlation between the cost and revenue of the project with those of the parent company. The participants should have a sound understanding of cost of and time required to complete the project, pattern of cash flows and risks involved. As project finance involves complex contractual arrangements and documentation between the participants, the advantages of risk pooling and sharing of expertise should be high enough to warrant the setting up of a separate project company.

The differences between corporate finance and project finance are outlined as follows.

Corporate Finance	Project Finance
Lend to existing entity	Lend to new entity
Full recourse (access to corporate assets as security for loans)	Limited recourse (access to assets of the project or transaction)
Lend against the balance sheet of the company	Lend against the income stream

In the financial structuring of projects, World Bank guarantees can complement loans from IFC and IBRD, and insurance from MIGA. Guaranteed debt is often arranged at lower cost and longer maturities than would otherwise be possible.

APPENDIX 19A.1: TAXONOMY OF RISKS

'Completion risk' refers to the risk that the project might not be completed due to, say, unexpected delay in construction schedule or shortage of critical inputs. A higher than expected input costs or lower than anticipated output price might reduce the profitability of the project.

The risk that the proposed technology will become obsolete or less efficient is called 'technological risk'. This is particularly important for hi-tech industries where the technology is rapidly evolving.

The risk that the raw material or other factors of production may become unavailable during the life of the project is called 'raw material supply risk'. This is especially important where natural resources are critical inputs.

The risk that the demand for the project's product will not be sufficient to meet all expenses and provide a satisfactory return to equity investors is called 'economic risk'.

When floating rate debt is used to finance a project, there is a risk that rising interest rates could jeopardize the viability of the project and the ability to service debt. This is referred to as 'financial risk'.

'Currency risk' arises when the project's revenues stream or its costs are denominated in different currencies or in more than one currency. Changes in the foreign exchange rate will affect the profitability of the project.

In some international projects, there is a possibility that political leaders in the host country may interfere in the execution of the project and in extreme cases the cost overrun will be so high that the project may no longer be viable. This is referred to as 'political risk'. The case of Enron Corporation in India serves as a good example.[11]

[11] Rangan et al., 'Enron Development Corporation'.

EXERCISES

1. List out the difference between corporate finance and project finance.
2. Write a brief note on valuation in project finance settings.
3. Describe the role of bilateral and multilateral institutions in funding projects.
4. What are the benefits and costs of project finance?
5. Describe the key risks in infrastructure projects.

REFERENCES

Brealy, Richard R., Ian A. Cooper and Michael A. Habib. 'Using Project Finance to Fund Infrastructure Investments'. *Journal of Applied Corporate Finance* (1996 Fall).

Esty, Benjamin C. 'Improved Techniques for Valuing Large-Scale Projects'. *The Journal of Project Finance* (1999 Spring).

Esty, Benjamin and Mathew Mateo Millet. 'Petrolera Zuata, Petrozuata C.A' (HBS Case No 9–299–012, 1998 Dec).

Gerrard, Michael. 'Financing Pakistan's Hub Power Project' (RMC Discussion Paper Series 118, Washington DC: World Bank, 1997).

Mandron, Alix. 'Improved Techniques for Valuing Large Scale Projects: A Follow Up'. *Journal of Project Finance* (2000 Spring).

Rangan, V. Kasturi, Krishna G. Palepu, A. Bhasin and Mihir A. Desai. 'Enron Development Corporation: The Dabhol Power Project in Maharashtra, India' (Harvard Business School Case 9–596–099, Boston, MA, 1998 July).

World Bank. 'Bidding for Private Concessions: The Use of World Bank Guarantees' (RMC Discussion Paper Series 120, Washington DC: World Bank, 1998).

SUGGESTED READINGS

Benoit, Philippe. 'The World Bank Group's Financial Instruments for Infrastructure' (World Bank Research Paper No. 101, Washington, DC, 1997 Jan).

Benoit, Philippe. 'Mitigating Project Risks—World Bank Support for Government Guarantees, Private Sector' (Note No. 79, May).

Biedelman, Carl R., Donna Fletcher and David Veshosky. 'On Allocating Risk: The Essence of Project Finance'. *Sloan Management Review* (1990 Spring).

Brennan, Michael J. and Eduardo Schwartz. 'Evaluating Natural Resource Investments'. *Journal of Business* 58, no. 2 (1985).

Diamonte, Robin, John Liew and Ross Stevens. 'Political Risk in Emerging and Developed Markets'. *Financial Analysts Journal* (1996 May–June).

Esty, Benjamin and Fuaad Qureshi. 'Financing the Mozal Project' (Harvard Business School Case No 9–200–005, Boston, MA, 2000 February).

Esty, Benjamin and Michael Kane. 'Chase's Strategy for Syndicating the Hong Kong Disneyland Loan' (HBS Case No. 9–201–072, Boston, MA, 2001 March).

Esty, Benjamin, Suzie Harris and Kathy Krueger. 'An Overview of the Project Finance Market' (Harvard Business School Case Study No 200–028, Boston, MA, 1999 December).

Finnerty, John D. *Project Financing: Asset Based Financial Engineering*. Hoboken, NJ: John Wiley & Sons, 1996.

Henderson, Wallace. 'Case Studies of Project Finance in Latin America'. *The Journal of Project Finance* (1999 Winter).

Hoffman, Scott L. *The Law and Business of International Project Finance*. London: Kluwer Law International, 1998.

International Finance Corporation. 'Project Finance in Developing Countries' (Lessons of Experience No. 7, Washington, DC, 1999).

Jensen, Michael C. 'Agency Costs of Free Cash Flow: Corporate Finance and Takeovers'. *American Economic Review* 76 (1986 May).

Kensinger, John and John Martin. 'Project Finance: Raising Money the Old Fashioned Way'. *Journal of Applied Corporate Finance* (1988 Fall).

Lake, Thomas and Henry Davis. 'Termo Emcali'. *The Journal of Project Finance* (1999 Winter).

Mao, James C. T. 'Project Financing: Funding the Future'. *Financial Executive* (1982 April).

Nevitt P. *Project Financing*. London: Euromoney Publications, 1989.

Percopo, Bob and Peter Haller. 'Insurance Solutions for Project Finance'. *The Journal of Project Finance* (1999 Summer).

Qureshi, Fuaad A. and Benjamin Esty. 'Financing the Mozal Project' (Harvard Business School Case Study No 200–005, 2000 February).

Rhodes, Tony, ed. *Syndicated Lending: Practice and Documentation*. London: Euromoney Publications PLC, 1996.

Shah, Salman and Anjan V. Thakor. 'Optimal Capital Structure and Project Financing'. *Journal of Economic Theory* 42 (1987 June).

Shou Qing Wang, Robert Tiong, S. K. Ting and D. Ashley. 'Risk Management Framework for BOT Power Projects in China'. *The Journal of Project Finance* (1999 Winter).

So, Jae and Ben Shin. 'The Private Infrastructure Industry—A Global Market of $60 Billion a Year'. *Private Sector* (1995 Oct).

Wells, Louis T. and Eric S. Gleason. 'Is Foreign Infrastructure Investment Still Risky?' *Harvard Business Review* (1995 Sep–Oct).

West, Gerald. 'Political Risk Investment Insurance: A Renaissance'. *The Journal of Project Finance* (1999 Summer).

Wynant, Larry. 'Essential Elements of Project Financing'. *Harvard Business Review* (1980 May–June).

CHAPTE

20

The Leasing Decision

LEARNING OBJECTIVES

- Leasing as an alternative to borrow and buy
- Provide a rationale for leasing
- Highlight theoretical issues in the valuation of leasing

A lease is a contract between the owner, called the lessor, and the user of the asset, called the lessee. The lease bestows the right of use on the lessee for a specific period of time for which the lessee makes periodic lease payments. The lease payments are made at regular intervals—quarterly, monthly or semi-annually. The timing of lease payments could be tailored to match lessee's cash flows. At the end of the lease term, the asset reverts back to the lessor unless there is a provision for the renewal of the contract or transfer of ownership to the lessee. In the Indian context, a lease contract cannot provide for a transfer of ownership from the lessor to lessee.

A lessee can be a company or an individual. Lessors may be leasing companies or equipment manufacturers. If the lessor is an independent company, it must buy the asset from the manufacturer and then deliver the asset to the lessee. Typically, the lessee first decides on the asset needed and then negotiates a lease contract with a lessor. The distinction between leasing and buying is depicted in Figure 20.1. Since the lessee is not the owner of the asset, the lessee cannot claim depreciation.

TYPES OF LEASES

Two important classes of lease exist: finance and operating lease. The distinction is based on the extent to which the risks and rewards of ownership are transferred from the lessor to the lessee. Operating leases are short-term, cancellable lease agreements running for 3–5 years. The lessor is generally responsible for maintaining and insuring the asset. Typically, the lease term will not cover the useful life of the asset or fully amortize the cost of the asset. Therefore, the lessor must recover the cost of the asset by renewing the contract or by selling the asset in the second-hand market for its residual value. The lessee will have the option to cancel the lease agreement. This shifts the risk of product obsolescence to the lessor. Computers, cars, trucks and office equipment are some of the general candidates for operating leases. Finance lease, on the other hand, is a long-term, non-cancellable lease.

The technical difference between finance lease and operating lease is that if the lease term exceeds 75 per cent of the useful life of the asset or the present value of the minimum lease payments exceeds 90

FIGURE 20.1
Lease Versus Buy

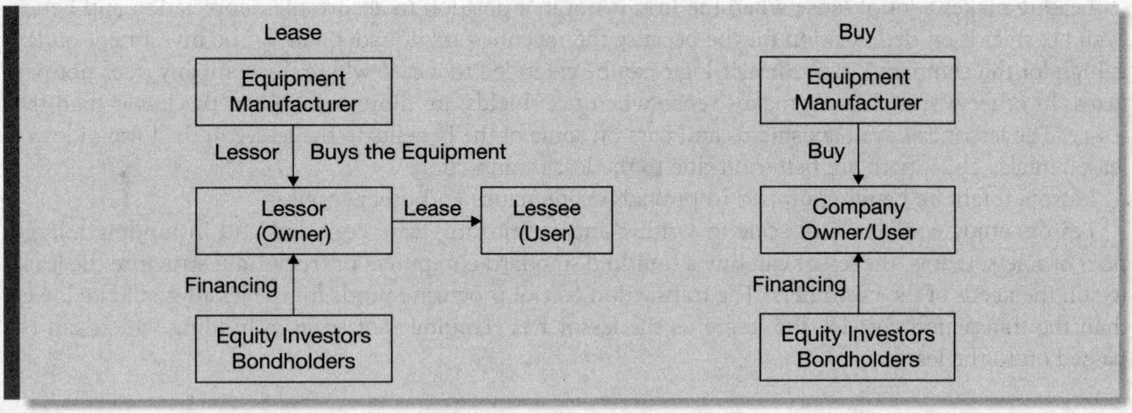

per cent of the fair market value of the asset at the inception of lease, the lease will be classified as a finance lease. Any lease other than finance lease is an operating lease. Two special types of finance lease exist: sale and lease back, and leveraged lease. In a sale and lease back arrangement, a company sells an asset it owns to another company (leasing company) and immediately leases it back. The lessee receives cash from the sale of the asset but gets to use the asset for the lease term. The lessee makes regular lease payments to the lessor. A leveraged lease is similar to any other lease except that the asset is funded by 50–60 per cent debt. The creditors will have the first charge on the asset and in the event of default by the lessor, the lease payments are made directly to the creditors.

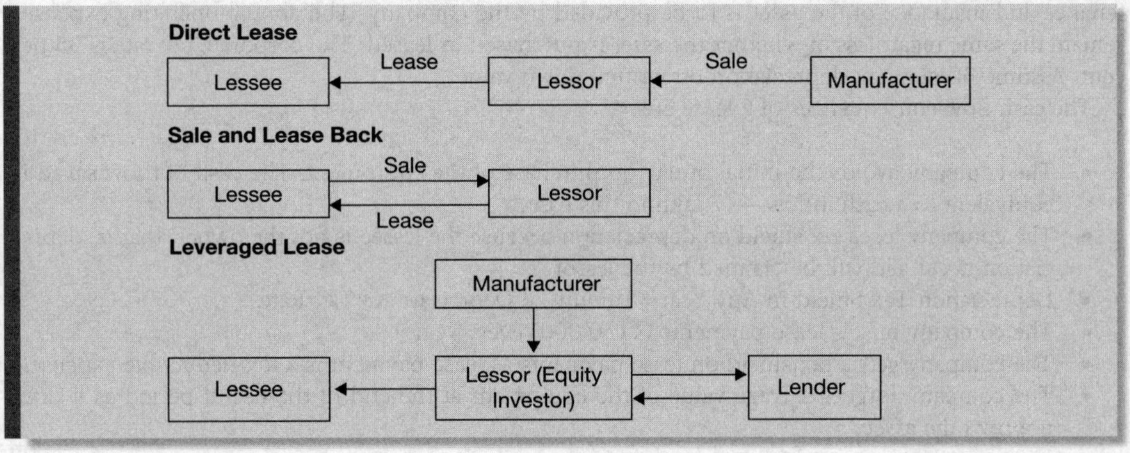

RATIONALE FOR LEASING

Leasing exists primarily due to information asymmetry between lessors and lessees regarding the market for the asset in question. Lessors can specialize in particular asset categories (e.g., computers, aircrafts) and enjoy economies of scale in gathering information relating to technical characteristics, product obsolescence and second-hand market for the asset. A lessee might not be able to find a suitable buyer at the end of the useful life due to lack of knowledge of second-hand market or make realistic estimate of asset's life or salvage value.

Leasing makes a lot of sense when the firm is not in a position to absorb the depreciation and hence avail tax shields on depreciation maybe because the revenues are not adequate or the investment outlay is high for the company's size. Similar logic can be extended to a case where the company does not pay taxes. In other words, leasing makes sense when tax shields are more valuable to the lessor than the lessee. The lessor can avail tax shields and pass on some of the benefits to the lessee in the form of lower lease rentals. Thus, both are better off due to the lease transaction.

Lessors might be better equipped to provide maintenance and other services.

Lessors enjoy economies of scale in writing and monitoring lease contracts and in funding a large pool of assets, that is, the lessor can buy a hundred standard computers or trucks and structure the lease to suit the needs of the customers. The transaction cost of procuring funds for the lessor would be lower than the transaction cost for the lessee as the lessor has economies of scale in funding which can be passed on to the lessee.

CASH FLOWS OF A LEASE

Suppose a company is in need of equipment. The company can either purchase it outright or lease it. Consider the following data.

Equipment Cost = ₹700,000
Asset's Useful Life = 7 Years

The company can lease the equipment for seven years at an annual lease rental of ₹150,000. The maintenance and insurance of the asset is to be provided by the company. The annual operating expenses remain the same regardless of whether the asset is purchased or leased. The corporate tax rate is 35 per cent. Assume 30 per cent depreciation on written down value.

The cash flow consequences of a lease are:

- The company avoids the initial outlay on purchase of the equipment. The cash outflow saved is equivalent to a cash inflow—₹7 lakh in this case.
- The company loses tax shield on depreciation because the lessee is not the owner, that is, depreciation tax shield will be claimed by the lessor.
- Depreciation Tax Shield in Any Year = Amount of Depreciation × Tax Rate
- The company makes lease payments (₹150,000) every year.
- The company gets a tax shield on lease payments as lease payment is a tax-deductible expense.
- The company forgoes salvage value of the equipment at the end of the useful period as it does not own the asset.

LEASE–DEBT EQUIVALENCE

Lease is akin to debt as the lessor is essentially making a loan to the lessee. The lease contract binds the lessee to a series of contractual lease payments. In short, lease displaces debt. Suppose a company currently has debt and equity in equal proportion. The total capital employed is ₹100,000. The company has an equipment in mind, which requires an outlay of ₹10,000. The firm can either purchase it or lease it. In order to purchase, the company will have to sell debt and equity in equal proportion (₹5,000) to maintain the debt–equity ratio of 1.0. Under the lease alternative, the company has a liability of ₹10,000, the present value of lease rentals. To maintain the capital structure, the company should reduce existing debt by ₹5,000. We established the fact that lease displaces debt. But how much of debt is equivalent to leasing? Define equivalent loan as the amount of loan that commits a firm to exactly the same stream of fixed obligations as does the lease liability.

Consider a single period situation. You have two options.

Borrow an amount ₹D @ i per cent and buy the asset.

Lease the asset and pay a lease rental of ₹L and forgo depreciation tax shield.

Let us ignore salvage value for the sake of simplicity.

The cost of borrowing is the after-tax interest payment and principal payment. The cost of leasing is the after-tax lease payment and the depreciation tax shield lost. The equivalent loan is the value of D at which the costs of the two alternatives are same.

Verify that

$$D = [L(1-T) + DT]/[1 + i(1-T)]$$

that is, equivalent loan is the present value of after-tax lease payments and depreciation tax shield. The result holds good for a multi-period situation as well.

Consider the cash flows.

	Years					
	0	1	2	3	4	5
Lease Cash Flows ₹	119,400	–36,720	–30,195	–26,280	–26,280	–23,340
Debt Cash Flows ₹	120,015	–36,720	–30,195	–26,280	–26,280	–23,340

The cash flows from the two alternatives are the same. ₹120,015 is the loan amount equivalent to lease. How did we arrive at this equivalent loan? It is the present value of lease cash flows discounted at the after-tax cost of debt. The difference between the initial cash flows gives the NPV of the lease, namely (₹119,400 – ₹120,015) –₹615 in this case. Since the NPV of the lease is negative, the company should borrow and buy. Stated in a different fashion, the lease cash flows service an equivalent loan of ₹120,015 while the lease finance is only ₹119,400. The company would be better off by taking a loan of ₹119,400. If the equivalent loan is more than the lease finance, borrow and buy; else lease.

NET ADVANTAGE OF LEASE

The cash flows from buying the asset as opposed to leasing it are as follows:

Cash Flows from Borrow and Buy

Year	Purchase Price Operating Saving	After-Tax Tax Shield	Depreciation	Salvage Value	Total
0	(P)	________	________	________	(P)
1		X_1	$D \times T$	________	$X_1 + DT$
2		X_1	$D \times T$	________	$X_1 + DT$
3		X_1	$D \times T$	________	$X_1 + DT$
N		X_1	$D \times T$	S	$X_1 + DT$

Cash Flows from Lease

Year	Lease Rentals	After-Tax Operating Saving	Tax Shield on Lease Rentals	Total
0		———	———	
1	L	X_1	L×T	X_1+L (1−T)
2	L	X_1	L×T	X_1+L (1−T)
3	L	X_1	L×T	X_1+L (1−T)
N	L	X_1	L×T	X_1+L (1−T)

For our analysis, it is the incremental cash flow from leasing in lieu of buying is what matters. In other words, the direct cash flows of buying the equipment are subtracted from those of leasing it. The incremental cash flows are shown in Table 20.1.

Let us go back to our earlier example.

$$\text{Purchase Price} = ₹700{,}000$$
$$\text{Lease Rentals} = ₹150{,}000$$

Tax rate for the company=35 per cent. Ignore salvage value. The cost of debt is 14 per cent. After-tax cost of debt=9.1 per cent

The depreciation tax shield for the equipment is shown in Table 20.2. The incremental cash flows are shown in Table 20.3.

If the NPV of the incremental cash flows (lease minus buy), called net advantage of lease (NAL), is positive, the company should prefer leasing for buying. The lease analysis begins with the assumption that the company has convinced itself that the equipment is financially worthwhile (by applying standard capital budgeting techniques). The issue, therefore, is to find out if the company should buy it or lease it. The appropriate discount rate is the after-tax cost of borrowing.

The decision rule is

$$\text{If NAL} > 0, \text{ lease}$$
$$\text{NAL} < 0, \text{ buy provided NPV of the equipment is} > 0$$

TABLE 20.1
Incremental Cash Flows

Year	Purchase Price Avoided	After-Tax Lease Rentals	Depreciation Tax Shield Foregone (–)	Salvage Value Foregone (–)	Total
0	+P				(P)
1		L (1−T)	D×T		L (1−T)+DT
2		L (1−T)	D×T		L (1−T)+DT
3		L (1−T)	D×T		L (1−T)+DT
4		L (1−T)	D×T		L (1−T)+DT
5		L (1−T)	D×T		L (1−T)+DT
N		L (1−T)	D×T	S	L (1−T)+DT

TABLE 20.2
Depreciation Tax Shield

Year	BV of the Asset	Depreciation	Dep Tax Shield
0	700,000	______	______
1	490,000	210,000	73,500
2	343,000	147,000	51,450
3	240,100	102,900	36,015
4	156,065	84,035	29,506
5	109,246	46,819	16,386
6	76,473	32,773	11,470
7	0	76,473	26,765

TABLE 20.3
Incremental Cash Flows (₹)

	Years							
Component	0	1	2	3	4	5	6	7
Purchase Price	700,000							
After-Tax Lease Payment		97,500	97,500	97,500	97,500	97,500	97,500	97,500
Depreciation Tax Shield Lost		73,500	51,450	36,015	29,506	16,386	11,470	26,765
Net Cash Flow	700,000	–171,000	–148,950	–133,515	–127,006	–113,886	–108,970	–124265

The PV of the incremental cash flows is as follows.

Year	Cash Flow ₹	PV @9.1% ₹
0	700,000	700,000
1	–171,000	–156,737
2	–148,950	–125,168
3	–133,515	–103,100
4	–127,006	–90,011
5	–113,886	–74,048
6	–108,970	–64,979
7	–124,265	–67,978

NPV=₹19,979

The lease has a positive NAL. The company would be better off leasing the equipment. Suppose the equipment in itself is not worthwhile. Can leasing make it worthwhile? Let us suppose the NPV of the project is –₹10,000. The NAL is ₹19,979.

Adjusted Present Value=–₹10,000+19,979=₹9,979. Leasing makes the project worthwhile.
The lease evaluation may be specified as:

$$NAL = P - \Sigma L_t/(1+X_1)^t + \Sigma L_t \times T/(1+X_2)^t - \Sigma D_t \times T/(1+X_3)^t + \Sigma O_t(1-T)/(1+X_4)^t - \Sigma S_n/(1+X_5)^n$$

where

P = purchase price avoided
L_t = lease payments at the end of period t
D_t = Depreciation charge relevant for tax payment at the end of period t
O_t = cash operating expenses expected to occur in period t if the asset is purchased but not if it is leased
t = tax rate
n = no. of periods covered by the lease agreement
S_n = Expected after-tax salvage value of the asset at the end of the last period covered by lease

X_1, X_2, X_3, X_4 and X_5 are discount rates appropriate for the respective cash flow components.

Since lease is similar to debt, the discount rate applicable to lease cash flows is cost of debt. But should cost of debt be the discount rate for all the components or just lease payments? Tax shields can be availed only when the company makes money. No company can be 'sure' of making money and hence avail tax shields. So tax shields might deserve a higher discount rate.

Some academics point out that the loss of interest tax shields (on borrowing) should be incorporated in the analysis. That is

$$NAL = P - \Sigma L_t(1+X_1)^t + \Sigma L_t \times T/(1+X_2)^t - \Sigma D_t \times T/(1+X_3)^t + \Sigma O_t(1-T)/(1+X_4)^t - \Sigma S_n/(1+X_5)^n - \Sigma I_t \times T/(1+X_6)^t$$

where I_t is the interest payment in period t.

The after-tax borrowing rate recognizes the interest tax shield lost on displaced debt. The PV of lease for 1 year

$$PV_L = [L(1-T) + TD + (I \times B \times T)]/(1+i)$$

where B is the debt displaced by lease; i is the interest rate; T is the tax rate; and TD is the depreciation tax shield.

If we assume that one rupee of lease displaces one rupee of debt, then $PV_L = B$

$$PV_L = [L(1-T) + TD + (i \times PV_L \times T)]/(1+i)$$
$$PV_L\{1 - [i \cdot T/(1+i)]\} = [L(1-T) + TD]/(1+i)$$
$$PV_L(1+i-iT) = (1-T)\,L + TD$$
$$PV_L = [L(1-T) + TD]/[1+i(1-T)]$$

This is precisely the lease valuation formula we used. One general observation is that, if interest tax shields are considered, then the appropriate discount rate is the before-tax cost of debt; else after-tax cost of debt should be used.

LEASE EVALUATION: LESSOR'S PERSPECTIVE

The cash flows to the lessor are simply the mirror image of that for lessee. When both of them are in the same tax bracket, the outflow to the lessee is the inflow to the lessor and vice versa. The value of the lease to the lessor in the previous example would be:

$$\begin{aligned} NPV &= -₹700{,}000 + 156{,}737 + 125{,}168 + 103{,}100 + 90{,}011 + 74{,}048 + 64{,}979 + 67{,}978 \\ &= -₹19{,}979 \end{aligned}$$

So a lessor would not be willing to lease the equipment. Suppose the lessee has a tax rate of 25 per cent and lessor has a tax rate of 35 per cent. The cash flows for the lessee would be:

Year	Purchase Price	After-Tax Lease Payments	Depreciation Tax Shield Lost	Total
0	700,000			700,000
1	112,500	52,500	(165,000)	
2	112,500	36,750	(149,250)	
3	112,500	25,725	(138,225)	
4	112,500	21,008	(133,508)	
5	112,500	11,704	(124,204)	
6	112,500	8,193	(120,693)	
7	112,500	19,118	(131,618)	

Post-Tax Cost of Debt = 14 (1 − 0.25) = 10.5 per cent

$$NAL = ₹29{,}331$$

The lessor gets ₹19,979.

When the lessee does not pay any tax,

$$\text{NPV of Lease} = 700{,}000 - [1.5\,L \times \text{PVIFA}\ (14,\ 7)] = ₹56{,}800$$

The important observation is that when the parties are in different tax brackets, the lease transaction can be structured in such a way that they share the gains in some agreeable proportion.

BREAK-EVEN LEASE RENTALS

The lease rental at which the NAL is zero is called break-even lease rental, that is, the lessee will be indifferent between leasing and purchasing when lease rental equals break-even rental. Consider the same example.

$$\begin{aligned} \text{Purchase Price Avoided} &= ₹700{,}000 \\ \text{PV (Depreciation Tax Shield)} &= 73{,}500 \times \text{PVIF}(9.1,\ 1) + 51{,}450 \times \text{PVIF}(9.1,\ 2). \\ &= ₹190{,}889 \\ \text{PV (After-Tax Lease Rentals)} &= L_t(1 - 0.35) \times \text{PVIFA}(9.1{,}7) = 3.26L_t \end{aligned}$$

Setting NAL=0

$$700{,}000-190{,}889-3.26L_t=0$$
$$L_t=₹156{,}169$$

Similarly, the break-even lease rental when tax rate is zero,

$$NAL=700{,}000-L_t\times PVIFA(14,7)=0$$

Lt=₹163,246. If the lessor is in the 35 per cent tax bracket, BELR=₹156,169

When the lessor is in the higher tax bracket than the lessee, the minimum lease rental required by the lessor turns out to be lesser than the maximum rental affordable by the lessee, thereby making NAL positive for both.

As the break-even rental for the lessee is lower than the break-even rental for the lessor, the transaction will be successful. Suppose the rental is ₹160,000.

Lessee's Gain=163,246−160,000=₹3,246
Lessor's Gain=160,000−156,169=₹3,831

CHOICE OF DISCOUNT RATE

Finance theorists generally agree that the discount rate for after-tax lease payments and depreciation tax shelter is the post-tax cost of debt and that for after-tax salvage value and operating savings is the WACC. Probably, post-tax cost of debt is too low a discount rate for tax shelters. Tax rates do change; income may not be available to be offset in every year. This makes tax shelters riskier. So it might be better to discount tax shields at cost of capital rather than cost of debt.

Obviously, the NAL is a function of discount rate. The higher the discount rate for outflows, the higher is the NPV. Applying inappropriate discount rate will lead to erroneous conclusions.

Consider the same cash flows. The WACC for the company is 17.05 per cent. Let us change the discount rate to WACC for the depreciation tax shield.

$$NAL=700{,}000-[97{,}500\times PVIFA(9.1,7)]-(D_tT)PVIF(17.05,7)$$
$$=₹51{,}924$$

Contrast this with the earlier figure of ₹19,979. Suddenly, leasing has become more attractive. It is useful to draw a graph of NAL versus discount rate and visually see the sensitivity of NAL to changes in discount rate.

UNEQUAL ASSET AND LEASE LIVES

So far, we assumed that the asset's business life specific to the lessee equals the period covered by the lease, that is, the lease term coincides with the period for which asset is being employed. There is no reason why they cannot be different. For instance, the asset's life might be 10 years, the asset's useful life eight years and the lease term, seven years. It implies that the lease will have to be replaced at the end of seventh year. So the lessee will have to make a forecast of lease rentals that are likely to prevail at the end of seven years. The difference between the lease term and asset holding period should be accounted for in comparing lease and purchase alternatives. To illustrate, if X is the asset life and Y is the lease term, and if X>Y, the two options cannot be compared (as they have different lives) without considering what happens after the shorter option expires. One could compare the option to purchase equipment that has a life of 10 years with two five-year back-to-back leases. In other words, the shorter option should be replicated to cover the life of the longer option. It is important to understand that the asset and lease lives are not only unequal but also uncertain. Typically, firms make estimates of asset lives on the basis of past experience with similar assets.

AN ILLUSTRATION

A company is contemplating on purchasing equipment for ₹8 million. The company has an option to lease the equipment for five years. The rentals are ₹550,000 p.a. after tax. At the end of five years, the company will have to replace the lease or purchase the equipment. The company's executives have forecasted the lease rentals that are likely to prevail starting from Year six.[1] Tax rate=34 per cent. Long-term borrowing rate=13 per cent. After-tax borrowing rate=8.6 per cent, WACC=15 per cent, salvage value=0, asset life=10 years. Tax and depreciation rates are forecasts. The lease rentals for Years six through 10 are ₹6.9 million p.a. The cash flows under purchase and lease alternatives are as follows.

	Purchase			Lease
Year	Purchase Price	Dep. Tax Shield	Net C.F. Payments	After-Tax Lease Payments
0	–800		–800	
1		22	22	–55
2		38	38	–55
3		33	33	–55
4		27	27	–55
5		27	27	–55
6		27	27	–69
7		24	24	–69
8		24	24	–69
9		24	24	–69
10		24	24	–69

Net present value:

	Purchase	Lease
At Borrowing Rate	–619	–395
At Cost of Capital	–660	–337
First Five Years at Borrowing Rate; Last Five Years at Cost of Capital		–369

[1] Cason, 'Leasing, Asset Lives and Uncertainty'.

The post-tax cost of debt is the discount rate for the first five years of the lease term. For the next five years, either cost of debt or cost of capital could be used as discount rate. But it is better to use cost of capital because the forecast of lease payments carry normal business risk like any other economic element.

EFFECT OF RESTRUCTURING LEASE RENTALS

The lessor has the discretion of structuring the lease rentals to match the cash flows of the lessee. Given below are two situations: in the first case, the lessor charges uniform rentals and in the second, a major portion of lease payments is recovered in the later part of the term.

Situation 1	Situation 2
Asset Cost = ₹1,000	Asset Cost = ₹1,000
N = 5 Years	N = 5 Years
T = 0.35	T = 0.35
Cost of Debt = 16%	Cost of Debt = 16%
L = 250 p.a.	75, 75, 300, 400 and 400
D = 30%	D = 30%

Ignore salvage value.

The NAL increases as lease rentals are deferred. The reason is fairly obvious. When lease rentals are bunched towards the end, the present value of outflow falls. The NPV increases.

MONTHLY LEASE PAYMENTS, ANNUAL DEPRECIATION AND MONTHLY DISCOUNT RATES

Usually, lease payments are made monthly in advance or in arrears, whereas depreciation tax shields are availed annually. So the basic model needs to be adjusted.

$$NAL = A_o - \sum L_t(1-T)/[1+(r \times /12)^t] - \sum D_t \times T/(1+r^*)^t$$

r^* = after-tax cost of debt
L = monthly lease payment
M = no. of months

The annual rate is to be converted into a monthly rate. If the annual rate is 12 per cent, the monthly rate is 1 per cent if compounding is done annually.

The monthly rate equivalent to 12 per cent compounded semi-annually:

$$\text{Effective Rate} = (1+0.12/2)^2 - 1 = 12.36 \text{ per cent}$$
$$\text{Monthly Rate} = 12.36/12 = 1.03 \text{ per cent}$$

Similar logic applies for other compounding periods as well.

CONCLUDING COMMENTS

The value of a lease is a function of tax rates for lessor and lessee. If the lessee cannot avail tax shield on depreciation, it makes sense to pass on to someone who can. Indeed, many lease transactions are either credit or tax motivated deals. Sometimes a company will lease because it has a weak credit rating and wants to use the lessor's ability to borrow money at a lower rate. The value of leasing increases when the

- Lessor's tax rate is substantially higher than the lessee's
- Lease period is extended
- Lease payments are bunched towards the end of the lease term
- Lessee uses a higher discount rate (wrongly).

The asset's holding period, the lease term and the asset's useful life need not coincide. This should be explicitly built into the analysis. Elementary capital budgeting theory tells us that two projects with unequal lives cannot be compared but their equivalent annuities can be.

There are two approaches to lease evaluation—equivalent loan approach and NPV (some compute IRR of lease). If the equivalent loan is higher than the lease finance, the company should borrow. Under the NAL method, leasing should be opted if NAL > 0. The implicit assumption is that the asset NPV > 0. The lease evaluation attempts to assess the financing side effect.

The estimate of the equipment's residual value plays a significant role in how the company values the lease. Neither the lessor nor the lessee will know with any certainty what the market for the equipment would be after the useful life of the asset or lease term. If inflation turns out to be higher than anticipated during the term of the lease, the value of the equipment would also be high and vice versa. The uncertainty is more pronounced in case of long-lived assets like land and buildings. Finally, lease flows are slightly more risky than debt flows because lenders get priority in bankruptcy. So the discount rate for lease payments should be slightly higher than the cost of debt.

EXERCISES

1. What are the different types of leases?
2. Write a brief note on lease evaluation.
3. Refer to the following data:
   Asset Cost = ₹22 million
   Lease Payments for the First 7 Years = ₹2.3 million
   –Lease Payments for the Next 8 Years = ₹2.8 million
   Salvage Value = 0
   Lease payments are made at the end of the year.
   Cost of debt for the lessee is 9 per cent after tax. Depreciation is charged at 25 per cent. Tax rate is 35 per cent. Find the NAL. Would you lease?
   Rework with 35 per cent tax rate for lessor and zero tax rate for lessee. What is the break-even lease rental?

4. The annual lease rental is ₹150,000 p.a. The after-tax borrowing rate is 7 per cent. The lease term is eight years. Find the monthly lease rental.
5. If the salvage value of the equipment in Question 1 is 10 per cent, how would your answer change? Cost of capital is 17 per cent.
6. Some argue that leasing becomes viable because of lower cost of capital for the lessor because lessor's primary source of finance is low-cost fixed deposits. The lessor uses his/her cost of capital as discount rate, which makes leasing viable. Do you agree? Why or why not?
7. Can leasing become viable because of better credit rating of the lessor? How? Why or why not?
8. Lease payments are usually quoted as a fraction of ₹1,000 of asset cost on a monthly basis. Convert lease rentals in Question 1 to this format.
9. An airline company needs an aircraft. It has two options:
   - Buy the aircraft for ₹500 million at a post-tax cost of debt of 8.5 per cent. The aircraft has a life of 15 years at the end of which it can be salvaged for ₹140 million. Annual maintenance expenses are ₹600,000.
   - Lease it for 15 years by paying ₹60 million per year.

   Assume straight line depreciation. Tax rate is 35 per cent. WACC is 18.5 per cent. Calculate NAL.

REFERENCE

Cason, Roger L. 'Leasing, Asset Lives and Uncertainty: A Practitioner's Comments'. *Financial Management* (1987 Summer).

SUGGESTED READINGS

Bower, R. S.. 'Issues in Lease Financing'. *Financial Management* (1973 Winter).
Franks, J. R. and S. D. Hodges. 'Valuation of Financial Lease Contracts: A Note'. *Journal of Finance* (1978 May).
Lewellen, W. G., M. S. Long and J. J. McConnell. 'Asset Leasing in Competitive Capital Markets'. *Journal of Finance* (1976 May).
McConnell, J. J. and J. S. Schallheim. 'Valuation of Asset Leasing Contracts'. *Journal of Financial Economics* (1983 Aug).
Miller, M. H. and Charles Upton. 'Leasing, Buying and the Cost of Capital Services'. *Journal of Finance* (1976 June).
Myers, S. C., David A., Dill and A. Bautista. 'Valuation of Financial Lease Contracts'. *Journal of Finance* (1976 June).
Pandey, I. M. 'Myths and Realities about Leasing'. *Vikalpa* 11, no. 4 (1986 Dec).
Schall, L. D. 'The Lease or Buy and Asset Acquisition Decision'. *Journal of Finance* (1974 Sep).
Weingartner, H. M. 'Leasing, Asset Lives and Uncertainty'. *Financial Management* (1987 Summer).

SECTION 5

Dividend Policy

CHAPTER

21

The Dividend Policy

LEARNING OBJECTIVES

- Highlight the theoretical debate surrounding the dividend policy of a firm.
- Provide a rationale for stock repurchases and bonus shares.
- Shed light on dividend policy around the world.

Dividend policy involves the decision to pay out earnings or retain for reinvestment in the business. Dividends are cash payments made by companies to shareholders either annually or semi-annually or even quarterly. The objective of this chapter is to figure out if dividends have a bearing on equity and firm value. The fraction of earnings paid out as dividends, that is, the dividend/profit after tax ratio, is an important measure of dividend policy. Two related metrics are dividend per share (DPS) in rupees and the dividend yield (i.e., dividend in rupees divided by stock price). The dividend payout metrics (five-year average for the period 2013–2017) of some of the major Indian companies are shown in Table 21.1.

Why do companies pay dividends? Why do investors pay attention to dividends? Should managers care for the amount of dividends they pay?

Consider a company whose balance sheet reads as follows.

TABLE 21.1
Dividend Payout at Major Indian Companies

Company	Divided Per Share ₹	Dividend Yield (%)
Coal India	21.68	7.85
HCL Technologies	53.11	6.25
HPCL	22.38	5.44
SBI	13.83	4.20
Infosys Technologies	32.69	3.44

			(₹)
Share Capital	100	Assets	120
Reserves	20		
	120		120

The company has issued one share @ ₹100. For the sake of simplicity, assume that the company has cash in hand as assets. The market value of the share is ₹120. If the company were to pay out all its earnings as dividends, the balance sheet would be:

			(₹)
Share Capital	100	Assets	100
Reserves	–		
	100		100

The market value of the share is ₹100. Add ₹20 of dividends. The investor is in the same final position. What the investor gets as dividends is offset by capital loss. He/she is neither better off nor worse off.

ARE DIVIDENDS IRRELEVANT?

An all-equity-financed firm has two sources of funds—current and future earnings and/or new equity. Since changing the amount of retained earnings varies the amount of dividends that the firm pays to its stockholders, it is important to understand the relationship between market value of the firm and its dividend policy. MM demonstrated that in a perfect market case dividends are irrelevant for the valuation of a firm. In other words, dividend policy does not affect stock price. Their proposition is based on certain assumptions.

- Dividends and capital gains (difference between selling price and purchase price) are taxed at the same rate.
- There are no transaction costs.
- Investment policy of the firm remains unchanged.
- Firms can issue new equity with no flotation or transaction cost.
- There are no information effects associated with dividends.

To prove their proposition, let us go back to our earlier example. The company generates earnings the following year. It can do two things with it.

- Invest in the business and skip dividends.
- Pay dividends to current shareholders and sell new shares to meet the investment requirement.

We are interested in the second situation. When the company sells new shares, existing shareholders suffer a capital loss because more shareholders share the pie. But an equal amount in dividends compensates them. What do new shareholders get? They participate in the existing earnings as well as the future earnings. High dividends today serve to spread the total earnings, including growth, over a larger number of shares. Cutting a pie into six or eight pieces will not 'increase' the size of the pie. The same is true for companies also.

We assumed that the company has access to equity alone to keep the discussion simple although the firm can sell both debt and equity. We have also assumed that shares can be sold with no flotation costs, the company's shares are fairly priced and so on. The important message is that a company can make money by good 'investment' decisions and not good dividend decision. If abundant cash is available to finance projects, a company need not worry about dividend policy.

DIVIDEND IRRELEVANCE: ALTERNATIVE EXPLANATION

The price of a share is equal to the present value of the expected future dividends. If dividends are expected to grow at a constant rate in perpetuity g, and the discount rate is k

$$P = D/(k-g) \tag{1}$$

If the firm retains a constant fraction, b, of its earnings per share and earns a constant average rate of return, r, on its investment, then

$$g = b \times r \tag{2}$$

Further, dividend,

$$\begin{aligned} D &= \text{Payout Ratio} \times \text{EPS} \\ &= (1-b) \times E \end{aligned} \tag{3}$$

Substituting in Equation (1)

$$P = [(1-b)E]/[k-br] \tag{4}$$

What would happen to P if retention ratio were to be changed?

Differentiating Equation (4) partially with respect to b

$$\partial P/\partial b = [(r-k)E]/[k-br]^2$$

For price to be independent of retained earnings, $\partial P/\partial b = 0$, that is, $r = k$

Simply put, dividend policy is irrelevant if the rate of return on the marginal investment is equal to the discount rate, that is, NPV = 0 and if r and k are independent of payout ratio.

ARE DIVIDENDS 'GOOD'?

Prior to the MM paper, most believed that higher dividends are good because the value of equity is the present value of dividends. Some theorists and practitioners believe that higher dividends have a favourable impact on stock price. The more generous the dividend policy, the higher will be the share price. The debate is whether investors value growth (retained earnings) or dividends. The effect is not too clear. Will an increase in dividends have the same (favourable) impact on stock price for a declining company as that for a growing company? When dividends are changed, firms may have to change their investment policies as well. So the change in stock price is probably a result of change in investment policy and not dividend policy.

ARE DIVIDENDS 'BAD'?

In many countries, dividends are taxed at a higher rate than capital gains. The tax on capital gains will be paid only when the investors sell shares. So a company that pays no dividends should be more attractive to investors than a similar company that pays dividends. This, at least in theory, should increase the price of the non-dividend paying company's stock. To sum up, in a world with taxes, investors would prefer smaller dividends or no dividends to high dividends.

Higher marginal tax rates on dividend income versus capital gains should make taxable investors prefer a rupee of pre-tax capital gain to a rupee of dividends. Therefore, some argue that holding risk constant, the higher is a stock's dividend yield higher is the before-tax return to compensate taxable investors for the higher tax liability. The counterargument is that the tax code has provisions that permit investors to transform dividend income into capital gains.

BIRD-IN-THE-HAND FALLACY

Argument: Dividends are better than capital gains because dividends are certain and capital gains are uncertain. So risk-averse investors prefer dividends.

Response: Firm value is determined by the cash flows from the project. If a firm increases dividends, it will have to sell new shares to satisfy investment requirements. What is received as dividends will be offset by loss of price appreciation. The new investors who bear the risk that the old investors avoid need to be compensated.

Argument: The price of a stock is the present value of future dividends.

$$P = D_1/(1+k) + D_2/(1+k)^2 + \cdots + D_n/(1+k)^n$$

Clearly, dividends received in earlier years are more valuable.

Response: The amount and timing of dividends may change but the present value of the stream does not. In other words, dividends do not affect value of equity.

WHY MIGHT DIVIDENDS MATTER?

The MM hypothesis is based on certain assumptions such as no taxes or transaction costs, no information asymmetry and so on. We can figure out why dividends may matter in real-life situations by relaxing these assumptions one by one.

TAXES

The investor who receives interest payments or dividends must pay personal tax and therefore, cares about after-tax receipts. Hence, managers should try to arrange their firms' capital structure to minimize the total taxes paid after earnings are distributed to their owners. In real life, not every investor faces the same tax rate. Low tax investors pay no or low personal taxes on dividend or interest receipts. High tax investors pay lower taxes when they receive income as capital gains instead of as interest or dividend income. Since capital gains tax is paid only when the gain is realized and if there is no offsetting loss, the investor can defer the tax payment (and weaken the impact). The combined effect of corporate and personal taxes is that there should be dividend clienteles.

The proponents of clientele effect contend that dividends matter because of the tendency of investors to buy shares in companies that have dividend policies that match their preferences for high, low or no dividends. The investors of high payout companies are there because they prefer high dividends, and the investors of low payout companies are there because they prefer low dividends. Stockholders in high tax bracket who do not need current income may choose low payout companies, and investors in low tax brackets may choose high payout companies. So firms hate to change their dividend policies due to the clientele effect lest they incur investors' wrath.

Miller and Modigliani (1961) were the first to recognize the clientele effect. In their words:

> If for example the frequency distribution of corporate payout ratios happened to correspond exactly with distribution of investor preferences for payout ratio, then the existence of these preferences would clearly lead ultimately to a situation whose implications were different, in no fundamental respect, from the perfect market case. Each corporation would tend to attract to itself a 'clientele' consisting of those preferring its particular payout ratio, but one clientele would be as good as another in terms of the valuation it would imply for firms.

If investors are mobile and the search and transaction costs are not high then dividend policy is still irrelevant, as new investors whose preferences match the new dividend policy of the firm would replace old investors.

TAXES AND CLIENTELE EFFECT

Given the tax disadvantage of dividends, it makes sense for companies to figure out who their marginal stockholders are and how they view dividends. Suppose an investor buys a share before the ex-dividend date (i.e., the date by which the investor should buy shares in order to be eligible for dividends). He/she can either collect dividends, sell shares after the ex-dividend date or sell the shares just before the ex-dividend date and forego dividends.

Let Purchase Price $= P_A$
Dividends $= D$
Price Just Before the Ex-Div Date $= P_B$
Ex-Dividend Price $= P_C$

Strategy A: Sell After the Ex-Dividend Date

Dividend Received $= D$
Tax on Dividend $= t_d \times D$
Capital Gain $= P_C - P_A$
Tax on Capital Gain $= T_{cg}(P_C - P_A)$

Strategy B: Sell Just Before the Ex-Dividend Date

Dividends $= 0$
Capital Gain $= P_B - P_A$
Tax on Capital Gain $= T_{cg}(P_B - P_A)$

To prevent arbitrage, the gain from each course of action must be the same.

$$P_B - T_{cg}(P_B - P_A) = P_C - T_{cg}(P_C - P_A) + D(1 - t_d)$$

By simplifying, we get:

$$(P_B - P_A)/D = (1 - t_d)/(1 - t_{cg})$$

For the investor to be indifferent between selling before or after the ex-dividend date, the price drop on the ex-dividend day should reflect the investor's tax differential between dividends and capital gains. By observing the price drop and the dividends, we can get some insight into marginal tax rates of shareholders. Elton and Gruber[1] point out that if the price drop is a larger proportion of dividends for firms in the high dividend class, it can be inferred that the investors in these firms are in lower tax bracket. But their critics dismiss this argument on the grounds that much of the activity around ex-dividend date is restricted to speculators and therefore, not indicative of real shareholders.

It is interesting to note that if an investor is indifferent between dividends and capital gains (i.e., tax exempt) and the price drop is lower than dividends, the investor can make riskless profit. An illustration will clarify the point.

$D = ₹10$

$(P_B - P_A) = ₹6$

$T_d = 0$ and $T_{cg} = 0$

Capital Loss = ₹6, Dividend Income = ₹10. Net Position = ₹4

Such a strategy is called dividend capture. Of course, the transaction costs should be factored into the analysis and the investor should be sure of amount of dividends and capital loss.[2]

Transaction Costs

When companies pay dividends, they may have to raise external equity to fund projects. Raising equity or debt entails transaction costs such as fees paid to merchant bankers, lawyers and other intermediaries. In Chapter 16, I pointed out that the cost of raising equity could be about 4–6 per cent of net proceeds if issued in India. The presence of transaction costs suggests that dividend policy is not trivial because paying out more forces a company to raise external capital. Of course, bank loans can be arranged at much lower costs.

Agency Conflicts

A firm is a collection of assets that are jointly owned. The shareholders of a firm appoint managers to take decisions on their behalf. There could be potential conflict of interests between managers and shareholders, and between shareholders and bondholders.

Mangers have discretion over the residual cash flow left over after meeting contractual payments. They may pay out residual cash flow as dividends or reinvest. Positive NPV projects create value for shareholders. Managers expropriate shareholders by overinvesting in value-destroying projects or increasing their perks and benefits. So such firms should pay more dividends. In other words, dividends are good news for shareholders of such firms because they resolve agency problems.

[1] Elton and Gruber, 'Marginal Stockholder Tax Rates and the Clientele Effect'.

[2] The solution is to sell a call option when the stock is purchased. This strategy is termed hedged dividend capture. See Brown and Lummer (1986).

Modern finance theory hypothesizes that investors are worried about systematic risk alone as they can diversify unsystematic risk by holding diversified portfolios. Managers, on the other hand, are concerned with total risk, which includes diversifiable risk like default risk as their careers and fortunes are tied to the fortunes of the company. Risk-averse managers may choose projects that are safe but have lower expected returns. But shareholders would want them to take on business gambles. Dividends serve the useful purpose of driving firms to competitive capital markets where the affairs of the company are scrutinized by financial intermediaries and investors.

Stockholders can transfer wealth from bondholders by choosing policies that increase the risk of the outstanding bonds. The transfer of wealth can be achieved in two ways. First, stockholders can reduce investment or sell off assets and pay dividends. Second, stockholders can sell new debt of same or higher priority and pay generous dividends. Both the acts increase the risk of existing bonds and bond price falls, thereby causing wealth loss to bondholders. Bondholders realize the incentives faced by stockholders and place restrictions on the level of future dividend payments and the usage and seniority of future debt issues. Based on this analysis, we would expect dividends to be constrained by the existing loan covenants.

Now let us suppose managers act in the interest of shareholders.

Consider a firm that currently has a debt/equity ratio of 1.0. The firm's balance sheet is as follows.

			(₹)
Equity	50	Assets	100
Debt	50		
	100		100

The company generates earnings amounting to ₹200 over a period of time, which it ploughs back into the business. The retained earnings increase equity.

			(₹)
Equity	250	Assets	300
Debt	50		
	300		300

The debt equity ratio is 0.20. The creditors have more cushion (security) than before and the shareholders are paying the creditors an interest rate more than that warranted by the default risk of the company. In other words, there is a wealth transfer from shareholders to bondholders. Shareholders can correct the situation by paying dividends of ₹100 and issuing debt worth ₹100 to revert to the original situation. In other words, managers acting in the interest of existing shareholders (or shareholders themselves) will not give away wealth to bondholders. They can achieve this by paying dividends. So dividend policy is a function of not only earning prospects but also agency considerations.

Information Asymmetry

At times, the managers of a company may know more about the true prospects of the firm than outside investors. They may convey future prospects by changing financial policies. In other words, changes in dividend policy convey information to stock markets.

There is a popular belief that firms increase dividends only when they are relatively certain that the higher payout could be maintained. So it is likely that investors will interpret an increase in dividends as a signal that management anticipates higher future earnings. Given the information signalling quality of dividends, we would expect the stock price to go up whenever dividends are increased. Empirical evidence supports this notion.

It is the information content that affects stock price and not dividends per se. It is not clear as to what dividends signal, why or how. Do changes in dividends signal the future or the 'past'? Moreover, a firm can convey information by resorting to a cheaper means of signalling. Dividends are an expensive means of signalling. We do not know if dividends are better signals than press reports or stock repurchases or some such thing. Companies may skip dividends because internal financing is cheaper than external equity due to issue costs that could be as high as 7 per cent of the issue size. The business press and equity research analysts are active enough to identify performers even if they do not pay dividends. A firm will be better off by 'telling the truth' than pay dividends to prop up the stock price.

The increase in dividends may mean two things: The firm expects a permanent increase in profits and cash flows, or the firm is in a declining stage and it opts to distribute dividends to liquidate the company. So an outsider cannot distinguish between positive dividends and negative dividends. So dividends are not the answer.

The Empirical Evidence

If dividends changes have information content in them, we would expect dividend changes to be followed by earnings changes in the same direction and unanticipated dividend changes to be followed by stock price changes in the same direction. Empirical tests of dividend initiations and omissions in the USA suggest that stock market react positively to dividend initiations and negatively to omissions. Likewise, dividend cuts, in general, are greeted negatively. As pointed out earlier, shareholders can expropriate wealth from bondholders by funding dividends with new debt. Bondholders protect themselves by inserting protective covenants or me-first rules. If security holders view these covenants as insufficient, unexpected changes in dividend payments can still result in wealth transfers. For these reasons, we would expect the stock price to go up and the prices of bonds and preferred stock to go down when there is a positive unexpected dividend change (and vice versa for unexpected negative dividend changes). Academic studies of security price reaction to unexpected dividend changes do not support the wealth transfer hypothesis.[3]

HOW DO MANAGERS SET DIVIDENDS?

The most direct way to find out what managers think of dividends is to ask them. One of the earliest surveys on dividends (a classic) is by John Lintner.[4] He conducted a survey of management views on dividend policy in the USA. His study concluded that:

- Firms have long-run target dividend payout ratio.
- Firms avoid reducing dividends in a lean period and move gradually towards the target payout ratio in much the same way as they move towards optimal capital structure even if earnings rise

[3] Randall Woolridge (1985).

[4] Lintner, 'Distribution of Income of Corporations among Dividends'.

rapidly. Dividends are increased only after managers are reasonably sure that they will be able to maintain them permanently at the new level.

- Firms make charges in DPS slowly and these changes lag behind changes in EPS by one or more periods on the belief that shareholders prefer gradual progression in dividends vis-à-vis erratic changes.
- Investment requirements have little influence on the dividend policy.

His model suggests that DPS is a function of current earnings, existing dividend rate, target payout ratio and speed of adjustment. If his model is correct, then the next year dividend would be (target ratio × next year earnings) and the change in dividends would be adjustment rate × (next year dividend − current dividend). The speed of adjustment depends on the conservatism of the company's managers and the outlook for the industry.

DIVIDEND TAX AND DIVIDEND POLICY

Countries differ in their tax treatment of dividends. Some countries tax both the company and the investor at the marginal rate. Some countries prefer to keep dividends tax-free.

In 1997–1998, the Government of India eliminated the double taxation of dividends (i.e., at the company and investor level) and introduced a new system of taxation in which dividends are taxed at a uniform rate of 10 per cent at the company level. Thus, a company contemplating on paying 25 per cent dividend will pay 22.73 per cent as dividend and 2.27 per cent as tax. This law was repealed in 2002 and reintroduced in 2003 at a tax rate of 12.5 per cent at the company level.

INTERNATIONAL COMPARISON

Based on the discussion so far, we would expect firms operating in countries with better protections of minority shareholders to pay higher dividends because dividends are an outcome of legal protection to shareholders which enables them to extract dividends from corporate insiders. A study of dividend policies of firms from 33 countries around the world confirms this expectation.[5] Table 21.2 presents the level of dividends in select countries. La Porta et al.[6] find that firms operating in countries with better protection of minority shareholders pay higher dividends, and faster growing firms pay lower dividends than slower growing firms consistent with the idea that legally protected shareholders are willing to wait for dividends when investment opportunities are good. The median dividend to cash flow ratio for common law countries like the USA and UK is 18.28, whereas for Civil Law countries it is 9.24. Similarly, other measures of dividend policy such as dividend/earnings and dividend/sales are also higher for companies from Common Law countries.

[5] La Porta, Lopez-de-Silanes, Shleifer and Vishny, 'Agency Problems and Dividend Policies Around the World'.

[6] Ibid.

[7] Ibid.

TABLE 21.2
Dividend Policy Around the World[7]

Country	Dividend/CF	Dividend/Earn	Dividend/Sales
Civil Law Countries			
Argentina	12.65	27.36	4.32
Belgium	11.77	39.38	1.09
Denmark	6.55	17.27	0.71
France	9.46	23.55	0.63
Germany	12.70	42.86	0.83
The Netherlands	11.29	30.02	0.74
Sweden	5.59	18.33	0.78
Median	**9.74**	**25.11**	**0.83**
Common Law Countries			
Australia	22.83	42.82	2.22
Canada	8.00	19.78	0.78
Hong Kong	35.43	45.93	7.51
India	25.69	49.34	1.55
Singapore	22.28	41.04	2.14
UK	16.67	36.91	1.89
USA	11.38	22.11	0.95
Median	**18.28**	**37.42**	**2.02**

STOCK REPURCHASES

An alternative to paying dividends is a stock repurchase by the firm. If some of the outstanding shares of the company are repurchased (by the company), fewer shares will be outstanding. If the stock repurchase is not expected to affect earnings, the EPS on the reduced equity base will go up. Further, if the P/E multiple of the stock is unaffected by stock repurchase, the stock price increases providing capital gains to shareholders. The firm can either extinguish shares or hold the shares as treasury stock. To illustrate, suppose a company buys back 10 million shares (face value is ₹10) at ₹100 each and cancel them.

The equity base of the company will be reduced by ₹100 million, while the reserves shrink by ₹900 million. The company can reissue at a later date. Many stock repurchase programmes are part of a corporate restructuring exercise where divisions or subsidiaries are sold off or leverage is increased. The inflow of capital due to debt issuance or asset sales is used for a one-time major stock repurchase. The regular stock repurchase, of course, is an alternative method of paying dividends.

Stock repurchases are a major corporate event in the USA. This trend is spreading to other parts of the world.

Stock repurchases are carried out in three ways.

Fixed Price Tender Offer: In a tender offer, the management offers to repurchase a certain number of shares either at the market price or at a premium to the market price. The company announces the tender price and the period for which the tender offer is open. Shareholders, at their own instance, can tender shares to the company.

Open Market Repurchases: In an open market repurchase, the company announces in a press release its intention of repurchasing but makes no commitments about price or amount. The company can execute trades at its will thereafter. Since the number of shares that can be repurchased in any given day is limited, the repurchase runs to several weeks or even months.[8] While there are legal restrictions on the volume of shares that can be purchased, this method offers the greatest degree of flexibility. Because of lack of a firm commitment on the company's part may send weak or negative signal to the market. To that extent, open market repurchases are not very effective.

The third route is to negotiate with large shareholders privately.

In a fixed price tender offer, a company invites its shareholders to tender shares to the company within a stipulated time period at a preset price premium, say 15 per cent over the prevailing market price. In a Dutch auction tender offer, a company announces its intention of buying shares within a specified price band. The shareholders are required to inform the company how many shares they are willing to tender and at what minimum price within the price band. Once all the tenders are received, the clearing price is set at the minimum price needed to purchase the desired number of shares from those shareholders who agreed to sell at or below that price. All shares transfer at the clearing price. The following table illustrates the way a Dutch auction would work for a company wishing to repurchase 2.5 million shares at an offered range of ₹35 to ₹45 per share. In this case, the clearing price is ₹40.

Price (₹)	Shares Tendered (Thousands)	Cumulative Shares Tendered (Thousands)
35	200	200
36	250	450
37	400	850
38	500	1,350
39	600	1,950
40	550	2,500
41	300	2,850
42	200	3,050
43	150	3,200
44	100	3,300
45	100	3,400

The advantages and disadvantages of different methods of repurchase are presented in Table 21.3.

[8] Regulators in some countries limit daily repurchases. In the USA, it is 25 per cent of the average daily traded volume in the previous four weeks.

TABLE 21.3
Pros and Cons of Various Share Repurchase Methods

	Benefits	Drawbacks	Strength of Signal to the Market
Open Market Purchase	1. Most flexible 2. Timing possibility to offset dilution from stock options 3. Inexpensive	May be announced but not completed	Weak
Dutch Auction	1. Results in permanent increase in stock price 2. Lower risk of undersubscription 3. Better price discovery	Possible wealth transfer from remaining shareholders	Strong positive
Tender Offer	1. Results in permanent increase in stock price 2. Often used to increase value via leveraged recap	Possible wealth transfer	Strong positive

RATIONALE FOR STOCK REPURCHASES

Stock repurchases are generally viewed as temporary substitutes for cash dividends. Since dividends are sticky, that is, managers hate to cut dividends, stock purchases can substitute cash dividends if the increase in cash flow is temporary. In other words, cash dividends are long-term commitments that managers like to maintain, whereas stock repurchase is a one-time affair.

Since managers and investors both expect a given level of dividends to be maintained, dividend payments are relatively inflexible. While higher dividends probably are the most attractive method for distributing a moderately and consistently increasing surplus of cash flow, they are not appropriate when the surplus arises in a sporadic pattern of large amounts. The important message is that stock repurchase is an alternative to making investment in the company's operations. Shareholders would be better off by receiving cash rather than investing in less profitable outlays in investment in productive facilities. If the internal rate of return of the investment is less than cost of capital, shareholders would be better off with stock repurchases.

Stock repurchase is the ideal tool to reduce redundant liquid assets and use unused debt capacity and move towards the firm's optimal capital structure. The value creating potential is more if the repurchase is financed with debt. The interest expense on debt is tax deductible leading to cash savings.[9]

Repurchase announcements may be viewed as positive signals by investors as repurchases are initiated when the company's shares are undervalued. This may prop up share price. The flip side of the coin is that stock repurchase can convey an adverse signal to the stock market that the increase in company's cash flows is not permanent. This may affect the company's stock price. In general, stock markets react positively to repurchases.

In sum, stock repurchases are used to:

[9] Of course, leverage can be increased by simply funding projects with debt. In other words, the leverage increasing property is not specific to repurchases.

- Increase reported earnings per share
- Make changes in capital structure
- Distribute cash to stockholders
- Reduce outflow due to dividends
- Buy out an irritating shareholder
- Send signal to the stock market that the company's shares are undervalued

Assume that a company currently has a BB capital structure. The company's management decides to buy back 40 per cent of shares at a 12 per cent premium to the previous market price resulting in a 54 per cent reduction in shareholders equity. The impact of the repurchase is shown in Table 21.4. The repurchase is to be financed with debt. Earnings may decline due to the increase in interest expense if the new facility carries a higher rate of interest compared to the existing facility. But the earnings are spread over a fewer number of shares. The net impact is that EPS and stock price rise.[10] But bondholders need not be better off. The increase in debt-to-capital ratio and a decrease in earnings coverage lead to a rating downgrade. In other words, shareholders can win at the expense of bondholders.

TABLE 21.4
Impact of a Stock Repurchase on Securities Prices

	Before		After	
Capitalization	₹ million	(%)	₹ million	(%)
Bank Loan	50	11.1	158	35.1
Debentures	200	44.4	200	44.4
Equity	200	44.4	92	20.4
Total	450	100	450	100
EBIT	50		50	
Interest Expense:				
Bank Loan	3.5 @ 7%		12.6 @8%	
Debentures	18 @ 9 %		18 @9 %	
EBT	28.5		19.4	
–Tax @ 34%	9.7		6.6	
PAT	18.8		12.8	
Market Valuations				
Shares Outstanding	10 million			6 million
EPS ₹	1.88		2.13	
P/E	12.0×		12.0×	
Price Per Share		22.5		25.5
Credit Rating	BB		B	
YTM (On Bonds)	9%		11%	

[10] The actual increase depends on the P/E multiple applied by investors after the buyback.

Once a company has decided that it will repurchase shares, the next step is to figure out how large the buyback should be. The size of the buyback depends on the purpose of the buyback. If the objective is to make changes in capital structure, then the number of shares is a function of the company's market value, its share price and the percentage of debt the company wants to reach. The calculation is not trivial because the stock price rises due to (expected) tax shields and other information effects. One should factor this in order to arrive at the number of shares.

If dividends and share repurchases are equivalent and when dividends are taxed at a higher rate than capital gains, as in many countries, why do companies prefer to pay dividends? John and Williams[11] present a theory where dividends are a costly signal because they are taxed more heavily than stock repurchases. Their starting point is the assumption that shareholders have liquidity needs that they must satisfy by selling some of their shares. The firm's managers, who act in the interest of the original shareholders, know the true value of the firm. Outside investors do not. If the firm is undervalued when the shareholders' liquidity needs arise, they would be selling shares at below the true value. However, suppose the firm pays a dividend that is taxed. If outside investors take taxed dividends to be a good signal, then the share price will rise; the shareholders will have to sell less equity to meet their liquidity needs and will maintain a higher proportionate share in the firm.

In Canada, firms must receive an approval from the exchange where the company's stock is listed before initiating a buyback.[12] Once authorized, the programme typically lasts one year and is restricted to 10 per cent of public float or 5 per cent of shares outstanding. A firm may commence repurchase two days after receiving approval from the stock exchange. The programme is to be executed through a broker. Cumulative repurchases over the trailing 30 days must not exceed 2 per cent of the outstanding shares.

Buyback of shares was introduced in India in 1998. Stock repurchases are carried out with the assistance of a merchant banker.

The SEBI guidelines relating to share buybacks is given in Appendix 21A.1.

BONUS SHARES

Bonus shares, also called stock dividends, are shares issued by a company to its shareholders free of cost by capitalizing reserves. Thus, stock dividend of 5 per cent means five shares are distributed to the investor for every 100 shares held. Bonus shares, like cash dividends, are considered valuable.

Suppose a company's balance sheet reads as given below. The company has issued one share at ₹10.

			(₹)
Share Capital	10	Assets	20
R&S	10		
Total	20	Total	20

For the sake of simplicity, let us assume that market value of share equals book value (₹20). The company pays one bonus share. The balance sheet after payment would be:

[11] John and Williams, 'Dividends, Dilution and Taxes'.

[12] Ikenberry, Lakonishok and Vermaelen (1999).

	(₹)		
Share Capital	20	Assets	20
R&S	–		
Total	20	Total	20

Market Value of Share = ₹20
No. of Shares = 2
Price per Share = ₹10

Now two shares are worth what one share was worth earlier. The investor is neither better off nor worse off. The investor's share in the pie remains the same. Bonus shares may be preferred when dividends are taxed at a higher rate than capital gains realized on selling bonus shares. It is quite possible that bonus shares may have favourable impact on stock price in real life. Indeed, academic studies of stock market reaction to stock dividends in the USA report positive abnormal return. Several plausible explanations have been suggested:

- Signalling: Due to information asymmetry, a company's management may choose stock dividends to signal the company's future financial policies, say a dividend rise or an increase in earnings.
- Liquidity Stock: Dividends may enhance liquidity by increasing the number of shares traded and the transaction cost (i.e., bid–ask spread).
- Making Changes in Trading Range: The stock dividend brings the share price down to a lower, more affordable, range. This may attract new investors.

Though academicians have been arguing that stock dividends do not have economic value, companies continue to pay stock dividends. The SEBI guidelines relating to issue of bonus shares is given in Appendix 21A.2.

INTEGRATING INVESTMENT, FINANCING AND DIVIDEND DECISIONS

It is important to understand that the investment, financing and dividend decisions are interrelated. How much you pay as dividends affects the amount retained and thus growth. To fund growth, you need cash. The cash should come from new shareholders or bondholders. But the company has a target debt equity mix to maintain. Moreover, in real-life situations, dividends may have impact on stock prices either due to perception of growth or lack of it. The typical sequence of decisions include:

- Determine capital expenditure and working capital requirements for the planning horizon (say five years).
- Determine the target debt–equity mix.
- Estimate cash flow available to pay out as dividends.
- Analyse the effect of various dividend policies on growth and stock price.

An Illustration

A company's current income statement is as follows:

	(₹10 million)
Net Sales	204.69
Other Income	6.39
Total Income	211.08
Cost of Materials	138.61
Total Variable Expenses	169.84
Total Fixed Expenses	21.85
EBIT	19.39
Depreciation	2.13
EBIT	17.25
Interest	1.11
PBT	16.14
Tax	5.649
PAT	10.49

The company spent ₹64.4 million on working capital and ₹630,000 on fixed assets. Sales and expenses are expected to grow at 15 per cent. Gross fixed assets (capital expenditure) are expected to grow at 5 per cent a year and depreciation is 7.5 per cent of gross fixed assets.

Tax rate is 35 per cent. The company currently has ₹79.2 million in debt and ₹389.7 million in equity. Interest rate on debt is 14 per cent.

Current Cash Flow = EBIT − Taxes + Depreciation − Capital Expenditure − Working Capital Investment = ₹62.8 million

Cash Flow to Equity = Cash Flow from Operation − After-Tax Interest − Principal Repayment

During the year, there was no principal repayment or borrowing

Cash Flow to Equity = Free Cash Flow − After-Tax Interest
= ₹62.8 − ₹7.2 = ₹55.5 million

The company currently has a payout ratio of 31 per cent.

Dividends Paid = ₹35 million Dividend/Cash Flow to Equity = 0.63
Retained Earnings = ₹76 million

The company is currently earning 37 per cent on capital employed. The cost of capital for the company is 14.62 per cent.

Cash Flow after Paying Dividends = ₹55.5 million − ₹35 million = ₹20.5 million, that is, the company is retaining ₹20.5 million for further investment. Since the company is earning more than the cost of capital, the company can retain cash assuming that the company will continue to earn more than the cost of capital on new projects and maintain the spread. The company is contemplating on growing at

15 per cent a year. To grow at 15 per cent, the company needs to spend ₹23.6 million on fixed assets and ₹41.2 million on working capital. The next year financials according to forecast is:

(₹10 million)

Net Sales	=235.39	Total Income	=242.27
EBIT	= 17.19	Net Income	= 11.17
− Taxes on EBIT	= 6.02		
+ Depreciation	= 2.68		
Gross Cash Flow	= 13.85		

Since Sources of Cash = Uses of Cash

Cash Balance Now + Cash Flow after Paying Dividends This Year + Gross Cash Flow During Next Year + Increase in Debt = Capital Expenditure + Increase in Working Capital + After-Tax Interest Payments + Dividends Next Year + Desired Cash Balance Next Year

Ignoring current cash balance and rearranging terms:

Cash Available Next Year to Pay Dividends = Current Residual Cash Flow + Gross Cash Flow − Capital Expenditure Next Year − Increase in Working Capital − After-Tax Interest Payment + New Debt

= ₹(20.5 + 138.5 − 23.6 − 8.475 − 41.2) million

= ₹ 857.2 million

The company has excess cash flow that can be paid out as dividends. Notice that the company can increase leverage substantially and improve return on equity. In short, the dividend payment next year is a function of

- Current cash balance
- Gross cash flow, that is, NOPAT + Depreciation
- Management policy on debt financing
- Required expenditure on upgradation of existing projects and capital expenditure on new projects
- Interest on new debt raised to finance expenditure on fixed assets and working capital
- Quality of projects in hand
- Cost of capital

This analysis helps in determining the cash flow available to pay dividends next year. But how much you 'can' pay and how much you 'should' pay are two different things. If management wants to increase dividends smoothly, the earlier equation helps in finding out how smooth it can be.

CONCLUDING COMMENTS

Some say dividends are good. Some say dividends are bad. MM declared it irrelevant. Since the formulation of the MM dividend irrelevance proposition, many academicians have been arguing that dividends do not matter, that is, whether a company pays 10 per cent or 100 per cent of its earnings in the form of dividends is likely to have no material effect on its long-run market value.

To say that investors collectively do not care whether they receive their returns in the form of dividends or capital gains is not the same as saying dividend policies of individual companies do not matter. In fact, dividend policy may matter greatly in some circumstances. For mature companies with highly stable cash flows paying out too little may cause managers to overinvest (free cash flow problem). On the other hand, for companies in high growth or riskier business paying out too much may reduce financial flexibility to the point that management is forced to pass up valuable investment opportunities.

According to its own financial projections, a company might not be expecting a sharp increase in its investment requirements in the foreseeable future. But if greater competition does not increase a company's investment requirements, it might lead to significant increase in business risk and, hence, to variability of its earnings and operating cash flows. An increase in cash flow variability due to an increase in business risk implies reduction in optimal capital structure and dividend payout. In such circumstances, a company may set a dividend level that would increase in tandem with earnings and that the company would be able to maintain in almost any business environment. At the same time, the payout should be designed to preserve management's ability to invest in growth opportunities in preparation for a competitive future. But what if a company's management significantly underestimates its own future earning power and, as a consequence of cutting dividend, became awash in cash? The company may simultaneously announce a stock repurchase programme for the next two–three years. The idea is to return any excess cash to shareholders through stock repurchases. Besides potential tax benefits for investors, a policy of substituting stock repurchases for dividends increases a company's financial flexibility to respond to increased competition.

APPENDIX 21A.1: SEBI (BUYBACK OF SECURITIES) REGULATIONS, 2018

The summary of SEBI guidelines relating to stock repurchases is given as follows:

- The maximum limit of any buyback shall be 25 per cent or less of the aggregate of paid-up capital and free reserves of the company:
- The ratio of the aggregate of secured and unsecured debts owed by the company after buyback shall not be more than twice the paid-up capital and free reserves
- All shares or other specified securities for buyback shall be fully paid-up.
- A company may buy back its shares or other specified securities by any one of the following methods:
    - from the existing shares or other specified security holders on a proportionate basis through the tender offer;
    - from the open market through (a) book building process and (b) stock exchange;
    - from odd lot holders.

Provided that no offer of buyback for 15 per cent or more of the paid-up capital and free reserves of the company shall be made from the open market.

- A company shall not buy back its shares or other specified securities so as to delist its shares or other specified securities from the stock exchange.

- A company shall not buy back its shares or other specified securities from any person through negotiated deals, whether on or off the stock exchange or through spot transactions or through any private arrangement.
- A company shall not make any offer of buyback within a period of one year reckoned from the date of expiry of buyback period of the preceding offer of buyback, if any.
- A company may undertake a buyback of its own shares or other specified securities out of (a) its free reserves; (b) the securities premium account or (c) the proceeds of the issue of any shares or other specified securities:
- Provided that no such buyback shall be made out of the proceeds of an earlier issue of the same kind of shares or same kind of other specified securities.

General Compliance and Filing Requirements for Buyback:
The company shall not authorize any buyback (whether tender offer or from open market or odd lot) unless:

- The buyback is authorized by the company's articles;
- Except otherwise specified in this regulation, a special resolution has been passed at a general meeting of the company authorizing the buyback;

Every buyback shall be completed within a period of one year from the date of passing of the special resolution at general meeting, or the resolution passed by the Board of Directors of the company, as the case may be.

The company shall, after expiry of the buyback period, file with the Registrar of Companies and the Board, a return containing such particulars relating to the buyback within 30 days of such expiry, in the format as may be specified.

APPENDIX 21A.2: SEBI GUIDELINES ON ISSUE OF BONUS SHARES

- The bonus issue is made out of free reserves built out of the genuine or share premium collected in cash only.
- Reserves created by revaluation of fixed assets are not capitalized.
- The declaration of bonus issue in lieu of dividends is not made.
- The bonus issue is not made unless the partly paid shares, if any existing, are made fully paid up.
- The company:
    - Has not defaulted on payment of interest or principal in respect of fixed deposits and interest on existing debentures or principal on redemption thereof
    - Has sufficient reason to believe that it has not defaulted in respect of the statutory dues of the employees such as contribution to provident fund, gratuity, bonus and so on.
- A company that announces its bonus issue after the approval of the Board of Directors must implement the proposals within a period of six months from the date of such approval and shall not have the option of changing the decision.
- There should be a provision in the Articles of Association of the company for capitalization of reserves and so on, and if not, the company shall pass a resolution at its general body meeting making provisions in the Articles of Association of capitalization.

- Consequent to the issue of bonus shares, if the subscribed and paid-up capital exceed the authorized share capital, a resolution is to be passed by the company at its general body meeting for increasing the authorized capital.

EXERCISES

1. How would you choose between dividends and stock repurchases as a CFO? What considerations might affect your decision?
2. What do you think would be the impact of dividend distribution tax on cost of equity?
3. There are four companies in an industry group other than your company. Their payouts are: 30 per cent, 28 per cent, 45 per cent and 35 per cent. How would you compare your dividend policy with that of competitors? The payouts of these companies are different. Why might they be different?
4. Some financial economists do not accept that investors and managements who pay attention to dividends are irrational. Consequently, they try to build regression models to explain differences in payout ratios. Intuitively, we would expect companies requiring large amounts of capital expenditure to choose lower dividend payout. Higher payout reduces retained earnings and drive companies to capital markets every now and then.
   Second, we would expect highly leveraged companies to have low payout ratios. These highly leveraged companies may view dividends as fixed costs and, accordingly, may keep the payout ratio low in order to maintain dividends continuously.
   Third, we would expect companies with riskier operation, that is, high business risk, to maintain low payout.
   In sum, payout is a function of growth rate, financial leverage and beta (proxy for business risk). The following data are available for an industry group.

Company	Expected Growth (%)	Beta	Payout Ratio
1.	20	1.05	–
2.	13	1.1	40.0
3	21	1.0	22.0
4	33	1.45	9.0
5	11	0.80	25.0
6	12	0.95	36.88
7	16	1.0	22.0

   Estimate a regression equation.
5. The income statement of a company is given as follows:

EBIT ₹	2,000
Interest₹	400
Tax ₹	560
PAT ₹	1,040

No of Shares Outstanding=100
Dividends Paid=₹400
Current Stock Price=₹12
Calculate dividend payout and dividend yield.

6. A company is currently earning 12 per cent return on equity. The following stock market data are available. R_f=12 per cent, beta=1.1 and risk premium=10 per cent. Would you force the company to pay more?
7. The following data are available for a company.

	(₹ million)
Debt @ 15%	500
Equity	500
EBIT	283.0
Interest	750
Tax	83.0
PAT	125.0

The company has a project with an outlay of ₹90 million. The company intends to maintain its debt–equity ratio. How much can the company pay out?

8. A company currently has a PAT of ₹400 million; depreciation is ₹200 million and capital expenditure is ₹1,000 million. If the PAT is expected to grow at 30 per cent and capital expenditure at 10 per cent, when will the company be able to pay dividends?

REFERENCES

Brown, K. and S. Lummer. 'A reexamination of the Covered Call Option Strategy for Corporate Cash Management'. *Financial Management* 15, (1986: 13–17).

Elton, E. J. and M. J. Gruber. 'Marginal Stockholder Tax Rates and the Clientele Effect'. *Review of Economics and Statistics* (1970 Feb).

Ikenberry, L. and Vermaelen. 'Stock Repurchases in Canada: Performance and Strategic Trading'. *Journal of Finance* (2000 October).

John, K. and J. Williams. 'Dividends, Dilution and Taxes: A Signaling Equilibrium'. *Journal of Finance* 40, no. 4 (1985).

La Porta, R., F. Lopez-de-Silanes, A. Shleifer and R. Vishny. 'Agency Problems and Dividend Policies Around the World'. *Journal of Finance* (2000 February).

Lintner, J. 'Distribution of Income of Corporations among Dividends, Retained Earnings and Taxes'. *American Economic Review* (1956).

Miller, M. H. and Franco Modigliani. 'Dividend Policy, Growth and Valuation of Shares'. *Journal of Business* (1961 Oct).

Randall, W. and C. Ghosh. 'Dividend Cuts: Do They Always Signal Bad News?'. *Midland Corporate Finance Journal* (Summer 1985: 20–32).

SUGGESTED READINGS

Allen, F. and R. Michaely. 'Pay Out Policy'. In *North-Holland Handbook of Economics*, edited by George Constantinides, Milton Harris and Rene Stulz, Netherlands: Elsevier BV, 2002.

Asquith, P. and D. W. Mullins. 'The Impact of Initiating Dividends on Shareholders' Wealth'. *Journal of Business* (1980 January).

Bagwell, L. and J. Shoven. 'Cash Distributions to Shareholders'. *Journal of Economic Perspectives* 3, no. 3 (1989 Summer).

Baker, K. H., G. E. Farrelly and R. B. Edelman. 'A Survey of Management Views of Dividend Policy'. *Financial Management* 14, no. 3 (1985).

Baker, K. H. and A. Phillips. 'Why Companies Issue Stock Dividends'. *Financial Practice and Education* (1993 Fall).

Bartov, E., I. Krinski and J. Lee. 'Evidence on How Companies Choose Between Dividends and Open Market Repurchases'. *Journal of Applied Corporate Finance* 11, no. 1 (1998 Spring).

Barclay, M. J., C. Smith and R. Watts. 'The Determinants of Corporate Leverage and Dividend Policies'. *Journal of Applied Corporate Finance* 7, no. 4 (1995 Winter).

Bernstein, P. 'Dividends: The Puzzle'. *Journal of Applied Corporate Finance* 9, no. 1 (1996 Spring).

Bertoneche, M. 'Share Buy-Backs: The European and Japanese Experience' (Harvard Business School Case No 9–298–134, Boston, MA, 1998 12 June).

Black, F. 'The Dividend Puzzle'. *Journal of Portfolio Management* (1976 Winter).

Black, F. and Myron Scholes. 'The Effects of Dividend Yield and Dividend Policy on Common Stock Prices and Returns'. *Journal of Financial Economics* (1974 May).

Dann, L. Y. 'Common Stock Repurchases: What Do They Really Accomplish?' In *The Revolution in Corporate Finance*, 2nd ed., edited by Joel M. Stern and Donald H. Chew Jr. Hoboken, NJ: Blackwell, 1992.

Easterbrook, F. H. 'Two Agency Cost Explanation of Dividends'. *American Economic Review* (1984 Sep).

Feldstein, M. and G. Jerry. 'Why Do Companies Pay Dividends?' *American Economic Review* (1983 March).

Grullon, G. and D. Ikenberry. 'What Do We Know about Stock Repurchases'. *Journal of Applied Corporate Finance* 13 (2000).

Hausch, D., D. Logue and J. Seward. 'Dutch Auction Share Repurchases: Theory and Evidence'. In *The New Corporate Finance: Where Theory Meets Practice*, edited by Donald Chew. New York, NY: McGraw Hill, 1999.

Mauboussin, M. and B. Hiler. 'To Buy or Not to Buy: Issues and Considerations Surrounding Share Repurchase'. *C S First Boston Equity Research* 5 (1998, 7 August).

Michaely, R., R. Thaler and K. Womack. 'Price Reactions to Dividend Initiations and Omissions: Overreaction or Drift?' *Journal of Finance* 50, no. 2 (1995 June).

Petit, Justin. 'Is Share Buyback Right for Your Company'. *Harvard Business Review* (2001 April).

Woolridge, Randall and Chinmoy Ghosh. 'Dividend Cuts: Do They Always Signal Bad News?' In *The Revolution in Corporate Finance*, edited by Joel Stern and Donald Chew Jr. Oxford: Basil Blackwell, 1992.

SECTION 6

Financial Policy, Competitive Strategy and Shareholder Value

CHAPTER

22

Growth and Shareholder Value

LEARNING OBJECTIVES

- Provide a link between growth and shareholder value
- Understand the determinants of sustainable growth

Corporate finance theoreticians generally agree that the objective of the firm is to maximize wealth, although there may be some disagreement as to whether the objective is to maximize the wealth of shareholders or the wealth of the firm, which includes bondholders and preferred stockholders. For years, growth has been only second to profits in the pantheon of corporate virtues. In recent years, however, there are increasing signs that some management must finally face the fact that unrestrained growth may be inconsistent with established financial policies. Empire building might be out of fashion but high growth is still in vogue. The question is: Is growth something that is to be maximized? Is there an ideal growth rate for a firm? What are the implications of faster growth? Finally, what relationship exists between financial policy that determines growth and corporate strategy?

SUSTAINABLE GROWTH

Define sustainable growth for those companies which have target payout ratio and capital structure as the annual percentage increase in sales that is consistent with the firm's established financial policies.

Let

p = the profit margin on existing and new sales

d = the target payout ratio

$(1-d)$ = retention ratio
L = target debt – equity ratio
S = sales at the beginning of the year
ds = increase in sales during the year

The increase in sales is preceded by an increase in asset base. Retained earnings, new debt or new equity can finance the increase in asset base. If we assume that the firm is unable or unwilling to sell new equity, the option reduces to retained earnings or new debt. Since the firm has a target debt–equity ratio to maintain, the increase in debt has to be proportional to the increase in retained earnings. So under stable conditions, retained earnings determine increase in sales.

Increase in Sales = Addition to Retained Earnings + Increase in Debt
Sustainable Growth g' = Change in Equity During the Period/Beginning Equity
= (Retention Rate × Earnings)/Beginning Equity
= Retention Rate × (Earnings/Beginning Equity)
= Retention Rate × ROE
But ROE = PAT/Equity = [PAT/Sales] × [Sales/Assets] × [Assets/Equity]
that is,

g' = Retention Rate × [PAT/Sales] × [Sales/Assets] × [Assets/Equity]

Let us plug in some numbers into the equation and see how it works. Consider the following data.

Sales = ₹8,730 million
PAT = ₹1,323 million
Total Assets = ₹19,536 million
Net Worth = ₹8,471 million
Debt = ₹7,626 million
Beginning Equity = ₹8,405 million
Sustainable Growth = $0.15 \times 0.47 \times 0.45 \times 2.32 = 7.3$ per cent

This equation suggests that g' is the only growth rate consistent with the stable values of the four ratios. Sustainable growth is a number. If the actual growth rate is not equal to g', one of these ratios will change. If actual growth is greater than g', the firm should improve operations or change financial policies. The firm has four options:

- Improve profit margin
- Improve asset turnover
- Decrease payout
- Increase leverage

A firm can improve asset turnover by cutting down finished goods inventory or being harsh on credit terms. This may either hurt service or drive bargaining customers away reducing the actual growth rate. A firm may or may not have much scope for improving the profit margin depending on the product differentiation, perceived value and nature of competition in the industry group.

The traditional argument is that a firm can always sell new equity. This may not be true of private firms either because of shortage of personal funds or fear of dilution of control if the firm goes public. Many firms may not be able to go public at all. Public companies may postpone public issue because of procedural hassles or underpricing of new issues or high issue costs or prolonged bearish market sentiment. Some firms may have the option of tapping overseas capital markets. But the number is small. Moreover, profit in real terms will be small due to high inflation in many countries. The other option is to decrease payout or increase leverage or resort to some combination.

DECREASE DIVIDENDS

From the stockholders viewpoint, there may be no real difference among dividend plans but may have different impact on stock price, maybe because investors do not see the similarity. It is quite possible that an increase in cash dividends would have a favourable impact on stock prices. Unexpected cuts in dividends can have dramatic impact on stock prices.

INCREASE LEVERAGE

The other alternative is to increase leverage. Probably, no other topic has attracted as much scholarly attention as the search for the optimal level of debt. Most of us believe that there are gains from leverage although we may debate on the magnitude. At one extreme, some conservative managers keep the debt levels too low, thereby foregoing increase in firm value. At the other extreme, some take on too much debt for the size and operating characteristics of the company probably because of lack of understanding of corporate debt capacity. Managers may not realize the risk associated with debt while making large capital investments financed with debt. It is possible to generate probability distribution of changes in earnings and cash flows based on historical patterns and current industry data to set debt levels with acceptable risk. Analysis of debt policy in real-life situations often lack probabilistic inputs because of which the estimates turn out to be point estimates, probably with large variance leading to unrealistic estimates of risk.

INCORPORATING BUSINESS DYNAMICS

Many growth plans that look good on paper go bad on execution. The reason could be anything: wrong product, wrong market, wrong strategy and competitive reaction. The list can go on. The most difficult part of growth analysis is incorporating competitive reaction, which executives may fail to take note of. It is indeed a challenge to balance growth drivers and restraining forces. Over time, it is possible to track the strategic degrees of freedom that are available to competitors on various dimensions such as pricing, new product introduction and so on. The growth analysis should ascertain how sensitive the pay-offs are to differing degrees of competition and competitive reactions. The growth plan analysis should incorporate soft issues such as motivation and productivity. Too rapid a growth may heighten pressure on executives resulting in defections, sagging morale and lower productivity. Quite often, skill development does not keep pace with growth. Executives get bogged down firefighting; organization development takes a back seat. The time to market and develop new product get extended.

PRODUCT MARKET VERSUS CAPITAL MARKET

It is a well-known fact that the executives' decision-making is guided by financial ratios—either their own or that of competitors. At times, financial intermediaries may also impose such norms on them. This probably explains the similarity in financial policies across industry groups. Policies are not supposed to be extraneously determined. They are supposed to reflect the firm's strategic choice. Executives caught between financial standards and strategic choice choose to adhere to financial standards. It is likely that projects that improve the competitiveness of the firm in the long run may be shelved because of conservative financial policy. Since managerial reward is proportional to the extent to which one beats forecasts, there is an incentive for downward biasing. This may also contribute to not taking up a project that is otherwise worthwhile. One should distinguish between not implementing the right strategy in conformance with accepted financial policy, implementing wrong strategy in conformance with accepted financial policy and not implementing right strategy not in conformance with financial policy. They are, obviously, not the same. The questions one should ask are:

- Who has valid market knowledge? Who makes investment decisions? Who decides on the package of securities that we sell? How do we ensure coordination among these interest groups?
- What financial policies are conducive for good growth in this industry? What are the assumptions underlying our financial policy and capital expenditure decisions? How do we allocate resources to projects that differ in importance and risk levels?
- What relationship exists between financial policy, competitive strategy and stock prices?

Ironically, a firm that goes totally by ratios (that determine growth) becomes a victim of blurred vision and focus, thereby curtailing its own growth. Consider a firm in a declining market. It will probably cut down assets, prune work force size and retire debt in anticipation of lower earnings and cash flows in the future. This might be a wise move. This exercise will not 'improve' the position of the firm although it may help sustain the recession. What is really required is a fundamental rethinking on strategy, industry condition and customer value. The company's assets or capabilities, if need arises, should be recreated. So growth is not something that can be explained by a set of balance sheet and income statement numbers alone but soft issues like strategic logic.

SENSITIVITY OF SUSTAINABLE GROWTH

To better understand the relationship between sustainable growth rate and the four determinants, a sensitivity analysis can be conducted. Let us suppose,

$$P=0.15,\ (1-d)=0.5,\ T=1.0 \text{ and } L=1.8$$

$$\text{Sustainable Growth}=0.15\times0.5\times1.8\times1.0=13.5 \text{ per cent}$$

Holding profit margin and asset turnover constant, increase retention ratio by 10 per cent and financial leverage to 2.0

$$\text{Sustainable Growth}=0.15\times0.6\times1.0\times2.0$$
$$=18 \text{ per cent}$$

Sustainable growth increased from 13.5 to 18 per cent. Suppose, profit margin improves by 1 per cent and asset turnover increases to 1.2.

$$g' = 0.16 \times 0.5 \times 1.2 \times 1.8$$
$$= 17.3 \text{ per cent}$$

BRINGING THEM ALL TOGETHER

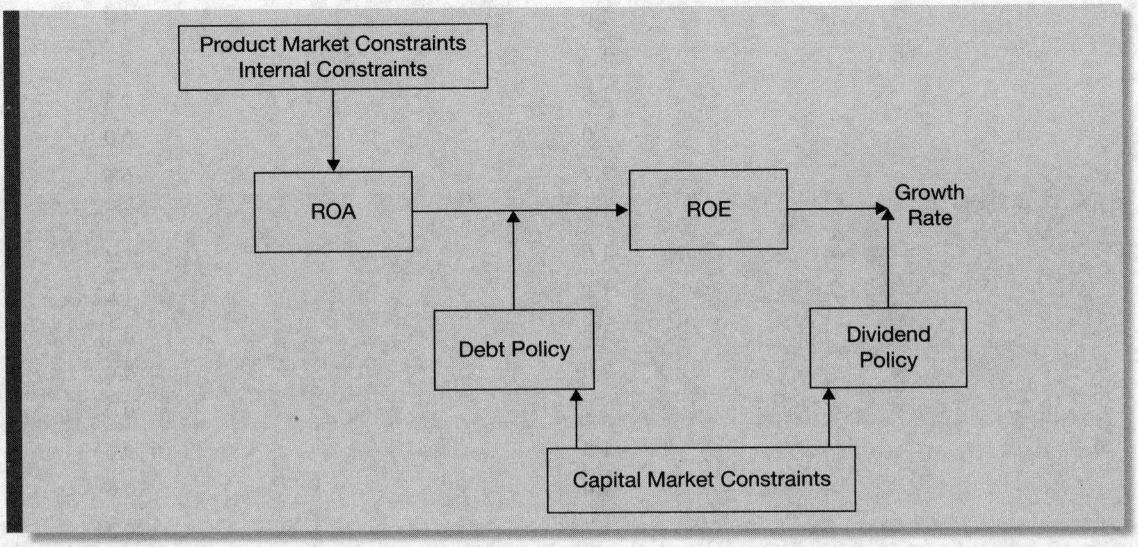

A graph of sustainable growth can be plotted for various combinations of two of the determinants (say P and T) holding the other two constant. The sensitivity of g' for various values of retention ratio and financial leverage is shown in Table 22.1. When P=15, T=1.0, (1−d)=0.4 and L=1.8, g'=10.8 per cent. Similar calculations have been made for other combinations. Suppose the current g' is 15 per cent and the company is contemplating on increasing it to 18 per cent. For the growth to increase, one or more ratios should change. Work backwards to arrive at 'realistic' values of the four ratios, say P=15 per cent, T=1.0, retention=0.6 and leverage=2.0.

GROWTH VERSUS VALUE

Sustainable growth is a function of return on assets, retained earnings and financial leverage.

$$g' = \text{Retention Rate} \times \text{ROE}$$
$$g' = (1-d)\ [\text{ROA} + \text{D/E}\ \{\text{ROA} - i(1-T)\}]$$

where

$$i = \text{interest rate on debt}$$
$$T = \text{tax rate}$$
$$\text{D/E} = \text{debt–equity ratio}$$
$$\text{ROA} = \text{EBIT}(1-T)/\text{Book Value of Total Capital}$$

TABLE 22.1
Sustainable Growth Rates for Various Combinations of p, A, T, L P=15%, T=1.0

Retention Ratio	Leverage	Sustainable Growth (%)
0.2	1.5	4.5
	1.6	4.8
	1.7	5.1
	1.8	5.4
	2.0	6.0
	2.2	6.6
0.3	1.5	6.75
	1.6	7.2
	1.7	7.65
	1.8	8.1
	2.0	9.0
	2.2	9.9
0.4	1.5	9.0
	1.6	9.6
	1.7	10.2
	1.8	10.8
	2.0	12.0
	2.2	13.2
0.5	1.5	11.25
	1.6	12.0
	1.7	12.75
	1.8	13.5
	2.0	15.0
		16.5

Injecting debt could increase sustainable growth. Injecting debt will increase the actual return on equity as long as ROA is greater than the after-tax cost of debt by an amount equal to

$$D/E\ ROA - i(1 - T)]$$

But the systematic risk of the stock and hence expected return increase with leverage.

$$\text{Expected Return} = R_f + \beta_L[E(R_M) - R_f] \quad (1)$$

The relationship between levered and unlevered beta is:

$$\beta_L = \beta_U[1+(1-T)D/E] \tag{2}$$

(i.e., leverage increases beta)
where β_U = unlevered beta of the stock (beta without debt)

Given the beta at the current level of debt β_L, the unlevered beta of the stock can be calculated as follows:

$$\beta_U = \beta_L/[1+(1-T)D/E] \tag{3}$$

The new beta, after increasing leverage, could be estimated using Equation (2). The new beta can be plugged in the CAPM to arrive at the new expected return. After quantifying the change in required return (cost of equity [COE]) due to increase in beta and actual return due to injecting debt, the percentage change in value can be calculated as follows:

$$\% \text{ Change in Value} = [(\text{PV of Increased Return/PV of Existing Return}) - 1] \times 100$$

If we assume that the stream of returns is a growing perpetuity, the present value of returns reduces to

$$[\text{Return}/k - g]$$

where k = COE
g = sustainable growth in equity

It should be noted that the increase in actual return should be more than the increase in expected return (COE) for value to increase. We will apply our new-found knowledge to two situations and figure out what creates value and why. Consider two companies. The first company has an investment opportunity with 25 per cent ROE in amounts sufficient to produce 10 per cent sustainable growth rate in sales for 10 years. The second company has an investment opportunity with 10 per cent ROE in amounts sufficient to produce 10 per cent sustainable growth rate in sales for 10 years. Both the companies have 20 per cent COE. The market value of the two hypothetical companies is shown in Tables 22.2 and 22.3.

At the end of 10 years, the stock is expected to sell at the book value of ₹2,593.70. In other words, ROE = COE. The second company retains all the profits it generates (i.e., retention rate is 100%) to produce a growth of 10 per cent p.a. The theoretical market price for the second company is shown in Table 22.3.

The PV of cash returned to stockholders ₹1,290.5 is ₹290.5 more than the initial investment of ₹1,000 for shareholders in Company A. So the M/B ratio of Company A is greater than 1.

The PV of cash returned to stockholders ₹418.9 is lower than the initial investment of ₹1,000 for shareholders in Company B. So the M/B ratio of Company B is less than 1. The moral of the story is that how fast a company 'can' grow and how fast a company 'should' grow are two different things. Growth is desirable if expected ROE is greater than COE and if the spread can be maintained. If not, growth will destroy value. The value creation model shown in Figure 22.1 depicts the concept.

TABLE 22.2
Market Price of Company A

Beg of year	BV of inv	ROE	PAT	R.R.*	Retained Earnings	Div	PV@ 20%
1	1,000	25%	250	40%	100	150	125
2	1,100		275		110	165	114.6
3	1,210		302.5		121	181.5	105
4	1,331.0		332.8		133.1	199.7	96.3
5	1,464.1		363		146.4	219.6	88.3
6	1,610.5		402.6		161.1	241.5	80.9
7	1,771.6		442.9		177.2	265.7	74.2
8	1,948.7		487.2		194.9	292.3	68.0
9	2,143.6		535.90		214.4	321.3	62.3
10	2,357.9		589.5		235.8	353.7	57.1
11	2,593.7					2,593.7	418.8
*RR=Retention Rate						Total=1,290.5	

TABLE 22.3
Market Price of Company B

Beg of year	BV of inv	ROE	PAT	R.R.*	Retained Earnings	Div	PV@ 20%
1	1,000	10%	100	100%	100	0	0
2	1,100		110		110	0	0
3	1,210		121		121	0	0
4	1,331.0		133.1		133.1	0	0
5	1,464.1		146.4		146.4	0	0
6	1,610.5		161.1		161.1	0	0
7	1,771.6		177.2		177.2	0	0
8	1,948.7		194.9		194.9	0	0
9	2,143.6		214.4		214.4	0	0
10	2,357.9		235.8		235.8	0	0
11	2,593.7					2,593.7*	418.8

Note: *Market Price at the End=Book Value.
Market Price/Book Value=1,290.5/1,000=1.29 for company A.
Market Price/Book Value=418.8/1,000=0.42 for company B.

The purpose of value analysis is twofold. First, evaluate the performance of current strategy. Second, evaluate potential strategies for each of the business units. For instance, a company may have the following options for a business unit: modernize the plant, hold, harvest or sell out. Even if the unit is currently losing money, it might make sense to invest in the unit if the spread between ROE and COE is expected to become positive in the foreseeable future implying that executives will have to take a

FIGURE 22.1
Value Creation Model

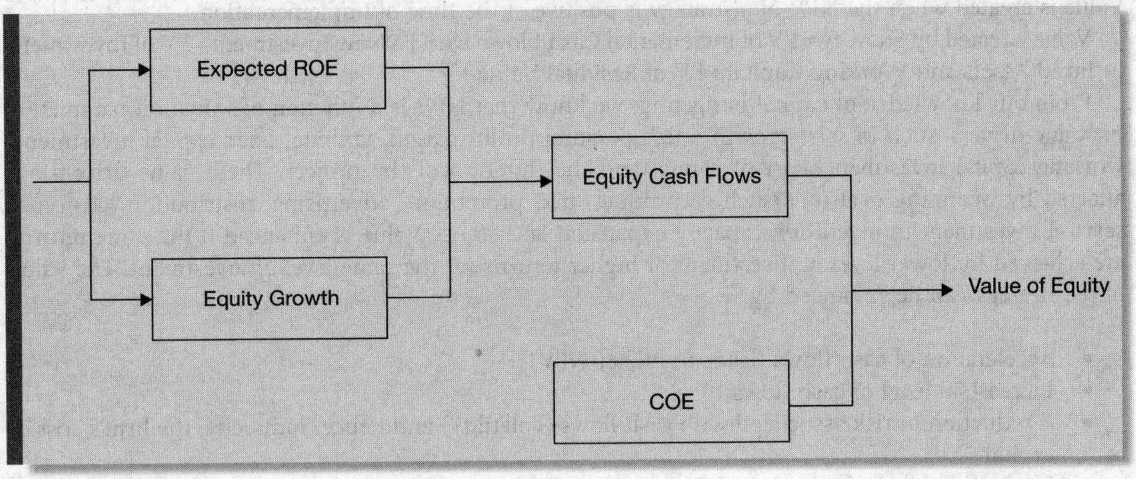

long-term view of business prospects before a strategic decision is made. Value creation should be the guiding factor in executive decision-making. But how do you measure value? This is important for two reasons. First, managers need to know how their performance will be evaluated and second, how to work towards that goal.

MEASURING VALUE

Shareholder value analysis (SVA) is the process of analysing how business decisions affect the company's economic value (i.e., NPV of cash flows discounted at WACC). One of the measures of shareholder value is the total shareholder return (TSR). It is the rate (IRR) that equates the purchase price (cash outflow), and dividends and sales proceeds (cash inflows) at the end of the holding period.[1]

If the holding period is one year,

$$TSR = [Div + (P_1 - P_0)]/P_0 \text{ ignoring time value of money}$$

The TSR of the company may be compared with that of the peer group to evaluate performance. More important, executives may be encouraged to be in the top 10 per cent of the peer group year after year. Another measure of value is the cash flow return on investment (CFROI). It is similar to the IRR of a project. It compares the cumulative cash invested in a business with the cash the business is producing while recognizing the importance of asset ages, asset lives and inflation.

[1] One must compare risk-adjusted returns or market-adjusted returns. It is inappropriate to compare raw returns. Further, a business group cannot be compared with a stand-alone company. The comparison is inexact.

VALUE DRIVERS

Value is created when the NPV of a strategy is positive at the time of implementation.

Value Created by Strategy = PV of Incremental Cash Flows Due To New Investment − PV of Investment in Fixed Assets and Working Capital + PV of Residual Value

From our knowledge of capital budgeting, we know that NPV is a function of valuation parameters or 'value drivers' such as sales growth rate, operating profit margin, tax rate, fixed capital investment, working capital investment, cost of capital and the duration of the project. These value drivers are affected by operating decisions such as product mix, promotion, advertising, distribution, customer service, investment in inventory, capacity expansion and so on. Value is enhanced if the same returns are achieved for lower level of investment or higher returns for the same level of investment. The value of the strategy can be enhanced by:

- Acceleration of cash flows (leads to higher NPV)
- Increase in level of cash flows
- A reduction in risk associated with cash flows (volatility) and hence, indirectly, the firm's cost of capital
- Increasing the residual value of the business

Total shareholder value is the sum of NPVs of all projects undertaken by the firm. This beautiful characteristic of NPV (i.e., additivity) provides us some useful insights into value creation:

- Whenever a loss-making project is terminated, the value of the firm goes up.
- Whenever a firm accepts a positive NPV project, the value of the firm goes up.
- Whenever a firm acquires another firm for a price greater than the PV of the expected cash flows, the value of the firm drops.

Market-based assets like customer and channel partner relationships also contribute to the four drivers of value. For instance, faster response to marketing efforts and earlier brand trials accelerate cash flows, while brand extensions and development of new uses enhance cash flows. The important point is that shareholder value is driven by 'both' tangible and intangible assets.

The value creation model presented earlier has three components: profitability, spread between COE and return on equity, and the advantage horizon during which the firm generates abnormal returns.

In any industry group, more profitable firms—those able to generate higher earnings per rupee of earnings—should have higher M/B ratios. Conversely, firms that are unable to generate positive abnormal returns should sell for lower M/B ratios.

$$ROE > K_e, \ M/B > 1$$
$$ROE < K_e, \ M/B < 1$$
$$ROE = K_e, \ M/B = 1$$

The period for which a firm can maintain a positive ($ROE - K_e$) spread is called advantage horizon. The greater the abnormal return, the longer the advantage horizon, the sooner the abnormal returns, the higher the M/B ratio.[2]

[2] One of earliest studies of value creation and destruction by US firms is by Professor William Fruhan of the Harvard Business School. This model is based on his study.

The market value of equity can be obtained by discounting equity cash flows at an appropriate discount rate.

$$M=[ECF/(1+k)^1+ECF/(1+k)^2+....]$$

If we assume that cash flows and discount rate are constant, the series reduces to a perpetuity.

$$M=ECF/k$$

Further, if we assume that ECF = Net income, that is, retention is zero,

$$M=\text{Net income}/k$$

$$\text{But Net income}=ROE\times\text{Book Value of Equity}$$

$$M=[ROE\times B]/k$$

$$\text{Or } M/B=ROE/k$$

Thus, market-to-book ratio is a function of ROE and COE.

If all earnings are returned to shareholders and earnings are constant

$$M=(ROE\times B)/(1+k)+(ROE\times B)/(1+k)^2+\cdots.$$

Divide both sides by B

$$M/B=(ROE)/(1+k)+(ROE)/(1+k)^2+\cdots.$$

Add and subtract k from each of the terms

$$M/B=[(ROE+k)-k]/(1+k)+[(ROE+k)-k]/(1+k)^2+\cdots.$$

The first term (ROE − k) is the abnormal earnings and the second term, k, is the normal earning.

It can be proved that the present value of this series is:

$$PV=1+(ROE-k)\ [(1/k)-\{1/k(1+k)^n\}\qquad(4)$$

This model assumes that retention is zero. Allowing for different rates would yield a more realistic model.

$$M=D_1/(k-g)=(\text{Net Income}\times\text{Payout})/(k-g)$$

But

$$\text{Payout}=(1-\text{Retention})=1-r$$

$$g=\text{Sustainable Growth Rate}=ROE\times r$$

$$\text{Net Income}=ROE\times B\qquad(5)$$

$$M=[ROE\times B\times(1-r)]/[k-(r\times ROE)]$$

$$M/B=[ROE\times(1-r)]/[k-(r\times ROE)]$$

If a firm pays out all its earnings as dividends, r is zero. Those firms that generate positive abnormal returns can increase value by retaining a larger fraction of earnings and invest in business.

Equations (4) and (5) can be combined as:

$$M/B = [1 + (ROE \times r)]/(1 + k) + [ROE(1 - r)/(k - r \times ROE)]\ [1 - (1 + r \times ROE)/(1 + k)^n]$$

Thus, M/B is a function of ROE, retention rate and the advantage horizon, n.

Competitive advantage period (CAP) is defined as the time period for which the company earns returns in excess of cost of capital.[3] Over time, competitive pressures drive returns to the cost of capital. Although a company's CAP is affected by a multitude of internal and external factors, only a few key factors such as current return on capital, rate of industry change and barriers to entry have a significant bearing. Companies with high P/E multiples tend to have a long CAP and those with low P/E multiples tend to have low CAP.

MANAGING FOR SHAREHOLDER VALUE

In small companies, where a small group of people or the head takes a decision, marshalling all the resources is not difficult. But in large companies where the decision-making is delegated to operating managers, there is a need for a shared framework that provides guidelines regarding how operating decisions need to be made and how they affect the overall value creation effort because value created in one part of the company may get destroyed elsewhere in the company. The management processes and measures relating to strategic planning, capital investments, budgets and executive compensation should be designed to encourage value-creating behaviour in the organization. Once the goal of value creation is set (e.g., in terms of shareholder return), one can work backwards to arrive at strategies that can achieve it. Managers should be encouraged to strive to beat minimum acceptable value and move towards the maximum value that the best owner could deliver through improved operations, reduced cost, lower working capital and so on. The planning process should generate intense discussion and debate on the value drivers and the process of delivering value. The end product of such a discussion is a value creating strategy. Value-based management requires a new way of thinking among executives, especially the top level managers. Often top managers who have authority to take decisions on major issues such as dividends, mergers and acquisitions, debt policy, corporate restructuring and so on can create tremendous value. The implementation process typically starts at the top and percolates downwards. It is hard to link actions at lower levels of hierarchy to shareholder value. But the company can benchmark the processes that characterize an ideal organization.

LIMITATIONS OF SHAREHOLDER VALUE ANALYSIS

It is usually easy to manipulate SVA calculations and show value creation on paper. SVA is a function of financial variables such as cash flows, sales volume, price and cost. Quite often, the forecasts are made by financial managers but are controlled by other line managers. The forecast may be nowhere near product market realities or not in line with the strategic thrust. Another limitation of SVA is that it does not capture the value of future growth opportunities.

[3] Mauboussin and Johnson, 'Competitive Advantage Period'.

CONCLUDING COMMENTS

Growth in itself is not bad. Individual firms may exhibit sustained high growth by creative fine-tuning of financial policies specific to the circumstances of the company. But then, no company can grow at fantastic rates forever. If it does, it will take over the national economy in a few decades. Too much growth can destroy value because of sheer complexity of operations, bureaucracy and lack of analytical support to important projects. Given a choice between growth and value, it is value that must win.

REFERENCE

Mauboussin, Michael and Paul Johnson. 'Competitive Advantage Period: The Neglected Value Driver'. *Financial Management* 26, no 2 (1997, 14 Jan).

CHAPTER 23

Mergers and Acquisitions

LEARNING OBJECTIVES

- Provide a rationale for mergers and acquisitions
- Provide an overview of valuation approaches in an acquisition
- Introduce valuation of brands
- Summarize the empirical findings on mergers
- Highlight some commonly adopted takeover defences

During the 1990s, there were over 11,500 acquisitions in the USA for a total value exceeding US$1.75 trillion; non-US firms acquired nearly US$250 billion worth of high technology assets in the USA, 60 per cent of which were acquirers from the European Union. In 2017, companies announced over 50,600 transactions with a total value of more than US$3.5 trillion (EUR 2.9 trillion). Compared to 2016, the numbers of deals grew only marginally by 2.9 per cent, while the value declined by 2 per cent. Obviously, these numbers are staggering and suggest that mergers and acquisitions (M&A) are very popular. Why do companies merge? Is it possible to create value by acquiring companies? Why do some mergers miscarry? What are the characteristics of a successful merger programme?

Mergers are defined as the combining of two or more companies into one, usually with only one company retaining its identity. Typically, the larger firm is the one whose identity is maintained. The term merger is generally used to indicate friendly joining of companies, while the term acquisition is used for unfriendly takeovers or combinations where one company is much larger than the other. Mergers can be classified as horizontal, vertical or conglomerate. A horizontal merger is one that takes place between two firms in the same line of business. A vertical merger is one in which the buyer expands towards the source of raw material or forwards towards the end customer. A conglomerate merger is one in which companies in unrelated lines of business merge. Firms merge due to variety of reasons:

- Lower production and distribution costs by combining facilities
- Gaining access to new distribution channels
- Tax benefit
- Gaining a favourable raw material position
- Gaining access to new markets
- Faster growth

WHY DO COMPANIES MERGE?

The most commonly cited reasons are economies of scale and synergy. Economies of scale are enjoyed when the average unit cost of production decreases as production increases. The fixed costs are spread over a larger volume of production when companies merge. There are numerous examples where economies are never realized. The combined entity might become so large that the complicated organization structure that usually follows a merger may increase costs due to bureaucratization. Small companies are generally acquired with the idea that the small company lacks something—say, managerial talent—which the acquirer can provide and use the small company's strength, say, product, in return. Thus, the acquisition tries to make use of complementary resources better. Put two companies together. What emerges is bigger and better.

At times, the acquired company may have potential tax shields but cannot avail them as the profits are not adequate. The company with tax loss carry forwards can merge with a profitable entity so that the tax shields may be availed.

Synergy could be expected in production, marketing, finance and operations due to sharing of R&D know-how, transferring of technology, more efficient usage of machinery, selling of complementary products through a common distribution channel, lower borrowing costs due to scale economies in borrowing and so on. Some cash-rich companies prefer to use cash for acquisitions under the premise that diversification reduces unsystematic corporate risk, that is, downturn in one company's fortune will be offset by upturn in another company's earnings. Modern finance theory hypothesizes that unsystematic risk is not priced in markets and hence irrelevant. So a diversifying company can create value only by providing a better risk–return trade-off that is unavailable through simple portfolio diversification. There are six ways in which diversification can create value.[1]

- By applying one merger partner's knowledge of the industry and skills to the competitive problems and opportunities of the other
- Investing in markets closely related to current fields of operation, thereby reducing the long-run average cost
- By achieving a critical mass in an area of competence
- Reducing systematic risk by diversifying into related product markets
- By profitable allocation of cash among units to maximize efficiency
- By lowering cost of debt and WACC due to risk pooling

[1] Salter and Wolf, 'Creating Value via Diversification'.

GAINS FROM MERGER

The first step in merger analysis is to identify the economic gains from the merger. There are gains if the combined entity is more than the sum of its parts.

That is, combined Value > (Value of Acquirer + Stand-Alone Value of Target)

The difference between the combined value and the sum of the values of individual companies is usually attributed to synergy.

Value of Acquirer + Stand-Alone Value of Target + Value of Synergy = Combined Value

There is also a cost attached to an acquisition. The cost of acquisition is the price premium paid over the market value plus other costs of integration. Therefore, the net gain is the value of synergy minus premium paid. Suppose,

$$V_A = ₹100$$
$$V_B = ₹150$$
$$V_{AB} = ₹175$$
$$\text{Synergy} = V_{AB} - (V_A + V_B) = ₹25$$
If premium is ₹10, net gain = ₹25 − ₹10 = ₹15

Acquisition need not be made with synergy in mind. It is possible to make money from non-synergistic acquisitions as well. Operating improvements are a big source of value creation. Better post-merger integration could lead to abnormal returns even when the acquired company is in unrelated business. Obviously, managerial talent is an important instrument in creating value by cutting down costs, improving revenues and operating profit margin, cash flow position and so on. Many a time, executive compensation is tied to the performance in the post-merger period. Providing equity stake in the company induces executives to think and behave like shareholders.

There are five principal steps in a successful M&A programme.

- Manage the pre-acquisition phase.
- Screen candidates.
- Eliminate those who do not meet the criteria and value the rest.
- Negotiate.
- Post-merger integration.

During the pre-acquisition phase, the acquirer should maintain secrecy about its intentions. Otherwise, the resulting price increase due to rumours may kill the deal.

TARGET VALUATION

One of the essential steps in M&A is determining the value of the target company. There are several valuation frameworks for measuring the value of the target firm. One of the popular approaches is the DCF methodology described under capital budgeting. In the DCF approach, the value of the business is the future expected cash flow discounted at a rate that reflects the riskiness of the projected cash flows. This methodology is used to value companies since firms are essentially collection of projects. The steps involved in the valuation are:

Step 1: Determine Free Cash Flow

Free cash flow is the cash flow available to both shareholders and bondholders after consideration for taxes, capital expenditure and working capital investment.

Free Cash Flow = NOPAT + Depreciation − Capital Expenditure − Working Capital Investment

Estimate the most likely incremental cash flows to be generated by the target company with the acquirer as owner (and not on as-is basis). Note that financing is not incorporated in the cash flows. Suitable adjustments for the specific financing of the acquisition will be made in the discount rate.

Step 2: Estimate a Suitable Discount Rate for the Acquisition

The acquiring company can use its WACC based on its target capital structure only if the acquisition will not affect the riskiness of the acquirer. If the acquirer intends to change the capital structure of the target company, suitable adjustments for the discount rate should be made. The discount rate should reflect the capital structure of the company after the acquisition.

Step 3: Calculate the Present Value of Cash Flows

Since the life of a going concern, by definition, is infinite, the value of the company

= PV of cash flows during the forecast period + Terminal value

We can set the forecast period in such a way that the company reaches a stable phase after that. In other words, we are assuming that the company will grow at a constant rate after the forecast period.

Step 4: Estimate the Terminal Value

The terminal value (TV) is the present value of cash flows occurring after the forecast period. If we assume that cash flows grow at a constant rate after the forecast period, then

$$TV = [CF_t(1+g)]/k-g$$

where CF_t = cash flow in the last year

g = constant growth rate

k = discount rate

Step 5: Add present value of TV

Step 6: Deduct the value of debt and other obligations assumed by the acquirer.

An Illustration

Clariant is a Dyes and Chemicals manufacturer. Analysts expect the company to grow at 15 per cent per annum. The analyst forecast of free cash flow is shown in Table 23.1. The cost of capital for the company is 14.62 per cent. The present value of cash flows amounts to ₹390.9 million. We are assuming that the company acquiring Clariant will not make any operating improvements or change the capital structure.

Analysts expect the cash flows to grow at 10 per cent forever after 2025.

TABLE 23.1
Free Cash Flow Forecast for Clariant

(₹10 million)

	Years							
	2017	2018	2020	2021	2022	2023	2024	2025
Sales	162.13	204.69	235.39	270.7	311.31	358.01	411.71	473.46
NOPAT	10.62	11.22	11.72	12.72	14.41	16.21	18.13	20.11
+Depreciation	3.14	2.13	2.68	2.82	2.96	3.11	3.26	3.42
Less:								
Capital exp.	0	0.63	2.36	1.79	1.88	1.97	2.07	2.17
Increase in WC	0	6.44	4.12	6.10	9.45	11.67	12.97	14.32
Free Cash Flow 13.76	6.28	7.37	7.65	6.04	5.68	6.35	7.04	

Approach 1: Terminal Value Is a Growing Perpetuity

$$TV = FCF_t (1+g)/(k-g)$$
$$= 70.4\ (1.10)/(0.1462-0.10)$$
$$= ₹1,676 \text{ million}$$
$$\text{Present Value of TV} = 1676 \times PVIF\ (14.62, 7)$$
$$= 1,676 \times 0.384 = 644.6$$
$$\text{Total Value} = ₹(390.6+644.6) = ₹1,035.2 \text{ cr.}$$

Since we are interested in buying only the shares of the firm, the value of outstanding debt should be deducted from the firm value to arrive at the value of equity. Clariant has debt amounting to ₹79.2 million.

$$\text{Value of Equity} = ₹1,035.2 - ₹79.2 = ₹956.0 \text{ million}$$

As is evident, much of the target company's value comes from TV, which is sensitive to the assumption made about the growth rate of cash flows in perpetuity. There are three other ways in which TV can be estimated.

Approach 2: Terminal Value Is a Stable Perpetuity

If there is no capital expenditure or capital expenditure exactly equals depreciation after the forecast period, meaning that the total capital does not grow anymore, cash flow equals profit after tax. In other words, when we assume that the company earns a rate of return on capital equal to the cost of capital irrespective of growth in sales,

$$TV = [\text{Free Cash Flow/Discount Rate}] = FCF/k$$
$$= [70.4/0.1462] = ₹481.5 \text{ million}$$

Value of the Firm = 390.9 + 481.5 = ₹872.4 million. The difference in value is almost ₹162.8 million.

Approach 3: Terminal Value as a Multiple of Book Value

The TV can also be estimated by multiplying the forecasted book value of capital by an appropriate market-to-book ratio (P/BV). Normally, the current M/B ratio is taken as proxy for future.

Consider the following example.

	Market Value	Book Value	M/B
Debt ₹	7.92	7.92	1.0
Equity ₹	15.0	10.0	1.50
Total Capital ₹	22.92	17.92	1.28

The current M/B ratio is 1.28. If the book value of capital at the end of forecast period is ₹300 million, TV = 300 × 1.28 = ₹384.0 million.

Approach 4: Terminal Value as a Multiple of Earnings

The TV under this method is established by multiplying the forecasted terminal year profits by an appropriate price–earnings multiple. As usual, the current P/E multiple can be used as proxy for future.

Current P/E Multiple = [Current Market Value of Company/Current Profit after Tax]

To illustrate, if the current market value is ₹576.2 million and profit after tax is ₹82.3 million,

P/E = 57.62/8.23 = 7

TV = Last Year Profits × P/E Multiple = 201.1 × 7 = ₹1,408 million

Obviously, the method adopted by the analyst affects the final value placed on the company's equity. These four methods might give four different answers. The DCF approach can capture the value of assets in place. Some components of the acquisition are hard to quantify. Consequently, the final price paid by the acquirer might be much higher than the DCF value obtained. But the premium paid for the so-called synergy should not be out of proportion. We could think of the target company's value as:

Value to buyer = value to seller + value added by buyer + change in value to buyer if target firm is acquired by competitor.

The first component is the DCF value of the target firm in its current form with the current growth rate, current financial plan and so on.

The second component, value added by acquirer comprises of synergy to acquirer, cost savings, value of new strategy after the acquisition, proceeds from sale of redundant assets adjusted for taxes, benefits from improvement in credit rating and other financing side effects.

The third component is the gain or loss to the acquirer if the competition manages to acquire the target. The sum total of these three components gives the maximum value of the target.

A sensitivity analysis may be conducted for pessimistic and optimistic values of key financial variables such as sales growth rate, profit margin, working capital investment, capital expenditure, period of high growth and so on. The end product of such an analysis is a range of prices within which the acquisition price may lie. Obviously, the acquirer would want to lower the price as much as possible and the opposite is true for the target. The important message is that the acquirer should consider not only what the target may be worth to the buyer but also what the target's next best alternative is likely to be. For example, suppose that when valued as a stand-alone, a target is worth ₹100, whereas, due to synergies, the target is worth ₹150 as part of the buying firm. A key element in the negotiation process is the value of target to another bidder. If the synergy is unique to the buyer, the buyer may purchase the company for one buck more than the stand-alone value (₹101). On the other hand, if the synergy is available to other bidders as well, the buyer may have to raise the bid closer to ₹150. In other words, the valuation must take into account the uniqueness of synergy and the likely range of prices affordable by other bidders. To sum up, valuation has three elements—estimation of cash flows, estimation of discount rate and sensitivity analysis.

Let us look at an extended example. ABC is in the process of purchasing XYZ. The pre-merger financial statements of both the companies are given in Table 23.2. Forecasting cash flows for XYZ under ABC's management involves suitable assumptions regarding sales growth rate, profit margin, capital expenditure and net working capital for every rupee of sales increase. The relevant assumptions for the forecast period are as follows.

	Years		
	1–5	6–7	8–10
Sales Growth Rate, g%	15	12	12
EBIT/Sales %	0.18	0.15	0.12
Tax Rate %	46	46	46
Capex per Rupee of Sales Increase (C)[2]	0.20	0.20	0.20
Working Capital per Rupee of Sales Increase (W)	0.15	0.15	0.15

TABLE 23.2
Pre-merger Financial Statements

(₹10 million)

Income Statement		
	ABC	XYZ
Sales	600	50
Operating Income	522	42.50
EBIT	78	7.5
Interest	4.50	0.40
PBT	73.50	7.10
Net Income	37.50	3.55
No. of Shares Outstanding (million)	10.00	1.11
Balance Sheet		
Debt	56.00	5.10
Equity	272.00	17.00
	328.0	22.10
Fixed Assets	216.00	20.00
Less: Accumulated Depreciation	(95)	(8.00)
Net Working Capital	180.00	7.50
Investments	25.00	1.00
Other Assets	2.00	1.60
	22.10	

[2] Net of depreciation.

TABLE 23.3
Forecast of Cash Flows

(₹10 million)

Sales	57.50	66.12	177.23
EBIT	10.35	11.90	21.27
NOPAT	5.59	6.43	11.48
Cash Flow	2.96	3.41	4.84

$$\text{The Cash Flow in any Year} = CF_t = S_{t-1}(1+g_t)(p_t)(1-T_c) - (S_t - S_{t-1})(C_t + W_t)$$

where p = EBIT/Sales
S = sales
T_c = tax rate

Thus, cash flow in year 1 = 50 (1 + 0.15)(0.18)(1 − 0.46) − (57.5 − 50)(0.20 + 0.15) = 2.96

The projections for the first 10 years are shown in Table 23.3.[3]

If we assume that the company generates normal returns from Year 10, that is, the company's value is unaffected by growth, the terminal value can be estimated as a perpetuity.

$$TV = \frac{NOPAT_{10}}{\text{Discount rate}}$$

PV of TV = TV × Discount Rate

Assuming that the discount rate is 13 per cent, the present value of TV = ₹26.02.

The Total Present Value of All Cash Flows	48.61
+ Investments	1.00
– XYZ's Debt Assumed	5.10
Value of XYZ Equity ₹ Crore	44.51
Value/Share ₹	40.10

The next step in the analysis is to find out if a cash purchase is indeed possible at the current offer price. The acquirer's equity is unchanged in a cash offer. So the post-merger debt capacity of the combined entity is ABC's equity (₹2,720 million) multiplied by the target debt–equity ratio (say, 30%). ABC and XYZ currently have pre-merger debt balances of ₹560 million and ₹51 million. The unused debt capacity is:

Post-merger Debt Capacity − Sum of Pre-merger Debt Balances of the Two Companies[4]
= ₹ 272 × 0.4 − (56 + 5.1) crore = ₹47.7 crore

[3] The sales growth rate and the assumptions regarding margins, capex and working capital investment are extrapolated from the current year (as base year) based on the assumption that current year is a normal year. One might take the average of past two or three years if there is a reason to believe that current year is too good or too bad so that the trend is not unrealistic.

[4] One might add the investments to this number assuming that the acquirer can liquidate such temporary investments.

If the post-merger debt capacity is more than the total offer price (number of shares acquired × acquisition price), a cash purchase financed with debt is possible. In this case, the purchase price of ₹44.51 crore is less than the post-merger debt capacity. So a cash purchase is feasible.

VALUATION IN PARTS

The APV approach described in earlier chapters can be used for valuing acquisition targets. WACC works reasonably well when the company targets a constant debt to value ratio. The corporate WACC used in many valuations is based on the assumption that the cash flows of the target are about as risky as that of the acquiring company and the target company will maintain a similar capital structure as that of the acquiring company. Both are restrictive assumptions. A better approach for valuation is to

- Value the company as if it were financed entirely with equity.
- Estimate the value of financing side effects such as tax shields and bankruptcy costs and so on.
- Add the two to arrive at APV.

The first step in calculating APV requires the calculation of present value of target company's cash flows assuming all equity financing. Consider a hypothetical example. The cash flows of a company are as follows.

(₹10 million)

Year	NOPAT	Capital Exp.	Depreciation	ΔWC	Net Cash Flow
1	65.00	30	20	20	35.00
2	70.20	32	22	22	38.20
3	75.40	35	24	23	41.40
4	80.60	37	26	25	44.60
5	87.10	40	28	27	48.10

Cash flows are expected to grow at 7 per cent forever thereafter.

$$\text{PV of TV} = \frac{48.10\,(1.07)}{(k - 0.07)\,(1+k)^5}$$

The unlevered value is obtained by discounting all the cash flows at the unlevered cost of equity. Assume that there are four comparable firms. Their betas and D/E ratios are as follows:

Firm	Beta	D/E
1	1.0	0.50
2	0.6	0.0
3	0.8	0.4
4	0.9	0.45

Company 2 has no debt. The cost of equity for this company can be taken as proxy for unlevered cost of equity.

Assume the following parameters: $R_f = 12.2$ per cent, beta = 0.60, market premium = 10 per cent

Cost of Unlevered Equity = 12.2 + 0.60 (10) = 18.2 per cent

The PV of Cash Flows = [35 × PVIF (18.2,1) + ··· + 48.1 × PVIF (18.2,5) + Present Value of TV]

TV = [51.47/0.112] = ₹459.50 crore

All Equity Value = ₹325.51 crore

The acquisition price of ₹330 crore will be financed with ₹99 crore of debt. It will be brought down to ₹66 crore in five years. The indebtedness is expected to remain at that level forever.

End of Year	Debt
0	99.00
1	92.40
2	85.8
3	79.20
4	72.60
5	66.00

Present Value of Interest Tax Shields = PV of Tax Shields During the First Five Years + PV of Perpetual Tax Shields after Year 5.

Tax Shield = Interest Rate × Amount of Debt Outstanding × Tax Rate

Assume a tax rate of 35 per cent and interest rate of 14 per cent.

$$\text{PV of Tax Shield During First 5 Years} = [0.14 \times 99 \times 0.35 \times \text{PVIF}(14,1)] + \cdots + [0.14 \times 72.60 \times 0.35 \times \text{PVIF}(14,5)]$$

$$= ₹14.70 \text{ crore}$$

$$\text{TV of Tax Shields} = \frac{0.14 \times 66 \times 0.35}{0.14(1.14)^5}$$

$$= ₹12 \text{ crore}$$

The cost of debt is used as discount rate on the assumption that tax shields are about as uncertain as debt payments generating them. If tax shields are considered riskier than interest payments, a higher rate may be used.

Present Value of Tax Shields = ₹(14.70 + 12) crore = ₹26.7 crore

APV = Base Case Value + PV of Tax Shield

Adjustment for incremental bankruptcy cost can be made either subjectively or taking suitable proxies. The acquisition price of ₹330 crore compares well with the base case value. An acquirer should look for making money from incremental improvements in operations rather than good financing. If tax shields evaporate or bankruptcy cost exceeds tax shields, the value will never be realized.

VALUATION OF BRANDS

Brand equity is created by combination of brand loyalty, consumer awareness, perceived quality and brand associations. Brand valuation quantifies the benefits of brand equity to the owner of the brand. Though companies have long recognized the importance of brands, interest in placing a value on them is a relatively recent phenomenon—mostly a result of the recent M&A wave in which brands play an important role.

There are four approaches for measuring the value of a brand.

- Cost Based: According to this approach, the value of a brand is the present value of all expenditure incurred on the brand till date (which an acquirer will have to incur in building a brand of comparable equity). It is, however, difficult to trace all brand-related costs throughout the life of the brand.
- Market Based: The market value of a brand is the amount for which a brand can be sold which is simply the present value of the benefits from owning the brand.
- Income Based: This involves determining future revenues directly attributable to the brand and then discounting them to the present at a suitable rate. In order to estimate net revenues, the brand's price premium and volume are compared to those of generic product.
- Interbrand Approach:The Interbrand approach is the most popular methodology for estimating the value of brands.[5]

  A brand's value is the product of:
  - Average annual after-tax profits of the brand adjusted for earnings of an equivalent unbranded product
  - A multiple reflecting the brand's strength

  Interbrand takes seven factors into account to arrive at a brand strength multiple. They are:

  Leadership: A brand which has the ability to influence the market in setting price points and commanding distribution gets a higher score (max 25).

  Stability: Those brands which enjoy a strong consumer franchise are considered stable and awarded a higher score (max 15).

  Market: Brands in markets such as foods and soft drinks are less vulnerable to shifts in fashion and technology (max 15).

  Geographic spread: Brands that have an international appeal are stronger then regional brands (max 25).

  Trend: The long-term appeal to consumers (max 10).

  Support: Consistency in investment and strength of communication (max 10).

  Protection: Legal protection available to the brand owner (max 10).

To assess the brand strength, Interbrand conducts a detailed audit of trade and retail outlets among other things. The final multiple assigned to the brand depends on the brand strength score. To illustrate, if the brand score is 56, Interbrand may apply a multiple of 8.42.

[5] Birkin, 'Assessing Brand Value'.

Brand valuation involves the following steps.

- Collect most recent profit data (3 years)
- Restate the prior period (Year 2, Year 1) profits to present-day values by inflating at a suitable rate
- Attach a weighting factor to the restated profit figures. Usually, a simple weighting of three times the current year, twice the previous year and once before is used. These aggregate earnings are divided by the sum of the weighting factors (3+2+1=6)
- Deduct operating income of an equivalent unbranded product
- Deduct taxes at the medium-term effective tax rate
- Apply a suitable multiple depending on the brand strength

SELLER'S PERSPECTIVE

It is necessary to remember that for every buyer there must be a seller. Although the methods of analysis for selling are the same as for buying, the selling process is termed divestiture. The decision to sell a company is at least as important as buying one. But selling generally lacks the kind of planning that goes into buying. Quite often, the decision and the choice of the buyer is arbitrary resulting in a raw deal for the selling company's shareholders. It is important to understand that selling needs the same set of skills required for buying. At some point in time, the executives of a company may have to take the decision to divest a division. There is nothing wrong in selling a division if it is worth more to someone else. The decision to sell may be prompted by poor growth prospects for a division or consolidation in the industry. Given the fact that the need to sell may arise any time, it makes sense for executives to be prepared. More specifically, executives need to know their company's worth. Consideration may be given to strengths and weaknesses in production, marketing, general management, value of synergy to potential buyers, value of brand equity, skill base of the organization and so on.

THE EMPIRICAL EVIDENCE ON MERGERS

Academic studies indicate that success in creating value through acquisitions in a competitive market is extremely difficult. Jensen and Ruback[6] highlight this point by summarizing results from M&A over a period of 11 years. They found that in case of a merger, the average return, around the date of announcement, to shareholders of the acquired company is 20 per cent, whereas the average return to the acquiring company is 0 per cent. Another study by McKinsey indicates that 61 per cent of the 116 acquisitions studied were failures, 23 per cent were successes. Yet another study suggests that more than half the deals—amounting to US$1.5 trillion—fall short of value creation targets. To assess the profitability of M&A, academic studies have adopted two approaches (excluding clinical studies of one or a small group of companies). Event studies examine the abnormal returns to shareholders in the period surrounding the announcement of the transaction. The raw return for one day is simply the change in the share price and any dividends paid, divided by the closing share price the day before. The abnormal return is obtained by deducting a benchmark of what investors

[6] Jensen and Ruback, 'The Market for Corporate Control'.

TABLE 23.4
Returns to Target Firm Shareholders[7]

Study	Cumulative Abnormal Return	Sample Size	Period
Lang et al. (1989)	+40.3%	87	1968–1986
Healy et al. (1992)	+45.6%	50	1979–1984
Bradley et al. (1988)	+31.77%	236	1963–1984

TABLE 23.5
Returns to Acquiring Firm Shareholders[8]

Study	Cumulative Abnormal Return	Sample Size	Period
Asquith et al. (1987)	–0.85%	343	1973–1983
Healy et al. (1992)	–2.2%	50	1979–1984
Morck et al. (1990)	–0.70%	326	1975–1987

required that day (as estimated by CAPM or any benchmark index return, say S&P 500). Accounting studies examine the reported financial results of acquirers before and after acquisitions to see how financial performance changed. These studies match acquirers and non-acquirers in the same industry of similar size.

These studies attempt to find out if acquirers outperformed the non-acquirers. The results of event studies of returns to target and bidding firms are presented in Tables 23.4 and 23.5. Note that most studies have documented negative returns to bidding firms.[9] Despite such statistics, why do companies acquire? Why do mergers fail? The reasons for merger failures can be numerous. Some of the key reasons are:

- Acquirers generally overpay
- Poor due diligence
- The value of synergy is overestimated
- Poor post-merger integration
- Psychological barriers

Companies often merge in the fear that the bigger competitors have economies of scale and may destroy them by exercising stranglehold on raw material supply, distribution and so on. What they do not realize is the drawbacks of being big. The acquiring company's executives would have drawn up elaborate plans for the target without consulting its executives which leads to resentment and managerial attrition. This can be avoided by honest discussions with the target company's executives. Most companies merge with the hope that the benefits of synergy will be realized. Synergy will be there only if the merged entity is

[7] Ibid.

[8] Ibid.

[9] Some studies have documented zero or positive returns.

managed better after the acquisition than it was managed before. It is the quality of the top management that determines the success of the merger. Quite often the executives of the acquiring company lose interest in the target company due to its smallness.[10] The small company executives get bogged down preparing vision and mission statements, budgets, forecasts, profit plans that were hitherto unheard of.

The elaborateness of the control system depends on the size and culture of the company. To make a merger successful:

- Define merger objectives.
- Decide what tasks need to be accomplished in the post-merger period.
- Install an on-site integration manager to coordinate all activities. This person could be from a finance background because they are often considered less intimidating.
- Choose managers from both the companies (and from outside).
- Make them a part of the solution rather than the problem.
- Establish performance yardstick and evaluate the managers on that yardstick. Put them on an attractive P&L incentive compensation plan.
- Motivate them to the hilt.

Once a company is acquired, the acquirer should decide whether the target should be left alone or adhere to the acquiring company's culture and control system. This is not an easy question to answer. If the target is a broken company, the answer is yes. If the target is a successful company and the acquisition motive is getting a foothold in other markets or some such thing, one should exercise one's judgement in changing existing systems because the exercise may destroy the unique culture and systems that contributed to the success of the company.

Integration has been cited as the most important process in an M&A deal. As mentioned earlier, many mergers have fallen through because of poor integration. The first 100 days is a time of anxiety and uncertainty for both the acquirer and the target. This is where care must be taken to avoid the iceberg syndrome that will sink all efforts. Executives often feel uncomfortable communicating with key employees after a merger because so many of their questions cannot be answered.

But not meeting with key employees can be fatal. Key employees who are made to feel a part of the process, allowed to make a case for their candidacies and reassured that their company of origin would not be counted against them are less likely to fall through the cracks. If key employees do not feel that they are in the loop, they will probably be busy looking for career opportunities elsewhere.

According to Michael Porter, acquisitions will most likely be profitable if:

- The floor price created by the seller's alternative of keeping the business is low, as when the seller feels great compulsion to sell or the seller is not optimistic about its prospects if it continues in the business.
- The market for companies is imperfect and does not eliminate above-average returns through the bidding process, as when the buyer has superior information, the number of bidders is low, the condition of the economy is bad, the selling company is sick and the seller has objectives besides maximizing the price received for the business.

[10] Kitching, 'Why Do Mergers Miscarry?

- The buyer has a unique ability to operate the acquired business, as when the buyer has a distinctive ability to improve the operations of the seller, the firm buys into an industry and can use the acquisition as a base from which to pursue an internal or grass-roots development and the acquisition will uniquely help a buyer's position in its existing business.

Nevertheless, there is only one test of the success or failure of a merger or acquisition—whether or not the per share value of the acquiring company rises after the deal is done. It is believed that astute companies can use the current M&A wave to deliver substantial value for their shareholders.

Finally, companies will have to act decisively to build the three capabilities that build a successful strategy—local networks, the capability to manage uncertainty and the ability to distinguish prime targets.

Those that move quickly, that understand the long-term potential, that have the courage to dip a toe in what may be the unknown and turbulent waters and that have the staying power, will be in the best position to capitalize on the M&A opportunities in the coming decade.

TAKEOVER DEFENCES

Studies indicate that only 25 per cent of all targets are successful in remaining independent. Another 25 per cent are saved and acquired by a 'white knight'. The remaining 50 per cent ultimately fall prey to the hostile acquirer. There are several defensive measures available to the managers of target companies to save their firm from the hands of an acquirer. Some of these defensive measures are discussed further:

Dual Class Recapitalization: In this, equity is restructured into two classes with different voting rights with the goal of providing management or family owners with voting rights disproportionately greater to their holdings.

Staggered or Classified Board: Directors are broken into classes with only one class being elected each year. This makes it difficult for a substantial shareholder to:

- Change all of the board at once without approval of the existing board
- Lowers the effectiveness of cumulative voting

Poison Pills: These are triggered by a tender offer or accumulation of shares by a single shareholder beyond a certain threshold. The trigger allows target shareholders with rights to purchase additional shares making acquisition difficult.

Greenmail: In a greenmail, the target repurchases at a premium the hostile bidder's target's block. Greenmails typically result in reduced shareholder value.

CONCLUDING COMMENTS

This chapter outlined some of the sensible reasons for mergers, action areas and the valuation approaches. The post-merger period is the most important phase in the merger process. Some quantify the number of changes in the working of the company at 2000 and non-routine decisions at 10,000!

All the decision areas may be clubbed under important headings such as Finance, Personnel & HR, Marketing and Technology, and a checklist be prepared so that the acquirer is better prepared to handle the complexity of the process. Acquisitions work only if:

- There are operating and financial improvements.
- The acquisition price is not too high.
- The incumbent management is competent.
- There is top management involvement in the process.

APPENDIX 23A.1: PROCEDURE FOR MERGERS

- Prepare scheme of merger.
- Get approval of Board of Directors of both companies.
- Get approval from banks and financial institutions which have lent money and the trustees of debenture holders.
- Intimate stock exchange about the proposed merger.
- Apply to high court (HC) having jurisdiction over the registered office of the company.
- HC gives direction for calling a meeting of members.
- HC approves the notice.
- Despatch notices to shareholders and creditors.
- Advertise the meeting in newspapers 21 days before the meeting.
- Hold the shareholder general meeting and pass resolutions.
- File resolutions with the registrar of companies within 30 days.
- Submit the report of the chairman of the meeting with HC.
- Within seven days of filing, both companies should make a joint petition to the court for approving the scheme.
- The court issues a notice to the Regional Director, Company Law Board.
- Hearing of petition and confirmation of scheme.
- File the court order with Registrar of Companies.
- Dissolution of transferor company.
- Transfer of assets and liabilities.
- Allotment of shares to shareholders of transferor company.
- Listing of shares at stock exchange.

APPENDIX 23A.2: PROCEDURE FOR TAKEOVERS

- Appoint a Category 1 merchant banker to advise on the acquisition.
- Collection of relevant information on the target.
- Examine shareholder profile.
- Investigation of title and indebtedness.
- Examine articles of association.
- Public announcement is to be made within four days of finalization of negotiation or entering into an MOU.

- Make all public announcements in one national English daily, one Hindi newspaper and one regional language newspaper of that place where the shares of the company are listed and traded.
- The public announcement should contain the following:
  - o Identity of the acquirer
  - o Purpose of the acquisition
  - o Total number of shares proposed to be acquired
  - o Offer price
  - o Method of payment
  - o The highest and the average price paid by the acquirer, if any, to shares of the target company during the 12-month period before the announcement
  - o Date of opening and closure of the offer
  - o Date by which the payment would be made
  - o Details of financial arrangements made for the purpose of acquisition
- Prepare a letter of offer with the help of the merchant banker within 14 days of announcement and get it approved by SEBI.
- Send a copy of the draft letter of offer to the target company at its registered office and to all the stock exchanges where the company is listed.
- Send the offer letter to all the shareholders of the company whose names appear in the register of members of the company as on the date of public announcement and the offer letter should reach them within 45 days.
- Open an escrow account and deposit the required amount as security for performance.
- Make payment and complete all other procedures within 30 days of the closure of the offer.
- Upward revision of price can be made any time up to seven days before the closure of the offer.

EXERCISES

1. Refer to the following data.
   Beta = 1.40, market premium = 10 per cent, long-term T-bond rate = 12 per cent. Pre-tax cost of debt = 13.5 per cent, tax rate = 35 per cent, target debt-to-value ratio = 0.45
   The working results for the past three years are as follows:

(₹10 million)

	2015	2016	2017
Sales	9.0	9.9	11.0
EBIT	4.5	4.95	5.5
Depreciation	0.72	0.72	0.72

The company has made capital expenditure of ₹0.72 crore each year in the last three years. It is expected to grow at 10 per cent for the next three years and drop to 5 per cent thereafter in line with growth in sales. Working capital is expected to be 15 per cent of sales. Additional depreciation for the next three years on the new equipment will be provided on straight line basis. Free cash flows are expected to grow at 5.5 per cent in perpetuity after three years. Determine the value of the company.

2. The adjusted present value approach and the WACC approach should yield same results. Can you think of a situation when they diverge?
3. For the illustration given in the chapter (Clariant), conduct a sensitivity analysis for the following factors.
   Discount rate
   Sales
   Growth rate in sales
   Investment in working capital and capital expenditure
   Terminal growth rate
   Draw suitable graphs.
4. Write essays on the following topics:
   - Role of top management in acquisitions
   - Post-merger integration
   - Non-synergistic acquisitions
   - Post-acquisition performance appraisal
5. The executives of Babur Chemicals are evaluating a potential acquisition candidate—Arathi Chemicals. The forecast of free cash flow under the current management is as follows.

(₹ million)

	0	1	2	3	4	5	6
Revenues		455	551	800	1,080	1,195	1,255
COGS		341.3	414.9	596	811.10	893.9	941.3
SGA Exp.		110.4	130	219.2	251.6	280.3	287.4
NOPAT							
+Depreciation		19	21	21	46.3	48.1	50
– Capex	100	8.1	9.5	13	16	16.3	17
– Working Capital	25	4.1	5.5	6.0	7.1	8	9.7
Free Cash Flow							

Cash flows are expected to grow at 6.5 per cent after Year 6.

The executives of Babur believe that NOPAT margin can be improved by 8 per cent and working capital investment can be cut by 20 per cent. Arathi chemicals has a strong marketing network which could be used to sell Babur's existing products. The arrangement is likely to generate savings of ₹1 million per annum for eight years.

	For Babur (%)	For Arathi (%)
COE	20	22
Tax Rate	35	35
Cost of Debt	12.5	13.5
Target D/V	30	20

- Estimate the value of Arathi under current management.
- Estimate the value of Arathi for Babur.
- Can Babur's cost of capital be used to discount cash flows of Arathi? If yes, when? If not, why not?
- Babur intends to increase debt by ₹2.5 million. What is the value of interest tax shields to Babur? Assume that debt is permanent.
- Conduct a sensitivity analysis.

6. ABC Ltd is considering the acquisition of XYZ Ltd. The management of ABC believes that cost of goods sold could be reduced by 1.5 per cent over the next three years (due to purchasing economies) and administrative expenses could be brought down by 3 per cent. The forecast of income statement of XYZ under ABC is as follows:

(₹ Thousands)

Year	1	2	3
Sales	60,000	63,000	66,000
COGS	30,000	31,000	33,000
Depreciation	4,000	4,200	4,300
SGA	21,000	22,000	22,500

Assume that cash flow increases at 7 per cent after Year three. ABC needs to incur expenditure on fixed assets and working capital to make operational improvements to XYZ, the details of which are as follows.

Year	1	2	3
Capex	4,900	5,100	5,300
WC	510	540	550

At a discount rate of 13 per cent, what is the maximum price that ABC should pay? Assume a tax rate of 30 per cent.

REFERENCES

Birkin, Michael. 'Assessing Brand Value'. In *Brand Power*, edited by Paul Stobart. New York, NY: New York University Press, 1994.

Bruner, Robert F. 'Does M&A Pay? A Survey of Evidence for the Decision Maker'. *Journal of Applied Finance* (2002 Spring/Summer).

Kitching, John. 'Why Do Mergers Miscarry?' *Harvard Business Review* (1967 Nov–Dec).

Jensen, M. C. and R. S. Ruback. 'The Market for Corporate Control: The Scientific Evidence'. *Journal of Financial Economics* 11 (1983 April).

Salter, M. and W. Wolf. 'Creating Value via Diversification'. *Harvard Business Review* (1978 July).

SUGGESTED READINGS

Anslinger, P. L. and T. E. Copeland. 'Growth Through Acquisitions: A Fresh Look'. *Harvard Business Review* (1996 Jan–Feb).

Asquith, P. 'Merger Bids, Uncertainty and Stockholder Returns'. *Journal of Financial Economics* 11 (1983 April).

Bradley, M., A. Desai and E. H. Kim. 'The Rationale Behind Interfirm Tender Offers: Information or Synergy?' *Journal of Financial Economics* 11 (1983 April).

Myers, S. C. 'The Evaluation of an Acquisition Target'. In *The Revolution in Corporate Finance*, edited by Joel Stern and Donald Chew. Hoboken, NJ: Blackwell, 1992.

Inselbag, I. and J. Kaufold. 'Two DCF Approaches for Valuing Companies under Alternative Financing Strategies'. *Journal of Applied Corporate Finance* (1997).

Jensen, Michael C. 'Takeovers: Folklore and Science'. *Harvard Business Review* (1984 Nov–Dec).

Leuherman, Timothy. 'What's It Worth: A General Manager's Guide to Valuation'. *Harvard Business Review* (1997 May–June).

Rappaport, Alfred. 'Strategic Analysis for More Profitable Acquisitions'. *Harvard Business Review* (1979 July–August).

CHAPTE

24

EVA and Divisional Performance Measurement

LEARNING OBJECTIVES

- Introduction to a financial metric called economic value added (EVA)
- Highlight the characteristics of a sound performance measure
- Summarize the empirical findings on EVA
- Provide an overview of leveraged equity purchase plan

The term divisional performance measurement refers to the organizational rules that consist of performance measurement and evaluation, and reward and punishment system. Performance measurement includes the objective and subjective measurement of both individuals and sub-units/divisions of the organization, whereas performance evaluation is the process of attaching values to various measures of performance to represent the importance of achievement. The rewards and punishment system prevailing in the organization attempts to encourage certain types of behaviour and discourage certain other types by linking rewards to results measured by the performance measurement system.

Since the objective of a firm is to maximize shareholders wealth, a performance measure should have high correlation with changes in shareholders wealth. Managers are commonly appraised on measures such as ROAs, EPS and ROE that do not capture value. Managers focus on cash flows while evaluating capital investments; but when it comes to performance measurement, accounting measures take over. If a company changes its accounting method from FIFO to LIFO during a period of high inflation, cash flow increases but earnings fall. Similarly, when a company acquires another company, there may be special write-offs like amortization of goodwill that is non-cash in nature. The EPS falls but cash flow is unaltered. Moreover, these measures can be easily manipulated due to denominator management: one can increase the value of these ratios by simply cutting down whatever that appears in the denominator.

Profit itself is not an appropriate measure of performance because it does not capture either the amount of capital used to generate those earnings or the required rate of return on capital. A good performance measure is one that incorporates all three.

Economic value added (EVA)[1] is an accounting-based measure of operating performance. The period could be a month, quarter, half-year or a year. The entity whose performance is being measured could be a division or the firm itself. EVA is the difference between accounting earnings—with suitable adjustments for interest and some accounting methods—and the cost of capital used to generate these earnings.

Expressed as a formula,

$$EVA = NOPAT - (WACC \times \text{Net Assets})$$

where NOPAT = Net Operating Profit After Tax

$$= EBIT(1-T)$$

$$\text{Net Assets} = \text{Adjusted Book Value of Net Capital at the Beginning of the Period}$$

$$WACC = \text{Weighted Average Cost of Capital}$$

$$= D/V(1-T)\ K_d + E/V\ K_e$$

where D = Market Value of Firm's Debt

$$E = \text{Market Value of Equity} = \text{Number of Shares} \times \text{Current Market Price}$$

Convertible debt/preferred securities must be treated as converted if they are in-the-money and options must be included in the calculation of equity if they are in-the-money

$V = D + E$

T = Marginal Tax Rate

K_d = marginal cost of borrowing long term after adjusting for offering discount and issuance cost.

K_e = cost of equity estimated by CAPM.

EVA has certain characteristics:

- It provides greater accountability for investor capital as it measures the required return on all investments.
- It is custom-made to a company's specific circumstances making only those accounting adjustments that are necessary.
- It is easy to communicate.
- It aligns managerial and shareholders' interests by tying management compensation to improvements in EVA.

[1] EVA is the registered trademark of Stern Stewart & Co.

COMPETITORS TO EVA

The purpose of value analysis is twofold. First, evaluate the performance of current strategy. Second, evaluate potential strategies for each of the business units. For instance, a company may have the following options for a business unit: modernize the plant, hold, harvest or sell out. Even if the unit is currently losing money, it might make sense to invest in the unit if the spread between ROE and COE is expected to become positive in the foreseeable future implying that executives will have to take a long-term view of business prospects before a strategic decision is made. Value creation should be the guiding factor in executive decision-making. But how do you measure value? This is important for two reasons. First, managers need to know how their performance will be evaluated, and second, how to work towards that goal.

Shareholder value analysis is the process of analysing how business decisions affect the company's economic value (i.e., NPV of cash flows discounted at WACC). One of the measures of shareholder value is the TSR. It is the rate (IRR) that equates the purchase price (cash outflow) and dividends and sales proceeds (cash inflows) at the end of the holding period.

If the holding period is one year:

$$TSR = Div + (P_1 - P_0)/P_0$$

The TSR of the company may be compared with that of the peer group to evaluate performance. More important, executives may be encouraged to be in the top 10 per cent of the peer group year after year.

The top 50 companies in the S&P 500 delivered an average TSR of 23.8 per cent between July 2013 and June 2016. The bottom 50 companies' TSR averaged 1.4 per cent, while the average for all of the scored S&P 500 companies was 12.2 per cent. The top 50's median TSR was 18.7 per cent; the bottom 50's was 2.1 per cent.[2]

Another measure of value is the CFROI. It is similar to the IRR of a project. It compares the cumulative cash invested in a business with the cash the business is producing while recognizing the importance of asset ages, asset lives and inflation. HOLT Value Associates measures CFROI in two steps: First, the inflation-adjusted cash flow available to all capital owners is compared with the inflation-adjusted gross investment made by the capital owners. HOLT then translates the ratio of gross cash flow to gross investment into an IRR.

The Balanced Scorecard popularized by Kaplan and Norton recognizes the fact that executives do not focus on one set of measures, as no single measure can provide a clear performance target or focus attention on the critical areas of business.[3] The Balanced Scorecard allows managers to look at their business from the perspective of customers, shareholders and employees. A typical Balanced Scorecard shown in Figure 24.1 considers goals and measures from various perspectives and tries to bring all the elements of the business together in a single management report.

The Balanced Scorecard could serve as the focal point for the organization's efforts communicating priorities to managers, employees, investors and customers. It is important to understand that performance measurement is an important aspect of strategy. What gets measured gets managed. The Balanced Scorecard tries to measure the capital allocation efficiency of executives from various perspectives. From a purely financial perspective, ROI, cash flow, project profitability and sales booking might be the relevant measures, whereas from a customer's perspective, customer satisfaction index, customer

---

[2] www.chiefexecutive.net

[3] Kaplan and Norton, 'The Balanced Scorecard'; 'Putting the Balanced Scorecard to Work' and 'Linking the Balanced Scorecard to Strategy'.

FIGURE 24.1
The Balanced Scorecard

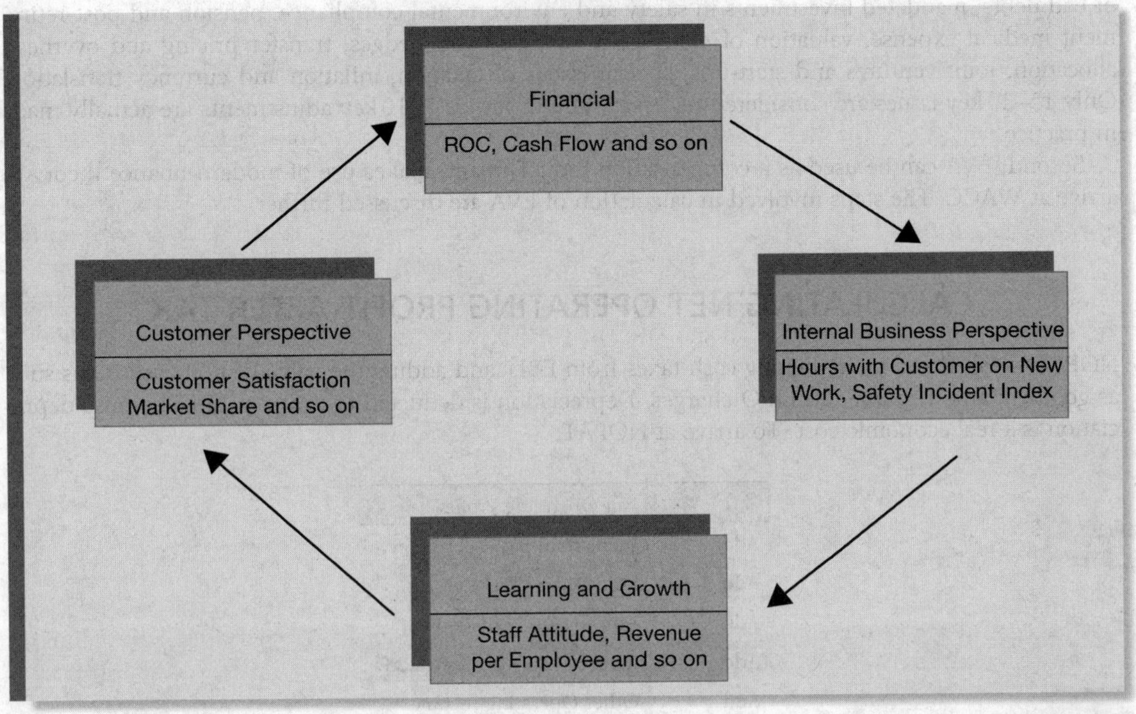

ranking survey, market share might be the relevant measures. A company can start by assessing its current position on these perspectives and arrive at the priority areas where attention is required. The question is: Are Balanced Scorecard and EVA substitutes or complementary? The answer is: they are complementary and are very effective when used together. The Balanced Scorecard is an excellent tool that can help managers track the many factors that influence performance. But it lacks a single focus for accountability. EVA provides it. The Balanced Scorecard broadens the view of performance and EVA provides a link between decisions, performance measures and rewards.

Under the 'residual income' (RI) method, an explicit cost of capital is specified for the investment centre and is applied on the investment base to arrive at the capital charge. To illustrate, if the invested capital is ₹100,000 and EBIT is ₹40,000, the RI at a capital cost of 15 per cent would be:

$$\begin{aligned} RI &= EBIT - (\text{Cost of Capital} \times \text{Invested Capital}) \\ &= 40{,}000 - (0.15 \times 100{,}000) \\ &= ₹25{,}000 \end{aligned}$$

EVA differs from RI method in several ways. First, it does not take balance sheet numbers directly since a balance sheet is prepared on historical cost basis. Accounting adjustments are made to produce a balance sheet that reflects economic values of assets in place and remove the effect of managers' focus on current earnings. Stern Stewart & Co. considers about 250 accounting adjustments in moving to EVA. In defining and refining its EVA measure, Stern Stewart & Co has identified over 120 shortcomings in conventional accounting. In addition to GAAP's inability to handle R&D and other corporate investments, Stern Stewart & Co has addressed performance measurement problems associated with accounting treatments of inventory costing and valuation, depreciation, revenue recognition, write-off of bad debts, mandated investments in safety and environmental compliance, pension and post-retirement medical expense, valuation of contingent liabilities and hedges, transfer pricing and overhead allocation, joint ventures and start-ups, special issues of taxation, inflation and currency translation. Only 15–20 key issues are considered necessary and as few as 5–10 key adjustments are actually made in practice.

Second, EVA can be used as a compensation tool. Third, it makes use of modern finance theory to arrive at WACC. The steps involved in calculation of EVA are discussed further.

CALCULATING NET OPERATING PROFIT AFTER TAX

NOPAT is calculated by deducting cash taxes from EBIT and adding the value of non-cash items such as goodwill amortization and LIFO charges. Depreciation is deducted to arrive at EBIT because depreciation is a real economic cost. To arrive at NOPAT:

	Net Operating Profits
Add	Increase in Bad Debt Reserve
Add	Increase in LIFO Reserve
Add	Amortization of Goodwill
Add	Increase in Capitalized R&D
Add	Other Operating Income
Deduct	Cash Operating Taxes

Where cash operating tax is defined as provision for income taxes less the increase in the deferred income tax reserve, plus the tax saved by unusual loss (gain), plus the tax saved by deducting interest expense.

That is, NOPAT = Net Sales − Cost of Sales − SG&A + Goodwill Amortization − Deferred Taxes + Tax Shield from Interest Expense − Taxes on Interest Income

CALCULATING INVESTED CAPITAL

The capital charge is to be applied on the economic book value of cash invested in business activities. To arrive at invested capital:

Total Assets
Less: Non-Interest Bearing Current Liabilities
Less: Marketable Securities and Construction in Progress
Add: Present Value of Non-Capitalized Leases
Add: Equity Equivalent Reserves[4]

[4] LIFO reserve is added to inventories, bad debt reserves are added to receivables, the cumulative amortization of goodwill is added back to goodwill, R&D expense is capitalized as a long-term asset and smoothly depreciated over five years.

EVA is a useful tool for divisional performance appraisal. The objective of divisional performance appraisal is to trace the overall performance to its constituent units. By separately measuring the performance of individual business units, operating managers can be held responsible for operations that are directly under their control and hence for creation or destruction of value. Rewarding divisional managers using company-wide measures will allow them to have free lunch at the expense of others. EVA can be calculated for each of the divisions and used as a performance measure. Computation of EVA involves calculation of NOPAT and WACC for each of the divisions. The WACC for the division could be calculated based on the division's target debt to value ratio, if it has one, or the firm's target may be taken as proxy for each of the divisions. Since, almost by definition, divisions are unlisted, stock market data will not be available to estimate cost of equity. The pure play technique can be used to estimate divisional cost of capital. The cost of debt could be estimated using prevailing yields on comparable debt instruments.

One might be tempted to reward those divisional managers who are reporting positive EVA and penalize those reporting negative EVA. A negative divisional EVA by itself does not tell us the whole story. One division might be subsidizing the other and hence reporting lower earnings and profits. The divisional EVA does not take synergies between divisions into account.[5]

EVA CENTRES

A positive EVA or an improvement in EVA does not happen by chance or luck. It is the product of concentrated effort by all functions in the organization. EVA can be used to measure the efficiency of each department and the department's contribution towards firm-wide EVA. In real-life situations, however, measuring departmental EVAs could be difficult. Manufacturing, almost by definition, does not have revenues but the investment in assets will be higher than that in other departments. Consequently, EVA will be negative. Marketing, on the other hand, will have lower investment needs but has revenues and profits. EVA will obviously be positive. The solution to this problem is to set transfer prices for interdepartmental transfers of goods and services. An external party's quoted price may be taken as proxy after making some adjustments. If the organization's costs are more than the price at which it can be outsourced, then there is clear incentive to outsource rather than make it in house. It is possible to treat each department as contracting with each other just as the firm would have contracted with an external party.[6] Each party is required to make payments for the services availed. The contract is enforced even if conditions change. For instance, marketing department cannot hold production department responsible for increases in cost due to volume shortfall. It should continue to buy capacity.

In general, an EVA centre represents a separate business unit. Selecting EVA centres could be problematic, especially for multinationals. Such companies will have to restate balance sheet and income statements of all subsidiaries in the home currency. In addition, there could be transfer–pricing issues. One solution is to organize the company along businesses rather than location.

In summary, internal departments behave like independent companies. The transfer price is the opportunity cost of the product or service, or the value foregone by not using the product or service transferred in its next best alternative use. In practice, however, it is difficult to obtain or costly to estimate transfer prices for all goods. Also, in real-life situations it might be difficult to find the next best

---

[5] Zimmerman, 'EVA and Divisional Performance Measurement'.

[6] Glassman, 'Contracting for Value'.

use for the resource. Often, all concerned parties negotiate a price. It should be noted that there could be internal resistance to such an exercise because of greater accountability.

EVA AND MVA

Another reliable measure of management's long-run success in adding value is market value added (MVA). The aim of management is to maximize the amount by which the company's market value exceeds the capital supplied by the firm's investors. MVA is the difference between the company's current market value, as determined the market price of its securities and its economic book value.

$$\text{MVA} = \text{Market Capitalization} - \text{Invested Capital}$$

where Market Capitalization = Market Value of Debt and Equity

Invested Capital = Book Value of Debt and Equity Including Equity Equivalent Reserves Like R&D Expenses

Thus, if a company's market value of debt and equity are ₹100 million and the adjusted book value of capital is ₹50 million, the MVA is ₹50 million. A negative MVA implies that the company will generate returns below its cost of capital, whereas a positive MVA implies the opposite. If MVA is a better indicator of performance, why calculate EVA? MVA has a limitation. MVA cannot be calculated for privately held firms and non-profit organizations as they are not listed on stock exchange.

Studies in the USA have shown that there is a high degree of correlation between EVA growth and MVA. Since EVA is correlated with MVA, increase in EVA results in higher MVA. At the company level, MVA is simply the present value of future EVAs.

The relationship between EVA and NPV

EVA is defined as

$$\text{EVA} = \text{NOPAT} - (\text{WACC} \times \text{Net Assets})$$

The present value of this equation is:

$$\sum_{i=1}^{\infty}\{\text{EVA}/(1+k)^t\} = \sum_{i=1}^{\infty}\{\text{NOPAT}/(1+k)^t\} - \sum_{i=1}^{\infty}\{k \times \text{NA}\}/(1+k)^t \quad (1)$$

where k = WACC

If we assume that the net asset base of the company remains constant, that is, depreciation equals capital expenditure and increase in working capital requirement,

$$\text{NOPAT}_t = \text{Cash Flow}_t \text{ and Net Assets}_{t-1} = \text{Net Assets}_t = \text{Net Assets (a constant)}$$

The present value of Equation (1) can be written as:

$$\text{PV of EVA} = \text{PV of Cash flows} - \sum_{i=1}^{\infty}\{(\text{K} \times \text{NA})/(1+\text{K})^t\}$$

Since, net assets, NA is a constant,

$$\text{PV of EVA} = \text{PV of Cash Flows} - \text{NA} \sum\{(K)/(1+K)^t\}$$
$$\text{PV of EVA} = \text{PV of Cash Flows} - \text{Net Assets} = \text{NPV}$$

At a project level, the present value of the future EVAs equals the NPV derived from the DCF methodology. The difference between the two is that EVA is a flow measure and NPV is a stock measure. Further, NPV is a summary measure based on projected cash flows and not realized performance. Compensation is to be tied to actual (periodic) performance as and when it is realized and not projected cash flows. Consequently, NPV cannot be used as an executive compensation tool.[7]

CONTROVERSY SURROUNDING EVA

A financial performance measure must be highly correlated with changes in shareholder wealth where shareholder wealth is defined as the abnormal return (also called alpha) earned by shareholders in any given period, that is,

$$\text{Abnormal Return} = \text{Actual Return} - \text{Expected Return (As Measured by CAPM)}$$

A firm derives its value from two sources: Assets in place and future growth opportunities. Balance sheets prepared by accountants capture the value of assets in place. Stern Stewart & Co considers a number of accounting adjustments to produce an economic balance sheet which reflects the value of assets in place more accurately than the balance sheet prepared by accountants. But it still does not produce a market value balance sheet that would capture the value of future growth opportunities. Further, EVA is calculated by deducting a capital charge on the 'economic book value' of assets using WACC based on 'market value weights' (from NOPAT). Apparently there's a problem. Bacidore et al.[8] propose that a variant of EVA, called Refined EVA (REVA), be used in which the capital charge is applied on the 'market' value of the firm. They conclude that:

- Both EVA and REVA are positively correlated with abnormal returns.
- The market rewards the unexpected increases in EVA. So rewarding managers for total EVA results in rewarding managers for inferior performance.
- REVA contains information not captured in EVA that is relevant for predicting abnormal returns.
- REVA could be used to compensate senior executives and EVA could be used to compensate those at lower levels.

But, according to finance theory, no single measure of operating performance is supposed to be correlated with abnormal stock returns. An operating decision can add substantial value in the period in which it is made even if it reduces that period's operating performance and there is no reason to expect an appropriate measure of one period's operating performance to be significantly correlated with the same period's abnormal stock returns.[9]

---

[7] Bacidore et al., 'EVA and Total Quality Management'.

[8] Bacidore et al., 'The Search for the Best Financial Performance Measure'.

[9] Ferguson and Leistikow, 'Search for the Best Financial Performance Measure'.

IS EVA CORRELATED WITH STOCK RETURNS?

If EVA is indeed the magic bullet that captures something net income and cash flow from operations do not, we would expect EVA to be more closely associated with stock returns and firm values than net income and CFO. Academic research does not support this hypothesis.[10] The researchers examined a sample of 6,174 firm-years over the period 1984–1993. As a test of association, they use adjusted R^2 from a regression of stock returns on each performance metric. Their study indicates that current period accounting earnings is significantly more highly associated with market-adjusted annual stock returns than are RI and EVA. Another study of 274 US companies suggests that the correlation between EVA with shareholder value is only 17.66 per cent; 60 companies (in the sample) had negative EVA but created positive shareholder value; 64 companies had positive EVA but destroyed shareholder value!

DOES IMPLEMENTING EVA RESULT IN BETTER PERFORMANCE?

Companies contemplating on implementing EVA or any other metric would want to make sure that they get their money's worth. If the experience of some of the companies that have implemented EVA is any indication, then EVA seems to be the answer. Herman Miller is a US$2 billion office furniture company. Between 1990 and 1995, the company's sales grew at an annual rate of 4.2 per cent and EVA was a negative US$127 million. Herman Miller adopted EVA as the primary performance metric and compensation tool in 1996 (Glassman 2001). EVA has grown from –US$23 million in 1995 to US$88 million in 2000. Sales have grown by 12.3 per cent and stock price by 28.4 per cent. It is important to understand that refining performance measurement alone will not help a company. Often underperforming companies may have to change other key business processes such as manufacturing, marketing and procurement. A company may have to reinvent a business model if there is a need.

Obviously one cannot generalize the benefits of implementing EVA by observing one company. To find out whether firms adopting RI-based measures create more wealth for shareholders by changing their operating, investing and financing decisions, researchers have compared the actions of companies that have adopted RI-based incentives with those of non-adopters.[11] The percentage relative change, that is, average percentage changes in selected actions of firms that adopt RI-based incentives is given further:

% Relative Change In				
Asset Turnover	Asset Dispositions	Asset Investments	Share Repurchases	Dividends per Share
14	100	–20	112	1

Operating decisions that use invested capital more efficiently will boost NOPAT. So we would expect companies resorting to RI-based incentives to increase asset turnover, reallocate capital to more profitable activities by increasing divestitures and decreasing new investments. Academic findings are consistent with these expectations.

[10] Biddle, Bowen and Wallace, 'Does EVA Beat Earnings?'

[11] Wallace, 'Adopting Residual Income Based Compensation Plans'; Biddle, Bowen and Wallace, 'Evidence on EVA'.

EVA AND EXECUTIVE COMPENSATION

The objective of incentive compensation is to make managers behave like owners. They should identify themselves with the fortunes of the company. Incentive compensation plans are usually administered by consultants. There are as many types of plans as there consultants. One of the measures of managerial performance is the appreciation in the stock price or stock returns derived from stock prices. Tying executive compensation to stock prices requires managers to take on too much risk. Moreover, stock prices are affected by extraneous factors not controllable by executives. EVA does not suffer from this drawback. It is a useful tool for executive compensation. Indeed, EVA is more a compensation tool than a financial management tool. Executives can be paid for the performance of the entire company or of their own division. For instance, at Eastman Chemical Company, compensation is determined by the performance of the entire company. But this leads to the free lunch problem. Some companies form groups of business units and managers are responsible not only for their own divisional EVA but also that of entire group. Some companies link divisional pay to other divisions' performance. Some supplement objective measures with subjective criteria. Executives should understand the need to maximize the value of not only their division but also that of other divisions that complement their resources and efforts. In a group incentive scheme, a plant or business unit sets financial or operational performance target. If the unit hits the target, everybody gets a payout. If the unit exceeds the target, the payout increases. Typically, executives get several times the incentive opportunity for rank and file employees.

The EVA compensation system has two components—cash bonus plan and leveraged stock option plan.[12] The cash bonus plan rewards improvements in EVA rather than absolute EVA in order to reward value addition due to managerial efforts as in the case of a business turnaround. The EVA bonus does not have a ceiling. Executives can earn unlimited amounts depending on their performance. A part of the annual bonus award is held in a bonus bank, which is distributed only if there is a continuous improvement in EVA. Usually two-thirds of the bonus is carried forward. The EVA targets are set by a predetermined formula and not by annual negotiation. EVA compensation encourages performers to stay on and pursue their business plans aggressively and forces under performers to leave.

Under the leveraged stock option plan, managers are given the option to buy shares (unlimited) at a discount to the prevailing market price. But the managers are not allowed to exercise their option immediately. The option is held in a bank. The exercise price of the option increases at a rate that reflects the cost of capital for the company. To illustrate, the strike price increases by 15 per cent if the cost of capital is 15 per cent during the planning period. Managers win only if the stock price rises at a faster rate than strike price. Managers use a part of their cash bonus awards to make leveraged purchase of stock.

A leveraged equity purchase plan has three features (Stewart 1990):

- Most of the purchase price for the shares is financed through a loan from the company secured solely by a pledge of the stock.
- The rest of the purchase price (say, 10%) comes from managers' personal wealth.
- The loan from the company accrues interest at a rate equal to the company's cost of capital.

The leveraged equity purchase plan is not to be confused with executive stock options which many companies grant their employees. Executive stock options are call options which give the holder the

[12] Stern, Stewart and Chew Jr, 'The EVA Financial Management System'.

right but not the obligation to purchase a company's shares at a specified exercise price. These are mostly at-the-money options, which means that the exercise price matches the stock price at the time of grant. The options usually come with certain restrictions: They cannot be sold to a third party and they must be exercised before a stipulated period of time (say, 10 years). Many of them also have a vesting period (say, 3–5 years) before which the executive cannot exercise the option.

Calculation of incentive compensation under the EVA system involves four steps:

- Establish a bonus target equal to a certain percentage of base pay (say, 35%). The executive earns the target bonus if the bonus unit is valued at US$1.0
- Establish a baseline EVA level. The EVA for the following year changes by a specified percentage of the difference between the actual EVA achieved and the baseline EVA for the prior year. This makes the system self-adjusting.
- A base unit value is established for each ensuing year. The base unit value indicates the target bonus amount an executive can earn by hitting the baseline EVA. To illustrate, if the base unit value is US$0.8 in a year, simply repeating the EVA baseline performance will produce only 80 per cent of the target bonus.
- Establish a bonus sensitivity factor (say, US$1,500,000) which is added to or subtracted from the base unit value to create a total unit value.

REASONS FOR FAILURE

Not all incentive plans succeed in achieving their objectives. Most of them end up causing more harm than good. There could be several reasons for such failures depending on the specific circumstances under which the plan is administered. Some of the common reasons are:

- Inadequate Incentives: If the incentives are not sufficiently high, employees might not be adequately motivated to achieve the target.
- Delinking Pay and Performance: Some companies set the bonus as a per cent of salary regardless of performance under the belief that short-term individual performance of executives cannot be measured. This is not true. Profitability indeed depends on a number of short-term decisions such as make versus buy made by individuals and these are not group decisions. This is especially true of managers in any well-run company with decentralization of powers.
- Complexity of the Performance Metric:

  Given below is a plan

  Bonus = 0.8 [SQRT {0.982 + (1.16 PAT × 0.8 Sales Growth)}] + [0.2 × Base Salary] if PAT is in between US$650 million and US$750 million

  Bonus = 0, if PAT is less than US$650 million and if sales growth is less than the average for the industry.

  Bonus = 120 per cent of normal if PAT is more than US$750 million and if sales growth rate beats the average growth for the industry by 10 per cent.

  Does this make sense? One of the prerequisites of a performance metric is that it should be simple and well understood by all.
- Too many Measures: All too often, companies insist on one set of measures such as profit after tax, sales growth, cash flow, inventory turns and so on all through the year but tie compensation to totally different set of measures. In so far as these measures are correlated with each other and

with the objective of the firm, that is, creating shareholder value, there is no problem. Too many measures simply confuse managers and employees, and lead the company astray. The EVA compensation plan does not suffer from this shortcoming.

Some companies tie compensation to a matrix built around sales growth and profitability. To illustrate, if the target bonus for an executive is 40 per cent, and the unit provided return on assets of 23 per cent and sales growth of 10 per cent, the manager might receive the target bonus of 40 per cent, else he/she may receive bonus according to a pre-specified formula.

- Rewarding Employees for the Means Rather than the End Result and Concentrating

  High Value Activities in the Hands of Few: Common sense suggests that human beings tend to maximize 'their' earnings. In those organizations, where compensation is tied to activities (that are supposed to lead to results), demand for high value activities will obviously be high and those entrenched in the organization will simply not allow newcomers to contribute leading to heart burns and employee defection.

IMPROVING EVA

There are three ways to improve EVA. The first is to grow the business by taking on new investments that promise to earn more than the cost of capital. The second way is to improve the efficiency of the existing business and increasing the return on existing capital. The third way is to get rid of those parts of the business that are not promising. EVA encourages managers to change behaviour by improving profits, investing money in projects with positive ROIC–WACC spread, eliminating investment in projects where returns are inadequate, focusing on cash flows.

Stern Stewart & Co has developed a management tool called 'EVA drivers' that helps management to trace EVA through the income statement and balance sheet to key operating and strategic levers available to the company. This tool is useful in diagnosing performance, benchmarking peer's planning and helping employees understand their role in creating value. The manufacturing EVA drivers, for instance, are:

- Reduce inventory
- Improve yields
- Reduce waste
- Improve labour efficiency
- Improving process

Likewise, marketing EVA drivers are:

- Increase market share/revenue
- Advertising
- Sales promotion
- Brand awareness

CONCLUDING COMMENTS

Choosing that metric that has the highest correlation with shareholder value is a good idea. But the benefits from implementing the metric should exceed the potential costs. The obvious benefit from implementing the metric is the additional shareholder value created (assuming that managers deliver goods). Some of the metrics require training of all executives involved in the process. The training entails cash outlay. Additional records need to be maintained apart from the normal accounting records; periodic audits are necessary; managers may resort to 'gaming', that is, increase their payoff without adding any value to shareholders. A company should choose a metric that has the highest benefit to cost ratio.

Implementation of EVA incentive system proceeds in three steps:

- Analyse businesses on EVA parameters, benchmark them against peers understand shareholders expectations and work out historical and future EVAs.
- Train managers to optimize EVA.
- Introduce an incentive compensation plan for all employees.

The characteristics of a sound compensation plan are:

- It should be perceived as fair.
- Employees should find it exciting.
- It should be linked to the business strategy.
- It should encourage ideas from employees to boost performance.

EXERCISES

1. The following data are available for a company for the period 1985–1989.

(₹ 000)

	2014	2015	2016	2017	2018
NOPAT	235,029	270,140	281,950	296,642	362,744
Beginning Capital	1,430,280	1,981,285	2,551,826	2,901,126	3,465,870
Long-Term Debt	1,013,967	2,152,208	2,577,134	1,546,824	3,255,236
Avg Shares Outstanding	46,970	49,840	51,905	52,670	52,272
Share Price	58	66	44	49	45
Tax Rate (%)	45	46	34	34	34
T-bond Rate (%)	10.74	8.14	8.76	9.11	8.62
Yield on the Company's Bond (%)	12.19	10.37	10.55	10.75	10.35
Beta	1.35	1.3	1.15	1.10	1.10

Calculate EVA, cumulative annual EVA and percentage change in cumulative EVA between 2014 and 2018. If the book value of equity is US$815,000 in 1985, calculate MVA.

2. A company is in the process of estimating EVA for two of its divisions—Beverages and Restaurants. The estimation of EVA requires an estimate of divisional cost of capital. The industry beta and average debt ratio for several industry groups is given further.

Industry	Industry Lev. Beta	Cost of Equity (%)	Cost of Debt %	Debt/ Capital (%)	Cost of Capital %
Aerospace	0.68	8.6	9.1	38.6	7.3
Airlines	0.89	10.8	9.8	70.4	7.4
Beverages	0.89	10	8.1	45.7	9.3
Cars & Trucks	1.03	12.4	8.5	46.6	8.7
Computers &	1.36	12.9	8.6	30.7	12.7
Peripherals Electronics	1.51	14.1	10.6	39.1	13.5
Oil & Gas	0.60	7.9	8.6	46.7	6.9
Restaurants	0.80	9.5	10	46.4	8.6

The Beverages division has a target debt/value ratio of 40 per cent and the Restaurants division has a target debt ratio of 35 per cent. Calculate the cost of equity for the divisions assuming a risk-free rate of 6 per cent and a risk premium of 7.5 per cent.

REFERENCES

Bacidore, J., J. M. Bacidore, J. A. Boquist, T. T. Milbourn and
A. V. Thakor. 'EVA and Total Quality Management'. *Journal of Applied Corporate Finance* 10, no. 2 (1997a Summer).

Bacidore, J. M., J. A. Boquist, T. T. Milbourn and A. V. Thakor. 'The Search for the Best Financial Performance Measure'. *Financial Analysts Journal* (1997b May–June).

Biddle, G., R. Bowen and J. S. Wallace. 'Does EVA Beat Earnings? Evidence on Associations with Stock Returns and Firm Values'. *Journal of Accounting and Economics* 24, no. 3 (1997 Dec).

Biddle, G. C., R. M. Bowen and J. S. Wallace. 'Evidence on EVA'. *Journal of Applied Corporate Finance* 12, no. 2 (1999 Summer).

Ferguson, R. and D. Leistikow. 'Search for the Best Financial Performance Measure: Basics Are Better'. *Financial Analysts Journal* (1998 January/February).

Fernandez, P. 'Shareholder Value Creators and Shareholder Value Destroyers in USA: Year 2000' (IESE Research Papers D/485, IESE Business School, 2001, 4 June).

Glassman, D. 'Contracting for Value: EVA and the Economics of Organizations'. *Journal of Applied Corporate Finance* 10, no. 2 (1997 Summer).

Glassman D. and H. Miller. 'Growth in the new economy'. *EVAluation*, 3, no. 1 (2001 February).

Kaplan, R. S. and D. Norton. 'The Balanced Scorecard—Measures That Drive Performance'. *Harvard Business Review* (1992 Jan–Feb).

Kaplan, R. S. and D. Norton. 'Putting the Balanced Scorecard to Work'. *Harvard Business Review* (1993 Sep–Oct).

Kaplan, R. S. and D. Norton. 'Linking the Balanced Scorecard to Strategy'. *California Management Review* 39, no. 1 (1996).

Stern, Joel, Bennett Stewart and Donald Chew Jr. 'The EVA Financial Management System'. *Journal of Applied Corporate Finance* 8, no. 2 (1995 Summer).

Stewart B. G. 'Rethinking Rewards'. *Harvard Business Review* (1993 November–December)

Wallace, J. 'Adopting Residual–Income Based Compensation Plans: Do You Get What You Pay For?' *Journal of Accounting and Economics* 24, no. 3 (1997 Dec).

Zimmerman, J. L. 'EVA and Divisional Performance Measurement: Capturing Synergies and other Issues'. *Journal of Applied Corporate Finance* 10, no. 2 (1997 Summer).

SUGGESTED READINGS

Baker, G., M. C. Jensen and K Murphy. 'Compensation and Incentives: Practice Versus Theory'. *Journal of Finance* 43, no. 3 (1988 July).

Brickley, J., C. Smith and J. L. Zimmerman. 'Transfer Pricing and the Control of Internal Transactions'. *Journal of Applied Corporate Finance* 8, no. 2 (1995 Summer).

Brennan, M. J. 'Executive Compensation in UK'. *Journal of Applied Corporate Finance* 9, no. 1 (1996 Spring).

Ehrbar, Al. *EVA: The Real Key to Creating Wealth*. Hoboken, NJ: John Wiley and Sons, 1998.

Glassman, D. 'Twelve Ways to Strengthen Your Incentive Plan'. *Journal of Applied Corporate Finance* 12, no. 2 (1999 Summer).

Jensen, M. C. and W. H. Meckling. 'Divisional Performance Measurement'. In *Foundations of Organizational Strategy*, edited by M. C. Jensen. Cambridge, MA: Harvard University Press, 1998.

Murphy, K. J. 'Executive Compensation'. In *Handbook of Labour Economics*, vol. 3, edited by Orley Ashenfelter and David Card. Amsterdam: North Holland, 1999.

Rappaport, A. 'New thinking on How to Link Executive Pay with Performance'. *Harvard Business Review* (1999 March–April).

Salter, M. 'What is Fair Pay for the Executive'. *Harvard Business Review* (1972 May–June).

Stern, Joel, Bennett Stewart and Donald Chew Jr. 'EVA: Fact and Fancy'. *Journal of Applied Corporate Finance* 7, no. 2 (1994 Summer).

Teaching Cases

MODULE 1

Risk and Return

1

ICICI Prudential*

LEARNING OBJECTIVE

The case can be used to discuss the risk and return of investing in stocks, mutual fund performance measurement and hedging using derivative instruments.

Description: The case highlights the performance of a mutual fund and the need to lock in the fund's alpha. Students are introduced to two derivative instruments to manage the volatility of fund returns and are asked to evaluate these alternatives.

INTRODUCTION

In January 2017, the manager of ICICI Prudential Value Fund Series 7 (D), was concerned with protecting the value of his fund portfolio. High volatility in equities (see Figure M1.1 and Table M1.1), uncertainty in the political and economic environment posed challenges to delivering abnormal returns. Over the previous three years, the fund had delivered spectacular returns both in relation to market indices (Nifty Index and S&P BSE 500 index) and other comparable funds (Table M1.2).[1] From the fund manager's perspective, the issue whether the fund had indeed outperformed relevant benchmarks and how he could hedge the risk of stock market volatility, and what impact it would have on the fund's performance.

COMPANY BACKGROUND

ICICI Prudential Asset Management Company (AMC) Ltd. was one of the top AMCs in India. ICICI Prudential provided investment solutions by creating simple and relevant investment solutions. The AMC was a joint venture between ICICI Bank, a top bank in India and Prudential Plc, one of UK's largest players in the financial services sector. The AMC managed significant assets in the mutual fund segment.

---

* This case was prepared by Durga Prasad and Kaushik Bhattacharjee of T. A. Pai Management Institute and Vishwanath S. R. from publicly available sources. Cases are not meant to demonstrate effective or ineffective handling of administrative situations. They are meant for class discussion.

[1] The standard deviation of ICICI's fund returns was 21.8 per cent.

FIGURE M1.1
Historical Performance of the Nifty Index[2]

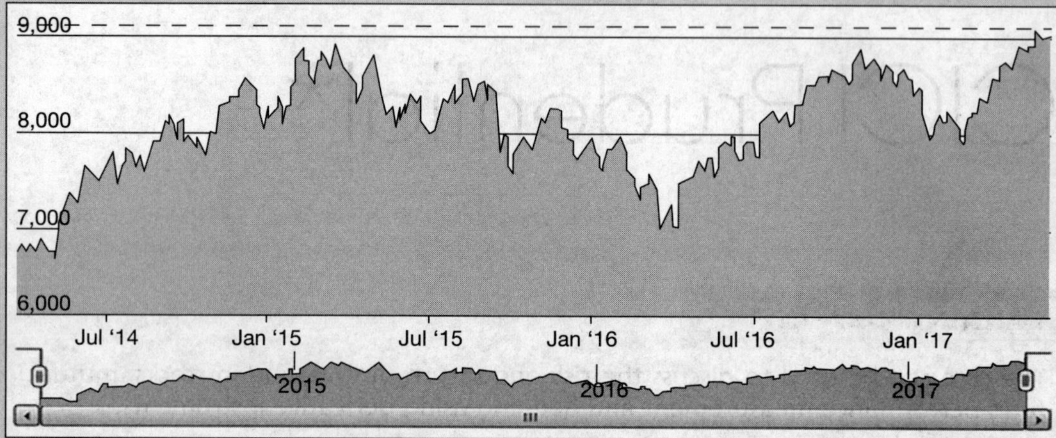

Source: http://profit.ndtv.com/market/domestic-index-nse_nifty/chart - 3 year horizon-date of retrieval January 30, 2017.

TABLE M1.1
Index Nifty 50 Closing Monthly Values (2016, Monthly)[3]

Month/Year	Jan	Feb	Mar	Apr	May	Jun
Nifty 50	7,563.55	6,987.05	7,738.4	7,849.8	8,160.1	8,287.75
Month/Year	Jul	Aug	Sep	Oct	Nov	Dec
Nifty 50	8,638.5	8,786.2	8,611.15	8,625.7	8,224.5	8,185.8

Source: Prowess IQ (1.4) http://www.moneycontrol.com/india/mutualfunds/mfinfo/portfolio_holdings/MPI2626, date of retrieval from the database 01/30/2017.

TABLE M1.2
Returns from icici fund and Its Peer Group (%)[4]

	1 Year	3 Years
ICICI Fund Series 7 (%)	17.83	44.96
Nifty Index Return (%)	3.0	10.1
BSE S&P 500 Index (%)	13.51	27.09
Category Funds, Average (%)	13.74	32.55
Fund Rank Within Category	8	2

[2] http://profit.ndtv.com/market/domestic-index-nse_nifty/chart (accessed 30 January 2017). Nifty was an acronym of the National Stock Exchange 50 Index. The index was widely used by the investment community.

[3] Prowess IQ (1.4) (accessed on 30 January 2017 from the database).

[4] https://www.valueresearchonline.com/funds/newsnapshot.asp?schemecode=30292 (accessed on 30 January 2017).

	1 Year	3 Years
HDFC Equity Fund (G)	25.8	19.4
ICICI Prudential Value Discovery Fund (G)	16.2	26.7
Reliance Equity Opportunities—Direct (G)	8.8	17.8
Franklin India Prima Plus	17.2	22.3
ICICI Prudential Recovery Series 2	33.09	NA
	1 Year	3 Years
ICICI Prudential Value Fund Series 7	17.83	44.96
ICICI Prudential Value Fund Series 6	30.08	NA
Reliance Capital Builder Fund II Series C	35.52	NA
Reliance Capital Builder Fund III Series A	29.08	NA

Source: https://www.valueresearchonline.com/funds/newsnapshot.asp?schemecode=30292 date of retrieval January 30, 2017.

The AMC provided portfolio management services by investing in different asset classes such as debt, equity and real estate. The AMC had witnessed substantial growth in scale. It had grown from two offices with six employees in 1998 to the present level of 153 offices with more than 1,100 employees reaching out to an investor base of more than 3 million investors.[5] The AMC focused more on providing products that yielded assured returns.

ICICI BANK

ICICI Bank, a wholly owned subsidiary of ICICI Limited, was initially promoted in 1994. ICICI was formed in 1955 at the initiative of the World Bank and the Government of India. The goal of ICICI was to provide project finance to businesses in India. In the 1990s, ICICI diversified its business from project finance to a variety of products and services through a number of subsidiaries and affiliates such as ICICI bank. In October 2001, the Boards of Directors of ICICI and ICICI Bank approved the merger of ICICI and two of its wholly owned retail finance subsidiaries, ICICI Personal Financial Services Limited and ICICI Capital Services Limited, with ICICI Bank. Consequent to the merger, the ICICI group's financing and banking operations, both wholesale and retail, were integrated into a single entity.[6] ICICI Bank was one of the leading banks in the private sector with total assets of ₹6,461.29 billion (US$103 billion) as on 31 March 2015 and a net income of ₹111.75 billion (US$1.78 billion) for the year ending 31 March 2015. ICICI Bank offered its services through its subsidiaries in the area of investment banking, personal and general insurance, venture capital and asset management.[7]

MUTUAL FUND INDUSTRY IN INDIA

The mutual fund industry India started in 1963 with the formation of Unit Trust of India, at the initiative of the Government of India and Reserve Bank of India. As on 30 April 2016, the assets under

[5] https://www.icicipruamc.com/AboutUs/CorporateProfile.aspx (accessed on 23 January 2017).
[6] https://www.icicibank.com/aboutus/history.page (accessed on 23 January 2017).
[7] https://www.icicipruamc.com/AboutUs/CorporateProfile.aspx (accessed on 23 January 2017).

management (AUM) in open-ended income schemes were ₹445.563 billion, and in close ended schemes ₹148.383 billion. According to the Associated Chambers of Commerce and Industry of India, 44 AMCs had set up operations since the liberalization of the Indian economy in 1993. The top seven AMCs had 70 per cent of the industry AUM. As on 31 March 2016, ICICI Prudential Mutual Fund was one of the largest fund houses in India.[8]

ICICI PRUDENTIAL VALUE FUND SERIES 7 REGULAR PLAN (D)

ICICI[9] Prudential Mutual Fund was a closed-ended fund.[10] The objective of this fund was to provide capital appreciation by investing in a well-diversified portfolio of stocks through fundamental analysis. The fund was launched in May 2015 with a face value of ₹10. The fund had ₹116.7 million worth of AUM as on 31 December 2016. Mr Atul Patel and Mr Shalya Shah managed this fund since May 2015. The fund focused on equities. The minimum investment in the fund was ₹5,000. The scheme would have a tenure of 1,100 days from the date of allotment of units.

Asset Allocation Pattern:[11] The fund was allowed to invest 80–100 per cent of the corpus in equity and equity-related instruments and up to 20 per cent in debt, money market instruments. The fund could also invest in derivatives up to 50 per cent of the net assets of the scheme. The scheme did not envisage investments in (a) repos in corporate debt securities,[12] (b) short selling of securities, (c) credit default swaps[13] and (d) equity-linked debentures. However, the fund was allowed to invest in American depository receipts/global depository receipts/foreign debt securities as permitted by Reserve Bank of India and Securities Exchange Board of India. Table 1.3 presents the details of portfolio holdings.

Investment Strategy:[14] The scheme aimed at providing long-term capital growth by investing in a well-diversified portfolio of equity and equity-related securities. The fund manager proposed to concentrate on business and economic fundamentals driven by in-depth research techniques and employing the full potential of the research team at the AMC. The stock selection process proposed to be adopted was generally a bottom approach seeking to identify companies with long-term sustainable competitive advantage. The fund would also use a top-down discipline for risk control by ensuring representation of companies from select sectors. As part of stock selection process, the fund studied parameters such as the price-to-book (P/B) ratio, price-to-earnings (P/E), dividend yields (D/Y) of companies. The scheme also examined companies with low P/B and P/E ratios. These companies had consistently paid dividends and were expected to pay attractive dividends in future too. The fund also studied other quantitative parameters such as ROE and Return on Capital Employed (ROCE) to identify stocks.

[8] https://mutualfundindia.com/Images/Research/PdfPaths/7a11b786a2c942b690db34e7c39db743Mutual%20Fund%20Screener%20-%20Mar%202016.pdf (accessed on 23 January 2017).

[9] http://www.moneycontrol.com/mutual-funds/nav/icici-prudential-value-fund-series-7-regular-plan/MPI2626 (accessed on 25 January 2017).

[10] Closed-ended funds issue a fixed number of shares at the time of inception and closes subscription for new investors at a specified date. In contrast, open-ended funds remain open to investors throughout the life of the fund. Once the initial capital is raised, fund managers invest the proceeds to buy a basket of securities. Shares in a closed-ended fund are not redeemable. They trade in the secondary market just like shares.

[11] Key information memorandum of the scheme which was publically available document.

[12] A repo is a repurchase agreement in which a dealer in government securities sells the securities to investors usually on an overnight basis and buys them back the following day.

[13] A credit default swap is an option where the risk seller pays a premium (measured in basis points of the nominal amount) to the risk buyer. In the case of a credit event, the risk buyer is paying a credit event payment. Common credit events include failure to pay, bankruptcy, cross-default, restructuring, merger and downgrading.

[14] Key information memorandum of the scheme which was publically available document.

TABLE M1.3
Portfolio Holdings as on 30 december 2016[15]

Equity	Sector	Qty.	Value (₹ million)	% Holding	Beta
HDFC Bank	Banking and Financial Services	7,942.00	9.6	0.10	1.00
KNR Constructions	Cement and Construction	49,825.00	8.5	0.09	0.78
ICICI Bank	Banking and Financial Services	29,069.00	7.4	0.08	1.96
Power Grid Corp	Utilities	33,215.00	6.1	0.06	0.81
Maruti Suzuki	Automotive	1,138.00	6.1	0.06	1.87
Tata Chemicals	Chemicals	11,280.00	5.7	0.06	1.79
Thomas Cook	Miscellaneous	30,085.00	5.6	0.06	0.28
Sundaram Finance	Banking and Financial Services	4,322.00	5.0	0.05	1.14
HCL Tech	Information Technology	5,786.00	4.8	0.05	0.09
Cipla	Pharmaceuticals	8,288.00	4.7	0.05	0.44
Bata India	Consumer Non-durables	9,958.00	4.5	0.05	1.14
Federal Bank	Banking and Financial Services	61,388.00	4.1	0.04	0.69
Mayur Uniquoters	Manufacturing	11,552.00	3.9	0.04	0.87
JK Lakshmi Cement	Cement and Construction	9,952.00	3.5	0.04	2.04
Bajaj Corp	Consumer Non-durables	9,157.00	3.4	0.04	0.33
GlaxoSmithKline Consumer	Food and Beverages	614	3.1	0.03	1.06
SRF	Manufacturing	1,787.00	2.8	0.03	1.83
Rallis India	Chemicals	14,248.00	2.7	0.03	1.49
Axis Bank	Banking and Financial Services	4,638.00	2.1	0.02	1.53
Coal India	Metals and Mining	6,770.00	2.0	0.02	0.13
(Weighted) Average					1.07

Source: http://www.moneycontrol.com/india/mutualfunds/mfinfo/portfolio_holdings/MPI2626 date of retrieval 01/30/2017; portfolio holding in Derivatives, CBLO, Net Current Assets not considered for this case; and Case writer estimates.

THE SITUATION IN EARLY 2017

The fund generated 17.83 per cent the last year and 44.96 per cent over the three-year period that the fund had operated. More recently, the fund had been ranked second from a universe of 40 funds. However, the fund returns were negative during the last quarter of 2016. Since poor performance reduced AUM, the fund manager was contemplating on minimizing market risk and locking in 'alpha'. In general, portfolio insurance appealed to 'safety first' investors and well-diversified funds that their managers believed to have positive alpha.[16]

To control the portfolio risk, the fund manager could go short on National Stock Exchange Nifty Index futures contracts. The lot size for a futures position was 75. Nifty 50 futures contracts had a maximum of three-month trading cycle—the near month (one), the next month (two) and the far month

[15] http://www.moneycontrol.com/india/mutualfunds/mfinfo/portfolio_holdings/MPI2626 (accessed on 30 January 2017; portfolio holding in derivatives, CBLO, net current assets not considered for this case; and case writer estimates).
[16] Leland, 'Who Should Buy Portfolio Insurance'.

(three). A new contract is introduced on the trading day following the expiry of the near month contract. The new contract would be introduced for a three-month duration. This way, at any point in time, there would be three contracts available for trading in the market, that is, one near month, one mid-month and one far month duration, respectively. Nifty 50 futures contracts expired on the last Thursday of the expiry month.

In preparing a hedging strategy, the fund manager's team prepared an analysis of price movements of his portfolio relative to the Nifty index. By regressing historical returns on ICICI's portfolio against movements in Nifty, the team determined the beta of the portfolio, which would be used in determining a hedge ratio (see Table 1.4).

TABLE M1.4
Statistical Analysis of ICICI'S Portfolio Versus the Nifty Index

Nifty = Nifty Weekly Price Returns

BSE 500 = BSE 500 Weekly Price Returns

ICICI = ICICI's Weekly Price Returns

Results of Regression:

ICICI = 0.032 + 0.234 × (BSE 500)

Adjusted R-Squared = 4.3%

ICICI = 0.01 + 0.075 × (Nifty)

Adjusted R Squared = –0.007

In addition to Nifty index futures, the fund manager could also buy a put option on the Nifty index. Nifty 50 options contracts have three consecutive monthly contracts, additionally three quarterly months of the cycle March/June/September/December and five following semi-annual months of the cycle June/December would be available, so that at any point in time there would be options contracts with at least 3-year tenure available. Table 1.5 presents the details of futures and put option contracts available as of 30 January 2017. Table 1.6 provides capital market data.

TABLE M1.5
Futures and Option Market Quotes[17]

Nifty Index Futures Prices (Contract Price = 75 Times the Index)					
Delivery Date	Open	High	Low	Settle	Open Interest
30 March 2017	8,669	8,708	8,682.8	8,682.8	1,057,575

TABLE M1.5 (*Continued*)
Options Quotes on Nifty Index[18]

Date	Expiry	Strike Price	Open	High	Low	Close	Settle Price	No. of Contracts	Open Interest	Underlying Value
30 Jan 2017	30 Mar 2017	9,100	448.05	448.05	448.05	448.05	448.05	2	6,675	8,632.75
30 Jan 2017	30 Mar 2017	9,500	800	800	800	800	800	1	10,050	8,632.75
30 Jan 2017	30 Mar 2017	7,500	12.65	13.1	12	12.85	12.85	883	470,400	8,632.75

17 National Stock Exchange.

18 The Nifty index had a dividend yield of 1.35 per cent.

Date	Expiry	Strike Price	Open	High	Low	Close	Settle Price	No. of Contracts	Open Interest	Underlying Value
30 Jan 2017	30 Mar 2017	7,600	13.75	16	13.75	15.2	15.2	165	143,625	8,632.75
30 Jan 2017	30 Mar 2017	7,700	17	18.5	16.7	18	18	599	358,950	8,632.75
30 Jan 2017	30 Mar 2017	7,800	22.1	23	20.55	22.05	22.05	729	339,075	8,632.75
30 Jan 2017	30 Mar 2017	7,900	27.35	29.95	25.55	28.15	28.15	2,149	354,825	8,632.75
30 Jan 2017	30 Mar 2017	8,000	34.45	36.25	31.85	35.15	35.15	3,655	944,475	8,,632.75
30 Jan 2017	30 Mar 2017	8,100	45.15	45.55	40.45	44.45	44.45	2,349	385,950	8,632.75
30 Jan 2017	30 Mar 2017	8,200	55.5	58	51.75	56.75	56.75	7,852	748,650	8,632.75
30 Jan 2017	30 Mar 2017	8,300	73.6	75.15	68.15	72.85	72.85	2,805	455,025	8,632.75
30 Jan 2017	30 Mar 2017	8,400	96.65	97.6	88	94.8	94.8	2,785	485,400	8,632.75
30 Jan 2017	30 Mar 2017	8,500	121.25	125.2	113.2	121.95	121.95	2,204	629,175	8,632.75
30 Jan 2017	30 Mar 2017	8,600	153.65	159.15	145.4	155	155	1,991	372,600	8,632.75
30 Jan 2017	30 Mar 2017	8,700	196.6	201.05	181.25	195.85	195.85	1,526	354,300	8,632.75
30 Jan 2017	30 Mar 2017	8,800	244.1	250.25	229.85	242.85	242.85	3,487	654,975	8,632.75
30 Jan 2017	30 Mar 2017	8,900	308.4	310	283.15	301.65	301.65	3,371	515,175	8,632.75
30 Jan 2017	30 Mar 2017	9,000	378.25	379.55	350.6	370.5	370.5	903	261,825	8,632.75

Source: National Stock Exchange.

TABLE M1.6
Capital Market Data (%)[19]

91-Day T-Bill (Primary) Yield	6.27
182-Day T-Bill (Primary) Yield	NA
364-Day T-Bill (Primary) Yield	6.25
10-Year Government Securities Yield	6.86

Three-month Nifty Index Volatility=9%
One-month Nifty Index Volatility=6%
Source: Reserve Bank of India, National Stock Exchange.

[19] Reserve Bank of India, National Stock Exchange.

EXERCISES

1. How has ICICI performed historically? In answering this question, you may estimate total and systematic risk, value at risk, market and risk adjusted portfolio returns.
2. Why manage risk? Why should ICICI Prudential manage the market risk?
3. What risks can the fund manager eliminate by shorting the index futures contracts? What futures position should ICICI take to hedge its position? How effective will this hedge be?
4. What return can the fund manager expect to earn assuming he adopts your hedging strategy?
5. Estimate the value of a put option on Nifty index at a strike price of 9,100 (see Table M1.5).

REFERENCE

Leland, Hayne. 'Who Should Buy Portfolio Insurance'. *Journal of Finance* 35 (1980).

MODULE 2

Cost of Capital, Capital Budgeting and Capital Structure

2

The Bolivian Tropical Wood Consortium*

LEARNING OBJECTIVE

To introduce estimation of discount rates in emerging markets, issues in capital budgeting

Description: The Tropical Wood Consortium spearheaded by Tahuamanu, the world leader in nut production, was formed in 2004 to explore investment opportunities in one of the most diverse and largely untapped forests of the world—the Bolivian Amazon. The project, if implemented, would give birth to the country's largest and technologically most advanced processing plant to produce 'ecologically sustainable' wood products. Students are asked to evaluate this prospective opportunity against the risk of investing in a country undergoing a severe political crisis.

> The blockades prevent us from meeting our contracts and we can soon be excluded from our main markets. Regaining them will be a hard task… we are losing clients, sales and overall exports are declining.
>
> —Osvaldo Barriga, President of the Bolivian Chamber of Exporters

> We really have the best of both worlds; access to the forestry resources and low production costs of Bolivia on the one hand, and the stability and more advanced infrastructure of Brazil on the other.
>
> —Enrique Nelkenbaum, Head of the Tropical Wood Consortium

This case was written by Irina Antsiverova, Nijat Valivev, Canan Avdemir and Oscar Farfan under the supervision of Professor Campbell Harvey of Fuqua School of Business, Duke University, USA.

On the morning of 15 January 2005, the boardroom of Tahuamanu's headquarters in La Paz looked more anxious than usual. Three days earlier, a riot had broken out in the city of Santa Cruz and several government buildings, including the city council and the airport, were taken by protesters. The Board was about to discuss a strategy to attract potential partners to invest in a forestry development project in the northern region of Bolivia. For Tahuamanu, the project was an opportunity to diversify into the profitable wood industry and create synergies with its core nut processing business. The ambitious endeavour, however, required an investment that was beyond the company's capacity. Tahuamanu had therefore decided to reach out to potential lenders including the Inter-American Investment Corporation (IIC) and International Finance Corporation (IFC), and equity partners who would be interested in investing in the Tropical Wood Consortium (TWC). The Consortium was also a way to diversify investment risks and foster strategic alliances with other companies within the industry. In an effort to promote the largely untapped forestry sector in Bolivia, the government, together with the International Forest Stewardship Council, had certified a large extension of forest to be exploited, thus attracting the interest of other potential competitors. The company's biggest challenge ahead was to put forward a convincing project that would persuade international partners and potential lenders to invest in a country undergoing severe political turmoil.

BOLIVIA

With a population of 8 million and a per capita GDP of US$900, Bolivia stood out as one of Latin America's smallest and poorest countries. Its economy was still highly dependent on minerals and hydrocarbon resources, which accounted for nearly 40 per cent of total GDP and 63 per cent of total exports. Bolivia had, nonetheless, agricultural and forestry potential, as it enjoyed one of the world's most diverse climates and a largely untapped forest in the Amazon region. Lack of productive infrastructure—including transportation, irrigation and electricity—along with poor financial intermediation had traditionally been the main roadblocks constraining the growth in these sectors. In the past two decades, World Bank support schemes along with the privileged access to Andean markets granted by the Comunidad Andina de Naciones (CAN) had allowed agriculture to flourish. With a threefold output increase in the 1990s, soybean was the fastest-growing product and had become the largest agricultural export earner. Other products such as sugar cane, maize and sunflower had also found profitable niches in neighbouring markets. Contrasting this dynamism was the largely untapped forestry sector, contributing to only 3.5 per cent of total exports. The World Bank estimated that the output of timber and manufactured wood products in Bolivia was 'far from realizing its full potential'. With over 1,000,000 hectares of forest recently certified by the Forest Stewardship Council, the Bolivian wood industry had the opportunity to expand in unprecedented proportions. Figure M2.1 presents the map of Bolivia.

ECONOMIC POLICY

After nearly three decades of military regimes and central planning, Bolivia introduced democracy in 1982 and embraced free market reforms in 1985. The abandonment of the state-led model was precipitated by an economic crises triggered by the collapse of international tin prices and a large-scale withdrawal of foreign loans. The orthodox policy package that initiated economic reforms came to be known as the New Economic Policy (NEP). The NEP was first introduced as a 'shock therapy' under an IMF-led

FIGURE M2.1
Map of Bolivia

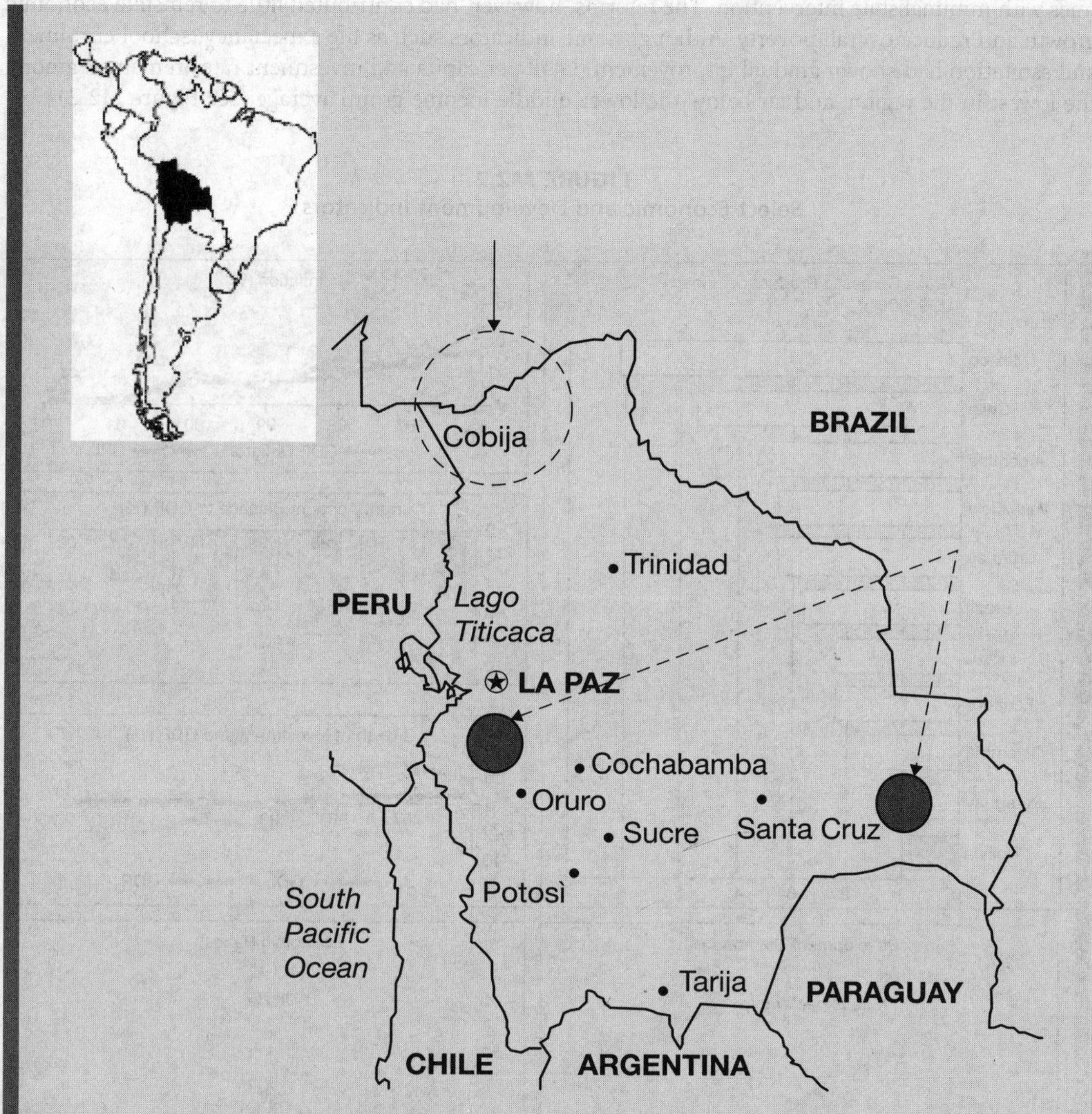

Note: This figure is not to scale. It does not represent any authentic national or international boundaries and is used for illustrative purposes only.

structural adjustment programme, consisting in the simultaneous elimination of price controls, contraction of public spending and liberalization of both trade and capital markets. After successfully curbing inflation and restoring fiscal health, the NEP continued throughout the 1990s with a wide-ranging privatization programme that included all major state-owned enterprises.

In the past 20 years, Bolivia had managed to maintain low inflation rates, a stable exchange rate and a controlled trade balance. The NEP had also turned Bolivia into one of the region's most open economies with minimal state intervention. The reforms, however, had contributed little to reinstate economic growth and reduce overall poverty. Although some indicators such as life expectancy, school enrolment and sanitation had shown gradual improvement, GDP per capita and investment rates remained among the lowest in the region, and far below the lower middle income group average (see Figure M2.2).

FIGURE M2.2
Select Economic and Development Indicators

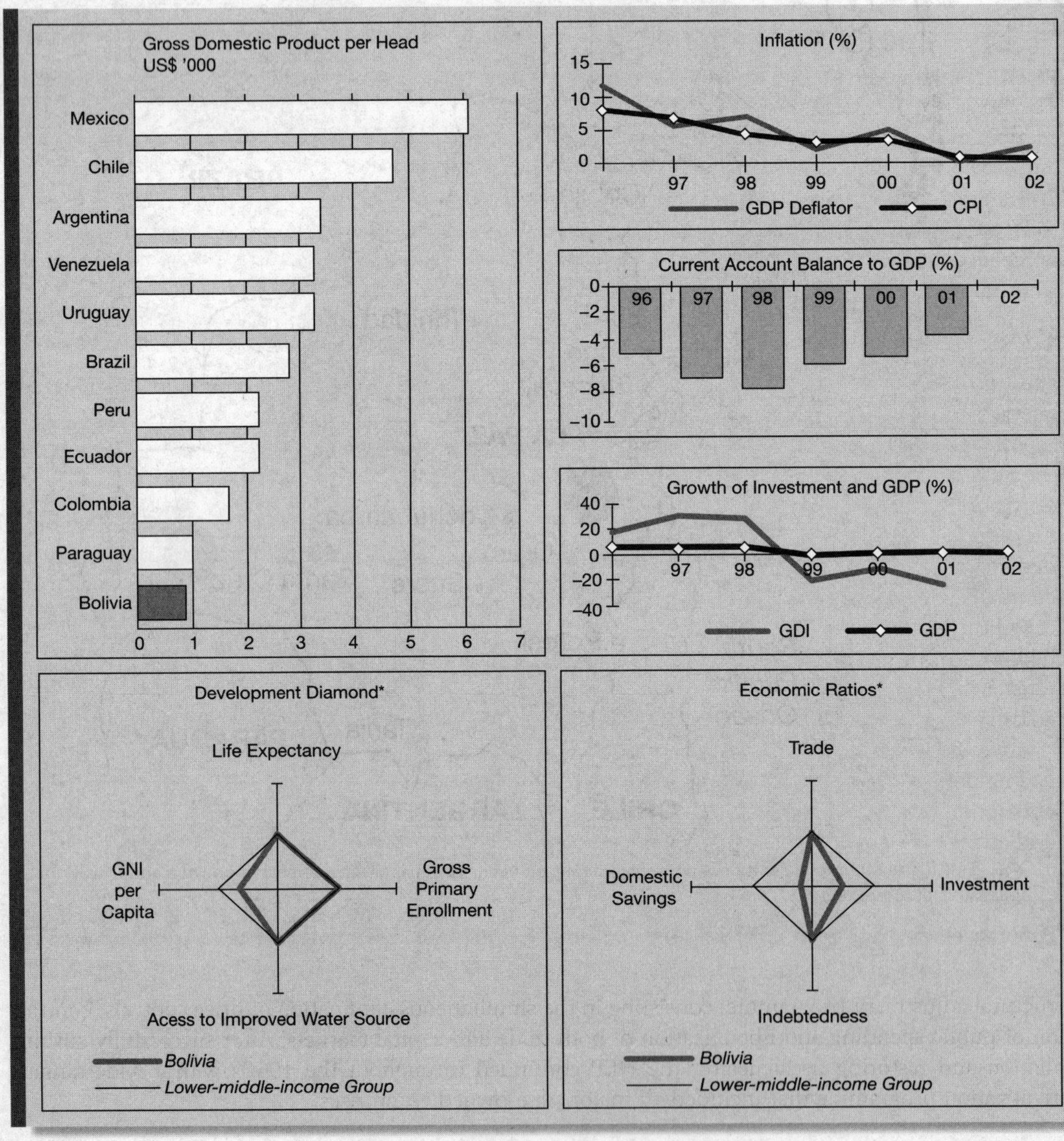

In spite of market-oriented policies, the economy lacked the dynamism necessary to reduce unemployment and significantly reduce overall poverty, which still affected more than 60 per cent of the population. Most of the foreign investment driven by the privatization process was directed to capital-intensive sectors, especially hydrocarbon and mining, which had little potential to create employment and bore no link with other domestic industries. The concentration of investment in these sectors had reinforced Bolivia's 'dual economy' characterized by a thriving resource-based/capital-intensive industry coexisting with a precarious informal sector supporting the largest portion of the population. As a result, income inequality, unemployment and informality had been growing to unprecedented levels, which in turn had been nurturing social unrest and political instability (see Figure M2.3).

BUSINESS ENVIRONMENT

The persistent failure to initiate a process of sustained development and address the country's major economic and social problems had progressively fostered a social backlash against the economic model and exacerbated political instability. In recent years, social turmoil had become violent. In October 2003, President Gonzalo Sanchez de Lozada, an unconditional supporter of market reforms, was forced to step down after a month of violent protest that left more than 80 casualties. Sanchez de Lozada was succeeded by his Vice President Carlos Mesa, who distanced himself both politically and ideologically from reforms in an effort to appeal to the prevailing 'anti-systemic' national sentiment.

Far from taking a conservative posture, Mesa ventured into implementing wide-ranging reforms. Among the most controversial ones were: *Asamblea Constituyente* that would redefine the national constitution and *Nueva Ley de Hidrocarburos*, which aimed at modifying the investment framework for the energy sector to allow higher government control.

After enjoying one year of popular support and relative stability, President Mesa started experiencing the cost of political isolation. The lack of control over a fragmented and polarized Congress slowed down his reforms and to a large extent eroded his popularity. A recent government measure increasing the price of gasoline had triggered another wave of violent protests. The social pressure that started demanding the policy's derogation escalated into other demands such as the removal of a French utility company, and 'political autonomy' for Santa Cruz—the country's most prosperous region. Mesa conceded the first two and was now struggling to keep protests in Santa Cruz under control. In recent days, however, different social sectors, including universities and members of the Congress, joined the separatist movement led by Santa Cruz's *Comite Cívico*. Mesa's biggest challenge ahead was to bring the country together and restore investment confidence.

Investors were becoming increasingly concerned about the operational risks resulting from the prevailing political instability. Governance indicators in Bolivia had worsened in terms of political stability, corruption, rule of law and government effectiveness. Persistent roadblocks and disruption of highways and airports had become a serious burden for doing business.

On account of escalating events, the World Markets Research Centre had recently revised the country's risk from moderate to medium, which placed Bolivia in a risk category higher than the Latin American average (Figure M2.3).

THE TROPICAL WOOD INDUSTRY

Processed tropical wood was a US$6.6 billion industry that had shown a vigorous growth over the past decade. A combination of lower trade barriers, increasing demand for wooden furniture and a buoyant

FIGURE M2.3
Main Drivers of Political Instability

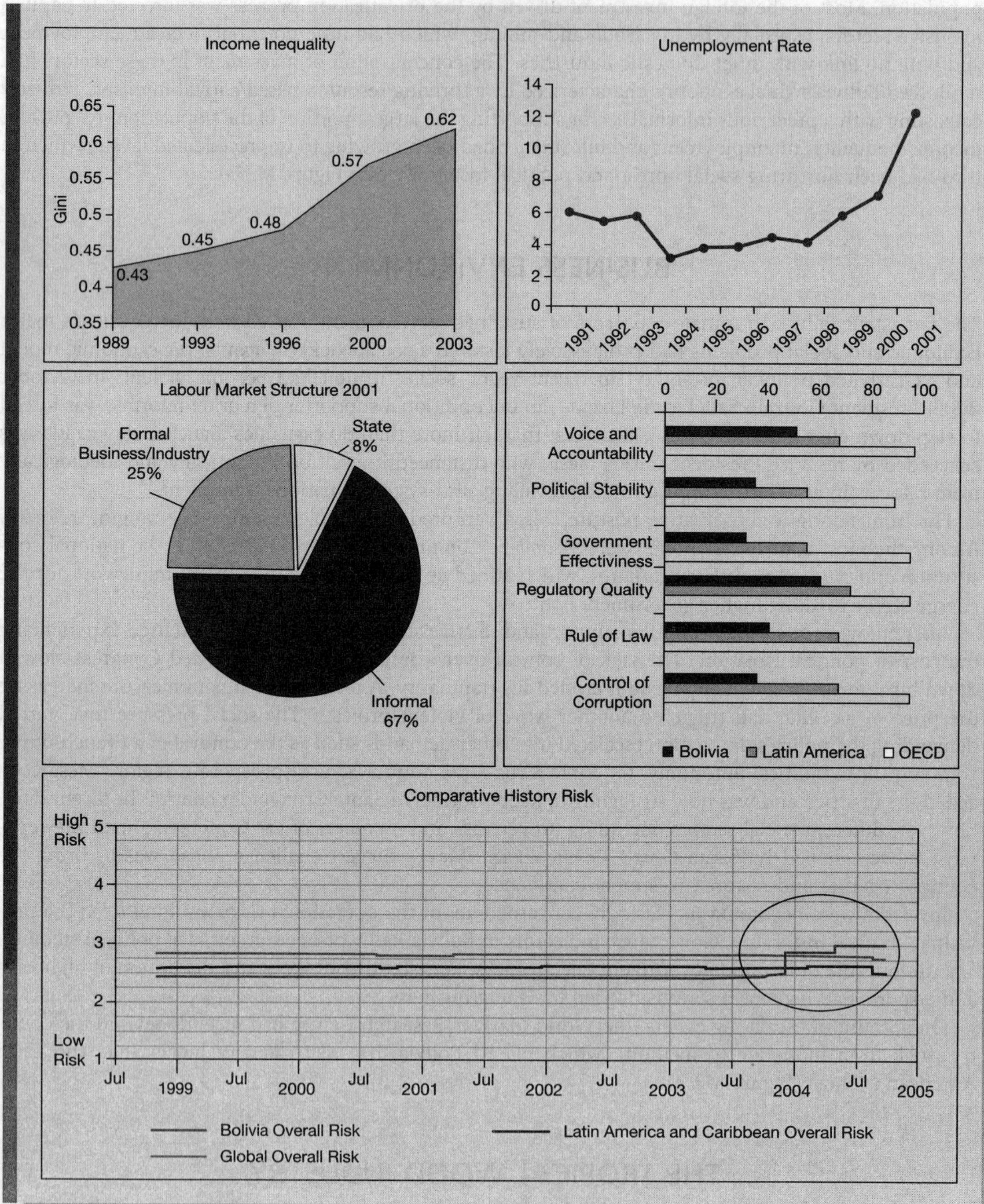

construction and renovation activity in developed markets, had kept tropical timber exports on the rise. Despite the gradual tendency to substitute wood for non-wood materials, the International Trade Centre estimated that demand for tropical wood products would increase at a healthy annual rate of 10 per cent in the medium term. Global exports in this industry were still dominated by Asian countries (83%) followed by Latin America (16%) and Africa (1%). In spite of its lead, however, Asia had been gradually losing market share to Latin America. The latter had experienced and average export growth of 24 per cent per year, increasing its global share from 7 per cent to 16 per cent in less than 10 years. The relative decline of Asian exports was largely explained by the saturation of its forestry potential and substantial deforestation. Latin America on the other hand had a significantly greater forestry potential and had been adopting sustainable practices in an effort to avoid the Asian experience and comply with stricter environmental standards imposed by importing markets (Figure M2.4).

Tropical wood exports from developing countries were not only growing in volume but also increasingly moving into value-added segments. The share of both processed furniture and semi-processed builders' joinery had increased relative to profiled wood, with Asia showing a significantly higher share of value-added exports than Latin America. Due to the growth of Asian economies and problems associated with deforestation, Asian wood processors were expected to gradually abandon wood extraction and move up to value-added products.

The Bolivian tropical forest offered one of Latin America's greatest growth potential for the wood industry. With over 49 million hectares and more than 360 wood species, Bolivia had the seventh largest and the most diverse tropical forest in the world. It was the second largest exporter in Latin America after Brazil (Figure M2.3), but much of its potential remained largely untapped. It was estimated that forestry operated at less than 1 per cent of full capacity, with local production still dominated by low value-added commercial timber.

Among the major obstacles inhibiting the development of this industry were lack of investment, poor infrastructure—including transportation and energy—and low entrepreneurial drive. However, in recent years, the government had been promoting investment in the sector by establishing a tax-free export processing zone in the tropical region and enacting one of the world's most modern and complete forestry law. In addition, with the support of the International Forest Stewardship Council, the government had recently certified more than 1 million hectares of forest ready to be exploited.

TAHUAMANU AND THE TROPICAL WOOD CONSORTIUM

In 1989, a group of entrepreneurs led by Enrique Nelkenbaum embarked on a project to develop a processing plant of Brazil nuts in the northern city of Cobija. The ambitious venture was aimed at creating the country's largest mechanized plant to tap into the (growth potential of) forestry sector in Bolivia. Tahuamanu, named after the largest river crossing the Bolivian Amazon, was then created with the support of several partners and lenders, including the Bolivian Export Foundation, the Andean Development Corporation and the Inter-American Development Bank. The company followed an aggressive growth strategy based on continuous technological upgradation and exports, and quickly became the largest producer of processed Brazil nuts in Bolivia, with revenues averaging US$6 million a year. After nearly 15 years of operations, Tahuamanu had successfully positioned itself in European and North American markets, reaching a diversified range of buyers that included the US food processor Planters and British chocolate maker Cadbury (Figure M4.5). The company had not only thrived in international markets but had also contributed to the development of the region and become a model for social corporate responsibility. It was estimated that over one half of the 57,000 inhabitants living in the city of Cobija

FIGURE M2.4
Processed Tropical Wood Industry

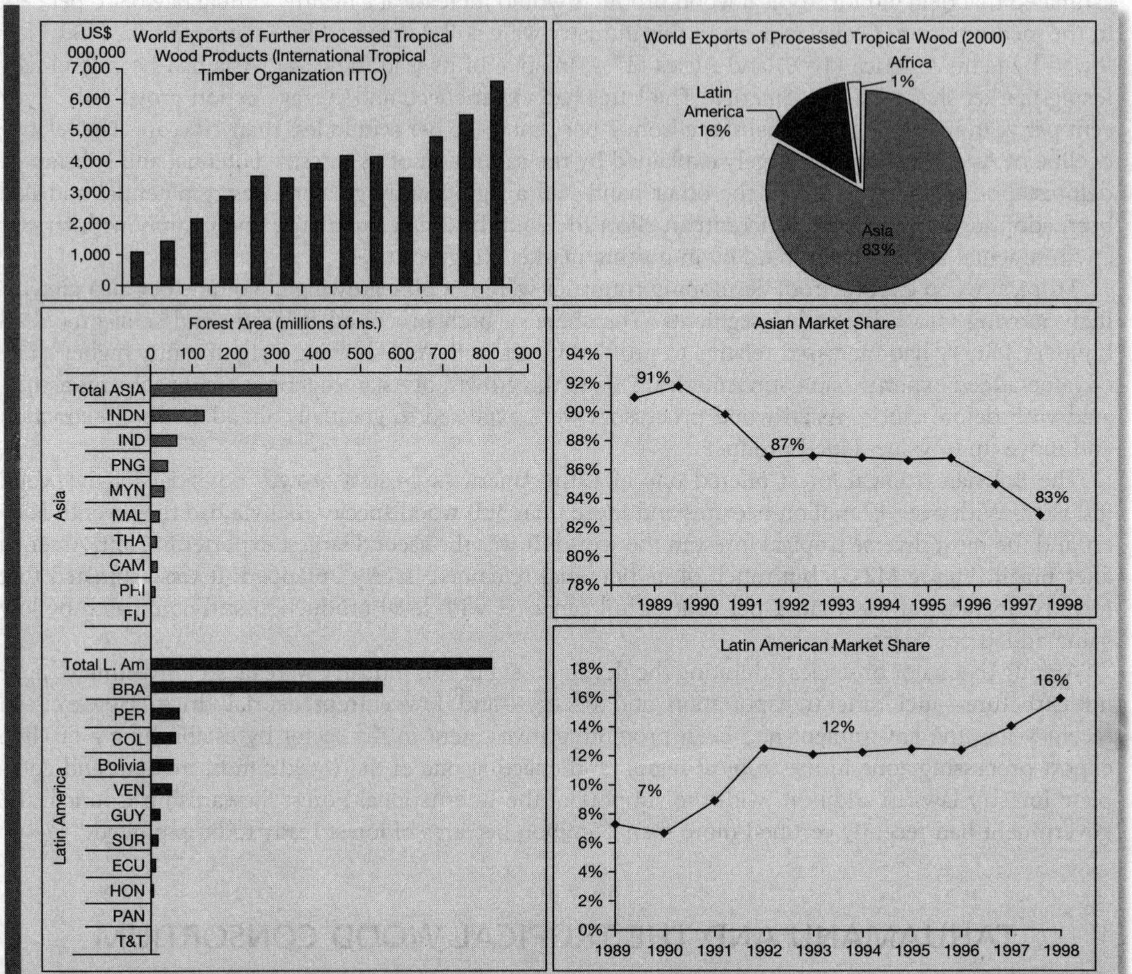

Latin America: Exports of Further Processed Tropical Wood 1999

US$ 000,000

Brazil	Bolivia	Honduras	Colombia	Others	Total
458.8	27.8	22.1	16.3	27.1	552.1

was direct or indirectly involved with the Brazil nut business. Tahuamanu's commitment to maintaining excellent working conditions using environment-friendly practices had earned the respect of both the local and the international community.

At the brink of reaching a saturation point in Brazil nut production, Tahuamanu started exploring new business opportunities in forestry. The most obvious choice was the wood industry, not only because of the region's potential and favourable market conditions but also because of the synergies that could potentially be created with the nut industry. In order to successfully undertake this new venture,

FIGURE M2.5
Tahuamanu in the Brazil Nut Industry

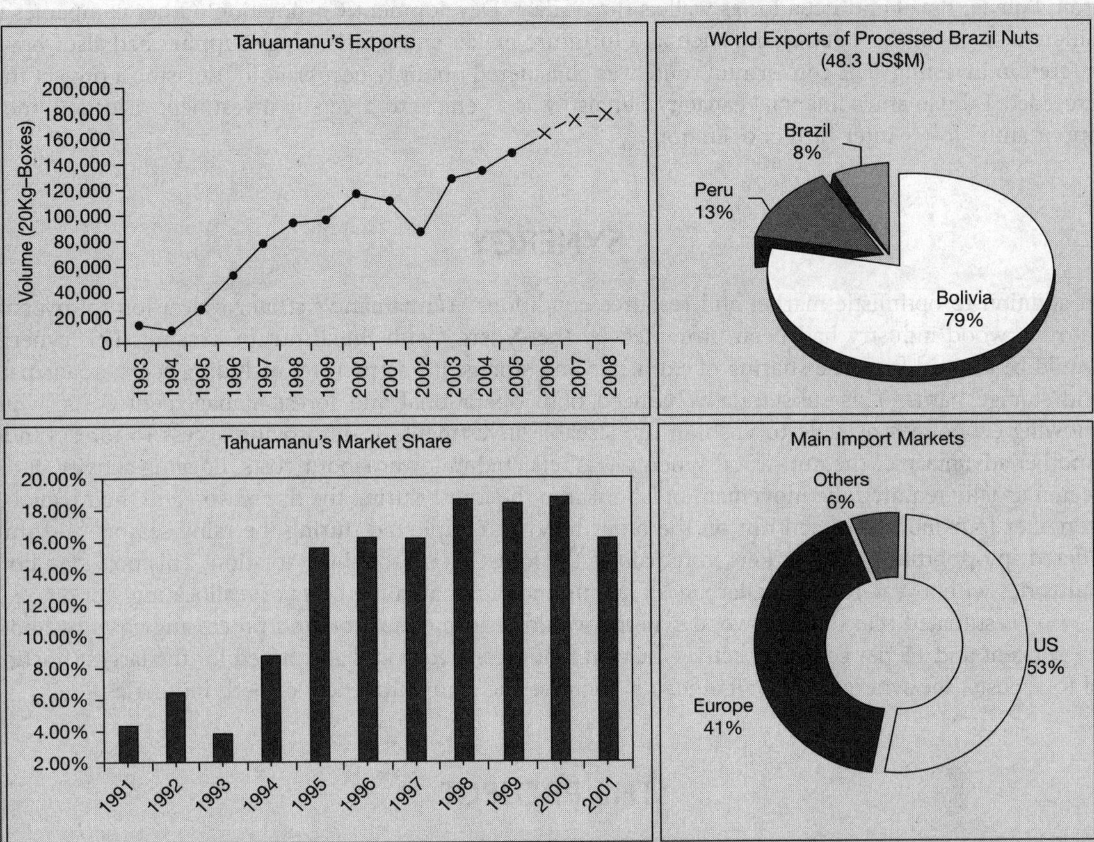

US$	2003	2004	2005e
REVENUES			
Containers	80	160	176
Exports (pounds)	5,607,848	5,620,000	5,620,000
Price (container FOB)	1.0	8.0	2.0
Revenues	5,798,515	11,240,000	11,240,000
EXPENSES			
Direct Cost (per pound)	0.9	6.8	1.7
Total Costs	4,928,738	9,554,000	9,554,000
Gross Margin	869,777	1,686,000	1,686,000
OPERATIONAL EXPENSES			
Overhead	360,000	360,000	396,000
Marketing		15,000	15,000
Certification HACCP		10,000	
Total Operational Expenses	360,000	385,000	411,000
		-	
EBIT AD	509,777	1,301,000	1,275,000
EBIT AD margin	59%	77%	76%

Tahuamanu had decided to spearhead the formation of the TWC. This business group was still in a phase of consolidation but was likely to include a number of small- and medium-sized wood processors from Bolivia, Brazil and Ecuador as well as the Andean Development Corporation. Other companies in different stages of the value chain, such as a furniture maker and a technology supplier had also shown interest in investing. The consortium route was considered not only necessary for devising a project that exceeded Tahuamanu's financial capacity but also was a vehicle to diversify investment risks and, most importantly, foster inter-firm cooperation.

SYNERGY

In addition to optimistic market and resource conditions, Tahuamanu's strategic decision to diversify into the wood industry had been prompted by the synergy with Brazil nut processing. This synergy would be derived from the sharing of extractive and storage infrastructure, including access roads/path and storage barns. This substantially reduced both operational and forest management costs, while allowing economies of scale to cushion the sizeable investments in improving access to forest lands. Another advantage of the nut–wood synergy was reflected in lower labour costs. Logging activity in the region usually required the movement of labour into the forest during the dry season and their reallocation after four months. Brazil nut on the other hand was exploited during the rainy season, and thus offered an opportunity for workers to remain in the forest for seasonal job rotation. This provided both industries with a year-round availability of labour and eliminated the costs of reallocating workers.

TWC estimated that the nut–wood synergy would reduce extraction and processing costs by about 35 per cent and 15 per cent, respectively. Given that these two stages accounted for the largest fraction of total costs, the synergy could significantly increase the competitiveness of both industries.

THE PROJECT

After nearly one year of extensive studies, TWC had come up with a US$13 million development project, which, if implemented, would give birth to the country's largest and most modern wood processing plant. The project would be located in a tax-free export processing zone in the northern city of Cobija with an area of influence of 186,000 hectares (a radius of 70 to100 km from the plant) to produce approximately 58,000 cubic metres of processed wood per year. The large extension was necessary to comply with sustainable forest management practices that recommend a 20-year rotation system, whereby the forest was completely replanted after a cycle of 20 years.

Annual production would need an estimated 130,000 cubic metres of raw material that would come from two sources: 50 per cent from private concessionaries and 50 per cent from community-based suppliers, organized in either the Indigenous Community Forest Land Association or the Land Forestry Association. This combination would provide both the reliability and flexibility necessary to manage demand fluctuations, while assuring a significant social and economic impact in the form of income earnings and employment creation throughout local communities.

In order to optimize forest management and leverage economies of scope in the extraction process, TWC would exploit 35 different species of hard, soft and precious wood. Around 70 per cent of the extraction and transportation to the plant would be outsourced to specialized Brazilian companies. Rough wood would then be processed with three different types of technologies—sawing, laminating and slicing—to finally produce plywood, veneer and sliced panels. The end uses included floors, frames, construction and furniture parts.

Road infrastructure in Bolivia was a major obstacle in transporting goods to final markets. The project was located far from major maritime ports with transportation costs averaging 12 per cent of total operational costs (depending on the product). In addition to distance, the country's main highways were still precarious and unreliable during rainy seasons. Restrictions on high-tonnage loads required for transporting wood products were often imposed. The project had, however, two major advantages that could largely reduce the high incidence of transportation costs. First, it concentrated on value-added processed products that were significantly less costly to transport. Second, the project was located near the border with Brazil, which offered a year-round road infrastructure with higher tonnage limits and lower freight rates. The Brazilian ports of Belen, Santos and Paranagua were therefore the most cost effective to reach North American and European markets. The data on transportation alternatives are presented in Figure M4.6. Ongoing investments in road infrastructure in both Bolivia and Peru would make the ports of Arica and Matarani viable alternatives in future.

FIGURE M2.6
Transportation Alternatives

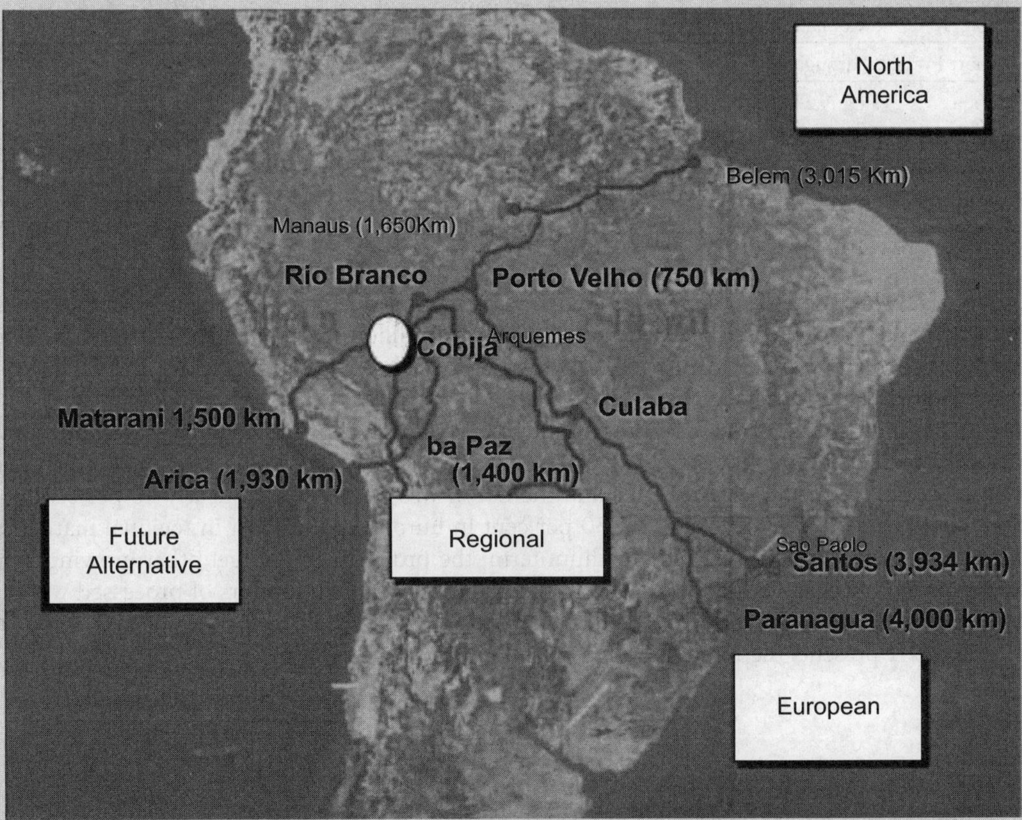

Note: This figure is not to scale. It does not represent any authentic national or international boundaries and is used for illustrative purposes only.

FIGURE M2.6
(Continued)

Export Freight Through Brazil				
		Distance Kilometres	Fright USS/Ton	Freight US Cents/Km × Ton
Cobija	Route Porto Velho	750	14.32	1.909
Porto Velho	Manaus	910	20.13	2.212
Total	Cobija – Manaus	1,660	34.45	2.075
Cobija	Porto Velho	750	14.32	1.909
Porto Velho	Belen	2,265	36.47	1.61
Total	Cobija – Belem	3,015	50.79	1.685
Cobija	Sao Paolo	3,300	63	1.909
Total	Cobija – Santos	3,934	75.1	1.909
Arquimes	Paranagua	3,300	68	2.061
Rio Branco	Paranagua	3,970	57.72	1.454
Total	Cobija – Paranagua	4,000	58.19	1.455
Export Freight Through Chile				
Cobija	La Paz	1,460	61.76	4.23
La Paz	Arica	460	30	6.522
Total	Cobija – Arica	1,920	91.76	4.779

Lack of a reliable source of energy was another obstacle for operating the plant in Cobija. To overcome this problem, the project had considered a US$1.5 million investment in a wood-based power generating plant. A proposed investment to construct a public hydroelectric plant in the region was expected to lower energy costs in the medium term.

Due to the limited size of the domestic economy, TWC was expected to direct its efforts towards international markets. In the first stage, the project would target the largest markets currently importing Bolivian wood, that is, the USA, Argentina and the UK. It was estimated that nearly 40 per cent of production would be sold in North America, 30 per cent in Europe and the rest in regional markets such as Argentina, Brazil and Bolivia. In the medium term, the project would target other growing markets like China and other Asian countries that were likely to become net importers of processed wood. The project was expected to generate US$11 million in annual revenues after the first four years of consolidation. Table M2.1 presents the forecast of free cash flows from the project.

FINANCING

It was estimated that a total investment of US$12.9 million was required for setting up the industrial complex with four different technologies for sawing, brushing, slicing, laminating and the power

TABLE M2.1
Project Cash Flow

US$ 000											
Year	0	1	2	3	4	5	6	7	8	9	10
CASH IN	0	1,932	2,760	6,823	8,733	9,606	10,471	11,204	11,876	12,232	12,477
Sales - Sawed	0	1,932	2,760	5,519	5,519	6,071	6,617	7,080	7,505	7,730	7,885
Sales - Laminated	0	0	0	1,304	1,863	2,049	2,234	2,390	2,534	2,610	2,662
Sales - Sliced	0	0	0	0	1,351	1,486	1,620	1,733	1,837	1,892	1,930
CASH OUT	4,630	2,000	4,643	8,935	6,047	7,020	6,845	7,230	7,571	7,642	7,700
Total Investments	4,630	579	2,725	4,047	289	652	0	0	0	0	0
Sawer	3,130	579	193	715	0	0	0	0	0	0	0
Laminator	0	0	2,532	502	175	634	0	0	0	0	0
Slicer	0	0	0	2,830	114	18	0	0	0	0	0
Energy	1,500	0	0	0	0	0	0	0	0	0	0
Total Operational Costs	–	1,406	1,856	4,701	5,460	5,951	6,428	6,813	7,154	7,225	7,283
Operational Costs - Sawing	0	1,406	1,856	3,537	3,537	3,855	4,164	4,414	4,634	4,681	4,718
Operational Costs - Laminating	0	0	0	1,164	1,551	1,691	1,826	1,935	2,032	2,052	2,069
Operational Costs - Slicing	0	0	0	0	372	405	438	464	487	492	496
Other Costs	0	15	62	187	298	417	417	417	417	417	417
Depreciation/ amortization	*0*	404	404	630	887	887	887	887	887	887	887
Sawing	0	404	404	404	404	404	404	404	404	404	404
Laminating	0	0	0	225	225	225	225	225	225	225	225
Slicing	0	0	0	0	257	257	257	257	257	257	257
Working Capital	0	0	0	0	0	0	0	0	0	0	0
Net Cash Flow	–4,630	–68	–1,883	–2,112	2,686	2,586	3,626	3,974	4,305	4,590	4,777

generating plant. Financing was expected to come primarily in the form of equity provided by TWC's different partners. The Consortium was still in a process of consolidation but was likely to include a number of wood processors from Bolivia, Brazil and Ecuador, a German technology supplier interested in a technology/equity swap as well as the Andean Development Corporation. As estimated, 35 per cent of the project was expected to be financed with loans provided by the IIC, the IFC and other commercial banks. The details of the proposed financing structure are shown in Table M2.2.

KEY SUCCESS FACTORS

After a thorough analysis of the main competitive forces in the processed wood industry, TWC identified four key success factors that would provide a competitive edge against other competitors: price advantage, growth potential, flexibility and internal capabilities.

The project's most important success factor was its price advantage derived from the interaction of four major cost drivers: (a) the nut–wood synergy, (b) optimization of economies of scope and scale in the extraction and processing of 35 different varieties of wood, (c) an estimated 20 per cent savings in operational costs due to tax and duty exemptions and (d) low labour and production costs in the region, including subsidized water and other services.

A second success factor stemmed from the region's large forestry potential. As discussed earlier, Latin America was expected to benefit the most from the rising world demand as well as saturation in Asia. Currently realizing less than 1 per cent of its full potential, the Bolivian forest offered one of the region's most attractive opportunities to expand. In addition, ongoing integration efforts with regional markets under MERCOSUR and the Free Trade Area of the Americas (FTAA), as well as the prospective extension of the Andean Trade Preference Act (ATPA), could further promote exports of Bolivian wood products.

TABLE M2.2
Financing Structure

	US$000	%
Total Investment	12,922	1.00
Debt	4,523	0.35
IIC-IADB	2,500	0.19
IFC-WB	1,500	0.12
Commercial	523	0.04
Equity	8,399	0.65
Tahuamanu	3,877	0.30
Brazil/Ecuador Partners	1,034	0.08
SMEs	775	0.06
International Furniture	646	0.05
Technology Supplier	646	0.05
USAID-GDA	646	0.05
PUMA Foundation	388	0.03
Andean Development Corporation*	388	0.03

Note: *Subordinated loan (quasi-equity).

Flexibility was another key competitive characteristic of the project. Since no land would be acquired and a large number of activities were to be outsourced, TWC would have the flexibility to more effectively manage demand fluctuations and concentrate on its core competences such as coordinating the value chain, adapting technologies, ensuring product quality and marketing the final product. In addition, the location of the plant near the border with Brazil and Peru added to the flexibility to draw upon existing infrastructure and supporting industries in these countries.

Being situated far away from regions prone to social conflict also insulated the project from major operational risks posed by political tensions.

The final success factor was Tahuamanu's extensive experience in forest management and international export marketing. In addition, inter-firm cooperation within the consortium was expected to help TWC move up the industry's learning curve more quickly.

CONCLUSION

After spending several hours discussing both the technical and strategic aspects of the wood processing project, the Board of Tahuamanu seemed more convinced about its viability.

CEO Enrique Nelkenbaum said:

Even though we have many obstacles ahead, we are taking all the necessary steps to overcome them. It is true that this is a new business for us and there will be some learning costs, but I am not worried about it. We are not just a Brazil Nut company, we are an Industrial Forestry Firm and our core competencies lie in mastering industrial technologies, managing the value chain and commercializing the products. I am confident that we can quickly become important players the same way we did in the nut industry.

The group of engineers present in the meeting agreed that most of the operational risks were largely mitigated.

The proximity to Brazil gives us access to more reliable transport infrastructure and more advanced supporting industries, which are largely absent in Bolivia. We will reduce the high incidence of energy and transportation costs by investing in our own generating plant and concentrating on high value-added processed products. The cost savings derived from the wood-nut synergy however is our greatest advantage and none of our competitors will ever match that.

The biggest challenge ahead was to convince potential partners to invest in a country undergoing political turmoil.

Tahuamanu's CEO added:

We have to convince them that, being located far from the regions prone to political conflict, Cobija is largely insulated from the operational risks affecting other industries in Bolivia, including our potential competitors. We really have the best of both worlds; access to the forestry resources and low production costs of Bolivia on the one hand, and the stability and more advanced infrastructure of Brazil on the other.

Exercises

1. What are the merits and demerits of investing in the project?
2. Estimate the project cost of capital using the ICCRC.
3. Would you accept the project? Why or why not? Assume a cost of capital of 11.2 per cent.
4. Estimate the impact of real options on the cost of capital determined by ICCRC.

ONLINE SOURCES

1. Central Intelligence Agency www.cia.com
2. Instituto Nacional de Estadística www.ine.gov.bo
3. Inter-American Development Bank Database www.iadb.org
4. Transparency International. *Corruption Perceptions Index 2003.* https://www.transparency.org/research/cpi/cpi_2003/0 (accessed on 4 January 2019).
5. Unidad de Analisis de Politicas Economicas y Sociales UDAPE. www.udape.gov.bo
6. World Bank Database www.worldbank.org
7. World Bank. 2005. *Doing Business Report.* http://rru.worldbank.org/DoingBusiness/ExploreEconomies/BusinessClimateSnapshot.aspx?economyid=25 (accessed on 4 January 2019).
8. World Development Report 2001/2002 www.worldbank.org/poverty/wdrpovrty (accessed on 4 January 2019).
9. UNCTAD/WTO International Trade Centre. www.intracen.org
10. International Tropical Timber Organization. www.itto.org
11. Tahuamanu SA. www.tahuamanu.com

3

Hutchison Whampoa and the Shanghai Deep Water Project*

LEARNING OBJECTIVE

To introduce estimation of cost of capital in emerging markets using the ICCRC model; real options analysis

Description: Starting with the second phase of the Shanghai Yangshan Deep Water Port Project, the Shanghai government lifted restrictions on foreign and domestic private investment. Hong Kong-based Hutchison Whampoa Limited (HWL), the world's leading port developer and operator, is faced with the decision of whether or not to invest in the project. The Phase II Shanghai Deep Water Port Project would almost double the size of Shanghai's first deep-water port and further alleviate the bottleneck that has constrained Shanghai's growth as an economic and shipping centre. However, it also comes with various external and internal risks and a total cost of US$800 million. The purpose of the case is to analyse HWL's investment decision.

Subjects Covered: Financial management, capital budgeting, discounted cash flow analysis

---

This case was written by Vidya Vishal, Jerry Wang, Grace Qingyun Zhao and Gaobo Zhou under the supervision of Professor Campbell Harvey, Fuqua School of Business, Duke University.

INTRODUCTION

On 30 September 2004, Hutchison Whampoa Limited (HWL) signed a contract with Shanghai International Port Group (SIPG), the state-owned company focusing on port-related business in the Shanghai region, for the Waigaoqiao Phase-5 project. HWL, controlled by Hong Kong tycoon Li Ka-shing, the richest man in Asia, would form a joint venture company with SIPG and hold 50 per cent equity. The total cost of the project was expected to be US$482 million.

> Since 1998, we have co-operated with Shanghai on a much larger scale and in greater depth. I believe there will be a better future, particularly through our efforts to develop Shanghai into an international port and trading center.
>
> —Li Ka-shing, Chairman, HWL

The Waigaoqiao Phase-5 project would equip Shanghai to handle the increasing shipping demand. But the solution to transport bottlenecks caused by the lack of a deep-water port was the Yangshan Deep Water Port Project, the Phase-1 of which was under construction. Several overseas port and shipping services operators including HWL had expressed interest in investing in the Phase-2 part of the project. But the US$800MM investment cost, increasing competition in the port industry and the port's long-term profitability were causes for concern.

HUTCHISON WHAMPOA LIMITED

The beginning of HWL goes back to the 1800s. In 1880, John Hutchison, a British expatriate in Hong Kong, formed the John D Hutchison and Company Ltd, taking over an existing firm. During an acquisition programme in the 1960s, this company took control of a diverse set of companies, including the Hong Kong and Whampoa Dock (the first registered company in Hong Kong, owned dry docks in Whampoa in China's Guangdong province since 1861). Hutchison International saw tumultuous times in the 1970s, and had to be rescued by the Hongkong and Shanghai Bank, which bought the entire company and eventually renamed it the HWL in 1977.

In 1979, Cheung Kong Holdings acquired HWL, making its founder Li Ka-Shing the first Chinese to control a British-style *hong* (trading company). In the 1980s, HWL started its diversification into energy, mining and telecommunications, and other businesses. By 2004, HWL had holdings in five core businesses: ports and related services, telecommunications, property and hotels, retail and manufacturing, and energy and infrastructure. For the year ending 31 December 2004, the Group's consolidated turnover was approximately HK$179 billion (US$23 billion). HWL had operations in 54 countries and employed over 200,000 people worldwide. Meanwhile, Li Ka-Shing came to be known as Superman in Hong Kong circles and was named Asia's richest and most influential businessman by the *Fortune* in 2004.

HWL, through its subsidiary Hutchison Port Holdings (HPH), was the world's leading port developer and operator, operating 242 berths in 41 ports spread over 20 countries in Asia, Africa, the Middle East, Europe and the USA.

HWL was the first foreign firm to invest in and operate container terminals in Shanghai in the early 1990s. Twenty years ago, private companies were not allowed to invest in key infrastructure projects such as ports and bridges. Even for Phase-1 of the Shanghai Yangshan Deep Water Port, the construction and operation of the port were handled by government-controlled subsidiaries—Tongsheng for construction, and Shengdong for operations. Presently the government was opening up Phase-2 for private sector partnership. Shanghai's importance as an import–export gateway to China was rising, and this made a presence in the Yangshan Deep Water Port all the more desirable. HWL was interested in an equity stake in the Yangshan Phase-2 Project. Table M3.1 presents the income statements of HWL.

TABLE M3.1
Hutchison Whampoa Limited Income Statement

	US$ millions	HK$ millions	HK$ millions
	2004	2004	2003
Turnover			
Company and subsidiary companies	17,256	134,595	104,921
Shares of associated companies and jointly controlled entities	5,746	44,820	40,688
Total	**23,002**	**179,415**	**145,609**
Company and Subsidiary Companies			
Turnover	17,256	134,595	104,921
Cost of inventory sold	–6,667	–52,006	–45,295
Staff costs	–2,760	–21,525	–16,856
Prepaid 3G telecommunication customer acquisition expense	–1,080	–8,423	–917
Depreciation and amortization	–3,880	–30,263	–13,166
Other operating expenses	–4,959	–38,680	–30,595
Change in fair value of investment properties	672	5,244	–1,809
Profit on disposal of investment and others	2,459	19,181	8,893
Operating Income	**1,041**	**8,123**	**5,176**
Share of profits less losses of associated companies	1,132	8,822	8,796
Share of profits less losses of jointly controlled entities	310	2,422	2,627
EBIT	**2,483**	**19,367**	**16,599**
Interest and other finance costs, including share of associated companies and jointly controlled entities	–1,630	–12,712	–9,568
Profit before Taxation	853	6,655	7,031
Current taxation charge	–484	–3,776	–2,758
Deferred taxation credit	874	6,818	5,854
Profit after Taxation	**1,243**	**9,697**	**10,127**
Minority interests	825	6,431	1,550
Profit Attributed to Shareholders	**2,068**	**16,128**	**11,677**
Dividends	946	7,375	7,375
Earnings per share	0.485	3.78	2.74

CHINA'S ECONOMY

Although China was still a developing country with a relatively low per capita income, it had experienced tremendous economic growth since the late 1970s. The GDP had doubled every seven years since 1987 largely due to economic liberalization policies. In 2004, the GDP reached US$1.65 trillion with growth rate of 9.5 per cent.[1]

The strong economic performance attracted foreign investments, which started to soar during the 1990s and continued to rise during 2000s. In 2004, China surpassed the USA and became the most attractive destination for FDI. During 2004, FDI inflows totalled US$60.6 billion, 13.3 per cent higher than the previous year.

Exports in 2004 rose 35.4 per cent to US$593.4 billion, while imports surged 36.0 per cent to US$561.4 billion.[2] FDI was estimated to increase another 30 per cent by the 2008 Olympics to US$80 billion. China's challenge in the twenty-first century was to balance its highly centralized political system with an increasingly decentralized economic system. The overall business and trade environment in China for the development of the national economy was positive. However, economic growth was under the pressure of both further adjustment and over-supply due to excessive production capacity.

CHINA'S PORT INDUSTRY

With the acceleration of the world economic integration and the continued rapid development of the Chinese economy and foreign trade, the port industry in China was growing fast and broke record in 2004. The cargo handling capacity of major coastal ports reached 1.8 billion tonnes with a growth rate of 13.5 per cent year on year. The container handling capacity was more than 60 million TEU (Twenty-Foot Equivalent Unit).

There were 3,300 productive berths in the coastal ports of China. Of these, 745 berths were deep-water berths with capacity of over 10,000 tonnes each. More than 130 ports were open to foreign vessels and accommodated more than 60,000 ships from over 100 countries each year. The eight key mega ports were divided into three economic regions: Bohai Bay region, Changjiang Delta region and Zhujiang Delta region. Table M3.2 presents operating data of these key ports.

The development of China's port industry was closely related to foreign trade: imports and exports. Handling capacity and foreign trade cargo throughput of major ports increased by 11.29 per cent and 14.70 per cent per year on average, respectively, during the period 1991–2004. The average increase in container throughput reached 30.05 per cent, higher than the 18.38 per cent rise in foreign trade and the 9.69 per cent increase in GDP.[3] Because foreign trade, the main driver of port industry, increased at a lower growth rate than container throughput, the high growth rate (more than 30%) of container throughput was hard to sustain. It was estimated that annual increase of container throughput would be 10–20 per cent for the next 10 years.

The overall trend was that nationwide container throughput would increase at a declining rate, while the handling capacity of most coastal ports still increased at a significantly high level, around 20 per

---

[1] National Bureau of Statistics of China. *China Statistical Yearbook 2004*.

[2] WMRC Country Report: China.

[3] Beijing Okokok Information Consulting Co. *Investment Study in China's Port Industry*.

TABLE M3.2
Operating Data on China's Key Ports

PORT	Throughput Capacity (2004) (Million TEU)	New Capacity (2005–2010) (Million TEU)	Average Growth Rate Per Year (%)
Dalian Port	2.2	6.2	30.73
Tianjin Port	4.8	6	17.61
Qingdao Port	6.5	4.5	11.10
Bohai Bay Subtotal	13.5	16.7	17.47
Shanghai Port	8.35	15	22.83
Ningbo Port	3	11.4	36.85
Changjiang Triangle Subtotal	11.35	26.4	27.17
Xiamen Port	3.7	4.6	17.54
Shenzhen Port	6.2	8.05	18.11
Guangzhou Port	4.2	4.2	14.87
Zhujiang Triangle Subtotal	14.1	16.85	16.84
Total	**38.95**	**59.95**	**20.49**

Source: Huatai Securities Co Ltd.

cent per year. The competition among ports was expected to intensify following the low utilization rate and excess capacity. Some ports were expected to lower their charges for container loading and unloading services.

SHANGHAI PORTS

The Shanghai ports, an aggregated term for all the shipping ports in Shanghai, boasted a cargo handling capacity of 8.14 million TEU. The importance of the port was growing, particularly as a gateway for container transport. As a result of the accelerated export demand, the growth rate at the ports averaged 29 per cent per year in the past three years and was expected to continue once China was accepted into the World Trade Organization (WTO). Table M3.3 presents the projections of container throughput for 2005–2007.

However, the port faced three major constraints:

- Water depth at the Yangtze River estuary and Huangpu River was only 7–8 meters. Because of this, third- and fourth-generation container ships could only enter and leave the port at high tide. Fifth- and sixth-generation ships needed 15 m to move freely.
- The Huangpu River was not wide enough for large ships. Container ships could not turn freely within the port. Large ships need to unload cargo to smaller ships prior to entering the port, resulting in increased shipping costs.
- The port lacked modern logistics to provide comprehensive services.

TABLE M3.3
Shanghai Ports Container Throughput and Projection (MM TEU)

	2004 A	2005 E	2006 E	2007 E
Huangpu River Port	3.83	3.75	3.3	3
Waigaoqiao Port	4.31	5.17	5.44	5.71
Yangshan Deep Water Port Phase-1			2.7	3.24
Yangshan Deep Water Port Phase-2				2
Shanghai Ports Total	**8.14**	**8.92**	**11.44**	**13.95**

Source: Huatai Securities Co Ltd.

To overcome these constraints and evolve into a key navigation hub in Asia, the construction of a deep-water port with wide berths became critical for Shanghai. Having no suitable place for such a harbour in its own area, the Shanghai Municipal Government (SMG) found that the Big Yangshan and Little Yangshan islands in the Hangzhou Bay, 27.5 km from Shanghai's southern coast, with water depths of 15 m and a stable geological structure, made a good site for Shanghai's deep-water port. Figure M3.1 presents a picture of the site.

THE YANGSHAN DEEP-WATER PORT PROJECT

The SMG had conducted massive feasibility studies of the Yangshan Deep-Water Port Project since the mid-1990s. In August 1999, when the Shanghai government submitted the Yangshan Deep Water Port Phase-1 Project proposal to the State Economic Planning Commission, the Shanghai government had to use a container to store the proposal weighing two tonnes and shipped it with a Boeing 747!

In February 2001, the State Council of the People's Republic of China officially approved Shanghai government's move to initiate planning for Phase-1 of the project. In March 2002, the Yangshan Project proposal was approved by the Council and the State Economic Planning Commission, and the project began construction on 26 June 2002.

In 2002, the Shanghai government founded Yangshan Port Construction and Command Office to take full control of the Yangshan Port Phase-1 construction. At the same time, Shanghai Tongsheng Investment Group (SHTS) was founded. SHTS was owned by three state-owned entities: Shanghai International Investment Group, Shanghai Port Authority and Shanghai State-Owned Asset Management Company. Figure M3.2 shows the complete deal structure for the Phase-1 project. Shanghai Tongsheng was to be the entity in charge of construction and operation of the Yangshan Phase-1 project. However, it was widely considered that Shanghai Tongsheng and the Yangshan Port Construction and Command Office were one entity with two official titles. The name of Tongsheng Investment was used to handle the financing of the project, and the name of the Command Office was used to coordinate relationships with other political entities, such as the Zhejiang Provincial Government.

After the completion of Phase-1 of the project, the port would be managed and operated by the Shanghai Port Container Co. Ltd (SPCCO). Table M3.4 presents the projected income statements of SPCCO.

The Phase-1 project was expected to cost US$1.7 billion financed with US$907 million of debt. The debt would be provided by a consortium of five domestic banks: China Construction Bank, the State

FIGURE M3.1
Location of the Shanghai Yangshan Deep Water Port

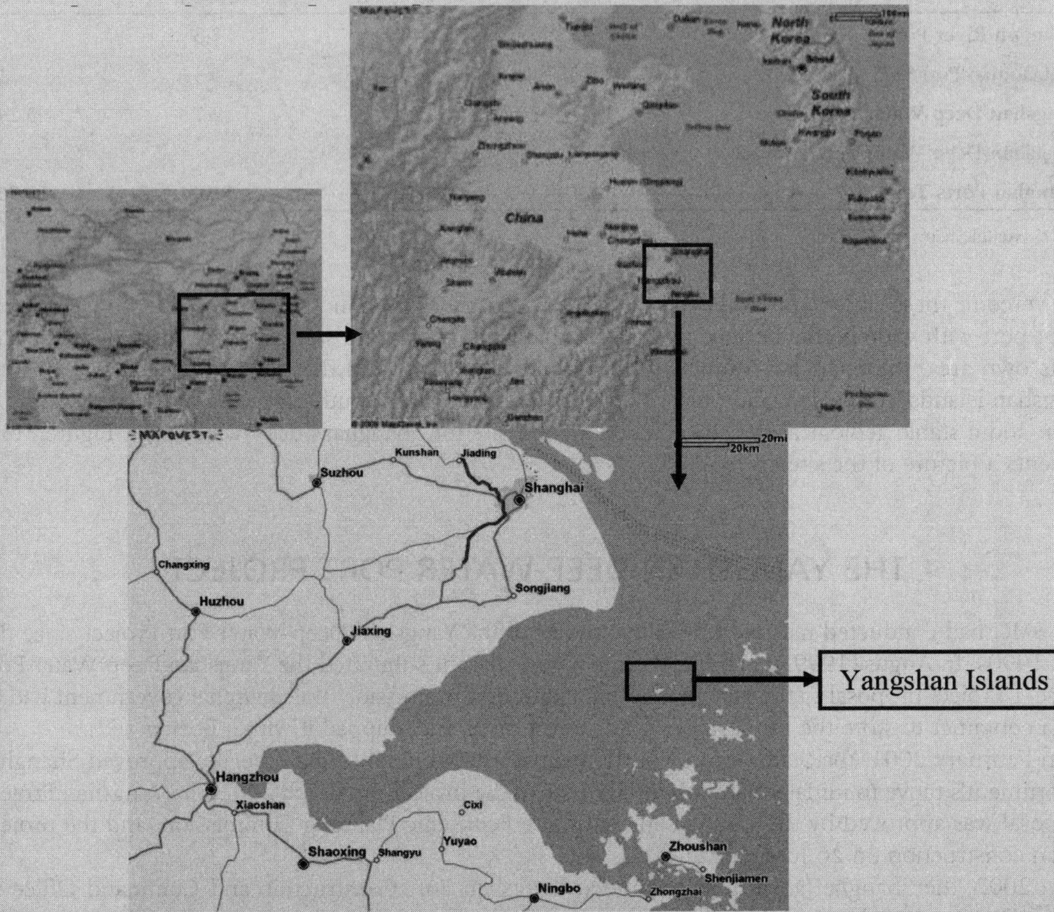

Source: www.mapquest.com.

Note: This figure is not to scale. It does not represent any authentic national or international boundaries and is used for illustrative purposes only.

Development Bank, the Bank of China, the Industrial and Commercial Bank of China and the Shanghai Pudong Development Bank. A (larger) US$2.06 billion line of credit was offered by these banks and five others until the year 2020 to be used for the entire Yangshan Deep Water Port Project.

Yangshan Deep Water Port Project had four separate components: Yangshan Deep Water Port Zone, Donghai Bridge, Lu-Hu Freeway and Luchao District.

Yangshan Deep Water Port Zone was the Phase-1 port area with the first five container berths. The total handling capacity of the five berths would be 2.2 million TEUs. It was projected to be completed

FIGURE M3.2

Deal Structure of the Phase-I Shanghai Yangshan Deep Water Port

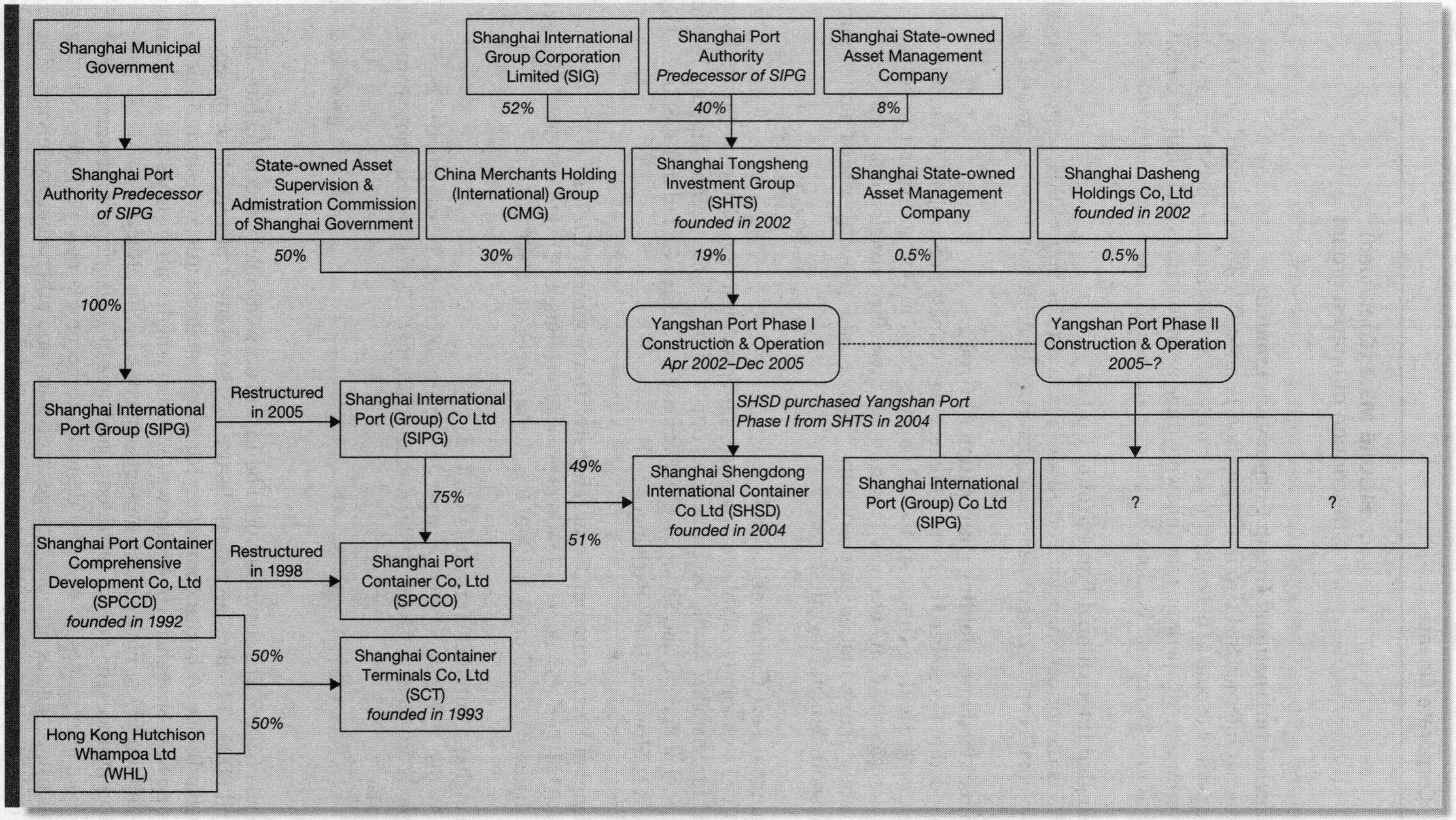

FIGURE M3.2 (*Continued*)
Description of Interest groups

Shanghai International Group Corporation Limited
Shanghai International Group Corporation Limited (SIG) was founded on 20 April 2000, with a registered capital of 6.3 billion Yuan currently. Authorized by the Shanghai Municipal People's government, SIG performs the following three main functions on behalf of the Shanghai government: investment and holding, capital operations and state assets management.

Shanghai International Port (Group) Co Ltd
SIPG is the former Shanghai Port Affair Bureau. In December 2004, approved by the Shanghai Municipal People's government, Shanghai Port Affair Bureau was restructured into SIPG.

China Merchants Holding (International) Group
Founded in December 1872 and commencing business in Shanghai in January 1873, the China Merchants Holding (International) Group has been in operation for 130 years. Headquartered in Hong Kong, CMG has now grown into a diversified conglomerate with expertise in sectors covering transportation infrastructure, finance and property-related utility services, energy transportation and logistics.

Shanghai Port Container Co Ltd
SPCCO was jointly established by Shanghai Port Authority, Shanghai Ocean Shipping Agency Co Ltd, Shanghai Traffic Investment (Group) Co Ltd, China Ocean Shipping Tallying Company (Shanghai Branch) and Shanghai Qifan Scientific Industry Co Ltd in 1998. In 2000, SPCCO was listed at Shanghai Stock Exchange.

Shanghai Port Container Comprehensive Development Co Ltd
Shanghai Port Container Comprehensive Development Co Ltd (SPCCD) was set up by the Shanghai Port Authority in 1992. It is the predecessor of SPCCO.

Shanghai Container Terminals Co Ltd
In August 1993, Shanghai Container Terminals Co Ltd (SCT) was founded by SPCCD and Hong Kong HWL. Each invested 1 billion Yuan to set up SCT, the largest joint venture at that time in China.

by the end of 2005. The channels would be 15.5 m deep capable of accepting fifth- and sixth-generation ships and 8000-TEU ultra-large ships. Figure M3.3 presents a picture of the project.

Donghai Bridge: A bridge connecting Big Yangshan and Little Yangshan to Luchaogang, the closest onshore point in Shanghai. The bridge was 32 km in length with six lanes and annual throughput capacity of 5 million TEUs. Figure M3.4 presents a picture of the project.

Luchao District: The district provided a land area of 1.5 sq. km, with storage area of 720,000 sq. m and 15 container cranes. It was also designed to become a new port city in Luchaogang to provide comprehensive logistics support, storage, processing and other auxiliary services. The district was connected to the Yangshan Deep Water Port via the Donghai Bridge.

TABLE M3.4
Shanghai Port Container Co Ltd (Operator and Manager of Shanghai Yangshan Deep Water Port Phase-1) Income Statement and Projection

	2004 A	2005 E	2006 E	2007 E
Revenue (000' Yuan)	4,043,460	4,763,550	6,271,400	6,730,110
Less Cost of Sales	1,792,960	2,301,950	3,077,610	3,489,520
Less Revenue Adjustment	121,440	142,910	188,140	201,900
Gross Profit	2,129,060	2,318,690	3,005,650	3,038,690
Other Business Profit	125,570	213,870	213,870	213,870
SG&A	335,950	404,900	627,140	572,060
Other Overhead	96,200	235,160	215,280	151,020
Operating Profit	1,822,480	1,892,500	2,377,100	2,529,480
Operating Margin (%)	45.07	39.73	37.90	37.58
Other Investment Income	47,540	50,000	80,000	80,000
Non-Operating Income	390	30000	50000	50000
Taxable Income	1,870,410	1,972,500	2,507,100	2,659,480
Tax	–281,720	–295,880	–376,070	–398,920
Minority Interest	–433,210	–400,000	–583,230	–557,190
Net Income	1,155,480	1,276,620	1,547,800	1,703,370
Capital Ex	1,863,680	3,287,130	6,500,000	200,000
Capital Ex % of Revenue	46.09	69.01	103.65	2.97

Source: Huatai Securities Co Ltd.

Lu-Hu Freeway: A freeway connecting Luchao and Shanghai, 43 km in length.

The Phase-1 Yangshan Deep Water Port would price container process fees competitively at RMB 350 per TEU, while the price at the Waigaoqiao Port would be increased from RMB 460 to RMB 506 to divert container throughput to the new port.[4] This price was significantly lower than the charges at Singapore Port and Busan port in Korea. Future competition from neighbouring ports was expected to further exert downward pricing pressure on the port.

THE PHASE-2 YANGSHAN DEEP WATER PORT EXPANSION PROJECT

Construction

The Yangshan Deep Water Port's Phase-2 expansion project would add four berths on the north-west side of the island next to the five berths constructed during Phase-1. The expanded portion was

[4] China Business Post, No. 648.

FIGURE M3.3
Shanghai Yangshan Deep Water Port (Phase-1)

Source: https://www.sinoptic.ch/shanghaiflash/texts/pdf/200303_Shanghai.Flash.pdf.

FIGURE M3.4
Donghai Bridge (Connecting Yangshan Deep Water Port and Shanghai City)

Source: https://www.sinoptic.ch/shanghaiflash/texts/pdf/200303_Shanghai.Flash.pdf.

FIGURE M3.5
Shanghai Yangshan Deep Water Port (Phase-2)

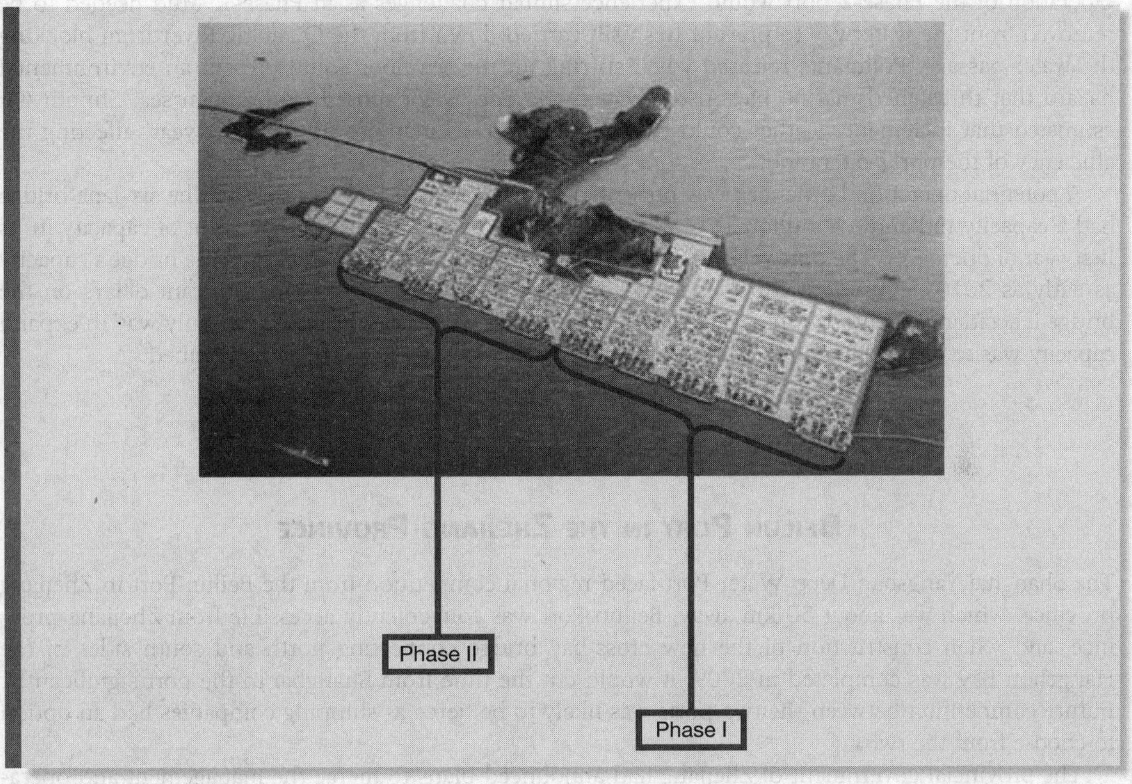

designed for container shipping and was expected to be completed in late 2006. It would add 1,400 m to the length of the quay and increase annual operation capacity by 2.1 million TEU. With average waterway depth of 15 m, it would also be able to accommodate up to 8,000 TEU container ships. Figure M3.5 presents the picture of the Phase-2 project.

The project was expected to take up 0.64 sq km of land; more than what was available on the Yangshan Island. To accommodate the project, the north-west section of the island's coastline was to be expanded into the sea by a 'sea-fill' by dumping rocks and sand into the sea. Using estimations published by Shimin Qu, former senior engineer at the Shanghai Institute of Port Design, it was estimated that applying this method to obtain the 0.64 sq. km of land would cost US$76.8 million.[5]

At the same time, geographical surveys found that the Phase-2 expansion site contained a thick mud layer, which was more difficult to prepare for construction than the sandy foundation found in Phase-1 site. Construction workers were to apply five different techniques to dry and strengthen the foundation before it could be readied for construction. The Phase-2 expansion project, including land creation, port construction and supporting infrastructure, was estimated to cost US$805 million.

[5] China Maritime, No. 68, P.56.

Operation

Operation of the Phase-2 port would experience similar challenges as in Phase-1. Mud needed to be removed from the waterway to prevent fresh silt carried down from the Qiantang River from blocking the water passage. Pollutants released when stirring up the sea floor could present an environmental hazard that threatened marine life. Also, because the port was exposed to the open sea, Shimin Qu estimated that inclement weather could close the port for as many as 50 days per year, affecting the efficiency of the port's operation.

A potential operation bottleneck was presented on the 32.5 km East Sea Bridge. The six-lane bridge had a capacity to handle 5 million TEU a year and was expected to reach 50 per cent of capacity in its first year of operation. The port was projected to reach 5.5 million TEU and exceed the bridge's capacity as early as 2010. Shipping companies were concerned that there would be significant delays on the bridge if accidents occurred. The bridge was also designed without railways, so the only way to expand capacity was to construct a new cross-sea bridge, which was not currently being planned.

COMPETITION

Beilun Port in the Zhejiang Province

The Shanghai Yangshan Deep Water Port faced regional competition from the Beilun Port in Zhejiang province, which was about 50 km away. Beilun Port was conveniently accessible from Zhejiang province, and when construction of the new cross-bay bridge connecting north and south sides of the Hangzhou Bay was completed in 2009, it would cut the time from Shanghai to the port significantly. Future competition between the two ports was likely to be fierce as shipping companies had an option to choose from the two.

The provincial government of Zhejiang had announced plans to merge the management and operations of the Ningbo (including Beilun Port) and Zhoushan ports to create the Ningbo–Zhoushan Port. Ningbo port was estimated to have handled 270 million tonnes of cargo during 2005, while Zhoushan had processed 80 million tonnes by the end of the year. Governor Lu Zushan had been quoted as saying that once the 100 billion Yuan (US$12.6 billion) integration and expansion was completed, the Ningbo–Zhoushan Port would be an integral part of the Shanghai International Shipping Center, although many speculated that Zhejiang did not want to be left behind due to the completion of Yangshan Deep Water Port complex being constructed 40 km from downtown Shanghai. Officials in Zhejiang estimated that the Ningbo–Zhoushan facility could handle 22 million TEU by 2020, the planned capacity of Shanghai Yangshan project.

Singapore Port

Singapore was favoured by its location at the outlet of Strait of Malacca, which made it a point of convergence, attracting 140,000 vessels every year. The Port of Singapore claimed the status of the world's busiest port in terms of shipping tonnage since 1986, reaching a container throughput reached 21.33 million TEUs in 2004. The booming world trade, general trend towards bigger ships and improvements in services offered at the port combined to keep up the top status in terms of tonnage.

Until 2002, the Singapore Port charged up to 50 per cent more than neighbouring ports by providing greater efficiency and value-added services to its customers. However, customer switching and stiff competition from ports in Southeast Asia forced the port to update its business model and discount its port dues in May 2002. The port signed a 10-year contract with Hanjin, a South Korean shipping company, and gained competitive advantage over rival ports by becoming the first foreign port to sign the Container Security Initiative (CSI) with the USA, allowing on-site US personnel to screen US-bound cargo containers for weapons of mass destruction.

Busan Port

Busan Port, located in the southeast of the Korean peninsula, was the gateway connecting the Pacific Ocean and the Asian continent. Within the Port, ships enjoyed a still water surface and only a small difference between high and low tides. The port also enjoyed proximity to an international arterial route and attracted 50,000 vessels annually, and handled 40 per cent of the total overseas cargo (imports and exports) and 80 per cent of container cargo. The Busan Port consisted of the North Port, South Port, Gamcheon Port and Dadaepo Port. Together, the ports could handle 169 vessels simultaneously and process 91 million tonnes of cargo annually. The Busan New Port, which was under construction, was scheduled to be operational by 2011. It could handle 30 vessels simultaneously and had an annual processing capacity of 8 million TEU per year.

Other Potential Investors

The Phase-2 expansion project of the Yangshan Deep Water Port was the first time the government had agreed to open the Yangshan Deep Water Port Project to foreign and domestic private investment. It was believed that the government would allow a higher percentage of foreign investment than domestic investment.

Due to the rapid rise of Shanghai in becoming the third largest container shipping port in the world, many foreign and domestic companies had expressed interest in investing in the project.

- **COSCO Group**
  The China Ocean Shipping (Group) Company (COSCO) was a diversified service company focusing mainly on shipping and logistic business.
- **China Shipping (Group) Company**
  China Shipping Group (China Shipping) was a shipping conglomerate that operated across different regions and sectors. It was a state-owned enterprise under the direct administration of China's central government and had assets totalling $5 billion.
- **OOCL**
  The Orient Overseas Container Line Limited (OOCL) was a wholly owned subsidiary of the Orient Overseas (International) Limited (OOIL), a public company listed on the Hong Kong Stock Exchange. OOCL was one of the world's largest integrated international container transportation, logistics and terminal companies.
- **AP Moller–Maersk**
  The AP Moller–Maersk Group was an international enterprise with activities covering diverse areas such as shipping, oil drilling, shipbuilding, industry and retail. It was headquartered in Esplanaden, Copenhagen, and had total assets exceeding $32 billion.

- **Port of Singapore Authority**
  The Port of Singapore Authority (PSA) was the world's largest container terminal operator. It operated 19 ports in 11 countries around the world, the largest of which was the world's number 1 container shipping port, the Singapore Port, with a designed capacity of 22.6 million TEU a year.

FUTURE EXPANSION

In total, the Yangshan Deep Water Project would consist of seven phases to be completed in 2020. By then, it would include 30 berths with an annual container handling capacity of 20MM TEU. The first four phases of the Yangshan Project would be constructed on the same island, while future phases would involve other neighbouring islands. Future expansion projects were likely to be open to foreign and domestic investment. Table M3.5 presents the timeline diagram of the seven phases of the project. Table M3.6 shows container handling volume and growth projections for the Yangshan Deep Water Port.

Shimin Qu pointed out that while the 15 m deep waterway at Yangshan Deep Water Port was sufficient to handle the world's existing largest container ships (8,000 TEU), the trend of building even larger vessels presented a challenge. Four ships of 10,000 TEU were being built by Hyundai Heavy Industries for COSCO.

A potential location for a new deep-water port that could accommodate bigger ships was Daqushan, an island located approximately 30 km from the Yangshan Island, with 20 m deep waterways. However, as Daqushan was under the jurisdiction of Zhejiang province, political intervention similar to that changed Yangshan's jurisdiction from Zhejiang to Shanghai would be needed.

THE INVESTMENT DECISION

The Phase-2 Shanghai Yangshan Deep Water Port Project presented a significant investment opportunity for HWL. The port was designed to both satisfy Shanghai's existing container handling needs and

TABLE M3.5
Shanghai Yangshan Deep Water Port Project Timeline

	Phase 1	Phase 2	Phase 3	Phase 4	Phase 5	Phase 6	Phase 7	Total
Completion Time	2005	2006	2008	2010			2020	2020
Total Investment (billion)	1.25	0.8			11.75 (Phases 3–7)			12.2
Accumulated Annual Capacity (TEU, million)	2.2			15			20	20
Number of Berths	5	4	4	3		14 (Phases 5–7)		30

TABLE M3.6
Projections of Container Handling Volume and Growth of Yangshan

Year	Container Handling Volume	CAGR
2005	2.2 m TEU	
2010	5.5 m TEU	20.1% (2005–2010)
2020	13.4 m TEU	9.3% (2010–2020)

Source: Shanghai Port Container Co Ltd.

attracted additional international cargo shipments. However, the project also faced significant risks and competition. HWL needed to decide whether these risks are worth the potential reward and whether or not to invest in the project.

Exercises

1. What are the merits and demerits of investing in the project?
2. Estimate the cost of capital for the project using the ICCRC model.
3. Estimate the IRR/NPV of the project by making suitable assumptions.
4. Is this NPV likely to understate the true value of the project? Why?

REFERENCES

Beijing Okokok Information Consulting Co. *Investment Study in China's Port Industry*. Available at https://faculty.fuqua.duke.edu/~charvey/Teaching/BA456_2006/Port/Port_case.doc (accessed on 4 January 2019).

China Maritime, No. 68, P.56. Available at https://repub.eur.nl/pub/6943/14.pdf (accessed on 4 January 2019).

National Bureau of Statistics of China. *China Statistical Yearbook 2004*. Available at http://www.stats.gov.cn/tjsj/ndsj/yb2004-c/indexeh.htm (accessed on 4 January 2019).

WMRC Country Report: China Available at www.worldmarketanalysis.com (accessed on 4 January 2019).

SUGGESTED READINGS

China International Capital Corporation. *Chinese Port Industry* (Beijing, issued 22 Feb 2006).

CITI Orient Securities Co. *SPCCO (600618)* (Shanghai, issued 15 Feb 2006).

Consulate General of Switzerland in Shanghai. 'Commercial Section', no. 3 (2003).

Goldman Sachs. *Dreaming With BRICs: The Path to 2050*. Global Economics Paper No: 99. Available at https://www.goldmansachs.com/insights/archive/archive-pdfs/brics-dream.pdf (accessed on 4 January 2019).

Guotai Junan Securities Co. *SPCCO (600618)* (Shanghai, issued 15 Feb 2006).

Huatai Securities Co. *SPCCO (600618)* (Nanjing, issued 17 Nov 2005).

Huatai Securities Co. *Chinese Port Industry* (Nanjing, issued 12 Dec 2005 and 20 Jan 2006).

Hutchison Whampoa Limited. Annual Report 2001. Available at http://202.66.146.82/listco/hk/hutchison/annual/2001/ar2001.pdf (accessed on 7 January 2019).

Hutchison Whampoa Limited. Annual Report 2004. Available at http://202.66.146.82/listco/hk/hutchison/annual/2004/ar2004.pdf (accessed on 7 January 2019).
Orient Securities Co. *SPCCO (600618)* (Shanghai, issued 16 Feb 2006).
Shanghai Port Container Company Limited Annual Report 2004 (Shanghai).
Consulate General of Switzerland in Shanghai. 'Research on the Investing and Financing System in the Yang Shan Deep-Water Port Construction'. *Journal of Shanghai Maritime University* 23, no. 4 (2002, Dec).
http://www.sigchina.com (accessed on 18 December 2005)
http://www.portshanghai.com.cn (accessed on 18 December 2005)
http://www.cmhico.com (accessed on 18 December 2005)
http://www.spcco.com (accessed on 18 December 2005)
http://www.sctport.com.cn (accessed on 18 December 2005)
http://www.shsict.com/ (accessed on 18 December 2005)
http://www.hutchison-whampoa.com (accessed on 18 December 2005)
http://www.htsc.com.cn/ (accessed on 18 December 2005)
http://www.research.kgi.com (accessed on 18 December 2005)
http://www.postel-cabling.com/jszc/gongchenanli/003.htm (accessed on 18 December 2005)
http://www.cna.tv/stories/corporatenews/view/34868/1/gb/ (accessed on 18 December 2005)
http://www.tianyablog.com/blogger/post_show.asp?blogid=140166&postid=3845171&idwriter=0&key=0 (accessed on 18 December 2005)
http://www.sunfed.com.cn/news/view.asp?NewsID=217&classID=1 (accessed on 18 December 2005)
http://news.sina.com.cn/z/yangshanshenshuigang/index.shtml (accessed on 18 December 2005)
http://zhidao.baidu.com/question/2183647.html (accessed on 18 December 2005)
http://www.yangshanterminal.com/ysportal/ (accessed on 18 December 2005)
http://www.fayhoo.com/servlet/info.F211newschina?id=20051211:1482784 (accessed on 18 December 2005)
http://roomx.blogchina.com/3833705.html (accessed on 18 December 2005)
http://www.moc.gov.cn/05news/0505/t20050526_18042.htm (accessed on 18 December 2005)
http://www.phoenixtv.com/phoenixtv/72631551992528896/20050527/557653.shtml (accessed on 18 December 2005)
http://www.shipbuilding.com.cn/news_show.php?newsid=3393 (accessed on 7 February 2006)
http://www.taxchina.cn/news/200308/t104214.html (accessed on 7 February 2006)
http://news.cnfol.com/051211/101,1281,1586405,00.shtml (accessed on 7 February 2006)
http://www.civil.edu.cn/news/02053101.htm (accessed on 7 February 2006)
http://www.investzj.com.cn/sanji.asp?id_forum=005613 (accessed on 7 February 2006)
http://www.hget.com.cn/cn/index/show_News.asp?id=397&classid=8 (accessed on 7 February 2006)
http://house.focus.cn/news/2004-09-18/77525.html (accessed on 7 February 2006)
http://www.sino56.com/sino/zjm/news/786.htm (accessed on 7 February 2006)
http://www2.mianyang.net.cn/news/china/20040626/286.htm (accessed on 7 February 2006)
http://www.hitwing.com/bbs/dispbbs.asp?BoardID=16&id=381 (accessed on 7 February 2006)
http://photo.eastday.com/eastday/node80808/node80840/node100721/userobject1ai1653727.html (accessed on 7 February 2006)
http://www.boraid.com/darticle3/list.asp?id=48487 (accessed on 7 February 2006)
http://news.sol.com.cn/special_msg.asp?id=152 (accessed on 7 February 2006)
http://www.p5w.net/p5w/home/industry/200512120668.html (accessed on 7 February 2006)
http://www.zjol.com.cn/gb/node2/node138665/node140578/userobject15ai1541226.html (accessed on 7 February 2006)
http://news.hexun.com/detail.aspx?lm=1715&id=1442380 (accessed on 7 February 2006)
http://www.xhby.net/xhby/content/2005-10/31/content_1004454.htm (accessed on 7 February 2006)
http://www.cccwto.org/tw3cccc/560.html (accessed on 7 February 2006)
http://www.ila571.com/new_view.asp?id=1465 (accessed on 7 February 2006)

4

Shanghai Disneyland*

LEARNING OBJECTIVE

To introduce issues in capital budgeting, cost of capital estimation in emerging markets and the economics of investing in China.

Description: The case highlights the economics of the Shanghai Disneyland theme park. Students are asked to evaluate the project and assess its viability.

I only hope that we don't lose sight of one thing—that it was all started by a mouse.

—Walt Disney

On a beautiful day in March 2003 in Orlando, Andy Berst strolled down the Main Street at the Magic Kingdom contemplating on a new project proposal. Andy, the Director of Finance for Hong Kong Disneyland, had spent the last four years preparing for the launch of Disney's newest park in Lantau Island in 2005. As he prepared to move to his new office in Hong Kong, he received a call from CEO Michael Eisner's office to discuss the possibility of a new venture in Shanghai.

Berst, like many senior executives with the company, knew that Disney was interested in breaking into mainland China for several years. On the other hand, he also knew that Disney had never built a park in a communist country, or what could be considered an emerging market. However, with the recent announcement from Universal Vivendi, a rival, confirming its intention to open a theme park in Shanghai around the same time as the Hong Kong Disneyland, Disney executives were anxious about their own response in mainland China. As he walked towards Cinderella's Castle, Andy's mind began to work out the details of the Shanghai Disneyland.

This case was prepared by Tera Ferguson, Kristy Harris, Scott Yancey, Wenny Tung and Jose Guerrero under the supervision of Professor Campbell Harvey, Fuqua School of Business, Duke University.

THE WALT DISNEY COMPANY'S THEME PARK AND RESORTS DIVISION

Disneyland will never be completed. It will continue to grow as long as there is imagination left in the world.

—Walt Disney

History

In 1955, Walt Disney opened the company's first theme park constructed at a cost of US$17.5 million in Anaheim, California, after just one year of construction. The partially completed park attracted over 28,000 visitors on its first day. More recently, Disneyland had recorded approximately 12 million visitors annually and had opened another park California Adventure in 2001.

Frustrated with space constraints after the first phase of Disneyland was completed, Walt Disney secretly purchased land in Orlando, Florida, after an extensive search around the country. Although Disney passed away before its launch, the Magic Kingdom became the first of four parks that opened Walt Disney World in 1971. Epcot, The Disney-MGM Studios and Disney's Animal Kingdom later added over 19 resorts, three water parks, 3 golf courses and a night-time entertainment complex.

Disney's first foray into international waters came in 1982 with the launch of Tokyo Disneyland. Reflective of the Walt Disney Company's financial situation in the early 1980s, the Tokyo Disneyland project was fully funded and wholly owned by the Oriental Land Company. Oriental Land Company had approached Disney about the construction of a theme park in Tokyo at a time when Disney could not financially support the project. Unlike its previous theme parks, the company's only revenue from this project came from royalties and management fees; Disney would not hold any equity stake. Despite a strong relationship with the Oriental Land Company, Disney's executive committee vowed never to enter into a similar project again without a substantial equity stake. They viewed Disney's brand as its greatest asset and the delivery of services at Disney parks as a critical element in maintaining the integrity of that brand.

As the overall financial health of the company improved, the push to expand internationally again culminated in the opening of Euro Disneyland (now Disneyland Paris) in 1992. Unwilling to let go of an equity stake as it had with the Tokyo project, Disney established a 39 per cent equity stake in the Euro Disneyland through a subsidiary and worked extensively with the French government to gain special tax breaks. Aside from its equity stake in the project, Disney would also receive regular royalties in the form of 'management fees' from Euro Disneyland. Despite a well-published rocky start, Disneyland Paris turned out to be profitable for Disney. Table M4.1 presents the timeline of Walt Disney's history. Table M4.2 presents data on annual attendance in Disney's theme parks and resorts. Table M4.3 presents data on ticket prices and disposable income of the local population at various locations.

REVENUES AND OPERATIONAL EXPENSES

Operating revenue for each of Disney's theme parks traditionally came from four areas: admissions charges, merchandise sales, food and beverage, and other miscellaneous 'main entrance' fees such as stroller and locker rentals. Table M4.4 presents the break-up of revenues.

TABLE M4.1
Timeline of Walt Disney's History

Year	Event
1901	Walter Elias Disney born in Chicago, Illinois
1928	Mickey Mouse is born
1952	Walt Disney announces plans to build Disneyland. Incorporates WED Enterprises
1953	Anaheim, California, selected as site after consulting with the Stanford Research Institute
1954	Disneyland excavation begins
1955	Disneyland opens to 28,154 visitors on 17 July. 90 million watch on ABC
1964	Universal Studios Hollywood opens
1966	Walt Disney dies
1971	Walt Disney World opens with the Magic Kingdom Park and two resorts
1982	Walt Disney World opens Epcot
1983	Tokyo Disneyland opens in Tokyo, Japan
1989	Walt Disney World opens the Disney–MGM Studios
1990	Universal Studios Orlando opens
1992	Euro Disneyland opens, name changed to Disneyland Paris later on
1994	Universal Studios Spain opens near Barcelona, Spain
1998	Walt Disney World opens Disney's Animal Kingdom Universal Studios opens Universal Studios Beijing (an indoor entertainment project)
1999	Hong Kong Disneyland Project announced in November Universal Studios Orlando opens Islands of Adventure
2001	Disneyland opens Disney California Adventure Tokyo Disneyland opens Tokyo DisneySea Universal Studios Japan Opens
2002	Disneyland Paris opens the Walt Disney Studios Park

Operating expenses were also fairly standard across all of Disney's theme parks. Table M4.5 presents the break-up of operating expenses for the Magic Kingdom Park in Orlando, Florida.

In addition to the aforementioned costs, regular capital expenditures were built into the financial projections of all parks to keep guests returning to Disney's theme parks. As a rule, Disney attempted to bring online an 'e-ticket'[1] attraction every three years.

Resorts

Disney theme parks had been traditionally marketed as vacation destinations. In line with this approach, every Disney theme park had a Disney theme resort hotel. The Disney resort hotels offered services such

[1] These involved a high level of financial investment (e.g., Space Mountain, Splash Mountain). An average e-ticket attraction costed approximately $100 million.

TABLE M4.2
Walt Disney Theme Parks and Resorts Annual Attendance 1992–2002 (in million)

	1992	1993	1994	1995	1996	1997	1998	1999	2000	2001	2002*
Disneyland	11.6	11.4	10.3	14.1	15	14.2	13.7	13.5	13.9	12.3	12.7
California Adventure										5	4.7
Magic Kingdom	11.5	12	11.2	12.9	13.8	17	15.6	15.2	15.4	14.7	14
Epcot	10	9.5	9.7	10.7	11.2	11.8	10.6	10.1	10.6	9	8.3
Disney-MGM Studios	8	8	8	9.5	10	10.4	9.5	8.7	8.9	8.3	8
Disney's Animal Kingdom							6	8.6	8.3	7.7	7.3
Tokyo Disneyland	16	15.8	16	15.5	17	17.4	16.7	17.5	16.5	17.7	13
Tokyo DisneySea										4	12
Disneyland Paris	10	9.8	8.8	10.7	11.7	12.6	12.5	12.5	12	12.2	12

Note: Estimated.

Source: http://www.scottware.com.au/theme/feature/crowds.htm.

TABLE M4.3
Ticket Prices and Disposable Income at Various Locations

	Orlando	Paris	Anaheim	Tokyo	Hong Kong	Shanghai
City Population (2000) (in Millions)	0.185984	2.1	3.7	28	7.116	13.216
Ticket Price (1 Day 1 Park Adult) No Tax Included ($)	50	39	47	46	N/A	N/A
Ticket Price Multi-Day, No Tax Included ($)	307		166	143	N/A	N/A
Ticket Price (Annual Pass), No Tax Included ($)	369	248	225	332	N/A	N/A
Annual Income (2000; $)	42,148	32,660	42,148	37,661	20,832	5,542
Annual Disposable Income (2000; $)	25,939	5,128	25,939	3,924	13,244	1,400

TABLE M4.4
Break-Up of Revenue for Disney Theme Parks

Average Revenue Breakdown	
Admissions	50%
Merchandise	24.5%
Food and Beverage	24.5%
Main Entrance	1%

TABLE M4.5
Break-Up of Operating Expense for the Magic Kingdom Park

Operating Expenses	US$ (in millions)
Park Labour (Salaried & Hourly)	50
Costs Associated w/Park Labour	25
Maintenance	15
Entertainment[2]	25
Food and Beverage[3]	32.43
Merchandise	53.58
Support Labour	5
Miscellaneous	5
Total Expenses[4]	211.01

as early morning entrance to the park and transportation services. While they were not highly profitable, they were considered necessary to the Disney vacation experience.

HONG KONG DISNEYLAND

We believed in our idea—a family park where parents and children could have fun together.

—Walt Disney

After months of deliberation, in November 1999, the Walt Disney Company was able to secure a deal with the Hong Kong Special Administrative Region Government to build a theme park, two hotels and a retail, dining and entertainment complex on Penny's Bay, Lantau Island. Because land was so scarce in Hong Kong, 280 hectares of land was dredged to make space. Disney planned to occupy 126 hectares of land during Phase-1 in 2005–2006. The proposed construction would include a 400-room Disney resort hotel. Hong Kong Disneyland's projected attendance in the first year totalled 6 million visitors.

The Hong Kong Disneyland was expected to create an estimated 18,000 new jobs in the first year (a projected 35,800 jobs over 20 years) and an approximate present economic value of US$19 billion. The US$1.8 billion Disney venture would be supported heavily by the government from a fiduciary prospective. The Hong Kong government's investment of US$22.5 billion not only included equity but also a substantial portion of project debt and US$13.6 billion contribution towards land formation and infrastructure improvement.

[2] Built-into entertainment costs are labour hours associated with entertainment. Of this $25 million, 28 per cent was assumed to go towards labour.

[3] Food and beverage, and merchandise expenses were based on 'per cap'. In the case of Magic Kingdom Park, it was assumed that for every admission, the park would receive $12.00 per person for food and beverage, and $12.00 per person for merchandise.

[4] Does not include start-up costs; start-up costs for a new theme park were estimated at $20 million (including opening costs for marketing, etc.).

The financial structure of the Hong Kong Disneyland deal was greatly in favour of Disney. The project was to be financed with 60 per cent debt, with 80 per cent of the debt covered by the Hong Kong government and 20 per cent of the debt covered through commercial means. Disney would provide 43 per cent of equity with the government contributing the balance.[5]

CHINA: BACKGROUND

We are not trying to entertain the critics. I'll take my chances with the public.

—Walt Disney

The Chinese government appeared to be embracing capitalism at an impressive pace. China concluded negotiations with the WTO in September 2001 committing to a large number of improvements to support business and trade development. There were still many limitations on foreign-owned enterprises, particularly in industries such as entertainment, but the government was beginning to make concessions. In 2002, China attracted a record US$52.7 billion in FDI, 14.8 per cent from the previous year and expected to continue climbing. About 26,700 foreign companies signed investment contracts in China in 2002, boosting the number of jobs created for Chinese workers by foreign companies to more than 23 million. Still, with many state-owned enterprises, China's total private sector only accounted for about 50 per cent of the country's economic output.

With a population of 1.26 billion people, China was the most populated country in the world, accounting for 20 per cent of the world's population. Population was expected to stabilize at 1.5 billion in 2050, as the current population growth rate of 1 per cent declined over the years. A change in the birth limitation policy could have a significant shift in the population growth. Although China's One-Child policy limited families to one child per household in order to increase natural resources per capita and stabilize the economic foundation, a New Population Law enacted in September 2002 eliminated the need for approval to have more than one child in urban areas. Many believed that the One-Child policy would quietly fade away in the coming years. Various projections and revisions for population growth are presented in Tables 4.6 and 4.7.

SHANGHAI

Located in the middle of China's east coast, Shanghai, was one of the four centrally administered municipalities. The city had four distinctive seasons with sufficient sunshine and rainfall. Average temperatures in Shanghai ranged from 2–3.5°C (36–38°F) in January to 27–28°C (81–82°F) in July.

The city was considered an economic centre in China, contributing approximately 5 per cent to China's GDP and continued to develop steadily. It had the highest per capita GDP in the country, amounting to US$4,512 in 2001 and US$3,327 as of September 2002. In addition, Shanghai was the largest recipient of FDI in the country, accounting for 9.4 per cent of China's total FDI. Shanghai was making substantial infrastructure improvements as it would be the venue for World Expo in 2010.

With a population of 14.15 million in 2002, Shanghai was one of the largest cities in the world. According to the 2002 National Bureau of Statistics of China, Shanghai had an average household size

[5] Disney speculated that the Chinese government would eventually sell its stake in the project.

TABLE M4.6
Population Projections for China

Source:	1995	2020	2025	2040	2050	2060
Zeng Yi/Vapel, 1989/1						
Scenario 1		1,534			1,690	
Scenario 2		1,496			1,557	
Scenario 3		1,422			1,431	
Lutz, W. (IIASA) 1994/2		1,605			1,873	
UN, 1994/3	1,222	1,488	1,526	1,591	1,606	
UN, 1996/3	1,220		1,480		1,517	
UN, 1998/3	1,227		1,488		1,484	
IPC/Oct., 1995/4	1,203	1,425		1,453	1,411	
Lutz, W. (IIASA) 1996/5	1,223	1,494	1,536	1,494	1,649	
IPC/ Sept., 1996/6	1,198	1,413	1,435	1,440	1,398	
IPC/Jul., 1998/6	1,203	1,397	1,408	1,385	1,322	
Shen/Spence, 1996/7						
Scenario A	1,229	1,530		1,604		1,540
Scenario B	1,223	1,466		1,516		1,469
Scenario C	1,223	1,454		1,430		1,250
Max Difference		208	128	219	551	290

Source: Zeng and Vaupei (1998), US Bureau of Census (1995), Shen and Spence (1996).

TABLE M4.7
China's Population by Age Group, 1950–2050[6]

	United Nations Population Projection, 1998 Revision, Medium Variant (million)				
	1950	1995	2010	2025	2050
Total	556.7	1,226.7	1,380.5	1,488.1	1,484.4
0–4	76.2	103.7	92.7	86.3	78.1
5–19	165.0	319.6	290.4	278.1	245.6
20–49	228.4	594.7	665.0	597.9	529.7
50+	87.1	208.8	332.4	525.8	631.0

Note: These estimates and projections include the population of Mainland China and Hong Kong.

[6] United Nations Population Division. *World Population Prospects*.

Population Increase or Decrease in China by Age Group, 1950–2050[7]

	United Nations Population Projection, 1998 Revision, Medium Variant (million)				
	1950–1995	1995–2010	2010–2025	2025–2050	1995–2050
Total	670.0	153.7	107.7	–3.7	257.7
0–4	27.5	–11.0	–6.4	–8.2	–25.6
5–19	154.6	–29.2	–12.3	–32.5	–74.0
20–49	366.3	70.3	–67.1	–68.2	–65.0
50+	121.7	123.6	193.4	105.2	422.2

Note: These estimates and projections include the population of Mainland China, Taiwan and Hong Kong.

of 2.89. It was the first city in China to record a negative fertility growth rate. However, despite this decrease, the total population and number of registrants were increasing due to 'floating' population. In 2000, 1.35 million women of childbearing age (15–49) were included among the 3.87 million floating population. This migration of women could potentially have a significant impact on the fertility growth in Shanghai. Additionally, as the metropolitan area expanded to suburban areas, the overall urban population would increase, impacting the wealth distribution of intra-urban households. Table M4.8 presents information on Shanghai's demographics.

The uneven distribution of wealth in China was considered worse than any other country in the world. In addition to the wealth disparity among rural and urban residents, there existed an uneven distribution of wealth within Shanghai. Of the urban with an annual income greater than 100,000 Yuan (US$12,066), 9.41 per cent lived in Shanghai. Furthermore, 10 per cent of the urban population lived in poverty, with an average annual income of only 2,676 Yuan (US$323). Tables 4.9–4.11 present information on income and expenditure of urban and rural households in Shanghai.

In an attempt to improve its wealth distribution, the Chinese government developed the Great Western Development plan. It restructured policies to develop and benefit a stable 'middle- income' group. This group would consist of a set of educated consumers earning between US$3,000 and US$12,000 a year. To achieve this, the government considered expanding teachers' salaries; pension and health care plans for urban residents; as well as tax breaks, loans and benefits for entrepreneurs. However, many believed that it would take some time before this plan reduced income disparity to Western standards. Table M4.11 and Figure M4.1 –14 present more demographic information on the urban and rural residents of China.

Many domestic tourists visited Nanjing Road, a shopping district in Shanghai, to capture the latest trends in the Chinese market. Shanghai consumers were considered trendsetters in fashion and lifestyle products across China. As a result, many merchandisers and distributors travelled to Shanghai to preview the latest fashion and product designs that were about to enter in order to gain a first mover advantage. Furthermore, Shanghai had experienced a surge in the number of domestic tourists and businessmen. Shanghai expected this to continue, especially with the launch of the 2010 World Expo. Figure M4.1 presents a map of the location.

[7] Ibid.

TABLE M4.8
Shanghai Demographic

	1997	2000	2001	2002
GDP (Million Yuan)	336,000	455,100	495,100	
Per Capital GDP	25,750	34,600	37,300	
Population (Million)	13.06	12.87		14.15
Including Floating Population	15.30	16.74	16.73	
Urban	10.19			
Rural	2.87			
Population by Age (Million)				
0–14	7.57	2.04		
15–60	3.89	12.77		
65+	1.60	1.93		
Average Urban Disposable Income (Yuan)		11,718	12,883	
Average Rural Disposable Income (Yuan)		5,100		
Average per Capita Income				
Urban	8,439			
Rural	5,277			
Average Value of Consumption				
Urban	6,820	8,868		
Rural	4,953			
Tourists (Million)			66.7	
Local			64.7	
Overseas			2	
Foreign			1.5	

THE SHANGHAI DISNEYLAND PROJECT

It's kind of fun to do the impossible.

—Walt Disney

Disney had long been interested in entering mainland China. With a foothold gained in the Chinese government through the addition of Hong Kong Disneyland, Berst and his finance team were now faced with evaluating the viability of a fourth international Disney theme park. While Berst understood that an existing relationship with the Chinese government would bestow significant benefits, he also realized that there was a great deal of uncertainty in a Communist country.

TABLE M4.9
Disposable Income of Rural and Urban Households in Shanghai

Year	Per Capita Annual Net Income of Rural Households (Yuan)		Per Capita Annual Disposable Income of Urban Households (Yuan)	
	Value (Yuan)	Index	Value (Yuan)	Index
1978	133.6	100	343.4	100
1980	191.3	139	477.6	127
1985	397.6	268.9	739.1	160.4
1986	423.8	277.6	899.6	182.5
1987	462.6	292	1,002.2	186.9
1988	544.9	310.7	1,181.4	182.5
1989	601.5	305.7	1,375.7	182.8
1990	686.3	311.2	1,510.2	198.1
1991	708.6	317.4	1,700.6	212.4
1992	784	336.2	2,026.6	232.9
1993	921.6	346.9	2,577.4	255.1
1994	1,221	364.4	3,496.2	276.8
1995	1,577.7	383.7	4,283	290.3
1996	1,926.1	418.2	4,838.9	301.6
1997	2,090.1	437.4	5,160.3	311.9
1998	2,162	456.2	5,425.1	329.9
1999	2,210.3	473.5	5,854.02	360.6
2000	2,253.4	483.48	6,280	383.69

Source: www.china.org.

TABLE M4.10
Income and Expenditure of Urban Households (Yuan)

Item	1985	1990	1995	1997	1998	1999	2000
Total Per Capita Annual Income	749	1,523	4,288	5,189	5,458	5,889	6,316.8
Lowest Income Households	483	860	2,178	2,456	2,505	2,647	2,678.3
#Households in Difficulties	438	783	1,985	2,186	2,229	2,357	2,350.8
Low-Income Households	599	1,077	2,778	3,246	3,329	3,518	3,658.5
Lower Middle-Income Households	692	1,267	3,364	3,988	4,135	4,392	4,651.7
Middle-Income Households	805	1,489	4,074	4,922	5,149	5,543	5,930.8
Upper Middle-Income Households	936	1,757	4,958	6,074	6,405	6,942	7,525
High-Income Households	1,098	2,072	6,036	7,495	7,918	8,675	9,484.7
Highest-Income Households	1,384	2,676	8,231	10,297	11,021	12,148	13,390.5

Item	1985	1990	1995	1997	1998	1999	2000
Per Capita Consumption Expenditure	673	1,279	3,538	4,186	4,332	4,616	4,998
Lowest-Income Households	456	782	2,061	2,333	2,398	2,523	2,540.1
#Households in Difficulties	418	725	1,904	2,148	2,214	2,328	2,320.4
Low-Income Households	551	961	2,516	2,895	2,979	3,137	2,374.9
Lower Middle-Income Households	627	1,098	2,934	3,427	3,503	3,695	3,947.9
Middle-Income Households	724	1,275	3,446	4,065	4,180	4,433	4,794.6
Upper Middle-Income Households	830	1,457	4,046	4,822	4,981	5,347	5,894.9
High-Income Households	963	1,685	4,666	5,710	6,003	6,443	9,102.3
Highest-Income Households	1,163	2,040	6,033	7,315	7,594	8,262	9,250.6

Source: www.china.org.

TABLE M4.11
Income and Expenditure of Rural Households (Yuan)

Item	1985	1990	1995	1998	1999	2000
Number of Households Surveyed per Capita Annual Income (Yuan)	**66,642**	**66,960**	**67,340**	**68,300**	**67,430**	**68,116**
Total Revenue	547.31	990.38	2,337.87	2,995.48	2,987.44	3,146.17
Net Income	397.6	686.31	1,577.74	2,161.98	2,210.34	
Cash Income	357.39	676.67	1,595.56	2,163.61	2,206.69	2,381.56
Percentage of Households Grouped by per Capita Annual Net Income (%)						
Under 100 Yuan	0.95	0.3	0.21	0.18	0.17	
100–200 Yuan	11.2	1.78	0.36	0.14	0.13	
200–300 Yuan	25.64	6.56	0.78	0.27	0.24	
200–300 Yuan	24.1	12.04	1.47	0.48	0.48	
300–400 Yuan	15.94	14.37	2.3	0.81	0.86	
500–600 Yuan	9.13	13.94	3.37	1.21	1.35	
600–800 Yuan	7.99	20.8	9.54	4.05	3.99	
800–1,000 Yuan	2.85	12.49	11.63	6.23	5.77	
1,000–1,200 Yuan	1.76	12.25	11.83	7.79	7.04	
1,200–1,300 Yuan	1.76	12.25	5.38	4.05	3.8	
1,300–1,500 Yuan	1.76	12.25	9.74	8.29	8.08	
1,500–1,700 Yuan	0.29	3.48	7.92	8.14	8.05	
1,700–2,000 Yuan	0.29	3.48	9.39	11.43	11.15	
2,000–2,500 Yuan	0.15	1.99	10.29	14.63	15.18	

(Continued)

TABLE M4.11
(Continued)

Item	1985	1990	1995	1998	1999	2000
2,500–3,000 Yuan	0.15	1.99	5.89	10.54	10.33	
3,000–3,500 Yuan	0.15	1.99	3.49	6.93	7.05	
3,500–4,000 Yuan	0.15	1.99	1.95	4.28	4.67	
4,000–4,500 Yuan	0.15	1.99	1.34	3	3.18	
4,500–5,000 Yuan	0.15	1.99	0.86	2.06	2.13	
5,000 Yuan and Over	0.15	1.99	2.26	5.5	6.35	
Per Capita Annual Expenditure (Yuan)						
Total Expenditure	485.51	903.47	2,138.33	2,457.17	2,390.37	2,652.38
Expenditure for Household Business	121.39	241.09	621.71	652.48	599.72	
Expenditure for Consumption	317.42	584.63	1,310.36	1,590.33	1,577.42	1,670.11
Other Non-Productive Expenditures	9.57	18.8	55.28	53.35	55.62	
Cash Expenditure	389.19	741.17	1,766.67	2,316.35	2,338.08	2,140.34
Productive Costs	98.93	183.35	517.06	565.97	528.36	
Taxes and Payments to Collective Units	16.35	33.38	76.96	98	93.06	
Expenditure for Consumption	194.68	374.74	859.43	1,128.16	1,144.61	
Expenditure for Savings and Credit	57.96	102.11	220.86	385.37	420.85	

Source: www.china.org

FIGURE M4.1
Project Location

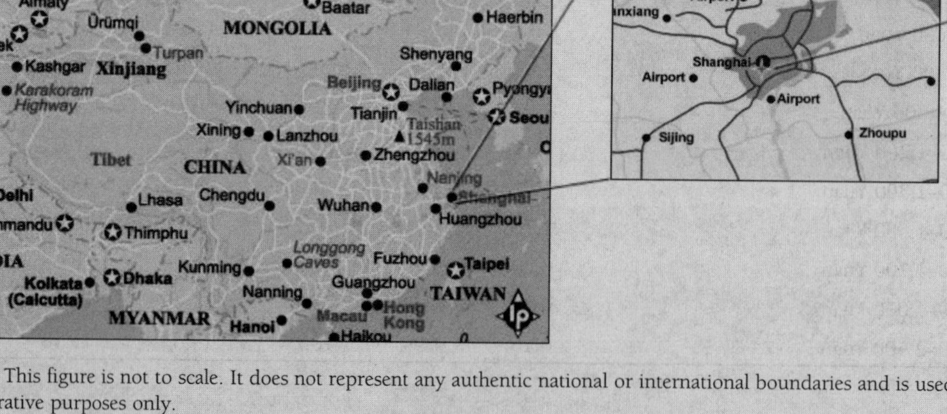

Note: This figure is not to scale. It does not represent any authentic national or international boundaries and is used for illustrative purposes only.

Shanghai, however, seemed to be an optimal entry location in China for many reasons. Brand recognition of Disney's core characters such as Mickey Mouse was strong, and an initial exploratory research suggested that there would be sufficient demand to sustain the park's existence over a number of years. Additionally, Berst knew that labour costs in China would be about two-thirds lower than other theme parks.

Berst knew that a sound evaluation of the Shanghai project would be dependent on his ability to accurately project demand. Off the cuff, Berst knew that such a project would cost about US$1.2 billion to complete, and he would need to take into consideration the implications of taxes. From his knowledge of Chinese tax laws, Berst knew he could expect 30 per cent taxes, but he could carry forward losses up to five years and carry back losses two years and utilize depreciation for 20 years. In addition, Disney typically used a 20- to 25-year time frame for evaluating returns on investments from similar theme parks.

Regardless of the numbers, Berst knew that the company needed to have a bigger presence in China to directly compete with Universal Vivendi, as well as take advantage of the largely untapped Chinese market.

Exercises

1. Would you invest in the project? Why or why not?
2. What are the risks in investing in the project?
3. Estimate the market size for the project; forecast revenues, expenses and cash flows for the project.
4. Estimate a suitable discount rate for the project, NPV and IRR.

REFERENCES

Statistical Abstract of the United States. (1995, Washington D C)

Shen J. and N. A. Spence. 'Modelling Urban-Rural Population Growth in China, Environment and Planning A: Economy and Space'. (1996 August).

United Nations Population Division. *World Population Prospects: The 1998 Edition*. New York, NY: United Nations Population Division, 1999.

Zeng, Yi and James W. Vaupel. 'The impact of Urbanization and Delayed Childbearing on Population Growth and Aging in China'. *Population and Development Review* 15, no. 3 (1989: 425–445).

MODULE 3

Financing Young and Mature Firms

5

Iceland Submarine Cable Project*

LEARNING OBJECTIVE

To introduce project financing in emerging markets, issues in capital budgeting and financing

Description: The case highlights a €6.3 billion project to export electricity from Iceland to the EU through a submarine cable. Students are asked to assess risks involved in the project, estimate a suitable discount rate, undertake a valuation exercise and evaluate the financial plan put together by the sponsors.

In January 2001, after several years of deliberation and debate, the Iceland government finally decided to pursue the Iceland Submarine Cable Project (ISCP). This project proposed to export 25 per cent of the country's electricity generated to the European continent. In order to undertake this €6.3 billion project, which represented over 80 per cent of the annual GDP, the prime minister of Iceland and the president of the state-owned energy company, Landsvirkjun, first needed to arrange the project's financing.

The Iceland government put together a financial plan so that they could pitch the idea to an investment bank that could help identify potential investors in the project. Their greatest concern involved identifying a lead equity investor who could attract additional equity capital while improving the possibility of issuing an investment grade bond for this monumental project. The magnitude of the project was such that it would take at least five years to complete the initial stages of construction. Arranging a financial structure attractive to all investors was necessary if the sponsors were to realize their dream.

This case was prepared by David Helgerson, Paul Timm, Tom Cowhey, Jason LaRose and Bill Wiseman under the supervision of Professor Campbell Harvey, Fuqua School of Business, Duke University.

* Reproduced with permission from Professor Campbell Harvey. Some of the images may be of poor quality. They are for representation purpose only.

THE REPUBLIC OF ICELAND

Iceland is a volcanic island located in the North Atlantic Ocean, lying approximately 2,600 miles northeast of New York and 500 miles northwest of Scotland, just south of the Arctic Circle. Most of Iceland's land is uninhabited (nearly 99%) as it consists largely of lakes, rivers, glaciers and a mountainous lava desert.

Although the country is a member of the North Atlantic Treaty Organization (NATO), it was the only member without its own military. Since 1951, Iceland had been protected by the Iceland Defense Force, which was controlled by the United States Military.

Iceland's population of 285,000 was growing at an annual rate of 1.1 per cent, with a 99.9 per cent literacy rate and less than 2.0 per cent unemployment.[1] In 2000, Iceland had a gross domestic product (GDP) of only US$8.6 billion with forecasted annual growth of 1.6 per cent in 2001.[2] Recent historic inflation had averaged 3.1 per cent. Table M5.1 presents additional macroeconomic data. Iceland maintained no national budget deficit, but its annual trade deficit was US$600 million. Although Iceland's recent €200 million bond issue received a rating of A+, Standard & Poor's (S&P) continued to be concerned about high external debt and weak external liquidity which compared unfavourably with A and AA rated countries. S&P maintained that the current levels might prove challenging if there was a sudden shift in confidence in the banking system or if the current account deficit was not reduced.[3] Table M5.2 presents the credit rating history of Iceland.

Over 70 per cent of Iceland's exports were marine products. However, there had been a recent push to diversify the country's exports and reduce their dependence on marine and fishing industries. Notably, the aluminium smelting industry was growing rapidly within Iceland, primarily to take advantage of the island's excess electricity capacity. Figure M5.1 presents data on Iceland's electricity sales. To

TABLE M5.1
Iceland Economic Data

	1995	1996	1997	1998	1999(1)	2000(2)	2001(3)
Population	267,806	269,727	272,069	275,264	278,575	281,691	284,785
Population growth (%)	0.5%	0.7%	0.9%	1.2%	1.2%	1.1%	1.1%
GDP, billion US$	$6.97	$7.26	$7.39	$8.12	$8.62	$8.61	$8.46
GDP per capita US$, current exchange rate	$26,014	$26,909	$27,169	$29,494	$30,960	$30,575	$29,705
GDP growth (% change from previous year)	0.1%	5.2%	4.8%	4.5%	4.4%	4.0%	1.6%
GDP by Sectors (%)							
Agriculture	2.3%	2.1%	1.8%	2.0%	2.0%	–	–
Fisheries and Fish Processing	14.9%	14.3%	12.7%	11.8%	11.1%	–	–
Manufacturing, Construction and Utilities	23.0%	23.1%	24.9%	24.0%	24.3%	–	–

[1] National Economic Statistics, Iceland, January 2001.
[2] Ibid.
[3] Standard & Poor's Ratings Services, 6 March 2000.

	1995	1996	1997	1998	1999[1]	2000[2]	2001[3]
Private Services	40.8%	41.3%	41.7%	43.3%	43.5%	–	–
Public Services	19.1%	19.3%	18.9%	18.9%	19.1%	–	–
Inflation (% change in CPI)	1.7%	2.3%	1.8%	1.7%	3.4%	5.2%	5.8%
Unemployment[3]	4.9%	3.7%	3.9%	2.8%	1.9%	1.5%	1.8%
Youth unemployment[4]	11.0%	8.4%	7.7%	6.1%	4.4%	–	–
Wages (% change in the Wage Index)	4.5%	6.4%	5.4%	9.4%	6.8%	6.7%	6.5%
Current Account Balance (billion US$)	$0.06	$(0.12)	$(0.11)	$(0.56)	$(0.60)	$(0.78)	$(0.79)
Current Account Balance (% of GDP)	0.8%	(1.7)%	(1.6)%	(6.9)%	(6.9)%	(9.1)%	(9.3)%
Main Export Categories (%)							
Marine Products	52.0%	52.4%	49.0%	48.5%	45.4%	–	–
Energy Intensive Products	9.6%	9.0%	9.9%	10.6%	11.9%	–	–
Tourist Revenues	12.3%	11.7%	11.6%	12.9%	12.9%	–	–
Other	26.1%	26.9%	29.5%	28.0%	29.8%	–	–
Export Shares (%)							
United States of America	12.3%	11.7%	13.9%	12.9%	14.7%	–	–
European Economic Area (EEA)	66.0%	66.1%	66.1%	69.8%	68.9%	–	–
Other	21.7%	22.2%	20.0%	17.3%	16.4%	–	–
Import Shares (%)							
United States of America	8.4%	9.4%	9.4%	11.1%	10.9%	–	–
European Economic Area (EEA)	70.0%	69.9%	69.6%	65.4%	66.3%	–	–
Other	21.6%	20.7%	21.0%	23.5%	22.8%	–	–
Public Sector Balance (% of GDP)	(3.0)%	(1.6)%	0.0%	0.5%	2.0%	2.8%	2.5%
Central Gov. Fin. Balance (% of GDP)	(2.6)%	(1.5)%	0.5%	1.1%	2.5%	3.2%	2.9%
Short-Term Int. Rates (3-month T-Bills)	7.3%	7.1%	7.0%	7.4%	8.6%	–	–
Long-Term Int. Rates (5-year T-Notes)	–	9.2%	8.7%	7.7%	8.9%	–	–
Effective Ex. Rate of the Krona (% change)	(0.8)%	0.2%	(1.3)%	(1.8)%	(0.3)%	–	–
Exchange Rates							
USD	64.79	66.68	70.98	71.12	72.42	78.80	86.00
DEM	45.22	44.33	40.94	40.50	39.46	–	–
GBP	102.22	104.18	116.24	117.83	117.14	–	–
JPY	0.69	0.61	0.59	0.55	0.64	–	–

Note: (1) Estimate
(2) Forecast (December 2000)
(3) Labour Force Survey
(4) 16–24 years
Source: National Economic Institute, Iceland.

TABLE M5.2
Iceland Ratings Agency Data, 1989–Present

	Local Currency Rating			Foreign Currency Rating		
	Long-term	Outlook	Short-term	Long-term	Outlook	Short-term
14-Feb-1989				A	—	A-1
26-Jun-1989				A	Stable	A-1
20-Jan-1994				A	Stable	A-1
15-Mar-1996	AA+	Stable	—	A+	Stable	A-1+
20-May-1998	AA+	Stable	—	A+	Positive	A-1+
27-May-1998	AA+	Stable	A-1+	A+	Positive	A-1+
23-Feb-2000	AA+	Stable	A-1+	A+	Positive	A-1+

Source: S&P Ratings Agency.
On 23 February 2000, S&P assigned its 'A+' long-term rating to the Republic of Iceland's seven-year €200 million bond.

FIGURE M5.1
Iceland Electricity Sales, 1950–2002E

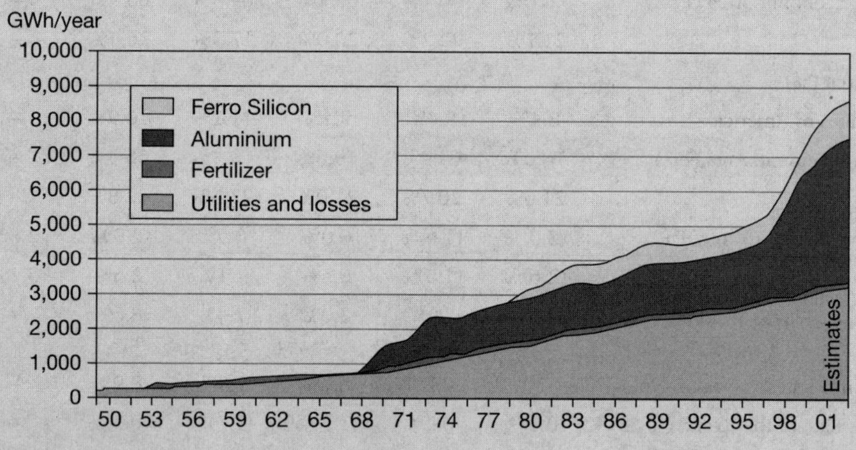

Source: Invest in Iceland.

bring this power-intensive industry to its shores, the government had constructed a US$1 billion power station although it had avoided granting tax relief.[4] This facility was selling electricity to the US-owned aluminium smelters at US$0.02/kWh, slightly above its variable cost. At the time, fossil fuels made up less than 0.1 per cent of Iceland's energy consumption, and no nuclear power was in use. But the country still produced more than 400 million excess kilowatt hours (kWh) annually.[5]

[4] www.rsk.is/skattyfirvold/annad/income.asp (accessed on 7 January 2019).
[5] Central Intelligence Agency. *CIA World Fact Book.*

Iceland's unique position straddling the Mid-Atlantic Ridge and its low population density (approximately 2.8 people per sq. km) provided the country a unique economic opportunity. Although Landsvirkjun, the national power company, controlled all 7 terawatt hours (TWh)[6] of annual electricity generation within Iceland, this represented only 17 per cent of the total renewable energy potential within the country.[7] It was estimated that at least another 35 TWh remained to be tapped annually from Iceland's geothermal and hydroelectric energy reserves (see Figure M5.2). It was a portion of this untapped potential that the ISCP wished to capture and supply electricity to the European Union (EU).

GEOTHERMAL AND HYDROELECTRIC ENERGY

Geothermal energy is heat derived from rocks and fluids contained in the earth's crust. The thermal energy from rocks is used to heat water to temperatures between 100°F and 300°F either directly or

FIGURE M5.2
Iceland Power Usage, Including Geothermal and Hydrogen Reserves

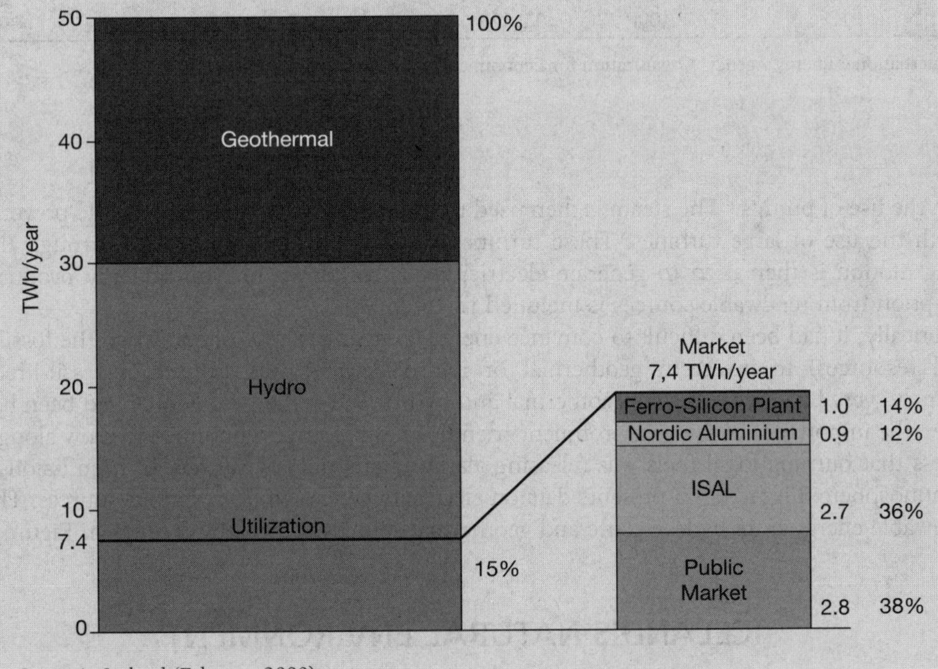

Source: Invest in Iceland (February 2000).

---

[6] One TWh = 1,000 megawatt hours = 1,000,000 kWh = 1,000,000,000 watt hours.

[7] www.lv.is/lv.nsf/pages/power_potential-ens.html (accessed on 7 January 2019).

TABLE M5.3
Energy Production and Consumption from Renewable Sources (1,000 Metric TOE)

	Production	Consumption					
	All Sources	All Sources	Biomass	Hydro	Geothermal	Solar	Wind
World	1,323,051	1,321,093	1,061,775	220,656	36,659	1,015	989
Europe	139,258	139,247	76,996	57,645	3,691	236	630
Germany	*5,569*	*5,569*	*3,816*	*1,493*	*0*	*3*	*258*
Iceland	*1,481*	*1,481*	*1*	*448*	*1,032*	*0*	*0*
United Kingdom	*2,097*	*2,097*	*1,685*	*355*	*0*	*0*	*57*
Asia	623,784	625,537	569,937	43,653	11,926	16	5
Middle East and N. Africa	18,597	18,613	11,562	6,275	179	597	0
Sub-Saharan Africa	NA	NA	NA	NA	NA	NA	NA
North America	150,068	150,027	78,240	58,590	12,820	77	297
C. America and Caribbean	35,432	35,432	25,641	3,815	5,968	0	7
South America	106,225	104,699	62,052	42,600	0	0	48
Oceania	11,098	11,098	5,924	3,437	1,646	89	1

Source: International Energy Agency, Organization for Economic Cooperation and Development.

through the use of pumps.[8] The steam is then used to generate electricity. Hydroelectric power is generated with the use of large turbines. These turbines spin as moving water passes through them; this spinning motion is then used to generate electricity. A breakdown of world energy production and consumption from renewable sources is included in Table M5.3.

Historically, it had been difficult to convince energy companies (who often owned the fossil fuel raw material resources) to invest in geothermal or hydroelectric plants instead of fossil-fired plants. Accordingly, very little of the earth's geothermal and hydroelectric energy potential had been harnessed. However, the importance of these environment-friendly energy sources continued to grow along with the awareness that burning fossil fuels was releasing alarming amounts of harmful CO_2 emissions into the earth's atmosphere. Figure M5.3 presents data on electricity generated from various sources. The potential renewable energy from hydroelectric and geothermal sources is listed by country in Figure M5.4.

ICELAND'S NATURAL ENVIRONMENT

Hydropower development, especially within Iceland, could have an environmental impact, most notably tied to the construction of the reservoirs needed for water storage.[9] Reservoirs often cover vegetated areas, which could reduce valuable grazing land for sheep while also visually impacting the land. Other

[8] www.geothermal.org/whatgeo.html (accessed on 7 January 2019).

[9] http://brunner.stjr.is/interpro/ivr/ivr.html (accessed on 7 January 2019).

FIGURE M5.3
World Electricity Generation, 1970–2020E

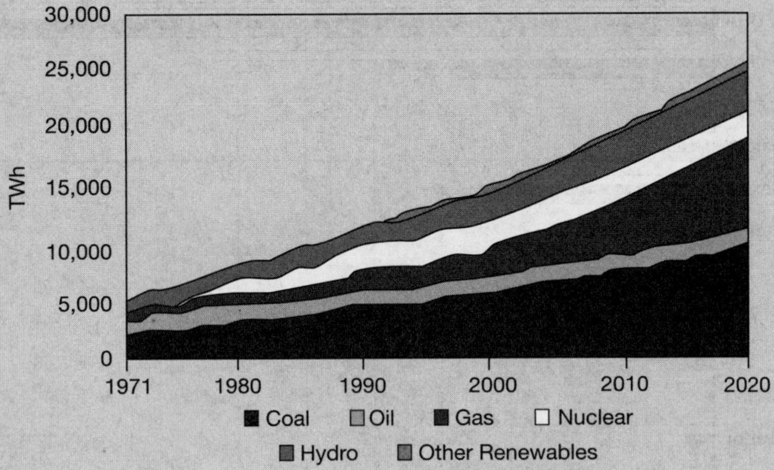

Source: International Energy Agency.

forms of impact involved reduced flow of waterfall and sediment transport in glacial rivers affecting freshwater fishing.

In addition, geothermal energy development within Iceland could negatively impact the natural environment. First, geothermal power plants could marginally increase air pollution although their impact was less than fossil fuel plants (Figure M5.5). For example, some countries with low quality geothermal reserves such as Italy experienced problems with mercury and sulphur emissions in the areas surrounding the power plants. These problems stalled the further development of geothermal plants. Second, tapping into geothermal reserves could lead to a drying up of natural hot springs. Finally, the high-temperature fields could cause air pollution themselves by increasing H_2S emissions from the fields.[10]

The Ministry of Environment in Reykjavik formulated the country's national environmental strategy to include the following top three objectives:[11]

- Reduce local pollution, waste generation and pollution of the atmosphere
- Complete improvements in waste management
- Attain sustainable use of natural resources

To drive home the point of these objectives, many citizens rallied against the government's recent decision to bring aluminium smelters to Iceland because of associated increase in local pollution and use of the country's natural power reserves by foreign-owned companies.

[10] www.lv.is/lv.nsf/pages/power_potential-ens.html (accessed on 7 January 2019).

[11] www.wri.org/wdces/ic93_721.html (accessed on 7 January 2019).

FIGURE M5.4
Selected Installed Geothermal Electricity Generation Capacity

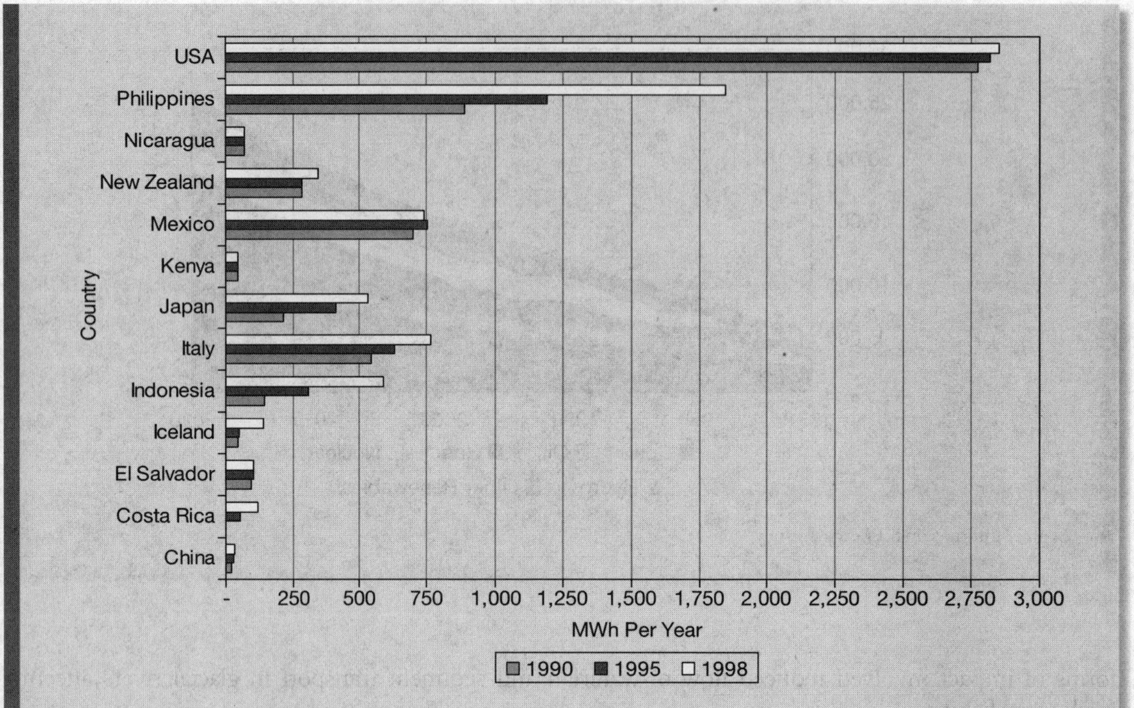

Source: World Energy Council.

Similarly, the World Wildlife Foundation's Arctic programme included a plan to escalate its campaign to establish a protective national park in a region that included some geothermal activity. The Ministry of Environment was scheduled to hear their case in March 2001 and vote on the issue within three months.[12]

ELECTRICITY IN THE EUROPEAN UNION

The EU was formed in 1993 to promote the economic and political integration of Europe. The EU consisted of 15 member countries: Austria, Belgium, Denmark, Finland, France, Germany, Greece, Ireland, Italy, Luxembourg, the Netherlands, Portugal, Spain, Sweden and the United Kingdom.[13] With the exception of the United Kingdom and temporarily Greece, the EU adopted the Euro as a single currency in 1999.

The EU played a significant role in its member's domestic energy policies. These countries collectively deregulated their energy industry in 1999 under the 1996 EU Directive on Electricity, mandating

[12] www.ngo.grida.no/wwfap/iceland.html (accessed on 7 January 2019).

[13] http://europa.eu.int/en/comm/dg17/wp_e.htm#h34 (accessed on 7 January 2019).

FIGURE M5.5
Gaseous Emissions from Electricity Production

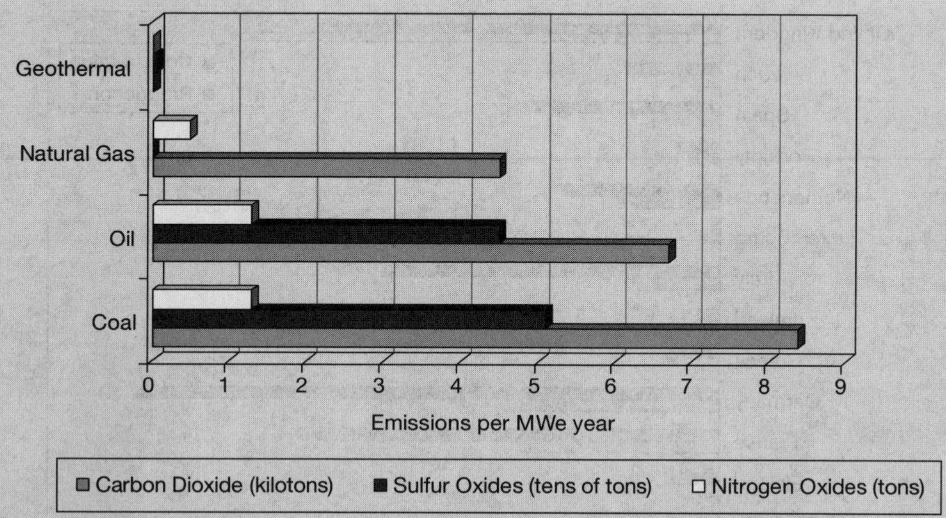

Source: World Energy Council; 'Survey of Energy Resources—Geothermal Energy Commentary'.

that countries completely open up their markets to competition within two years. Many countries liberalized their electricity markets ahead of the schedule, following which there was an immediate and precipitous decrease in electricity prices.[14] The data on domestic electricity generation capacity and usage in each of the member countries is presented in Figure M5.6.

On 11 December 1997, the Kyoto Protocol was introduced at a meeting of the United Nations in Japan. This protocol called for a 60 per cent reduction in worldwide CO_2 emissions by 2050 along with dramatic reductions in the use of nuclear power. The protocol was signed by all the EU member countries and its impact was already being felt in the energy market in early 2001. As a net importer of energy, the EU consumed 16 per cent of the world's energy, yet produced just 8 per cent. Heavily dependent on fossil fuels, EU member countries produced roughly 895 million metric tonnes of carbon dioxide in 1998.[15] They had collectively agreed to lower their emissions by 25 per cent before 2010.[16]

The demand for electricity had been particularly constant with a forecasted growth of 1.7 per cent p.a. The EU was expecting a major shift in the breakdown of its electricity sources over the next 20 years due to its environmental policies. Throughout the entire EU, electricity generated by nuclear energy was expected to drop from 33 per cent in 1997 to 25 per cent by 2020. Natural gas was expected to replace nuclear power as the dominant fuel in the EU accounting for 28 per cent of fuel in 2020. The use of coal and oil that accounted for 24 per cent and 8 per cent of power generation in Western Europe had been declining since 1970. Electricity from coal was expected to drop from 24 per cent to 16 per cent by 2020.[17]

---

[14] European Commission, 'Opening Up to Choice'.
[15] International Energy Agency, *Regional Indicators*.
[16] www.kyotoprotocol.de (accessed on 7 January 2019).
[17] US Department of Energy, Energy Information Administration, *International Energy Outlook 2000*.

FIGURE M5.6
European Energy Demand and Consumption, 1998 (Quadrillion Btu)

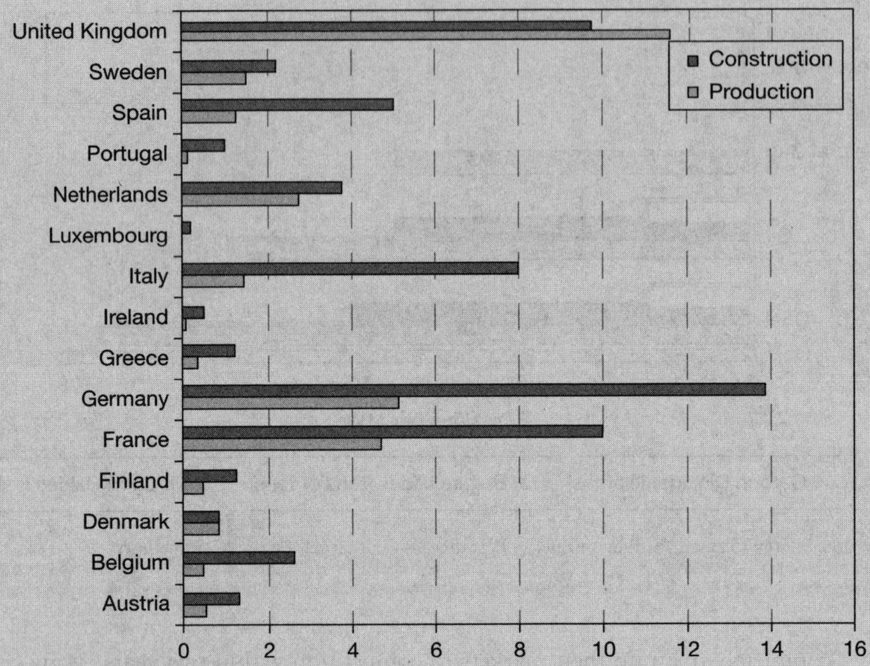

Source: Energy Information Administration.[18]

In accordance with the Kyoto Protocol, the EU also agreed to increase its total energy contributions from renewable sources (wind, hydroelectric and geothermal) from 6 per cent in 2000 to 14 per cent by 2001. To achieve this goal, the EU would have to raise its share of renewable sources of electricity from 14 per cent to 22 per cent over the next 10 years.[19] For every terawatt of electricity generated from a renewable source instead of a fossil fuel, CO_2 emissions would decline by nearly 0.3 million metric tonnes. In addition to these fossil fuel concessions, the union members agreed to build no additional nuclear capacity.[20]

To help drive its commitment to the Kyoto Protocol, the European Parliament discussed the implementation of an energy tax on all forms of non-renewable energy production including coal, lignite, peat, natural gas, mineral oils, ethyl and methyl alcohols. The tax would also likely apply to nuclear energy as well to provide incentive for member countries to accelerate the process of reducing their reliance on nuclear energy sources.[21]

---

[18] www.eia.doe.gov

[19] European Commission, 'Recent Progress with Building the Internal Electricity Market'.

[20] www.kyotoprotocol.de (accessed on 7 January 2019).

[21] http://europa.eu.int/.html (accessed on 7 January 2019).

THE SUBMARINE CABLE PROJECT

In the light of these trends in the EU, members of the ISCP were convinced that the timing to build their long researched cable project was right. Completion of the proposed energy export project involved three main components: building power capacity in Iceland, determining a European end point for the cable and laying the cable along the ocean floor from Iceland to the European continent.

At the time, Landsvirkjun was generating 7 TWh of electricity per year in Iceland, which represented nearly all of its installed capacity. The proposed submarine cable project would involve harnessing 10 TWh annually to export and would require the construction of additional power facilities. It was anticipated that these facilities could be constructed at a cost of approximately €1.9 billion. In addition, new infrastructure would have to be built to transport electricity to the cable end point within Iceland at an additional cost of €236 million.

The closest (and the most cost-effective) end point for the cable was in the United Kingdom, but the Iceland government was unsure if this was the best location for the cable since the UK was a net exporter of energy. Therefore, power shipped to the UK would have pass through the European power grid to other countries with greater demands for electricity. While the EU had recently begun initiatives to connect all the member state power grids (See Figure M5.7 for data on the status of the EU power grid), the ISCP members preferred to ship their power to a country that already had demand for their electricity. While a cable to Norway was another possibility, the ISCP members were hesitant as the country was not a member of the EU. Therefore, the next logical choice for the cable end point was Germany.

ENERGY SITUATION IN GERMANY AND EUROPE

Germany[22] had very limited domestic energy sources and was heavily import-reliant to meet its total energy needs. The German electricity market was the largest in Europe, consuming 488 billion kWh. Due to its heavy reliance on coal (50%) and nuclear resources (31%), Germany had been able to domestically generate enough electricity to meet its local demand, although its domestic demand had increased as deregulation lowered local prices.[23] However, Chancellor Gerhard Schroeder was a staunch advocate of eliminating Germany's nuclear energy plants. As a member of the majority Green party, he passed a decree that all domestic nuclear plants (generating 30% of German electricity)[24] would be closed by 2005, only to rescind his position in the wake of political backlash. His compromise was to eliminate all nuclear energy production by 2021,[25] which would still require dramatic increase in energy production from natural gas and renewable sources.

Germany had been particularly active in promoting renewable energy. The German Feed Law of 1991 required utilities to accept all electricity generated by renewable energy, at somewhat discounted prices. In 1998, the Feed Law was modified to require utilities' acceptance of just 5 per cent of total electricity from renewable sources. Soon thereafter, however, Chancellor Schroeder stated that Germany would reach the Kyoto Protocol emission target by levying 'eco-taxes' to advance renewable energy projects. On 1 April 1999, the first phase of the tax was implemented on gasoline and electricity. The second phase, currently underway, would raise energy prices about 10 per cent over the next three

[22] For the previous 10 years, German inflation had averaged 2.3 per cent (Source: Eurostat).

[23] www.eia.doe.gov/cabs/germany2/html (accessed on 7 January 2019).

[24] Ibid.

[25] Ibid.

FIGURE M5.7

European Union Power Grid and Proposed Electrical Infrastructure Projects

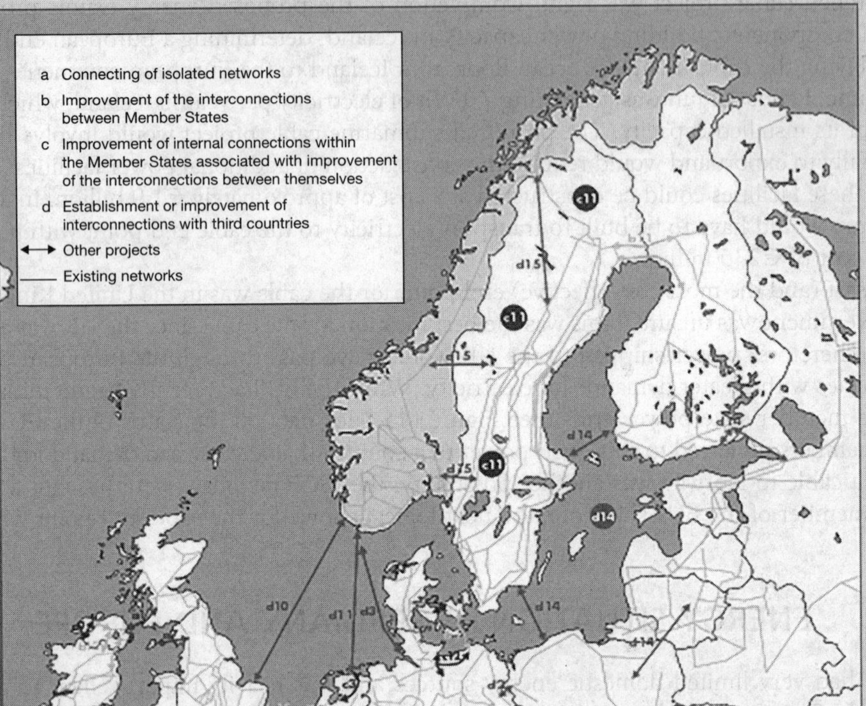

Source: European Commission—Directorate General for Energy (DG XVII).

Note: This figure is not to scale. It does not represent any authentic national or international boundaries and is used for illustrative purposes only.

years. Most analysts believed that this tax was imminent given Germany's existing 16 per cent VAT on energy consumption and the staggering 300 per cent tax on gasoline. Although renewable energy was not initially exempt from the tax, the revenue generated by the tax would be used to fund and aid renewable energy programmes.[26] Germany had been a leading proponent of EU-mandated carbon emissions taxes as well. Although previous attempts to mandate EU coal and natural gas excise taxes were narrowly defeated, they were still under consideration for the future.

The historic electricity prices in Germany and other parts of Europe are provided in Table M5.4 and Figures 5.8 and 5.9.

The Iceland government had already discussed the project with Pirelli, the worldwide leader in cable and rubber production. Pirelli had both the capacity to build the cable and expertise in laying sub-terrain and submarine power cables. They estimated the cost of producing and laying the cable to Germany at €3.5 billion.

In order to determine the feasibility of selling green energy to Europe, in 1993 Landsvirkjun conducted a study with Pirelli, Vattenfall Engineering AB of Sweden and the ABB Transmission Technology Institute in the USA. The study determined that it would be technically feasible to harness a portion of Iceland's untapped energy resources and transport electricity via a submarine cable to Europe. More recent studies by Scottish Hydro plc and the Icenet Gruppe (comprising of several European energy companies) also confirmed the project's feasibility. Total construction would take about 10 years with the first phase of power transportation in Year five. The project would involve three major developmental blocks:

- Harnessing up to an additional 20 per cent of Iceland's power reserves and building transmission lines to transport this electricity to a coastal site
- Laying a submarine cable from the coast to a site in the UK or mainland Europe
- Building converter stations at the cable destination

Landsvirkjun had vast experience in harnessing both hydro and geothermal power resources and would lead the development of the project in Iceland. Pirelli would construct and lay the submarine cable. Depending on the terminal point of the cable, a third party would oversee the development of converter stations at an estimated additional cost of €375 million and take on marketing responsibilities within the destination country.

A map detailing the expected cable route and estimated cost is contained in Figure M5.9.

HARNESSING ICELAND'S RENEWABLE ENERGY

Development of geothermal power sources represents one methodology for harnessing green energy for electricity generation. Wells are drilled into the earth's crust in locations where magma pockets rise near the surface. Water is pumped onto the magma pocket, generating steam, which in turn drives a turbine to generate electricity. A graphical depiction of this process is shown in Table M5.6.

Geothermal electricity generation facilities have significant operating leverage. Investment is required for exploration, well drilling, plant installation and creation of a steam field. The capital costs for geothermal generation are substantially higher on a per megawatt basis than fossil fuel-fired generating facilities. However, lack of input materials for geothermal facilities make them insensitive to volatile

[26] Ibid.

TABLE M5.4
Recent Historic Electricity Prices in Germany (Euros/100KWh)

	Price excluding taxes												
	Deusseldorf	Hamburg	Hanover	Western Zone	Frankfurt	Stuttgart	Munich	Southern Zone	Erfurt	Leipzig	Rostock	Average	% Change
Jan-1990	€8.37	€9.14	€8.30	€8.43	€7.68	€8.75	€7.94	€7.76	NA	NA	NA	**€8.30**	
Jan-1991	8.30	8.94	8.81	8.06	7.62	8.68	7.87	7.70	NA	NA	NA	**8.25**	
Jul-1991	8.27	9.24	8.80	8.04	7.81	8.67	7.86	7.69	NA	NA	NA	**8.30**	0.6
Jan-1992	8.33	9.36	8.85	8.09	8.10	8.72	7.90	7.74	NA	NA	NA	**8.39**	1.1
Jul-1992	8.62	9.73	8.85	8.09	8.10	8.72	7.90	7.74	8.55	8.29	8.60	**8.47**	1.0
Jan-1993	8.99	10.07	9.23	8.44	8.45	9.10	8.24	8.07	8.92	8.64	8.97	**8.83**	4.2
Jul-1993	9.03	10.05	9.26	8.47	8.48	9.13	8.27	8.10	8.95	8.67	9.08	**8.86**	0.4
Jan-1994	9.12	10.13	9.36	8.55	8.56	9.22	8.36	8.18	9.04	8.77	9.17	**8.95**	1.0
Jul-1994	9.17	10.14	9.41	8.48	8.95	9.27	8.40	8.23	9.09	8.82	9.22	**9.02**	0.7
Jan-1995	9.24	10.20	9.48	8.54	9.02	9.35	8.47	8.29	9.16	8.89	9.29	**9.08**	0.8
Jul-1995	9.42	9.59	9.66	8.70	9.19	9.52	8.63	8.45	9.34	9.06	9.47	**9.18**	1.1
Jan-1996	8.34	9.51	8.93	8.22	8.91	9.04	8.00	7.79	9.44	8.58	9.36	**8.74**	(4.9)
Jul-1996	8.25	8.27	8.16	8.12	8.81	8.94	7.91	7.70	9.34	8.48	9.26	**8.48**	(3.0)
Jan-1997	8.09	7.98	8.01	7.97	8.35	8.77	7.76	7.56	8.90	8.32	8.57	**8.21**	(3.2)
Jul-1997	7.96	7.55	7.61	7.84	8.22	8.63	7.64	7.44	8.76	8.19	8.43	**8.02**	(2.2)
Jan-1998	7.98	7.56	7.62	7.86	8.23	8.48	7.47	7.45	8.78	8.20	8.46	**8.01**	(0.2)
Jul-1998	8.00	7.58	7.64	7.87	8.25	NA	7.26	7.47	8.80	8.22	8.47	**7.96**	(0.7)
Jan-1999	8.06	7.64	7.09	7.14	8.31	NA	6.98	6.96	8.87	7.37	8.54	**7.70**	(3.3)
Jul-1999	8.26	7.64	7.09	7.14	6.94	NA	7.98	6.96	8.87	8.87	7.37	**7.71**	0.2
Jan-2000	5.04	6.64	5.85	4.97	5.48	NA	5.11	5.13	9.13	NA	7.45	**6.09**	(21.0)
Jul-2000	7.80	6.64	5.85	4.97	5.48	NA	5.11	5.13	9.13	5.90	7.45	**6.35**	4.2
Standard Dev	0.89	1.20	1.12	1.03	1.00	0.30	0.94	0.88	0.24	0.76	0.68	**0.80**	5.4
Average Change													(1.2)
Annual Standard Deviation (1991–1999)		1.6%											
Annual Standard Deviation (1999–2000)		7.9%											
Annual Standard Deviation (1990–2000)		3.8%											

Source: Eurostat.

EXHIBIT B

Recent Historic Electricity Prices in Germany (Euros/100KWh), 1990–2000

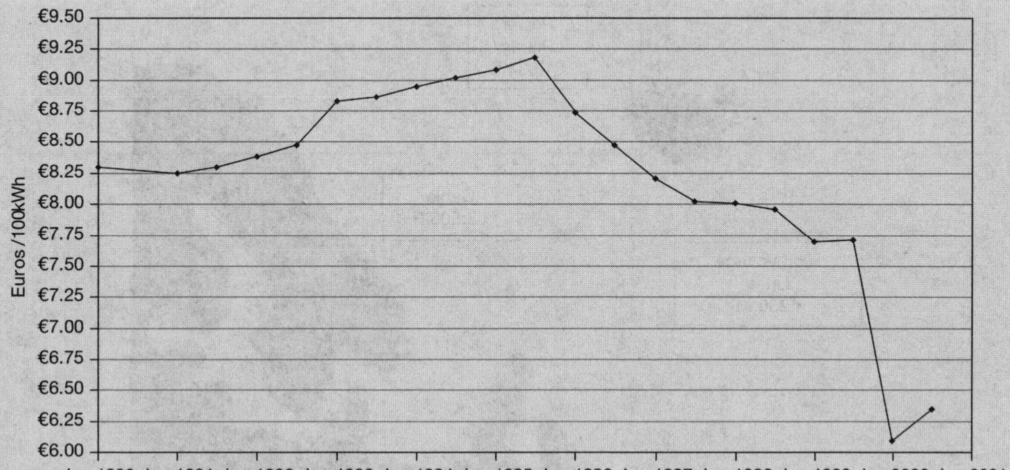

Source: Eurostat.

FIGURE M5.8

Cross-Section of Selected European Industrial Electrical Prices (10 MW), July 2000

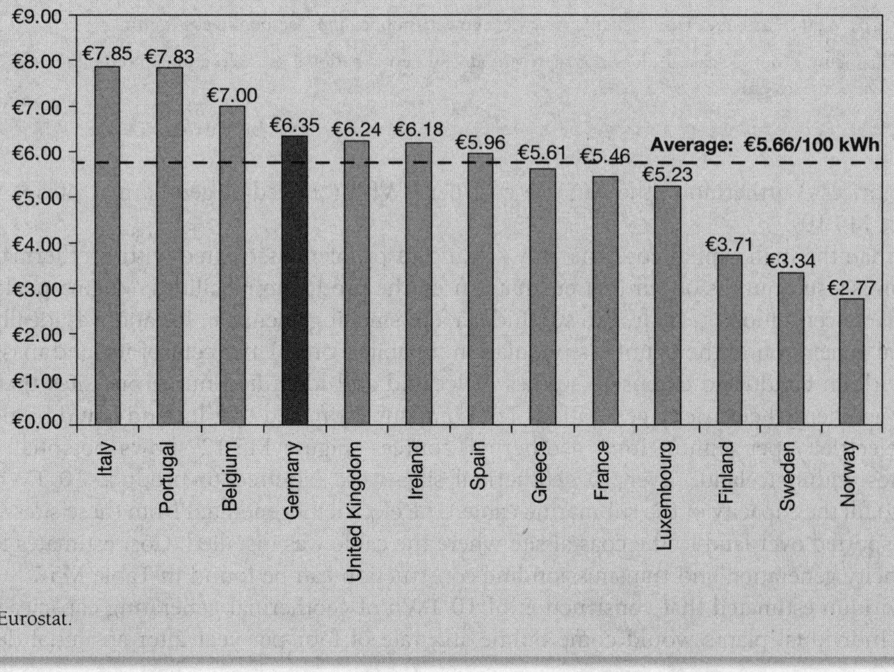

Source: Eurostat.

FIGURE M5.9
Proposed Submarine Cable Route and Summary Construction Cost Data

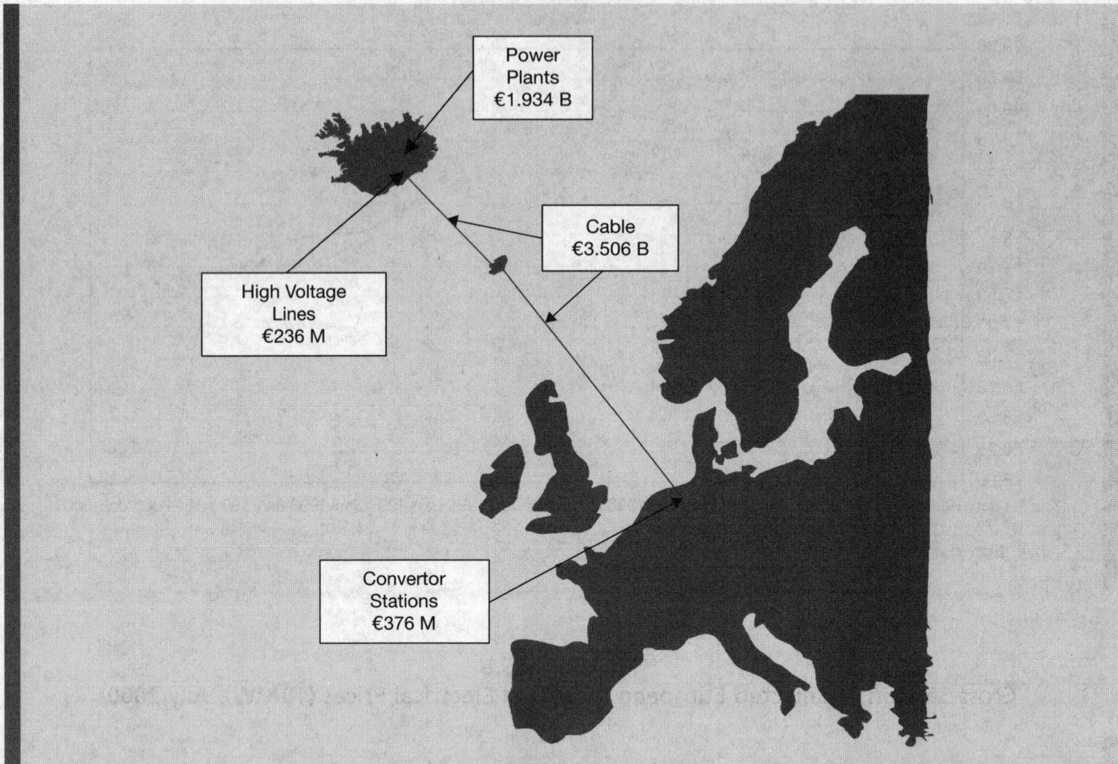

Source: CIA World Factbook, Faroe Islands (www.cia.gov/cia/publications/factbook/geos/fo.html).

Note: This figure is not to scale. It does not represent any authentic national or international boundaries and is used for illustrative purposes only.

fossil fuel prices. Furthermore, the variable cost per kWh produced at geothermal sites is nearly zero (see Figure M5.10).

Other than the high capital cost, the only significant problem associated with geothermal electricity production is a sulphurous odour that emanates from the production facilities. Magma pockets contain substantial concentrations of hydrogen sulphide, a foul smelling chemical. Iceland was ideally suited for geothermal generation as the country's population inhabited only 1 per cent of its land mass.

Landsvirkjun conducted extensive studies of Iceland and identified numerous sites that were well suited for geothermal electricity generation. The company estimated that Iceland could harness over 20 TWh of electricity per annum from geothermal sources. Figure M5.12 shows potential geothermal energy sites within Iceland. Over 30 geothermal sites were required to produce 10 TWh of power required to fill the capacity of the submarine cable. The electricity generated from these sites would need to be transported over land to the coastal site where the cable was installed. Cost estimates for geothermal electricity generation and transmission line construction can be found in Table M5.7.

Landsvirkjun estimated that construction of 10 TWh of geothermal generating capacity would take 10 years. Individual plants would come online at a rate of four per year after an initial development

TABLE M5.5
Macroeconomic Statistics for the Faroe Islands

- Population 45,296
- 90% of GDP comes from fishing industry
- Self-governing division of the Kingdom of Denmark since 1948
- GDP per capita: US$16,000
- Fish and fish products account for 92% of exports
- Territorial Sea—3 nautical miles
- Exclusive Fishing Zone—200 nautical miles
- External Debt—US$767 million

Source: CIA World Factbook, Faroe Islands (www.cia.gov/cia/publications/factbook/geos/fo.html).

TABLE M5.6
Variable Cost Comparison of Electricity Generation Facilities

(mUSD/kWh)			
	Capacity factor		
	40%	60%	80%
Hydropower	$39	$33	$30
Geothermal	58	39	29
Natural Gas	61	49	43
Coal-Fired	78	60	51
Nuclear	106	76	60

Source: The World Bank Group.

period of three years. The expected timing of capital expenditure can be found in Table M5.8. If construction of the submarine cable preceded completion of generation facilities, Landsvirkjun agreed to supply approximately 2 TWh of power from its existing infrastructure at the wholesale price of electricity in Iceland. Wholesale electricity in Iceland had historically been sold at €1.50 to €2.00 per 100 kWh and was not expected to change in the foreseeable future.

LAYING THE CABLE

The large-scale transmission of electricity from Iceland to Europe would require a massive submarine cable. This cable would be longer than any submarine cable in use at the time. Significant progress had been made in the manufacture and installation of such cables since the early 1990s, leading to reduced power losses. In 1993, a study by Pirelli showed such a project to be technically feasible, but not without its challenges.

Long-haul electricity transmission systems had undergone significant technological development since the 1950s. The preferred technology to transfer large amounts of electricity over long distances

FIGURE M5.10
Fundamentals of Extracting Geothermal Energy

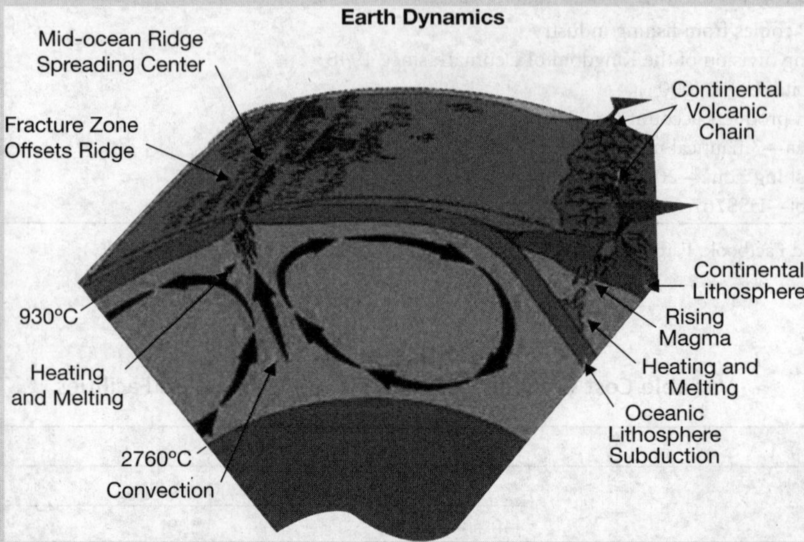

Source: Volcanoes: Crucibles of Change, Princeton University Press, 1997.

was the high-voltage direct current (HVDC) transmission system. HVDC was the preferred system as it was the most economically viable and provided for maximum flow control and flexibility. HVDC transmission systems were used on every continent in the world, save Antarctica.

The largest above-ground HVDC system in the world was the Itaipu project in Brazil, which connected a massive hydropower generating plant to the Sao Paulo electricity grid (approximately 785 km). The cable was rated at 6.3 gigawatts, providing an annual power transfer capacity of over 50 TWh. The most well-known submarine cable project connected the Swedish island of Gotland in the Baltic Sea to the city of Visby, some 70 km away. This cable provided an annual power transfer capacity of 0.4 TWh.[27]

In contrast, the Iceland project would transfer a maximum of 9.56 TWh per year over a distance exceeding 1,800 km. The cable would reach depths of up to 1,100 m under the North Sea. No submarine cable of comparable length had ever been laid before. In their 1999 study, Pirelli recommended using two cables, each rated at 550 MW, providing a total annual power transfer capacity of 9.56 TWh per year. However, given the likelihood of intermittent failures, Pirelli estimated that the cable would have an operating time of 94 per cent. Each cable would also incur transmission losses of approximately 48 MW, bringing the maximum transferable power down to 8.2 TWh per year.

[27] Rudervall, Charpentier and Sharma, 'High Voltage Direct Current Transmission Systems Technology Review Paper'.

FIGURE M5.11
Geothermal Plant Diagram

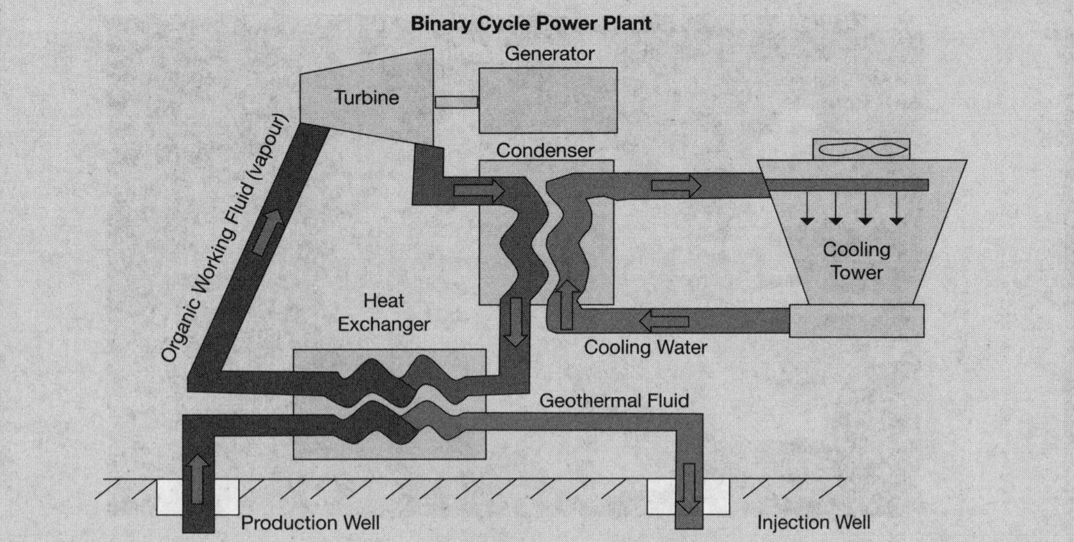

Source: Sustainable Development Information Service.

FIGURE M5.12
Estimated Geothermal Resources in Iceland

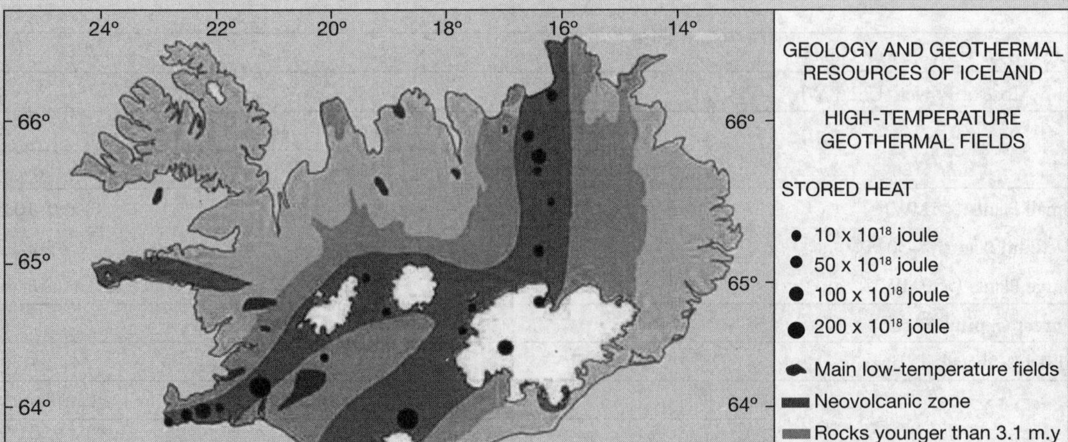

Source: Invest in Iceland.

Note: This figure is not to scale. It does not represent any authentic national or international boundaries and is used for illustrative purposes only.

FIGURE M5.13
Estimated Harnessable Hydropower in Iceland

Source: Landsvirkjun, Iceland National Power Company.

Note: This figure is not to scale. It does not represent any authentic national or international boundaries and is used for illustrative purposes only.

TABLE M5.7
Estimated Cost of Geothermal Energy Production

Levelised Unit Power Costs			
Unit Cost of Power (USc/KWh)			
	Quality of resource		
	High	Medium	Low
Small Plants (<5 MW)	5.0–7.0	5.5–8.5	6.0–10.5
Medium Plants (5–30 MW)	4.0–6.0	4.5–7.0	Not Suitable
Large Plants (>30 MW)	2.5–5.0	4.0–6.0	Not Suitable
Direct Capital Costs			
US$/kW Installed Capacity			
	Quality of resource		
	High	Medium	Low
Small Plants (<5 MW)			
Explotarion	400–800	400–1,000	400–1,000
Steam Field	100–200	300–600	500–900
Power Plant	1,100–1,300	1,100–1,400	1,100–1,800
Total	**1,600–2,300**	**1,800–3,000**	**2,000–3,700**

Medium Plants (5–30 MW)			
Explotarion	250–400	250–600	Not Suitable
Steam Field	200–500	400–700	
Power Plant	850–1,200	950–1,200	
Total	**1,300–2,100**	**1,600–2,500**	
Large Plants (>30 MW)			
Explotarion	100–200	100–400	Not Suitable
Steam Field	300–450	400–700	
Power Plant	750–1,100	850–1,100	
Total	**1,150–1,750**	**1,350–2,200**	
Indirect Costs			
Location A - Developed nation. Indirect costs = 5–10% of direct costs.			
Location B - Remote area of a developed nation. Indirect costs = 10–30% of direct costs.			
Location C - Developing nation. Indirect costs = 30–60% of direct costs.			
Operating & Maintenance Costs			
USc/kWh Installed Capacity			
		Size of plant	
	Small	Medium	Large
Steam Field	0.35–0.70	0.25–0.35	0.15–0.25
Power Plant	0.45–0.70	0.35–0.45	0.25–0.45
Total	**0.80–1.40**	**0.60–0.80**	**0.40–0.70**

Source: The World Bank Group.

Note: Excludes the cost for new makeup wells. Geothermal wells decline at a rate of 5–10% per annum.

Production and installation of one 550 MW cable would take 4–6 years, with the second cable following in 6–10 years after project commencement. This was dependent on Pirelli's manufacturing capacity and weather conditions in the North Atlantic. The total cost of both cables was estimated at €3,506 million, spread evenly over the duration of installation. Increased competition within the submarine cable industry made it unlikely to change over the next several years. Detailed technical and economic specifications of the Iceland (Europe) submarine cable are presented in Table M5.9. Table M5.8 presents the projected income statement and cash flows.

Converter Stations

Deregulation of the European power industry led to the construction of several grid extensions that would link all the EU countries together allowing easy transfer of energy between member nations. However, even with these additions, converter stations were required at the terminal point of the cable in order to convert HVDC electricity into an alternating current with a frequency matching that of the European power grid. These converter stations would cost approximately €50 million per TWh of capacity to construct. In addition, their construction would involve a private European energy company willing to participate in the project. The energy would then be sold through an independent transmission system operator (TSO).

TABLE M5.8
Projected Income Statement and Summary Cash Flows

	Projected																	
	2002	2003	2004	2005	2006	2007	2008	2009	2010	2011	2012	2013	2014	2015	2016	2017	2018	2019
Electricity Price (€/100 kWh)	€6.35	€6.49	€6.64	€6.79	€6.95	€7.11	€7.27	€7.44	€7.61	€7.79	€7.97	€8.15	€8.34	€8.53	€8.72	€8.93	€9.13	€9.34
Annual Electricity Price Growth/(Decline)		2.3%	2.3%	2.3%	2.3%	2.3%	2.3%	2.3%	2.3%	2.3%	2.3%	2.3%	2.3%	2.3%	2.3%	2.3%	2.3%	2.3%
Annual Capacity of Cable (TWh)	–	–	–	2.39	4.78	4.78	4.78	9.56	9.56	9.56	9.56	9.56	9.56	9.56	9.56	9.56	9.56	9.56
Up-Time	94.0%	94.0%	94.0%	94.0%	94.0%	94.0%	94.0%	94.0%	94.0%	94.0%	94.0%	94.0%	94.0%	94.0%	94.0%	94.0%	94.0%	94.0%
Effective Capacity (TWh)	–	–	–	2.25	4.49	4.49	4.49	8.99	8.99	8.99	8.99	8.99	8.99	8.99	8.99	8.99	8.99	8.99
Power Loss (%)	8.8%	8.8%	8.8%	8.8%	8.8%	8.8%	8.8%	8.8%	8.8%	8.8%	8.8%	8.8%	8.8%	8.8%	8.8%	8.8%	8.8%	8.8%
Power Loss (TWh)	–	–	–	(0.20)	(0.40)	(0.40)	(0.40)	(0.79)	(0.79)	(0.79)	(0.79)	(0 79)	(0.79)	(0.79)	(0.79)	(0.79)	(0.79)	(0.79)
Saleable Electricity (TWh)	–	–	–	2.05	4.10	4 10	4.10	8.20	8.20	8.20	8.20	8.20	8.20	8.20	8.20	8.20	8.20	8.20
Electricity Revenues (€MM)	**€0.0**	**€0.0**	**€0.0**	**€139.2**	**€284.8**	**€291.4**	**€298.1**	**€609.8**	**€623.9**	**€638.2**	**€652.9**	**€667.9**	**€683.3**	**€699.0**	**€715.1**	**€731.5**	**€748.3**	**€765.5**
Operating & Maintenance Costs																		
Steam Field																		
USD/100 kWh	0.20	*Source: World Bank*																
€/USD	1.10	*As of Feb 20, 2001*																
€/100 kWh	0.22	0.23	0.23	0.24	0.25	0.26	0.26	0.27	0.28	0.29	0.30	0.31	0.32	0.33	0.34	0.35	0.36	0.37
Inflationary Growth		3.1%	3.1%	3.1%	3.1%	3.1%	3.1%	3.1%	3.1%	3.1%	3.1%	3.1%	3.1%	3.1%	3.1%	3.1%	3.1%	3.1%
Steam Field Costs (€/MM)	–	–	–	*(5.8)*	*(11.9)*	*(12.2)*	*(12.6)*	*(26.0)*	*(26.8)*	*(27.7)*	*(28.5)*	*(29.4)*	*(30.3)*	*(31.3)*	*(32.2)*	*(33.2)*	*(34.3)*	*(35.3)*
Power Plant																		
USD/100 kWh	0.35	*Source: World Bank*																
€/USD	1.10	*As of Feb 20, 2001*																
€/100 kWh	0.38	0.40	0.41	0.42	0.43	0.45	0.46	0.48	0.49	0.51	0.52	0.54	0.55	0.57	0.59	0.61	0.63	0.65

Inflationary Growth		3.1%	3.1%	3.1%	3.1%	3.1%	3.1%	3.1%	3.1%	3.1%	3.1%	3.1%	3.1%	3.1%	3.1%	3.1%	3.1%	3.1%
Power Plant Costs (€MM)	–	–	–	*(10.1)*	*(20.8)*	*(21.4)*	*(22.1)*	*(45.5)*	*(46.9)*	*(48.4)*	*(49.9)*	*(51.5)*	*(53.0)*	*(54.7)*	*(56.4)*	*(58.1)*	*(59.9)*	*(61.8)*
Total O&M Costs	–	–	–	(15.8)	(32.6)	(33.7)	(34.7)	(71.6)	(73.8)	(76.1)	(78.4)	(80.9)	(83.4)	(85.9)	(88.6)	(91.4)	(94.2)	(97.1)
Start-up costs	(8.9)	(18.3)	(18.7)	(19.1)	-	-	-	-	-	-	-	-	-	-	-	-	-	-
SG&A	–	–	–	(4.2)	(8.5)	(8.7)	(8.9)	(18.3)	(18.7)	(19.1)	(19.6)	(20.0)	(20.5)	(21.0)	(21.5)	(21.9)	(22.4)	(23.0)
% of sales	3%	3%	3%	3%	3%	3%	3%	3%	3%	3%	3%	3%	3%	3%	3%	3%	3%	3%
Depreciation	(18.0)	(38.2)	(62.2)	(90.9)	(124.1)	(160.3)	(190.8)	(221.3)	(249.7)	(270.6)	(272.4)	(272.4)	(272.4)	(272.4)	(272.4)	(272.4)	(272.4)	(272.4)
Total Operating Expenses	€(27.0)	€(56.5)	€(80.9)	€(130.0)	€(165.3)	€(202.7)	€(234.5)	€(311.2)	€(342.2)	€(365.8)	€(370.4)	€(373.3)	€(376.2)	€(379.3)	€(382.4)	€(385.7)	€(389.0)	€(392.4)
Operating Profit	**€(27.0)**	**€(56.5)**	**€(80.9)**	**€9.2**	**€119.5**	**€88.6**	**€63.6**	**€298.6**	**€281.7**	**€272.4**	**€282.5**	**€294.6**	**€307.0**	**€319.7**	**€332.6**	**€345.8**	**€359.3**	**€373.1**
Tax Rate	30.0%	30.0%	30.0%	30.0%	30.0%	30.0%	30.0%	30.0%	30.0%	30.0%	30.0%	30.0%	30.0%	30.0%	30.0%	30.0%	30.0%	30.0%
Taxes	8	17	24	(3)	(36)	(27)	(19)	(90)	(85)	(82)	(85)	(88)	(92)	(96)	(100)	(104)	(108)	(112)
EBIAT	**€(18.9)**	**€(39.5)**	**€(56.6)**	**€6.4**	**€83.7**	**€62.1**	**€44.5**	**€209.1**	**€197.2**	**€190.7**	**€197.8**	**€206.2**	**€214.9**	**€223.8**	**€232.8**	**€242.1**	**€251.5**	**€261.2**
+ Depreciation	18	38	62	91	124	160	191	221	250	271	272	272	272	272	272	272	272	272
– Initial Capital Expenditures	(400)	(448)	(533)	(639)	(737)	(805)	(678)	(678)	(630)	(466)	(39)	–	–	–	–	–	–	–
– Maintenance Capital Expenditures	–	–	–	–	–	–	–	–	–	–	–	–	–	–	–	–	–	–
– Change in WC		–	–	(11)	(12)	(1)	(1)	(26)	(1)	(1)	(1)	(1)	(1)	(1)	(1)	(1)	(1)	(1)
Free Cash Flow	**€(401)**	**€(450)**	**€(527)**	**€(553)**	**€(542)**	**€(583)**	**€(443)**	**€(273)**	**€(184)**	**€(5)**	**€430**	**€477**	**€486**	**€495**	**€504**	**€513**	**€523**	**€532**
% Growth												11.0%	1.8%	1.8%	1.8%	1.8%	1.8%	1.8%
Maintenance CapEx % of Power Plant CapEx	0%	0%	0%	2%	3%	5%	7%	8%	8%	8%	8%	8%	8%	8%	8%	8%	8%	8%
Working Capital																		
Accounts Receivable	–	–	–	23	47	48	49	100	103	105	107	110	112	115	118	120	123	126
Days Receivable	*60*	*60*	*60*	*60*	*60*	*60*	*60*	*60*	*60*	*60*	*60*	*60*	*60*	*60*	*60*	*60*	*60*	*60*
Accounts Payable	–	–	–	(11)	(23)	(24)	(24)	(50)	(51)	(52)	(54)	(55)	(56)	(57)	(59)	(60)	(62)	(63)
Days Payable	*30*	*30*	*30*	*30*	*30*	*30*	*30*	*30*	*30*	*30*	*30*	*30*	*30*	*30*	*30*	*30*	*30*	*30*
Working Capital	–	–	–	11	23	24	24	50	51	52	54	55	56	57	59	60	62	63
Change In WC		–	–	(11)	(12)	(1)	(1)	(26)	(1)	(1)	(1)	(1)	(1)	(1)	(1)	(1)	(1)	(1)

TABLE M5.8
(Continued)

Capital Expenditures		
	USD	Euro
Power Plants	$1,760	€1,934
High-Voltage Lines	$215	€236
Submarine Cable	$3,190	€3,506
Converter Stations	$342	€376
Total Costs	$5,507	€6,053
€/USD	1.10	*As of 20 Feb 2001*

Capex Worksheet																		
Power Plant	€10	€48	€116	€203	€290	€358	€271	€280	€242	€77	€39	–	–	–	–	–	–	–
High Voltage Lines	€2	€12	€28	€47	€59	€59	€19	€9	–	–	–	–	–	–	–	–	–	–
% of construction, Cable 1	1%	5%	12%	20%	25%	25%	8%	4%										
Cumulative % of construction, Cable 1	1%	6%	18%	38%	63%	88%	96%	100%	100%	100%	100%	100%	100%	100%	100%	100%	100%	100%
% of construction, Cable 2				1%	5%	12%	20%	25%	25%	8%	4%							
Cumulative % of construction, Cable 2	0%	0%	0%	1%	6%	18%	38%	63%	88%	96%	100%	100%	100%	100%	100%	100%	100%	100%
Submarine Cable	€351	€351	€351	€351	€351	€351	€351	€351	€351	€351	–	–	–	–	–	–	–	–
Converter Stations	€38	€38	€38	€38	€38	€38	€38	€38	€38	€38	–	–	–	–	–	–	–	–
% of construction	10%	10%	10%	10%	10%	10%	10%	10%	10%	10%								
Cumulative % of construction	10%	20%	30%	40%	50%	60%	70%	80%	90%	100%	100%	100%	100%	100%	100%	100%	100%	100%
Total Initial CapEx	€400	€448	€533	€639	€737	€805	€678	€678	€630	€466	€39	–	–	–	–	–	–	–

Depreciation Schedule																				
		CapEx	Depreciation Expense																	
Depreciation %:	2002	400	18	18	18	18	18	18	18	18	18	18	18	18	18	18	18	18	18	18
5%	2003	448		20	20	20	20	20	20	20	20	20	20	20	20	20	20	20	20	20
Salvage Value:	2004	533			24	24	24	24	24	24	24	24	24	24	24	24	24	24	24	24
10%	2005	639				29	29	29	29	29	29	29	29	29	29	29	29	29	29	29
	2006	737					33	33	33	33	33	33	33	33	33	33	33	33	33	33
	2007	805						36	36	36	36	36	36	36	36	36	36	36	36	36
	2008	678							31	31	31	31	31	31	31	31	31	31	31	31
	2009	678								31	31	31	31	31	31	31	31	31	31	31
	2010	630									28	28	28	28	28	28	28	28	28	28
	2011	466										21	21	21	21	21	21	21	21	21
	2012	39											2	2	2	2	2	2	2	2
	2013	–												–	–	–	–	–	–	–
	2014	–													–	–	–	–	–	–
	2015	–														–	–	–	–	–
	2016	–															–	–	–	–
	2017	–																–	–	–
	2018	–																	–	–
	2019	–																		–
	Total Depreciation		18	38	62	91	124	160	191	221	250	271	272	272	272	272	272	272	272	272

TABLE M5.9
Technical and Economic Specifications for the Submarine Cables

Project Physical Specs, as of 1999					
		1 Cable		2 Cables	
		Scotland	Germany or Netherlands	Scotland	Germany or Netherlands
Length	km	1,170	1,950	2,340	3,900
Up-time	hours/annum	8,400	8,200	16,800	16,400
Up-time	% of year	96%	94%	96%	94%
Capacity	TWh/year	4.95	4.78	9.9	9.56
Power Losses	MW	27	48	54	96

Financial Summary, as of 1999 ***Millions of 1999 US$***				
	1 Cable		2 Cables	
	Scotland	Germany or Netherlands	Scotland	Germany or Netherlands
Power Plants	$916	$916	$1,760	$1,760
High-voltage Lines	$104	$104	$215	$215
Generating Subtotal	**$1,020**	**$1,020**	**$1,975**	**$1,975**
Submarine Cable	$965	$1,606	$1,915	$3,190
Converter Stations	$171	$171	$342	$342
Cable Subtotal	**$1,136**	**$1,777**	**$2,257**	**$3,532**
Total	**$2,156**	**$2,797**	**$4,232**	**$5,507**

Financial Summary, as of 1993 ***All Figures in Millions of Currency Units*** Exchange Rate 62.78 ISK/USD				
	1 Cable		**2 Cables**	
	Scotland	Germany or Netherlands	Scotland	Germany or Netherlands
Hydro Plant	67,800 kr.	67,800 kr.	132,200 kr.	132,200 kr.
High-voltage Lines	6,800 kr.	6,800 kr.	13,200 kr.	13,200 kr.
Generating Subtotal	**74,600 kr.**	**74,600 kr.**	**145,400 kr.**	**145,400 kr.**
Cable and Converter Stations	55,450 kr.	110,900 kr.	106,150 kr.	212,300 kr.
Total	**130,050 kr.**	**185,500 kr.**	**251,550 kr.**	**357,700 kr.**
Hydro Plant	$1,080	$1,080	$2,106	$2,106
High-voltage Lines	$108	$108	$210	$210
Generating Subtotal	**$1,188**	**$1,188**	**$2,316**	**$2,316**
Submarine Cable Converter Stations	$883	$1,766	$1,691	$3,382
Cable Subtotal	$883	$1,766	$1,691	$3,382
Total	**$2,072**	**$2,955**	**$4,007**	**$5,698**

Source: Submarine Cable from Iceland: Export of Electricity to Europe; Iceland Ministry of Industry and Commerce.

FUNDING THE PROJECT

Iceland had an investment grade bond rating in 2001. But the sheer size of the submarine cable project made it impossible for the government to consider funding it alone. In addition, the government was unwilling to take on all project risks.

The Iceland government knew that debt would be a significant portion of this project since project finance often involved debt to capitalization ratios of 60–70 per cent.[28] Even with such a capital structure, the project would still require €1.95 billion–€2.60 billion in equity capital. In addition, an investment grade bond rating would require that the holding company meet a debt service coverage ratio (DSCR) of 1.5 on average and not less than 1.2 in stress cases.[29]

Because the project involved three components—power plants, conversion stations and the cable itself—sole ownership of one component could harm an equity investor should the export of power be stalled at any time due to actions of investors in other components. Therefore, the proposed deal structure involved the formation of an offshore holding company whose assets included all of the project's components. The Iceland government would be one stakeholder in the holding company.

Instead of raising equity from unrelated institutional investors, the Iceland government felt that it should identify equity investors with a strategic interest in the submarine cable project. While no company had committed to the project, several partners made sense.

Pirelli, a world leader in cable systems, was one potential investor whose expertise in laying subterrain and submarine cables could add value to the project. The Icenet Gruppe, a European energy syndicate, could provide capital as well as a termination site for the cable and conversion station. Regional power companies such as Hamburg Electrical Works (HEW) AG in Germany, Scottish Hydro plc and the National Power Company of Norway were other entities that had been invested in project studies thus far. Finally, a global energy company whose portfolio included little or no renewable energy production might look to invest in a project that could provide it with positive environmental publicity and expertise for future renewable energy projects.

In addition to the above, the ISCP team was evaluating the possibility of European Investment Bank (EIB) funding. The EIB was the EU's term lending institution and had financed numerous, large, European infrastructure projects in the past in areas such as water management, air traffic control and electricity networks. Projects in the past had received up to 50 per cent of investment cost.[30]

THE DECISION

In order to present the submarine cable project to a potential lead investor, the Iceland government had to evaluate it from the other side of the table. Although there could be strategic value in the project, it understood that any lead investor would require a fair return on its equity.

---

[28] Esty, Ben. *Journal of Applied Corporate Finance.*

[29] S&P.

[30] http://eib.eu.int/ (accessed on 8 January 2019).

Could this project generate enough revenue to entice a large investor who could handle the size of such an investment? Could the risks be managed or mitigated to make this investment attractive? How much equity capital would be required to obtain an investment grade rating for the project debt? These were the questions facing the executives of the ISCP. In order to undertake a valuation of the project, they gathered data on beta and leverage for comparable European utility companies (Table M5.10) and US treasury and corporate bond yields (Table M5.11).

TABLE M5.10
Comparable European Integrated Electric Utility Firms

Company	Equity Beta	Debt/equity Ratio %	Asset Beta
Verbund	0.39	90.0	0.24
EVN	0.56	34.0	0.45
Fortum	0.48	82.0	0.30
RWE	0.73	10.0	0.68
EDP	0.56	42.0	0.43
Endesa	0.72	107.0	0.41
Sydkraft	0.33	55.0	0.24
Iberdrola	0.64	52.0	0.47
E.ON	0.74	21.0	0.65
Peer Average	**0.57**	**54.8**	**0.41**
Iceland Tax Rate	30.0%		

Note: Equity Betas represent 'Adjusted Equity Betas' using BE500 as Relative Index over four years.

Firms selected as comparables were European vertically integrated electric utilities, with divisions ranging from raw material extraction and electricity generation to distribution of power.

Source: Bloomberg.

TABLE M5.11
Corporate Bond Yields and Rating Comparisons

US Government Bond Ratings *5 March 2001*	
	Yield %
2-Year Bond	4.47
5-Year Bond	4.74
10-Year Bond	4.97
30-Year Bond	5.37

Source: Bloomberg.

US Utilities Corporate Bond Yields
5 March 2001

	Number of years			
	2%	5%	10%	30%
AA1/AA2	5.43	6.08	6.70	7.32
AA3	5.48	6.13	6.74	7.37
A1	5.53	6.18	6.81	7.45
A2	5.64	6.25	6.84	7.54
A3	5.70	6.33	6.91	7.66
BBB1	5.86	6.45	6.97	7.76
BBB2	5.89	6.48	7.01	7.82
BBB3	5.98	6.59	7.23	7.99
BB1/BB2	6.02	6.67	7.27	8.06
BB3	7.18	7.18	7.90	8.76

Source: Bloomberg.

Rating Scale Comparison

	Rating Scale Comparison		
	S&P	Moody	Comp
Investment Grade	AAA	Aaa	AAA
	AA+	Aa1	AA1
	AA	Aa2	AA2
	AA-	Aa3	AA3
	A+	A1	A1
	A	A2	A2
	A-	A3	A3
	BBB+	Baa1	BBB1
	BBB	Baa2	BBB2
	BBB-	Baa3	BBB3
Non-Investment Grade	BB+	Ba1	BB1
	BB+	Ba2	BB2
	BB-	Ba3	BB3
	B+	B1	B1
	B	B2	B2
	B-	B3	B3
	CCC+	Caa1	CCC1
	CCC	Caa2	CCC2
	CCC-	Caa3	CCC3

Source: Bloomberg.

Exercises

1. How can one best forecast the revenues from such a large project that has so many variables?
2. How can all of the risks associated with the ISCP be accounted for and mitigated in the financial forecasts?
3. What discount rate should be used to evaluate a project that involves multiple countries as well as the North Atlantic Ocean?
4. What is the optimal capital structure for financing this project and how will the syndicate raise the necessary debt?
5. Are there any real options or other extraneous sources of value that could make the ISCP more attractive to potential equity investors?

REFERENCES

Central Intelligence Agency. *CIA World Fact Book*. Available at http://www.cia.gov/cia/publications/factbook/geos/ic.html (accessed on 7 January 2019).

Esty, Ben. *Journal of Applied Corporate Finance* 12, no. 3 (1998 October).

European Commission. 'Opening Up to Choice: The Single Electricity Market' (1999, 1 January). Available at https://www.europeansources.info/record/opening-up-to-choice-the-single-electricity-market/ (accessed on 7 January 2019).

European Commission. 'Recent Progress with Building the Internal Electricity Market'. Communication from the Commission to the Council and the European Parliament, Commission of the European Communities (2000, 16 May).

International Energy Agency. *Regional Indicators: The European Union* (August 2000). Available at http://www.eia.doe.gov/emeu/cabs/euro.html (accessed on 7 January 2019).

National Economic Statistics, Iceland, January 2001.

Rudervall, R., J. P. Charpentier and Raghuveer Sharma. 'High Voltage Direct Current Transmission Systems Technology Review Paper' (ABB Power Systems, 2000). Available at https://www.researchgate.net/publication/266866179_High_Voltage_Direct_Current_HVDCTransmission_Systems_Technology_Review_Paper (accessed on 8 January 2019).

Standard & Poor's Ratings Services, 2000, 6 March.

US Department of Energy, Energy Information Administration. *International Energy Outlook 2000*. Available at https://rosap.ntl.bts.gov/view/dot/5104/dot_5104_DS1.pdf? (accessed on 7 January 2019).

6

Air Deccan Initial Public Offering*

LEARNING OBJECTIVE

To introduce issues in going public and IPO valuation.

Description: The case presents the initial public offering of shares by a rapidly growing airline company in India. Students are asked to evaluate the attractiveness of investing in the company's shares from the perspective of investors.

> If the Wright brothers were alive today, Wilbur would have to fire Orville to reduce costs.
>
> —Herb Kelleher, Southwest Airlines

> I believe that for India to be a developed country, every Indian should be able to fly. In all developed countries, the common man flies.
>
> —Captain G. R. Gopinath, Managing Director, Air Deccan

> We will have more seats at ₹1 than Air Deccan at ₹500.
>
> —Jehangir Wadia, Managing Director, GoAir

On a cold February morning in 2006, the cool breeze did little to soothe the fervour in the office of Mohan Kumar, the Finance Director of Air Deccan. Air Deccan had come a long way from having to abort its inaugural flight from Hyderabad to Vijayawada on 24 September 2003 due to an engine fire to revolutionizing the Indian aviation industry by being its first low-cost airline. And

This case was prepared by Ruchika Chinda, Anuj Sharma, Ruibin Chen and Rishi Gupta under the supervision of Professor Campbell Harvey, Fuqua School of Business, Duke University.

* Reproduced with permission from Professor Campbell Harvey.

now, merely two and a half years after its inception, plans of an IPO were on the horizon to raise the much needed capital to support the company's tremendous growth plans.

With only a few days left for Air Deccan to announce its offering price, Kumar pondered over the company financials repeatedly, his thoughts drifting over the many critical decisions to be made in the coming days. The recent announcement of the consolidation of two airline giants in India, Air Sahara and Jet Airways, further compounded his anxiety about Air Deccan's growth projections and the timing of its IPO.

THE INDIAN ECONOMY

India was the world's largest democracy in terms of population. India's Central Statistical Office estimated a population of 1.091 billion people as of 31 March 2005. According to the World Bank,[1] India was the 10th largest economy in the world in 2004 with a GDP in nominal terms estimated to be US$692 billion.

The Government of India initiated a series of major macroeconomic and structural reforms in 1991 to promote economic stability and growth. In part as a result of this reform programme, India's economy registered an average real GDP growth of 6.9 per cent for the year ending 31 March 2005—a compound annual growth of 120 per cent since 1991 (Table M6.1). Table M6.2 shows the annual percentage change in key economic indicators in recent years. Table M6.3 presents the demographic pattern.

As the Indian economy continued its growth, its middle class was also growing and enjoying an increasing disposable income. The service sectors had become increasingly important as a result of the growth in the Indian economy, which necessitated greater connectivity throughout India.

THE INDIAN AVIATION INDUSTRY

History

Before 1990, the Indian aviation sector was characterized by a high degree of government control. The Government of India nationalized the airline industry in 1953 through enactment of the Air Corporations Act. In accordance with this act, the two air corporations, namely Indian Airlines Corporation and Air India International, were established and the assets of all the then existing air companies (nine) were

TABLE M6.1
India's GDP Growth

As of, and for the Year Ended March 31					
	1995	2000	2003	2004	2005
Real GDP at factor cost (₹ million)	8,380,310	11,483,670	13,183,620	14,305,480	15,294,080
Real GDP (per capita ₹)	8,209	11,369	12,496	13,332	14,018

Source: CSO.

[1] www.worldbank.org

TABLE M6.2
Key Economic Indicators

As of, and for the Year Ended March 31 Annual Percentage Change, Except for Imports, Exports and Foreign Exchange Assets					
	2001	2002	2003	2004	2005
Industrial Production	5.1	2.6	5.8	7.0	8.4
Inflation Rate based on Wholesale Price Index (average)	7.1	3.7	3.4	5.4	6.4
Imports (% of GDP)	10.9	10.8	12.1	13.0	15.5
Exports (% of GDP)	9.6	9.2	10.4	10.6	11.5
Foreign Exchange Reserves (in US$ billions)	39.5	51.0	71.9	107.5	135.8

Source: CMIE; Monthly Economic Indicators, November 2005.

transferred to the two new corporations. The operation of scheduled air transport services was made a monopoly of these two corporations and the Act prohibited any person other than the corporations or their associates to operate any scheduled air transport services from, to or across India.

The liberalization in the Indian civil aviation industry began in 1986 with private sector players being permitted to operate as air taxi operators, but not being permitted to operate scheduled services. This air taxi scheme was introduced to boost tourism and augment domestic air services. A number of private companies commenced domestic operations as air taxi operators including Jet Airways, Air Sahara and Damania Airways. However, the carriers could not publish time schedules or issue tickets to public. In 1994, the Air Corporations Act was repealed and air transport in India was thus opened to the operation of scheduled services by any carrier that fulfilled the statutory requirements. The dormant Indian aviation industry has been revolutionized ever since.[2]

Industry Characteristics

Compared to other countries, the growth of the domestic aviation sector in India had been relatively resilient in the face of regular international disruptions such as terrorist attacks in various countries, health hazards and natural disasters. Indian Airlines flight IC 814 was hijacked on 24 December 1999 shortly after it entered the Indian airspace. The hijacking ended on New Year's Eve with the death on one passenger only after India released three terrorists in exchange for hostages. Such terrorist attacks in India had significant impact on domestic passenger traffic whenever they took place.

Based on statistics compiled by the Directorate General of Civil Aviation (DGCA) in India, the sector maintained a CAGR of 15.67 per cent from fiscal 2002 to 2005 in terms of domestic passengers. According to the DGCA, Indian domestic air traffic increased at a significantly higher rate in 2005 than the rates experienced over the previous 5 to 10 years (Tables 6.4 and 6.5).

Despite the recent growth in air passenger traffic, India continued to have relatively low penetration of air services. According to the Centre for Monitoring Indian Economy (CMIE), domestic air traffic reached 20 million in 2005. For a country with a billion plus population, this amounted to an average Indian making 0.02 trips per annum which is one of the lowest in the world compared to an average of

[2] Ministry of Civil Aviation, Government of India. *Domestic Air Transport Policy Document.*

TABLE M6.3
India's Demographic Pattern

Classification	US$ p.a.	No. of Households in 2000				Annual growth rate (%)		
		1995–96	2001–02	2005–06	2009–10	1995–96 to 2001–02	2001–02 to 2005–06	2005–06 to 2009–10
Deprived	<2,070	131,176	135,378	132,249	114,394	0.5	–0.6	–3.6
Aspirers	2,070–4,600	28,901	41,262	53,276	75,304	6.1	6.6	9.0
Seekers	4,600–11,500	3,881	9,034	13,813	22,268	15.1	11.2	12.7
Strivers	11,500–22,990	651	1,712	3,212	6,173	17.5	17.0	17.7
Near rich	22,990–45,980	189	546	1,122	2,373	19.4	19.7	20.6
Clear rich	45,980–114,940	63	201	454	1,037	21.3	22.6	22.9
Sheer rich	114,940–229,890	11	40	103	255	23.4	26.8	25.4
Super rich	>229,890	5	20	53	141	25.8	27.9	28.1
Total		**165,877**	**188,193**	**204,282**	**221,945**	**NA**	**NA**	**NA**

Note: Forecast data

Source: NCAER'sreport – 'The Great Indian Middle Class' 2004–05.

TABLE M6.10
Comparable Company Data

₹ millions

Company Name	Country	Year Ended	Sales	EBITDAR	PAT	P/E	Adj EV	EV/ EBITDAR	Mkt Cap/ Sales	EPS	RONW %	NAV
Jet Airways India Ltd	INDIA	March-2005	43,380	14,309	3,920	22.9	105,788.74	7.4	2.1	45.40	22	202.8
SpiceJet	INDLA	March-2005	20	NA	–287	40.1	14,204	NA	650.9	(1.90)	–78	–2.4
easyJet pic @	BRITAIN	September-2005	105,924	16,496	3,364	36.6	154,327.47	9.4	1.2	8.42	5	165.9
Ryanair Holdings PLC #	IRELAND	March-2005	72,597	24,960	14,488	21.9	321,860.44	12.9	4.4	19.01	15	123.1
JetBlue Airways Corp *	USA	December-2004	55,972	11,521	2,099	43.1	169,321.06	14.7	1.8	13.56	6	213.8
Gol Linhas Aereas Inteligentes^	BRAZIL	December-2004	38,290	15,487	7,512	27.9	241,602.99	15.6	6.0	42.03	38	104.5
AirAsia BHD**	MALAYSIA.	June-2005	7,856	2,602	1,316	30.7	45,945.10	17.7	5.7	0.62	12	4.8
Southwest Airlines Co	USA	December-2005	335,308	63,489	24,228	23.3	594,882.75	9.4	1.7	30.71	8	374.0

Note: Enterprise Value includes Market value of equity as of Jan 23, 2006 (Jan 22, 2006 for US companies) adj for Net Debt and Capitalized lease rental
Lease rentals for the Year have been capitalized by seven to calculate the capitalized lease rental as per industry practice
All currency conversions are as on January23, 2006
@ currency conversion considered: 1 Great Britain Pound = 78.96 Indian Rupees
# currency conversion considered: 1 Euro = 54.31 Indian Rupees
* currency conversion considered: 1 US$ = 44.21 Indian Rupees
^ currency conversion considered: 1 Brazilian Rigget = 19.52 Indian Rupees
** currency conversion considered: 1 Malaysian Real = 11.79 Indian Rupees

Source: Based on financials from Bloomberg and C line.

Proceeds from sale/disposal of fixed assets	–	–	–	–	51.83	44.19
Proceeds from transfer of aircraft/engine purchase rights	–	–	–	–	–	246.89
Investment in subsidiary company	–	–	–	–	(4.48)	–
Interest received	0.09	0.04	0.65	622	2.97	2.94
Purchase of Investments	(1.00)	–	–	–	–	–
Sale of Investments	–	–	0.61	–	–	–
Net cash used in investing activities	**(6.35)**	**(3.46)**	**(88.46)**	**(199.03)**	**(1,716.18)**	**(1,461.05)**
C. Cash Flows from Financing Activities						
Proceeds from issue of share capital	–	–.	0.80	206.48	87.40	–
Share debenture issue expenses					(27.15)	(024)
Proceeds from term loans (including hire purchase)	4.00	0.80	60.53	144.25	1,917.62	1,521.72
Repayment of term loans (including hire purchase)	(1.37)	(3.82)	(7.39)	(12.27)	(552.29)	(377.78)
Change in overdraft facility (including bode overdraft)	–	–	–	29.00	35.75	55.75
Change in cash credit facility	–	15.60	(0.43)	(7.70)	1.96	48.21
Finance lease obligation	–	–	–	–	(2.42)	(16.67)
Proceeds from convertible debentures	–	–	–	–	1,217.60	217.70
Unsecured loans received	7.00	6.00	38.90	114.38	128.00	40.00
Unsecured loans repaid	(7.65)	(0.15)	(21.65)	(24.50)	(218.00)	(33.00)
Interest paid	(3.20)	(4.63)	(9.34)	(28.03)	(60.98)	(21.83)
Dividends Paid	(0.18)	(1.00)	(1.00)	(1.00)	(1.74)	–
Tax on dividend paid	–	(0.10)	–	(0.13)	(0.23)	–
Net cash (used in) generated from financing activities	**(1.40)**	**12.70**	**60.42**	**420.48**	**2,525.52**	**1,433.86**
Net change in cash and cash equivalents (A-B-Q	**(21.85)**	**3.88**	**15.49**	**139.66**	**669.52**	**(271.23)**
Cash and cash equivalents at the beginning of the year period	22.58	0.73	4.61	20.10	159.76	829.28
Cash and cash equivalents at the aid of the year/ period	**0.73**	**4.61**	**20.10**	**159.76**	**829.28**	**558.05**

Notes

(1) Cash and cash equivalents induce margin money deposit against bank guarantees and letters of credit issued by banks.

(2) Assets taken under finance lease	–	–	–	–	30.59	26.31

TABLE M6.9
Cash Flow Statement

₹ millions	Year Ended 31 March 2001	Year Ended 31 March 2002	Year Ended 31 March 2003	Year Ended 31 March 2004	Year Ended 31 March 2005	Six Months Ended 31 September 2005
A. Cash Flows from Operating Activities Net Profit/(Loss) before tax, as restated Adjustments for:	11.50	15.31	4.83	(119.57)	(352.32)	(665.24)
Depreciation	0.95	1.07	3.27	11.47	30.59	24.55
Employee stock compensation cost	–	–	–	–	–	7.24
Provision for wealth tax	–	–	–	–	0.03	–
Preliminary expanses written off*	–	–	–	–	–	–
Amortization	–	–	–	–	24.54	15.67
Insurance claims	–	–	–	(12.70)	(25.96)	–
Profit on transfer of aircraft/engine purchase rights	–	–	–	–	(45.81)	(287.62)
Loss on sale/transfer of investments	–	–	0.39	–	–	0.34
Interest income	(1.27)	(1.21)	(1.83)	(1.92)	(5.80)	(3.84)
Sundry balances written back	–	–	–	(0.01)	(0.11)	(0.10)
Interest expense	2.65	5.24	15.18	31.68	55.70	23.19
Operating profit before working capital changes	**13.83**	**20.41**	**21.84**	**(91.05)**	**(319.14)**	**(885.81)**
Movements in working capital						
Decrease (increase) in sundry debtors	(10.86)	(3.32)	3.92	(16.15)	(22.34)	(22.85)
Decrease/(increase) in inventories	(6.18)	(11.54)	(16.70)	(80.89)	(244.41)	(88.92)
Decrease/(increase) in loans and advances	(2.61)	(15.19)	0.36	(43.60)	(162.70)	(248.85)
Decrease/(increase) in other current assets	–	(5.07)	2.53	(19.10)	(110.28)	13.36
(Decrease)/increase in current liabilities and provisions	(9.46)	12.12	30.98	169.31	721.54	990.68
Cash generated from/(used in) operations	**(15.28)**	**(2.59)**	**42.93**	**(81.48)**	**(137.33)**	**(242.39)**
Income tax (paid)/refund, including fringe benefit tax	1.18	(2.77)	0.60	(0.31)	(2.49)	(1.65)
Net Cash generated from/(used in) operations	**(14.10)**	**(5.36)**	**43.53**	**(81.79)**	**(139.82)**	**(244.04)**
B. Cash Flows from Investing Activities						
Purchase of fixed assets and changes in capital work in progress	(5.44)	(3.50)	(89.72)	(205.25)	(1,766.50)	(1,755.07)

Total (D)	71.71	109.69	134.56	480.81	1,760.37	1,830.97
E. Liabilities and Provisions						
a) Current liabilities and Provisions	35.63	43.32	74.24	257.23	1,082.00	2,157.88
b) Deferred Tax Liability, net	1.31	–	3.10	–	–	–
c) Secured Loans	6.69	19.89	73.05	226.21	1,594.17	2,792.85
d) Unsecured Loans	10.02	15.87	38.51	123.00	1,250.60	1,475.30
Total (E)	53.65	79.08	188.90	606.44	3,926.77	6,426.03
F. Net Worth [Refer Note F(2) in Annexure 4] (A+B+C+D–E)	37.06	52.24	52.56	141.19	(123.73)	(796.70)
Net Worth Represented						
Equity Share Capital	20.00	20.00	20.80	155.27	161.99	161.99
Employee Stock Options Outstanding (Net of Deferred Compensation Cost)	–	–	–	–	–	7.24
Reserves and Surplus:						
Securities Premium	–	–	–	79.20	159.88	159.88
Profit and Loss Account	17.06	32.24	31.76	(93.28)	(445.60)	(1,125.81)
Net Worth [Refer Note F(2) in Annexure 4]	37.06	52.24	52.56	141.19	(123.73)	(796.70)

Source: Company annual reports.

TABLE M6.8
Balance Sheet

	As At 31 March 2001	As At 31 March 2002	As At 31 March 2003	As At 31 March 2004	As At 31 March 2005	As At 30 September 2005
A Fixed Assets						
Gross Block	19.98	23.01	111.75	270.98	552.48	2,238.30
Less: Accumulated Depreciation	1.98	3.04	6.31	16.33	45.22	69.77
Net Block	18.00	19.97	105.44	254.65	507.26	2,168.53
Add: Capital Work-in-Progress, including Capital Advances	–	0.47	1.46	12.17	1,530.93	1,625.70
Total (A)	18.00	20.44	106.90	266.82	2,038.19	3,794.23
B. Investments (B)	1.00	1.00	–	–	4.48	4.13
C. Deferred Tax Asset, net (C)	–	0.19	–	–	–	–
D. Current Assets. Loans and Advances						
a) Inventories	10.44	21.98	38.68	119.57	363.98	452.90
b) Sundry Debtors	28.40	31.72	27.80	43.95	66.29	89.14
c) Cash and Bank Balances	0.73	4.61	20.10	159.76	829.28	558.05
d) Loans and Advances	32.12	46.29	45.43	134.66	340.94	588.84
e) Other Current Assets	–	5.07	2.54	21.64	131.92	118.56
f) Share/Debenture Issue Expenses and Preliminary Expenses	0.02	0.02	0.01	1.23	27.96	23.48

Provision for tax						
Current tax	1.08	0.63	0.88	0.64	–	–
Deferred tax expense/(credit)	–	–	4.14	2.07	(13.24)	–
Fringe benefit tax	–	–	–	–	–	14.97
Profit/(loss) after tax and before prior period items	7.17	9.08	6.24	5.97	(167.89)	(725.01)
Prior period income/(expenses)	–	–	–	(0.37)	(27.43)	–
Net profit/(loss) for the year/period as per audited accounts (A)	7.17	9.08	6.24	5.60	(195.32)	(725.01)
Adjustments – Increase/(decrease) in profits (Refer Annexure 4)						
Deferred revenue expenditure	(2.76)	0.93	(2.16)	(87.45)	(164.41)	44.80
Provision for maintenance expenses	5.13	3.56	(5.45)	(8.21)	(6.78)	–
Prior period income/(expense)	(0.30)	(0.07)	–	(27.06)	27.43	–
Other adjustments	1.18	1.18	1.18	(5.16)	–	–
Total impact of adjustments	3.25	5.60	(6.43)	(127.88)	(143.76)	44.80
Tax adjustments (Refer Annexure 4)						
Deferred tax (expense)/credit	(0.55)	1.50	0.84	5.18	(13.24)	–
Total of adjustments after tax impact (B)	2.70	7.10	(5.59)	(122.70)	(157.00)	44.80
Net profit/(loss), as restated (A+B)	9.87	16.18	0.65	(117.10)	(352.32)	(680.21)
Profit and Loss Account at die beginning of the year period	21.42	17.06	32.24	31.76	(93.28)	(445.60)
Amount available for appropriation as restated	31.29	33.24	32.89	(85.34)	(445.60)	(1,125.81)
Appropriations						
Proposed Dividend on Equity Share Capital	1.00	1.00	1.00	1.74	–	–
Tax on Dividend	0.10	–	0.13	0.23	–	–
Issue of Bonus Shares	13.13	–	–	5.97	–	–
	14.23	1.00	1.13	7.94	–	–
BALANCE CARRIED FORWARD, AS RESTATED	17.06	32.24	31.76	(93.28)	(445.60)	(1,125.81)

* Less than ₹ lacs

The above statement should be read with the significant accounting policies appearing in Annexure 4A and Notes to the Summary Statement of Assets and Liabilities, Profits and Losses and Cash Flows as restated, appearing in Annexure 4.

Source: Company annual reports.

TABLE M6.7
Income Statement

₹ millions	Year Ended 31 March 2001	Year Ended 31 March 2002	Year Ended 31 March 2003	Year Ended 31 March 2004	Year Ended 31 March 2005	Six Months Ended 31 September 2005
Income						
Sale of airline tickets and related income (Refer note F(1) in Annexure 4)	–	–	–	314.18	2,669.46	3,085.69
Helicopter charter and other services	147.17	195.48	234.15	315.21	386.08	202.97
	147.17	195.48	234.15	629.39	3,055.54	3,288.66
Other income	0.12	0.52	0.77	44.18	147.29	329.61
Total Income	147.29	196.00	234.92	673.57	3,202.83	3,618.27
Expenditure						
Aircraft fuel expenses	4.14	5.60	12.54	92.44	929.85	1,400.02
Aircraft/Engine repairs and maintenance	12.10	11.55	3.10	88.43	492.76	497.14
Aircraft/Engine lease rentals	47.97	54.09	57.22	106.45	451.17	558.13
Other direct operating expenses	36.83	56.61	58.11	167.64	736.54	942.78
Employee remuneration and benefits	14.70	20.34	26.40	71.46	317.65	431.40
Administrate and general expenses	13.68	21.95	34.56	75.57	203.06	295.72
Employee stock compensation cost	–	–	–	–	–	7.24
Advertisement and business promotion expenses	3.36	4.48	5.40	3.18	62.95	41.20
Finance and banking charges	2.65	5.24	15.18	38.69	102.14	70.68
Amortization	2.66	5.36	7.8S	9.87	57.25	59.45
Depreciation	0.95	1.07	3.27	11.16	30.59	24.55
Preliminary expenses written off	–	–	–	–	–	–
Total Expenditure	139.04	186.29	223.66	664.89	3,383.96	4,328.31
Profit/(Loss) before taxation and prior period items	8.25	9.71	11.26	8.68	(181.13)	(710.04)

TABLE M6.6
Key Events and Milestones

Year	Key Events, Milestones and Achievements
September 1997	Launch of first Helicopter by Deccan Aviation. First base opened at Jakkur.
January 1998	Introduction of second helicopter into Deccan Aviation fleet.
June 1998	Opening of second base in Hyderabad.
October 1998	Long-term contract signed with Cairn Energy for exploration and opening of third new base at Yanam.
December 1998	Commencement of Offshore flying operations.
May 1999	Conclusion of arrangement with Helicopter Leasing Corporation and introduction of four helicopters.
June 2001	First fixed wing aircraft introduced into Deccan Aviation fleet.
November 2001	Second fixed wing aircraft introduced into Deccan Aviation fleet.
November 2002	Commencement of Vaishno Devi operations.
August 2003	• Launch of Air Deccan; first ATR 42 320 aircraft acquired. • First Air Deccan flights take place on Bangalore–Hubli and Bangalore–Mangalore sectors.
April 2004	• Induction of fifth aircraft (ATR 42-500) into fleet. • Launch of flights on Mumbai–Ahmedabad, Mumbai–Chennai and Mumbai–Kolhapur–Belgaum sectors.
August 2004	• Induction of First Airbus A 320 into fleet. Launch of ₹500 ticket schemes. • Launch of flights on Delhi–Mumbai, Delhi–Bangalore and Mumbai–Bangalore sectors.
September 2004	Induction of second Airbus A 320 and launch of flights on Chennai–Delhi flights.
November 2004	Launch of travel agent credit cards.
December 2004	Launch of flights on Chennai–Kolkata sector
March 2005	Introduction of Fourth and Fifth Airbus A-320. Air Deccan enters into tie up arrangement with Club HP.
September 2005	Fleet strength reaches 20 Aircraft.
October 2005	Crossed 2.5 million passengers
December 2005	Connected the most number of destinations in India (46)

Source: Company website.

haul routes such as Delhi–Mumbai, Delhi–Bangalore and Chennai–Delhi. In Captain G. R. Gopinath's words,

> We have major expansion plans and are going to increase our operations four times by April 2004. The airline is also going to break the image of a regional low frills airline and enter the trunk route market.[3]

Table M6.6 lists the key events and milestones in the history of the company. Tables 6.7–6.10 present financial information on Air Deccan and its comparables.

[3] http://www.domain-b.com/news_review/200312dec/20031226newsa.htm (accessed on 8 January 2019).

2.02 trips per person per year in the USA. While penetration rates are expected to be low for a country with significantly low per capita GDP, India's aviation market was still well below where it could be.

India received only a fraction of international tourists that smaller countries received. Infrastructure issues and poor marketing ensured that India remained a fringe player in the world tourism industry. Tourism accounted for only 2.5 per cent of India's GDP versus 6 per cent in Asia Pacific and 5.3 per cent in China. In the recent past, however, the government had given a much needed impetus to the tourism industry through various schemes and organized events. According to the World Travel and Tourism Council India 2004 report, domestic tourist visits in India grew by 19 per cent from 309 million to 367.6 million in fiscal 2004. They also forecasted that India would be the second fastest-growing travel and tourism economy in the world with an annualized real growth rate projected at 8.8 per cent between 2005 and 2014.

Aviation turbine fuel (ATF) prices and airport charges in India are among the highest in the world. Fuel prices in India were 80 per cent higher (120% higher two years ago) than international base prices. Thus, despite high levels of efficiency and productivity and relatively lower manpower costs, air fares for travel within India remained higher than comparable international travel. For most international carriers, fuel costs as a percentage of revenue was 15–20 per cent, whereas for Indian carriers, it was nearly 25 per cent and as high as 35 per cent for low-cost carrier's (LCCs). Although the government has taken steps to reduce exercise and custom duties and also removed the Indian air travel tax (IATT) and foreign travel tax (FTT), fuel costs borne by Indian carriers were still 60 per cent higher than their international counterparts.

Airport congestion was a debilitating infrastructure problem faced by the industry. While India had over 450 airports, only 62 of them were in use. Moreover, Delhi and Mumbai accounted for more than 40 per cent of the total traffic. This situation was exacerbated through outdated infrastructure, inadequate ground handling systems, night landing facilities and poor passenger amenities. Due to the poor asset utilization, only 10 out of the 62 airports in India were profitable. Consequently, the government had limited funds to improve existing airports or to invest in new ones.

While the domestic aviation sector in India continued to be highly regulated, the government had in the recent past taken initiatives to ease the underlying constraints faced by the industry. It had agreed to partially privatize the two major airports of Mumbai and Delhi, allowing 49 per cent of the equity to be held by foreign airports, up from 40 per cent. Moreover, it had also facilitated the setting up of a new privately held Greenfield airport in Bangalore (74% held by Unique Zurich, L&T and Siemens Project). Exploratory studies on the modernization of the airports in Chennai, Hyderabad and Calcutta had also begun. The government also reduced excise duty on ATF from 16 per cent to 8 per cent on 9 January 2004. However, India had been led by coalition governments since 1991 with the Leftist parties still enjoying considerable power in the government and support in sections of the society. A recent decision by the government to privatize airports in an effort to modernize them was met by a four-day long nationwide airport employee strike backed by the leaders of the Leftist parties of India.

The changing regulatory environment, a growing but underpenetrated aviation market, the need to establish geographic connectivity throughout the country and the opportunity to capitalize on a growing economy were some of the factors that had contributed to the birth of several new airlines in recent years including Air Deccan.

COMPANY BACKGROUND

Air Deccan began scheduled operations in August 2003, with a single ATR turboprop aircraft, flying a single route between Bangalore and Hubli. Soon thereafter, Air Deccan announced plans to fly on long

TABLE M6.4
Domestic Air Traffic

Year ended March 31	Domestic Sector Passengers (millions)[1] %	Year-on-Year Growth %
1996	10.4	
1997	11.2	7.70
1998	11.55	−1.30
1999	12.0	4.30
2000	12.7	5.80
2001	13.7	7.90
2002	12.8	−6.60
2003	13.9	8.60
2004	15.7	12.90
2005	19.9	26.80

Note: (1) Information does not include air taxi operators.
Source: DGCA, CMIE Monthly Economic Indicator, November 2005.

TABLE M6.5
Domestic Passenger Traffic

Air Traffic (Passengers in Millions) Data:											
Month	2002	2003	% Growth	2004	% Growth	2005	% Growth	2006E	% Growth	2008E	% Growth
JAN	2.24	2.67	16.1	3.06	14.6	3.68	20.3	4.46	21.2	5.40	21.2
FEB	2.08	2.45	15.2	2.96	20.8	3.32	12.2	4.02	21.2	4.87	21.2
MAR	2.16	2.34	7.9	2.82	20.5	3.41	20.9	4.13	21.2	5.01	21.2
APR	2.15	2.25	4.4	2.92	29.8	3.41	16.8	4.13	21.2		
MAY	2.53	2.68	5.8	3.39	26.5	4.00	18.0	4.85	21.2		
JUN	2.11	2.56	17.5	3.23	26.2	3.82	18.3	4.63	21.2		
JUL	2.17	2.43	10.9	3.01	23.9	3.64	20.9	4.41	21.2		
AUG	2.30	2.40	4.2	3.00	25.0	3.73	24.3	4.52	21.2		
SEP	2.20	2.33	5.6	2.96	27.0	3.66	23.6	4.43	21.2		
OCT	2.52	2.70	6.7	3.31	22.6	4.25	28.4	5.15	21.2		
NOV	2.50	2.82	11.4	3.67	30.1	4.47	21.8	5.42	21.2		
DEC	2.81	3.11	9.6	3.95	27.0	4.99	26.3	6.05	21.2		
Sum (Calender Year)	**27.76**	**30.74**	**10.7**	**38.28**	**24.5**	**46.38**	**21.2**	**56.19**	**21.2**		
Sum (Fiscal Year)		**28.75**	**-**	**32.12**	**11.7**	**39.85**	**24.1**	**48.58**	**21.9**	**58.86**	**21.2**

Source: Airport Authority of India website.

Air Deccan was India's first airline to follow a no-frills, low-cost scheduled passenger airline business model. Counter-intuitive to a general LCC strategy, which had only one aircraft type, Air Deccan followed a two aircraft type fleet strategy with the aim of effectively serving both the highly travelled routes between major Indian urban centres and the routes to and from regional locations. Air Deccan used the ATR turboprop aircraft, in both 48 seat and 72 seat sizes, for its regional routes which had lower passenger volumes per sector and involved short flights. On its trunk routes, Air Deccan used the 180 seat Airbus A320 jet aircraft. Table M6.11 presents information on the type of aircrafts that Air Deccan operated as of 30 November 2005.

Air Deccan created history on 25 August 2004 by flying passengers to Delhi from Bangalore for a fare of only ₹700, virtually half the price of a railway ticket in many destinations.[4] The company offered 75 per cent of the seats at rates ranging between ₹500 and ₹5,000 and the remaining 25 per cent at around ₹7,500, which was 25 per cent less than the normal fare of ₹10,500 on any other airline.[5] Sceptics cited the reason as hidden costs, but regardless, this provided a means for air travel to be accessible to the average middle income bracket customer, something which was previously unheard of. An estimated 40 per cent of Air Deccan's passengers were first-time flyers.

COST STRUCTURE AND OPERATIONS

Air Deccan's business model was inspired by the low-cost business models adopted by successful, no-frills, low-cost airlines in other parts of the world. Air Deccan's target customer base included those who travelled by train or other ground transportation means as well as those who already travelled by air. It aimed to turn non-fliers into fliers and occasional fliers into more frequent fliers. Overall, Air Deccan's flight fares were as much as 50 per cent lower than those of other leading airlines in the country.[6] To sustain these low fares, Air Deccan used innovative techniques to keep overall costs of the company low. For example, in-flight food and drinks were served for a price. An estimated 5 per cent of the revenue came from these in-flight services. The company had also removed the business class section and reduced overall leg space on its aircrafts. This helped increase the seating capacity by another 22 per

TABLE M6.11
Aircraft Composition as of November 2005

Aircraft Type	Number of Passenger Seats	Model	Number of Aircrafts	Average Age (in years)$^{(1)}$
ATR	48	42-320	5	11
	48	42-500	8	7
Air Bus	72	72-500	3	*
	180	A320-200	7	2.86

Notes: $^{(1)}$ Calculated based on year of manufacture.
* New aircraft recently acquired.
Source: Company website, annual reports and IPO prospectus.

[4] http://us.rediff.com/money/2004/nov/20spec.htm (accessed on 8 January 2019).
[5] http://specials.rediff.com/money/2004/aug/25deccan.htm (accessed on 8 January 2019).
[6] http://www.quillem.com/node/368 (accessed on 8 January 2019).

TABLE M6.12
Air Deccan's Load Factor and Revenue

	Year Ended 31 March 2003	Year Ended 31 March 2004	Year Ended 31 March 2005	Six Months Ended 30 September 2005
Available seats flown[(1)]	–	244,091	1,292,738	1,497,106
Passengers flown[(2)]	–	152,910	987,104	1,070,047
Passenger Load Factor[(3)]	–	63%	76%	71%
Revenues (₹ millions)[(4)]	–	314	2,669	3,086
Revenues per Passenger (₹)	–	2,055	2,704	2,884

Notes: (1) Defined as aircraft seating capacity over all flights flown during the period.
(2) Defined as number of passengers flown.
(3) Defined as passengers flown expressed as a percentage of available seats flown.
(4) Income from sale of airline tickets and related income.

Source: Company website, annual reports and IPO prospectus.

cent.[7] Distribution costs were kept low by selling tickets through websites and call centres. Additionally, Air Deccan increased its aircraft utilization by investing in technology to reduce airport turnaround time between flights significantly. On average, an Air Deccan aircraft flew for about 12 hours a day compared to 8–9 hours for its competitors.[8] Table M6.12 presents information relating to Air Deccan's load factors and revenue.

A significant portion of the company's expenses such as fuel, aircraft and engine maintenance services, interest and principal obligations under the terms of foreign debt and aircraft lease payments were denominated in or linked to US dollars. In Fiscal 2005, 35.96 per cent of Air Deccan's expenses were incurred in currencies other than the Indian Rupee.

GROWTH STRATEGY AND FINANCING

Air Deccan's main competitive advantage was due to the fact that it was a first mover. While other airlines competed on major routes of the network, Air Deccan aimed to increase its presence in underdeveloped areas and create a first mover advantage by setting up infrastructure in these locations at very competitive costs.

In order to help satisfy anticipated demand from existing routes as well as to add new routes and grow flight frequencies across the route network, the company had placed orders for the future delivery of 101 aircrafts. Table M6.13 presents details of the number and types of aircraft on order as of 30 November 2005. Air Deccan was also vulnerable to aircraft design and mechanical defects because of its dependence on limited suppliers. Overall, the additional aircraft orders represented approximately ₹133.50 million in amounts payable in the current fiscal year as pre-delivery payments and deposits, plus approximately ₹44,056.62 million in additional commitments. To satisfy these huge capital needs, the management made the decision to offer 25 per cent stake of the company via an IPO. Table M6.14

[7] http://us.rediff.com/money/2004/nov/20spec.htm (accessed on 8 January 2019).
[8] http://us.rediff.com/money/2004/nov/20spec.htm (accessed on 8 January 2019).

TABLE M6.13
Aircrafts on Order as of November 2005

Period/Year	Mode of Acquisition	Aircraft Type & Number: A 320	ATR 42–500	ATR 72–500	Number of Aircrafts to be Acquired
01 December 2005–31 March 2006	Outright purchase				
	lease	4	2	1	7
	Hire purchase			2	2
	Subtotal	4	2	3	9
2006–2007	Outright purchase				
	Lease	5		1	6
	Hire purchase			2	2
	Yet to be decided	2		5	7
	Subtotal	7		8	15
2007–2008	Yet to be decided	6		6	12
	Lease			1	1
	Subtotal	6		7	13
2008–2009	Yet to be decided	9		6	15
	Subtotal	9		6	15
2009–2010	Yet to be decided	12		6	18
	Subtotal	12		6	18
2010–2011	Yet to be decided	12			12
	Subtotal	12			12
2011–2012	Yet to be decided	10			10
	Subtotal	10			10
2012–2013	Yet to be decided	9			9
	Subtotal	9			9
	Grand total	**69**	**2**	**30**	**101**

Source: Company website, annual reports and IPO prospectus.

presents details of the proposed uses of the IPO. Around the same time, two other competing airlines (Kingfisher and SpiceJet) announced their plans of an IPO as well.

Historically, Air Deccan had tapped private equity (PE) and internal accruals for financing its growth. Air Deccan promoters led by Captain G. R. Gopinath held 64 per cent of the stock, while 27 per cent was with PE funds, which included ICICI Venture Funds Management Co. that invested US$40–50 million in January 2005. The airline was also offering 10 per cent of its stock as ESOPs, which would vest in four annual instalments. Most of the PE investor firms were not under a lock-up agreement and, hence, could choose to reduce their exposure by means of an IPO. Table M6.15 presents the ownership structure before and after the IPO.

TABLE M6.14
Proposed Uses of the IPO

Description	Estimated Funds Requirement (₹ million)
Setting up a training centre	656.69
Setting up a hangar facility	400.20
Setting up infrastructure at airports	170.83
Market development initiatives	452.20
Debt repayment	1,327.50
General corporate purposes	....
Issue expenses	....
Total	

Source: IPO prospectus.

TABLE M6.15
Ownership Structure

	Equity Shares owned before the Issue		Equity Shares owned after the Issue #	
Shareholder Category	No. of shares	%	No. of shares	%
Promoter				
Capt G.R. Gopinath*	10,950,000	14.87	10,950,000	11.15
Capt K.J. Samuel*	8,349,000	11.34	8,349,000	8.50
Vishnu Singh Rawal*	2,863,500	3.89	2,863,500	2.92
Subtotal (A)	**22,162,500**	**30.01**	**22,162,500**	**22.57**
Other existingshareholders				
Subria CIPEF Limited	13,574,356	18.43	13,574,356	13.83
Subria CGPE Limited	451,463	0.61	451,463	0.46
The Western India Trustee and Executor Company Ltd (India Advantage Fund-I)	14,025,818	19.05	14,025,818	14.29
Eureka Venture Fund	5,400,000	7.33	5,400,000	5.50
Golden Venture Limited	3,716,880	5.05	3,716,880	3.79
Brindavan Breweries Limited	9,027,660	12.26	9,027,660	9.19
Lachman Dass Ladhani	1,063,530	1.44	1,063,530	1.08
Prakash Ladhani	912,000	1.24	912,000	0.93
Sumant Kapur	912,000	1.24	912,000	0.93

Shareholder Category	Equity Shares owned before the Issue		Equity Shares owned after the Issue #	
	No. of shares	%	No. of shares	%
Kenichi Miyagawa	705,000	0.96	705,000	0.72
Sudhir Choudhrie	456,000	0.62	456,000	0.46
Kaushalya Devi Ladhani	455,850	0.62	455,850	0.46
Naresh Ladhani	455,835	0.62	455,835	0.46
Rajesh Ladhani	151,980	0.21	151,980	0.15
Monica Ladhani	75,990	0.10	75,990	0.08
Shalini Ladhani	75,990	0.10	75,990	0.08
S.N.Ladhani	13,155	0.02	13,155	0.01
SubTotal (B)	**51,473,507**	**69.90**	**51,473,507**	**52.43**
Public (C)			**24,546,000**	**25.00**
Total share capital (A+B+C)	**73,636,007**	**100.00**	**98,182,007**	**100.00**

Notes: ∞ The above shareholding pattern does not take into account the transfer of Equity Shares to the Promoters and other shareholders pursuant to the escrow agreement with the investors For details see
* History and Corporate Structure – Escrow Agreement on page [•].
• Promoter Directors.
Assuming the existing Shareholders do not participate in the issue.

Source: IPO prospectus.

FINANCIAL OUTLOOK

Due to a strong growth in the domestic market driven by affordability, a booming economy, and an increase in capacity, the aviation sector in India was expected to flourish in the years ahead. Analysts expected airline passenger growth to slow down to 12 per cent per annum by 2012 and 10 per cent per annum by 2013.

Air Deccan increased its market share from 6.5 per cent in March 2005 to 11 per cent in October 2005. Even though it was unlikely that Air Deccan would continue to gain market share at the same rate, management expected the firm to further strengthen its position and gain market share of about 19 per cent by 2013.

Fuel expenses are the most significant part of operating expenses for an airline company. Fuel costs for Air Deccan were 38.7 per cent of sales in 2005 due to an increase in international crude oil prices. Thus, Air Deccan's fuel cost was expected to be around 35 per cent of sales in 2006 and come down (in line with most oil analysts' forecast) to 30 per cent by 2013 with government initiative to bring airline fuel costs in line with what they were for international carriers.

Air Deccan incurred more costs on operating expenses and on repairs and maintenance partly due to the age of its fleet and partly due to the start-up costs of establishing maintenance facilities. Together, these costs accounted for 39.8 per cent of revenue in the six months ending September 2005. However, as Air Deccan acquired new fleet, these costs would settle at around 24 per cent.

Administrative and general expenses for Air Deccan had been lower compared to competitors and were likely to remain low due to its low-cost operational model. The employee remuneration cost for Air Deccan was higher at 12 per cent of sales compared to 7–8 per cent for its peers. These costs were significantly higher internationally and were likely to go up in India as the Indian economy opened up more. However, due to its emphasis on cost reductions, Air Deccan was likely to keep these costs at around 8.5 per cent of sales in the long run.

CHALLENGES

After years of dormant competitive dynamics, the Indian aviation market was witnessing a large number of new entrants in addition to aggressive fleet expansion and modernization plans from incumbents. Kingfisher Airlines launched its airline with a fleet of 30 new planes in 2005. The same year, SpiceJet began operations with three new Boeing aircrafts. GoAir was next in line among others. While growth in demand was estimated to keep pace, if further new players come in or if demand growth did not sustain, there could be excess capacity that could lead to price wars, once fleet additions gained momentum. Figure M6.1 presents the details of market share for leading domestic airlines in October 2005.

Skilled labour had not kept pace with the industry growth. With aggressive fleet additions by new entrants as well as incumbents, the industry was witnessing a shortage of pilots and skilled crew. This imbalance in supply and demand could cause crew costs to rise sharply.

Starting up an airline in India was fairly easy, capital being the main constraint. Other barriers to entry were mandatory coverage of certain routes and the lack of adequate airport infrastructure. Execution was a major hurdle for all the new players due to a host of internal and infrastructure issues. A new private airline would have to compete with established players that had the network, time slots and a brand name in place. Network would be a key challenge due to the limited size of operations and the regulatory requirements on route dispersal norms. Lack of a good network would also mean lower utilization of the aircraft. Therefore, cost structures would necessarily be inferior. This would be further accentuated by higher labour costs. Moreover, infrastructure issues on landing and parking slots would limit choices on time slots. However, the government seemed keen to encourage competition and was addressing infrastructure and regulatory issues.

FIGURE M6.1
Market Shares of Leading Airlines in October 2005

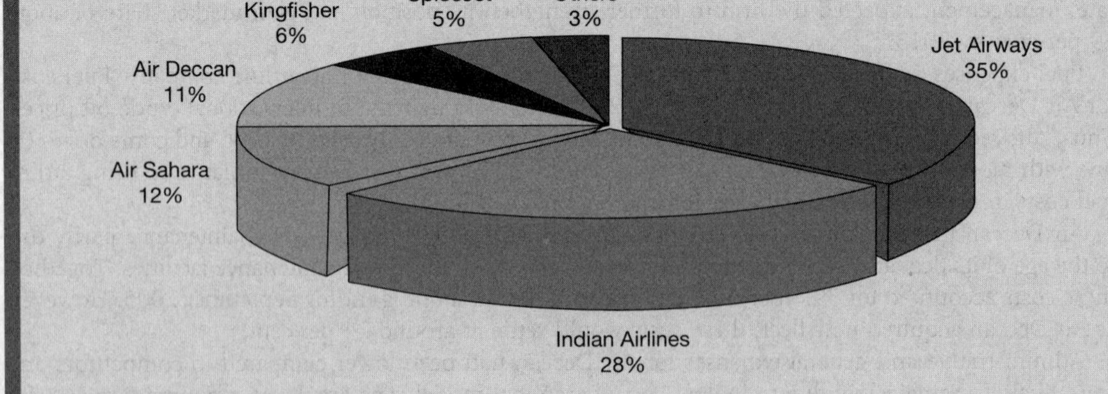

Source: Center for Asia Pacific Aviation.

Despite the market having expanded at 27 per cent in 2005, there was a consistent shortage in capacity in major routes, especially at peak flying hours. Thus, a part of the new fleet coming in could cater to this unmet demand. New carriers would also expand the market, either by flying to new destinations or by lowering price points.

Many of the new entrants as well as incumbents were positioning themselves as LCCs in an attempt to gain market share through aggressive pricing. Industry experts reckoned that average fares would drop by 30 per cent due to increased competition. Already Air Deccan has fired the first salvo by dropping its cheapest fare to ₹1 on all routes. But that might not be enough as GoAir's Managing Director Jehangir Wadia claimed:

> We will have more seats at ₹1 than Air Deccan at ₹500.

The airline had a quasi-hub and spoke route strategy that included linking smaller towns with metros as well as intra-metro connections. However, it did not provide connecting services. Experts felt that this strategy was responsible for its higher costs. According to an industry expert,

> Air Deccan's inventory and maintenance costs are higher because it has both ATRs and Airbus aircrafts—low cost carriers never do that. As a result, its cost per seat per km on an ATR is 2.5 times higher than it should be.

But Captain G. R. Gopinath had a counterpoint.

> In India, if you want the masses to travel, you have to connect small towns and cities to the metros. I have a twin cost model so my ATR fares are 60% higher than Airbus fares. Thus, I am not losing money.

But competitive pressure was already beginning to show in the industry. Jet Airways announced its acquisition of Air Sahara the previous month, thereby sending ripples in the industry. The merger of two established airline giants in India sent a strong signal to the market, indicating the possibility of a massive price war. Even though Air Deccan was currently by far the leader in LCCs, whether it could sustain its position in the long run given increased competition and recent skyrocketing oil prices was questionable.

THE OFFERING

As the breeze outside Kumar's office increased in intensity, it bought him back to reality. Air Deccan needed to raise capital fast and Kumar could only hope that the decision to do an IPO now was well justified.

PREPARING TO GO PUBLIC

The process of preparing the company to go public was time-consuming. Air Deccan had hoped to take the company public in order to build the brand and raise additional capital. The senior management at Air Deccan was aware that the IPO would be the first day of its public life and believed that it was very important to meet the company's responsibilities to its new shareholders and for life in the public spotlight. The company's executives spent several months preparing the company to take it public, developing the infrastructure and systems that would enable it to meet the demands placed on public companies. While the IPO brought additional capital a stock market listing entailed costs such as investment banker's fees, stock exchange listing fees, IPO grading fee[9] and so on. The issue expenses could be as high as 6 per cent of net proceeds. In addition to the explicit cost of going public, there was also an implicit cost in going public: public issues often list at a price much higher than the issue price, a phenomenon called IPO underpricing. In the early 1990s, an average IPO produced 35.3 per cent returns upon listing.[10]

Market Conditions

Apart from the costs of going public, other issues included possibility of poor response from investors and the issue getting listed below the issue price. Seventeen PE & VC-backed companies raised about US$950 million via IPOs during 2005.[11] The largest PE-backed IPO during 2005 was that of wind energy turbine maker Suzlon Energy, which raised US$342 million. The oversubscribed IPO fetched spectacular returns for Suzlon's PE backers including Citicorp and ChrysCapital. Citicorp, which had invested US$22.5 million in Suzlon in April 2004, sold shares worth US$29.9 million as part of the IPO. Other top PE-backed IPOs during the year included that of Punj Lloyd, HT Media, YES Bank, Shoppers Stop and PVR Cinemas.

Preparing the Prospectus

Having selected lead managers, the company's officials turned their attention to the preparation of the prospectus. The Securities and Exchange Board of India (SEBI) (Act) required all companies to prepare a prospectus for distribution of securities to investors. The contents of the prospectus and supplemental financial information were governed by SEBI regulations. The prospectus was an important document. The company and its management team were liable for information provided in the prospectus and for omission of any material information. The company's investment banker drafted the prospectus after conducting due diligence investigation of the firm in consultation with the accountant and the legal counsel. The prospectus gave the details of the company's business and management, names of principal shareholders and their level of ownership, audited financial statements, underwriting agreement, information on the use of proceeds, dividend policy and capitalization. A discussion of management's perception of all risk factors and competitive position was also included. The company had to file the draft prospectus with SEBI through a merchant banker. After the preparation of prospectus, the merchant banker, along with the due diligence certificates and other compliances, sent the same to SEBI for vetting. On receiving the same, the Board scrutinized it and could suggest changes within 21 days of receipt of prospectus. A company could come out with a public issue any time within 365 days from the date of the letter from SEBI or if no letter was received from SEBI, within 365 days from the date of expiry of 21 days of submission of prospectus with SEBI. If the issue size was up to ₹20 crores,[12] then the merchant bankers were required to file prospectus with the regional office of SEBI falling under the

[9] In 2007, the SEBI made it mandatory that all IPOs must get a grading from one of the credit rating agencies such as CRISIL, ICRA, CARE and Fitch. The grading is on a five-point scale with one indicating poor fundamentals and five indicating strong fundamentals. The cost of grading works out to ₹500,000 and takes about 3–4 weeks. Air Deccan chose not to get the IPO graded as it was not mandatory at that point in time.

[10] Loughran, Ritter and Rydqvist, 'Initial Public Offerings'.

[11] www.vccircle.com (accessed on 8 January 2019).

[12] ₹1 crore=₹10 million. In India amounts are quoted in crores rather than millions and billions.

jurisdiction in which registered office of the company was situated. If the issue size was more than ₹20 crore, merchant bankers were required to file prospectus at SEBI, Mumbai office. A prospectus was also filed with the concerned stock exchanges along with the application for listing its securities. After making changes, if any, made by SEBI/stock exchanges, the final prospectus duly signed by all the directors (or by authorized representatives through its Power of Attorney) had to be filed with the Registrar of Companies (ROC) along with the copy of all material documents. The ROC could suggest changes which had to be reported to SEBI/stock exchanges. The date on which ROC card was obtained is the date of the prospectus. The draft offer document filed with SEBI had to be made public for a period of 21 days from the date of filing the offer document with SEBI. Once the registration statement was approved by the SEBI, the marketing of the offering began.

After the preparation of the prospectus, the company set out on a road show to address potential investors. A typical road show lasted 3–4 weeks. A timeline diagram of the IPO process is given in Table M6.16. Once the stock was listed, the underwriter had the obligation to stabilize the price and provide analyst recommendations.

TABLE M6.16
IPO Timeline

S. No.	Day No.	No. of Days	Event
A			
1	T-0	1	Share Transfer to increase number of members to 7
2	T-1	1	Board Meeting and Resolution
3	T-2	21	Notice for shareholders meeting
4	T-23	1	Shareholders meeting and special resolution
5	T-24	1	Filing of Form 23 with ROC
6	T-25	1	Filing of Statement in Lieu of Prospectus with ROC
7	T-26	1	Amendment of MOA and AOA
8	T-27	5	Conversion into a Public Limited Company
9	T-32	1	Notice for Statutory Meeting
10	T-33	30	Statutory Meeting and Statutory Report
11	T-63	1	Copy of Statutory Report to ROC
B			Preparation and Regulatory Approvals
1	T-64	1	Board Resolution for issue of shares
2	T-65	21	Shareholders Resolution
3	T-86	1	Filing Form 23 with ROC
4	T-87	10	Appointment of merchant banker
5	T-97	30	Due diligence audit by the merchant banker
6	T-127	10	Preparation of prospectus
7	T-137	5	In principle approval for listing

(Continued)

TABLE M6.16
(Continued)

S. No.	Day No.	No. of Days	Event
8	T-142	25	Vetting of prospectus
9	T-167	7	SEBI compliance
10	T-174	5	ROC card
11	T-179	2	1% security deposit and promoters contribution
C			Marketing & Research
1	T-181	3	Investor targeting
2	T-184	7	Research and sales calls
3	T-191	7	Marketing efforts
D			Execution
1	T-198	10	Book open and close for book building
2	T-208	3	Price discovery
3	T-211	10	Public offer opens
E			Post-Issue Obligations
1	T-221	10	Registry works
2	T-231	7	Allotment of shares
3	T-238	5	Administrative duties
4	T-243	3	Return of allotment
5	T-246	5	Listing and trading of securities
6	T-251	–	Commencement of trading
7	–	–	Investor grievance handling
8	–	–	Refund of security deposit

PRICING AND VALUATION

Finally, the company had to make sure the issue price was right. If the price were to be low, the issue would be hopelessly oversubscribed, whereas if the price were to be high there was a possibility that the stock would list at below the issue price.

In determining the initial public offering (IPO) price, the factors that would be considered were the prevailing market and general economic condition, the history of and prospects for the company and industry, an assessment of the company's management and its operating results and the market prices of securities and certain financial and operating information as they relate to market valuations of companies engaged in activities similar to those of the company. The company could either perform a discounted cash flow valuation or compare the valuation multiples with those of the peer group companies. The DCF approach involved forecasting of cash flows to equity and estimation of appropriate discount rate to discount cash flows. The value of equity thus arrived was divided by the number of shares outstanding to arrive at the intrinsic value.

Under the relative valuation approach, the objective was to find out if Air Deccan was under or over-valued relative to peer companies.

The airline business was touted to be a tricky business the world over, let alone in an emerging economy such as India. Even though the future looked promising for Air Deccan, Kumar could not help but wonder if he could do anything else to strengthen Air Deccan's attractiveness to both domestic and foreign investors. And finally, of course, he was yet to come up with a price for the offering.

Finally, in early 2006, when the SEBI started scanning an entire spectrum of IPOs launched over 2003, 2004 and 2005, it unearthed manipulation of the primary market by financiers and market players by using fictitious demat accounts. The IPO scam came to the light in 2005 when the private Yes Bank launched its IPO. Roopalben Panchal of Indiabulls Securities, a brokerage firm, had allegedly opened several fake demat accounts and subsequently raised finances on the shares allotted to her through Bharat Overseas Bank branches. While investigating the Yes Bank scam, SEBI found that certain entities had illegally obtained IPO shares reserved for retail applicants through thousands of demat accounts. They then transferred the shares to financiers, who sold on the first day of listing, making windfall gains from the price difference between the IPO price and the listing price.

Kumar wondered what these events implied to Air Deccan's IPO.

Exercises

1. Why does Air Deccan need to go public?
2. What are the benefits and costs of going public?
3. Should Air Deccan be worried about IPO underpricing?
4. Can the offer price be justified?
5. On a relative basis, how attractive or unattractive is the issue price (vis-à-vis industry peers)?
6. As an investor would you invest in the company?

REFERENCES

Loughran, Tim, Jay Ritter and Kristian Rydqvist. 'Initial Public Offerings: International Insights'. *Pacific Basin Finance Journal* 2 (1994 June).

Ministry of Civil Aviation, Government of India. *Domestic Air Transport Policy Document*. Available at http://civilaviation.nic.in/moca/acvl.htm (accessed on 8 January 2019).

SUGGESTED READINGS

Datamonitor. 'Airlines in India' (October 2005).

Datamonitor. 'Jet Airways' (February 2006).

Duetsche Bank. 'Jet Airways' (Duetsche Bank report, 11 May 2005).

JP Morgan. 'Jet Airways' (JP Morgan report, 24 January 2006).

Morgan Stanley. 'Jet Airways' (Morgan Stanley report, 23 January 2006).

Morgan Stanley. 'Jet Airways' (Morgan Stanley report, 25 January 2006).

Morgan Stanley. 'Jet Airways' (Morgan Stanley report, 15 March 2006).

7

Wockhardt Limited: Will It Rise from the Ashes?*

LEARNING OBJECTIVE

The case provides an introduction to how currency mismatches create exposures, why and how companies hedge (or do not hedge) those exposures, alternate valuation models and the use of foreign currency convertibles in funding a global expansion programme.

Description: The case highlights the ambitious growth strategy of Wockhardt, a global biopharmaceutical company. In a bid to dominate the biopharmaceutical market, Wockhardt grew aggressively by acquiring companies all over the world. This expansion was funded by a mix of secured loans (bank borrowings) and unsecured loans including foreign currency (US$ denominated) convertible bonds (FCCBs). Due to deteriorating business and economic conditions, the Company experienced a sharp decline in profitability and stock price resulting in a debt overhang. The Company had to restructure its capital structure to escape bankruptcy. The company's management is faced with several options to deal with financial distress. The case asks students to evaluate those options.

On 31 March 2009, in view of the adverse market conditions, liquidity constraints and debt burden, the Board of Directors of Wockhardt Ltd,[1] a global pharmaceutical and biotechnology company from India, agreed to make a reference to corporate debt restructuring (CDR) cell

* Reproduced with permission from *The CASE Journal*, Emerald Publishing.

[1] In German language, Wockhardt means 'work hard'.

through ICICI Bank, one of the lending banks, for financial restructuring of the company through the CDR mechanism. Investors were surprised by the sudden development at the company.

Wockhardt said in a press release:

> Restructuring of debt, release of working capital and fresh priority debt by banks pending divestment of non-core assets is a positive step forward and will provide a great impetus to the core operations of the company.[2]

In particular, Mr Khorakiwala, the chairman of the company, was faced with the task of determining a possible solution to the debt overhang problem caused by foreign currency convertibles. His options included issue of new securities aimed at paying down debt, sale of one or more businesses and, finally, a full liquidation.

COMPANY BACKGROUND

Wockhardt was India's leading research-based global health care enterprise with businesses in the fields of pharmaceuticals, biotechnology and super specialty hospitals. Wockhardt was a multinational company with a workforce of 8,600 employees belonging to 14 nationalities. It had three research centres and 12 manufacturing plants, with businesses ranging from manufacturing and marketing of pharmaceutical and biopharmaceutical formulations, active pharmaceutical ingredients and vaccines. Headquartered in Mumbai, India, Wockhardt had full-fledged operations in the USA, UK, Ireland and France. It also had a marketing presence in several emerging markets such as Russia, Brazil and Mexico. Through Wockhardt Hospitals Ltd, it operated a chain of super specialty hospitals.

Wockhardt was founded by Habil Khorakiwala in the 1960s. The Company was incorporated as a limited liability public company in 1999.[3] Wockhardt was one of the earliest domestic entrants in the biopharmaceuticals sector. The Company marketed a portfolio of three products and their analogues in India, which included Hepatitis B vaccine Biovac, Wepox and Wosulin. Wockhardt's businesses ranged from R&D to manufacturing and marketing. Traditional biopharmaceutical companies faced challenges arising from patent expiration, generic competition and poor development pipeline. Contract manufacturing offered a way to rationalize costs, cut assets and streamline manufacturing processes. On a contract basis, the Company manufactured Exenatide for Amylin Pharmaceuticals. It also had contracts with Pfizer, Cephalon, Johnson & Johnson, AstraZeneca and several other leading pharmaceutical companies.

The total biotechnology market was estimated at US$75 billion. US$10 billion worth of biological drugs were expected to go off patent by 2010, and an additional US$10 billion by 2015.[4] However, the market for biopharmaceuticals was challenging with strong entry barriers. The cost and technical challenges in manufacturing biopharmaceuticals were a lot higher than those involved in traditional pharmaceutical generics. A study by the industry indicated that developing a biosimilar could cost between US$10 and US$40 million, against a development cost of under US$5 million in case of pharmaceutical

---

[2] Das Gupta, Surajeet and P. B. Jayakumar, *Wockhardt gets CDR lifeline with riders.*

[3] The founder owned 73.4 per cent of the Company's stock. The Company's website contains details of its businesses (www.wockhardt.com)

[4] This section is based on the information in Joshi, *Avendus India Equity Research*, Wockhardt, 22 October 2008; Joshi, *Avendus India Equity Research*, Wockhardt, 27 April 2009.

generics.[5] Success in this business was determined by funding options related to clinical trials and regulatory submissions, speed with which a company took its products to the market and distribution strategies. The Company's strategy was to expand globally by leveraging on its domestic market experience in products and delivery systems.

The global insulin market was estimated at over US$4 billion and another US$6 billion was contributed by insulin analogues. Of the global insulin market, US$750 million was accounted for by the Rest of the World (RoW, i.e., ex-USA, EU and Japan). It is this market that industry observers felt Wockhardt could address over the medium term. In FY07, the Company received 45 regulatory approvals for recombinant insulin from RoW, taking the total approvals to 73. Wockhardt was expanding its geographical reach in new markets. These included Mexico, Brazil, Colombia and Venezuela. The company was also targeting expansion of its product basket by including Glargine (long-lasting insulin) and Lispro (fast-acting insulin), though these opportunities would materialize only over the long term. Tables M7.1–7.5 present financial data and board composition of Wockhardt, and Table M7.6 presents key ratios and indicators for its competition.[6]

TABLE M7.1
Income Statements (₹ '0M)

	2008	2007	2006	2005	2004	2003
Net Sales	1,472.13	1,355.66	1,223.84	1,050.85	898.13	740.24
Expenses						
Raw Materials	662.31	606.03	481.49	432.23	362.35	322.39
Power & Fuel	36.41	29.72	33.18	18.54	14.48	12.43
Employee Cost	139.2	111.5	107.39	81.05	67.29	59.95
Other Manufacturing Expenses	27.3	23.29	33.86	20.72	14.25	9.35
Selling and Administrative Expenses	191.56	173.84	128.47	107.52	96.06	95.11
Miscellaneous Expenses	704.73	66.77	141.36	74.08	68.89	68.4
Total	**1,761.51**	**1,011.15**	**925.75**	**734.14**	**623.32**	**567.63**
Operating Profit	–289.38	344.51	298.09	316.71	274.81	172.61
Interest	121.67	36.85	10.62	27.07	16	10.5
Gross Profit	–411.05	307.66	287.47	289.64	258.81	162.11
Depreciation	46.03	34.54	34.84	24.22	18.41	16.08
Profit Before Tax	–457.08	273.12	252.63	265.42	240.4	146.03
Net Income	–348.76	213.88	213.55	238.47	207.78	133.36
Extraordinary Items	–443.83	0	–43.97	0.11	–0.45	0.23
Adjusted Net Income	95.07	213.88	257.52	238.36	208.23	133.13

Source: CAPITALINE database.

[5] Jacoby, R. and D. Iyer, *Winning with Biosimilars*.

[6] Wockhardt changed its accounting period from the existing January through December period to an April through March period beginning in 2009. Consequently, the fiscal year ending 31 December 2009 was extended by three months to 31 March 2010 and the annual report was released in 2010.

TABLE M7.2
Balance Sheet (₹ '0M)

	2008	2007	2006	2005	2004	2003
Equity Capital	677.27	1,026.03	956.56	805.19	620.62	473.32
Secured Loans	749.15	253.98	222.16	315.63	333.16	296.18
Unsecured Loans	1,071.49	554.83	485.34	494.08	483.22	4.81
Total Debt	1,820.64	808.81	707.5	809.71	816.38	300.99
Total Liabilities	**2,497.91**	**1,834.84**	**1,664.06**	**1,614.9**	**1,437**	**774.31**
Gross Fixed Assets	958.95	764.42	706.13	487.35	408.34	282.89
Less: Accumulated Depreciation	244.17	194.67	157.88	121.73	98.1	80.51
Net Fixed Assets	714.78	569.75	548.25	365.62	310.24	202.38
Capital Work-in-Progress	399.15	340.92	153.01	231.14	152.4	149.52
Investments	302.6	302.47	159.89	184.28	175.16	154.78
Current Assets, Loans & Advances						
Inventories	257.08	262.42	214.98	156.15	89.38	90.37
Sundry Debtors	459.45	346.98	254.38	206.68	144.38	146.83
Cash and Bank Balances	474.08	177.15	519.22	646.07	669.09	147.43
Loans and Advances	891.76	261.27	212.3	153.43	184.12	101.18
Total Current Assets	2,082.37	1,047.82	1,200.88	1,162.33	1,086.97	485.81
Less: Current Liabilities and Provisions						
Current Liabilities	417.12	257.45	233.63	198.53	168.53	144.39
Provisions	583.87	56.55	82.66	75.86	68.64	37.08
Total Current Liabilities	1,000.99	314	316.29	274.39	237.17	181.47
Net Deferred Tax	0	−112.12	−81.68	−54.08	−50.6	−36.71
Total Assets	**2,497.91**	**1,834.84**	**1,664.06**	**1,614.9**	**1,437**	**774.31**

Source: CAPITALINE database.

TABLE M7.3
Cash Flow Statements (₹'0M)

	2008	2007	2006	2005
Cash and Cash Equivalents at Beginning of the Year	174.22	519.22	646.08	669.09
Net Cash from Operating Activities	**66.77**	**127.48**	**154.64**	**175.24**
Net Cash Used in Investing Activities	−947.28	−401.97	−117.58	−96.69
Net Cash Used in Financing Activities	742.61	−70.5	−163.92	−101.56
Net Increase/(Decrease) in Cash and Cash Equivalent	−137.9	−344.99	−126.86	−23.01
Cash and Cash Equivalents at End of the Year	36.32	174.23	519.22	646.08

TABLE M7.4
Key Ratios of Wockhardt

	2008	2007	2006	2005	2004	2003
Debt–Equity Ratio	1.54	0.76	0.86	1.14	1.02	0.4
Long-Term Debt–Equity Ratio	0.96	0.67	0.86	1.13	0.96	0.33
Current Ratio	1.27	2.16	3.17	3.49	2.69	1.65
Total Asset Turnover Ratio	0.66	0.71	0.7	0.65	0.81	1.3
Interest Coverage Ratio	0.89	8.41	30.1	10.8	16.03	14.91
EBDIT Margin (%)	10.74	27.87	31.05	31.74	30.69	22.5
EBIT Margin (%)	7.54	25.07	28	29.31	28.63	20.41
PAT Margin (%)	6.61	17.3	22.55	23.9	23.2	17.39
ROCE (%)	0	17.72	19.5	19.17	23.19	26.48
ROE (%)	0	21.58	29.23	33.45	37.99	31.66
Payout (%)	0	63.81	26.58	23.71	27.2	20.98
Price Earning (P/E)	0	23.67	18.63	21.07	19.21	20.13
Price to Book Value (P/BV)	1.75	4.45	4.01	6.04	6.21	5.52
Enterprise value/EBIDTA	0	15.09	13.5	15.87	14.56	16.04
Market Capitalization/Sales	0.82	3.69	3.36	4.87	4.31	3.41

Source: CAPITALINE database.

TABLE M7.5
Board of Directors and Their Remuneration (in Brackets)

1. Rajiv Gandhi Executive Director-Corporate Finance (₹10.32 million)
   CFO of Wockhardt; a chartered accountant and a company secretary
2. Bharat Patel, Director (₹100,000), Independent
   Mr Patel is an economics graduate from the University of Notre Dame and an MBA from the University of Michigan in the USA. He has more than 40 years' management experience in marketing, sales, exports, manufacturing and buying functions. He served as chairman and managing director of Procter & Gamble India Limited for several years.
3. Aman Mehta, Director (₹100,000), Independent
   An economics graduate, he has over 35 years of experience in various positions with the HSBC Group. He headed HSBC operations in the Middle East, USA, Australia and Asia-Pacific.
4. Habil Khorakiwala, Chairman (₹17.6 million)
   Founder of Wockhardt; he is an alumnus of Purdue University and Harvard Business School.
5. Abid Hussain, Director (₹80,000), Independent
   He is a former Indian Ambassador to the USA. He is a great scholar and has vast experience in various walks of life. He was appointed Vice Chairman, Rajiv Gandhi Foundation, New Delhi, and was also the chancellor of Central University, Hyderabad. He was Secretary, Ministry of Heavy Industries, Commerce Secretary, Government of India, and Chairman, IIFT. He became a member of the Planning Commission in 1985. In 1988, he was honoured with the Padma Bhushan, the second highest civilian award in India.

6. Murtaza Khorakiwala, Managing Director (N.A)
A medical doctor and an MBA from University of Illinois.

7. R. A. Shah, Director (₹100,000), Independent
He is a senior partner of M/s Crawford Bayley & Co., a leading Mumbai firm of solicitors and advocates. He sits on the boards of various multinational and Indian companies. He has rich experience in the field of law and corporate affairs with special focus on foreign investments, JVs, technology and license agreements, intellectual property rights, mergers and acquisitions, industrial licensing, anti-trust laws, company law and taxation.

8. Huzaifa Khorakiwala, Executive Director (N.A)
An MBA from Yale University and serves as the CEO of Wockhardt Foundation.

9. Shekhar Datta, Director (₹80,000), Independent
A mechanical engineering graduate, Mr Datta has served as Managing Director of Greaves Cotton Limited, Chairman of Bombay Stock Exchange and held directorships of Crompton Greaves Limited, Industrial Development Bank of India Limited and other corporates. Mr Datta is former member of the International Business Advisory Board of UNIDO, former president of the Confederation of Indian Industry (CII), Bombay Chamber of Commerce and Industry, and Indo-Italian Chamber of Commerce and Industry.

Source: Company Annual Report 2007–2008.

OPERATING HISTORY AND ACQUISITIONS

With an objective of reaching US$1 billion sales by 2009, Wockhardt had been an active acquirer throughout the 2000s. Starting with the Wallis Laboratory of the UK, Wockhardt grew through a series of acquisitions in the UK, Germany, USA and France. Wockhardt's global expansion strategy had been primarily funded through secured loans and (convertible) public debt. The Company's recent overseas acquisitions over the past three years—Pinewood, Ireland (October 2006 for US$150 million); Negma Laboratories, France (May 2007 for US$265 million) and Morton Grove, USA (October 2007 for US$37 million)—had a cumulative cost of US$450 million.[7]

Pinewood had a portfolio of over 200 prescriptions and over the counter (OTC) products licensed in various markets globally. The Company had a presence in various therapeutic categories including antibiotics, analgesics, dermatology and rheumatology. The Company also marketed and distributed branded generics in Ireland and supplied a wide range of services and pharmaceuticals to hospitals. In hospital services, Pinewood was a leading supplier of renal health care products including dialysis monitors, dialyzers, bloodlines, vascular access devices, pharmaceutical and dietary supplements. The Company enjoyed a 60 per cent market share in the renal business in Ireland. At the time of acquisition, Pinewood had reported net sales of EUR54 million (or US$70 million) for the year ending June 2006, and an EBITDA margin of over 20 per cent. In 2007, the Company reported a 15 per cent growth in sales (EUR62 million; ₹3.6 billion) and a 3 per cent expansion in operating margins. Pinewood reported a net profit of ₹526 million for 2007. Analysts expected Pinewood to grow between 5 and 8 per cent during 2008–2010.

On 3 May 2007, Wockhardt Ltd announced the acquisition of Negma Laboratories, the fourth largest independent, integrated pharmaceutical group in France in an all-cash deal worth US$265 million. At the time of acquisition, Negma had reported annual net sales of US$150 million. Negma owned fully integrated manufacturing capabilities spanning Active Pharmaceutical Ingredients (APIs) to formulations (liquids, gels, vials, capsules and powders) and the Company's therapeutic presence spanned osteoarthritis/rheumatology, hypertension and the phlebotonic segment. The Company's portfolio

[7] In addition, the Company had acquired Esparma GmbH of Germany in 2004 for US$11 million (₹490 million).

TABLE M7.6
2008 Peer Financial Data (Indian Rupees in Millions Except Ratios)

Ratio	Wockhardt	GlaxoSmithKline	Torrent Pharma	Glenmark	Alkem Lab	Ajanta Pharma	Abbott India	Pfizer	Sanofi India	Cadila Healthcare	Divis Labs
Sales			15,865.2	21,160.3						28,624	
Profitability Ratios											
Earnings Before Interest and Tax Margin (%)	19.98	33.24	19.35	34.11	10.32	13.93	9.65	--	18.82	11.09	38.29
Gross Profit Margin (%)	20.53	35.32	19.4	34.31	10.83	13.97	9.95	--	19.77	11.83	38.71
Net Profit Margin (%)	–22.55	32.36	15.56	28.03	14.86	6.22	8.62	37.59	15.33	13.17	33.77
Return on Capital Employed (%)	13.73	45.06	21.14	31	13.53	13.56	41.04	--	31.45	17.31	42.94
Return on Equity (%)	–51.49	37.41	26.57	37.83	17.13	13.25	27.95	--	20.4	22.41	40.45
Liquidity And Solvency Ratios											
Current Ratio	1.02	1.94	1.42	1.45	4.89	1	2.31	1.87	3.71	1	2.12
Debt–Equity Ratio	2.69	--	0.58	0.51	0.34	1.23	--	--	--	0.7	0.1
Debt Coverage Ratios											
Interest Coverage	2.82	1,326.05	9.39	11.03	10.23	2.69	4,556.50	--	752.5	7.96	50.28
Total Debt to Equity	2.69	0	0.58	0.51	0.34	1.23	0	--	--	0.7	0.1
Financial Charges Coverage Ratio	1.58	1,357.13	10.95	11.71	11.56	3.15	4,905.50	--	805.99	8.82	44.02
Management Efficiency Ratios											
Inventory Turnover Ratio	7	7.85	6.45	5.55	4.97	3.65	7.74	--	6.17	5.78	3.89
Debtors Turnover Ratio	3.73	35.03	5.47	2.72	--	3.59	22.18	12.04	14.03	6.45	5.47
Fixed Assets Turnover Ratio	1.64	5.94	1.65	3.42	2.25	2.33	7.04	--	3.51	1.62	1.61
Total Assets Turnover Ratio	0.6	1.08	1.08	0.94	0.86	0.95	3.13	--	1.31	1.06	1.08
Asset Turnover Ratio	0.69	1.15	1.19	0.95	--	1.08	3.06	0.94	1.34	1.08	1.25
Number of Days In Working Capital	266.77	149.15	87.7	199.07	217.8	208.19	88.73	401.32	235.56	100.54	119.59
Valuation Multiples											
P/E	NA	NA	6.14	20.46	NA	NA	NA	NA	NA	12.23	NA

Source: http://www.moneycontrol.com/financials (accessed on 2 February 2016).

comprised of three key patented products: ART 50 (sales of US$100 million and growing at a rate of 7–8% p.a.; enjoyed patent protection up to 2016), Nebilox (revenues of US$25 million, growing at a rate of 100% p.a.) and Urispas (sales of US$20 million). The Company had high selling, general and administrative expenses (SG&A), which resulted in low operating margins. Given that the company manufactured and marketed patented drugs, EBITDA margins of 18 per cent (at the time of acquisition) seemed low. Wockhardt saw an opportunity to improve margins. Analysts expected the Company to grow sales at 8–10 per cent (in EUR). The acquisition transaction was valued at 1.8 times sales and 9.7 times the EBITDA. With this acquisition, the Company became the largest Indian pharmaceutical company in Europe with more than 1,500 employees based in the continent.

The Company's Chairman Habil Khorakiwala said:[8]

> France-based Negma is a unique acquisition for Wockhardt. It is a research based pharmaceutical company with 172 patents. The acquisition will allow Wockhardt to extend this patented portfolio to other European markets where Wockhardt enjoys a strong presence. Further, it will provide us the right entry vehicle to enter the French generics market valued at US$2 billion, leveraging Wockhardt's robust EU portfolio and impressive pipeline. With this acquisition, Wockhardt will enjoy a pan-European presence, covering all the key markets of Europe—namely Germany, UK, Ireland and now France.

With the Negma acquisition, the Company's European business would account for more than 60 per cent of the Company's total revenues. Wockhardt had a portfolio of 130 products in the European market. In the next one year, it expected to launch 24 more products in Europe.

'We have a proven track record of successful value-creation post acquisitions. We expect to demonstrate the same integration momentum with Negma as with our other acquisitions', said Khorakiwala.[9]

Pinewood and Negma were together expected to have revenues of ₹12.1 billion in FY 2009.

Morton Grove was a liquid generic and specialty dermatology company in the USA with a manufacturing facility in Chicago. The Company marketed a basket of 31 generics in the US market, of which 13 products occupied the No. 1 position in the applicable reference group. However, with an annual sales of US$52 million it was relatively small. It also had a pipeline of 16 products under development, including some niche therapies (a nasal spray platform addressing a US$1.2 billion opportunity). Analysts expected Morton Grove to report a top line of ₹2.7 billion, followed by a 12–17 per cent growth over the following two years. Martin Grove was expected to have revenues of ₹3,164 million and the RoW operations to have ₹15,329 million in 2009; sales from domestic formulations were expected to be ₹9,340 million.

Wockhardt had also expanded in the domestic market by acquiring Dumex India from Royal Numico NV in June 2006. Dumex brought with it two strong nutrition brands: Protinex and Farex. Protinex was the market leader and the largest prescribed brand in its category and was growing at a rate of 20 per cent in volumes, while Farex was the third largest selling infant nutrition formula in the cereals category. At the time of acquisition, the two brands together reported sales of ₹600 million. The Dumex portfolio aptly complemented Wockhardt's own infant nutrition basket which consisted of brands such as 'Dexolac', 'Nusobee' and 'First Food'. These acquisitions put the Company on a rapid growth trajectory. Sales and operating profit rose five times during 2001 and 2008.

To allay concerns relating to the efficacy of the Company's acquisitions, the Company clarified that it had been able to demonstrate tremendous value creation in all the acquisitions that were done in the

[8] Business Standard, Wockhardt Buys French Firm Negma for $265 million.

[9] OneIndia, Wockhardt Acquires Negma Laboratories for US$265 million.

past. The Company claimed that it was synonymously linked with value creation via acquisitions.[10] In additions to these acquisitions, Wockhardt also formed majority joint ventures (JVs) in Mexico and South Africa and established a wholly owned subsidiary in Brazil in 2008.

Financing

Wockhardt raised debt from domestic banks as well as international markets to fund its expansion. This debt was raised as a mix of secured loans and unsecured loans including the FCCBs. FCCBs are dollar-denominated bonds that could later be converted to shares of the company at a predetermined price. On 21 September 2004, the Board of Directors of Wockhardt Ltd approved the issuance of FCCBs amounting to US$100 million with a green shoe option of US$10 million.[11] The proposed issue was for a zero coupon instrument, with a 50 per cent premium, five-year tenor with a yield of 5.25 per cent compounded semi-annually. The issue was approved by shareholders on 20 October 2004. In October 2005, the Company allotted 141,397 equity shares of ₹5 each at an issue price of ₹486.075 per share to Taib Securities Mauritius Ltd on conversion of 1,500 FCCBs amounting to US$1,500,000. The Company raised US$110 million (₹4,779.94 million) through FCCBs for acquisitions in Europe. The Company claimed that it was the first company in India to issue FX convertibles, thereby setting a new trend for other companies. Issuers of FX convertibles justified the issuance on the basis of lower interest rates in foreign currencies. Table M7.7 presents the interest rates, inflation and exchange rates during 2007 and 2012.

In March 2006, the Company received shareholders' approval to raise up to US$800 million (₹37 billion), in one or more tranches, to fund overseas acquisitions through an issue of equity-related securities. An extraordinary general meeting (EGM) of shareholders also authorized the Company to increase the foreign institutional investment (FII) cap in the Company to 49 per cent.

'Wockhardt's ability to create value through acquisitions is well known. These approvals reaffirm our shareholder's confidence in our expertise and empower us to seize global opportunities quickly', said the Company's Chairman Mr Habil Khorakiwala.[12]

The Company's debt grew from ₹9.1 billion in 2005 to ₹30 billion in 2008, which translated into an approximate incremental debt of US$506 million. Of this, the outstanding FCCB of US$108.5 million, along with the premium payable on maturity at 29.6 per cent (US$32 million), would entail a total outflow of US$140 million by September 2009.

Recent Financial Performance and Restructuring

The Company posted a net profit of ₹2.13 billion for the year ending 31 December 2007 as compared to ₹2.57 billion for the year ending 31 December 2006. Total income increased from ₹12.23 billion for the year ending 31 December 2006 to ₹13.55 billion for the year ending 31 December 2007. The sales of the Company on a consolidated basis for the year 2008 grew to ₹14.77 billion and profit before depreciation, interest and tax declined from ₹3.44 billion to ₹2.89 billion between 2007 and 2008. Due to mark-to-market (MTM) and derivative losses of ₹5.81 billion and provision of ₹1.295 billion towards

[10] Company Press Release, 14 June 2007 accessible at http://www.wockhardt.com/media/press-releases.aspx

[11] Upon announcement, the share price rose from ₹330.85 to ₹333.95.

[12] Domain-b.com, 'Wockhardt to Raise Up to $800 million to Fund Overseas Acquisitions'.

TABLE M7.7
Historical (Monthly) Inflation, Interest Rates and Exchange Rates, 2007–2012

Date	90-Day Rupee Lending Rate (%)	90-Day Euro Dollar Rate (%)	India CPI Inflation Rate (%)	US CPI Inflation Rate (%)	Forward Ex Rate 90-Day (₹/US$)	Spot Exchange Rate (₹/US$)
Dec 2012	8.92	0.3095	11.17	–0.04	55.53	54.99
Nov 2012	8.73	0.311	9.55	–0.2	55.27	54.26
Oct 2012	8.66	0.3305	9.6	0.24	54.67	53.81
Sep 2012	8.81	0.3856	9.14	0.49	53.54	52.86
Aug 2012	8.95	0.4323	10.31	0.51	56.42	55.53
Jul 2012	9.24	0.4536	9.84	–0.02	56.73	55.65
Jun 2012	9.41	0.4656	10.05	–0.03	56.46	55.64
May 2012	9.78	0.4665	10.16	–0.13	57.48	56.11
Apr 2012	9.64	0.4668	10.22	0.2	53.76	52.74
Mar 2012	11.09	0.4733	8.65	0.26	51.88	50.88
Feb 2012	10.28	0.5032	7.57	0.21	50.28	49.02
Jan 2012	9.91	0.5659	5.32	0.25	50.54	49.46
Dec 2011	9.84	0.5557	6.49	–0.02	54.57	53.06
Nov 2011	9.63	0.4753	9.34	0.17	52.61	52.21
Oct 2011	9.57	0.4065	9.39	0.04	49.49	48.69
Sep 2011	9.51	0.3502	10.06	0.23	50.08	48.97
Aug 2011	9.5	0.2932	8.99	0.26	46.45	46.1
Jul 2011	9.41	0.2499	8.43	0.25	44.57	44.19
Jun 2011	9.43	0.2478	8.62	0.03	45.18	44.7
May 2011	9.7	0.2607	8.72	0.38	45.59	45.06
Apr 2011	9.06	0.2814	9.41	0.49	44.94	44.22
Mar 2011	10.15	0.3084	8.82	0.51	45.26	44.58
Feb 2011	9.66	0.3119	8.82	0.33	46.02	45.27
Jan 2011	9.3	0.3034	9.3	0.29	46.7	45.9
Dec 2010	9	0.3027	9.47	0.41	45.3	44.71
Nov 2010	8.19	0.2869	8.33	0.24	46.54	45.88
Oct 2010	7.85	0.2888	9.7	0.34	44.97	44.43
Sep 2010	7.49	0.2914	9.82	0.12	45.4	44.94
Aug 2010	6.9	0.3626	9.88	0.15	47.72	47.08
Jul 2010	6.53	0.5103	11.25	0.18	47.02	46.41

(Continued)

TABLE M7.7
(Continued)

Date	90-Day Rupee Lending Rate (%)	90-Day Euro Dollar Rate (%)	India CPI Inflation Rate (%)	US CPI Inflation Rate (%)	Forward Ex Rate 90-Day (₹/US$)	Spot Exchange Rate (₹/US$)
Jun 2010	6.5	0.5369	13.73	–0.01	47.31	46.45
May 2010	5.33	0.4585	13.91	–0.04	46.75	46.37
Apr 2010	5.01	0.3116	13.33	0.03	44.67	44.37
Mar 2010	5.69	0.2684	14.86	0.02	45.12	44.92
Feb 2010	4.97	0.2505	14.86	–0.1	46.3	46.08
Jan 2010	4.59	0.2501	16.22	0.05	46.46	46.18
Dec 2009	4.6	0.2531	14.97	0.05	46.78	46.53
Nov 2009	4.44	0.2681	13.51	0.33	46.59	46.51
Oct 2009	4.61	0.2831	11.49	0.3	47.51	46.97
Sep 2009	4.67	0.298	11.64	0.19	47.96	48.11
Aug 2009	4.58	0.4245	11.72	0.33	48.75	48.83
Jul 2009	4.52	0.5153	11.89	–0.03	48.19	47.94
Jun 2009	4.72	0.6207	9.29	0.83	48.44	47.9
May 2009	5.29	0.8166	8.63	0.15	47.45	47.09
Apr 2009	5.64	1.1062	8.7	0.1	50.17	50.09
Mar 2009	7.64	1.2667	8.03	–0.1	51.69	50.73
Feb 2009	7.64	1.2426	9.63	0.36	52.44	51.16
Jan 2009	7.83	1.2108	10.45	0.25	49.76	48.88
Dec 2008	8.89	1.8294	9.7	–0.82	49.9	48.8
Nov 2008	10.43	2.2791	10.45	–1.77	52.32	50.11
Oct 2008	11.73	4.0586	10.45	–0.86	51.95	49.46
Sep 2008	11.86	3.1217	9.77	0.09	47.63	46.96
Aug 2008	11.22	2.8063	9.02	–0.15	44.45	43.94
Jul 2008	10.39	2.7921	8.33	0.71	43.13	42.57
Jun 2008	9.94	2.7654	7.69	1.05	43.91	43.04
May 2008	8.87	2.6924	7.75	0.59	42.32	42.46
Apr 2008	8.77	2.7947	7.81	0.23	40.82	40.49
Mar 2008	9.82	2.7825	7.87	0.36	40.17	40.12
Feb 2008	9.61	3.0876	5.47	0.24	40.13	40.01
Jan 2008	8.54	3.9176	5.51	0.34	39.56	39.37
Dec 2007	8.56	4.9794	5.51	0.29	39.6	39.41

Date	90-Day Rupee Lending Rate (%)	90-Day Euro Dollar Rate (%)	India CPI Inflation Rate (%)	US CPI Inflation Rate (%)	Forward Ex Rate 90-Day (₹/US$)	Spot Exchange Rate (₹/US$)
Nov 2007	8.5	4.9621	5.51	0.79	39.9	39.6
Oct 2007	7.9	5.1465	5.51	0.31	39.41	39.33
Sep 2007	8.45	5.4939	6.4	0.42	39.91	39.85
Aug 2007	8.47	5.4837	7.26	0.03	41.4	40.93
Jul 2007	7.54	5.3597	6.45	0.18	40.63	40.37
Jun 2007	9.31	5.3593	5.69	0.23	40.98	40.72
May 2007	9.72	5.3595	6.61	0.41	40.67	40.61
Apr 2007	11.12	5.3555	6.67	0.3	41.69	41.18
Mar 2007	11.65	5.3479	6.72	0.52	43.61	43.47
Feb 2007	10.22	5.3598	7.56	0.39	44.75	44.29
Jan 2007	9.19	5.3601	6.72	0.17	44.38	44.18

Source: Bloomberg database.

premium on FCCBs for the period October 2004 to December 2008, the Company incurred a loss of ₹1.389 billion.[13] The Company's risk management policy was to hedge the interest risk on 50 per cent of long-term loans.[14]

Reacting to media speculations suggesting that Wockhardt would book significant losses in its first quarter of 2008 because of fluctuations in the values of derivative contracts, Wockhardt Ltd announced that it would not incur any loss arising out of derivatives either in the first quarter or thereafter. Wockhardt had a significant business presence outside India, mainly in Europe and in the USA, to the extent of 60 per cent of its annual sales. In the past one year, there had been considerable currency fluctuation. Wockhardt claimed that it had a professional team that undertook hedging of currency and interest rate risks. In addition, its financial performance over the past few years, the Company claimed, clearly demonstrated that there had been no losses on account of hedging activities. As of 31 March, the Company had entered into one, US$20 million (₹981 million) forward contract on the US dollar.[15] In addition, the Company had FX option positions for various amounts in several currencies such as the

[13] The Company entered into currency option contracts and interest rate options with banks to hedge the currency exposure and to bring down its interest cost on foreign loans. MTM is an accounting practice of assigning a value to an asset, based on current market price and not at the price at which it was acquired. The evaluation was in line with guidelines on accounting for derivatives issued by the Institute of Chartered Accountants of India in March 2008. The Company maintained that some of the banks, based on the early termination clause in their agreement, had ended certain forex contracts and claimed an amount of ₹4,895 million. Its Board took the stand that the forex transactions were unilaterally cancelled by banks and the MTM losses were on account of the counter-positions advised by the banks. Wockhardt was in the process of obtaining a legal opinion on whether these contracts could be disputed. If the Company had provided for the entire MTM charges, loss incurred in 2008 would have been higher.

[14] The Telegraph, *Derivative Loss Hurts Wockhardt Bottomline.*

[15] The Company had not hedged any exposure in the previous year. Nor did it reveal its risk management philosophy in its annual reports.

US$, Euro, GBP, Yen and Australian Dollar as well as interest rate options in US$ and Euro.[16] However, the Company also had substantially unhedged positions in many of these currencies too (see Table M7.8).[17]

This news came at a time when the Company became the target of an insider trading inquiry by SEBI, the stock market regulator. In May 2008, the Securities Appellate Tribunal (SAT) upheld an order by SEBI that charged Mr Rajiv Gandhi, the CFO of the Company and a board member, his wife and sister for insider trading.[18] The SAT order alleged that the appellants traded in Wockhardt stock before and after board meetings held to consider financial results in January and April 1999. The appellants, however, argued that a law that came into effect in 2002 could not be applied to transactions done in 1999.

During the year 2008, due to global meltdown, there had been significant volatility in currencies and interest rates.[19] Major currencies such as EURO, GBP, CHF had significantly depreciated against the US Dollar. Besides, in line with the interest rate cuts carried out by the US Federal Reserve, EURO and UK zones, the LIBOR of all major currencies collapsed, resulting in an increase in MTM losses from October and November of 2008. As of March 2009, there were claims to the tune of ₹4,900 million due to forex contracts.

At the height of its expansion, Wockhardt also considered restructuring options such as spin-offs to create value for shareholders. On 18 January 2008, Wockhardt Ltd informed Bombay Stock Exchange that WPL had considered in principal to demerge its R&D business into a separate entity. The new company would house the new drug discovery programme and the innovative new technologies being developed by the R&D team. The Company would be a listed company and was scheduled to come into effect from 1 January 2009.

Wockhardt Chairman Habil Khorakiwala said:[20]

> The R&D business has great potential and needs to be a focused entity for carrying out unrelenting research activities for the future. At Wockhardt we recognise this fundamental need and are re-structuring our R&D business to unlock true value for all our stakeholders. This will ease the Company to invite strategic investors interested in the R&D Business.

A total of 110,000 zero coupon FCCBs issued in 2004 were redeemable on the maturity date at 129.578 per cent of its principal amount, only if there were no conversion of bonds on or before 25 September 2009. Wockhardt proposed to negotiate with FCCB holders to extend the due date of payment. The FCCBs of US$108.50 million and certain term loans were due during the year 2009. Given the precarious position it was in, Wockhardt approached domestic lenders for CDR led by ICICI Bank in April 2009.[21] In a couple of months, the lenders proposed to restructure existing loans. The lenders

---

[16] Wockhardt, *Annual Report, 2007–2008 available at* http://www.wockhardt.com/investor-connect/annual-reports.aspx.

[17] The Company's Board comprised an audit committee, investors grievance committee and remuneration committee. However, it did not have a risk management committee.

[18] Dandekar, Vikas and Payal Bhattar, 'Wockhardt CFO Found Guilty of Insider Trading'.

[19] The ₹/US$ exchange rate increased from 45 in January 2004 to 50.95 in March 2009 and the ₹/Euro rate increased from 57.4 to 67.48 (https://rbi.org.in/scripts/ReferenceRateArchive.aspx). In 2008 alone, the ₹/US$ rate increased from 39 to 48.

[20] *The Economic Times*, 'Wockhardt to Spin Off R&D Business'.

[21] In order to protect the interests of lenders to firms in distress, the Reserve Bank of India (India's central bank) issued guidelines relating to CDR for implementation by financial institutions and banks. The guidelines came into effect in 2001. The CDR mechanism was a voluntary non-statutory system based on debtor–creditor agreement (DCA) and inter-creditor agreement (ICA).

TABLE M7.8
Extent of Hedging By Wockhardt (In millions)

(a) The Company enters into forward exchange contracts being derivative instruments, which are not intended for trading, or speculative purposes, but for hedge purposes, to establish the amount of reporting currency required or available at the settlement date of certain payables and receivables.

	2008		2007	
No. of contracts	1		-	
Notional principal in foreign currency	Foreign currency	₹	Foreign currency	₹
US$	20	981.3	-	-

(b) Outstanding currency swaps and interest rate swaps (other than forward exchange contracts stated above) to hedge against fluctuations in changes in exchange rate and interest rate changes:

	2008		2007	
No. of contracts	136		2	
Notional principal in foreign currency	Foreign currency	₹	Foreign currency	₹
Interest rate options:				
US$	232.5	11,325.08		
EUR	56	3,764.82		
Currency options:				
US$	988.05	48,127.92		
JPY	4,130.00	2,207.07	100	3,941
CHF	10	452.13		
AUD	10	333.63		
GBP	106	7,487.84		
EUR	345.8	23,247.79		

(c) The year-end foreign currency exposures that have not been hedged by a derivative instrument or otherwise are given below:

		2008		2007	
	Currency	Foreign Currency	₹	Foreign Currency	₹
Loan Availed	US$	263.6	12,839.89	300	11,823.00
Interest Payable	US$	0.47	22.8	1.25	49.16
Sundry Debtors	ACU	0.05	2.47	0.16	6.42
	AUD	0.01	0.46	0.01	0.48
	CHF	0.43	19.54	0.04	1.54
	EUR	1.69	113.62	55.89	3,239.78
	GBP	26.24	1,853.59	31.68	2,500.75
	US$	26.7	1,300.60	71.66	2,823.99
Loans and Advances	EUR	44.51	2,992.25	59.81	3,467.26

(Continued)

TABLE M7.8
(Continued)

	Currency	2008 Foreign Currency	2008 ₹	2007 Foreign Currency	2007 ₹
	US$	0.72	35.07	22.11	871.19
	CHF	0.05	2.25	0.04	1.29
	GBP	0.02	1.75		
	JPY	6.41	3.42		
	SEK	0.23	1.45		
Sundry Creditors	ACU	0.001	0.03	0.001	0.05
	AUD	–	–	0.0002	0.01
	CAD	0.01	0.27	0.01	0.22
	CHF	0.02	0.69	0.08	2.68
	EUR	5.19	348.92	3.49	202.17
	GBP	9.16	647.1	10.21	805.86
	JPY	3.05	1.63	15.83	5.56
	SEK	0.23	1.45	0.23	1.44
	US$	2.51	122.26	10.1	397.88
FCCB	US$	108.5	5,285.04	108.5	4,275.99
Time Deposit	US$	16.63	809.84	45.64	1,798.67

Source: Wockhardt 2008 Annual Report.

included domestic lenders, FCCB holders and other foreign lenders. Most of the secured loans were given by domestic lenders. The plan was to sell some of the assets and raise ₹7.9 billion and repay secured lenders by 2015. The promoters also agreed to get ₹700 million as fresh equity.

The Company had a net debt of about ₹34 billion in FY09. The company's debt-to-equity ratio was close to 3.0. Wockhardt's then auditor S. R. Batliboi and Company noted that the Company had defaulted to the extent of ₹50 million and ₹130 million owed to two banks in December. They had earlier said the Company would have to repay loans and related liabilities worth ₹14.144 billion before the end of 2009, if the CDR failed to go through.[22]

In February 2009, the stock price of Wockhardt was trading at a low of ₹70 and was down 80 per cent that year. At this stage, the future looked bleak and whether WPL would sail through the restructuring process was anybody's guess. The Company had several generic options such as sale of long-term domestic debt or equity to pay down foreign currency debt, partial or full liquidation. Figure M7.1 presents the stock price history.[23]

[22] Das Gupta and Jayakumar, *Wockhardt Gets CDR Lifeline with Riders*. Wockhardt changed its auditors in May 2009 by replacing S. R. Batliboi and Co. with BDO Haribhakti. The audit firm was due for review and Khorakiwala said the change was to ensure greater 'transparency'.

[23] The stock price had risen from ₹151 in January 2003 to ₹506 in March 2006 and then climbed down to ₹85 in early 2009.

FIGURE M7.1
Stock Market Reaction to Major Events (In ₹)

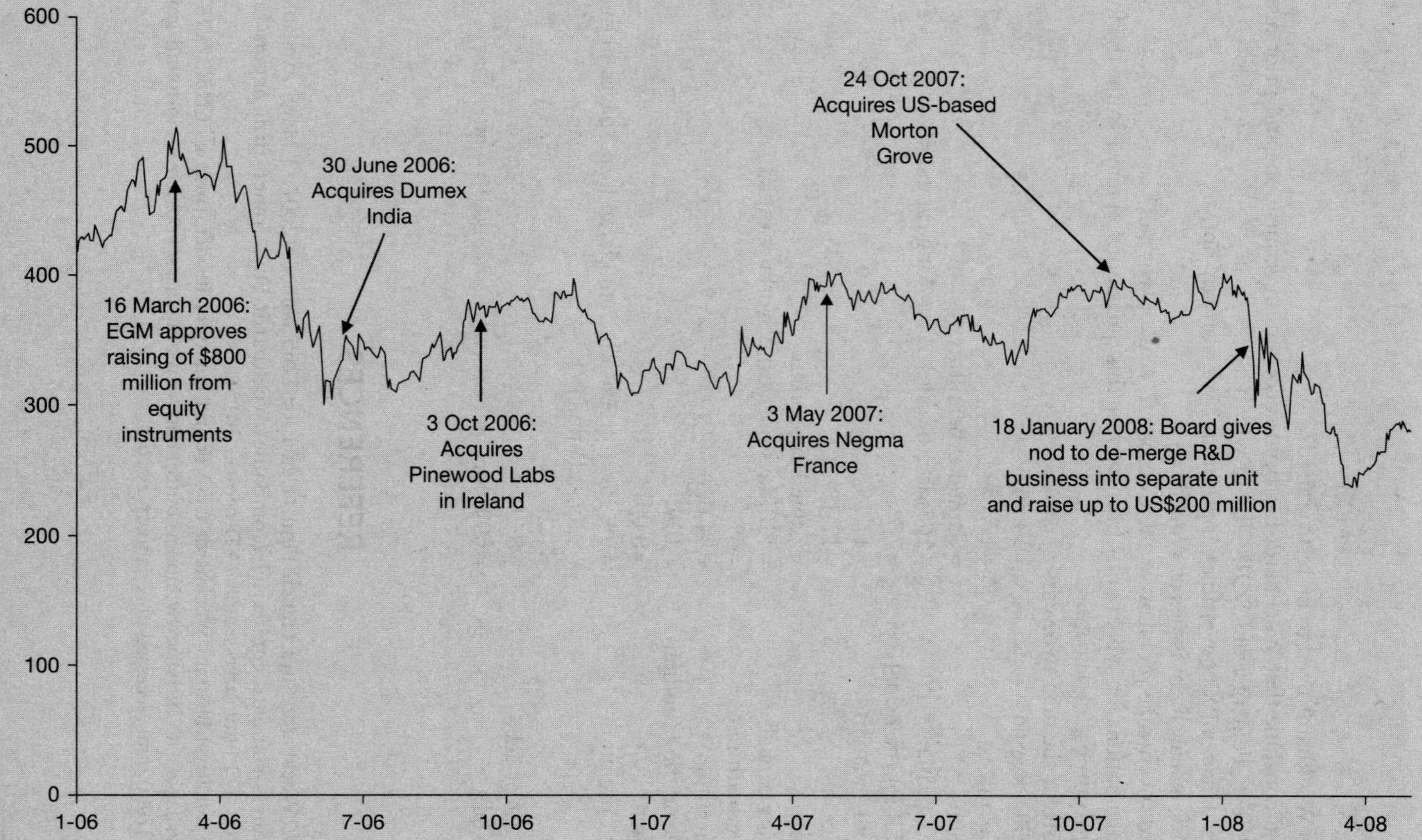

Source: Created by case writer using data available in google finance (http://www.google.com/finance?q=NSE%3AWOCKPHARMA&ei=Nh-0VsnWBYHXuATi-IOgBA).

EXERCISES

1. Why does Wockhardt need to be restructured?
2. Would you conclude that Wockhardt has been successful in acquisitions and prior restructuring efforts (e.g., demerger of R&D)? Why or why not?
3. Was the issuance of FX convertibles appropriate? Why or why not?
4. Identify risk management issues at Wockhardt.
5. Were there governance problems at the Company? Why or why not?
6. What are the options for Wockhardt? In answering this question, you may assume the following data for the purpose of valuation:

Sales CAGR for the next two years	=7.2%
Average EBIT margin	=19.5%
Average tax rate	=17.1%
Depreciation	=Capital expenditure
Net working capital	=107 days of sales; Δ working capital=0
Sales CAGR for the next 10 years	=7.7%
Average EBIT margin	=17.1%
Average tax rate	=17.1%
Depreciation	=Capital expenditure
Net working capital	=110 days of sales; Δ working capital=0
Terminal growth rate	=5%
Net debt (million)	=34,000
Shares outstanding (million)	=109
Risk-free rate	=8.0%[24]
Equity risk premium	=9% (*Source*: Aswath Damodaran http://pages.stern.nyu.edu/~adamodar/)
Beta	=1.25
Post-tax cost of debt	=8.2%[25]
Debt/Capital	=60% for the next two years and 45% after that

REFERENCES

Business Standard. 'Wockhardt Buys French Firm Negma for $265 Million' (2007, 3 May). Available at http://www.business-standard.com/article/companies/wockhardt-buys-french-firm-negma-for-265mn-107050300031_1.html (accessed on 14 December 2015).

Dandekar, Vikas and Payal Bhattar. 'Wockhardt CFO Found Guilty of Insider Trading'. *CNBC TV18* (2008, 14 May). Available at http://www.moneycontrol.com/news/business/wockhardt-cfo-found-guiltyinsider-trading_337990.html (accessed on 2 January 2016).

[24] *Source*: Reserve Bank of India; 10-year T-bond rate.

[25] *Source*: Case writer estimate using yields on comparable bonds and the company's effective tax rate.

Das Gupta, Surajeet and P. B. Jayakumar. *Wockhardt Gets CDR Lifeline with Riders* (2009, 10 July). Available at http://www.rediff.com/money/report/wockhardt-gets-cdr-lifeline-with-riders/20090710.htm (accessed on 15 December 2015).

Domain-b.com. 'Wockhardt to Raise Up to $800 Million to Fund Overseas Acquisitions'. *Hindustan Times* (2006, 16 March). Available at https://www.domain-b.com/companies/companies_w/wockhardt/20060316_million.html (accessed on 9 January 2019).

Jacoby, R. and D. Iyer. *Winning with Biosimilars: Opportunities in Global Markets*. Deloitte (2015).

Joshi, M. *Avendus India Equity Research*. Wockhardt (2008, 22 October).

Joshi, M. *Avendus India Equity Research*. Wockhardt (2009, 27 April).

OneIndia. *Wockhardt Acquires Negma Laboratories for USD 265 Million* (2007, 3 May). Available at http://www.oneindia.com/2007/05/03/wockhardt-acquires-negma-laboratories-for-usd-265-million-1178194083.html (accessed on 18 December 2015).

The Telegraph. 'Derivative Loss Hurts Wockhardt Bottomline' (2008, 29 April). Available at http://www.telegraphindia.com/1080429/jsp/business/story_9202396.jsp (accessed on 4 January 2016).

Wockhardt. Company Press Release (2007, 14 June). Available at http://www.wockhardt.com/media/press-releases.aspx (accessed on January 2010).

Wockhardt. *Annual Report, 2007–2008*.

The Economic Times. 'Wockhardt to Spin Off R&D Business' (2008, 19 January). Available at http://articles.economictimes.indiatimes.com/2008-01-19/news/27714732_1_wck-wockhardt-habil-khorakiwala (accessed on 12 December 2015).

MODULE 4

Project Finance

8 The Dalian Water Supply Project

9 AES Corporation: Building an LNG Power Plant in Honduras

8

The Dalian Water Supply Project*

LEARNING OBJECTIVE

To demonstrate project analysis and financing in emerging markets; role of multilateral institutions; to demonstrate financial and economic analysis of non-profit projects

Description: The case presents a proposal considered by the ADB to invest US$160 million in a water supply project in China in 1994. The case focuses on the role of the ADB in emerging market projects, project financing and. risk mitigation in emerging markets.

In early 1994, Alyona Dubrovina, Henning Hummervoll and Jim Horiuchi, new recruits at the ADB, Manila, Philippines, received their first assignment. They had to make a recommendation to the president and the Board of Directors whether to invest US$160 million in the Dalian Water Supply Project in the People's Republic of China (PRC).

If approved, this would be the Bank's 33rd loan to the PRC and the first loan to the water supply sector in the PRC. The amount of funding was considered significant by ADB's standards as an average loan approved in the previous year amounted to US$68 million per transaction. The loan would be used to finance an expansion of the water supply system in the Dalian city and rural towns in the Liaoning Province. The Dalian region experienced a severe shortage of water supply and was expected to deteriorate with the rapid population growth. If the Project was approved, it would provide water to 2.2 million residents and commercial users.

[1] This case was written by Alyona Dubrovina, Jim Horiuchi and Henning Hummervoll under the supervision of Professor Campbell Harvey, Fuqua School of Business, Duke University.

* Reproduced with permission from Professor Campbell Harvey. Some of the images may be of poor quality. They are for representation purpose only.

At the time, ADB was developing new guidelines for financial and economic analysis of projects and was looking for new ideas. The new recruits were asked to not use any of the existing guidelines of the bank in their analysis.

Alyona, Henning and Jim faced a dilemma. Typically, one would select a project with the highest net present value. What investment criteria were they to use? How would one place a value on the benefits of 2.2 million people having access to fresh water?

PROJECT DESCRIPTION

With an estimated population of 1.19 billion in 1994 (1.29 billion in 2003), China had the highest population in the world.[1] Although more than 90 per cent of the population living in urban areas had easy access to water supply,[2] many parts of the country, particularly Northern provinces, including the Liaoning Province, had been experiencing a shortage of freshwater due to outdated municipal water supply system and low rainfall.

In general, the water supply system in China was state-owned. Since these state-owned water utilities did not have a policy of cost recovery and tariff adjustment, they always ran into deficits and hence relied on government subsidies to operate. Given the limited financial resources available, the water utilities could not expand or even maintain the existing operation at a satisfactory level. As the quality of the existing system deteriorated without capital investments, the water utilities throughout China failed to provide the end users with adequate quality and quantity of water.

The water consumption for Dalian in 1993 was 155 litres per capita per day (LPCD), while the Chinese national average consumption was 170 LPCD. This shortage in Dalian appeared even more severe when compared to the consumption level of 300 LPCD in large cities in Asia.[3]

Water is an absolute necessity for human lives. In Dalian, the water shortage in 1994 was so severe that many areas of the city had water only for a few hours a day, usually in the middle of the night, and the pressure in the system was sometimes insufficient to provide water to elevated places in the city for periods of several days. In addition to the physical and economic inconvenience and cost, this frequent interruption had major impact on public health, since contamination from the surrounding drains and ground was possible. The Project would lead to improved living conditions, improved public health, increased productivity and economic opportunities for the people in the municipality as agricultural and industrial activities would increase with the availability of water.

DALIAN WATER SUPPLY PROJECT

The 1978 reforms, including relaxation of control over migration from rural to urban areas, brought about rapid growth of cities. Between 1983 and 1991, the population of cities grew at the rate of 8 per cent per year. This rural to urban migration generated an enormous demand for urban services, including water supply. The water shortage was particularly acute in the northern PRC with scarce rainfall, where Dalian Municipality was located.

The Dalian Water Supply Project (the Project) was to provide supplemental water in the Dalian Municipality, a major seaport town in Liaoning Province in Northeast China (Figure M8.1). The

[1] *Source*: EIU Country Data; Economist Intelligence Unit.

[2] *Source*: Asian Development Bank.

[3] Source of statistics: Asian Development Bank.

shortage in water supply in the Dalian region was no different from the situation in other parts of China. This was mainly attributed to outdated and inefficient water supply system. This water shortage, combined with the anticipated increase in demand due to growth in population and commercial activities

FIGURE M8.1
Project Location in Liaoning Province

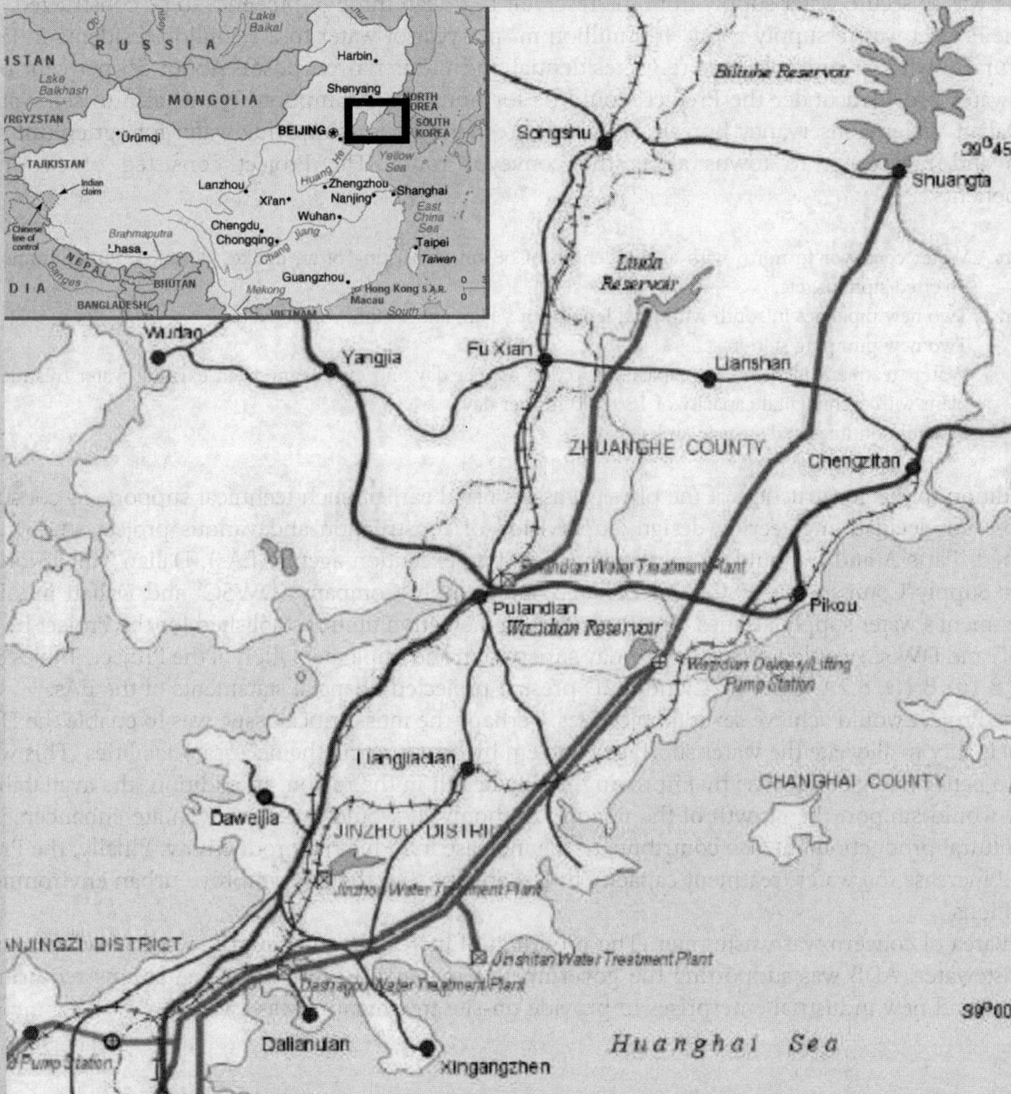

Note: This figure is not to scale. It does not represent any authentic national or international boundaries and is used for illustrative purposes only.

on account of growing industry and port capacity, had prompted the Dalian Municipality to launch a water supply project to meet the projected demand.

In the past, the municipal government had contemplated on a water supply project several times. However, it never reached the point of actual implementation, as the outcome of various technical analyses, including a survey conducted by the ADB, suggested that water resources in the Dalian region had been fully exploited. Upon further investigating other practical and feasible water resources, the Municipality sought water supply from the Biliuhe Reservoir located 160 km (100 miles) north of Dalian. Thus, the Project was to secure water supply from the reservoir to Dalian through pipelines to be constructed.

The Project was to supply about 400 million m^3 per year of water to 2.2 million residents in Dalian and rural towns for multiple uses (e.g., residential and industrial purpose). About 55 per cent of the total water provided under the Project would be for human consumption. It was also to sell water to the Dalian Water Conservancy Bureau, which was responsible for supplying water for agricultural purposes and raw water to towns along the conveyor route. The Project consisted of two major components:

Part A: Water conveyor in north with a total length of 68 km, consisting of an intake, closed conduits, tunnels, inverted siphons, etc.

Part B: Two new pipelines in south with total lengths of 94 km and 79 km, respectively.
Two new pumping stations.
Water treatment plant with a capacity 150,000 m^3 per day and expansion of an existing water treatment plant with incremental capacity of 180,000 m^3 per day.
Distribution lines and storage tanks.

In addition to the construction of the physical assets listed earlier, such technical supports as consulting services for detailed engineering design, supervision of construction and various project studies were required. Parts A and B would be implemented by two execution agents (EAs), Dalian Yinbi Northern Water Supply Company (NWSC) and Dalian Water Supply Company (DWSC) and Dalian municipal government's water supply utilities. The Project implementation units, established for the Project by both NWSC and DWSC, would execute day-to-day supervision and implementation of the Project. Tables 8.1A, 8.1B, 8.1C, 8.1D, 8.2A, 8.2B, 8.2C and 8.2D present projected financial statements of the EAs.

The Project would achieve several objectives. Perhaps the most critical issue was to enable the Dalian Municipality to alleviate the water shortage problem by constructing the necessary facilities. This would lead to better living conditions by improving public health in the region. In addition, the availability of water would support the growth of the region's economy. It would not only facilitate enhancement of agricultural production but also contribute to the increase in industrial productivity. Finally, the Project would increase the water treatment capacity in Dalian city, and thereby, improve urban environmental conditions.

An area of concern was wastewater. The provision of increased water supply would lead to increase in wastewater. ADB was supporting the government's initiative to introduce regulations requiring all existing and new industrial enterprises to provide on-site treatment of wastewater.

PEOPLE'S REPUBLIC OF CHINA

China had a long and rich history and was, for centuries, a leading civilization outpacing the rest of the world in arts and sciences. In the 19th and early 20th century, however, the country was plagued by civil unrest, famine, military defeats and foreign occupation. After the Second World War, Mao Zedong

TABLE M8.1A

Dalian Water Supply Company: Water Demand and Sales Projections

Item	1992	1993	1994	1995	1996	1997	1998	1999	2000	2001	2002	2003	2004
	Actual												
Population	1,808.0	1,852.5	1,898.2	1,945.0	1,993.5	2,043.3	2,094.2	2,146.5	2,200.0	2,227.4	2,255.2	2,283.3	2,311.7
Population Increase (%)	2.47%	2.46%	2.47%	2.47%	2.49%	2.50%	2.49%	2.50%	2.49%	1.25%	1.25%	1.25%	1.24%
Domestic Water Demand {mil. m^3}	44.84	52	50.3	54.6	58.32	62.3	66.55	71.09	75.94	79.37	82.96	86.71	90.63
Industrial (mil. m^3)	78.28	77.21	107.9	121.18	128.89	137.08	145.8	155.08	164.94	170.79	176.86	183.14	189.64
Institutional and Others {mil. m^3)	52.16	61.22	57.4	62.78	67.66	72.92	78.58	84.69	91.27	95.59	100.13	104.89	109.85
Bulk Water to DETDZ (mil. m^3)	13	17.71	25.55	31.77	42.6	62.41	84.39	86.56	89.46	93.14	94.85	94.85	94.85
Total Water Demand (mil. m^3)	188.28	208.14	241.15	270.33	297.47	334.71	375.32	397.42	421.61	438.89	454.8	469.59	484 97
Domestic Water Sales (mil. m^3}	44.84	47.82	58.45	59.85	61.25	62.65	64.05	65.45	66.8	69.55	70.83	70.83	70.83
Industrial Water Sales (mil. m^3)	78.27	77.21	77.21	82.24	87.61	93.32	99.4	105.88	112.79	117.41	119.58	119.58	119.58
Institutional Water Sales (mil. m^3)	29.42	29.88	20.18	22.49	25.07	27.94	31.14	34.71	38.69	40.28	41.02	41.02	41.02
Commercial Water Sales (mil. m^3)	9.74	13.63	13.73	15.16	18.28	22.05	26.59	32.07	38.68	40.27	41.01	41.01	41.01
Bulk Water to DETDZ (mil. m^3}	13	17.71	25.55	31.77	42.6	62.41	84.39	86.56	89.46	93.14	94.85	94.85	94.85
Total Water Sales (mil. m^3)	175.27	186.25	195.12	211.51	234.81	268.37	305.57	324.67	346.42	360.65	367.29	367.29	367.29

(Continued)

TABLE M8.1A
(Continued)

Item	1992	1993	1994	1995	1996	1997	1998	1999	2000	2001	2002	2003	2004
	Actual												
Nonrevenue Water (mil. m^3)	44.11	38.9	45.78	37.75	40.36	43.25	46.45	45.24	48.82	50.83	51.76	51.76	51.76
Raw Water Supply(mil. m^3)	219.38	225.15	240.9	249.26	275.17	311.62	352.02	369.91	395.24	411.48	419.05	419.05	419.05
NRW Rate (excl. Bulk Water) (%)	21.4%	18.8%	21.3%	17.4%	17.4%	17.4%	17.4%	16.0%	16.0%	16.0%	16.0%	16.0%	16.0%
Domestic Water Charge (Y/m^3)	0.4	0.4	1	1	1.25	1.84	1.97	2.17	2.32	2.49	2.66	2.85	3.04
Industrial (Y/m^3)	0.6	0.6	1.02	1.32	1.65	2.42	2.59	2.86	3.06	3.27	3.5	3.75	4.01
Institutional and Others (Y/m^3)	0.4	0.8	0.94	1.21	1.52	2.22	2.38	2.63	2.81	3.01	3.22	3.44	3.68
Average Water Charge (Y/m^3)	0.52	0.59	0.93	1.20	1.50	2.20	2.35	2.60	2.78	2.98	3.19	3.41	3.65
Bulk Water Rate to DETDZ (Y/m^3)	0.52	0.8	0.8	1.00	1.00	1.20	1.80	1.80	1.80	1.80	1.80	1.80	1.80
Treated Water Revenue (Y/million)	28.28	99.44	157.70	215.69	288.32	453.11	519.77	619.09	714.35	797.18	869.08	929.02	994.41
Bulk Water Revenue (Y/million)	6.76	14.17	20.44	31.77	42.60	74.89	151.90	155.81	161.03	167.65	170.73	170.73	170.73
Total Water Revenue (Y/million)	35.04	113.61	178.14	247.46	330.92	528.00	671.68	774.89	875.38	964.83	1,039.81	1,099.75	1,165.14

TABLE M8.1B

Dalian Water Supply Company: Projected Income Statement (million Yuan)

Item	1992	1993	1994	1995	1996	1997	1998	1999	2000	2001	2002	2003	2004
	Actual												
Revenue													
Water revenue	35.0	111 8	178.1	247.5	330.9	528.0	672.6	774.9	875.9	963.9	1,038.5	1,099.2	1,164.2
Other Revenue (Net)	44.9	33.3	36.6	39.2	41.9	44.8	48.0	51.3	54.9	58.8	62.9	67.3	72.0
Operating revenue	79.9	145.1	214.7	286.7	372.8	572.8	720.6	826.2	930.8	1,022.7	1,101.4	1,166.5	1,236.2
Expenses													
Salaries	8.4	17.2	20.0	21.4	22.9	24.5	26.2	28.0	30.0	32.1	34.3	36.7	39.3
Power	62.9	81.4	110.6	118.3	126.6	135.6	145.1	155.3	166.2	177.8	190.3	203.6	217.8
Raw Water	26.0	28.4	68.3	100.4	119.9	149.4	184.1	207.8	238.0	267.5	291.9	310.8	333.6
Chemicals	1.6	1.7	2.0	2.2	2.6	3.2	3.8	4.3	4.9	5.5	6.0	6.4	6.8
Maintenance	4.8	13.1	14.5	15.5	16.5	17.6	34.0	36.8	36.8	36.8	36.8	45.8	45.8
Administration/overhead	14.7	15.9	11.0	13.2	15.3	17.4	21.4	23.5	25.6	27.8	29.8	32.5	34.5
Repairs	0.0	4.9	4.9	6.6	17.6	17.6	34.0	36.8	36.8	36.8	36.8	45.8	45.8
Total Operating Expenses	118.4	162.6	231.3	277.6	321.4	365.3	448.6	492.5	538.3	584.3	625.9	681.6	723.6
Overhead Expenses (Subcompanies)	47.2	28.7	31.6	33.8	36.1	38.7	41.4	44.3	47.4	50.7	54.2	58.0	62.1
Depreciation	30.2	30.7	30.6	30.6	82.0	82.0	115.1	124.8	124.8	124.8	124.8	155.2	155.2
Net Income Before Interest/Tax	(115.9)	(76.9)	(78.8)	(55.3)	(66.7)	86 8	115.5	164.6	220.3	262.9	296.5	271.7	295.3
Interest	0.0	0.0	11.7	17.6	32.3	53.0	68.1	128.3	125.6	122.6	119.3	115.6	111.6
Tax	2.3	3.7	3.9	7.6	14.2	32.8	44.6	52.8	60.0	65.8	70.6	74.3	78.0
Net Income before Subsidy	(115.9)	(76.9)	(90.5)	(72.9)	(99.0)	33.8	47.4	36.3	94.7	140.3	177.2	156.1	183.7
DMG Subsidy	120.5	69.2	95.0	80.0	120.0	0.0	0.0	0.0	0.0	0.0	0.0	0.0	
Net Income	2.3	(11.4)	0.6	(0.5)	6.8	1.0	2.8	(16.5)	34.7	74.5	106.6	81.8	105.7
Operating Ratio		1.33	1.22	1.08	1.08	0.78	0.78	0.75	0.71	0.69	0.68	0.72	0.71
Power Rate(Y/Kwh)		0.40	0.40	0.42	0.45	0.48	0.51	0.55	0.59	0.63	0.67	0.72	0.77
Average Charge Of Raw Water		0.16	0.34	0.48	0.51	0.55	0.59	0.63	0.67	0.72	0.77	0.82	0.88
			112.5%	41.2%	6.3%	7.8%	7.3%	6.8%	6.3%	7.5%	6.9%	6.5%	7.3%

Source: Dalian Economic and Technological Development Zone.

Note: Net Revenue on subcompanies and interest on government bonds and securities value-added tax starting from 1994 at about 11.5 per cent on taxable items.

TABLE M8.1C

Dalian Water Supply Company: Projected Source and Use of Funds (million Yuan)

Item	1992	1993	1994	1995	1996	1997	1998	1999	2000	2001	2002	2003	2004
	Actual												
Sources													
Net Income	2.3	(11.4)	0.6	(0.5)	6.8	1.0	2.8	(16.5)	34.7	74.5	106.6	81.8	105.7
Add Back: Depreciation and interest	30.2	30.7	42.3	48.2	114.3	135.0	183.2	253.1	250.4	247.4	244.1	270.8	266 8
Net Internal Cash Generation	32.5	19.3	42.9	47.7	121.1	136.0	186.0	236.6	285.1	321.9	350.7	352.6	372.5
Grant from Central Government	0.0	0.0	18.6	11.5	16.5	13.6	0.0	0.0	0.0	0.0	0.0	0.0	0.0
DMG Contribution	0.0	0.0	251.1	155.2	223.5	184.0	0.0	0.0	00	0.0	0.0	0.0	0.0
DTEDZ Contribution	0.0	0.0	0.0	0.0	46.4	46.4	46.4	0.0	0.0	0.0	0.0	0.0	0.0
Bank Loan	0.0	0.0	258.6	159.8	230.2	189.5	0.0	0.0	0.0	0.0	0.0	0.0	0.0
World Bank Loan	0.0	0.0	0.0	20.0	20.0	20.0	20.0	20.0	20.0	0.0	0.0	0.0	0.0
OECF Loan	0.0	0.0	0.0	0.0	153.7	153.7	153.7	0.0	0.0	0.0	0.0	0.0	0.0
Construction Bank of China	0.0	0.0	97.7	55.2	125.9	111.8	46.4	0.0	0.0	0.0	0.0	0.0	0.0
Subtotal	0.0	0.0	626.0	401.7	816.2	719.0	266.5	20.0	20.0	0.0	0.0	0.0	0.0
Total Sources	32.5	19.3	668.9	449.4	937.3	855.0	452.5	256.6	305.1	321.9	350.7	352.6	372.5
Uses													
Capital Expenditures	0.0	11.0	626.1	401.7	816.3	719.0	266.5	220.0	220.0	200.0	200.0	200.0	200.0
Amortization	0.0	0.0	0.0	0.0	0.0	0.0	6.8	29.5	32.2	35.2	38.5	42.2	46.2
Interest Payment	0.0	0.0	11.7	17.6	32.3	53.0	68.1	128.3	125.6	122.6	119.3	115.6	111.6
Total Debt Service	0.0	0.0	11.7	17.6	32.3	53.0	74.9	157.8	157.8	157.8	157.8	157.8	157.8
Changes in Working Capital	1.2	(7.7)	47.8	(4.3)	(3.2)	(2.6)	(12.1)	(1.7)	(1.5)	(0.9)	0.8	(2.0)	2.2
Appropriation of Reserves	0.0	21.9	0.0	0.0	0.0	0.0	0.0	0.0	0.0	0.0	0.0	0.0	0.0
Total Uses	1.2	25.2	685.6	415.0	845.4	769.4	329.3	376.1	376.3	356.9	358.6	355.8	360.0
Net Flow of Funds	31.3	(5.9)	(16.7)	34.4	91.9	85.6	123.2	(119.5)	(71.2)	(35.0)	(7.9)	(3 2)	12.5
Accumulated Net Funds	31.0	24.9	8.5	42.8	134.7	220.7	344.0	224.6	153.4	118.5	110.6	107.5	120.0
Debt–Service Ratio	0.0	0.0	0.0	2.7	3.7	2.6	2.5	1.5	1.8	2.0	2.2	2.2	2.4

Source: Dalian Economic and Technological Development Zone.

TABLE M8.1D
Dalian Water Supply Company: Projected Balance Sheet (million Yuan)

Item	1992	1993	1994	1995	1996	1997	1998	1999	2000	2001	2002	2003	2004
	Actual												
Assets													
Gross fixed assets	580.8	612.6	612.6	612.6	1,640.3	1,640.3	3,175.6	3,442.1	3,442.1	3,4421	3,442.1	4,282.1	4,282.1
Accumulated Depreciation	193.3	218.7	249.3	280.0	362.0	444.0	559.1	683.9	808.7	933.4	1,058.2	1,213.4	1,368.7
Net fixed assets	387.5	393.9	363.3	332.6	1,278.3	1,196.3	2,616.5	2,758.2	2,633.4	2,508.7	2,383.9	3,068.7	2,913.4
Work-in-progress	20.8	0.0	626.1	1,027.7	816.3	1,535.2	266.5	220.0	440.0	640.0	840.0	200.0	400.0
Cash	31.0	24.9	8.5	42.8	134.7	220.7	344.0	224.6	153.4	118.5	110.6	107.5	120.0
Accounts receivable - sales	0.4	1.1	2.0	2.9	3.9	4.8	5.7	6.6	7.5	8.4	9.4	10.3	11.2
Other receivables	48.5	91.7	91.7	98.1	105.0	112.3	120.2	128.6	137.6	147.3	157.6	168.6	180.4
Inventories	7 8	45.8	57.8	69.4	80.4	91.3	112.1	123.1	134.6	146.1	156.5	170.4	180.9
Current Assets	87.7	163.5	160.0	213.2	324.0	429.1	582.0	482.9	433.1	420.3	434.1	456.8	492.5
Total assets	496.0	557.4	1,149.4	1,573.5	2,418.6	3,160.6	3,465.0	3,461.1	3,506.5	3,569.0	3,658.0	3,725.5	3,805.9
Liabilities and Equity													
Accounts payable	60.9	150.5	115.6	138.8	160.7	182.5	224.2	246.3	269.2	292.1	312.9	340.8	361.8
Short-term loans	0.0	0.0	0.0	0.0	0.0	0.0	0.0	0.0	0.0	0.0	0.0	0.0	0.0
Taxes payable	0.0	0.0	0.0	0.0	0.0	0.0	0.0	0.0	0.0	0.0	0.0	0.0	0.0
Total Current Liabilities	60.9	150.5	115.6	138.8	160.7	182.5	224.2	246.3	269.2	292.1	312.9	340.8	361.8
ADB Loan	0.0	0.0	258.6	418.4	648.6	838.1	838.1	818.7	798.0	775.9	752.3	727.2	700.4
OECF Loan	0.0	0.0	0.0	0.0	153.7	307.4	461.1	461.1	461.1	461.1	461.1	461.1	461.1
World Bank Loan	0.0	0.0	0.0	20.0	40.0	60.0	80.0	100.0	120.0	120.0	120.0	120.0	120.0
Construction Bank Loan	0.0	0.0	97.7	153.0	278.9	390.7	430.3	420.2	408.8	395.7	380.7	363.7	344.3
Total Long-term Debt	0.0	0.0	356.3	591.4	1,121.2	1,596.2	1,809.5	1,800.0	1,787.9	1,752.7	1,714.1	1,672.0	1,625.8
Total Liabilities	60.9	150.5	471.9	730.2	1,281.9	1,778.7	2,033.7	2,046.3	2,057.1	2,044.8	2,027.0	2,012.8	1,987.6
Equity and Reserves	435.1	406.9	677.3	843.5	1,136.6	1,381.9	1,431.2	1,414.8	1,449.5	1,524.1	1,630.8	1,712.5	1,818.3
Total Liabilities and Equity	496.0	557.4	1,149.2	1,573.7	2,418.5	3,160.6	3,464.9	3,461.1	3,506.6	3,568.9	3,657.8	3,725.3	3,805.9

Source: Dalian Economic and Technological Development Zone.

TABLE M8.2A

Dalian Yinbi Northern Water Supply Company: Water Demand and Sales Projections

Item	1992	1993	1994	1995	1996	1997	1998	1999	2000	2001	2002	2003	2004
	Actual												
Billable Water Demand (mil. m^3)	144.8	144.8	163.05	192.35	192.35	192.35	289.56	333.36	364.56	364.56	364.56	364.56	364.56
Average Water Charge (Y/m^3)	0.16	0.16	0.34	0.48	0.51	0.55	0.59	0.63	0.67	0.72	0.77	0.82	0.88
Water Revenue (Y million)	23.17	23.17	55.44	92.33	98.79	105.71	170.27	209.74	245.43	262.61	280.99	300.66	321.71
Other Sales (Y million)	0	0	0	0	0	0	0	0	0	0	0	0	0
Water Revenue (Y million)	23.17	23.17	55.44	92.33	98.79	105.71	170.27	209.74	245.43	262.61	280.99	300.66	321.71
Local Price Escalation Factor		10.0%	10.0%	7.0%	7.0%	7.0%	7.0%	7.0%	7.0%	7.0%	7.0%	7.0%	7.0%
Cumulative Factors		1.0000	1.1000	1.1770	1.2594	1.3475	1.4419	1.5428	1.6508	1.7664	1.8900	2.0223	2.1639
Raw Water Charge (Y/m^3)													
- At 1993 Constant Price		0.16	0.31	0.41	0.41	0.41	0.41	0.41	0.41	0.41	0.41	0.41	0.41
Increase Rate			93.2%	31.9%	0.0%	0.0%	0.0%	0.0%	0.0%	0.0%	0.0%	0.0%	0.0%
-At Current Prices		0.16	0.34	0.48	0.51	0.55	0.59	0.63	0.67	0.72	0.77	0.82	0.88
Increase Rate			112.5%	41.2%	6.3%	7.8%	7.3%	6.8%	6.3%	7.5%	6.9%	6.5%	7.3%

Source: Dalian Economic and Technological Development Zone.

TABLE M8.2B

Dalian Yinbi Northern Water Supply Company: Projected Income Statements (million Yuan)

Item	1992	1993	1994	1995	1996	1997	1998	1999	2000	2001	2002	2003	2004
	Actual												
[Revenue]													
Water Revenue	25.6	27.2	55.4	92.3	98.8	105.7	170.3	209.7	245.4	262.6	281.0	300.7	321.7
Other Revenue	0.0	0.0	0.0	0.0	0.0	0.0	0.0	0.0	0.0	0.0	0.0	0.0	0.0
Total Revenue	25.6	27.2	55.4	92.3	98.8	105.7	170.3	209.7	245.4	262.6	281.0	300.7	321.7
[Expenses]													
Salaries	0.6	0.7	0.8	0.8	0.9	1.5	1.6	1.7	1.8	1.9	2.0	2.2	2.3
Power*	25.9	27.5	34.1	43.0	46.0	0.0	0.0	0.0	0.0	0.0	0.0	0.0	0.0
Raw Water	6.7	7.1	31.1	36.7	36.7	34.2	51.4	59.2	64.8	64.8	64.8	64.8	64.8
Chemicals	0.0	0.0	0.0	0.0	0.0	0.0	0.0	0.0	0.0	0.0	0.0	0.0	0.0
Maintenance	3.2	3.5	3.9	4.1	4.4	0.7	0.7	0.7	0.8	0.9	0.9	1.0	1.0
Admin/Overhead Expenses	2.5	2.8	3.1	3.3	3.5	3.6	5.4	6.2	6.7	6.8	6.8	6.8	6.8
Repairs	0.0	0.0	0.7	0.7	0.7	0.7	0.7	0.7	0.8	0.9	0.9	1.0	1.0
Subtotal	38.9	41.6	73.7	88.6	92.2	40.7	59.8	68.5	74.9	75.3	75.4	75.8	75.9
Depreciation	1.9	1.9	1.9	1.9	1.9	1.6	34.0	34.0	34.0	34.0	34.0	46.5	46.5
Operating Income	(15.2)	(16.3)	(20.2)	1.8	4.7	63.4	76.5	107.2	136.5	153.6	171.6	178.5	199.2
Operating Interest	0.0	0.0	0.0	(3.6)	(11.1)	(18.9)	(22.8)	(59.2)	(57.8)	(56.2)	(54.4)	(52.5)	(50.4)
Value-Added Tax	0.0	0.0	0.0	0.0	0.0	0.0	0.0	(8.5)	(8.5)	(8.5)	(8.5)	(11.6)	(11.6)
Net Income before Subsidy	(15.2)	(16.3)	(20 2)	(1.8)	(6.4)	44.5	53.7	39.5	70.2	88.9	108.7	114.4	137.2
DMG Subsidy	13.3	16.5	20.0	2.0	6.5	0.0	0.0	0.0	0.0	0.0	0.0	0.0	0.0
Net Income	–1.9	0.2	–0.2	0.2	0.1	44.5	53.7	31	61.8	80.4	100.2	102.8	125.6
Operating Ratio	1.52	1.53	1.33	0.96	0.93	0.38	0.35	0.33	0.31	0.29	0.27	0.25	0.24
Inflation Factor		1.10	1.10	1.07	1.07	1.07	1.07	1.07	1.07	1.07	1.07	1.07	1.07

Source: Dalian Economic and Technological Development Zone.

Note: *Gravity flow after Project completion

TABLE M8.2C

Dalian Yinbi Northern Water Supply Company: Projected Source and Uses of Funds (million Yuan)

Item	1992	1993	1994	1995	1996	1997	1998	1999	2000	2001	2002	2003	2004
	Actual												
[Sources]													
Net Income	(1.9)	0.2	0.0	0.2	0.1	44.6	53.8	31.0	61.8	80.4	100.2	102.8	125.6
Add back: Depreciation and Interest	1.9	1.9	1.9	5.5	13.0	20.5	56.7	93.2	91.7	90.1	88.4	99.0	96.9
Net Internal Cash Generation	0.0	2.1	1.9	5.7	13.1	65.1	110.5	124.2	153.5	170.5	188.6	201.8	222.5
DMG Contribution	0.0	0.0	37.3	155.2	175.6	169.8	0.0	0.0	0.0	0.0	0.0	0.0	0.0
Bank Loan	0.0	0.0	38.4	159.8	180.5	174.9	0.0	0.0	0.0	0.0	0.0	0.0	0.0
Grant from Central Government	0.0	0.0	2.8	11.5	13.0	12.6	0.0	0.0	0.0	0.0	0.0	0.0	0.0
Construction bank of China	0.0	0.0	0.4	50.4	56.3	55.0	0.0	0.0	0.0	0.0	0.0	0.0	0.0
Subtotal	0.0	0.0	78.9	376.9	425.8	412.3	0.0	0.0	0.0	0.0	0.0	0.0	0.0
Total Sources	0.0	2.1	80.8	382.6	438.9	477.4	110.5	124 2	153.5	170.5	188.6	201.8	222.5
[Uses]													
Capital Expenditures	0.0	0.0	78.8	376.8	425.8	412.3	0.0	100.0	100.0	150.0	150.0	100.0	100.0
Amortization	0.0	0.0	0.0	0.0	0.0	0.0	3.7	17.0	18.5	20.1	21.8	23.7	25.8
Interest Payment	0.0	0.0	0.0	3.6	11.1	18.9	22.8	59.2	57.8	56.2	54.4	52.5	50.4
Total Debt Service	0.0	0.0	0.0	3.6	11.1	18.9	26.5	76.2	76.3	76.3	76.2	76.2	76.2
Changes in Working Capital	0.0	(1.4)	2.5	(2.5)	(3.5)	(7.8)	(17.2)	(16.3)	(17.0)	(16.3)	(16.8)	(20.5)	(21.1)
Total Uses	0.0	(1.4)	81.3	377.9	433.4	423.4	9.3	159.9	159.3	210.0	209.4	155.7	155.1
Net Flow of Funds (cash)	0.0	3.5	(0.6)	4.7	5.5	54.0	101.2	(35.7)	(5.8)	(39.5)	(20.8)	46.1	67.4
Accumulated Net funds (cash)	0.0	3.5	2.9	7.6	13.1	67.1	168.3	132.6	126.8	87.3	66.5	112.6	180.0
Debt–Service Ratio						3.45	4.18	1.63	2.01	2.24	2.47	2.65	2.92

Source: Dalian Economic and Technological Development Zone.

TABLE M8.2D

Dalian Yinbi Northern Water Supply Company: Projected Balance Sheets (million Yuan)

Item	1992	1993	1994	1995	1996	1997	1998	1999	2000	2001	2002	2003	2004
	Actual												
[Assets]													
Gross Fixed Assets	65.2	65.2	65.2	65.2	65.2	65.2	1,359.0	1,359.0	1,359.0	1,359.0	1,359.0	1,859.0	1,859.0
Less: Accumulated Depreciation	(6.7)	(8.5)	(10.4)	(12.3)	(14.2)	(15.8)	(49.8)	(83.8)	(117.8)	(151.7)	(185.7)	(232.2)	(278.7)
Net Fixed Assets	58.5	56.7	54.8	52.9	51.0	49.4	1,309.2	1,275.2	1,241.2	1,207.3	1,173.3	1,626.8	1,580.3
Work-in-Progress	0.0	0.0	78.8	455.7	881.4	1,293.8	0.0	100.0	200.0	350.0	500.0	100.0	200.0
Cash	0.0	3.5	2.9	7.5	12.9	67.0	168.2	132.6	126.9	87.4	66.6	112.7	180.0
Accounts Receivable - Sales	0.0	0.0	0.0	0.0	0.0	0.0	0.0	0.0	0.0	0.0	0.0	0.0	0.0
Other Receivables	0.0	0.0	0.0	0.0	0.0	0.0	0.0	0.0	0.0	0.0	0.0	0.0	0.0
Inventories	0.0	0.0	19.5	23.5	24.4	10.1	10.8	11.6	12.4	13.3	14.2	15.2	16.3
Total Current Assets	0.0	3.5	22.4	31.0	37.3	77.1	179.0	144.2	139.3	100.7	80.8	127.9	196.3
Total assets	58.5	60.2	156.0	539.6	969.7	1,420.3	1,488.2	1,519.4	1,580.5	1,658.0	1,754.1	1,854.7	1,976.6
[Liabilities and Equity]													
Accounts Payable	0.0	0.0	14.7	17.7	18.5	8.1	12.0	13.7	15.0	15.0	15.1	15.1	15.2
Short-Term Bank Loans	0.0	0.0	0.0	0.0	0.0	0.0	0.0	0.0	0.0	0.0	0.0	0.0	0.0
Taxes Payable	1.3	2.7	5.0	8.4	12.2	16.0	30.1	45.4	61.9	79.0	96.7	118.2	140.3
Total Current Liabilities	1.3	2.7	19.7	26.1	30.7	24.1	42.1	59.1	76.9	94.0	111.8	133.3	155.5
(Long-term Liabilities)													
ADB Loan	0.0	0.0	38.4	198.2	379.0	553.9	553.9	541.1	527.4	512.8	497.3	480.7	462.9
Construction Bank Loan	0.0	0.0	0.4	50.8	107.1	162.1	158.4	154.2	149.4	144.0	137.7	130.6	122.5
Other Long-term Loans	0.0	0.0	0.0	0.0	0.0	0.0	0.0	0.0	0.0	0.0	0.0	0.0	0.0
Total Long-term Debts	0.0	0.0	38.8	249.0	486.1	716.0	712.3	695.3	676.8	656.8	635.0	611.3	585.4
Total Liabilities	1.3	2.7	58.5	275.1	516.8	740.1	754.4	754.4	753.7	750.8	746.8	744.6	740.9
Equity and Reserves	57.2	57.5	97.5	264.4	453.0	680.1	733.8	764.9	826.7	907.1	1,007.3	1,110.1	1,235.6
Total liabilities and Equity	58.5	60.2	156.0	539.6	969.7	1,420.3	1,488.2	1,519.4	1,580.5	1,658.0	1,754.1	1,854.7	1,976.6

Source: Dalian Economic and Technological Development Zone.

and his communist party established a dictatorship exercising strict control and censorship. Millions of lives were lost through political oppression and failed economic reform programmes. In 1978, Mao was succeeded by Deng Xiaoping, who gradually started introducing market-oriented reforms and decentralized decision-making.

China's population was approximately one-fifth of the world's population at 1.19 billion in 1994. Although per capita GDP was very low, with an estimated 75 million people living in poverty, there were strong signs of an increasing middle class and improved overall quality of life.

Ever since the reforms started, the economy had grown by an average rate of 9 per cent per year. In 1992 and 1993, the economy grew even faster at 13 per cent per year. As a result, foreign investors were increasingly looking towards China for future opportunities. At the third plenum of the Chinese Communist Party in November 1993, a landmark decision was made to implement a range of reforms in order for China to make the transition to a socialist market economy. Reforms were wide-ranging and included fiscal, financial and enterprise reforms, including changes to foreign exchange and taxation systems and economic, foreign trade and securities laws. Many of these changes were believed to be a result of the demands placed on China to be accepted into the WTO.

China continued its growth momentum throughout the 1990s. However, the focus on economic reforms and growth had its direct and indirect side effects and many pressing issues competing priorities had to be tackled. Although the boom increased the national income and improved living standards, problems of an overheated economy such as high inflation, excessive monetary expansion and speculative investment emerged. The national cost of living was up to 24 per cent in 1994 due to inflation. There was a huge gap in living standards between the rural and urban population; the reforms of the private sector came at great social cost. Bottlenecks appeared in key sectors, such as energy, transport and communications. Basic infrastructure was underdeveloped, pollution was high in many urban centres and rural municipalities had inadequate water, sewage and power systems to sustain the increased demand from its industries and citizens.

In line with the economic reforms, the PRC government promoted the idea of privatization to keep the state-owned entities away from financial troubles and to push China to the next level of economic development. The government encouraged industrial consolidation among inefficient state-owned companies in various sectors ranging from banking to automotive manufacturing. It resorted to bankruptcy only as a last resort. Thus, rather than plunging into true capitalism through privatization, the government tried developing industrial conglomerates using the Korean model.

In the 1990s, the government eventually decided to allow foreign and private investors to purchase majority stakes in large state-owned enterprises. In order to underline its political inclination, the government officials insisted on referring to it as 'ownership transformation', refusing to call it 'privatization'.[4] In reality, due to restrictions on foreign ownership many potential foreign investors were discouraged from taking part in the privatization programme.

Table M8.3 presents the credit ratings of China and other select countries. Table M8.4 presents the sovereign bond spreads above US treasury bonds.

DALIAN CITY

The Dalian Municipality was located in the Liaoning Province in Northeast China. It included the seaport town of Lushun, the offshore Changshan Islands, the main city Dalian and the adjacent agricultural

[4] Pan, 'China Accelerates Privatization'.

TABLE M8.3
Country Credit Ratings

Period	South Korea	China	Mexico	Argentina	Brazil	Venezuela
Sep 1993	68 9	57.3	45.6	32.6	27.8	37.6
March 1994	69.5	58	46.9	35.6	28.8	37.6

Source: 'Standard and Poor', Moody's.

TABLE M8.4
Sovereign Bond Spreads

Date	Spread	Country
Dec-1993	352	Argentina
Jan-1994	339	Argentina
Feb-1994	462	Argentina
Mar-1994	739	Argentina
Apr-1994	712	Argentina
May-1994	570	Argentina
Jun-1994	773	Argentina
Apr-1994	1,127	Brazil
May-1994	1,087	Brazil
Jun-1994	1,186	Brazil
Dec-1993	266	Mexico
Jan-1994	315	Mexico
Feb-1994	402	Mexico
Mar-1994	484	Mexico
Apr-1994	547	Mexico
May-1994	424	Mexico
Jun-1994	532	Mexico
Dec-1993	91	South Korea
Jan-1994	93	South Korea
Feb-1994	96	South Korea
Mar-1994	110	South Korea
Apr-1994	99	South Korea
May-1994	115	South Korea
Jun-1994	104	South Korea
Dec-1993	617	Venezuela
Jan-1994	688	Venezuela
Feb-1994	998	Venezuela

(*Continued*)

TABLE M8.4
(Continued)

Date	Spread	Country
Mar-1994	1,481	Venezuela
Apr-1994	1,512	Venezuela
May-1994	1,217	Venezuela
Jun-1994	1,713	Venezuela
Mar-1994	126	China
Apr-1994	123	China
May-1994	137	China
Jun-1994	114	China

Source: 'Standard and Poor', Moody's.

regions. The city of Dalian had a population of 4.7 million and was the main commercial port for industrialized north-eastern China.

Given its location as gateway to both Beijing and Tianjin, facing the Shandong Peninsula in the south and neighbouring Japan, Korea and Russia, Dalian was the first area to be chosen for technology development. This occurred in 1984 as the city was declared an open coastal city and was given a larger degree of autonomy. On account of its freedom in economic planning, industrial growth and increased international trade, the Dalian Economic and Technology Development Zone had become one of the most successful precedents in China.

Dalian had a rich variety of resources including a range of agricultural products, fruits and seafood. Mineral resources included limestone and diamond. Industrial output included machinery, electronics, petrochemical, household, textiles, garment, metallurgical, building material, food processing and pharmaceutical products.

Constraint on water supply and delivery would limit growth in the region. In 1993, the average consumption of water in Dalian was 155 LPCD compared to a national average of 170 LPCD. Dalian and few other northern cities had been implementing water conservation measures, including pricing policies linking tariff to the marginal cost of water supply in order to discourage water wastage and encourage more efficient use of water. These policies were in line with guidelines issued by PRC in 1992 calling for full cost recovery from industrial and commercial users and recovery of O&M costs from residential users by 2000.

The population in Dalian Municipality was projected to be 5.2 million in 2000. The project studies showed that surface water resources within the city's limits were fully exploited and underground resources were overexploited, resulting in an increase in water salinity. The only practical source of additional water was the Billiuhe Reservoir, 160 km north of the city. The Project would supply water from Billiuhe Reservoir.

PROJECT COSTS AND FINANCING PLAN

The estimated total project cost was about the equivalent of US$380 million.[5] It consisted of foreign currency and local currency components of US$164 million (or 43%) and US$216 million (57%),

[5] The average exchange rate between 1 January and 31 July 1994: US$1 = Chinese yuan 8.60722 (Source: ONDA Corporation, www.onda.com).

respectively. The foreign currency portion was to mainly cover the purchase of equipment and materials, and interest during construction, whereas the local currency portion would cover civil works at the project site. In addition, they would adequately provide for the costs during construction and contingencies (e.g., cost overrun). The details of project cost are shown in Table M8.5.

The Project would be funded by a combination of loans, grant from the central government and Dalian Municipality's internal resources. While the two utility units NWSC and DWSC acted as EAs of the Project, the central government of the PRC would be the borrower. The government would then hand over the entire loan proceeds to NWCS and DWSC based on two separate subsidiary loan agreements supported by the Dalian Municipality's guarantee.

The proposed loan of US$160 million would be ADB's first loan to the water supply sector in the PRC. It would be the largest source of financing for the Project accounting for 42.1 per cent of the Project's cost (Figure M8.2). The ADB loan would be denominated in US$ and amortized semi-annually over a 25-year period, including the grace construction period of five years. The floating interest rate would be based on ADB's pool-based rate lending system with a commitment charge of 0.75 per cent per annum. The entire loan amount of US$160 million would be re-lent to the two EAs under two separate subsidiary loan agreements for US$60 million and US$100 million, respectively.

As EAs, NWSC and DWSC would be responsible for planning, organizing and implementing the Project. NWSC was created by the Dalian municipal government in 1993 to provide water from Biliuhe

TABLE M8.5
Sources and Uses of Cash (US$ million Equivalent)

Uses of Cash				Sources of Cash			
Major Components	Foreign Currency Cost	Local Currency Cost	Total	Major Components	Foreign Currency Cost	Local Currency Cost	Total
I. Base Cost				Loans			
Civil Works	$15.0	$124.9	$139.9	Asian Development Bank Loan	$160.0	–	$160.0
Equipment and Materials	$112.8	$8.8	$121.7	Ministry of Water Resources	–	$23.0	$23.0
Consulting Services and Training	$2.2	$7.6	$9.8	PRC State Planning Commission	–	$11.5	$11.5
Others (land, resettlement, etc.)	–	$16.8	$16.8	Commercial Banks	–	$18.5	$18.5
Subtotal	$130.0	$158.1	$288.1	**Total Loans**	$160.0	$53.0	$213.0
II. Physical and Price Contingencies	$17.5	$40.0	$57.4	Central Government Grant	–	$11.5	$11.5
III. Interest During Construction	$16.6	$17.5	$34.2	Dalian Municipal Government	$4.1	$151.2	$155.3
Total Project Cost	$164.1	$215.6	$379.7	**Total Project Cost**	$164.1	$215.6	$379.7

Source: Asian Development Bank.

FIGURE M8.2
Break-Up of Financing Sources

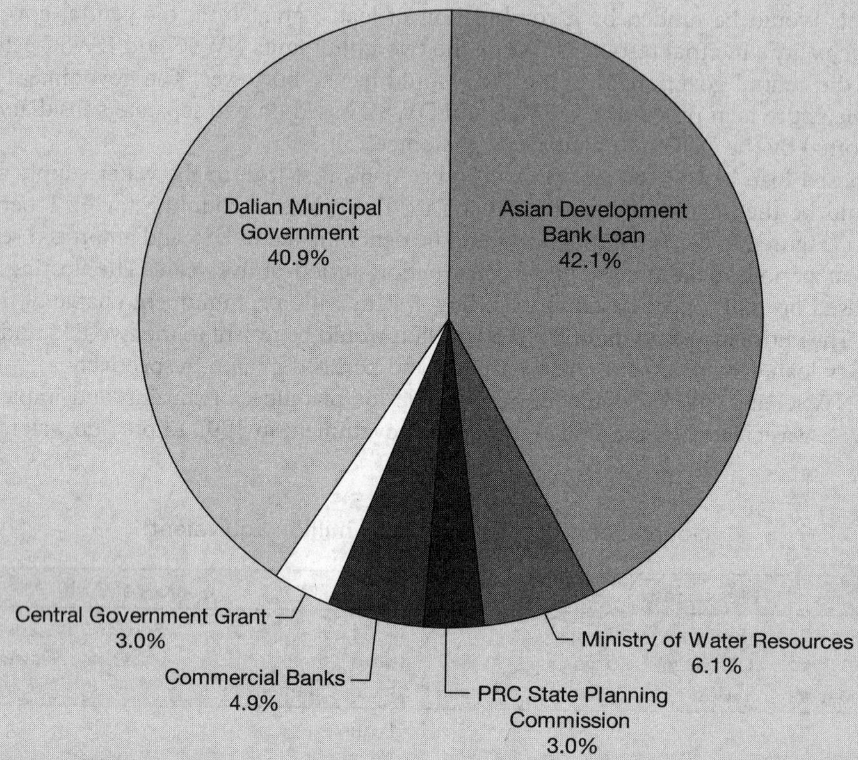

Source: Asian Development Bank.

Reservoir to cater to the needs of agriculture and small towns along the northern conveyor and to Dalian city at Wazidian Reservoir. NWSC was independent from Dalian city responsible for water resource management/allocation for all of Dalian Municipality, which included rural areas, villages, small towns as well as the Dalian city. DWSC had been the water supply company for Dalian city for more than 80 years and was responsible for the treatment, distribution and sale of water. DWSC would purchase the raw water from NWSC at Wazidian Reservoir and convey it through the southern conveyors to Dalian Economic and technological development zone (DETDZ), Jinzhou district, Lushun district and to its own water treatment plants in Dalian city for distribution and sale to urban customers. Both NWSC and DWSC were legal entities and registered as state enterprises under the country's state industrial enterprise law.

The detailed design of the southern conveyor had already been completed utilizing DWSC's own funds. One of the two pipelines included in this portion of the Project was already under construction and financed by DWSC. The remaining portion of the pipeline was expected to be completed by the end of 1994 utilizing the proceeds of the bank loan in accordance with advance action and retroactive financing approved by the bank. The physical implementation of the Project was expected to be completed by the end of September 1998.

FINANCING BY ASIAN DEVELOPMENT BANK

ADB was a multilateral development finance institution dedicated to reducing poverty in Asia and the Pacific. ADB was established in 1966 by 31 founding members. In 1994, ADB was owned by 53 members: 37 from Asia-Pacific and 16 from other parts of the world. The largest shareholders of ADB were the USA and Japan with 15.84 per cent and 16.4 per cent stake, respectively.

ADB's principal tools were loans, which it mainly provided to governments for specific projects and programmes. Other ADB's activities included technical assistance grants and equity investments, whose volumes were significantly lower than loans. A summary of ADB's operational activities is presented in Table M8.6. In 1993, the bank had lent US$5.2 billion. The average size of an approved loan was US$68 million. China, with receipts of US$1.29 billion, was the second largest borrower in 1993, following Indonesia with US$1.05 billion.

ADB's operations were financed by issuing bonds, recycling repayments and receiving contributions from members. The bank had a net income of US$570 million in 1993. ADB had AAA rating and typically raised US$1–US$3 billion a year from bond issues. The 'after-swap' weighted average cost of funds for the bank was 5.15 per cent per annum. In 1993, the average life of a loan was 10.5 years.

Nearly 75 per cent of ADB's lending was from ordinary capital resources (OCR) comprising of paid-in capital, reserves, funds raised through borrowings and accumulated retained earnings. OCR loans were usually for 15–25 years and typically carried an interest rate close to the 10-year T-bond rate in the disbursement currency. OCR loans were generally made to members with a higher level of economic development. At the end of 1993, OCR investment portfolio amounted to US$5.64 billion. The realized rate of return on these investments was 7 per cent.

The rest of the lending was from Asian Development Fund (ADF) dedicated to reduction of poverty and improvement in the quality of life of poor people throughout Asia and the Pacific. It was available to countries with lower levels of economic development. ADF investment portfolio amounted to US$725 million. Of the portfolio, 60 per cent was held in securities issued or guaranteed by governments of member countries. The return on ADF investments was 5.48 per cent.

Of the US$5.3 billion loans granted in 1993, 78 per cent was to energy, transportation and communication and social infrastructure.

Table M8.7 presents the composition of 1993 loan portfolio by sector.

TABLE M8.6
Summary of ADB's Operational Activities In 1993

	$ million	% of Total
Energy	1,775	34
Transportation and Communication	1,555	29
Social Infrastructure	781	15
Agriculture and Agro-Industry	361	7
Industry and Non-Fuel Materials	333	6
Finance	310	6
Multisector	167	3
Total:	**5,282**	**100**

TABLE M8.7
Loan Approvals by Sector in 1993

	1996–1993	1990	1991	1992	1993
Total Lending (Amount)	477,102	39,722	47,507	51,094	52,813
Number of Projects	1,179	57	74	65	78
OCR Loans (Amount)	328,484	24,917	24,035	39,544	39,838
Number of Loans	678	27	42	35	38
Disbursements	163,799	16,891	20,662	18,796	20,162
ADF Loans (Amount)	148,618	14,805	13,472	11,550	12,975
Number of Loans	609	36	33	32	40
Disbursements	84,158	10,626	10,374	8,875	9,251
Government and Government Guaranteed Loans (Amount)	470,028	38,933	45,939	50,594	50,402
Number of Projects	1,127	50	62	64	66
OCR Loans (Amount)	321,550	24,188	32,467	39,044	37,427
Number of loans	631	22	30	34	26
Disbursements	163,830	16,073	19,939	18,199	19,172
ADF Loans (Amount)	148,473	14,745	13,472	11,550	12,975
Number of loans	604	34	33	32	40
Disbursements	84,007	10,621	10,320	8,813	9,243
Private Sector Loans (Amount)					
Number of Projects	52	7	12	1	12
OCR Loans (Amount)	6,929	729	1,568	500	2,411
Number of loans	47	5	12	1	12
Disbursements	3,563	818	723	597	990
ADF Loans (Amount)	145	60			
Number of loans	5	2			
Disbursements	151	05	54	62	08
Equity Investments (Amount)	1,927	316	205	106	227
Number of Investments	69	15	6	4	9
Equity Underwriting (Amount)	457	43		52	
Number of Commitments	7	1		1	
Technical Assistance (Amount)	36,689	2,931	3,694	4,777	5,240
Number of Projects	3,155	255	241	278	287
Co-Financing (Amount)	173,635	12,666	14,320	30,242	34,946
Number of Projects	387	26	21	21	24

Only 31 per cent of ADB's projects were co-financed. For every dollar lent by ADB in 1993, an additional 66 cents were mobilized from other sources. Co-financing originated primarily from official sources (41%) and export credit agencies (46%). Only 12 per cent of co-financing originated from commercial institutions.

Interest rate on the bank's loan was determined by adding a spread (around 0.4% per annum in 1993) to the average cost of bank's outstanding qualified borrowings to cover administrative expenses and cost of carrying liquidity. The rates were adjusted on 1 January and 1 July each year. On 1 January 1994, the lending rate in US$ was 6.67 per cent per annum and that for multi-currency loans was 6.26 per cent per annum.

THE DECISION

If approved, this would be the bank's 33rd loan to the PRC and the first loan to the water supply sector in the PRC. Beginning in 1991, the World Bank Group's (WBG) Overseas Economic Cooperation Fund (OECF) and a number of bilateral agencies sponsored 11 projects, which included major water supply components for a total loan amount of US$1,078 million. ADB collaborated with WBG and OECF in the water supply sector, sharing project and economic information to prevent duplication of effort.

The bank conducted seven studies spending US$6.19 million to address critical issues involving water resource and water supply. These studies and previous projects in China demonstrated that PRC engineers possessed adequate capabilities in design and construction, and local contractors had proved to be generally competent.

ADB's overall objective (in the PRC) was to help the country achieve sustainable and equitable growth. In the infrastructure sector, macroeconomic policy dialogue centred on increasing efficiency, recovering costs and mobilizing financial resources to meet investment requirements.

The issue of financial sustainability was a particular challenge in the PRC, where water supplies had been perceived as a social benefit with only a nominal user charge, often unchanged for 30 years, and heavily subsidized from general revenues. Because of these historical factors, an immediate shift to full cost recovery was not feasible. In 1993, total domestic, public and industrial tariffs were increased 300, 800 and 550 per cent, respectively, in Dalian. After these increases, water tariff recovered only 30 per cent of O&M costs. With these increases, O&M costs would be fully recovered by 1995 and the future tariff increases would enable full cost recovery at project completion in 1998. The domestic water tariff would be increased 250 per cent in 1994 with further increases planned for all categories as service improved.

To understand whether the bank should make the investment, Alyona, Henning and Jim had to find an answer to several questions: Was the financial return from the Project sufficient to make the investment worthwhile? Did the economic benefits of the Project justify the lower return? How should the economic benefits of the Project be captured? What would happen if the bank did not invest? Could the Dalian Municipality carry out the Project on its own? What were the risks associated with the Project? Was the Project structured effectively to address the risks? Was the Project structure effective to ensure sustainability of the Project?

EXERCISES

1. As ADB, would you invest in the Project? Why or why not?
2. Identify the key risks in the Project. Have they been adequately addressed?
3. Estimate cost of debt, cost of equity and WACC for the Project using the Erb–Harvey–Viskanta model.
4. What are the economic costs and benefits of this Project?
5. Perform a sensitivity analysis.

REFERENCE

Pan, Philip. 'China Accelerates Privatization, Continuing Shift from Doctrine'. *The Washington Post* (2003, 12 November). Available at https://www.globalpolicy.org/component/content/article/213/45729.html (accessed on 9 January 2019).

9

AES Corporation: Building an LNG Power Plant in Honduras*

LEARNING OBJECTIVE

To introduce project financing in emerging markets; highlight the role of multilateral institutions in structuring and funding projects in developing countries.

Description: The case presents the financing of a power project in Honduras. United Energy's (a private equity fund) executives considering an equity investment in the project must determine the value of the project. The case considers the economics of the project from the perspective of various participants.

INTRODUCTION

On a cold winter morning in January 2001, Carlos Garcia looked across the table at his United Energy colleague, Stan Johnson, and asked, 'Well, what do you think?' Carlos had been recently hired as senior advisor for Latin American investments at United Energy, the New York City-based private equity fund.[1] AES, a US-based power company, was selling a 12.5 per cent stake (US$25 million) in its planned liquefied natural gas (LNG) fired power plant, the 'El Faro Project', in

* Reproduced with permission from Professor Campbell Harvey. Some of the images may be of poor quality. They are for representation purpose only.

This case was written by Stan Brunson, Rachel Fefer, Andrew Frankel and Carlos Sanchez under the supervision of Professor Campbell Harvey, Fuqua School of Business, Duke University.

[1] The names of persons and entities have been disguised to preserve confidentiality.

Honduras. While Carlos had extensive knowledge of Latin America, he depended on Stan for his energy sector expertise. Carlos was feeling nervous, as he considered his first big recommendation. Carlos had many questions like how much the proposed LNG plant was worth; and the appropriate cost of capital for a project generating revenues in five emerging market countries.

HONDURAS BACKGROUND

The Republic of Honduras lies at what had been the south-eastern tip of the Mayan Civilization. A republic of approximately 6.6 million inhabitants, it had an area of 112,492 sq. km comprising of a mountainous terrain, narrow coastal strips, the Bay Islands and several other smaller islands in the Caribbean Sea and the Pacific Ocean. A majority of the population lived in the mountainous interior of the country.

Honduras' history could be summarized as an uneven process of political and economic modernization. For the most part, the country had been a democracy with brief periods of military rule, the last of which lasted nine years and ended in 1981. Since then, there had been six democratic elections. The emphasis of the recent administrations had been to modernize and globalize the economy, as well as to integrate it with other Central American countries, with which it shared not only a common history but also a customs union, the Central American Common Market. Table M9.1 presents economic indicators for Central American countries.

Economic development showed consistent progress until October 1998, when Hurricane Mitch struck Central America with devastating consequences. Extremely heavy rainfall caused severe flooding and mudslides, killing some 7,000 people in one week. The replacement cost of the damage to the social and economic infrastructure was estimated at around US$5 billion, equivalent to 95 per cent of GDP in 1998. Following an international humanitarian relief effort reconstruction became a priority. In 1999, many bilateral creditors wrote off debts that Honduras owed to them and the Paris Club group of creditors deferred debt service payments for three years. In 2000, the World Bank and the International

TABLE M9.1
Economic Indicators for Central American Countries

	Honduras	Guatemala	Nicaragua	Costa Rica	El Salvador
GDP (US$ Billion)	5.9	19.1	2.5	15.8	13.2
GDP per Head (US$)	899	1,673	477	4,127	2,127
Consumer Price Inflation (Average %)	11.1	6	11.5	11	2.2
Current Account Balance (US$ Billion)	–0.3	–0.9	–0.5	–0.9	–0.4
% of GDP	–4.4	–4.5	–19.2	–5.4	–3.2
Exports of Goods fob (US$)	2	3.1	0.6	5.9	3.0
Imports of Goods fob (US$)	–2.7	–4.5	–1.6	–6.1	–4.7
External Debt (US$ billion)	5.5	4.7	7	4.3	4.4
Debt–Service Ratio, Paid (%)	10.6	8.5	31.8	8.9	8

Source: Economist Intelligence Unit, Country Data.

Monetary Fund qualified Honduras for debt relief under the heavily indebted poor countries (HIPC) initiative. As a result of these efforts, the Lempira, the local currency, strengthened by almost 15 per cent in real terms between 1998 and 2001. However, concerns that the currency was overvalued were increasing due to large fiscal and external imbalances.

The administration of former President Carlos Roberto Flores tried to pursue market-oriented policies in order to encourage private sector investment. Though it had progressed slowly in privatization, several major advances were made: the role of the armed forces in politics all but disappeared; the judiciary had gained greater independence from politics, reducing the scope for corruption.

Ricardo Maduro Joest of the National Party was elected president and was sworn in to office on 27 January 2002. A Stanford graduate with a degree in economics, Maduro was a pro-market businessman who, in a previous administration, served as president of the Central Bank. His main challenges included fighting crime (his own son was killed in an attempted kidnapping in 1999) and attracting foreign investment. He had also signalled his intention to improve political and trade links with other Central American countries. Table M9.2 presents a forecast of some of the economic indicators for Honduras.

TABLE M9.2
Economic Forecast for Honduras

	2000	2001	2002	2003
Real GDP Growth	4.8	2.0	3.2	4.0
Gross Agricultural Production Growth	7.6	0.5	3.0	3.0
Gross Fixed Investment Growth	–4.7	3.0	8.0	8.8
Unemployment Rate (Average)	28.0	28.5	28.0	27.5
Consumer Price Inflation				
Average	11.1	9.7	7.9	9.4
Year-end	10.1	8.8	8.9	9.4
Weighted Average Commercial Bank Lending Rate	26.8	23.9	21.2	21.7
NFPS Balance (% of GDP)	–2.0	–3.1	–3.5	–2.6
Exports of Goods fob (US$ m)	1,984.2	1,955.5	2,118.5	2,421.6
Imports of Goods fob (US$ m)	2,697.6	2,729.2	2,811.8	3,130.8
Current Account Balance (US$ m)	–259.0	–281.7	–274.1	–246.4
% of GDP	–4.4	–4.5	–4.3	–3.8
External Debt (year-end; US$ Billion)	5.5	5.6	5.6	5.6
Exchange Rates				
La: US$ Average	14.84	15.51	17.26	19.35
La: US$ Year-end	15.14	15.93	18.18	20.33
La: SDR Average	19.57	19.73	22.43	25.82

Source: Economist Intelligence Unit, Country Data.

ELECTRICITY MARKET IN CENTRAL AMERICA

Soon after taking office in 2001, Mexico's President Vicente Fox put forth 'Plan Puebla–Panamá', a region-wide poverty fighting initiative intended to integrate the Central American isthmus with south-eastern Mexico. It comprised several social, economic and infrastructure projects, chief among them was the construction of a US$320.3 million regional electricity grid intended to establish a wholesale electricity market. This grid was a separate initiative to be financed largely by the Inter-American Development Bank (IDB). The IDB predicted a single market by January 2002, and the completion of the grid by 2006. Annexure 9.1 presents information on this regional initiative. Figure M9.1 presents a map of the proposed grid.

The El Faro Project was developed in anticipation of the creation of a single electricity market and completion of an electrical power grid in Central America. The El Faro Project would supply 25–35 per cent of its power to Honduras; 35–40 per cent to El Salvador; 10–20 per cent to Guatemala and 5–20 per cent to the rest of Central America. AES would be selling electricity to the national power companies in all these countries.

FIGURE M9.1
Map of the Proposed Central American Power Grid

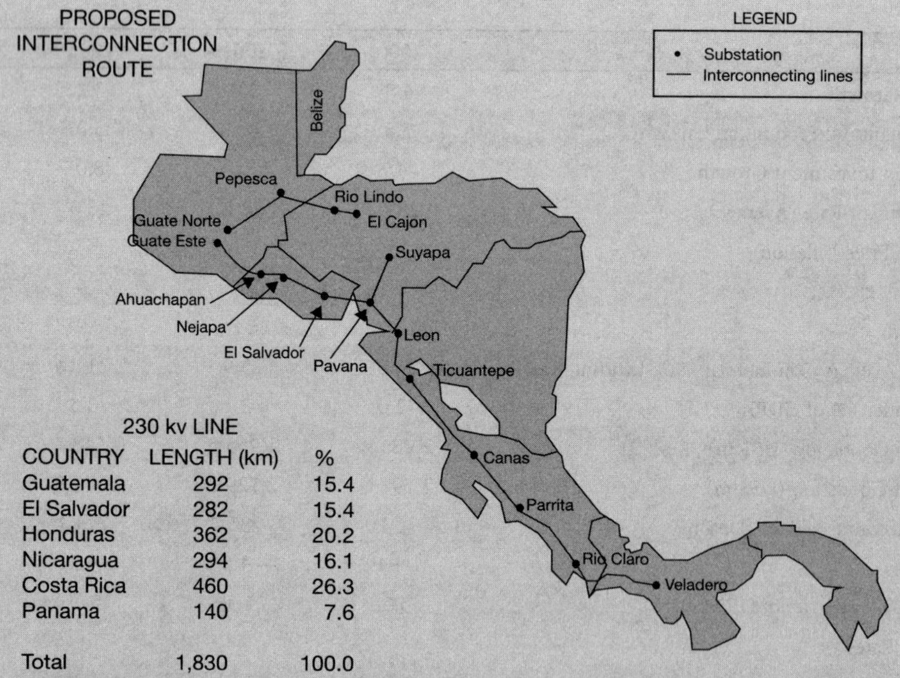

COUNTRY	LENGTH (km)	%
Guatemala	292	15.4
El Salvador	282	15.4
Honduras	362	20.2
Nicaragua	294	16.1
Costa Rica	460	26.3
Panama	140	7.6
Total	1,830	100.0

Source: Inter-American Development Bank.

Note: This figure is not to scale. It does not represent any authentic national or international boundaries and is used for illustrative purposes only.

THE EL FARO PROJECT

The El Faro Project involved the construction of an LNG[2] fired power plant located on the Atlantic Coast of Honduras in El Faro in Puerto Cortés. Its capacity, provided by three LNG turbines and a steam turbine,[3] was expected to reach 790 MW by 2008. The plant would occupy an area of approximately 20 hectares. It would include an upgradation of existing transmission lines in Honduras and the construction of an additional transmission line measuring 373 km, initially connecting San Pedro Sula, El Progreso, Santa Rosa de Copán in Honduras and the town of Nejapa in El Salvador, integrating El Faro into the regional initiative. Eventually, the line would be connected to Guatemala. Figure M9.2 presents a map of the transmission line upgrade.

The plant was the first gas-fired generator in the area. It would sell electricity to Honduras initially. Later on, electricity would be sold to El Salvador, Nicaragua, Guatemala and Costa Rica as the transmission line got completed and capacity became available. All of the electricity generated would be initially sold at a fixed price of US$0.05 per kWh, which was less than half the prevailing retail market price (US$0.11 to 0.18 per kWh). This price, however, would fluctuate with the price of LNG. When the grid was complete in 10 years, 30 per cent of production would be sold at spot prices (at US$0.01429 per kWh per MMBtu of LNG) in the local market. Table M9.3 presents data on electric prices and demand.

FIGURE M9.2
Transmission Line Upgrade

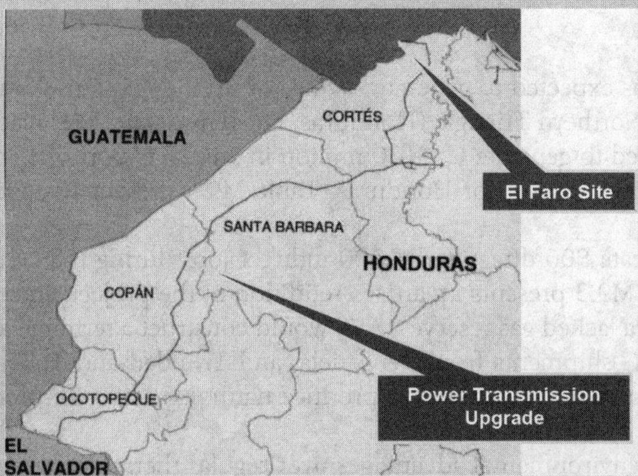

Source: Inter-American Development Bank.

Note: This figure is not to scale. It does not represent any authentic national or international boundaries and is used for illustrative purposes only.

[2] LNG is natural gas that has been liquefied for ease of storing and transporting. LNG takes up about (1/600)th the space that natural gas does in its gaseous form, and it can be easily shipped overseas. LNG is produced by cooling natural gas below its boiling point, –162°C (–259°F), and is stored in double-walled cryogenic containers at or slightly above atmospheric pressure. It can be converted back to its gaseous form by simply raising the temperature.

[3] A steam turbine and LNG turbine, with a capacity of 310 MW, were expected to be operational in 2002. In 2006, a second LNG turbine was expected to come on line, adding 230 MW of capacity. The third LNG turbine was expected to be operational in 2008.

TABLE M9.3
Electricity Prices and Demand Levels

NYMEX LNG Spot Prices	$/kWh	Production Demand for 70%	Production Demand for 30% (after yr 10)
$0.00	0.050	100%	100%
$3.50	0.050	100%	100%
$4.00	0.050	100%	100%
$4.50	0.055	100%	100%
$5.00	0.060	100%	80%
$5.50	0.065	100%	80%
$6.00	0.072	100%	80%
$6.50	0.078	90%	75%
$7.00	0.084	80%	75%
$7.50	0.090	70%	75%
$8.00	0.090	65%	65%

Note: Electricity prices will fluctuate with LNG prices in stepped increments for the initial 70 per cent of production capacity. The above table illustrates one possible contract scenario. It should be noted that when the price increases considerably, LNG-generated electricity will be more expensive than other sources and demand will fall depending on the availability of other supplies (coal, hydro, etc.).

The El Faro plant was expected to generate savings of up to US$75 million in Honduras, and up to US$210 million in the Northern Triangle (Honduras, Guatemala and El Salvador). Furthermore, the El Faro Project was expected to generate US$120 million in annual export of electricity and a US$90 million reduction in electricity import for Honduras. Table M9.4 presents data on consumption levels in Central America.

The entire would create 800 direct and 1,500 indirect jobs during the construction phase between 2002 and 2004. Figure M9.3 presents an artist's rendition of the project site.

Since Central America lacked gas reserves, AES would construct a terminal and storage facility beside the plant to receive LNG shipments from Venezuela, and Trinidad and Tobago. Trinidad and Tobago was a low-cost LNG producer. It was able to produce natural gas as a by-product from its oil refining activities.

LNG provided clear environmental advantages over regular thermoelectric plants, surpassing World Bank's environmental requirements for project financing. The El Faro plant would produce:

- 13.50 times less SO_2, 99.4 per cent less than World Bank standards
- 11 times less nitrogen oxide emissions, 58.9 per cent lower than World Bank standards
- 3 times less particles, 93.5 per cent lower than World Bank standards
- 3 times less CO_2 than World Bank standards

Both the US Environmental Protection Agency and the United Nations supported the use of natural gas. The El Faro Project received its environmental license from the Honduras government on 25 January 2002, the last day of the Flores administration.

TABLE M9.4
Electricity Consumption in Central America

	Energy Consumption							
	Total (Quadrillion Btu)	Petroleum (%)	Natural Gas (%)	Coal (%)	Nuclear (%)	Hydroelectric (%)	Other Electric (%)	Net Electric Imports (%)
Belize	0.004	100	0	0	0	0	0	0
Costa Rica	0.14	51	0	0	0	37	13	–1
El Salvador	0.10	73	0	0	0	15	10	3
Guatemala	0.15	85	0	0	0	17	0	–2
Honduras	0.08	74	0	2	0	23	0	2
Nicaragua	0.06	84	0	0	0	7	8	1
Panama	0.16	78	0	1	0	21	0	–0.4
Total	**0.70**	**74**	**0**	**0.4**	**0**	**21**	**5**	**0.2**

Source: Energy Information Administration, International Energy Annual 1999 and the International Energy Database (January 2001).

FIGURE M9.3
Artist's Rendition of Proposed Site

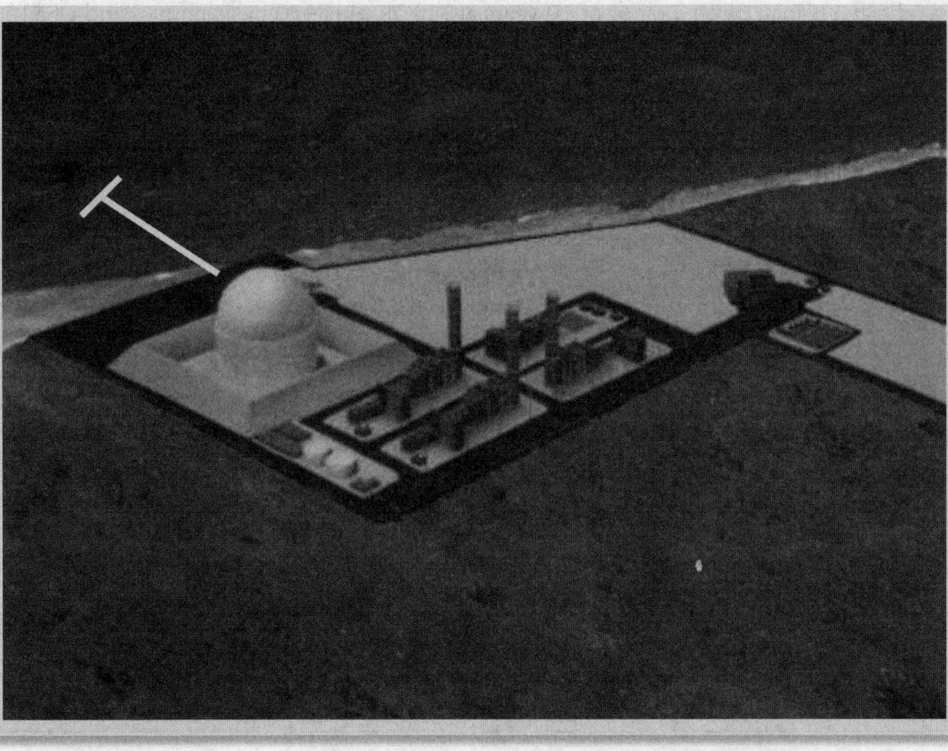

PROJECT SPONSOR

AES was founded in 1981 in Arlington, Virginia. AES owned all or part of 182 power plants worldwide, employing over 60,000 people. It was the world's largest independent power producing company, with an installed capacity of 50,000 MW in 32 countries that supplied electricity to over 20 million consumers. In Latin America, AES had a presence in Argentina, Brazil, Dominican Republic, Mexico, Puerto Rico and El Salvador. It also owned distribution companies that sold energy directly to commercial, industrial, residential and governmental consumers. Overall, AES generated 18,000 MW in the region. In El Salvador, it acquired four electricity distribution companies (CAESS, CLESA, DEUSEM and EEO) that were privatized by the Salvador government in the mid-1990s. Thus, AES would be selling some of the LNG-generated electricity from El Faro to AES-owned distribution companies in El Salvador.

FINANCING STRUCTURE

The total investment of US$640 million represented the largest foreign investment in the history of Honduras. The project would have an initial debt to equity ratio of approximately 1.9. The proposed financing structure included US$200 million of equity, of which AES was offering 12.5 per cent to United Energy. This US$25 million equity investment was projected by AES to have a 17 per cent annual return beginning in the 10th year of the project.

On the debt side, the project would be financed with US$440 million of senior debt, consisting of US$140 million of IFC A-loan (with a tenor of 12 years at LIBOR plus 450 basis points), US$150 million of IFC syndicated B-loan (with a tenor of 10 years at LIBOR plus 450 basis points) and US$150 million from Export Credit Agencies (ECAs; with a tenor of 10 years at 5.79%). Financial disbursements would match construction requirements. Table M9.5 presents the financial structure.

The mission of the IFC was to promote sustainable private sector development in developing countries, alleviate poverty and improve people's lives. As part of the World Bank Group, the IFC was required to consider the environmental and social impact of the projects it supported. IFC evaluated investments in terms of local development impact, allowing the organization to accept a higher level of

TABLE M9.5
Financing Structure (US$ million)

Sources and Uses of Cash (in US$ millions)

Uses of Cash		Sources of Cash	
Capital Expenditures	$621.50	Equity	
Working Capital	$18.50	AES	$175.00
		Other	$25.00
		Debt	
		IFC A Loans	$140.00
		IFC B Loans	$150.00
		ECA	$150.00
Total Uses	**$640.00**	**Total Sources**	**$640.00**

risk than most commercial lenders. The IFC had two internal rates of return measures for evaluating whether to support a project or not: the financial rate of return and the economic rate of return. The financial rate of return was based on constant price projections of pre-interest, after-tax free cash flows. Economic rate of return, which measured the economic impact of the project on the host country, was based on constant price projections of pre-interest, before-tax free cash flows adjusted for economic distortions and transfer payments.

While the IFC made direct loans from its own account (called A-loan), it also played a crucial role in mobilizing funds from other investors and lenders for private sector projects in emerging markets. The 'halo' effect of IFC's involvement and its reputation as an 'honest broker' tended to bring in other investors to the project. In its syndicated loan programme (called B-loan), participating banks provided their own funds and accepted their own commercial risk, while IFC remained the lender of record. This structure allowed B-loan participants to benefit fully from IFC's status as a highly creditworthy institution.

In valuing the project, Carlos and Stan had the following additional information to take into account:

- Each LNG turbine produced 220 MW, and steam turbine produced 180 MW of electricity. Annexure 9.2 presents the information on power conversion measures.
- Construction costs were projected at US$550 per installed kWh.
- Construction costs included US$80 million for the terminal facility, US$72 million for the storage facility and US$35 million for the transmission line upgrade.
- LNG would be delivered at NYMEX natural gas spot prices (plus a spread to cover liquefaction and delivery costs). LNG was currently trading at US$2.40 per MMBtu, but had ranged from US$1.20 to US$10.20 over the past four years. Figure M9.4 presents data on LNG spot prices.

FIGURE M9.4
LNG Spot Prices (US$/MMBTU)

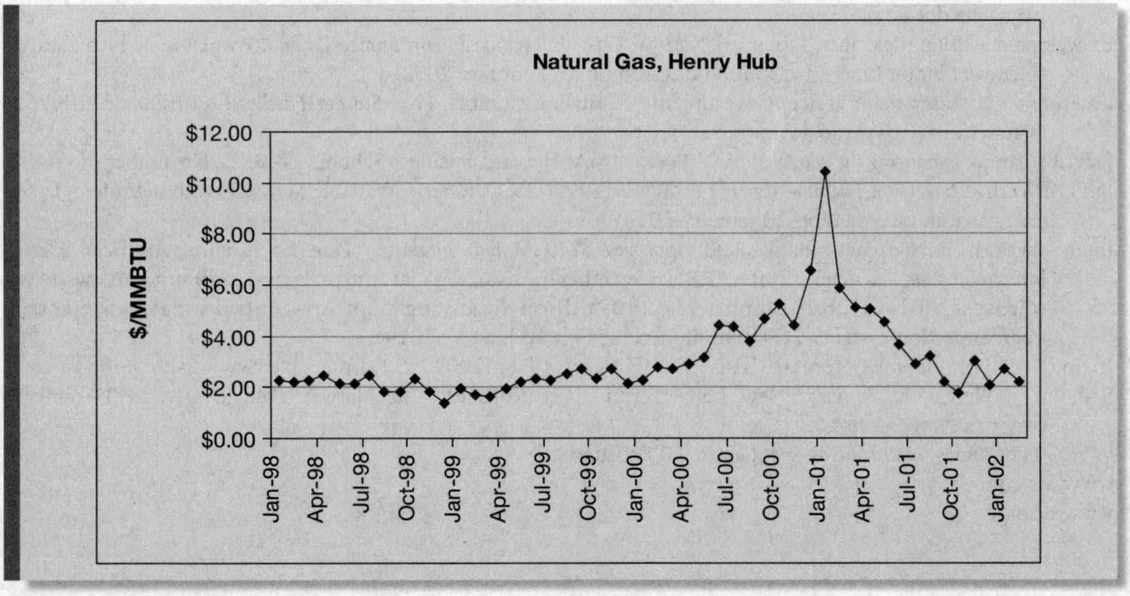

- Construction costs, operating expenses and revenue would be in US$.
- The project would have a dividend payout ratio of 70 per cent on positive net income.

AES has made a request to the Honduras government that it be allowed to operate under free trade zone conditions, granting it an exemption from all types of general taxes, income taxes, and other charges.

THE DECISION

Carlos and Stan looked at the spreadsheet they had created for the financial projections and reflected on what they knew of Honduras and other countries that would benefit from the El Faro Project. They had to decide whether or not this would be a smart investment by United Energy.

EXERCISES

1. What are the differences between corporate finance and project finance?
2. Identify the risks and options in the project.
3. Estimate a suitable discount rate for the project.
4. Draw a decision tree for the project.
5. Undertake a valuation of the project.

SUGGESTED READINGS

Department of Energy, Energy Information Administration. *Regional Indicators: Central America* (2001 June). (www.eia.doe.gov)

Encyclopædia Britannica, Inc. 'Liquefied Natural Gas'. *Encyclopædia Britannica Online*. Available at http://search.eb.com/bol/topic?thes_id=235403 (accessed on 26 February 2002).

Environmental Assessment Office, Government of British Columbia. *LNG Storage Facility Cost Estimate* (1997, 20 October 20). (www.eao.gov.bc)

Esty, Benjamin. *Financing the Mozal Project*. Boston, MA: Harvard Business School, 1999, 22 November.

INFO@WatB. *Conversion Factors—Energy or Work* (1999, 25 October). Available at www.watb.net/info/c_factor/energy.shtml (accessed on 10 January 2019).

Inter-American Development Bank. *IDB Approves $240 Million Financing Plan For Central American Electric Interconnection System* (2001, 28 November). Available at https://www.iadb.org/en/news/news-releases/2001-11-28/idb-approves-240-million-financing-plan-for-central-american-electric-interconnection-system%2C959.html (accessed on 10 January 2019).

Irwin, Neil. 'Formula for Corporate Crisis'. *The Washington Post* (2002, 25 February). (www.washingtonpost.com)

Solholm, Rolleiv. 'Oil & Gas: New LNG Terminal at Kollsnes'. *The Norway Post* (2001, 14 December). (www.norwaypost.no)

WTRG Economics. *Natural Gas Spot* (2002, 20 February).

www.aes.com

www.ifc.org

ANNEXURE 9.1: CENTRAL AMERICAN ELECTRIC INTERCONNECTION SYSTEM[4]

At an estimated total cost of US$320.3 million, the Central American Electric Interconnection System (SIEPAC) Project will develop Central America's first regional power grid and establish a regional wholesale electricity market including Costa Rica, El Salvador, Honduras, Guatemala, Nicaragua and Panama.

The Project seeks to bring the benefits of integration to those countries' efforts to improve their national power systems. The regional market will gradually allow qualified agents to buy or sell electricity no matter where they are located in the Central American isthmus.

In turn, the creation of a regional market with clear and uniform rules is expected to offer incentives for building larger and more efficient power plants, sparking investments that would help reduce the cost of electricity in the region and strengthen the reliability of their electricity systems.

'This project, which has roots that can be traced back to proposals floated nearly three decades ago, will become a milestone in the region's quest for integration and will establish a firm base to build on other initiatives under the Puebla-Panama Plan', said IDB President Enrique V. Iglesias.

Under the approved plan, the IDB will provide US$170 million in ordinary and soft loans to power utilities in Costa Rica, El Salvador, Guatemala, Honduras, Nicaragua and Panama. It will also grant the same firms US$70 million more in concessional financing from a special fund established by Spain and administered by the IDB.

One of the main elements in the SIEPAC project will be the construction of a 1,830 km (1,144-mile), 230-kilovolt power transmission line from Guatemala to Panama, with connections to substations and the national power grids of the six participating countries.

The new line will overcome the poor quality of the existing bilateral interconnections, which curtail the possibility of making firm transactions at a regional level.

The Project will also help establish two regional institutions: the Regional Electric Interconnection Commission (CRIE) and the Regional Operating Agency (EOR). CRIE will serve as regulator for the new regional wholesale market, while EOR will act as the system's operator and administrator of regional power transactions.

Under the financing plan, the six Central American utilities[5] will transfer loan resources to Empresa Propietaria de la Línea (ELP), a company that will own the SIEPAC transmission line. Under its charter, ELP will be able to open its capital to private sector investors.

As well, the IDB will provide a total US$9.9 million in technical cooperation resources to support Central American countries' efforts to establish the legal, regulatory and technical rules needed to consolidate the regional electricity market.

Under the Puebla–Panama Plan, future interconnections are planned to link the SIEPAC with the electricity grids of southern Mexico and Belize. The Puebla–Panama Plan was launched earlier this year to promote economic and social development and foster integration among Central American countries and the southern states of Mexico.

---

[4] Inter-American Development Bank Press Release (2001, 28 November).

[5] The participating Central American utilities are Costa Rica's Instituto Costarricense de Electricidad (ICE), El Salvador's Comisión Ejecutiva Hidroeléctrica del Río Lempa (CEL), Guatemala's Instituto Nacional de Electrificación (INDE), Honduras' Empresa Nacional de Energía Eléctrica (ENEE), Nicaragua's Empresa Nicaragüense de Electricidad (ENEL) and Panama's Empresa de Transmisión Eléctrica S.A. (ETESA).

The financing plan approved by the IDB includes four US$30 million, 25-year, variable interest rate loans for electricity companies in Costa Rica, El Salvador, Guatemala and Panama; and two US$25 million, 40-year, low-interest rate loans for power concerns in Honduras and Nicaragua.

The loans made with concessional resources provided by the Spanish government were granted in euros with a 35-year amortization period and at a variable interest rate. The utilities from Costa Rica, El Salvador, Guatemala and Panama received loans worth US$10 million each while the Honduran and Nicaraguan firms were given loans worth US$15 million each.

ANNEXURE 9.2: POWER CONVERSION MEASURES

1,030,000 Btu per 1,000 cubic feet

1 Btu	= 1.0002928 Kilowatt-Hours
1,000 Megawatts	= 1 Kilowatt

Btu (British thermal unit) is the quantity of heat that must be applied to one pound of pure water to raise its temperature 1° F.

MODULE 5

Dividends and Stock Repurchases

10

IVEY | Publishing

Dividend Policy at SRF Limited: Buyback of Shares*

Kulbir Singh, David Sharp and S. Ramanna Vishwanath wrote this case solely to provide material for class discussion. The authors do not intend to illustrate either effective or ineffective handling of a managerial situation. The authors may have disguised certain names and other identifying information to protect confidentiality.

On April 5 2012, Ritu Padma, a chartered accountant and financial analyst for SRF Limited (SRF), was asked by her chief financial officer (CFO) to analyze the company's cash dividend and share repurchase policy and provide recommendations for the next 12 to 24 months. SRF was a ₹38 billion[2] multi-business entity. Having completed its third round of share buybacks at ₹380 per share, SRF paid an interim and consistent dividend of ₹7 per share. The company had engaged in a series of share buybacks since 2006.

---

* Reproduced with permission from IVEY Publishing.

[1] This case has been written on the basis of published sources only. Consequently, the interpretation and perspectives presented in this case are not necessarily those of SRF Limited or any of its employees.

[2] ₹ = INR = Indian rupee; all currency amounts are in ₹ unless otherwise specified; US$1 = ₹51 on 5 April 2012.

In light of India's falling economic growth and pessimistic global economic outlook, Padma needed to analyze whether the company would be able to maintain its growth. Should the company go ahead with another round of share buybacks and increasing dividends? In order to conduct her analysis, Padma gathered the company's financial statements (see Exhibits 1A, 1B, and 1C) and relevant data on various important ratios (see Exhibit 2), on dividend and earnings per share (EPS) (see Exhibit 3), and on stock prices (see Exhibit 4). She also needed to know what the analysts' opinions were about SRF, but could find very few analyst reports. Based on these inputs and analyses, she had to give her recommendation to her CFO.

COMPANY BACKGROUND

Incorporated as Shri Ram Fibres in 1970, the company changed its name to SRF Limited in 1990, when it became a multi-business entity engaged in the manufacture and sale of chemical-based industrial intermediates in India and internationally. SRF operated in three broad business segments (see Exhibit 5). The technical textile business (TTB) comprised 52 per cent of fiscal year (FY) 2012's sale of products, the chemicals and polymers business (CPB) comprised 29 per cent of FY 2012's sale of products, and the packaging films business (PFB) comprised 19 per cent of FY 2012's sale of products.[3] Through these segments, SRF catered to various industries including automotive, infrastructure, consumer durables, pharmaceuticals and agrochemicals. SRF exported its products to nearly 60 countries across the globe.[4]

SRF was a global entity with operations in four countries: India, Dubai, South Africa and Thailand. The company had eight manufacturing facilities in India and one each in Dubai, South Africa and Thailand. The South Africa and Thailand facilities had been acquired the most recently and were fully integrated into the company's overall business.[5]

SRF was a market leader in India in technical textiles, refrigerants, engineering plastics, and industrial yarns. The company was controlled by Arun Bharat Ram Group, which consisted of various individuals and corporate bodies, with promoters holding 49.95 per cent of equity in the company.

INDUSTRY PROFILE[6]

TECHNICAL TEXTILE BUSINESS

The TTB segment was mainly diversified into tire cord fabrics, belting fabrics, coated fabrics and industrial yarn. It accounted for the largest share of business for the company, with a contribution to the sales of the firm in FY 2012, down from 48 per cent in FY 2011. In actual terms, however, sales of the TTB segment had increased during 2011–12 to over ₹16.7 billion from ₹14.5 billion in FY 2011–10 (see Exhibit 6).

[3] SRF Ltd Annual Report 2011–12, Schedule 19, p. 62 (excluding excise duty).

[4] Various SRF Ltd annual reports, accessed 8 July 2015, www.srf.com/investor-relations/investors.html#reports.

[5] Various SRF Ltd annual reports, accessed 8 July 2015, www.srf.com/investor-relations/investors.html#reports.

[6] Various facts and figures related to production, factories, and products are taken from the Management Discussion and Analysis (MDA) section of various annual reports of SRF Ltd., accessed 8 July 2015, www.srf.com/investor-relations/investors.html#reports.

EXHIBIT 1A
Balance Sheet (in ₹10 million)

Sources of Funds	2003–2012	2003–2011	2003–2010	2003–2009	2003–2008	2003–2007	2003–2006
Share Capital	58.44	61.52	61.52	61.71	68.91	68.91	65.55
Reserves Total	1,788.26	1,578.48	1,206.48	914.77	902.65	804.88	531.22
Total Shareholders' Funds	1,846.70	1,640.00	1,268.00	976.48	971.56	873.79	596.77
Secured Loans	532.99	460.53	750.20	750.15	425.5	483.41	602.46
Unsecured Loans	461.24	351.63	189.15	134.68	73.14	0.23	1.38
Total Debt	994.23	812.16	939.35	884.83	498.64	483.64	603.84
Other Liabilities	10.40	10.34	0.00	0.00	0.00	0.00	0.00
Total Liabilities	2,851.33	2,462.5	2,207.35	1,861.31	1,470.20	1,357.43	1,200.61
Application of Funds							
Gross Block	3,094.31	2,886.99	2,707.22	2,187.97	1,865.86	1,691.99	1,418.66
Less: Accumulated Depreciation	1,233.53	1,080.62	935.48	808.32	719.49	644.05	566.92
Net Block	1,860.78	1,806.37	1,771.74	1,379.65	1,146.37	1,047.94	851.74
Capital Work in Progress	414.26	113.07	127.07	280.80	89.30	114.50	245.50
Investments	218.70	201.90	164.62	133.60	147.53	99.07	96.07
Current Assets, Loans, and Advances							
Inventories	412.20	438.73	249.03	191.11	228.60	184.09	157.30
Sundry Debtors	408.03	441.78	340.23	230.24	233.00	204.93	120.07
Cash and Bank	129.21	63.86	65.35	3.10	7.23	17.91	8.43
Loans and Advances	82.91	114.16	167.30	147.64	93.87	96.95	92.28
Total Current Assets	1,032.35	1,058.53	821.91	572.09	562.70	503.88	378.08
Less: Current Liabilities and Provisions							
Current Liabilities	542.48	559.33	447.39	316.40	297.82	233.36	217.94
Provisions	13.40	9.07	24.69	15.13	29.45	47.38	44.79
Total Current Liabilities	555.88	568.40	472.08	331.53	327.27	280.74	262.73
Net Current Assets	476.47	490.13	349.83	240.56	235.43	223.14	115.35
Deferred Tax Assets	8.42	6.27	5.01	2.63	4.14	3.30	5.13
Deferred Tax Liability	225.51	215.69	210.92	175.93	152.57	130.52	113.18
Net Deferred Tax	−217.09	−209.42	−205.91	−173.30	−148.43	−127.22	−108.05
Other Assets	98.21	60.45	0.00	0.00	0.00	0.00	0.00
Total Assets	2,851.33	2,462.5	2,207.35	1,861.31	1,470.2	1,357.43	1,200.61

Source: Prepared by the authors with information from the Capitaline Database, accessed July 8, 2015, www.capitaline.com.

EXHIBIT 1B
Income Statement (in ₹10 million)

	2012	2011	2010	2009	2008	2007	2006
Income							
Sales Turnover	3,790.73	3,344.57	2,344.32	1,958.69	1,785	1,963.37	1,433.33
Excise Duty	260.48	281.30	163.24	153.46	169.67	161.38	141.06
Net Sales	3,530.25	3,063.27	2,181.08	1,805.23	1,615.33	1,801.99	1,292.27
Other Income	28.02	43.37	68.16	18.27	19.99	13.50	11.72
Stock Adjustments	6.52	44.80	26.17	–32.96	–8.53	29.38	11.62
Total Income	3,564.79	3,151.44	2,275.41	1,790.54	1,626.79	1,844.87	1,315.61
Expenditure							
Raw Materials	2,027.56	1,650.54	1,163.52	927.40	907.49	882.00	750.44
Power and Fuel Cost	267.00	213.23	166.33	137.95	139.99	143.99	121.42
Employee Cost	153.40	140.73	104.82	86.43	75.55	66.37	53.18
Other Manufacturing Expenses	86.77	75.82	63.49	51.73	50.17	46.88	41.70
Selling and Administrative Expenses	139.55	113.01	104.94	94.95	82.30	113.19	58.03
Miscellaneous Expenses	58.88	51.23	19.09	95.60	36.03	36.16	30.28
Total Expenditure	2,733.16	2,244.56	1,622.19	1,394.06	1,291.53	1,288.59	1,055.05
Operating Profit	831.63	906.88	653.22	396.48	335.26	556.28	260.56
Interest	104.09	77.69	68.05	51.11	36.07	36.40	39.28
Gross Profit	727.54	829.19	585.17	345.37	299.19	519.88	221.28
Depreciation	161.68	151.71	131.26	99.40	96.72	76.77	62.85
Profit Before Tax	565.86	677.48	453.91	245.97	202.47	443.11	158.43
Tax	168.47	184.04	119.65	56.07	41.14	134.87	47.41
Fringe Benefit Tax	0.00	0.00	0.00	1.75	1.39	0.00	0.00
Deferred Tax	10.01	10.00	24.84	24.87	21.21	19.17	6.25
Net Profit	387.38	483.44	309.42	163.28	138.73	289.07	104.77
Extraordinary Items	3.39	2.07	0.40	–53.23	–15.64	0.00	0.00
Adjusted Net Profit	383.99	481.37	309.02	216.51	154.37	289.07	104.77
Profit and Loss Balance Brought Forward	931.56	627.14	482.07	442.20	358.18	145.96	78.26
Appropriations	214.91	179.02	164.35	123.41	54.71	76.85	37.07
Profit and Loss Balance Carried Down	1,104.03	931.56	627.14	482.07	442.20	358.18	145.96

Source: Prepared by the authors with information from the Capitaline Database, accessed July 8, 2015, www.capitaline.com.

EXHIBIT 1C
Cash Flow Statement (in ₹10 million)

	2012	2011	2010	2009	2008	2007	2006
Cash and Cash Equivalents at Beginning of Year	56.65	18.40	3.10	7.74	17.91	8.43	9.08
Cash Flow from Operating Activities							
Net Profit Before Tax and Extraordinary Items	565.86	677.48	453.91	245.96	202.47	443.11	158.43
Adjustment for							
Depreciation	161.68	151.71	132.13	99.40	96.72	78.59	64.76
Interest (Net)	102.08	76.79	64.24	48.99	34.61	35.51	37.66
Dividend Received	(13.48)	(4.73)	(0.84)	(0.85)	(2.58)	(1.49)	(0.11)
P/L on Sales of Assets	(4.80)	(0.05)	(0.58)	(0.70)	0.38	0.49	0.23
P/L on Sales of Invest	(0.10)	(2.85)	0.00	(2.01)	(0.15)	0.00	0.00
Provisions (Net)	0.81	6.13	0.66	0.65	1.31	2.01	9.97
P/L in Forex	(5.68)	(10.23)	(46.32)	81.10	21.11	16.74	4.02
Others	0.00	0.00	(0.87)	0.00	0.00	(1.81)	(1.91)
Total Adjustments (PBT and Extraordinary Items)	240.51	216.77	148.42	226.58	151.40	130.04	114.62
Operating Profit Before WC Changes	806.37	894.25	602.33	472.54	353.87	573.15	273.05
Adjustment for							
Trade and Other Receivables	33.44	(113.05)	(111.09)	(6.74)	(27.09)	(90.62)	(50.95)
Inventories	26.34	(190.96)	(57.93)	61.50	(44.51)	(27.44)	17.13
Trade Payables	(39.15)	160.96	173.69	(73.24)	9.65	16.42	(10.68)
Loans and Advances	1.87	9.68	0.00	0.00	0.00	0.00	0.00
Others	1.76	2.11	0.00	0.00	0.00	0.00	0.00
Total (OP Before WC Changes)	24.26	(131.26)	4.67	(18.48)	(61.95)	(101.64)	(44.50)
Cash Generated from/(Used in) Operations	830.63	762.99	607.00	454.06	291.92	471.51	228.55
Interest Paid (Net)	0.00	0.00	0.00	0.00	0.00	(35.51)	(37.66)
Direct Taxes Paid	(165.18)	(192.71)	(112.55)	(57.16)	(63.69)	(127.74)	(45.31)
Others	0.00	0.00	16.02	(12.46)	(0.37)	(16.74)	(4.02)
Total Others	(165.18)	(192.71)	(96.53)	(69.62)	(64.06)	(179.99)	(86.99)
Cash Flow Before Extraordinary Items	665.45	570.28	510.47	384.44	227.86	291.52	141.56
Extraordinary Items							
Net Cash from Operating Activities	665.45	570.28	510.47	384.44	227.86	291.52	141.56

(Continued)

EXHIBIT 1C
(Continued)

	2012	2011	2010	2009	2008	2007	2006
Cash Flow from Investing Activities							
Investment in Assets							
Purchased of Fixed Assets	(495.37)	(202.02)	(356.39)	(385.47)	(173.87)	(145.97)	(334.33)
Sale of Fixed Assets	7.34	1.00	1.69	2.47	1.37	1.02	0.50
Financial/Capital Investment							
Purchase of Investments	(1,040.60)	(882.76)	(611.49)	(479.10)	(483.18)	(330.99)	(2.58)
Sale of Investments	1024.24	861.25	646.55	495.28	434.86	328.16	5.01
Interest Received	2.23	3.11	3.81	1.41	1.46	0.00	0.00
Dividend Received	13.48	4.73	0.84	0.85	2.58	1.49	0.11
Investment in Subsidiaries	(0.44)	(14.56)	(65.41)	0.00	0.00	0.00	0.00
Others	1.86	46.24	27.45	(71.57)	25.46	0.00	0.00
Net Cash Used in Investing Activities	(487.26)	(183.01)	(352.95)	(436.13)	(191.32)	(146.29)	(331.29)
Cash Flow from Financing Activity Proceeds							
Proceeds from Issue of Shares (Including Share Premium)	0.00	0.00	0.00	0.00	0.00	25.82	2.87
Proceeds from Other Long-Term Borrowings	416.34	144.90	261.40	200.00	0.00	0.00	223.22
Proceeds from Short-Term Borrowings	163.63	0.00	44.83	118.32	84.09	0.00	25.52
Payments							
Of Long-Term Borrowings	(419.61)	(75.59)	0.00	(106.69)	(57.91)	(40.28)	(71.67)
Of Short-Term Borrowings	0.00	(192.91)	(231.65)	0.00	0.00	(79.92)	0.00
Dividend Paid	(80.87)	(125.27)	(12.35)	(47.74)	(33.94)	(46.51)	(16.13)
Interest Paid	(88.81)	(78.88)	(84.44)	(40.53)	(33.64)	0.00	0.00
Others	(103.26)	(21.27)	(73.06)	(76.31)	(5.82)	5.14	25.27
Net Cash Used in Financing Activities	(112.58)	(349.02)	(95.27)	47.05	(47.22)	(135.75)	189.08
Net Income (December) in Cash and Cash Equivalent	65.61	38.25	62.25	(4.64)	(10.68)	9.48	(0.65)
Cash and Cash Equivalents at End of Year	122.26	56.65	65.35	3.10	7.23	17.91	8.43

Note: P/L=profit/loss; PBT=profit before taxes; WC=working capital; OP=operating profit

Source: Prepared by the authors with information from the Capitaline Database, accessed July 8, 2015, www.capitaline.com.

EXHIBIT 2
Key Ratios and Miscellaneous Information

	2012	2011	2010	2009	2008	2007	2006
Key Ratios							
Debt-to-Equity Ratio	0.54	0.63	0.86	0.75	0.57	0.81	1.07
Long-Term Debt-to-Equity Ratio	0.30	0.38	0.59	0.56	0.50	0.73	0.98
Current Ratio	0.89	0.88	0.80	0.85	1.07	1.00	0.89
Turnover Ratios							
Fixed Assets	1.29	1.22	0.98	0.99	1.04	1.31	1.14
Inventory	8.91	9.73	10.65	9.33	8.65	11.50	8.59
Debtors	8.92	8.55	8.22	8.46	8.15	12.08	13.58
Total Asset Turnover Ratio	1.43	1.43	1.15	1.18	1.26	1.54	1.35
Interest Cover Ratio	6.44	9.72	7.67	7.35	7.24	13.17	5.03
Growth Ratios							
PBIDTM (%)	21.94	27.12	27.86	24.24	20.05	28.33	18.18
PBITM (%)	17.67	22.58	22.26	19.17	14.63	24.42	13.79
PBDTM (%)	19.19	24.79	24.96	21.63	18.03	26.48	15.44
CPM (%)	14.48	18.99	18.80	16.13	14.07	18.63	11.69
APATM (%)	10.22	14.45	13.20	11.05	8.65	14.72	7.31
ROE (%)	22.96	34.59	29.05	23.63	17.86	42.81	21.80
ROCE (%)	25.76	33.14	26.40	23.35	19.27	39.33	19.85
RONW (%)	22.96	34.59	29.05	23.63	17.86	42.81	21.80
Payout (%)	21.71	18.05	28.71	40.96	25.53	14.39	18.97
Valuation Ratios							
Shares Outstanding (in million)	57.42	60.50	60.50	60.69	67.89	67.89	64.53
EPS	75.86	79.72	50.21	26.76	19.88	43.63	16.35
Price-to-Earnings Ratio	3.97	4.16	3.92	3.56	5.39	2.96	21.72
Stock Market							
Beta	1.18	1.18	1.16	1.10	1.33	0.95	0.95
Standard Deviation Returns (%)	1.7	2.7	3.1	2.9	3.7	4.1	3.6
Standard & Poor's BSE Sensex							
Beta	0.93	0.93	0.93	0.93	0.93	0.93	0.93
Standard Deviation Returns (%)	1.25	1.10	1.91	2.78	1.92	1.74	1.02

Note: PBIDTM = profit before interest, depreciation, and tax margin; PBITM = profit before interest and tax margin; PBDTM = profit before depreciation and tax margin × 100; ROE = return on equity; ROCE = return on capital employed; RONW = return on net worth; EPS = earnings per share; BSE Sensex = Bombay Stock Exchange Sensitive Index (the oldest and most widely followed stock index in India, comprising 30 of the most actively traded and largest stocks on the BSE)

Source: Prepared by the authors with information from the Capitaline Database, accessed July 8, 2015, www.capitaline.com, and from the CMIE Prowess Database, https://prowess.cmie.com.

EXHIBIT 3
SRF Limited Dividend Per Share (DPS) and Earnings Per Share (EPs)

Year	Dividend Amount (₹)	DPS (₹)	Dividend Yield (%)	EPS (₹)
2012	81.23	14	5.50	64.03
2011	84.71	14	4.40	76.31
2010	84.71	14	7.09	47.96
2009	62.53	10	13.56	24.74
2008	33.94	5	4.96	19.30
2007	40.73	6	4.95	41.07
2006	19.36	3	0.91	15.57

Source: Prepared by the authors with information from the Capitaline Database, accessed July 8, 2015, www.capitaline.com.

EXHIBIT 4
SRF Limited Stock Price Chart, 2006–2012 (₹)

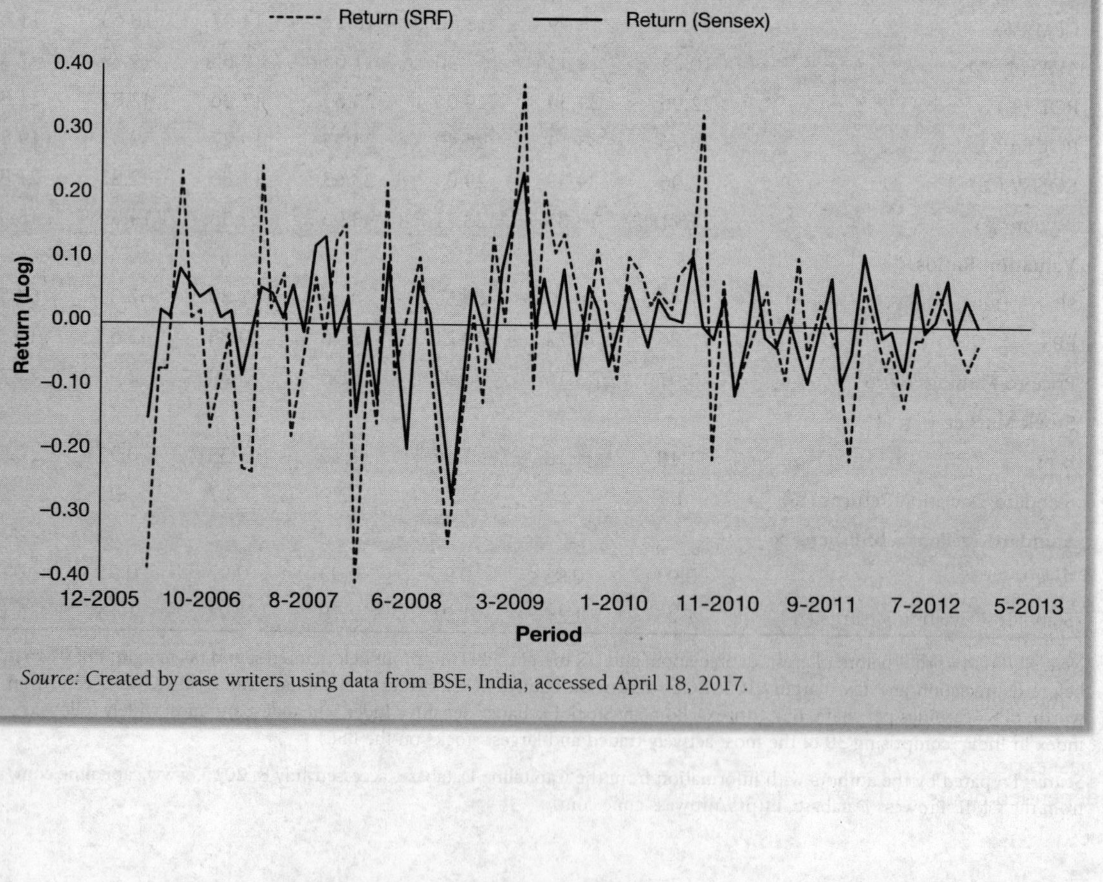

Source: Created by case writers using data from BSE, India, accessed April 18, 2017.

EXHIBIT 5
Business Segments of SRF Limited

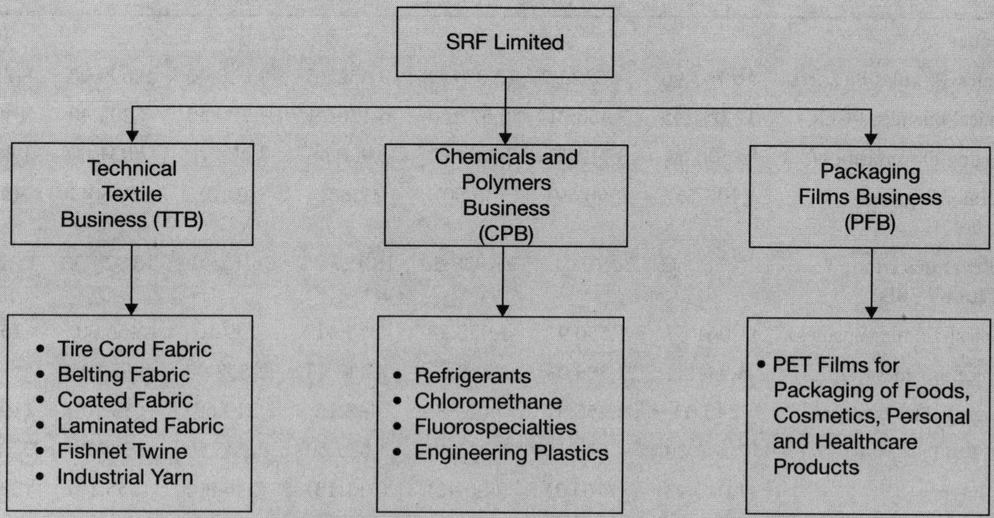

Note: PET = polyethylene terephthalate

Source: Prepared by the authors with information from SRF Limited annual reports.

Revenue for the TTB segment was mainly driven by the sale of tires to the auto industry for trucks, buses, multi-utility vehicles and two-wheelers.

Nylon Tire Cord Fabric and Polyester Tire Cord Fabric

Nylon tire cord fabric and polyester tire cord fabric were SRF's main products. These two products were used as a reinforcement material in the bias tires for all major categories, from two-wheelers to light and heavy commercial vehicles. As the market leader in Asia, SRF was the second-largest tire manufacturer of Nylon 6 tire cord and the fifth-largest tire cord producer in the world. SRF began its operational journey in 1974 with 2,500 million tonnes per annum (MTPA) and currently stood at 70,000 MTPA, after continuous periodical expansions and acquisitions. SRF was the only company with a fully integrated polyester tire cord plant with a capacity of 6,000 MTPA, and had become the only company in India to produce polyester tire cord fabric. Having set up India's only polyester industrial yarn plant in 2009–10, SRF had been the country's market leader in nylon tire cord fabric for decades.

Demand for nylon tire cord fabric and polyester tire cord fabric depended on the growth of the auto industry and the demand for replacement parts from original equipment manufacturers (OEMs).

According to industry estimates, tire production was expected to grow by 9.3 per cent in 2012–13 and 13.4 per cent in 2013–14. The OEM demand for tires, which consisted of 45 per cent of total tire sales, was expected to increase by 10 to 14 per cent each year during 2012–14. However, this demand depended on the growth in automobile production. Replacement parts demand was expected to rise by 7

EXHIBIT 6
Segment Revenue (in ₹ million)

	2012	2011	2010	2009	2008	2007	2006
Revenues							
Technical Textiles Business	16,743.98	14,512.00	12,034.88	9,052.36	9,088.00	8,699.90	8,757.40
Chemical Business+CER	12,052.45	7,466.71	6,577.60	6,176.74	4,789.40	7,294.40	3,490.50
Packaging Film Business	6,606.66	8,713.13	3,364.82	2,900.58	2,275.70	2,031.00	1,480.10
Less: Inter-Segment Revenues	(100.56)	(590.69)	(38.80)	(2.66)	(0.10)	(0.80)	(0.90)
Net Revenues from Operations EBIT	35,302.53	30,101.15	21,938.50	18,127.02	16,153.00	18,024.50	13,727.10
Technical Textiles Business	1,061.63	1,550.97	1,958.23	375.41	199.10	466.80	750.00
Chemical Business	5,941.34	2,888.08	2,768.07	3,238.43	2,552.80	4,834.20	1,546.60
Packaging Film Business	245.03	3,456.51	406.88	448.16	213.60	(53.40)	(193.20)
Total EBIT	7,248.00	7,895.56	5,133.18	4,062.00	2,965.50	5,247.60	2,103.40
Less: Interest	(1,040.93)	(776.92)	(680.48)	(511.13)	(346.80)	(355.10)	(388.80)
Other Unallocatable Expenditure	(548.43)	343.85	863.95	(1,091.30)	(565.30)	(461.40)	(160.50)
PBT	5,658.64	7,462.49	5,316.65	2,459.57	2,053.40	4,431.10	1,554.10
EBIT Margin (%)							
Technical Textiles Business	6.34	10.69	16.27	4.15	2.19	5.37	8.56
Chemical Business	49.30	38.68	42.08	52.43	53.30	66.27	44.31
Packaging Film Business	3.71	39.67	12.09	15.45	9.39	(2.63)	(13.05)

Note: CER = certified emissions reduction; EBIT = earnings before interest and taxes; PBT = profit before taxes

Source: Various annual reports of SRF Ltd, accessed July 8, 2015, www.srf.com/investor-relations/investors.html#reports.

to 11 per cent each year during 2012–14 due to the increase in vehicle sales in recent years. The demand for replacement tires was considered healthy. In March 2011, nearly 80 million automobiles had been sold in the previous six years. Exports were also expected to rise by 19.4 per cent during 2012–14.

However, raw material costs had been rising steadily, especially the cost of natural rubber. In response, tire manufacturers had raised their prices during 2011–12.

Belting Fabric

Belting Fabric was used as reinforcement material for conveyor belts. SRF was the second-largest manufacturer of conveyer belting fabric in the world. It was also the market leader in several countries, with a market share of 60 per cent in belting fabrics, and had a presence in Europe, Asia, the United States and Latin America. The overseas market accounted for 55 per cent of SRF's belting fabric business.

This segment's growth potential depended on growth in the domestic mining and infrastructure industry. However, this business segment was adversely affected in the second half of 2011–12 due to the fall in mining activity in the country and a freeze on key infrastructure and power projects.

During the previous five years, SRF had increased its belting fabric business at a compound annual growth rate of about 11 per cent.

Coated and Laminated Fabrics

Coated and laminated fabrics had a wide range of applications including protective covers, dynamic tarpaulins, static covers, auto canopies and awnings.

As India experienced changing lifestyles, urbanization and massive investments in infrastructure, products such as signage, awnings and hangar covers were expected to see double-digit growth. Increased use of tensile structures with fabrics, as evidenced in stadiums, homes and exhibition centres, was also expected to mean double-digit growth for SRF's high-end product sales.

The company's new state-of-the-art project was expected to produce 1.7 million square metres per year of coated fabric through a new coating line at its existing plant location in Gummidipoondi, in Tamil Nadu state. With a total investment of approximately ₹1.43 billion, work was progressing on schedule. Commercial production at the new plant had started in the second quarter of 2011–12. The new facility would offer a wide assortment of products, including hangar covers, auto canopies, awnings, lacquered tarpaulins and fabrics for tensile structures. Polyurethane-coated fabrics for various applications were also expected to be introduced.

Industrial Yarn (Nylon and Polyester)

Industrial yarn was used for conveyor belts, transmission belts, hoses, ropes, geo-textile applications, fishing nets and stitching threads. SRF continued to enjoy a substantial market share in this segment.

Chemicals and Polymers Business

The CPB segment included chloromethane, pharmaceuticals, certified emission reductions (CER) and allied products, refrigerant gases and engineering plastics.

During 2011–12, SRF posted record performance in this segment (including CER income), with sales growth of 61 per cent and earnings before interest and taxes (EBIT) growth of 106 per cent. The fluoro-specialties business had continued to grow at a brisk pace, with sales growth of 48 per cent and earnings before interest, depreciation and taxes growth of 99 per cent in this same period.

Chemicals—Refrigerant/Chloromethane/Fluoro-Specialties

Refrigerant/chloromethane/fluoro-specialties were primarily used as a cooling medium (refrigerants) in the air conditioning and refrigeration industry. The market for refrigerants was estimated to grow at about 20–25 per cent per year. SRF was the market leader in this area with about a 40 per cent share of the Indian domestic market. Exports accounted for 60 per cent of the volumes produced and were spread across 45 countries worldwide. In response to market concerns, the company had focused on producing and delivering new-generation hydrofluorocarbon (HFC) blends and HFCs in place of hydrochlorofluorocarbons and chlorofluorocarbons.

During 2012–13, the company planned to increase the production capacity of HFC-134a, an ozone-friendly refrigerant, and set up new production facilities for multi-purpose chemicals at Dahej, in Gujarat state. New projects were planned every year for the fluoro-specialties business.

Polymers—Engineering Plastics

Engineering plastics were used widely in the automotive and electrical industries. Performance in this area was mainly driven by those industries, which consisted of the user segments of engineering plastics.

Packaging Films

During 2011–12, the packaging films industry saw a drop in the domestic market of around 30 per cent. The drop in business was partly due to a ban on plastic laminates that were used in the packaging of gutka, an extremely harmful mixture of tobacco and other substances that was found to cause cancer.[7] The ban was issued by the Supreme Court of India. SRF's packaging films segment saw a decline of 92.91 per cent in EBIT, from almost ₹3.5 billion in 2010–11 to ₹245 million in 2011–12 (see Exhibit 6). SRF responded to this challenge by venturing into value-added product variants and two international projects at Thailand and South Africa to be commissioned in 2013–14.

SRF competed against several companies in major business segments (see Exhibit 7).

CAPITAL EXPENDITURES: GROWTH, EXPANSION AND RESEARCH AND DEVELOPMENT[8]

During 2006–2012, the company embarked on a journey of growth and expansion of its production facilities and market, both in India and overseas, through various organic and inorganic opportunities.

In 2008–09, SRF acquired Thai Baroda Industries Limited, a Thailand-based tire cord company, which enabled SRF to emerge as the third-largest tire cord fabric manufacturer in Asia, and fifth-largest in the world.

In 2008–09, SRF acquired the belting fabrics business of Industex Technical Textiles (Pty) Limited, in South Africa. The company was then renamed SRF Industex Belting (Pty) Ltd. The acquisition's price was ₹200 million.

In 2009–10, SRF set up the first and only producer plant of polyester industrial yarn in technological collaboration with Toray Industries, Japan. It would serve the growing segment of polyester tire cord

[7] Afshan Yasmeen, "Gutka More Harmful than Other Forms of Tobacco," The Hindu, 7 June 2016, accessed February 23, 2017, www.thehindu.com/news/national/karnataka/gutka-more-harmful-than-other-forms-of-tobacco/article4769653.ece.

[8] Details related to product, processes, production, plant locations, etc. are based on the Management Discussion and Analysis (MDA) sections of various annual reports of SRF Ltd., accessed July 8, 2015, www.srf.com/investor-relations/investors.html#reports.

EXHIBIT 7
SRF Limited and Competitors' Data

Company	Share Closing Price on the Bombay Stock Exchange (₹)	Market Capitalization (in ₹ million)	Sales Revenue (in ₹ million)	Profit After Tax (in ₹ million)	Total Assets (in ₹ million)
Aditya Birla Nuvo Ltd.	858.60	97,464.16	88,679.50	3,453.90	122,569.90
Century Enka Ltd.	120.85	2,640.64	18,256.30	87.80	13,321.50
Filatex India Ltd.	40.15	963.60	5,193.30	137.00	4,626.10
JBF Industries Ltd.	114.95	8,270.36	47,820.80	486.70	34,224.90
NRC Ltd.	3.95	147.09	0.10	(570.10)	3,789.50
Paras Petrofils Ltd.	0.48	160.43	1,209.90	(60.00)	692.90
SRF Ltd.	270.35	15,523.63	33,470.30	3,873.80	36,354.60
Shekhawati Poly-Yarn Ltd.	26.80	589.90	2,143.40	44.20	1,800.10
Sumeet Industries Ltd.	27.10	1,579.65	8,934.40	174.70	6,261.70
Vardhman Acrylics Ltd.			4,212.20	244.90	3,549.70

Note: Share closing price and market capitalization as on February 15, 2012; others as on December 31, 2011.

Source: Prepared by the authors with information from the Capitaline Database, accessed July 8, 2015, www.capitaline.com.

fabric used for radial tires for passenger cars and light commercial vehicles—a one-stop-shop for all kinds of fabric for tire manufacturers. It would also provide backward integration with the company's belting fabric and coated fabric businesses.

In 2008–09, SRF purchased two businesses—an engineering plastics business and an industrial yarn business—from the holding company SRF Polymers Limited.

Two international packaging films projects were started at plants in Thailand and South Africa. The plant at South Africa was expected to have a production capacity of 25,000 in biaxially oriented polypropylene film, with an investment of ₹2.5 billion. The African plant would begin its production in July 2013. Both units were scheduled to be commissioned during 2013–14.

In October 2010, SRF's board approved an 80:20 joint venture with Nitol-Niloy to establish a plant in Bangladesh for the production of biaxially oriented polyethylene terephthalate, a polyester film used for its high tensile strength. The plant had a capacity of 28,500 MTPA, with an estimated cost of ₹3.2 billion. The project was commissioned in 2012.

By the fourth quarter of 2011–12, production began at the multi-purpose chemical complex in Dahej, Gujarat state, for flourine-based specialty chemicals and hydrofluorocarbons, to be used as intermediates in the manufacture of drugs and pesticides for customers in Japan, Europe and the United States. During 2012–13, this plant was expected to increase its production capacity of HFC-134a. SRF would have invested over ₹2 billion by that time.

The commissioning of a state-of-the-art coating line plant was expected at an existing site in Gummidipoondi, with a total investment of approximately ₹1.4 billion. The plant had the capacity to produce 17 million square metres per year of coated fabric, starting in the second quarter of FY 2011–12.

SRF had also actively invested in research and development centres at Chennai and Bhiwadi for chemicals, and at Manali for TTB (see Exhibit 8). The company planned to spend another ₹1.4 billion for acquisition, new projects, research and development facilities and upgrading existing facilities.[9]

Carbon Emission Reductions

SRF's income also included receipts from the transfer of CER, also referred to as carbon credits, which were added to capital reserves (see Exhibits 9 and 10).

The United Nations Framework Convention on Climate Change, an international environmental treaty for stabilizing greenhouse gas in the atmosphere to prevent the deterioration of the earth's ozone layer, provided SRF with approval in principle for 3,833,566 CERs per year. However, income from CERs would be generated only until June 2014 and the amount would depend on CER value, which had seen a fall in price.

Dividend History—Buyback of Shares[10]

On 24 June 2006, the SRF board of directors decided to buy back the company's equity shares from the open market through stock exchanges. During FY 2006–07, the company purchased 16,084 equity shares at an average price of ₹194.29, resulting in the disbursement of ₹3,124,934 to its shareholders (see Exhibit 11).

On 25 April 2008, the company again decided to buy back its equity shares from the open market through stock exchanges. The buyback started on July 2, 2008, and ended on 16 April 2009. During this period, the company was able to purchase a total of 7,381,425 equity shares at an average market price of ₹94.83 per share. This buyback of shares cost the company nearly ₹700 million, reaching the maximum allowed buyback amount of shares for that time.

On 28 July 2009, the SRF board of directors announced another buyback of fully paid-up equity shares for an amount not exceeding ₹650 million, at a maximum price of ₹160 per share, from the open market through stock exchanges. However, the company was not eligible to make a second buyback offer before the completion of 365 days from the date of the preceding offer of buyback, according to the Securities and Exchange Board of India's Buyback of Shares Act. Consequently, SRF withdrew its buyback offer.

On 26 February 2011, SRF announced a buyback of fully paid-up equity shares for an amount not exceeding ₹900 million, at a maximum price of ₹380 per share, from the open market through stock exchanges. The buyback started on 6 April 2011, and remained open until 25 February 2012. A total of 3,083,080 equity shares, at an average market price of ₹291.89 per share, were bought back, for a total amount of approximately ₹900 million, by 10 February 2012. SRF's share buyback history included several different buyback events from 2008 to 2012 (see Exhibits 12A and 12B).

[9] "India Ratings Affirms SRF at 'IND AA'/Stable," money control, 26 September 2012, accessed 23 February 2017, www.moneycontrol.com/news/fitch-research/india-ratings-affirms-srf-at-%60ind-aa%60-stable_761993.html.

[10] Details related to stocks (such as number of buybacks, date of announcement, and price) mentioned here are based on various annual reports, accessed 8 July 2015, www.srf.com/investor-relations/investors.html#reports.

EXHIBIT 8

SRF Limited Capital Expenditures (in ₹ million)

	2012	2011	2010	2009	2008	2007	2006
Capital Expenditure	618	767	536	381	2,335	1,753	106
Recurring Expenditure	2,099	1,846	1,375	1,156	897	401	159
Total Expenditure	2,717	2,613	1,911	1,537	3,232	2,154	265
Total R&D Expenditure (% of Net Turnover)	0.77	0.88	0.88	0.85	2.00	11.90	0.21

Note: R&D = research and development

Source: Prepared by the authors with information from the Capitaline Database.

EXHIBIT 9

Certified Emissions Reduction Receipts

	2011	2010	2009	2008
CER Receipts (in million ₹)	1,369.80	2,595.60	3,483.74	2,677.11
% of Profit Before Tax	20%	57%	142%	132%

CER = certified emissions reduction

Source: Prepared by the authors with information from the Capitaline Database and SRF annual reports.

EXHIBIT 10

Generation and Receipt of certified Emissions Reductions from HFC2

Year	Generated	Received
2005–06	3,823,225	2,510,549
2006–07	4,828,337	5,369,088
2007–08	3,906,220	1,744,265
2008–09	3,950,689	3,903,416
2009–10	4,706,063	2,981,153
2010–11	2,861,580	871,079
2011–12	1,472,078	8,168,642
TOTAL	**25,548,192**	**25,548,192**

Source: "Project 0115: GHG Emission Reduction by Thermal Oxidation of HFC 23 at Refrigerant (HCFC-22) Manufacturing Facility of SRF Ltd," accessed July 8, 2015, https://cdm.unfccc.int/Projects/DB/DNV-CUK1129901204.48/view.

SRF IN 2012[11]

During FY 2011–12, the company was affected by a multitude of factors and combined effects, including an adverse demand–supply situation, higher energy costs, and higher input costs, which resulted in

[11] Some details mentioned here are based on various annual reports, accessed July 8, 2015, www.srf.com/investor-relations/investors.html#reports.

EXHIBIT 11A
SRF Limited Shareholding Information (as on March 31)

	Shareholding (%)					
	2012	2011	2010	2009	2008	2007
Promoters	49.95	47.44	47.25	46.20	42.39	42.42
Mutual Funds and UTI	8.80	8.35	7.04	6.35	5.96	5.76
Banks, FIs, Insurance Companies	4.07	3.87	4.18	4.42	4.24	4.25
Central Government/State Government	0.00	0.00	0.00	0.94	0.86	0.86
Foreign Institutional Investors	10.47	13.23	4.62	5.04	9.08	8.54
Private Corporate Bodies	4.42	5.02	9.31	10.77	10.23	12.30
Indian Public	20.78	21.37	26.41	25.22	26.38	24.98
NRIs/OCBs	0.61	0.65	0.74	0.53	0.58	0.49
Others	0.89	0.09	0.45	0.53	0.28	0.40

Note: UTI=Unit Trust of India (a mutual fund co. owned by the government of India); FI=financial institution; NRI=Non-Resident Indians; OCB=overseas corporate bodies

Source: Prepared by the authors with information from various of SRF Ltd.'s annual reports, accessed July 8, 2015, www.srf.com/investor-relations/investors.html#reports; National Stock Exchange, Mumbai; www.nseindia.com.

a decline of 36 per cent in its net profit after tax of ₹870 million compared to ₹1.36 billion the previous year. SRF's net sales also declined from ₹8.46 billion to ₹8.22 billion during the same period.

Unlike the CPB segment, both the TTP and PFB segments showed a decline in profitability.

The company's performance, in light of the global economic crisis, European economic problems, the falling index of industrial production data, and falling gross domestic product figures (see Exhibits 13a and 13b), raised many questions. With healthy cash balance reserves, a consistent dividend payment history, and many capital expenditure projects in the pipeline, could SRF maintain robust growth in the coming years? What was the strategy behind the past three buybacks of shares? Would the firm engage in such an endeavour again in the future? With SRF's zero share premium amount left in the reserves, Padma also had to determine if the company could reward its shareholders by paying a higher dividend in the coming years (see Exhibits 14 and 15), and understand why there were so few reports from analysts about the company. Based on her analyses, what should her recommendation be to the CFO for the next two years?

EXHIBIT 11B

Pattern of Shareholding by Share Class

Number of Equity Shares Held	31 March 2012		31 March 2011		31 March 2010		31 March 2009		31 March 2008		31 March 2007	
	Number of Shareholders (%)	Number of Shares (%)	Number of Shareholders (%)	Number of Shares (%)	Number of Shareholders (%)	Number of Shares (%)	Number of Shareholders (%)	Number of Shares (%)	Number of Shareholders (%)	Number of Shares (%)	Number of Shareholders (%)	Number of Shares (%)
Up to 500	93.08	10.27	92.95	9.98	92.65	12.11	93.09	12.84	92.53	12.67	92.88	12.97
501–1,000	3.95	3.24	3.96	3.15	4.13	3.83	4.10	3.93	4.29	4.01	4.07	3.90
1,001–2,000	1.53	2.47	1.57	2.48	1.67	3.02	1.52	2.86	1.67	3.03	1.65	3.10
2,001–3,000	0.46	1.30	0.45	1.21	0.49	1.54	0.45	1.45	0.51	1.63	0.51	1.63
3,001–4,000	0.24	0.94	0.25	0.93	0.21	0.90	0.19	0.85	0.24	1.03	0.21	0.97
4,001–5,000	0.16	0.82	0.19	0.93	0.21	1.17	0.15	0.91	0.18	1.03	0.14	0.84
5,001–10,000	0.29	2.20	0.30	2.27	0.32	2.84	0.15	2.24	0.28	2.40	0.26	2.34
10,001 & above	0.29	78.76	0.33	79.06	0.32	74.59	0.25	74.92	0.30	74.20	0.28	74.25

Source: Prepared by the authors with company information (annual reports).

EXHIBIT 12A

Share Buyback Details

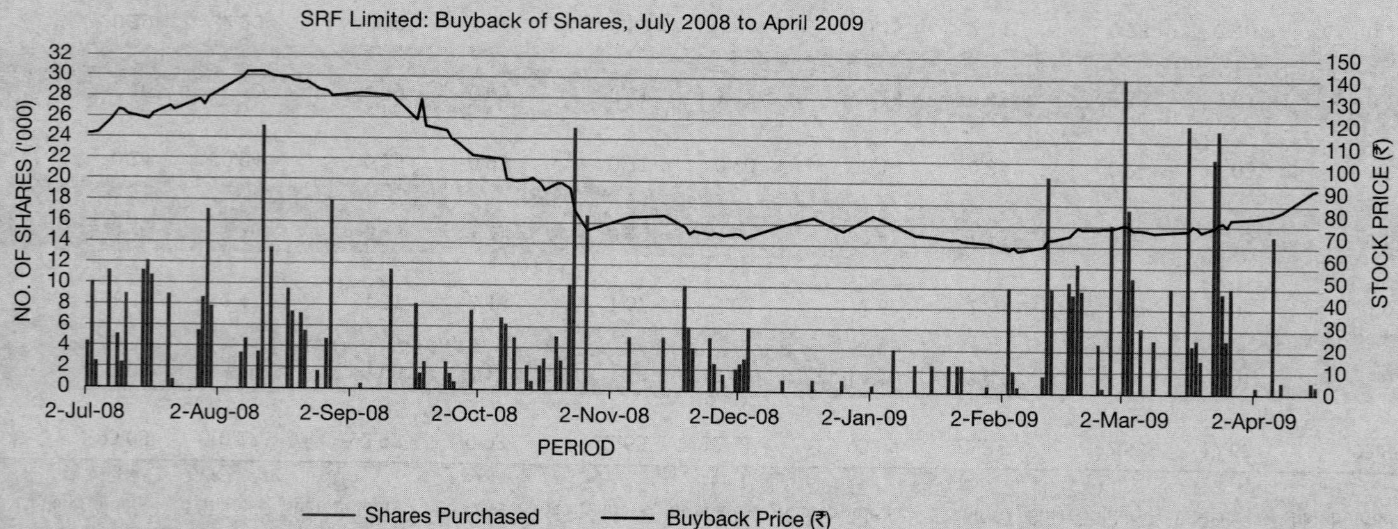

Source: Prepared by authors using data from accessed July 8, 2015, ProwessIO, https://prowessiq.cmie.com; National Stock Exchange, Mumbai, www.nseindia.com/live_market/dynaContent/live_watch/get_quote/GetQuote.jsp?symbol=SRF&illiquid=0&smeFlag=0&itpFlag=0#); Bombay Stock Exchange, www.bseindia.com/markets/equity/EQReports/StockPrcHistori.aspx?expandable=7&scripcode=503806&flag=sp&Submit=G.

EXHIBIT 12B
Share Buyback Details

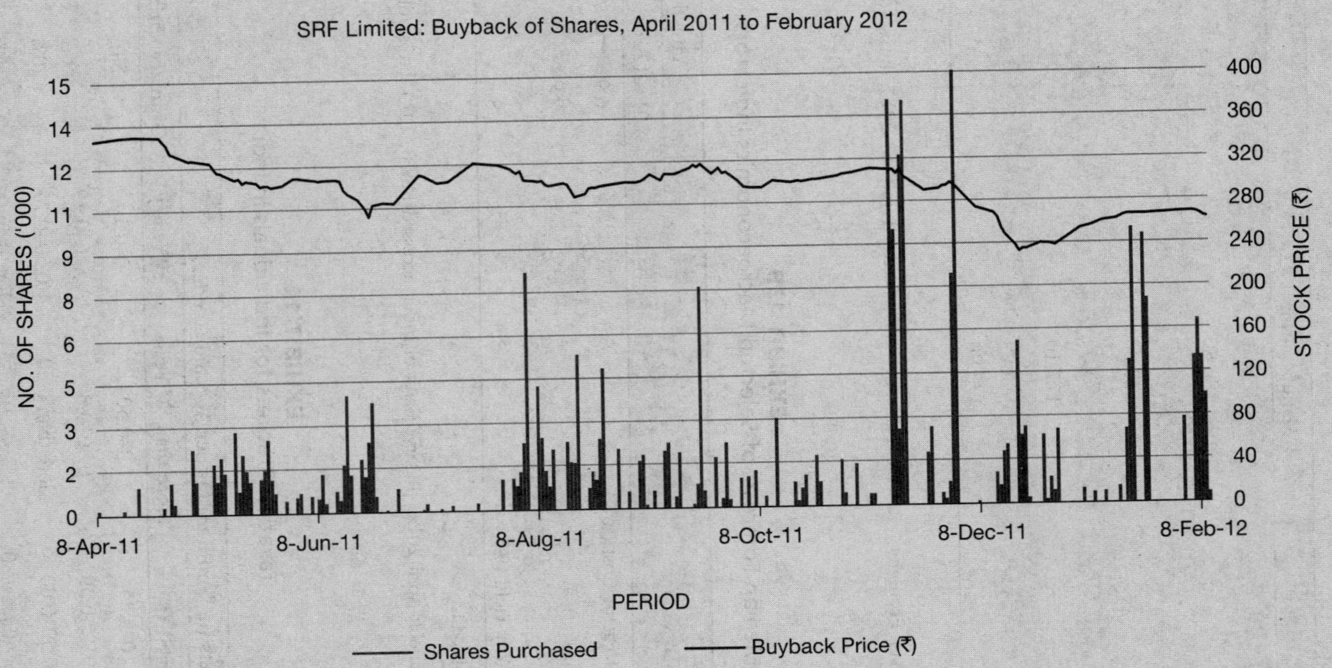

Source: Prepared by authors using data from accessed July 8, 2015, ProwessIO, https://prowessiq.cmie.com; National Stock Exchange, Mumbai, www.nseindia.com/live_market/dynaContent/live_watch/get_quote/GetQuote.jsp?symbol=SRF&illiquid=0&smeFlag=0&itpFlag=0#); Bombay Stock Exchange, www.bseindia.com/markets/equity/EQReports/StockPrcHistori.aspx?expandable=7&scripcode=503806&flag=sp&Submit=G.

EXHIBIT 13A
Index Of Industrial Production In India

Month	Manufacturing	Mining and Quarrying
January 2012	188.60	138.00
February 2012	186.80	135.00
March 2012	198.70	149.60
April 2012	173.00	124.80
May 2012E	178.30	128.40
June 2012E	177.10	121.20
July 2012E	174.30	114.00
August 2012E	173.90	110.10

Note: E=estimate

Source: "Database on Indian Economy," Reserve Bank of India, accessed July 8, 2015, https://dbie.rbi.org.in/DBIE/dbie.rbi?site=home.

EXHIBIT 13B
Median Forecasts of Selected Macroeconomics Indicators

		Annual Forecasts	
	Actual	2011–12	2012–13
Real GDP Growth Rate at Factor Cost (%)	8.4	6.9	7.2
Treasury Bill, 91 Days' Yield (% at Year-End)	8.2	8.8	7.9
10-Year Guaranteed Security Yield (%)	8.4	8.4	8.2

Note: GDP=gross domestic product

Source: "Macroeconomic Outlook April 2012," Reserve Bank of India, accessed July 8, 2015, https://dbie.rbi.org.in/DBIE/dbie.rbi?site=home.

EXHIBIT 14
Taxation Brackets for Individuals in India

Income Brackets (in ₹ million) (as per Age and Gender)				Tax Rates 2012	
Less than 60 Years	**60–80 Years**	**More than 80 Years**	**Women**	**Ordinary Citizen**	**Senior Citizen**
0–0.18	0–0.25	0–0.50	0–0.19	NIL	NIL
0.18–0.49	0.25–0.50	0.50–0.80	0.16–0.49	10%	20%
0.50–0.79	0.50–0.80	More than 0.80	0.50–0.79	20%	30%
More than 0.80	More than 0.80		More than 0.80	30%	

Income Brackets (in ₹ million)				**2011**
Less than 60 Years	**65–80 Years**	**More than 80 Years**	**Women**	**Ordinary Citizen**
0–0.16	0–0.24	Same	0–0.19	NIL
0.16–0.50	0.24–0.50	Same	0.16–0.50	10%
0.50–0.80	0.50–0.80	Same	0.50–0.80	20%
More than 0.80	More than 0.80	Same	More than 0.80	30%

Income Brackets (in ₹ million)				**2010**
Less than 60 Years	**65–80 Years**	**More than 80 Years**	**Women**	**Ordinary Citizen**
0–0.15	0–0.225	Same	0–0.18	NIL
0.15–0.30	0.225–0.30	Same	0.18–0.30	10%
0.30–0.50	0.30–0.50	Same	0.30–0.50	20%
More than 0.50	More than 0.50	Same	More than 0.50	30%

Note: Any individual age 80 years and above is classified as a senior citizen as per the government of India's Income Tax Act. This concept came into existence in 2012.

Source: Prepared by the authors with information accessed July 8, 2015 from Ministry of Finance, http://finmin.nic.in, and Income Tax Department, www.incometaxindia.gov.in/Pages/default.aspx.

EXHIBIT 15
Tax Rate on Dividend Income and Capital Gains in Sale of Equity Shares (India)

	Tax Rate		
Cash Dividend Income Received by	2012	2011	2010
Individuals and Firms (Less than or Equal to ₹1 million)	NIL	NIL	NIL
Individuals and Firms (More than ₹1 million)	10%	10%	10%
Tax on Cash Dividend Paid by Firms	16.608%	16.995%	16.995%
(Dividend Distribution Tax)			
Short-Term Capital Gains Effective Tax (Equity Shares)			
Individuals and Firms (Less than or Equal to ₹1 million)	15.450%	15.450%	15.450%
Individuals and Firms (More than ₹1 million)	16.950%	16.950%	16.575%
Long-Term Capital Gains Tax (Equity Shares)	NIL	NIL	NIL

Source: Prepared by the authors with information accessed July 8, 2015, Ministry of Finance, http://finmin.nic.in; Income Tax Department, www.incometaxindia.gov.in/Pages/default.aspx; and Raja Babu, "Special Income Tax Rates on Long Term-Short Term Capital Gain," www.itaxindia.org/2011/10/special-income-tax-rates-on-long-term.html.

MODULE 6

Acquisitions and Corporate Restructuring

11

Restructuring at Suzlon Energy Ltd*

LEARNING OBJECTIVE

To introduce issues in the use of FCCBs and corporate restructuring

Description: The case highlights the ambitious growth strategy of Suzlon, a global wind energy company headquartered in India. In 2007, Suzlon announced the acquisition of Repower of Germany, a leading wind turbine manufacturer. It issued zero coupon and coupon-bearing FCCB (US$) amounting to US$760 million to finance the acquisition. Due to deteriorating business conditions, the company experienced a sharp decline in profitability and stock price resulting in a debt overhang. At the same time, the Indian Rupee depreciated from ₹44/US$ to ₹55/US$ leading to losses on largely unhedged, foreign currency coupon payments. The company had to restructure its debt to escape bankruptcy. Since convertible bondholders did not agree to restructure the terms of the instrument, the company had to turn to senior lenders in 2012 to restructure debt. The case asks students to critically analyse the causes of financial distress, the company's financing strategy and decide whether they, as lenders, would restructure debt.

On 29 October 2012, Suzlon Energy Ltd, one of the top five wind energy companies in the world, announced that its senior secured lenders had agreed to restructure its debt. The plan was to get a moratorium on the payment of interest and principal. Upon announcement, Suzlon shares closed 10.7 per cent higher at ₹17.10.[1]

Kirti Vagadia, the chief financial officer of Suzlon Group, said:[2]

---

* Reproduced with permission from *The CASE Journal*, Emerald Publishing.

[1] The ₹to US$ exchange rate at that time way ₹55.7877/US$.

[2] Suzlon, *Suzlon Group Announces Formal Approval of Corporate Debt Restructuring Proposal.*

> Our senior secured lenders are supportive of our long-term business plan, and our efforts to consolidate our overall debt to achieve a sustainable capital structure. This is an important step towards stabilizing our business. Considering our overall business outlook, we recognize that despite strong business fundamentals and a $7.2 b order book, the timeline of the corporate debt restructuring process will continue to impact performance.

Under the debt restructuring plan, lenders agreed to enhance working capital facilities by ₹18 billion (US$350 million) and convert interest of ₹15 billion (US$270 million) during the moratorium period into equity over two years. From the perspective of the CFO and bankers at SBI Capital Markets (Suzlon's advisor), the task was to choose a plan of action from the available alternatives such as asset sales and raising equity to restore the financial health of the company.

COMPANY BACKGROUND

Suzlon Energy was set up in 1995 by Tulsi Tanti and his three brothers.[3] The company had its headquarters at Pune, India. The company had the vision of being one of the top three companies in wind energy. In 2011, it was the fifth largest wind turbine manufacture with an installed capacity of 20,000 MW across 30 countries and a workforce of more than 13,000 employees. The company had operations in Asia, Australia, Europe, Africa and North America. The company offered a product portfolio that ranged from 600 KW onshore turbines to 6.15 MW offshore turbines. The company had a vertically integrated manufacturing base. It had developed one of the largest wind farms in the western Indian states of Gujarat and Rajasthan with a cumulative capacity of over 1,000 MW.

During 2009–2011, the company's sales fell from ₹74,164.60 million to ₹47,183.60 but climbed back to ₹72,190.50 million in 2012 reflecting its product market difficulties soon after the Global Financial Crisis of 2007–2008. During the same period, the company accumulated losses of more than ₹25 billion (See Table M11.1). Its cash flow from operations dwindled from ₹21 billion to ₹5.4 billion during 2010–2012 (see Table M11.2).

INDUSTRY BACKGROUND

The Indian power sector had grown considerably over the past decade. The installed generation capacity of the power sector had increased to 181,500 MW at the end of August 2011.[4] The Indian power sector was largely coal based with the total installed capacity comprising of 99,503 MW (55%) coal-based and 20,162 MW (11%) renewable energy power plants. The capacity addition requirement during the 12th Five-Year Plan during 2012–2017 was expected to be 75,715 MW. Of this, 42,131 MW was to be generated by the private sector. Renewable sources of energy were becoming increasingly important in bridging the demand–supply gap.

Wind energy was the fastest-growing sector in India and had an installed capacity of more than 19 GW.[5] It accounted for more than 70 per cent of the total installed capacity in renewable energy. India was an energy-deficient nation because of which all power companies, including wind energy companies, had significant growth potential.[6] The demand–supply gap persisted due to delay in implementation of

[3] http://www.suzlon.com/about_suzlon/l2.aspx?l1=1&l2=1 (accessed on 10 January 2019).

[4] Government of India, Ministry of Power, 'Report of the Working Group on Power for Twelfth Plan'.

[5] Netscribes, 'Wind Energy Sector Update'.

[6] The power deficit was estimated at 9.1 per cent in July 2012.

TABLE M11.1
Financial Summary of Suzlon Energy (₹ million)

	2009	2010	2011	2012
Total Income	74,164.60	40,123.20	47,183.60	72,190.50
Revenue	72,544.70	35,057.20	43,586.60	68,719.90
Income from Financial Services	1,550.10	2,557.00	3,316.70	3,470.60
Change in Stock	683.7	–2,549.70	2,237.00	962.3
Total Expenses	79,530.50	51,714.40	51,277.20	78,206.60
Raw Materials, Stores and Spares	46,148.90	22,400.10	29,778.90	45,273.10
Power, Fuel and Water Charges	44.6	39.3	50.5	88.5
Compensation to Employees	1,990.70	1,810.10	2,152.30	3,374.30
Indirect Taxes	97.8	168.8	17.9	40.5
Selling and Distribution Expenses	9,727.10	2,976.80	2,174.90	3,925.40
Interest Paid	3,801.20	6,535.90	5,780.40	7,843.20
Depreciation	1,013.00	1,275.10	1,568.90	1,826.80
Profit				
EBDITA	6,251.60	5,294.80	9,015.40	13,993.80
PAT	–4,682.20	–14,140.90	–1,856.60	–5,053.80
Total Liabilities	179,140.60	172,920.20	174,930.80	206,630.30
Net Worth	65,803.20	56,043.10	67,019.20	54,197.60
Paid-up Equity Capital	2,996.60	3,113.50	3,554.70	3,554.70
Reserves and Surplus	61,856.60	52,929.20	64,390.10	51,424.40
Borrowings	73,294.80	76,012.20	66,773.30	87,332.40
Current Liabilities and Provisions	40,042.60	40,864.90	40,212.70	64,318.80
Total Assets	179,140.60	172,920.20	174,930.80	206,630.30
Net Fixed Assets	5,515.00	9,171.60	8,631.70	9,672.80
Investments	71,278.00	75,926.00	78,450.60	88,156.20
Current Assets	67,622.20	45,356.50	35,178.40	57,663.90
Loans and Advances	30,101.70	42,362.30	50,817.70	50,225.60

Source: Centre for Monitoring Indian Economy's Prowess Database.

power projects. The wind energy industry in India was expected to add another 15,000 MW during 2012–2017. The industry had grown rapidly in the past few years due to various incentives such as accelerated depreciation offered by the Government of India. However, some of the incentives were rolled back by the government in 2011. This limited the growth prospects and aggravated the situation for Suzlon, which had already been struggling due to a slowdown in overseas markets.[7]

[7] Vithlani and Singh, 'ENAM Securities India Research Report'.

TABLE M11.2
Cash Flow Statement of Suzlon Energy (₹ million)

	2009	2010	2011	2012
Net Cash Flow from Operating Activities	–3,703.80	21,070.60	7,248.50	5,443.60
Net Profit before Tax and Extraordinary Income	4,330.00	–7,996.50	–2,232.30	–1,498.40
Add: Adjustments for Non-cash and Non-operating Expenses	10,751.60	11,058.30	10,575.80	12,657.00
Depreciation	991.6	1,262.70	1,568.90	1,826.80
Amortization	70.4	84.6	22.9	19.8
Unrealized Foreign Exchange Losses	6.3	415.5		922.3
Other Provisions	5,882.10	2,745.50	3,126.20	1,992.00
Interest Paid	3,801.20	6,535.90	5,780.40	7,843.20
Loss on Sale of Assets		14.1	29.3	48.8
Other Non-Cash and Non-Operating Expenses			48	4.1
Less: Adjustments for Non-cash and Non-operating Income	1,527.90	2,229.00	3,357.80	3,470.60
Unrealized Foreign Exchange Gain			41.1	
Interest Income	1,224.30	2,227.90	2,927.40	3,466.70
Dividend Income	112.9	1.1	389.3	3.9
Profit on Sale of Investments	189.1			
Profit or Loss on Sale of Assets	1.6			
Operating Cash Flow before Working Capital Changes	13,553.70	832.8	4,985.70	7,688.00
Add: Cash Inflow Due to:	5,489.00	24,021.50	5,899.70	8,009.70
Decrease in Trade and Other Receivables		18,163.30	5,899.70	
Decrease in Inventories	996	5,858.20		
Increase in Trade and Other Payables	4,493.00			8,009.70
Less: Cash Outflow Due to:	16,641.80	656.1	3,947.10	10,172.10
Increase in Trade and Other Receivables	16,641.80			8,011.60
Increase in Inventories			2,171.50	2,160.50
Decrease in Trade and Other Payables		656.1	1,775.60	
Cash Flow Generated from Operations	2,400.90	24,198.20	6,938.30	5,525.60
Cash Outflow due to Direct Taxes Paid	644.1	77.5		82
Cash Outflow due to Dividend Tax Paid	243.9			
Cash Flow before Extraordinary Items	1,512.90	24,120.70	6,938.30	5,443.60
Cash Outflow due to Extraordinary Items	5,216.70	3,050.10		
Cash Inflow due to Extraordinary Items			310.2	

	2009	2010	2011	2012
Net Cash Inflow from Investing Activities	–35,831.80	–25,965.30	–7,515.20	–11,512.60
Less: Cash Outflow Due to Investing Activities	41,026.00	28,645.80	11,679.00	16,351.50
Add: Cash Inflow Due to Investing Activities	5,194.20	2,680.50	4,163.80	4,838.90
Net Cash Inflow or (Outflow) from Financing Activities	32,904.60	8,762.90	-3,136.30	7,399.10
Less: Cash Outflow Due to Financing Activities	5,627.30	28,809.00	13,082.00	8,585.10
Issue Expenses	50.5	163.8	93	130.9
Interest Paid	3,658.90	6,460.20	5,780.20	7,271.30
Dividend Paid	1,498.30			
Repayment of Borrowings	419.6	21,229.30	7,208.80	1,182.90
Repayment of Long-Term Liabilities	419.6	993.6	128.8	1,182.90
Repayment of Short-Term Liabilities		20,235.70	7,080.00	
Add: Cash Inflow from Financing Activities	38,531.90	37,571.90	9,945.70	15,984.20
Proceeds from Share Issue	1,019.40	5,231.30	10.1	
Proceeds from Borrowings	37,510.20	32,340.60	9,935.60	15,984.20
Proceeds from Long-Term Borrowings	8,900.00	32,340.60	9,935.60	9,562.70
Proceeds from Short-Term Borrowings	28,610.20			6,421.50
Net Increase or (Decrease) in Cash and Cash Equivalents	–6,631.00	3,868.20	–3,403.00	1,330.10

The Indian states of Tamil Nadu, Gujarat, Maharashtra, Karnataka and Rajasthan were among the leading states in terms of installed wind energy capacity. The quantum of energy generated from wind stood at 23.4BU in 2011–2012 registering a growth rate of 19.7 per cent since 2008.[8] Apart from generation, India was also a key player in the global wind energy equipment manufacturing. The wind power equipment production capacity stood at 8,000 MW in 2012. There were 19 wind turbine manufacturers in India and new companies were expected to enter the market. Vestas Wind Systems of Denmark was the industry leader. General Electric of the USA, Enercon of Germany and Gamesa Technologies of Spain occupied the next three positions. The top conventional power producers in India included NTPC, PGCIL, NHPC, Neyveli Lignite, Torrent Power and CESC. Power producers using coal and other fossil fuels such as oil and gas were exposed to fluctuations in not only the price of input but also the availability of input.[9] Wind energy, on the other hand, was more sustainable.

[8] e-Research and Publications India Private Limited, 'Renewable Energy Sector in India Report'.

[9] The Coalgate scandal in India concerned allocation of coal deposits to public and private enterprises. The Comptroller and Auditor General of India accused the government of inefficient allocation. In response to the report, the Supreme Court of India cancelled the mining rights given to several companies. As a result, coal-based power plants faced huge raw material supplies. Several of them had to temporarily shut down.

Tables M11.3 and M11.4 present key ratios for Suzlon and other power generation and equipment manufacturing companies.

OPERATING AND FINANCING HISTORY

Suzlon was known for its operational excellence and had received a number of awards such as the best manufacturer, best service provider and the best company in corporate social responsibility at the Wind India Conference held annually in India.[10] In 2006, the company expanded its geographical spread by signing a contract with Australian Gas Light (AGL) Company to manufacture the largest wind farm in Australia. It signed another contract with Tecnologias Energeticas (TECHNERIA) to build a high capacity turbine in Portugal. In December 2006, the company signed a turnkey contract with British Petroleum for setting up a 40 MW wind power plant in the Indian state of Maharashtra. In March 2007, it constructed a 2.1 MW turbine in Australia and a 150 MW plant for DLF Limited in India. To establish Suzlon as a key global player, Tulsi Tanti began acquiring key competitors worldwide. In 2006, Tanti acquired Hansen Transmissions of Belgium for US$565 million. The next year it made a bid for Germany's Repower AG.

Repower Acquisition

Repower was Germany's leading wind energy firm with forecasted revenues of €450 million in 2006. The company had established a strong presence in Europe and was seeking a position in China, India and the USA.

In January 2007, Areva S.A., the largest single shareholder of Repower Systems AG, declared its intention to acquire Repower and made an offer of €105 per share to its shareholders. The offer price was at a premium of 44 per cent to the three-month average stock price of Repower. However, soon after Areva's offer, Suzlon Windenergie GmbH, an affiliate of Suzlon, made a counter-offer at €126 per share (which corresponded to a premium of 72% to the three-month average stock price of Repower) and exceeded Areva's offer by 20 per cent. Suzlon Windenergie GmbH further revised its offer to €150 in response to the revised offer of €140 by Areva and completed the acquisition.[11] By May 2007, Suzlon had received 25.46 per cent of Repower's shares. Suzlon wanted to control 75 per cent of Repower and be the fourth largest wind turbine-maker after Eneron, ReGen Gamesa and Vestas. Suzlon ended up controlling 87.1 per cent of votes due to voting pool arrangements with Martifer and Areva. Upon announcement, Suzlon's stock price remained flat while the market rose marginally.

Suzlon hoped that the partnership with Repower would bolster Suzlon's R&D efforts. The combination was expected to not only bring together R&D and technology teams but also provide geographical expansion into European markets. In addition, the combined entity would be better positioned to make capital investments. The partnership would create products that were the most reliable with the best life cycle costs. Table M11.5 presents a forecast of free cash flow to equity shareholders of Repower.

[10] The information contained in this section is based on the company annual reports (http://www.suzlon.com/investors/annual_result.aspx?l1=6&l2=23&l3=42; accessed on 10 January 2019) and its website (www.suzlon.com; accessed on 10 January 2019).

[11] Reuters, 'India's Suzlon Energy Completes Repower Acquisition'.

TABLE M11.3
Key Ratios of Suzlon and Domestic Competitors

	Suzlon Energy Ltd						Bharat Heavy Electricals Ltd					
Year	2012	2011	2010	2009	2008	2007	2012	2011	2010	2009	2008	2007
Debt–Equity Ratio	1.23	1.14	1.23	0.77	0.4	0.23	0.01	0.01	0.01	0.01	0.01	0.04
Long-Term Debt–Equity Ratio	0.8	0.89	0.75	0.4	0.2	0.05	0	0.01	0.01	0.01	0.01	0.04
Current Ratio	0.84	1.23	1.36	1.49	1.93	2.12	1.78	1.56	1.37	1.4	1.45	1.47
Fixed Asset Turnover	4.27	3.12	3.07	8.54	10.29	11.12	5.66	6.02	5.86	5.89	5.07	4.78
Inventory Turnover	5.53	4.81	3.2	5.05	4.85	4.34	4.11	4.37	4.03	4.17	4.35	4.78
Debtors Turnover	2.4	1.65	0.9	1.8	2.62	3.03	2.16	2.16	1.89	2.04	2.01	2.27
Interest Cover Ratio	0.84	0.67	–0.09	1.98	12.52	12.03	201.9	165.54	197.73	158.89	126.08	87.22
EBDITA Margin (%)	13.45	13.65	1.72	13.22	26.48	24.06	22.19	21.82	20.47	18.3	21.92	21.31
EBIT Margin (%)	10.78	10.05	–1.9	11.85	25.23	22.69	20.6	20.58	19.14	17.13	20.55	19.87
EBDT Margin (%)	0.55	–1.45	–19.25	7.22	24.46	22.17	22.09	21.69	20.37	18.19	21.76	21.08
PAT Margin (%)	–2.21	–3.34	–29.69	6.83	21.95	19.72	14.01	13.66	12.46	11.01	13.16	12.7
ROCE (%)	0	3.28	–0.49	7.16	23.5	30.58	28.56	35.94	45.47	40.73	45.23	45.16
ROE (%)	0	–2.35	–17.01	7.31	28.55	32.61	30.93	33.33	29.88	26.47	29.23	30.02
Price Earning (P/E)	0	0	0	0	31.8	27.7	9.27	17.51	28.35	24.57	36.84	23.83
Price to Book Value (P/BV)	0.8	1.17	2	0.98	5.68	7.79	2.48	5.01	7.34	5.69	9.34	6.3
EV/EBIDTA	22.79	25.85	0	0	26.96	22.88	5.06	9.52	15.12	12.17	19.4	12.24
Market Cap/Sales	0.66	1.82	3.21	0.88	5.7	5.36	1.25	2.29	3.37	2.58	4.63	2.91

Source: Centre for Monitoring Indian Economy's Prowess Database.

TABLE M11.3
(*Continued*)

	Triveni Turbines Ltd						CESC Ltd					
	2012	2011	2010	2009	2008	2007	2012	2011	2010	2009	2008	2007
Debt–Equity Ratio	1.74	0	0	0	0	0	0.67	0.83	0.96	0.91	1.03	1.38
Long-Term Debt–Equity Ratio	1.13	0	0	0	0	0	0.51	0.73	0.9	0.85	0.93	1.29
Current Ratio	0.74	0.73	4.26	0.36	0.7	0.98	1.83	1.47	1.25	1.35	1.29	1.37
Fixed Asset Turnover	3.89	3.85	35.47	6.81	11.79	6.51	0.43	0.41	0.37	0.41	0.41	0.39
Inventory Turnover	7.59	6.55	25.13	8.25	8.08	6.51	16.16	15.93	14.9	15.91	16.47	14.94
Debtors Turnover	7.76	5.91	40.2	63.86	112.98	8.5	6.2	7.92	7.33	8.6	7.75	5.4
Interest Cover Ratio	13.12	12.42	0	–19.38	–8.41	23	3.04	2.83	3.22	3.41	3.22	2.64
EBITDA Margin (%)	23.74	22.95	–127.36	–21.92	–7.47	5.61	27.8	28.67	28.71	26.96	26.63	27.9
EBIT Margin (%)	22	21.08	–134	–23.21	–7.99	5.16	21.72	22.37	22.58	21.29	20.67	21.66
EBDT Margin (%)	22.07	21.25	–127.36	–23.12	–8.42	5.38	20.65	20.77	21.69	20.72	20.2	19.71
PAT Margin (%)	13.72	11.51	–125.87	–24.84	–8.72	2.02	11.65	11.51	12.92	13.27	12.56	11.88
ROCE (%)	138.36	0	0	0	0	76.67	10.33	11.1	10.71	10.82	11.62	12.68
ROE (%)	424.68	0	0	0	0	30	12.1	12.02	12.01	12.87	14.31	16.5
Price Earning (P/E)	18.02	0	0	0	0	0	6.28	8.13	11.3	6.58	14.91	10.86
Price to Book Value (P/BV)	23.88	0	0	0	0	0	0.72	0.93	1.28	0.79	1.75	1.62
EV/EBIDTA	10.15	0	0	0	0	0	4.25	4.98	7.65	5.52	8.93	7.09
Market Cap/Sales	2.37	0	0	0	0	0	0.72	0.92	1.43	0.85	1.83	1.27

Source: Centre for Monitoring Indian Economy's Prowess Database.

TABLE M11.4
Comparison with Broad Industry Peer Companies (Domestic and Global)

Panel A: Domestic Peer Group						
Year	2012	2011	2010	2009	2008	2007
No. of Companies	12	14	15	11	8	9
Debt–Equity Ratio	1.04	1.03	1.06	0.71	0.45	0.35
Long-Term Debt–Equity Ratio	1.01	0.86	0.67	0.38	0.22	0.12
Current Ratio	2.22	1.94	1.51	1.55	1.72	1.67
Fixed Assets Turnover	3.85	3.28	3.64	6.83	6.41	7.34
Inventory Turnover	4.83	4.69	4.37	5.6	4.55	5.08
Debtors Turnover	1.91	1.6	1.42	2.19	2.63	3.69
Interest Coverage Ratio	1.18	1.13	0.54	2.42	11.67	7.25
EBITDA Margin (%)	14.28	14.07	8.63	12.98	23.27	18.16
EBIT Margin (%)	12.05	11.54	6.23	11.7	22.08	16.85
EBDT Margin (%)	4.05	3.84	–2.97	8.15	21.37	15.83
PAT Margin (%)	0.84	1.38	–9.34	6.91	18.68	13.09
ROA (%)	6.72	5.45	2.85	8.62	21.69	28.43
ROE (%)	1	1.4	–9.25	8.88	26.61	29.85

Source: Centre for Monitoring Indian Economy's Prowess Database.

Panel B: Valuation Ratios of Global Peer Companies					
Gamesa Corp Tecnologica SA					
	2008	2009	2010	2011	2012
Price to Book Ratio	2.04	1.82	0.86	0.46	0.40
Price Earnings Ratio (P/E)	17.39	24.71	27.44	11.71	–
Market Cap to Revenue	0.802	0.8997	0.5125	0.2606	0.1562
Vestas Wind Systems A/S					
	2008	2009	2010	2011	2012
Price to Book Ratio	4.73	3.40	1.74	0.65	0.53
Price Earnings Ratio (P/E)	14.69	67.38	30.84	–	–
Market Cap to Revenue	1.24	1.70	0.69	0.28	0.11

Peer Group Averages (International)			
	2008	2009	2010
Price/Earnings	34.52	27.43	19.72
Price/Book Value	1.58	2.52	1.61
Market Cap/Sales	18.7	33.22	12.41

Source: Bloomberg.

TABLE M11.5
Forecast of Free Cash Flow to Equity of Repower (€)

	2008	2009	2010	2011	2012	Terminal Year
Sales	782,183,944.8	899,511,536.5	1,034,438,267	1,189,604,007	1,368,044,608	1,436,446,839
NOPAT/ Sales (%)	20	20	20	20	20	20
Depreciation/ Sales (%)	1	1	1	1	1	1
Capex/ Sales (%)	1.5	1.5	1.5	1.5	1.5	1.5
Δ Working Capital/ Sales (%)	15	15	15	15	15	15
Net Debt/ Sales (%)	–0.20	15	–0.20	–0.20	–0.20	–0.20
Free Cash Flow To Equity	33,633,910	175,404,750	44,480,845	51,152,972	58,825,918	61,767,214

Source: Case Writer.

The investment bankers for the transaction were ABN AMRO Bank, SBI and ICICI Bank. In February 2007, Suzlon and its associates entered into a credit arrangement with ABN AMRO Bank, wherein several tranches of debt were to be provided for funding the acquisition. The credit line was provided to cover the acquisition of 6,057,209 shares (amounting to €793,208,334) and transaction costs. This would increase the debt servicing burden from €669 million to €1,736 million.

After the Repower acquisition, Suzlon continued to consolidate its position by setting up subsidiaries and winning new orders throughout the world. In the ensuing years, Suzlon incurred capital expenditure amounting to ₹88.87 billion to fund the expansion.

Financing

Suzlon funded its acquisition by a combination of term loans from banks, non-convertible debentures, coupon-bearing and zero coupon FCCBs. During 2007–2012, the company issued FCCBs amounting to approximately US$760 million. Table M11.6 provides a snapshot of the company's financing programme.

Foreign Currency Convertible Bonds

An FCCB is a hybrid instrument that provides investors the option of converting the bond into equity shares on a specified date or after an initial lock-in period. The conversion price is usually set at a premium to the market price of the issuing company's stock at the time of issue.

TABLE M11.6
Financing History 2006–2012, Amounts Outstanding in ₹ million

Secured/ Unsecured	Instrument	2006	2007	2008	2009	2010	2011	2012
(a) Secured	12.5% Secured Redeemable Non-Convertible Debentures			0.0	3,000.0			
	Term loan							
	Banks	252.8	161.0	70.0	5,651.0	17,733.7	17,875.9	16,321.4
	Financial Institutions	1,373.1	1,061.8	150.6	148.4			14,020.6
	Others					6,094.1	1,436.4	
	Foreign Currency							
	Working Capital Facilities							
	Rupee Loans	1,140.2	4,015.8	983.5	20,556.7	12,616.3	8,815.1	
	Foreign Currency Loans	0.0	2,479.2	5,518.5	10,706.2	2,467.5	2,940.0	
(b) Unsecured								
Long-Term	Zero Coupon Convertible Bonds			20,055.0	25,355.0			
	Foreign Currency Convertible Bonds					21,508.9	21,362.7	13,481.9
	Term Loans							
	Banks					1,453.2	11,840.3	
	Financial Institutions	293.4	203.2	111.2	69.3			
	Loans & Advances							1,450
Short-Term	Banks	0.0	3,445.4	3,958.6	7,245.7	1.4	0.0	18,887.6
	Financial Institutions	294.2	0.0	0.0	562.5	3,750.0	0.0	

Source: Company Annual Reports.

Convertible bonds were popular among issuers because they carried lower coupon rate as compared to straight bonds and provided a possibility of accretion to share capital in the event of conversion of bonds into equity shares. FCCBs did not involve front-end equity dilution as is the case with equity shares. Investors found convertible bonds attractive because these instruments allowed investors to benefit from the upside potential of the company while retaining the safety of debt. These instruments carried attractive yields to maturity. As far as taxation was concerned, interest payments on bonds (until the conversion option was exercised) were subject to a withholding tax of 10 per cent. Dividends on the converted portion of the bond were subject to deduction of tax at source at the rate of 10 per cent. Investors were not liable to capital gains tax in India when FCCBs were converted into shares.

During 2004–2006, Indian companies mobilized US$10.6 billion by issuing FCCBs. Indian companies were able to issue FCCBs at low coupon rates. Out of the 78 issues made during 2004–2006, 41 were zero coupon bonds and another 26 carried coupon rates of less than 2 per cent.[12] The YTM on FCCBs, however, ranged between 4–8.5 per cent with an average of 6.1 per cent.[13] Most FCCBs were priced to yield 5–7 per cent. YTMs on FCCBs were favourable compared to straight debt issues. The coupon on FCCBs was 30–40 per cent less compared to straight bonds, foreign currency loans and external commercial borrowings. This translated into cost savings of 2–3 per cent p.a. One-third of the issuers could raise funds at yields lower than the sovereign yield. FCCBs carried fewer covenants than syndicated loans and debentures. Hence, these were more convenient to issuers.[14]

In most cases, the conversion price embedded in the bond involved a substantial premium to the market price at the time of issue. On average, FCCB issues commanded a premium of 44 per cent. FCCB bondholders who chose not to convert would receive the principal at an exchange rate fixed at the time of the issue.

As interest rate on foreign debt was considerably lower than the benchmark prime lending rate in India, it made sense for Indian firms to borrow in a foreign currency when the domestic currency strengthened relative to the foreign currency. This resulted in lower cash outflows due to interest and principal payments. Most FCCBs were denominated in US$. The bonds were mainly listed in Singapore, Luxembourg, London and Hong Kong.

During 2003–2007, the Indian stock market was experiencing a cyclical bull run. Indian FCCBs provided an attractive investment opportunity to international investors who were looking for international diversification opportunities without being exposed to emerging market equity risks.

FCCBs denominated in US$ appealed to Suzlon because its revenues were also mostly denominated in US$. In 2009, Suzlon had foreign exchange earnings of ₹41.115 billion and foreign currency expenses of ₹37.541 billion. Suzlon's coupon-bearing bonds carried a semi-annual interest rate of 7.5 per cent and a redemption premium ranging up to 150 per cent of the principal amount. These bonds were listed in Singapore. Top global corporations such as Tata Motors, Tata Steel, Reliance Communications and Larsen & Toubro were among the biggest issuers of FX converts.[15] Table M11.7 presents the details of FCCBs issued by Suzlon and the stock market reaction to securities issued by it.

Indian companies treated FCCBs as pure debt instruments. The income statements of companies did not account for debt service when they issued zero coupon convertibles. In case of coupon-bearing bonds, debt service was generally charged directly to reserves rather than to the income statement, thereby overstating profits and EPS. This was an anomaly in the accounting treatment.

Apart from FCCBs and term loans, Suzlon had issued 207,565,299 shares at a price of ₹61 on a rights basis to its existing shareholders to raise ₹3,528.60 million in June 2010. In the previous year, it had issued global depository receipts (GDR) at a price of US$7.40 per GDR to raise US$108.04 million.

Suzlon had a dedicated treasury team monitoring the foreign exchange fluctuations with the objective of minimizing the impact of adverse currency fluctuations. Exposures were managed and hedged on contractual basis. It used forward and option contracts to hedge its foreign exchange risk. However, the zero coupon convertible bonds issued in 2007 were 'unhedged'. So were debtors, creditors, loans given and received, and bank balances. These amounted to ₹24 billion in 2008 and ₹80 billion in

[12] Hajra and Sawant, 'FCCBs and Financial Position of Indian Companies'.

[13] In most cases, a redemption premium is payable at maturity if the bond is not converted. Redemption premiums ranged from 5 per cent to 60 per cent.

[14] Banka, S, 'Foreign Currency Convertible Bonds'.

[15] Nathwani and Sridhar, *Impact of Global Economic Meltdown on FCCBs Issued by Indian Companies*.

TABLE M11.7
Details of FX Convertibles Issued by Suzlon

Instrument Name	Currency/Amount	Issue Date	Maturity Date	Issue Price	Coupon/ Frequency	Convertible	Conversion Price	Conversion Dates	Floor Price	Redemption at Maturity	Name of Exchange
Panel A: FCCB Issues											
Convertible Bonds	US$35,592.000 Face Value US$1,000	8 May 2009	June 2012	100%	7.50% Semi-annual 12 June/ 12 Dec	Yes 100% Equity Shares of Par Value ₹10	₹76.6755 per share	18 June 2009–5 June 2012	₹62.0125	150.24% of the principal amount	SGX-ST
Convertible Bonds	US$20,796,000 Face Value US$1,000	8 May 2009	Oct 2012	100%	7.5% Semi-annual 11 April/ 11 Oct	Yes 100% Equity Shares of Par Value ₹10	₹76.6755 per share	18 June 2009–4 Oct 2012	₹62.0125	157.72% of the principal amount	SGX-ST
Zero Coupon Convertible Bonds	US$200,000,000 Face Value US$1,000	10 Oct 2007	11 Oct 2012	100%	Zero Coupon	Yes 100% Equity Shares of Par Value ₹10	₹1,859.40 per share	20 Nov 2007–4 Oct 2012	₹1,102.99	144.48% of the principal amount	SGX-ST
Zero Coupon Convertible Bonds	US$300,000,000 Face Value US$1,000	11 June 2007	12 June 2012	100%	Zero Coupon	Yes 100% Equity Shares of Par Value ₹10	₹1,800.00 per share	22 July 2007–5 June 2012	₹1,102.99	145.23% of the principal amount	SGX-ST
FCCB	US$ 200,000,000	21 Sept 2007	22 Sept 2012	100%	YTM 7.55% semi-annual	Yes 100% Equity Shares of Par Value ₹10	₹1,859.40 per share	20 Sept 2007–1 Oct 2012		130% of principal	SGX-ST
Zero Coupon Convertible Bonds	US$ 90,000,000	24 July 2009	25 July 2014	104.30%	Zero Coupon	Yes 100% Equity Shares of Par Value ₹2	₹90.38 per share	2 Sept 2009–18 July 2014	₹89.525	134.198% of the principal amount	SGX-ST

(Continued)

TABLE M11.7
(Continued)

Panel B: Stock Market Reaction to Security Issues		
Announcement Date	Instrument	Nifty Index Adjusted Return (%)
16 May 2007	FCCB	−1.04
21 September 2007	FCCB	−4.55
21 July 2009	GDR	−3.27
	ZCCB	

Source: Company Annual Reports.

2009.[16] Table M11.8 presents historical interest rates, inflation rates in Indian Rupee and US$, and exchange rates between the two currencies.

Operating and Financial Performance

In 2008, Suzlon's turbine blades developed cracks in the USA. This adversely affected orders from the USA and hence sales.[17] The Global Financial Crisis of 2008 led to a tight credit situation. This hurt Suzlon particularly more because it purchased Repower at stretched valuations. Due to competition from Enercon, ReGen, Gamesa and Vestas, Suzlon's market share fell from 58 per cent in 2008 to 35 per cent in 2012.[18] At its peak in 2007–2008, Suzlon had a net income of ₹10,170 million. In FY 2010 and FY 2011, it incurred losses of ₹9,820 million and ₹10.96 billion. However, in 2012, the company managed to reduce its losses to ₹4,780 million. The company's long-term debt had been downgraded from AA in 2009 to BBB in 2012 in line with the company's deteriorating financial position.

On 15 February 2010, due to poor financial performance, Suzlon announced its intention to reduce conversion prices of its US$300 million zero coupon bonds issued in June 2007 and US$200 million zero coupon convertible bonds issued in October 2007. On 18 May 2010, convertible bondholders agreed to:[19]

- Remove financial covenants
- Effect a reduction in (a) the conversion price of the US$300 million zero coupon convertible bonds from ₹359.68 per equity share to ₹97.26 per equity share, and (b) the conversion price of the US$200 million zero coupon convertible bonds from ₹371.55 per equity share to ₹97.26 per equity share
- Set the fixed exchange rate at US$1 = ₹44.60 and replace the respective fixed exchange rates in the terms and conditions of the US$300 million zero coupon convertible bonds due in June 2012 and US$200 million zero coupon convertible bonds due in October 2012.

[16] In 2009, Suzlon had foreign exchange earnings of ₹41.115 billion and foreign currency expenses of ₹37.541 billion.
[17] Stromsta, *Cracked Turbine Blades Drag Suzlon to Q3 Losses.*
[18] PANCHABUTA, *₹110 Billion Debt.*
[19] Suzlon Press Release, 18 May 2010, http://www.suzlon.com/media_center/press_release.aspx?l1=7&l2=31 (accessed in July 2015).

TABLE M11.8
Historical (Monthly) Inflation, Interest Rates and Exchange Rates, 2007–2012

Date	90-Day Rupee Lending Rate (%)	90-Day Euro Dollar Rate (%)	India CPI Inflation Rate (%)	US CPI Inflation Rate (%)	Forward Ex Rate 90-day (₹/US$)	Spot Exchange Rate (₹/US$)
Dec 2012	8.92	0.3095	11.17	–0.04	55.53	54.99
Nov 2012	8.73	0.311	9.55	–0.2	55.27	54.26
Oct 2012	8.66	0.3305	9.6	0.24	54.67	53.81
Sep 2012	8.81	0.3856	9.14	0.49	53.54	52.86
Aug 2012	8.95	0.4323	10.31	0.51	56.42	55.53
Jul 2012	9.24	0.4536	9.84	–0.02	56.73	55.65
Jun 2012	9.41	0.4656	10.05	–0.03	56.46	55.64
May 2012	9.78	0.4665	10.16	–0.13	57.48	56.11
Apr 2012	9.64	0.4668	10.22	0.2	53.76	52.74
Mar 2012	11.09	0.4733	8.65	0.26	51.88	50.88
Feb 2012	10.28	0.5032	7.57	0.21	50.28	49.02
Jan 2012	9.91	0.5659	5.32	0.25	50.54	49.46
Dec 2011	9.84	0.5557	6.49	–0.02	54.57	53.06
Nov 2011	9.63	0.4753	9.34	0.17	52.61	52.21
Oct 2011	9.57	0.4065	9.39	0.04	49.49	48.69
Sep 2011	9.51	0.3502	10.06	0.23	50.08	48.97
Aug 2011	9.5	0.2932	8.99	0.26	46.45	46.1
Jul 2011	9.41	0.2499	8.43	0.25	44.57	44.19
Jun 2011	9.43	0.2478	8.62	0.03	45.18	44.7
May 2011	9.7	0.2607	8.72	0.38	45.59	45.06
Apr 2011	9.06	0.2814	9.41	0.49	44.94	44.22
Mar 2011	10.15	0.3084	8.82	0.51	45.26	44.58
Feb 2011	9.66	0.3119	8.82	0.33	46.02	45.27
Jan 2011	9.3	0.3034	9.3	0.29	46.7	45.9
Dec 2010	9	0.3027	9.47	0.41	45.3	44.71
Nov 2010	8.19	0.2869	8.33	0.24	46.54	45.88
Oct 2010	7.85	0.2888	9.7	0.34	44.97	44.43
Sep 2010	7.49	0.2914	9.82	0.12	45.4	44.94
Aug 2010	6.9	0.3626	9.88	0.15	47.72	47.08
Jul 2010	6.53	0.5103	11.25	0.18	47.02	46.41

(Continued)

TABLE M11.8
(Continued)

Date	90-Day Rupee Lending Rate (%)	90-Day Euro Dollar Rate (%)	India CPI Inflation Rate (%)	US CPI Inflation Rate (%)	Forward Ex Rate 90-day (₹/US$)	Spot Exchange Rate (₹/US$)
Jun 2010	6.5	0.5369	13.73	-0.01	47.31	46.45
May 2010	5.33	0.4585	13.91	-0.04	46.75	46.37
Apr 2010	5.01	0.3116	13.33	0.03	44.67	44.37
Mar 2010	5.69	0.2684	14.86	0.02	45.12	44.92
Feb 2010	4.97	0.2505	14.86	-0.1	46.3	46.08
Jan 2010	4.59	0.2501	16.22	0.05	46.46	46.18
Dec 2009	4.6	0.2531	14.97	0.05	46.78	46.53
Nov 2009	4.44	0.2681	13.51	0.33	46.59	46.51
Oct 2009	4.61	0.2831	11.49	0.3	47.51	46.97
Sep 2009	4.67	0.298	11.64	0.19	47.96	48.11
Aug 2009	4.58	0.4245	11.72	0.33	48.75	48.83
Jul 2009	4.52	0.5153	11.89	–0.03	48.19	47.94
Jun 2009	4.72	0.6207	9.29	0.83	48.44	47.9
May 2009	5.29	0.8166	8.63	0.15	47.45	47.09
Apr 2009	5.64	1.1062	8.7	0.1	50.17	50.09
Mar 2009	7.64	1.2667	8.03	–0.1	51.69	50.73
Feb 2009	7.64	1.2426	9.63	0.36	52.44	51.16
Jan 2009	7.83	1.2108	10.45	0.25	49.76	48.88
Dec 2008	8.89	1.8294	9.7	–0.82	49.9	48.8
Nov 2008	10.43	2.2791	10.45	–1.77	52.32	50.11
Oct 2008	11.73	4.0586	10.45	–0.86	51.95	49.46
Sep 2008	11.86	3.1217	9.77	0.09	47.63	46.96
Aug 2008	11.22	2.8063	9.02	–0.15	44.45	43.94
Jul 2008	10.39	2.7921	8.33	0.71	43.13	42.57
Jun 2008	9.94	2.7654	7.69	1.05	43.91	43.04
May 2008	8.87	2.6924	7.75	0.59	42.32	42.46
Apr 2008	8.77	2.7947	7.81	0.23	40.82	40.49
Mar 2008	9.82	2.7825	7.87	0.36	40.17	40.12
Feb 2008	9.61	3.0876	5.47	0.24	40.13	40.01
Jan 2008	8.54	3.9176	5.51	0.34	39.56	39.37
Dec 2007	8.56	4.9794	5.51	0.29	39.6	39.41

(Continued)

Date	90-Day Rupee Lending Rate (%)	90-Day Euro Dollar Rate (%)	India CPI Inflation Rate (%)	US CPI Inflation Rate (%)	Forward Ex Rate 90-day (₹/US$)	Spot Exchange Rate (₹/US$)
Nov 2007	8.5	4.9621	5.51	0.79	39.9	39.6
Oct 2007	7.9	5.1465	5.51	0.31	39.41	39.33
Sep 2007	8.45	5.4939	6.4	0.42	39.91	39.85
Aug 2007	8.47	5.4837	7.26	0.03	41.4	40.93
Jul 2007	7.54	5.3597	6.45	0.18	40.63	40.37
Jun 2007	9.31	5.3593	5.69	0.23	40.98	40.72
May 2007	9.72	5.3595	6.61	0.41	40.67	40.61
Apr 2007	11.12	5.3555	6.67	0.3	41.69	41.18
Mar 2007	11.65	5.3479	6.72	0.52	43.61	43.47
Feb 2007	10.22	5.3598	7.56	0.39	44.75	44.29
Jan 2007	9.19	5.3601	6.72	0.17	44.38	44.18

Source: Bloomberg Database.

In 2012, Suzlon had debt amounting to more than ₹110 billion (US$2 billion). It needed US$360 million in June and US$206 million in October to redeem the FCCBs. Its high leverage, high financing costs and repeated business losses left very little cash to redeem the bonds. It had to urgently raise US$360 million before foreign currency convertible bonds matured in June 2012. The bondholders approved the proposal for a 45-day extension. The company had to arrange funds to pay the bondholders by 27 July. In 2012 alone, the company was obligated to repay debt amounting to ₹39.2 billion (US$700 million) and had to pay another US$250 million in the next financial year. To infuse equity capital, Suzlon had to either get the banks to restructure debt or sell its equity interest in Repower or merge Repower with itself[20] or sell its non-critical assets such as the wind farm in India or China. The sale of non-critical assets, however, was expected to fetch only US$100 million. The company's stock price fell from a high of ₹446 in January 2008 to ₹19.75 in July 2012 to reflect these concerns. At that valuation, the company's debt was three times its market capitalization of ₹35 billion. Figure M11.1 presents historical stock prices and Table M11.9 presents a timeline of events from 2007 to 2012.

CORPORATE DEBT RESTRUCTURING IN INDIA

Under the bankruptcy procedure in the USA, the debtor retains the possession of assets and operates the business under the supervision of a bankruptcy court. The debtor has a fiduciary responsibility towards the creditors. A trustee is appointed to oversee the business when the debtor is ineffective. This type of insolvency code was absent in India. The government was yet to bring out a legislation to deal with bankruptcies. The corporate restructuring mechanism in India left the responsibility of debt

[20] Repower was debt free and had cash balances of approximately ₹15,000 million.

FIGURE M11.1
Stock Price Chart (in ₹)

Source: Case Writer.

restructuring to banks themselves. In 2011, in order to protect the interests of lenders to firms in distress, the Reserve Bank of India (India's central bank) issued guidelines relating to CDR to be implemented by banks. The CDR was a voluntary non-statutory system which was based on the DCA and ICA. The arrangement provided for multi-banking accounts, syndication or consortium accounts, wherein all banks and institutions together could have an outstanding exposure of ₹100 million or more.

DCA had a legal binding on both the debtor and the creditor(s) to not take a recourse to any legal action during the period of the contract and take a 'standstill' position.

CDR in India had a three-tier structure comprising of a standing forum, an empowered group (EG) and a CDR cell.

- On the top of this three-tier system was the CDR forum, which was a representative general body comprising of chief executives of commercial banks and financial institutions. It laid down policies and guidelines to be followed by the other two tiers in debt restructuring.
- The second tier was the EG, which screened the preliminary reports of all cases reported by the CDR cell and deliberated on the individual cases of corporate structuring. After it concluded the

TABLE M11.9
Timeline of Events[21]

2 March 2007	Announced the acquisition of Repower Systems AG, Germany
16 May 2007	Launched US$300 million FCCBs with a tenor of five years and one day at a conversion premium of 59.59% and YTM of 7.6%
3 June 2007	Made an offer to acquire the entire outstanding equity share capital of Repower Systems AG to increase the equity stake from 33.85% to 100%
21 September 2007	Launched US$200 million FCCBs with a tenor of five years and one day at a conversion premium of 59.59% and YTM of 7.6%
11 October 2007	Company was awarded the Euromoney and Ernst & Young Global Renewable Energy Award for 'M&A of the Year' for the successful acquisition of Repower Systems AG of Germany
20 December 2007	Allotted 11,386,000 equity shares of ₹10/- each for cash at an issue price of ₹1,917 per equity share (inclusive of premium) aggregating to ₹21,827 million to the selected qualified institutional buyers (QIBs) pursuant to qualified institutional placement
6 June 2008	Signed a share purchase agreement with Areva for acquisition of Areva's total stake of approximately 30% in Repower Systems AG
6 June 2009	Increased the equity stake in Repower to 90.72% by purchasing shares held by Martifer with a final payment of ₹87.6 million
20 July 2009	The Securities Issue Committee of the Board of Directors of the Company was authorized to decide on the terms for appropriate mode of further issue of equity shares, GDRs, ADRs, FCCBS and/or any other security convertible into or linked to equity shares to the extent of ₹50 billion
21 July 2009	The issue of GDRs was priced on 21 July 2009 for a total amount US$108.04 million comprising of 14,600,000 GDRs. The price per GDR was fixed at US$7.40. Each GDR would represent four equity shares of the Company A fresh issue of US$90.00 million zero coupon convertible bonds was priced on 21 July 2009 for a total amount of US$93.87 million (issue price of 104.3%) and the initial conversion price was set at ₹90.38 per share The Company raised a total amount of US$201.91 million through both the issuances
19 November 2009	AE-Rotor Holding B.V. (AERH), Netherlands, a wholly owned subsidiary of Suzlon Energy Ltd, announced its intention to sell approximately 35% equity interest in Hansen Transmissions International NV, Belgium
15 February 2010	Announced the intention to reduce the conversion prices of its US$300 million zero coupon convertible bonds issued on 11 June 2007 and due June 2012 and US$200 million zero coupon convertible bonds issued on 10 October 2007 and due October 2012
18 May 2010	FX convertible bondholders agreed to: • Removal of financial covenants • effect a reduction in (a) the conversion price of the US$300 million zero coupon convertible bonds due June 2012 from ₹359.68 per equity share to ₹97.26 per equity share, and

(Continued)

[21] The timeline of events has been constructed by the information contained in company press releases (available at http://www.suzlon.com/media_center/press_release.aspx?l1=7&l2=31) on the respective dates.

TABLE M11.9
(Continued)

	(b) the conversion price of the US$200 million zero coupon convertible bonds due October 2012 from ₹371.55 per equity share to ₹97.26 per equity share • Revise the floor price in respect of the US$300 million zero coupon convertible bonds due June 2012 and the US$200 million zero coupon convertible bonds due October 2012 to ₹74.025 per equity share • The fixed exchange rate was set at US$1=₹44.6000 and replaced the respective fixed exchange rates in the terms and conditions of the US$300 million zero coupon convertible bonds due June 2012 and the US$200 million zero coupon convertible bonds due October 2012
6 July 2010	Tanti, Chairman and Managing Director, Suzlon Energy Limited, was conferred the title, 'Wind Visionary of Asia' during an international consultation—'Quantum Leap in Wind Power in Asia' held at the ADB headquarters in Manila, Philippines
18 May 2012	Sought an extension of 45 days to make the interest payment
18 September 2012	Notices to FX convertible bondholders were sent to grant an extension of maturity dates of each of the series of bonds from 11 October 2012 to 11 February 2013. The meetings of the holders of the bonds were proposed to be held on 10 October 2012
3 October 2012	Company issued a subsequent notice providing further information in relation to the incentive fee payable to holders of the bonds who consented to the proposed extension
10 October 2012	Bondholders did not approve extension of maturities. The company announced that it was actively engaged with key stakeholders to find a consensual solution Company defaulted on payment to FX convertible bondholders
29 October 2012	Initiated discussions with its senior secured lenders to restructure its debt with a maturity period of 10 years under the CDR mechanism, including a two-year moratorium on principal and interest payments on term debt

Source: Company Press Releases (various dates).

feasibility of the project, it along with the CDR cell prepared a detailed restructuring package. This task was to be completed within 90 days or a maximum of 180 days of reference to EG.

- The third tier—the CDR cell—issued the Letter of Approval (LOA), once the restructuring plan was approved and confirmed by the EG. The lenders were required to approve the restructuring plan within 45 days from the issue of LOA and execute the restructuring within next 45 days.

THE 2012 RESTRUCTURING

Suzlon defaulted on payment to FX convertible bondholders as bondholders did not agree to further extend the maturity dates. On 28 October 2012, the company commenced its discussions on CDR with its senior lenders. Suzlon requested an extended maturity period of up to 10 years, and a moratorium on the interest and principal payments for the next two years. The consortium of 19 domestic banks went through the CDR mechanism outlined earlier and approved the company's debt restructuring package of ₹95 billion (US$1.8 billion). The package included (a) two-year moratorium on interest and principal payments, (b) 3 per cent reduction in interest rates and (c) six-month moratorium on working capital interest. Further, to bring financial stability, US$270 million of two years' interest payments during moratorium was to be converted into equity over the next two years. The package included a 10-year end-to-end back-ended repayment plan. It also included increased working capital facilities of ₹18 billion (US$350 million) which would allow the company to accelerate the execution of its order book. The founders were required to bring in an additional equity of ₹2,500 million (US$50 million). As a consequence, Suzlon was to consolidate by selling few of its overseas subsidiaries. It was required to open an escrow account with the SBI. Suzlon appointed SBI Capital Markets (the investment banking unit of the SBI) to advise the company on the debt recast. In order to deal with distress, Suzlon could sell non-core assets that would fetch US$100 million or sell equity shares to the public or sell off its shareholding in Repower. It was not clear if any of these was a viable alternative.

Exercises

1. Is restructuring necessary?
2. Why is Suzlon in distress?
3. Was the purchase price paid to Repower high? You may answer this question by undertaking multiples and DCF valuation of Repower.
   In your valuation of Repower, assume the following:

R^f	= German 10-year Eurobond Rate = 3.81 per cent
Beta	= 0.88
Germany's Risk Premium	= 5.28 per cent[22]
Number of Outstanding Shares	= 8,993,576
Profit after Tax in 2007	= €7,053,555
Equity in 2007	= €187,829,789

4. Why did Suzlon choose to issue FX convertibles? In which currency has it been cheaper to borrow during 2007–2012?
5. What were the options for Suzlon in dealing with financial distress?
6. As a lender, would you approve the restructuring? Why or why not?

[22] Dimson, Marsh and Staunton, *The Worldwide Equity Premium.*

REFERENCES

Banka, S. 'Foreign Currency Convertible Bonds'. *The Chartered Accountant* (2005 November).

Dimson, Elroy, Paul Marsh and Mike Staunton. *The Worldwide Equity Premium: A Smaller Puzzle* (7 April 2006). Available at http://papers.ssrn.com/sol3/papers.cfm?abstract_id=891620 (accessed on 10 January 2019).

e-Research and Publications India Private Limited. 'Renewable Energy Sector in India Report'. Tamil Nadu: e-Research and Publications India Private Limited.

Government of India, Ministry of Power. 'Report of the Working Group on Power for Twelfth Plan' (2012 January). Available at http://planningcommission.gov.in/aboutus/committee/wrkgrp12/wg_power1904.pdf accessed in July 2015 (accessed on 10 January 2019).

Hajra, S. and P. Sawant. 'FCCBs and Financial Position of Indian Companies' (Anand Rathi Research Report, 2006 November).

Nathwani, A. and C. Sridhar. *Impact of Global Economic Meltdown on FCCBs Issued by Indian Companies* (CRISIL Research).

Netscribes. 'Wind Energy Sector Update' (Report, 2012). Gurugram: Netscribes.

PANCHABUTA. *₹110 Billion Debt: Can Suzlon Energy Weather the Big Storm?* Available at http://panchabuta.com/2012/07/08/rs-110-billion-debt-can-suzlon-energy-weather-the-big-storm/ (accessed on 10 January 2019).

Reuters. *India's Suzlon Energy Completes Repower Acquisition* (2 June 2007). Available at https://uk.reuters.com/article/repower-suzlon/indias-suzlon-energy-completes-repower-acquisition-idUKBOM474320070602 (accessed on 10 January 2019).

Stromsta, Karl-Erik. *Cracked Turbine Blades Drag Suzlon to Q3 Losses* (2 February 2009). Available at http://www.rechargenews.com/wind/article1277834.ece (accessed on 10 January 2019).

Suzlon. *Suzlon Group Announces Formal Approval of Corporate Debt Restructuring Proposal* (24 January 2013). Available at https://www.suzlon.com/press-release-detail/134/suzlon-group-announces-formal-approval-of-corporate-debt-restructuring-cdr-proposal (accessed on 10 January 2019).

Suzlon. (Suzlon Press Release, 18 May 2010). Available at https://www.suzlon.com/press-release-detail/87/suzlon-group-to-supply-98mw-to-mytrah-energy.

Vithlani, B. and C. Singh. 'ENAM Securities India Research Report' (29 May 2012). Pune: Suzlon.

12

Lanco Infratech Limited

LEARNING OBJECTIVE

The case can be used to teach factors that drive restructuring initiatives, the dangers of unhedged foreign currency exposures and the design of capital structure in utilities.

Description: The case highlights the ambitious growth strategy of Lanco Infratech Ltd (LITL), one of the top infrastructure and energy companies in India. The company grew aggressively by setting up power projects and bidding for infrastructure projects all over India. This expansion was funded by a mix of secured loans and foreign currency term loans. Due to deteriorating business and economic conditions, the company experienced a sharp decline in profitability and stock price resulting in financial distress. The company had to restructure to escape bankruptcy. The case asks students to analyse the company's operating and financial strategy and assess whether the proposed restructuring is sustainable.

On 10 August 2017, the National Company Law Tribunal admitted insolvency proceedings against Lanco Infratech Ltd (LITL), one of the 12 firms referred to the Tribunal following a directive by the Reserve Bank of India.[1] The insolvency petition was moved by IDBI Bank, one of the lenders to the company. Once a petition was admitted, a six-month moratorium period was provided to decide on a resolution plan in accordance with the Insolvency and Bankruptcy Code, 2016. During this period, the Board would be suspended and an interim insolvency resolution professional took charge. The existing proceedings against the borrower would be suspended. This moratorium could be extended up to 270 days. IDBI had granted loans amounting to ₹12,340 million under a prior master restructuring agreement in 2013. In addition, the Bank had also sanctioned a long-term working capital term loan of ₹1,700 million. As of 15 June 2017, LITL had defaulted on principal and interest payments amounting to ₹2,349.6 million. At the time of filing of the insolvency petition, LITL had an outstanding debt of ₹83 billion. It had an operating portfolio of more than 3,400 MW and was

[1] India's central bank.

constructing projects to generate 4,600 MW. The group was executing three coal-based power projects of 1,320 MW and two hydropower projects totalling 576 MW to which the lenders had a combined exposure of more than ₹280 billion. Macroeconomic and sectoral issues affected the performance of the company after 2012. Several under-construction projects were stranded for more than four years because of which there was a substantial increase in cost of these projects primarily due to interest during construction and Indian Rupee depreciation. In response to the insolvency petition, the company opined that a simultaneous resolution of LITL and the under-construction projects would be the best option for maximizing recovery for lenders not just in LITL but also the under-construction projects. At this stage, it was not clear whether the company would sink or swim and lenders, in general, and IDBI in particular, had to decide whether to accept LITL's proposal.

COMPANY BACKGROUND

LITL was a conglomerate involved in EPC, power, real estate, solar energy and natural resources. It was founded by Lagadapati Amarappa Naidu.[2] Lagadapati Madhusudhan Rao, one of his nephews, was the executive chairman. It was headquartered in Gurgaon close to New Delhi. LITL went public in November 2006 following an IPO of shares. LITL's gross revenue as on 31 March 2016 was ₹99.99 billion (about US$1.51 billion). The company's expertise was in building large civic and urban infrastructure projects, which it had extended to constructing thermal and hydropower projects across the country. LITL was one of the leading private sector power developers in India with 3,460 MW under operation and 4,636 MW under construction. In order to provide fuel security for its current power generating assets and its future power portfolio expansions, LITL, through its Australian subsidiary, Lanco Resources Australia, had acquired Griffin Coal Mining Company and Carpenter Mine Management. Griffin Coal owned the largest operational thermal coal mines in Western Australia, producing around 4 million tonnes per annum (mtpa) of coal which could be increased up to 18 mtpa in the near term. LITL had strategic global partnerships with leading power companies such as Genting, Harbin, GE, Dongfang Electric and Doosan. With an employee strength of over 3,734 people, LITL had a pan-India presence in strategic locations and was expanding its footprint in emerging markets.

The company diversified from construction to power generation in the early 1990s to capitalize on the opportunities provided by the liberalization of the Indian economy. In 1995, the Andhra Pradesh state government opened the power sector to private players. LITL entered the power sector against a power purchase agreement with the state government with a 368 MW gas power plant in Kondapalli, near Vijayawada in Andhra Pradesh. The plant was commissioned in 2000. Lanco Kondapalli Power Ltd (LKPL) was a joint venture between LITL and the Genting group of Malaysia. Over the next five years, LITL consolidated its position in the power sector by commissioning large projects, winning bids for several others and winning a range of business and industry awards such as the 8th Annual Construction World Award for Fastest Growing Construction Company and Golden Peacock Occupational Health & Safety Award. The completed projects included 2 × 600 MW Lanco Anpara Power Limited, 2 × 600 MW Udupi Power Corp Limited, 120 MW Lanco Tanjore Power Company Ltd, a gas-based combined cycle power plant located at Karuppur village of Tanjore district in Tamil Nadu. It had another 7,000+ MW of capacity under construction and 10,000+ MW under development and was heading towards successful completion of its vision of 15,000+ MW by 2015. The EPC business had orders worth more than

[2] Lanco is an acronym for **L**agadapati **A**marappa **N**aidu and **Co**mpany. The information on the company's background is from the company's website http://www.lancogroup.com

TABLE M12.1
Income Statement (In ₹10 million)

Year	2009	2010	2011	2012	2013	2014	2015	2016
Sales	4,051.24	5,797.94	5,793.56	8,591.78	4,729.41	2,229.9	1,388.83	2,671.34
Other Income	15.06	56.96	106.39	64.26	81.64	102.97	234.94	158.22
Total Income	4,097.65	5,998.21	5,915.15	8,669.25	4,822.75	2,339.37	1,630.46	2,829.56
Total Expenditure	3,515.48	5,020.4	5,085.03	7,956.43	4,084.71	2,554.39	1,454.5	2,239.06
Raw Material Consumed	3,548.95	0	0	5,413.94	0	1,798.46	764.67	1,323.47
Stock Adjustment	–276.55	73.82	–341.15	–207.73	–342.99	–151.47	3.65	67.74
Purchase of Finished Goods	9.24	0	0	49.82	289.06	0	0	143.39
Employee Expenses	160.19	272.98	416.47	507.91	365.66	185.6	181.51	205.28
Other Expenses	73.65	4673.6	1,842.46	191.25	3,576.69	127.76	102.33	–21.18
EBDIT	582.17	977.81	830.12	712.82	738.04	–215.02	175.96	590.5
Interest	138.61	197.94	337.74	505.12	600.32	627.73	772.31	932.53
EBDT	443.56	779.87	492.38	207.7	137.72	–842.75	–596.35	–342.03
Depreciation	40.53	59.77	72.06	101.44	127.49	117.24	121.28	110.5
Tax	138.16	233.72	152.62	–9.41	–3.11	0	–45.4	0.09
Deferred Tax	0	0	–10.62	0	0	0	0	0
Profit After Tax	264.87	486.38	278.32	115.67	13.34	–959.99	–672.23	–452.62
Gain/(Loss) on Cancellation of Foreign Exchange	0	0	0	–149.02	0	0	0	0
Other Extraordinary Income/(Expense)	0	0	0	0	0	–0.9	99.75	84.62
Adjusted Profit After Extraordinary Items	**264.87**	**486.38**	**278.32**	**264.69**	**13.34**	**–959.09**	**–771.98**	**–537.22**

Source: Prowess Database.

₹370 billion, including both internal and external projects.[3] Tables M12.1–M12.5 present the financial statements and key financial ratios for LITL and its competitors.

GROWTH STRATEGY

LITL,[4] a new holding corporate entity, was created in 2006 to consolidate LITL's diverse operations under a single brand. LITL decided to focus on its core business—energy and construction—and enter the infrastructure and property development sectors. As part of its business strategy, the organization had chalked out an ambitious growth plan in power and solar energy. LITL also envisaged aggressive

[3] Lanco also executed projects on behalf of other power producers.

[4] This section is based on information in company annual reports.

TABLE M12.2
Balance Sheet (₹10 million)

Year	2009	2010	2011	2012	2013	2014	2015	2016
Share Capital	219.83	238.55	238.72	238.97	239.24	239.24	245.09	273.78
Reserves	1,877.79	3,031.62	4,384.41	4,467.09	3,433.22	1,218.3	–692.86	–996.31
Total Shareholders' Equity	2,097.62	3,270.17	4,623.13	4,706.06	3,672.46	1,457.54	–447.77	–722.53
Minority Interest	703.28	710.82	845.32	951.88	934.18	837.48	1,339.19	1,479.21
Secured Loans	5,247.27	7,561.91	14,327.9	30,214.8	32,990.1	36,208.9	38,816.6	43,988.8
Unsecured Loans	349.71	799.47	2,325.13	1,015.13	990.47	496.45	374.5	375.85
Total Debt/Loan Funds	5,596.98	8,361.38	16,653	31,229.9	33,980.5	36,705.3	39,191.1	44,364.6
Total Liabilities	8,397.88	12,342.4	22,121.5	36,887.9	38,587.2	39,000.4	40,082.6	45,121.3
Gross Block	2,386.71	6,164.39	12,304	21,522.5	26,685.1	26,844.4	27,159.3	25,394.5
Less: Accumulated Depreciation	761.53	1,086.66	1,966.75	2,882.05	4,064.81	5,090.02	5,911.87	5,685.66
Net Block	1,625.18	5,077.73	10,337.2	18,640.4	22,620.3	21,754.4	21,247.4	19,708.9
Capital Work-in-Progress	3,788.67	1,923.73	5,237	13,880.1	12,134.5	14,034.9	16,004.6	21,176.5
Investments	983.69	2,014.14	3,194.94	2,764.26	2,901.6	3,006.09	3,155.55	1,778.47
Inventories	1,322.29	1,626.71	2,142.96	2,788.88	3,097.58	3,121.34	3,320.32	3,365.22
Sundry Debtors	1,194.35	2,226.99	1,458.5	3,764.19	4,657.62	3,959.36	3,353.99	2,988.34
Cash and Bank Balance	990.45	962.77	1,266.45	1,412.07	572.81	579.34	808.26	634.25
Loans and Advances	1,643.86	2,193	2,729.69	2,737.65	3,153.73	2,817.39	2,965.82	2,633.28
Total Current Assets	5,150.95	7,009.47	7,597.6	10,702.8	11,481.7	10,477.4	10,448.4	9,621.09
Current Liabilities	3,079.16	3,408.3	2,820.71	6,288.83	7,082.61	7,413.06	8,431.97	6,145.11
Provisions	53.97	99.5	69.2	168.27	184.25	196.72	83.39	99.21
Total Current Liabilities	3,133.13	3,507.8	2,889.91	6,457.1	7,266.86	7,609.78	8,515.36	6,244.32
Net Current Assets	2,017.82	3,501.67	4,707.69	4,245.69	4,214.88	2,867.65	1,933.03	3,376.77
Deferred Tax Assets	5.88	11.16	33.49	67.06	209.8	668.63	948.67	801.8
Deferred Tax Liability	23.36	111.46	570.31	756.66	814.2	1,087.35	1,232.87	822.47
Net Deferred Tax	–17.48	–100.3	–536.82	–689.6	–604.4	–418.72	–284.2	–20.67
Total Assets	8,397.88	12,417	22,940	38,840.9	41,266.9	41,244.3	42,056.4	46,020

Source: Prowess Database.

TABLE M12.3
Cash Flow Statement (₹10 million)

	2017	2016	2015	2014	2013	2012	2011	2010
Cash Flow Summary								
Cash and Cash Equivalents at the Beginning	24.89	303.68	113.3	36.84	111.17	304.82	345.69	60.19
Net Cash from Operating Activities	459.55	–1,592.66	43.1	–182.68	209.76	3,965.32	3,716.71	80.5
Net Cash Used in Investing Activities	–183.66	785.86	–210.69	60.8	–245.01	–4,079.64	–4,485.19	–1,702.06
Net Cash Used in Financing Activities	–268.02	528	357.96	198.34	–39.08	–79.33	727.61	1,907.06
Net Inc./(Dec) in Cash and Cash Equivalent	7.87	–278.8	190.37	76.46	–74.33	–193.65	–40.87	285.5
Cash and Cash Equivalents at the End	32.76	24.88	303.67	113.3	36.84	111.17	304.82	345.69

growth plans for EPC with a strong order book growth. By September 2010, it was in the list of top 10 companies published by Forbes Asia.[5]

In December 2010, the company's EPC division was awarded the EPC Contract by a Moser Baer group company for their 2×600 MW Coal-Based Thermal Power Project through an international bidding process. It was also successful in bidding for 278 KM, two-lane, road development project that connected the Indian cities of Aligarh and Kanpur in the State of Uttar Pradesh on a Design, Build, Finance, Operate and Transfer (DBFOT) basis. The scope of work involved repair, widening and reconstruction of three major and 29 minor bridges, construction of five new rail-over-bridges, four toll plazas and other wayside amenities. The project involved an investment of around ₹10 billion. The grant from National Highways Authority of India would be ₹2.87 billion. The concession period for the Project was 12 years, including a construction period of 18 months. In January 2011, Lanco Kondapalli Power Limited, a subsidiary company developing a 732 MW (2×366) gas-based power project in the state of Andhra Pradesh, achieved financial closure. The project, estimated to cost ₹26.1 billion, would be financed with a debt of ₹18.27 billion and equity of ₹7.83 billion. A consortium of six banks and financial institutions with Axis Bank in the lead provided the debt.

Around the same time, LITL was also aggressively pursuing its international expansion plans. The company through its step-down Australian subsidiary, Lanco Resources Australia Pty Ltd, concluded a binding agreement with Griffin Energy Group Pty Ltd and Carpenter Mine Management Holdings Pty Ltd to purchase 100 per cent shares of Griffin Coal Mining Company Pty Ltd and Carpenter Mine Management Pty Ltd (Griffin Coal). Griffin coal, based in Collie in Western Australia, owned the largest operational thermal coal mine in Western Australia. The mine produced over 5 mtpa of coal that could be ramped up to over 15 mtpa in the near term. The mining tenements contained over 1.1 billion tonnes of thermal coal resources. The mine was strategically located on the western coast of Australia closer to

[5] https://www.forbes.com/global/2010/0927/fab-50-10-asian-paints-crompton-greaves-companies-to-watch.html#1cebeca73e46 (accessed on 11 January 2019).

TABLE M12.4
Financial Ratios

	2017	2016	2015	2014	2013	2012	2011	2010	2009	2008	2007	2006
Debt–Equity Ratio	5.07	3.65	2.66	1.67	1.25	1.14	0.99	0.81	0.55	0.24	0.14	0.52
Long-Term Debt–Equity Ratio	3.08	2.7	2.01	0.81	0.29	0.31	0.51	0.6	0.35	0.18	0.11	0.44
Current Ratio	0.7	0.76	0.85	1.03	1.06	1	1.11	1.25	1.05	1.05	1.07	1.1
Turnover Ratios												
Fixed Assets	2.49	2.28	0.94	1.48	3.19	7.83	10.05	14.36	12.95	10.74	9.59	7.41
Inventory	1.15	1.89	0.98	1.64	4.1	9.77	9.61	13.67	14.13	15.38	17.59	12.61
Debtors	0.88	1.49	0.89	1.09	1.92	3.77	2.69	3.42	4.65	4.16	4.5	3.59
Total Asset Turnover Ratio	0.13	0.2	0.11	0.16	0.34	0.65	0.63	1.31	1.53	0.85	0.64	1.19
Interest Cover Ratio	0.14	0.41	–0.02	–0.53	1.02	1.21	2.24	4.64	3.91	9.62	5.77	4.18
EBDIT Margin (%)	13.97	18.46	7.4	–9.61	15.66	8.28	14.29	16.46	14.26	21.79	23.48	11.38
EBIT Margin (%)	8.6	14.32	–1.29	–14.86	12.97	7.1	13.05	15.45	13.27	21.06	22.79	10.12
EBDT Margin (%)	–49.04	–16.45	–47.94	–37.68	3	2.41	8.48	13.13	10.86	19.6	19.53	8.96
Net Income Margin (%)	–54.41	–20.59	–53.38	–42.93	0.36	1.34	4.79	8.19	6.49	12.71	13.64	5.79
Return on Capital Employed (%)	0	0	0	–2.41	4.36	4.63	8.21	20.18	20.25	18	14.55	12.08
Return on Net Worth (%)	0	0	0	–30.45	0.47	3.29	8.43	19.37	15.33	13.47	9.96	10.5

Source: Prowess Database.

India compared with the mines in New South Wales and Queensland. The Griffin coal mines were well connected to two ports through both rail and road.

In January 2011, Griffin had defaulted on debt amounting to US$475 million and was seeking buyers for the company. It was acquired by LITL for a total consideration of US$730 million. The deal was concluded on 28 February 2011. An amount of US$483 million was paid on the conclusion of the deal. Further, US$100 million and A$150 million would be paid at the end of the second and fourth year from the conclusion date as consideration in fulfilment of the conditions of the binding agreement. Suresh Kumar, the CFO of LITL, said:[6]

[6] https://www.indiainfoline.com/article/international-market/lanco-infratech-concludes-agreement-with-griffin-coal-and-carpenter-mine-113101703399_1.html (accessed on 11 January 2019).

TABLE M12.5
Peer Companies Industry Mean, Median and LITL Mean and Median

	Mar 2015		Mar 2016		Mar 2017	
Industrial infrastructure	Mean	Median	Mean	Median	Mean	Median
Pat (in millions)	–18.1691	0.6	–42.6519	0	–129.924	0.2
Sales (in millions)	5,400.071	795.85	5,348.434	871.55	6,564.322	1,177.85
Ncf from op act (in millions)	116.6773	12.05	237.4502	41	464.4955	1.7
Debt/equity (times)	17.19806	1.5	56.54347	1.56	11.45266	1.4
Current ratio (times)	14.54679	0.965	4.935903	0.9	6.966559	0.93
Return on net worth (%)	–12.1066	0	–0.29996	0	–2.23752	0.5
Roce (%)	–15.2909	0	–9.04201	0	0.79989	0.01
	Mar 2015		Mar 2016		Mar 2017	
LITL (infrastructure group)	Mean	Median	Mean	Median	Mean	Median
Pat (in millions)	–6,722.3	–6,722.3	–2,273.25	–2,273.25	–8,895.2	–8,895.2
Sales (in millions)	13,950.9	13,950.9	26,718	26,718	16,354	16,354
Ncf from op act (in millions)	221.1	221.1	–7,963.5	–7,963.5	4,595.5	4,595.5
Debt/equity (times)	11.015	11.015	14.355	14.355	8.19	8.19
Current ratio (times)	35.055	35.055	120.895	120.895	0.55	0.55
Return on net worth (%)	–30.7	–30.7	–26.655	–26.655	–70.54	–70.54
Roce (%)	–8.33	–8.33	–3.465	–3.465	–9.47	–9.47
	Mar 2015		Mar 2016		Mar 2017	
Power generation industry	Mean	Median	Mean	Median	Mean	Median
Pat (in millions)	405.5353	–0.1	421.669	–0.2	707.5698	–0.2
Sales (in millions)	12,934.16	442.9	13,289.29	587.85	17,784.32	886.85
Ncf from op act (in millions)	1,773.648	39.35	2,323.314	31.95	3,916.561	48.45
Debt/equity (times)	83.45871	1.97	23.46636	1.77	58.44348	1.46
Current ratio (times)	4.614872	0.63	2.463785	0.5	11.38777	0.495
Return on net worth (%)	–16.2351	0	–7.24547	0	–6.77562	0
Roce (%)	–1.11717	0	–2.46234	–0.03	–20.554	0
	Mar 2015		Mar 2016		Mar 2017	
LITL (power group)	Mean	Median	Mean	Median	Mean	Median
Pat (in millions)	–434.075	–113.05	528.6667	–2.1	–556.5	–21.3
Sales (in millions)	6,921.05	3,244.95	11,218.94	7,839	9,640	10,371
Ncf from op act (in millions)	–509	1.1	1,334.55	0.2	2,366.7	79.6
Debt/equity (times)	424.74	0.39	7.952143	0.995	21.92273	3.42
Current ratio (times)	1.329375	0.585	0.736429	0.365	0.477273	0.47
Return on net worth (%)	–1.63583	0	–5.94231	–0.01	–12.0036	–0.44
Roce (%)	–0.27385	0	–4.13643	0	–1.51818	–0.04

source: Prowess Database.

> The acquisition of Griffin Coal is an important component of our development strategy, providing increased fuel security for our current power generation assets and future power portfolio expansions. This acquisition also presents an opportunity to Lanco to participate in the burgeoning natural resources trading market.

The logic of the purchase was questioned in the business media, as the company had faced difficulties and had been forced to defer pension and other payments to suppliers. Two months later, Lanco Solar Holdings, Singapore, a subsidiary of LITL unveiled its solar plans. It was implementing a fully integrated business strategy as a developer of solar farms, EPC contractor and also integrated manufacturer of solar PV modules. Lanco Solar Holdings was present in both solar PV and solar thermal technologies. Under various policies of both state and central governments, Lanco Solar Holdings had already signed power purchase agreements to the extent of 140 MW and aimed to develop 200–300 MW of solar power over the next two years. It also offered turnkey EPC services to other solar power developers and was looking to build 300–500 MW of solar thermal and solar PV plants over the next couple of years. It had secured a contract for establishing solar power generation projects to be built on Parliament House and Science City in the state of Punjab. Lanco Solar Holdings had also established a global presence across the UK, Germany, France, Italy, Spain, the USA and Canada. It was developing solar power plants and providing turnkey EPC services in these countries. The first few projects in Europe are expected to be commissioned by April 2011. As part of its integrated business strategy, LITL was setting up India's first integrated Solar PV manufacturing special economic zone (SEZ) project in Rajnandgaon district of Chhattisgarh. The SEZ would have integrated facilities to manufacture polysilicon, ingots, wafers, PV cells and PV modules with an installed capacity of 250 MW/year. The first phase of the project involved an investment of ₹13.7 billion and would be completed by 2012. The state-of-the-art project was the first such integrated solar photovoltaic facility, putting the country and the state of Chhattisgarh on the global map of polysilicon production bases.

The project would provide the critical backward integration for solar projects undertaken by the company. LITL had signed power purchase agreements with NTPC Vidyut Vyapar Nigam Ltd (NVVN) for development of a 5 MW solar PV project and a 100 MW solar thermal project in the state of Rajasthan under the first phase of the Jawaharlal Nehru National Solar Mission (JNNSM). In addition, it had signed up with Gujarat Urja Vikas Nigam Ltd (GUVNL) for development of a 35 MW solar PV project in the state of Gujarat. The company had already commissioned a 5 MW solar PV project in Gujarat using its in-house EPC capabilities, while another 5 MW is under development.

Apart from the foreign subsidiaries, LITL also operated Lanco Vidarbha Thermal Power Ltd, another subsidiary that operated a 1,320 (2×660) MW coal-based super-critical thermal power project at Wardha in Maharashtra and Lanco Anpara Power Limited, a group company.[7] Throughout 2011 and 2012, the company continued to bag EPC contracts for both conventional and solar power plants in India and abroad.

LITL reported a loss of ₹2.6 billion (US$50 million) for the three months ending 30 Sep 2011, its first in four years. In November 2011, Suresh Kumar, the chief financial officer at LITL, quit becoming the second top executive to resign.[8] By the end of 2011, LITL's total debt stood at ₹190 billion (US$3.7 billion), a fivefold increase since 2007. Revenue from LITL's power business fell 26 per cent to ₹9.9 billion in the last quarter. At this stage, the sector was facing several problems relating to international coal pricing, domestic financing and interest rates. The company's shares plunged 61 per cent that year reflecting these concerns. Figure M12.1 presents the stock price history of the company.

[7] In all, Lanco had 89 subsidiaries and 10 associate companies.

[8] The CEO too quit in the same month.

FIGURE M12.1
Stock Price History (in ₹)

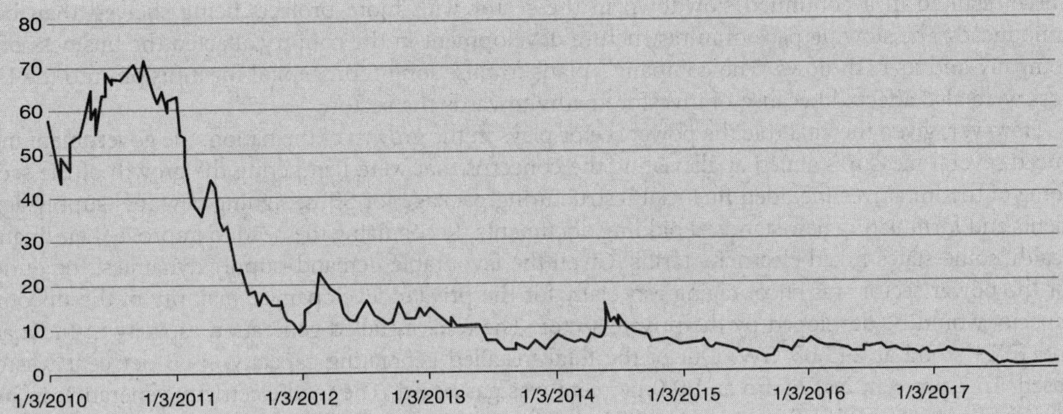

Source: Case writer.

Towards the end of 2012, LITL entered into a memorandum of understanding (MoU) with the China Development Bank (CDB), a bank owned by the government of PRC, to arrange US$2 billion debt for two power projects: Anpara Phase II and Himavat, each having capacity of 2 × 660 MW.[9] Out of the total amount of US$2 billion required, US$600 million would be contributed by CDB and the remaining amount would be syndicated.

INDUSTRY BACKGROUND AND MACROECONOMIC CONDITIONS

India's GDP grew at a modest rate of 4.7 per cent during the year 2013–2014. Continued struggle with high inflation, high interest rates, infrastructure constraints and lack of policy reforms pushed the nation's growth rate to sub-5 per cent for the second year. The growth rate in the previous year was 4.5 per cent. Agriculture grew at a pace of 4.7 per cent for the year whilst mining and manufacturing contracted by 1.4 per cent and 0.7 per cent, respectively. The country witnessed a continued slowdown in economic activity during the year 2012–2013 and LITL, being among the nation's largest players in the infrastructure sector, too got affected by the continued slowing economy.

LITL provided EPC services to the infrastructure sector with a primary focus on the power sector. The company was heavily involved in the construction of power plants and other infrastructure projects. The company's EPC revenues got affected due to various unresolved issues especially in the power sector. The envisaged growth in the power sector was affected due to factors such as unavailability of

[9] https://www.indiainfoline.com/article/general-others/lanco-infratech-to-raise-us-2-bn-from-chinese-banks-113110706311_1.html (accessed on 11 January 2019).

fuel (both coal and gas), unviable power tariffs not reflecting the true cost of generation, delays in obtaining vital clearances, poor financial and commercial health of the State Electricity Boards (SEBs) leading to lower power procurement by SEBs, high interest rates and a weakening of the Indian Rupee. These resulted in a continued slowdown in the sector with more projects being shelved than being announced. The slowing pace of infrastructure development in the country affected the business of the company and its cash flows. The company's plans to raise long-term capital for infusion into the business were also affected because of investor apathy towards the sector.

However, given the vital role the power sector plays in the growth of the nation, the government introduced several measures aimed at alleviating the concerns that were hampering the growth of the sector. Some of the initiatives included financial restructuring package for SEBs, signing new fuel supply agreements and formulating new standard bidding documents. Recognizing the need to improve their financial health, some states hiked electricity tariffs. Given the favourable demand–supply dynamics, the outlook for the power sector was encouraging especially for the private developers as majority of the upcoming capacity would be developed by the private sector. The total installed generation capacity in India as of end FY14 stood at 243.03 GW. Out of the total installed generating capacity, 59.8 per cent was coal based, 16.7 per cent was hydro and 9.0 per cent was gas based. The total electricity generation in India during FY14 was at 966.38 billion units (BUs) versus 912.06 BUs in FY13, an increase of 5.96 per cent.

The generating capacity addition during 2013–2014 stood at 17,825 MW as against 20,623 MW in 2012–2013, a decline of 13.57 per cent. The 12th Five-Year Plan of the Government of India targeted a capacity addition of 88,537 MW with 53 per cent of the capacity being added by the private sector. Among the various renewable energy resources, solar energy was considered to have the highest potential in the country. The JNNSM was launched in January 2010 to make India a global leader in solar energy. As per the National Tariff Policy of January 2011, solar-specific Renewable Purchase Obligation (RPO) was envisaged to increase from a minimum of 0.25 per cent in 2012 to 3 per cent in 2022. The nation would need an installed solar capacity of approximately 34,000 MW in order to achieve the 3 per cent RPO compliance by 2022.

Coal-generated power was expected to continue to be the major source of energy for the nation. With the current per capita commercial primary energy consumption in India at about 350 kgoe (kilograms of oil equivalent)/year well below that of developed countries, energy usage in India was expected to rise. The increasing demand for energy would be driven by an expanding economy, improvements in infrastructure, rising population and enhanced standard of living. As of April 2014, the geological resources of coal in the country were estimated to be a cumulative total of 301.56 billion tonnes with the state of Jharkhand having the highest resources at 80,716 million tonnes (MT) followed by the state of Orissa at 75,073 MT.

According to the Planning Commission of the Government of India, infrastructure investment had to be, on average, almost 10 per cent of GDP during the 12th Five-Year Plan in order to attain a 9 per cent real GDP growth rate. Projected investment in infrastructure during the 12th Five-Year Plan stood at ₹6.57 trillion at current prices and ₹4.09 trillion at 2007 prices.

THE 2013 RESTRUCTURING

In June 2013, LITL had won a contract for setting up two 300 MW power plants in Gujarat. However, the contract was cancelled in October 2013, when the company failed to furnish the 10 per cent guarantee required in the contract. On 23 July 2013, LITL announced that it had initiated the process of

CDR prescribed under the RBI guidelines by way of reference to CDR cell.[10] Under the CDR plan, more than ₹70 billion would be restructured by the company. There would be a moratorium on interest payments for fund-based facilities,[11] which would be in place for two years. ₹263 million of secured loans from banks and financial institutions and ₹5,662 million of unsecured loans had to be repaid in the near future. Further, the company had ₹353.9 million of secured hypothecation loans and that had to be repaid. Unsecured loans and advances included (a) intercorporate deposits from two subsidiaries bearing interest rate of 9 per cent p.a. and 15.50 per cent p.a. to be repayable on or before 4 September 2013 and 1 January 2014, respectively.

The proposal was only for LITL and not for any of its subsidiaries. CDR was a mechanism adopted in India which permitted viable companies additional time to meet debt obligations, subject to certain terms and conditions. The terms of CDR were:

- Reschedule term loans and short-term working capital loans and provide a moratorium period of two years from the cut-off date of 1 April 2013. These were repayable in 30 quarterly instalments starting from 30 June 2015.
- ₹25 billion priority loan to be sanctioned with a moratorium period of two years at an interest rate of 12.5 per cent. It would be repayable in 18 quarterly instalments starting from 30 June 2015.
- The rate of interest on restructured facilities would be 11 per cent p.a. initially and increase to 16 per cent p.a. for the financial year 2016–2017.
- The company should raise funds by sale of assets/divestment of shares in special purpose vehicles or qualified institutional placements or an IPO to repay the aforementioned restructured facilities under CDR scheme.

In relation to the loans restructured by the CDR lenders, a total amount to ₹22.24 billion would qualify for the conversion of 3,545 million shares at the sole discretion and on demand of the CDR lenders.

The Corporate Debt Restructuring Empowered Group (CDREG) in its meeting held on 11 December 2013 approved the CDR package submitted by the company and issued a letter of approval on 20 December 2013. In relation to the amount outstanding as at 31 March 2014 against the loans restructured by the CDR lenders, a total amount of ₹22.24 billion would qualify for the conversion into 3,545 million shares at the sole discretion and on demand of the CDR lenders. In terms of CDR package, the promoters brought into the company as unsecured loan a total amount of ₹1,520 million and the same would qualify for the conversion into 244 million shares at the sole discretion of the founders. Shareholders were expected to vote on the proposal in April 2014.

At the time of filing for debt restructuring, the company had an order book of ₹260 billion to be executed in the next two to three years. The company was of the view that macroeconomic conditions prevailing in India were responsible for the slowdown and the situation would reverse in 18–24 months. The proposed restructuring would help the company to execute the order book and generate ₹100 billion of revenues.

[10] The CDR was a voluntary non-statutory system which was based on the DCA and ICA. The arrangement provided for multi-banking accounts, syndication or consortium accounts, wherein all banks and institutions together could have an outstanding exposure of ₹100 million or more. DCA had a legal binding on both the debtor and the creditor(s) to not take a recourse to any legal action during the period of the contract and take a 'standstill' position.

[11] Banks provide two types of credit facilities. Fund-based facilities provide cash (e.g., working capital loan, overdraft), whereas non-fund based facilities do not provide cash (e.g., letter of credit, guarantee).

The power division had incurred a loss of ₹6,710 million for the year ending 31 March 2013 against an estimated profit after tax of ₹34,750 million for the same period. EPC revenues were down by 50 per cent to ₹47.41 billion as on 31 March compared with the previous year, despite a strong current order book. With this proposal, the company hoped to ensure timely completion of all existing projects with an installed capacity of 4,636 MW as well as efficiently execute the expansion plans of Griffin Coal. The current restructuring proposal would also address the timely development of 6,240 MW capacity in the pipeline. In addition, the company would get over ₹25 billion priority loans from its lenders. This would help the company in improving the EPC operations in different segments.

EVENTS DURING 2014–2017

In February 2014, LITL became the successful bidder of the prestigious EPC Contract for establishing 1 × 660 MW super-critical Ennore Thermal Power Station Expansion Project by Tamil Nadu Generation and Distribution Corporation Limited (TANGEDCO). The shareholders were allowed to vote for or against the proposed restructuring in April 2014. Of the 1,740,925,768 valid votes, 99.9 per cent of votes were polled for the resolution and 0.01 per cent voted against the resolution because of which the resolution was passed. The Board of Directors of the company passed circular resolution on 29 December 2014 approving the allotment of 54.574 million equity shares of ₹1 only each at an issue price of ₹6.23 per share to ICICI Bank, CDR lender, as per CDR package approved for the company. The shares allotted to ICICI Bank would be locked-in for a period of one year. The Board of Directors of the company at its meeting held on 30 December 2015 approved the issuance of 321,453,885 compulsorily convertible debentures (CCDs) of face value of ₹10 each at par, on preferential basis to IDFC Bank, subject to the necessary approvals in this regard.

The company continued to make losses for the next three years although losses were halved. Total debt increased by ₹80 billion over the next years with long-term debt/equity rising to three. Consequently interest expense rose 150 per cent and interest coverage fell to abysmal levels (0.14). The total debt of Griffin was close to US$900 million. LITL incurred a loss of US$300 million on account of Griffin Coal. The sale process of Griffin Coal in 2011 was overseen by KordaMentha—the administrator of Carpenter Mine. The Australian mine was continuously making cash losses ever since its acquisition. Production at the mine during the FY17 was 2.50 MT with sales of 2.45 MT. Production was less than optimal as the fall in international coal prices did not economically justify exporting a part of the production. In 2015, LITL alleged that KordaMentha misled the bidders by withholding two reports suggesting the Griffin coal deposits were smaller than disclosed first. Denying LITL's allegation, KordaMentha in turn made a counter allegation that LITL defaulted on its instalment to the tune of US$150 for the mine. The issue was settled out of court as the Australian advisory and investment firm agreed to pay about US$10 million as expenses and also waive US$150 million payment instalment by LITL.

A reorganization scheme was approved in FY 2017 by the steering committee of lenders to the group. It took into consideration all issues impacting LITL and the coal-based power projects under construction, covering 70 per cent of the debt exposure of the group. After much deliberations, it was vetted by lenders and IDBI Capital Markets, the lenders' investment bank. The scheme provided for:

- the EPC to be demerged into a 100 per cent subsidiary
- the lenders in LITL to convert ₹24,000 million of their debt into equity to acquire a majority stake of 60 per cent

- the balance debt of LITL to be transferred to a new power holding company along with the investments in operating and under construction coal-based power assets at an estimated value of ₹53,100 million
- lenders in under-construction projects to approve cost overrun proposals along with change in debt–equity ratio, reduction in interest rate to 10.25 per cent and elongation of repayment schedule to 17 years
- the under-construction projects to be completed and sold over four years to repay the debt transferred to the holding company

The scheme was subsequently sanctioned by a majority of lenders after a seven-month delay. However, some lenders to under-construction projects did not approve it because of their unwillingness to change the terms and conditions of their loans and the scheme could not be implemented. LITL was an EPC contractor in five under-construction projects and a substantial portion of its value was tied up in the form of equity invested in these projects. It felt that insolvency proceedings would bring the under-construction projects to a standstill resulting in further cost overruns and its EPC business would be affected. IDBI and other lenders had to decide whether to consider the proposal or not.

Tables M12.6–M12.8 present a snapshot of the structure of liabilities, extent of unhedged exposures and the board composition of LITL as of 31 March 2017. As of August 2017, the stock was trading at ₹1, even less than the face value of ₹10.[12]

TABLE M12.6
Structure of Liabilities (in ₹Hundred Thousands)

Rupee Term Loans	31 Mar 2017	Short-Term Borrowings	31 Mar 2017
Secured		Cash Credit and Working Capital Loan from Banks	2,480.04
From Banks	22,904.25	**Foreign Currency Loans and Advances Secured (From Banks)**	409.59
From Financial Institutions	9,623.02		
Unsecured			
From Banks	49.17		
Foreign Currency Term Loans			
Secured			
From Banks	7,054.49		
From Others	**388.31**		
Deferred Payment Liabilities	**743.32**		
Total	**40,752.58**		**2,889.63**

Note: The US$ to ₹exchange rate appreciated from ₹46.12/US$ in January 2010 to ₹44.25/US$ in April 2011 and then depreciated to ₹62.02/US$ in January 2015 and ₹67.87/US$ in January 2016. It had partially recovered to ₹64.86/US$ in March 2017.

Source: Company Annual Report 2016–2017.

[12] As of March 2017, Lanco had 3,314,063,857 shares outstanding.

TABLE M12.7
Details of Unhedged Foreign Currency Exposure

	Currency	Exchange Rate	Amount in Million	Amount in ₹ million
Trade Receivables	US$	601	145.9	8,769.7
	AU$	557.1	1.2	67.6
Trade Payables	US$	601	230.2	13,836
	Euro	825.8	0.7	54.3
Advance to Suppliers	US$	449.4	132.7	5,961
	Euro	681.8	0	1.7
	GBP	864.5	0	0.5
Advance from Customers	US$	451.5	346.5	15,646
Loans Receivable	US$	601	35.9	2,155.2
Foreign Currency Term Loan	US$	601	96.2	5,779.7
	Euro	825.8	1.7	141.2

TABLE M12.8
Board of Directors

Name	Director Category	# Directorships	# Chairmanships	# Committees	# Shares Held by Non-Executive Directors	Education
L. Madhusudhan Rao	Executive	14	2	1	NA	M Tech
G. Bhaskara Rao	Executive	14	2	4	NA	ME
L. Sridhar	Non-Executive	14	0	3	45,143,587	MS
G. Venkatesh Babu	Executive	14	0	8	NA	Chartered Accountant
S. C. Manocha	Executive	3	0	0	NA	MBA
Pamidi Kotaiah	Non-Exe and Independent	10	4	3	95,555	MA
P. Abraham	Non Exe and Independent	12	0	1	5,170	MA
Uddesh Kumar Kohli	Non-Exe and Independent	6	2	5	169,050	PhD
B. Vasanthan	Non-Exe and Independent	1	0	0	28,500	NA
R. Krishnamoorthy	Non-Exe and Independent	4	1	2	0	CMA

Source: Company Annual Report 2016–2017.

EXERCISES

1. Why is LITL in financial distress: is it bad strategy or bad luck?
2. What are the key risks faced by the company? How would you address them?
3. With regard to its capital structure, did the company have the wrong capital structure, issue wrong kinds of capital or issue capital in the wrong sequence?
4. As a lender, would you approve the proposed restructuring? Why or why not?

Index